The Home Voices
Speak Louder
Than the Drums

The Home Voices Speak Louder Than the Drums

Dreams and the Imagination in Civil War Letters and Memoirs

WANDA EASTER BURCH

McFarland & Company, Inc., Publishers
Jefferson, North Carolina

LIBRARY OF CONGRESS CATALOGUING-IN-PUBLICATION DATA

Names: Burch, Wanda Easter, 1947– author.
Title: The home voices speak louder than the drums : dreams and the imagination in Civil war Letters and memoirs / Wanda Easter Burch.
Description: Jefferson, North Carolina : McFarland & Company, Inc., Publishers, 2017. | Includes bibliographical references and index.
Identifiers: LCCN 2017018266 | ISBN 9781476665580 (softcover : acid free paper) ∞
Subjects: LCSH: United States—History—Civil War, 1861–1865—Psychological aspects. | Dreams—Social aspects—United States—History—19th century. | Dreams—United States—History—19th century.
Classification: LCC E468.9 .B889 2017 | DDC 973.7/1—dc23
LC record available at https://lccn.loc.gov/2017018266

BRITISH LIBRARY CATALOGUING DATA ARE AVAILABLE

ISBN (print) 978-1-4766-6558-0
ISBN (ebook) 978-1-4766-2525-6

© 2017 Wanda Easter Burch. All rights reserved

No part of this book may be reproduced or transmitted in any form or by any means, electronic or mechanical, including photocopying or recording, or by any information storage and retrieval system, without permission in writing from the publisher.

Front cover image: *Our heaven born banner*, William Bauly, Sarony, Major & Knapp lithograph, 1861 (Library of Congress)

Printed in the United States of America

McFarland & Company, Inc., Publishers
Box 611, Jefferson, North Carolina 28640
www.mcfarlandpub.com

For Ron and Evan, whose dreams
offer counsel and guidance.

For John Kenosian, whose music and dreams
heal the heart, the spirit and the soul.

Acknowledgments

I would like to thank my husband, Ron, and my son and his family, who have listened to my stories of dreams and the Civil War since my discovery of a book of soldiers' letters in Savannah, Georgia, in 2007. I would like to thank the female veterans who have shared their own military dreaming of "home" experiences at Creative Healing Connections' workshops on dreams and healing at Wiawaka Holiday House in Lake George, New York.

Archivists at universities, too numerous to mention by name, have been gracious and prompt in responding to my questions. Paul Mercer of the Special Collections Division of the New York State Library deserves special thanks for alerting me to the Charles Hagar collection, which led me to meeting the Reverend Hagar's descendants who shared additional material in the Clinton Historical Society in Clinton, New York. Thanks to the *Johnstown (NY) Leader Herald* for an article on my research, which led me to Delbert and Rosemary Pierce, of Fonda, New York, who gave me access to ancestral letters and papers and a self-published contemporary journal written by Civil War soldier David Lane. Thanks to John Quinn, bandleader, and the 77th New York Regimental Balladeers, whose programming and a 21-track CD, *Come Dearest the Daylight Is Gone*, includes excerpts from letters and journals and includes a booklet, *Dreaming of Home in the American Civil War* (Wanda Burch).

Special thanks to singer/songwriter and program partner on healing dreams and music, John Kenosian, whose dreaming is expressed in music and art and who generously gives back to those searching for healing for the soul and spirit.

Table of Contents

Acknowledgments   vii
Preface   1
Introduction   3

1. Playing for Keeps: Gods, Generals and Staff on the Battlefield   7
2. Artists and Music, Artists and Illustrators: Embedded Dreamers   31
3. Homesickness—"like fire in my bones"   41
4. Tenting Tonight: Dreaming of Home on the Old Campground   49
5. Dreaming of Children   79
6. "Just So" Dreams   84
7. Dreaming of Home—with a Smile   96
8. Precognitive Dreaming   100
9. "Sacred Soil is adhesive"   118
10. Families Dreaming at Home   125
11. Dreaming in Prison: Seven Occupants to Make a Shadow   140
12. Caring for the Wounded   161
13. Caring for Souls on the Battlefield   177
14. Dying Tonight on the Old Campground   185
15. Presentiment: I Have a Rendezvous with Death—or Life   198
16. Soldier's Heart   212
17. Slavery   218
18. Many Are the Hearts That Are Weary Tonight: Wishing for the War to Cease   232

Chapter Notes   235
Bibliography   263
Index   273

Preface

This book explores a little referenced but prevalent subject in the vast research on the Civil War: dreams and the imagination in the letters of Civil War soldiers and in the journals and diaries of their families writing from home.

The study of dreams and the use of the imagination at home and in the field in the Civil War has been a personal passion since I attended a "Vernacular Architecture Forum" in Savannah several years ago and picked up a journal compendium of letters from soldiers in Georgia. I opened it at random and the first words I saw were these: "soldier mortals would not survive if they were not blessed with the gift of imagination and the pictures of hope. The second angel of mercy is the night dream." Henry Graves wrote those words in Petersburg, Virginia, in 1862. He continued with a dream so evocative, so real, that he demanded when he awoke to know where his beloved was and why she had abandoned him to the horror and noise of battle. I began a search for similar letters that led me to archives, published journals, diaries and memoirs, genealogy Web sites, and poems written from battlefield dreams. The numbers of letters, journals and diaries recording dreams of home, precognitive dreams of battle, presentiment dreams and visions, and "just so" dreams of the conditions of the body and soul in camp or in a torn landscape of war were astonishing.

I was born in Cullman, Alabama, grew up in Memphis, Tennessee, and have spent the last several decades involved in historic preservation and regional history in the Mohawk Valley of upstate New York. My degrees are in history and museum management. I have recently retired after thirty-seven years as site manager of a New York State historic house museum [Johnson Hall] in Johnstown, New York. My interest in dreams was inspired by my grandmother who was a healer in the Alabama mountains. I have written about my own use of the imagery from my dreaming in a healing journey that shadowed me from my first dreams of a diagnosis of breast cancer through surgery, chemotherapy and beyond into "giving back" through work with advocacy and arts retreats for women. Dreaming and history and the possibility that dreaming *at* home and *of* home on the battlefields, in camp, and in the letters between family members in the Civil War could provide emotional well-being for the soldier and their families at home became my passion. I began a literary journey and several years of physical journeys into the landscapes of the Civil War, which also spoke to my root connectedness and led me back to battlefields and to my personal connection with the events that shaped my homeland. I have become invested in the lives of each of the soldiers and each of the families who shared their dreams and their lives on the pages of their letters and journals. One soldier, defending the length of his letters and the depth of his feelings, described his words as "soul on paper."

Dreams are in almost every soldier's letters but are rarely indexed in published works or acknowledged in the histories of the Civil War. Curious about the incidences of the word "dream," I typed that word into the search box on the "Documenting the American South" Internet site, which makes available the holdings of several university collections. I had 13,700,000 "hits" on the term. Expecting most of the entries to be the generic use of the word "dream," I chose twenty pages of ten entries each. Of those ten entries on each page, at least five and often more were soldiers' letters describing a night dream. I think that in itself says something about the prevalence, if not the importance, of dreaming in the Civil War.

Carl Jung was said to have believed the soldier on the battlefield should be removed from combat if he ceased to dream of home. It was the dream of home that left the soul intact and allowed the soldier to fight his enemy with a conscience and with humanity. That has been true since the beginning of time and is still true today. It is still the gift of the night dream of home, however "home" is defined, and the imagination that brings the soldier home safe and keeps the dream from becoming the nightmare.

Introduction

Soldiers' dreams dreamed in camp and dreams dreamed by families at home in the war were trusted advisors of life and death, war and peace. They were particularly relevant in nineteenth century American culture, where home was romanticized and revered. "Home," no matter what the actual reality, was an image of refuge and safety. Dreams in this period were printed as poems, written as songs, painted, scripted in journals and diaries and became the daily "news" in popular newspapers, one of them used as a prognosticator of how the war was going. The letters carrying those dreams back and forth in correspondence gave them the same quality of immediacy, the same flawlessness of revelation, as the increasing horror of the conditions of the reality of a war that began with hope for a short ending—and was occasionally seen even as a jolly adventure, an outing that would be over before it began—to the waking reality of a lengthy contest of grim terror that brought death, maimed bodies, disease and living conditions that deteriorated as the years wore on.

In 1864, the *Richmond (VA) Daily Dispatch* editors circumvented being asked "fifty times a day" when the war would end by turning to a "friend's" dream they felt "might throw some light on the subject." The "friend" dreamed he awoke from a fifty-year sleep and found himself on the south bank of the Rapidan River. He saw a corporal with seventeen men and a wheelbarrow and asked the corporal what all this meant: "'This,' replied the corporal, 'is the Army of Northern Virginia.' 'Where are the Yankees?' enquired the friend. 'They are on the other side of the river,' replied the corporal. 'They have the advantage of us in numbers and transportation—as they have twenty-one men and two wheelbarrows—but we expect to get the advantage in position, will whip them, and then the war will end.'" The editors of the *Richmond Dispatch* announced to their readers, a culture of men and women who believed in dreams, "This is the best and all the information we have about the probable duration of the war."[1] The dream had some truth in it. The South, undermanned and lacking the equipment and supplies of the Union army, used their superior knowledge of position to prolong the Civil War, believing till the end that they would win. They lost lives, towns, a built environment, and a flourishing landscape of people, places, and family structure in an effort to hold onto beliefs and systems that had long since ceased to thrive and which brought their own history of suffering and deprivation. The South both lost and won. Freedom was gained by those suffering in a torturous culture of slavery. And the South won a new beginning—although it came slowly and painfully and in many ways is still evolving—on the long road home that turned up again and again in their dreaming.

These dreams of home traveled across the landscapes of war—on the battlefield and

The Soldier's Dream of Home, Currier & Ives (Library of Congress, LC-USZC2-3014).

in camp—to families and loved ones waiting at home and then back again to the soldiers, waiting, longing and often homesick for contact with the homes they had left. Union general Joshua Chamberlain wrote that he could not imagine "*any body* would be *more glad* to see *any body*, that somebody to see somebody who is the constant center of his every dream & the soul of his every thought."[2] These letters recorded a time when the American culture accepted dreams as a valued indicator of life and death, of hope and sorrow, a hold on humanity that allowed them to survive horrible living conditions, loneliness, depression, and the bodily depravations of war, slavery, and prison. These dreams were, as Graves wrote, "angels of mercy."

*[S]oldier mortals would not survive if they were not blessed
with the gift of imagination and the pictures of hope.
The second angel of mercy is the night dream.*
—Henry Graves, to "Aunt Hattie,"
Petersburg, Virginia, August 7, 1862

CHAPTER 1

Playing for Keeps: Gods, Generals and Staff on the Battlefield

A great nation mourns, and a great man has fallen. Earth's best son is laid low in Death by the traitorous hand, of a demon, in human form.... The shock has paralyzed and exasperated the Nation.[1]

> Sleep hath its own world,
> A boundary between the things misnamed
> Death and existence: Sleep hath its own world
> And a wide realm of wild reality.
> And dreams in their development have breath,
> And tears and tortures, and the touch of joy;
> They leave a weight upon our waking thoughts,
> They take a weight from off our waking toils,
> They do divide our being.[2]

Major protagonists in the Civil War dreamed dreams and experienced presentiments of battle, of life, of victory, of loss, and of death. They queried husbands and wives and family and friends on the nature of their dreams, some protesting they did not believe in dreams while at the same time haunted by them, researching them in ways most comfortable for them and waiting and watching to see whether their own waking moments would validate or eradicate their messages. Men and women, no matter what their place in a regiment or their position in this terrible war, wanted to know more about dreams even when they wrote or said they didn't believe in dreams or an uncomfortable dream message caused them to say "dreams are by contraries, are they not?" They believed in dreams, intuition, omens, and the power of the imagination and the positive or negative word or feeling to turn the corner on death or life in the lonely environs of the battlefield camp or hospital. They paid attention to dreams both good and ill, watched expectantly if a dove flew through the window in a house harboring the sick or frail, and wondered if naming the bedposts brought a positive vision of a lover. Men publicly used night dreams and imaginary dreams as devices to prove a point, to drive a victory or to excuse a defeat. The most shocking and well-known "true" dream of presentiment—President Abraham Lincoln's dream of his own death—touched the hearts and minds of all who lived through the horrific events of April 14, 1865, and influenced future generations in America.

Abraham Lincoln's dream of death was not his first dream. He dreamed important dreams his entire life and often asked friends to help him unravel them. He referenced a history of dreams about his family, including one about his son Tad, an "ugly" dream that generated his sending a telegram to Mrs. Lincoln telling her to put Tad's pistol away.[3] He received dream visitations from his son Willie, who had died at the age of twelve (both Tad and Willie were ill at the same time, but Tad survived).

Lincoln was said to have shared with Colonel LeGrand Cannon of New York—a staff officer in the regular army, Department of Virginia, with headquarters at Fort Monroe—a dream about Willie. As chief of staff, Colonel Cannon had the privilege of spending time with President Lincoln, who had come to Fort Monroe to discuss the lack of harmony between the army and the navy. Lincoln occupied Colonel Cannon's room during his visit and the colonel performed the role of secretary during Lincoln's brief stay. Colonel Cannon viewed his own interesting position as the only gate open for communication with the rebel government. According to the story, the day after the president's arrival the president asked if the colonel had either the Bible or Shakespeare. Both were available. Lincoln chose Shakespeare that evening and read alone for several hours. Then he asked if he could read aloud and read to Colonel Cannon from *Macbeth*, *King Lear* and *King John*, finally "reading the passage where Constance bewails to the King the loss of her child." According to Colonel Cannon, Lincoln's voice trembled and he asked the colonel if he had ever dreamed of a lost friend and felt that in that dream he was "having a sweet communion with that friend and yet a consciousness that it was not a reality." Cannon admitted that most people had those dreams. "So do I," responded the president. "I dream of my dead boy, Willie, again and again." What struck the colonel was not the president's dreams but that Lincoln felt such total sorrow the president was "completely overcome" and "wept as only such a man in the breaking down of a great sorrow could weep." The colonel wept with him and then quietly left the room. Lincoln never spoke to him again of the dreams but the colonel felt he had been the recipient of a sacred trust that evening.[4]

The nation's best record of Abraham Lincoln's dreams is a memoir, *Recollections of Abraham Lincoln*, written by his friend and aide Colonel Ward Hill Lamon, who was confidant for what he called Lincoln's "kinship with the shades," a history of dreaming dreams and experiencing presentiments that both elated and disturbed Lincoln in "astonishing" ways. Lamon acknowledged that Lincoln's rapidly sliding scale of dreaming—from the high to the low—was part of a culture that accepted and believed in the "marvelous."[5] William Herndon wrote that Abraham Lincoln grew up in a culture that "believed in these things.... With them he walked, talked, and labored, and from them he also absorbed whatever of superstition showed itself in him thereafter." Lincoln's early Baptist training, according to Herndon, led him to his trust in dreams and visions but also instilled fatalism in him, leaving decisive action on his dreams unbalanced. Lincoln's birth culture embraced superstition, and Lincoln was impressed with the many varieties available. He visited voodoo fortune-tellers in New Orleans in 1831, and he took his son Robert to Terre Haute, Indiana, to be cured by the "mad-stone" of the bite of a mad dog.[6]

Lamon's story of Lincoln "dreaming through the veil that hides the future," in which Lincoln was given detailed warnings of his own death, began on the eve of his renomination to the office of president. Lincoln was in Baltimore at the War Department, so involved with telegraphic communication with General Grant in Richmond that he was unaware he had been renominated. When he was made aware of it, the occasion triggered a memory of a vision that had occurred just after his 1860 election. He shared a story with his secretary John Hay and later with Lamon of resting on a lounge in his chamber at Springfield and seeing two faces, each his own, in a mirror. One face was an image of himself full of good health and "hopeful life," the second revealed a ghostly presence, pale and lifeless. He played with the image, bringing it up at will, each time seeing the image and watching it vanish. He then unsuccessfully tried to force the image to appear when he was in the Executive Mansion. Lincoln believed the double image, visible only in Springfield, was a big vision, revealing safe passage through his first term as president but signifying death in the second, ghostly, image, which he interpreted to be his second term in office. This mirror vision, explained Lincoln, was why he was unaware of the renomination. Renomination, he believed, was foreordained by the vision of the two faces. Lamon wrote that from that time forward, Lincoln sealed his own fate and crippled his ability to change the forecasting of his subsequent dream of death. The president thus moved through his second term and all its pivotal events "awaiting the inevitable hour of his fall by a murderous hand."[7] Herndon wrote that Lincoln's dance with fatalism was one that "ran through his being like the thin blue vein through the whitest marble." (Mary Todd Lincoln, after her husband's death, told Herndon that Abraham's philosophy was "what is to be will be, and no prayers of ours can reverse the decree.") Lincoln shared his belief of doom with family and friends, telling Herndon, "I am sure I shall meet with some terrible end" and citing the case of Brutus and Caesar, arguing that Brutus was forced by laws "and conditions over which he had no control" to kill Caesar. Lincoln quoted a line to Herndon: "There's a divinity that shapes our ends, Rough-hew them how we will."[8]

Lincoln's most startling and accurate presentiment dream occurred only ten days before his assassination. Its detail, in hindsight, was extraordinary; and the level of concern it gave the president was notable. What was missing was the important and vital information on where and how Lincoln was to die. Could he—or would he—have made an effort to change the outcome of this dream if it had revealed the where and how? If Lamon's assessment of the mirror vision was accurate, it might explain that Lincoln, even after exhaustive self-interpretation, allowed the dream to manifest in such deadly fashion because he was paralyzed by the 1860 mirror vision, which he perceived as unchangeable destiny.

A lithograph published by Currier and Ives in 1864 might contradict that opinion. In the cartoon a sleeping image of Lincoln, tormented by dreams of defeat in the election year, is visited by "Liberty" brandishing the head of a black man at the door of the White House and driving Lincoln out with her foot. The caption reads: "Coming events cast their shadows before." Lincoln took warning and fled in this image, wearing the disguise of a Scotsman's cap and cape. The lithograph alluded to a waking incident prior to his 1861 inauguration in which he took a night train and disguised himself in similar attire.[9] Apparently heeding warnings in life and in dreaming was not a foreign notion to Lincoln. But buoyed by confidence and belief when the "good health" mirror image accurately predicted his winning the election, Lincoln then accepted the "ghostly ... lifeless" second image without question or effort to dispel it in any way.

Lincoln shared his memorable presentiment dream of someone dead in the White House with Lamon, and Lamon wrote in his memoir that he recorded the dream as shared, particularly noting the president's melancholy. Mary Lincoln was present and tried to cheer up President Lincoln. His response was that there was much in the "Bible about dreams." Lincoln had found sixteen chapters in the Old Testament and at least four or

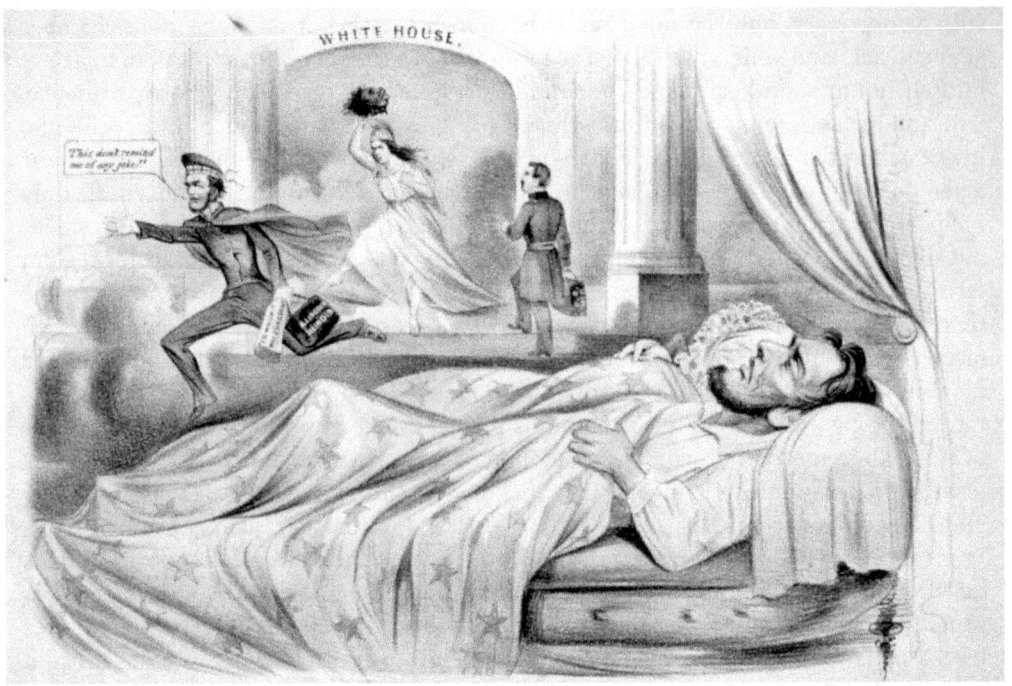

Currier & Ives, *Abraham's Dream* (Library of Congress, LC-DIG-ppmsca-19400).

five in the New Testament in which dreams were mentioned and many other chapters that referred to visions. He was looking for veracity in dreaming and was impressed that God and angels appeared to ordinary men in dreams, revealing significant information. In a conversation with Mary on whether or not *he* believed in dreams, Lincoln replied, "I can't say that I do." But he then revealed he had one that had "haunted me ever since." His search through the Bible had begun upon waking from that dream. He had opened the book again and again at random, a practice Robert Moss calls "Bibliomancy,"[10] checking for confirmation on the truth of the disturbing dream. The pages fell open to Genesis 28, and Lincoln's eyes fell on Jacob's important dream of Bethel. Lincoln closed the Bible and opened it again and again, each time encountering a new dream or vision: "I kept on turning the leaves of the old book, and everywhere my eye fell upon passages recording matters strangely in keeping with my own thoughts—supernatural visitations, dreams, visions, etc." This revelation frightened Mary; her husband revealed the depth of his own fears, referencing the menacing nature of the dream as being like "Banquo's ghost, it will not down."[11]

Mary insisted on hearing the dream. After some hesitancy, accompanied by deep melancholy, Lincoln began: "About ten days ago I retired very late." He had been awaiting dispatches from the front. He was weary but began to dream as soon as he slept. "There seemed to be a death-like stillness about me," he recalled, then he heard "subdued" sobs, "as if a number of people were weeping." He thought he left his bed and wandered downstairs, still hearing sobbing, but he could not see the mourners. He wandered from room to room, seeing no living person but still hearing the same terrible sounds of mourning. There was a light in the rooms, revealing familiar objects, but he still could not find the source of the sounds of such grieving "as if ... hearts would break." He became more alarmed, desperate to find the meaning and cause of such grief. Finally arriving at the East Room, he entered and saw before him "a catafalque, on which rested a corpse wrapped in funeral vestments. Around it were stationed soldiers who were acting as guards, and there was a throng of people, some gazing mournfully upon the corpse, whose face was covered, others weeping pitifully." He asked, "Who is dead in the White House?" The answer came from one of the soldiers: "The President ... was killed by an assassin!" At that response, the burst of grief was so loud it awakened him.[12]

He told Mary that although it was "only a dream" he had been concerned since then. Mary was horrified by the dream. Lincoln asked her to "try to forget it." Lamon said the East Room dream was "so in keeping with other dreams and threatening presentiments of" Lincoln's that he Lincoln was "profoundly disturbed by it." He referenced it frequently in conversation with others but tried to excuse it by saying it was not him in the dream that was killed but someone else, a dream person who was not really him at all.[13]

Lincoln also referenced a repetitive dream, one more accommodating because its timing became an omen for Union victory, dreamed always just before important engagements that ended in success: Antietam, Gettysburg, the night preceding the firing on Fort Sumter, the battles at Bull Run, Vicksburg, Stones River and others. In each of these dreams Lincoln saw a "ship sailing away rapidly, toward a dark and indefinite shore, badly damaged, and our victorious vessels in close pursuit." He saw "the close of a battle on land, the enemy routed, and our forces in possession of vantage ground of incalculable importance."[14] The last time he dreamed this dream was the night before his assassination. There was a cabinet meeting in which Grant was present. Seward was absent, in bed with serious injuries suffered from a carriage accident detailed by Elizabeth Blair Lee, wife of naval commander Samuel Phillips Lee.[15] Grant had not heard from General Sherman but was expecting hourly a dispatch announcing Johnson's surrender. Lincoln told him the news would come soon and would be important. When Grant asked him how he knew that, Lincoln told him about the recurring dream that happened before "every event of great national importance. It portends some important event that will happen soon." He shared many instances of the dream. Grant was said to question Stones River as a victory, but the president said facts did not matter, that the dream preceded the fight and if victory did not follow, the event and results were equally important. Lincoln insisted that this time the dream related to Sherman, for he knew "of no other very important event which is likely just now to occur" and he had the "strange dream again last night."[16]

Uncommonly cheerful, the president left the cabinet meeting and invited Mary for an afternoon carriage drive. He felt the war had come to a close and he told Mary they must try to be "more cheerful in the future." He laid out plans for that future, which included a return to Springfield and his old law practice. He was joyful. Mary Todd Lincoln recalled a similar joy just before their son Willie had died.[17]

John Hugh Bowers, a Lincoln biographer, wrote that Tad Lincoln agreed with his mother: "'Father has never been happy since we came to Washington.' His laughter had failed, he had aged rapidly, his shoulders were bent, dreadful dreams had haunted him, and on the night of the 13th he had one which oppressed him. But the next day was the fourth anniversary of the evacuation of Fort Sumter: Good Friday, April 14. And at last he was happy, sharing with his people the joy that came with the end of the war."

That evening the Lincolns went to Ford's Theatre, where at 10:20 p.m., April 14, 1865, John Wilkes Booth fired the shot that killed the president.[18] The Grants were to have been with them, but because of an urgent sense of presentiment of danger experienced by

Julia Dent Grant they changed their minds and left Washington that day. Thus a young officer, Major Rathbone, and the lady engaged to him, both of them thereafter ill-fated, went instead. The theatre was crowded; many officers returned from the war were there and eager to see Lincoln.

The play was *Our American Cousin*, in which the part of Lord Dundreary was afterwards developed and made famous. Sometime after 10 o'clock, at a point in the play it is said no person present could afterwards remember, a shot was heard in the theatre and Abraham Lincoln fell forward upon the front of the box, unconscious and dying. A wild-looking man who had entered the box unobserved struck a knife at Major Rathbone, who tried to seize him. Then the man jumped from the box to the stage, caught one of his spurs in the drapery and fell, breaking the small bone of his leg. He rose, shouted, "Sic semper tyrannis," the motto of Virginia, disappeared behind the scenes, mounted a horse waiting at the stage door, and rode away."[19]

That evening, just after the president was assassinated, Mary exclaimed, "His dream was prophetic."[20] Secretary Gideon Welles, present at the cabinet meeting, noted in his diary that great events did indeed follow his ship of state dream as Lincoln predicted, "for within a few hours the good and gentle as well as truly great man who narrated his dream closed forever his earthly career."[21]

President Lincoln understood dreaming on a far deeper level than he purported when he told Mary that he did not believe in dreams. He believed and understood dreaming. He confused his mirror image dream with fate or destiny, which paralyzed his thinking. But he believed that dreams and presentiments were part of the natural order and that they had an "extraordinary character he ascribed ... to the Almighty Intelligence that governs the universe." He also believed the "common people," in touch with their natural instincts and feelings, were the best interpreters of their own dreams.[22] He counted himself among those ordinary people. "Yet," as Robert Moss writes, "he was unable to take action based on his dream to avoid the tragedy that it portended ... one of the 'what ifs' of history."[23]

Dreams and Generals

Wandering to Those Dreadful Battlefields: General Robert E. Lee

Robert Edward Lee (1807–1870), the son of Revolutionary War officer Henry "Light Horse Harry" Lee III, graduated at the top of his class at the United States Military Academy in 1829. He was an officer and combat engineer in the United States Army for thirty-two years. During that time he married Mary Anna Randolph Custis (1808–1873). When the state of Virginia voted for secession from the union in April 1861, Lee followed his home state, despite his desire for the country to remain united. President Lincoln had invited Lee to command the Union army before Lee's decision to remain with the vote of his home state.

The most solid evidence to support the oft-quoted phrase that supposedly came from Lee's dying lips—"Strike the tent"—survived in the "recollections" of Captain Robert E. Lee, his son: "A southern poet has celebrated in song these last significant words ... and a thousand voices were raised to give meaning to the uncertain sound, when the dying man said, with emphasis, 'Tell Hill he must come up!' These sentences serve to show most touchingly through what fields the imagination was passing; but generally his words, though few, were coherent; but for the most part, indeed, his silence was unbroken."

What remained of Lee's recorded life was an astonishing treasure of journals, accounts, letters, and documents, all attesting to the boundless kindness and graciousness of Confederate general Robert E. Lee. After surrendering to General Ulysses S. Grant and relinquishing the Confederate army at Appomattox Courthouse on April 9, 1865, General Lee relinquished the life he had known before the war and poured his wisdom and considerable patience into the supervision of his college as the president of Washington and Lee University. Mary Custis Lee's ancestral home, Arlington, was lost in the vengeful decisions in the days of furious accountability. Mary fought relentlessly for Arlington, stunned that she would never see her beloved childhood home again. Her battle was won, far too late, after her death; and her son, devastated by the destruction of centuries-old trees and gardens felled for a cemetery of suffering and loss, chose to sell the house and move on with his life. Accounts of General Lee's last days, written by relatives, including those of his wife, Mary Custis Lee, and his son Captain Robert E. Lee, quoted above, supported the story of General Lee's returning home from Washington College on Wednesday, September 28, 1870, attending a vestry meeting at Grace Episcopal church, returning to his house, and sitting down at the table, where he found himself unable to speak. Physicians were called and Lee spoke a few words and short sentences off and on until the afternoon of October 10, when his pulse became more feeble and rapid. On October 11 he declined more rapidly and died on the morning of October 12, shortly after 9:00 a.m.

Mary wrote a letter to a dear friend, summing up his last hours. She felt a "sublime resignation" in him during his last hours, defined in his countenance. She wrote that she never forgot that look: "He never smiled, and rarely attempted to speak, except in dreams, and then he wandered to those dreadful battle-fields … [and] at last sank to rest with one deep-drawn sigh. And oh, what a glorious rest was in store for him."[24]

Dreaming to Inspire Union—Creative Visioning by Charles W. Alexander

In a culture that took dreams to heart, it was not surprising to find an entrepreneur creating dream "visions" to stir American memory and patriotism while at the same time financing a personal enterprise. This effort to dupe the American people, successful in part, spoke to the nineteenth century's quick belief in a dream but also, sadly, became a device that could undermine "real" dreams and play on the notion that dream information could be tossed aside as "only a dream."

A Philadelphia journalist, Charles W. Alexander (1836–1927), published *The Soldier's Casket*, a periodical for Union veterans of the Civil War. He used the pen name Wesley Bradshaw and wrote vision and dream pieces as broadsides, featuring famous American figures. The dream pieces bore remarkable similarities to one another, and they were offered for sale as advertisements in the periodical. Newspapers quickly picked them up and spread them across the country, giving mass credence to the "dreams" created by Wesley Bradshaw and their famous "dreamers": President George Washington, John C. Calhoun, and General George McClellan, and including various fictitious pieces by Abra-

GENERAL M'CLELLAN'S DREAM.

BY WESLEY BRADSHAW. (pseud.) Charles Wesley Alexander

(ORIGINALLY PUBLISHED IN THE DOLLAR WEEKLY NEWS.)

Two o'clock of the third night after General McClellan's arrival in Washington to take command of the United States Army, found that justly celebrated soldier poring over several maps, and reports of scouts.

As the hour came tolling through the night, together with the dull rumbling of army wagons and artillery wheels, the wearied hero, pushing from him his maps and reports, leaned his forehead on his folded arms upon the table before him, and fell into a sleep so deep that even the occasional booming of the heavy guns, being placed in position on the entrenchments, was insufficient to disturb it.

"I could not have been slumbering thus, more than ten minutes," said the General, to an intimate friend, to whom he related the strange narrative, "when I thought the door of my room, which I had carefully locked, was thrown suddenly open, and some one strode to me, and, laying a hand upon my shoulder, said, in a slow, solemn voice:

"'*General McClellan, do you sleep at your post? Rouse you, or ere it can be prevented, the foe will be in Washington!*'

"Never before in my life have I heard a voice possessing the commanding and even terrible tone of the one that addressed to me these fearful words. And the sensation that passed through me, as it fell upon my ears, and I coweringly shrunk into myself at the thought of my own negligence, I can only compare to the whistling, shrieking sweep of a storm of grape-shop, discharged directly through my brain. I could not move, however, although I tried hardly to raise my head from the table. As a sense of my willingness, and yet helplessness to make answer to the unknown intruder oppressed me, I once more heard that same slow, solemn voice repeat:

"'*General McClellan do you sleep at your post?*'

There was a peculiarity about it this time; it seemed as though I—a mere atom of matter—was suspended in the centre of an infinite space, and that the voice came from a hollow distance all around me. As the last word was uttered I regained, by some felt and yet unknown power, my volition, and with the change, the grape-shot-discharge sensation in my brain ceased, and a strange but new one seized my heart; one as of a huge, rough icicle being sawed back and forth through and through me.

"I started up, or rather I should say I thought I started up, for whether I was awake or asleep I am utterly unable to decide. My first thought was about my maps, and, before my eyelids had half opened my hand was grasping them. But this was all. The table was still before me, and the maps, all crumpled in my tightening clutch, were still before me; but everything else had disappeared. The furniture was gone, the walls of the apartment were gone, the ceiling was not to be seen. All I saw was the tableau I am about to describe to you.

"My gaze was turned Southward, and there, spread out before me, was a *living map*, yes a *living map*, that is the only expression I can think of as befitting the scene. In one grand *coup d'œil* my eye took in the whole expanse of country, as far south as the Gulf of Mexico, and from the Atlantic ocean on the east to the Mississippi river westwardly.

"Before fully fixing my attention upon the immense scene, however, I thought of the mysterious visitant, whose voice I had heard but a moment previous, and I looked toward him. An apparition stood on my left, somewhat in front, at a distance of about six feet from me. I sought for his features, hoping to recognize him. But I was disappointed, for the statue-like figure was naught but a vapor, a cloud, having only the general outlines of a man.

"This troubled me, and I was turning the matter over in my mind, when the shadowy visitor, in the same slow, solemn tone as before, said:

"'*General McClellan, your time is short! Look to the Southward!*'

"I felt unable to resist this command, even had I wished to do so, and again, therefore, my eyes were cast over the *living map*.

"Out on the Atlantic I saw the various vessels of the blockading squadron looming up with the most perfect distinctness in the bright moonshine, that illumined everything with a strong, but mellow light. I saw Charlestown Harbor and its forts, with their pacing sentinels, and their sullen looking barbette guns. My eyes followed the Ocean line all the way round into the Gulf, to New Orleans, and thence up the Mississippi. Fort Pickens, and, in fact, every fortification along this water boundary, I beheld with as much distinctness, as you, sir, see that Corporal's guard passing there.

"This sight filled me with delightful surprise; but it would be utterly impossible for me to describe the ecstatic amazement that followed, as, within the limits I mention, my eyes took in, in minute, but lightning-like detail, every mountain range, every hill, every valley, every forest, every meadow, every river, every rivulet, every city, every village, every camp, every tent, every body of men, every sentinel, every earthwork, every cannon, and, I may say, dispensing with further detail, every living and every dead thing, no matter what its height or bulk.

"My blood seemed to stop in its channels with joy, as I thought, that the knowledge, and thereby advantage, thus given to me, would insure a speedy and happy termination of the war. And this one idea was engrossing my mind, when, once more, that slow, solemn voice said:

"'General McClellan, take your map, and note what you behold. Tarry not; your time is short.'

"I started, and, glancing at the unearthly speaker, saw him extend his arm and point Southwardly.

"Still I saw no features.

"Smoothing out the largest and most accurate one of my maps, I seized a pencil, and once more bent my gaze out over the *living map*.

"As I looked this time, a cold, thrilling chill ran over me, and the huge, rough icicle again began its sawing motion through my heart. For, as, pencil in hand, I compared the map before me with the *living map*, I saw masses of the enemy's forces being hurried to certain points so as thwart movements that, within a day or two, I intended to make at *those identical points*; while on two particular approaches to Washington I beheld heavy columns of the foe posted for a concentrated attack, that I instantly saw must succeed in its object unless speedily prevented.

"'Treachery! treachery!' cried I, in despair. And, as before my blood seemed to stop in its channels for joy, it now did so for fear. Ruin and defeat seemed to stare me in the face. At this dreadful moment that same slow, solemn voice struck once more upon my ears, saying:

"'General McClellan, you have been betrayed! and, had not God willed otherwise, ere the Sun of to-morrow had set, the Confederate flag would have floated above the Capital and your own grave. But note what you see. Your time is short! Tarry not!'

"Ere the words had left the lips of my vapory Mentor, my pencil was flying with the speed of thought, transferring to the map before me all that I saw upon the *living map*. Some mysterious and unearthly influence was upon me, and I noted and recorded the minutest point I beheld without the slightest effort, delay or mistake.

"At last the task was done, and my pencil dropped from my fingers.

"For awhile previous to this, however, I had become conscious that there was a shining of light on my left, that steadily increased until the moment I ceased my task, when it became in an instant more intense than the noonday Sun.

"Quickly I raised my eyes, and never, were I to live forever, should I forget what I saw. The dim, shadowy figure was no longer a dim, shadowy figure, but the glorified and refulgent *Spirit of Washington, the Father of his country, and now a second time its Saviour*.

"My friend, it would be utterly useless for me to attempt to describe the mighty, returned spirit. I can only say that Washington, as I beheld him in my dream, or trance, as you may choose to term it, it was the most God-like being I could have ever conceived of.

"Like a weak, dazzled bird, I sat gazing at the heavenly vision. From the sweet and silent repose of Mount Vernon our Washington had risen, to once more encircle and raise up, with his saving arm, our fallen, bleeding country.

"As I continued looking, an expression of sublime benignity came gently upon his visage, and for the last time, I heard that slow, solemn voice, saying to me something like this:

"'General McClellan, while yet in the flesh, I beheld the birth of the American Republic. It was, indeed, a hard and bloody one, but God's blessing was upon the nation, and therefore, through this, her FIRST GREAT STRUGGLE for existence, he sustained her, and with His mighty hand brought her out triumphantly.

"'A century has not passed since then, and yet the Child Republic has taken her position, a peer with nations whose page of history extends for ages into the past. She has, since those dark days, by the favor of God, greatly prospered. And now, by very reason of this prosperity, has she been brought to her SECOND GREAT STRUGGLE. This is by far the most perilous ordeal she has to endure. Passing, as she is, from childhood to opening maturity, she is called on to accomplish that vast result, Self-conquest, to learn that important lesson, Self-control, Self-rule, that in the future, will place her in the van of power and civilization. It is here that all nations have hitherto failed, and she too, the Republic of the earth, had not God willed otherwise, would, by to-morrow's sunset, have been a broken heap of stones cast up over the final grave of human liberty.

"'But her cries have come up out of her borders like sweet incense unto Heaven, and she will be saved. Then shall peace once more come upon her, and prosperity fill her with joy. But her mission will not then be yet finished, for, ere another century shall have gone by, the oppressors of the whole earth, hating and envying her exaltation, shall join themselves together and raise up their hands against her.

"'But if she still be found worthy of her high calling, they shall surely be discomfited, and then will be ended her THIRD AND LAST GREAT STRUGGLE for existence!

"'Thenceforth shall the Republic go on, increasing in goodness and power, until her borders shall end only in the remotest corners of the earth, and the whole earth shall, beneath her shadowing wings, become a Universal Republic. Let her in her prosperity, however, remember the Lord, her God; let her trust be always in Him, and she shall never be confounded.'

"The heavenly visitant ceased speaking, and, as I still continued gazing upon him, drew near to me, and raised and spread out his hands above me. No sound now passed his lips, but I felt a strange influence coming over me. I inclined my head forward to receive the blessing, the baptism of the Spirit of Washington.

"The following instant a peal of thunder rolled in upon my ears, and I awoke. The Vision had departed, and I was again sitting in my apartment, with everything exactly as it was before I feel asleep, with one exception.

"The map, on which I had dreamed I had been marking, *was literally covered with a net-work of pencil marks, signs, and figures.*

"I rose to my feet, and rubbed my eyes, and took a turn or two about the room, to convince myself that I was really awake. I again seated myself; but the pencilings were as plain as ever, and I had before me as complete a map and repository of information as though I had spent years in gathering and recording its details.

"My mind now became confused with the strange and numberless ideas and thoughts that crowded themselves into it, and I voluntarily sank down on my knees to seek wisdom and guidance on high. As I arose, refreshed in spirit, the same solemn voice seemed to say to me, from an infinite distance:

"'*Your time is short! Tarry not!*'

"In an instant thought became clear and active. Hastening out couriers, with orders to have executed certain manœuvres at certain points, (*guiding myself by that, now, in my eyes, unearthly map,*) I threw myself into the saddle, and long ere daylight, galloping like the tempest from post to post and camp to camp, had the happiness to divert the enemy from his object, *which, my friend, I assure you, would have proved entirely successful, by reason of the last piece of treachery, had not Heaven interposed.*

"That map is locked upon by no human eye, save my own, and, therefore, treachery can do no harm. *I have on it every whit of information that I need, information that the enemy would give millions to keep from us.* The fate of the war is settled.

"The rebellion truly seems very formidable, but it is only struggling in the path of an avalanche. The mighty, toppling mass of National power and retribution will, until the proper moment comes, now and then let slip down upon its victim forerunners of its approach. And when the proper moment does come, it will sweep down upon, and forever annihilate treason with a thunder that shall reverberate throughout the world for ages upon ages to come.

"*Sir, there will be no more Bull Run affairs!*

"God has stretched forth his arm, and the American Union is saved! And our beloved, glorious Washington shall again rest quietly, sweetly in his tomb, until, perhaps, the end of the prophetic century approaches that is to bring the Republic to her THIRD AND FINAL STRUGGLE, when he may, once more laying aside the cerements of Mount Vernon, come, a messenger of succor and peace, from the Great Ruler, who has all the nations of the Earth in keeping.

"But the future is too vast for our comprehension; we are the children of the present.

"*When Peace shall again have folded her bright wings, and settled upon our land, that strange unearthly wonderful map, marked while the spirit eyes of Washington looked on, shall be preserved among American archives as a precious reminder to the American Nation, of what in their* SECOND GREAT STRUGGLE *for existence, they owed to God and the Glorified Spirit of Washington.*

"Verily, the ways of God are above the understanding of man."

***General McClellan's Dream*, broadside by Wesley Bradshaw (Duke University Libraries Digital Collections, Broadsides and Ephemera Collection, Folder DC1, #bdsdc10139).**

ham Lincoln, Jefferson Davis, Ulysses S. Grant, and others. In each of three dreams or visions of Washington, Calhoun, and McClellan, the protagonist falls asleep, dreams or has a vision in which a prophecy of great magnitude is presented in a form that gets the dreamer's undivided attention. In the George Washington vision, published in the *National Tribune* in 1880, the president falls asleep at Valley Forge and is visited by an angel who reveals a prophetic vision of America. The dream vision was not only a fraud, but George Washington had died before his dream made the rounds across America. To give credence to the dream, Bradshaw claimed that a soldier, Anthony Sherman, supposedly at Valley Forge during the winter of 1777–1778, heard and shared the dream story. No documents supported this account. The soldier *did* serve in the Continental Army, but his pension documents place him at Saratoga under the command of Benedict Arnold at the end of 1777 and in New Jersey in 1778 just before the Battle of Monmouth.

In the published dream vision, George Washington, not shown in any account of his life as being particularly religious, had gone into a thicket to pray and ask comfort from God. In words supposedly from Anthony Sherman, a pale and shaken Washington emerged from his quarters and related an extraordinary story of sitting at a table, engaged in a dispatch, and looking up to see a beautiful female. Having given orders not to be disturbed, the astonished Washington felt strange sensations coursing through his body as he asked her purpose. In an equally sensation-saturated environment, the presence finally made a statement: "Son of the Republic, look and learn." She extended her arm toward the east, where Washington was presented a vaporous vision of all the countries of the world. Saying "look and learn" again, the female visitor pointed toward a dark, shadowy being like an angel, floating in mid-air between Europe and America, sprinkling water, flashing lightning, repeating the vision two more times, adding more land, villages, battles, and finally a crown of light, on which was traced the word "Union," bearing the American flag, which he placed between the divided nation. The angel said, "Remember ye are brethren," and again, "Son of the Republic, look and learn." Then a trumpet blast, more battles, burning villages, a long bugle blast, and bright glowing suns bursting over America. Over the head of one of the angels shone the word "Union." The angel, holding the American flag in one hand and a sword in the other, descended among the people of America, who took courage and claimed victory in these battles. The burned villages were reborn, the people were restored, and the angel proclaimed, "While the stars remain, and the heavens send down dew upon the earth, so long shall the Union last."

To extend this vision into his next broadside versions of these political dreams, Bradshaw presented the angel announcing that three great perils would befall America before true Union was achieved, the greatest and most fearful being the third [revealed in the McClellan vision as the Civil War]. The angel exited at this point in the dream vision.[25]

Nullification and John C. Calhoun: The Dream of Union Continues

Bradshaw's John C. Calhoun dream bridged the gap between the Washington and McClellan dreams, which taken together were to bring full circle the Washington version of achieving "true Union." In the John C. Calhoun dream, political associates breakfasted with Calhoun and noticed him gazing at his right hand and nervously brushing it. When questioned about it, he supposedly revealed a dream in which he saw a large black spot on the back of his right hand. When pressed further—in this version by political associate

Robert Toombs of Georgia (the character role played by Anthony Sherman in the Washington dream)—Calhoun revealed the rest of the dream.

Calhoun's vision began, as with Washington in his dream, with Calhoun sitting in his room writing when he was astonished by the intrusion of a cloaked visitor who sat down opposite him and asked, "What are you writing, senator from South Carolina?" Calhoun responded that he was writing a plan for the dissolution of the American union. Then the visitor asked to look at Calhoun's right hand, revealing himself as General George Washington and asking if this would be the hand he would use to sign papers for the dissolution of the union and again addressing him as "senator from South Carolina." When Calhoun answered "yes," a large black blotch appeared on the back of his hand. "That," said the visitor, "is the mark by which Benedict Arnold is known in the next world." Saying no more, the visitor laid on the table a skeleton—the bones of Isaac Hayne, "who was hung at Charleston by the British. He gave his life in order to establish the Union." Hayne was a South Carolinian "and so was" Calhoun. "There was no blotch on his hand," the visitor said. With these words, the visitor disappeared and left Calhoun to ponder the vision.[26]

The background for this "dream" was the nullification crisis that erupted over the protective tariffs designed to raise import taxes on goods coming from foreign countries, making those goods more expensive than goods produced in the United States. This tariff would have benefitted new industry in the north but would have raised prices for goods purchased by those in the mainly agricultural south. When Congress passed the protective tax in 1828, Vice President John C. Calhoun wrote an anonymous protest declaring a state's right to nullify a law unproductive to its future. This position threatened the unity of the United States and split South Carolina's political system into a States Rights Party (the Nullifiers) and a Unionist Party. In a compromise the tariff was lowered; South Carolina repealed the nullification. States Rights, however, became a rallying cry for southern states against laws unsatisfactory to their economy. These events thirty years before the Civil War brought forward the idea of secession. John C. Calhoun tempered his arguments, but his death in 1850 left holding the reins a younger generation of reckless politicians known as the "fire-eaters," whose ties to the federal government were less strong and less rational.

McClellan's Dream of the Living Map: Advancing Toward True Union

Moving forward into the Civil War and the third "dream" in the Bradshaw series newspapers had reported that the Union cause was saved by McClellan's dreaming of Washington, bringing the dream cycle back to the first dream.[27]

The year 1862 had opened with the republic in dire straits. General George B. McClellan had taken command of the U.S. Army. In this "dream," he arrived in Washington and went to work studying maps and reports in the early morning hours when he fell asleep with his head resting over his folded arms. The door was thrown open, and a man walked in and demanded, "General McClellan, do you sleep at your post? Rouse you, or ere it can be prevented, the foe will be in Washington." Like the prior "dreamers," McClellan experienced strange feelings of being suspended in space, with everything except the maps vanishing. One map became a "living map" of America, showing troop movements and patterns of the Confederate lines that would enable McClellan to quickly end the war. Then he saw the enemy in positions known only to him, meaning his plans were known by the Confederates. The voice spoke again: "General McClellan, you have been betrayed! ... Your time is short." Taking heed of these dream words, McClellan drew what he saw on his paper map that was lying on the table. As he did so, the voice materialized into George Washington, who soliloquized (all of the words recalled by the dreaming McClellan) on a panorama of events, with God's blessing on the American Republic through early struggles and now to a "second great struggle ... until her borders shall end only in the remotest corners of the earth, and the whole earth shall ... become a Universal Republic."

A blessing was bestowed, thunder roared, and the general awoke to find the map covered with the marks and information he had recorded in the dream. According to the dream report, McClellan's actions taken as a result of the "living map" saved the capital and the union in 1862.

The war, as promised in this third dream, was *not* speedily won; and the July 19, 1862, edition of the *Richmond Daily Dispatch*, biased and itself not totally reliable on political news, questioned the veracity of the McClellan dream. However, the editors recognized the dream motif from the John C. Calhoun dream and, tongue firmly in cheek, doubted that any "Yankee" would be privy to any conversation from such a notable Virginian as George Washington. The editor pondered, "Wonder if the map embraced the Chickahominy swamp! We suspect the only spirit that visits McClellan is one that he is a little too fond of calling from the "vasty deep" of the distilleries; and that, in this condition, he mistakes Old Scott, (who considers himself equal to George Washington.) showing him a map of Virginia, for the Father of his Country. A man must certainly be very drunk to make that mistake."[28]

A more detailed investigation by the American Psychical Research Institute in the early twentieth century used the Portland, Maine, version of the McClellan dream for cycling back to the work of Wesley Bradshaw."[29]

The reality of that year was that dissolution of the union hung in the balance of the Civil War. In a stroke of luck, General Lee's orders detailing the Confederates' plan for the Antietam/Sharpsburg campaign near Frederick, Maryland, fell into General McClellan's hands on September 13, 1862, when the 27th Indiana camped on the site of a Confederate camp. Sergeant John Bloss and Corporal Barton Mitchell found a piece of paper wrapped around three cigars. The paper was addressed to General Hill and was headed "Special Order No. 191, Headquarters, Army of Northern Virginia." This would have been the pot of gold for McClellan but once again McClellan failed to act quickly. Bruce Catton, Civil War historian, observed that no general in the war "was ever given so fair a chance to destroy the opposing army one piece at a time." Caution destroyed action. McClellan overestimated the number of troops under Lee's command and took eighteen hours to set his troops in motion, giving Lee time to be alerted to the full situation. The war continued for three more years.

Broken Mirrors and Never Turning Back: Dreaming and Superstition in the Lives of General Ulysses S. Grant and Julia Dent Grant

Julia Dent married Lt. Ulysses Grant in 1848. In the years 1843 and 1844 Ulysses had begun an intense courtship that escalated to weekly visits when he was in the area of

Julia's home. He was aware of Julia's quick wit, intelligence and beauty, but he also became aware of Julia's attachment to folkloric precautions and fairies and her flawless track record of dreaming precognitively. On an early spring visit Ulysses had obtained a leave of absence to visit his home and say good-bye before he left the area. He visited Julia and brought her his class ring, formally asking her to wear it. In her reminiscences, Julia recalled Grant's saying that if he gave any ring to a lady it would be a stand-in as an engagement ring. The offer startled Julia and she recalled replying that her mama would not allow her to take such a gift from a gentleman. She was not thinking of him as a "lover" yet and her response put him off. He left her house but asked her to continue to think of him.

Ulysses, a lieutenant at that time, left with orders to go to Louisiana. Julia, aware he was away down the Mississippi, knew he would not be back in his usual barracks, but she rode out hoping that he was still nearby for their usual Saturday visit. She held her horse there for some time, waiting and listening, but sadly rode back home when no one came. Realizing that her handsome and attentive lieutenant meant more to her than a fleeting courtship, Julia consciously set a dream intent. She wanted to see him again. Julia had a new bed and believed in a popular superstition—naming the bedposts, a device sure to seal the dream intention and bring a dream of one's true love. The new bed had been set up in the morning and the superstition held that whatever the occupant dreamed the first night in a new bed would come true. Julia recorded that "Josephine S." (a friend who was spending the night) and she, "according to custom, named the bedposts, and of course my absent friend was not forgotten." The "naming" was of the one who was desired to appear in the first dream. Julia named a bedpost Ulysses and later said, "I did dream of Mr. Grant. I thought he came at Monday noon and was dressed in civilian clothes. He came in, greeted us all most cordially, and seated himself near me; when I asked him how long he would remain, he said: 'I am going to try to stay a week.'" Julia immediately shared the dream with friends, all of whom said it would come true; but Julia protested that it could not come true because Ulysses was sailing down the Mississippi, "far below the mouth of the Ohio."—or so she thought. Monday morning arrived. The day progressed into the afternoon and Julia's maid came to her and pointed toward the gate where Lt. Ulysses Grant was seen arriving, uncharacteristically in civilian clothing, just as she had seen him in her "bedpost" dream.

Julia pulled herself together and later wrote that she met Ulysses in the drawing room. Certainly aware of a dream coming to fulfillment, she tested its information and asked Ulysses how long he planned to remain. He replied that he would try to stay for a week. Julia's sister, apparently unable to contain herself, announced that these were the same words Julia had dreamed. Ulysses asked Julia if she had been dreaming of him and she confessed to naming one of the bedposts after him and that her entire dream was falling into place: "[H]e had returned at noontide, replied to my question as to how long he would remain, and was dressed in citizen's clothes. On inquiring how he happened to be dressed so, he told me he was wearing borrowed plumage; that he had plunged into Gravois Creek and was nearly drowned, was of course very wet and had to borrow dry clothing from brother John, who lived some two miles from us." What she was not told was that Ulysses was equally as superstitious as Julia. His men wrote that once he started forward, whether it be on a march or in a battle—or just crossing a creek—he believed it was bad luck to turn around on a path or during a journey and go back. So Ulysses would have never returned to camp and put on his own dry clothing. Thus, unwittingly, he played out a crucial element in Julia's dream: "Lieutenant Grant remained just a week in Missouri. Nearly all of the time was spent at our house ... [and] he declared his love and told me that without me life would be insupportable."[30]

Remaining with stories from the 1840s, Julia recalled a dream that in her mind was triggered by reading George Sand's description of a reception in Venice in *Consuelo*. She was also thinking about Mardi Gras in New Orleans. She wanted to go but her papa had not permitted the trip. She dreamed she was in New Orleans. She could hear the "hurrahs, salutes of cannon" and see the flags and carpets spread for her and her party. She recalled the dream many years later in 1880 when she and Ulysses returned from a hero's trip around the world, which brought them finally from Mexico to New Orleans. They were greeted by trains filled with people, loud salutations, a gun salute and shouts, as well as flowers, "flags, banners, and garlands." As in the dream from almost four decades earlier, carpets were rolled out for them to walk upon.[31]

In her reminiscences, Julia described her need to verify and validate dreams. She described her distress at not having heard from Ulysses for a month [in the 1840s]. Usually he sent letters out of Mexico so that they arrived in a consistent manner. Julia had dreamed "the Monday morning paper was handed me and there the second name in the D's in the list of advertised letters was Julia Dent-2. I was leaning out of the window when the paper was handed to Sister Nell, who had just gone to the front door. I called down to her not to open the paper until I told her my dream, that she must look at the second name in the D's in the list of advertised letters and see if it was Julia Dent-2; and sure enough, there it was, and I lost no time in sending for those two very nice letters."[32]

Julia confessed that belief in fairies was one of her more persistent superstitions. Her daughter Nellie was born on July 4, 1855, in a house owned by her brother Louis. Referring to her daughter as a "little fairy," she described the good wishes everyone heaped on her and the blessings of beauty, wealth, and good health called on her through the beneficence of "good fairies."[33] In a second story of fairies, Julia described being left churning butter with a dasher. She had asked a servant, Phyllis, to bring cold water for cooling the butter. Not gone ten minutes, Phyllis returned to find that the butter had "come"—equally superstitious Phyllis concurred that the fairies had been there and helped Julia with the churning.[34] As Julia wrote that story, she turned more serious, attributing her belief in fairies to handling a particular bout of despondency, lifting it from her heart so thoroughly that she never again lost courage, not even in the darkest hours of her life: " You will say I am superstitious, but once, soon after we had moved up to the new log house on the Captain's farm, I was feeling quite blue (which was rare with me), when a feeling of the deepest despondency like a black cloud fell around me, and I exclaimed (aloud, I think): 'Is this my destiny? Is this my destiny?' ... All at once the dark shadow passed away and a silvery light came hovering over me, and something seemed to say, 'No, no, *this* is not your destiny. Cheer up, be happy now, make the best of this. Up and be doing for your dear ones.' That was my last dark visitor."[35]

Ulysses took heed when intuition or dreams, folkloric superstition or fairies guided Julia's surroundings. Just after her marriage to him, Julia sobbed with fear when they moved into a new house and found an heirloom mirror broken when she opened the moving box. The mirror had been in her father's house for fifty years: "I cried and sobbed like a child when I saw this. The Captain, in place of being impatient with me, tried to soothe me, saying, 'It is broken, and tears will not mend it now.' I sobbed out: 'It has always been at home, and then it is such a bad sign.'" This meant someone would die within the year, a folk belief that dated to the Roman Empire.

According to Julia's reminiscences, Ulysses knelt gently beside her and suggested that perhaps the breaking of the mirror did not cause misfortune to come. She said "no," it did not cause the misfortune but foretold misfortune. The astute Captain Ulysses S. Grant carefully suggested that since the broken mirror did not bring the misfortune that Julia had no cause for such grief. He also suggested, even more astutely, that they take each fragment of the broken mirror and have them made into single and separate mirrors, thereby breaking the manifestation of the foretelling of bad fortune. Julia agreed.[36]

In the first year of the Civil War, Julia recalled a dream that followed a visit the "Captain" made to Kentucky to see his family and George McClellan. Ulysses had asked Julia to open his letters and forward those that seemed important. "One night," she wrote, "I dreamed at three separate and distinct times ... I received through the mail a peculiar package from which, upon opening, an old and familiar ring of my mother's (which I had always considered mine, but which was claimed by my sister at my mother's death) tumbled out, wrapped up in tissue paper, and, as I loosened the paper, the little ring flashed out bright stars on the surrounding paper." Julia interpreted the dream as meaning she would finally receive the ring. Instead of the ring, she received a letter addressed to "Colonel U.S. Grant, Official Business." She said she did not immediately recognize the difference in rank but opened the letter and found a sheet of vellum, "the face of which was entirely covered with tissue paper, and as I raised my hand to draw down the tissue covering, I exposed to view the great seal of the State of Illinois, which is spangled over with stars; just as in my dream, the little ring flashed out its starry light. A prophecy of mamma's, made long ago, now came vividly to my mind. This then was the meaning of my dream. Mamma had sent her little diamond ring as a reminder, and so I interpreted it." The letter contained the commission of U.S. Grant as colonel of the 21st Illinois Volunteer Infantry.[37]

Julia, always vigilant in supporting her husband's advances, added to this story, saying that her mother was present in the house in the summer of either 1856 or 1857 when the nation was in an uproar over admitting states as slave or free. Her mother had been resting in a room with Julia and her sister Nellie when she arose from her rest, pointed the finger with the same ring toward them, and said she had been given a prophecy that "that little man will fill the highest place in this government. His light is now hid under a bushel, but circumstances will occur, and at no distant day, when his worth and wisdom will be shown and appreciated. He is a philosopher. He is a great statesman. You will all live to see it, but I will not." Julia claimed that Nellie asked if their mother meant Nellie's husband and their mother said she meant Captain Grant.[38]

A significant dream captured a perilous moment in Ulysses' life after Colonel Grant moved to Missouri and then to Cairo, Illinois. He had asked Julia to visit him there and to bring the children, now four in number. Nervous and frustrated, Julia decided to go into a room alone and rest. As soon as she settled down she "saw Ulys" a few rods away but only his head and shoulders, as though he were on horseback. He also looked at her in what she thought was a reproachful manner. She awoke and called out his name: "Ulys!" Her friend in the next room answered her but assured Julia on hearing about the episode that Julia was just nervous about the journey. Before they left for the remaining leg of the trip they heard about the battle of Belmont. Ulysses met Julia at the train and she said that she had seen him in a dream on the day of the battle. He asked the hour of the vision, and when she told him the hour, he responded, "That is singular. Just about that time I was on horseback and in great peril, and I thought of you and the children, and what would become of you if I were lost. I was thinking of you, my dear Julia, and very earnestly too." Julia said, "I told him I thought the look was almost reproachful."[39] Julia was told that Richmond had fallen. She replied it had not, because it would not fall until her husband led his army through.[40]

Julia's stronger intuitive "feelings" saved her husband's life when he was invited and expected to accompany President Lincoln to the theater. The feeling was not the difficult relationship between Mary Lincoln and Julia Grant; it was a strong, abiding intuitive feeling of danger that drove Julia, according to her *Reminiscences*, to insist that Ulysses leave an important cabinet meeting immediately upon closing business and take a carriage for a train home rather than leave for the theater. Julia couldn't let go of a "freak" obsessive feeling of specific danger, and both Julia and Ulysses knew to trust her long-standing accurate association with her dreams, her feelings, and her intuition.

The series of events began unfolding when a strange young man took a position near the door to her room. His dress was an odd mixture of fabrics and he wore a shabby hat. Julia did not trust him. The young man said he was sent by Mrs. Lincoln and that she would call for Julia at 8:00 to go to the theater. In an instant flash of presentiment of danger, Julia declined and, without thinking further, said that she and General Grant would be leaving the city that afternoon. The young man reminded her that the newspapers had announced that General Grant would be with President Lincoln at the theater. Julia defiantly ordered the man to give Mrs. Lincoln her new message. She thought later that his demeanor and a strange parting smile should have clued her that he was part of something that was dangerous.

Julia sent a note to General Grant telling him she wanted to go home that evening and then she followed the note with three messengers from his staff. She was now desperately sure that they both needed to leave. Ulysses sent word back for her to pack her trunks and they would leave immediately for Philadelphia. At a late luncheon four men sat near Julia and her luncheon companions. She noticed odd eating behavior. One of them, for example, was holding a spoon near his mouth but never ate. The same man rode past the Grant's carriage later in the evening, glaring through the carriage glass.[41]

Long after Lincoln's assassination, Julia and Ulysses S. Grant took a year (1877) for a trip around the world. In her travelogue notes, Julia shared stories of riding elephants, eating unusual cuisine and giving and receiving elegant gifts. Climbing a rough mountain road, Julia watched General Grant in the advance and recalled an extravagant daydream from her youth in which she was reading "aloud *History of the Conquest of Mexico* by [William H.] Prescott."[42]

In one of her last dreams recorded in her reminiscences, Julia was back in America, where she sadly related a vision in Washington in which she "looked down upon a great throng surging up the avenue leading from Pennsylvania Avenue towards the White House. In the midst of this throng of moving people was an open carriage drawn by four prancing horses, and seated in this carriage with his pretty wife beside him was one dear to me. The carriage drove on and stopped at the portals of the White House. The trees were green and the air was balmy as I looked down on that pageant. After that, I gave no more thought to the subject, as I knew General Grant was not to be there, nor was I."[43]

These reminiscences shared a strong sense of Julia's belief in the destiny of Ulysses Grant and of her destiny alongside him as his wife. She envisioned success, warnings of danger, and safe passage through difficult times and onward through a grand hero's march around the world and back again to dreamed-of acclaim in the streets of New Orleans and, happily and sadly, in the halls—and not—of the presidential mansion.

"Let us cross over the river...": Thomas [Stonewall] Jackson

Much has been written about Thomas "Stonewall" Jackson—his life, his military prowess, his sense of duty and responsibility, the intense loyalty of those who fought and died for and with him and his devotion to God. Jackson supported his nation's flag until his state seceded; complicated politics changed the direction of his loyalties. Secession brought equal and intense devotion and an intense sense of duty to his state, to the position of the South, and to his personal role in General Lee's cause.

What is often not revealed in the accounts of the brief but critical role Jackson played in the Civil War South is the story of his adoration of his second wife, Mary Anna Morrison, and his devotion to his young daughter, Julia, including his moving dream of Julia's first steps. His first wife had died in childbirth just a year after their marriage. His letters to his second wife, whom he fondly called "my darling," "my little wife," and "my *esposa*," were filled with gratitude for her love, her life and their baby. His relief on the survival of both of them in childbirth was palpable. Jackson wrote letters to his wife during their courtship and continued writing whenever they were separated by any event, large or small. His first letter, dated April 1857, to Anna was from his home in Lexington to her home, Cottage Home, in North Carolina. Anna and Thomas had agreed to marry. He spoke of his gratitude to God "for all the sources of natural beauty with which he has adorned the earth," the songs of birds and "all animated nature," which disposed his thoughts toward meditation and ultimately to Anna, whom he described as "a gift from our Heavenly Father."[44]

After their marriage, his devotion to Anna continued unabated. When she was away for health reasons, Thomas wrote to his "little dove" about his "sad heart" at her absence in the house and spoke to her as though she were present, sharing his love for her, sending her flowers from her garden, specifically ones just opening so that they would arrive in a preserved state, ready to open and delight her.[45] When the war separated them, loneliness for Anna deepened, described by Thomas as a loneliness "for which he can hardly account, but he knows if his darling were here he wouldn't feel this.... I follow you in mind and heart."[46] Anna had moved in with neighbors after Thomas's departure but at his wishes closed their Lexington home and moved back to Cottage Home with her parents in North Carolina. Anna was able to make a brief visit to his camp in August 1861 and he wrote about the enduring memory of her "dear face" long after she was gone.[47]

By the fall of 1862 Thomas was in charge of over half the Army of Northern Virginia, had acquired the nickname "Stonewall," and was as popular as a rock star might be today. Men stopped what they were doing and cheered when he made an appearance. "A Georgia sergeant in one of Longstreet's regiment noted of the post–Antietam period: 'One day ... I heard cheering down the road in our front. Some of the boys thought it was Stonewall Jackson or a rabbit.... Everyone made for the road and sure enough, it was Gen. Jackson galloping along the road with his escort. He passed us with his cap off and the cheering continued down the line as far as we could hear.... He certainly creates more excitement than all of the rest of the officers put together."[48] However, praise and fame were not the highlight of Thomas Jackson's life; the birth of a healthy baby girl on November 23, 1862, was his shining star.

Anna sent a letter, "written" by his new baby, delighting Stonewall's imagination and charging his desire to hold her in his arms: "My own dear Father, as my mother's letter has been cut short by my arrival, I think it but justice that I should continue it. I know you are rejoiced to hear of my coming, and I hope that God has sent me to radiate your pathway through life. I am a very tiny little thing. I weigh only eight and a half pounds, and Aunt Harriet says I am the express image of my darling papa…. My hair is dark and long, my eyes are blue, my nose straight just like papa's…."[49]

He doted on his baby but had only a few chances to hold her in his arms. Letters revealed that he would not put her down on these few visits. He could not bear to let go of her. He wrote longing letters wishing to see her "funny little ways" and wishing he could hear her "squeal with delight" after Anna wrote him a story of her joy at seeing little chickens for the first time.

The last letters exchanged between Anna and Thomas included one from Thomas with a much-cherished dream of his daughter. Like most soldiers' dreams, this dream was so real he could see his baby taking her first steps, moving along from one table and chair to the next, making her way from her mother's arms into his and reaching out her arms to kiss him: "Last night I dreamed that my little wife and I were on opposite sides of a room, in the center of which was a table. And the little baby started from her mother, making her way along under the table, and finally reached her father. And what do you think she did when she arrived at her destination? She just climbed up on her father and kissed him! And don't you think he was a happy man? But when he awoke he found it all a delusion. I am glad to hear that she enjoys out-doors, and grows, and coos, and laughs. How I would love to see her sweet ways! That her little chubby hands have lost their resemblance to mine is not regretted by me."[50]

Thomas "Stonewall" Jackson was moved by this dream, by his child's kiss, which he could feel on his face, and saddened by the dream's disappearance upon his awaking. Anna sent her last letter on April 20, announcing her intention to come and visit. She later recounted her memory of this last visit:

> Little Julia was nearly five months old now, and was plump, rosy, and good, and with her nurse, Hetty, we set out upon this visit, so full of interest and anticipated joys…. [T]aking his baby in his arms, he caressed her with the tenderest affection, and held her long and lovingly. During the whole of this short visit, when he was with us, he rarely had her out of his arms, walking her, and amusing her in every way that he could think of…. He was frequently told that she resembled him, but he would say: "No, she is too pretty to look like me." When she slept in the day, he would often kneel over her cradle, and gaze upon her little face with the most rapt admiration, and he said he felt almost as if she were an angel, in her innocence and purity. I have often wished that the picture which was presented to me of that father kneeling over the cradle of that lovely infant could have been put upon canvas.[51]

Thomas died a month later, shot by his own men in early morning when it was still dark, in the post-battle confusion at Chancellorsville when "Stonewall" and several of his staff rode out in front of the Confederate lines to gather information about "enemy dispositions." Nervous pickets, thinking Jackson and his staff were a column of the Union army, opened fire, mortally wounding Stonewall Jackson and several others of his staff.[52] Journals written by men at Chancellorsville expressed mourning; words of men who knew Stonewall only by reputation described the loss of this great man. Two of hundreds wrote, "Today we were pained by the melancholy news of the death of our heroic & beloved leader Lieut. Gen. Jackson. He died this evening about 3 pm"; "I expect you have heard of the mourning … of the death of our brave General Jackson. He was shot by our own men. It is beyond all doubt. We all lament his loss."[53]

The image of his young daughter and sweet wife were engraved in Thomas's memory and he was comforted by his intense devotion to his God and to an eternity that sustained him and about which he wrote in every letter. There, blessed peace awaited him. He understood "presentiment" and felt the presentiment of survival on numerous occasions, a possible explanation of his extraordinary confidence on the battlefield. After the Battle of Sharpsburg [Antietam], Robert Lewis Dabney wrote, "During this terrible conflict, General Jackson exposed his life with his accustomed imperturbable bravery, and communicating his own indomitable spirit to his men. Yet he said to a Christian comrade that on no day of battle had he ever felt so calm an assurance that he should be preserved from all personal harm through the protection of his Heavenly father."[54] Jackson also understood both the earthly finality and the promise of last days. His final words were said to have been, "Let us cross over the river, and rest under the shade of the trees."

The Heart of a Soldier: General George Pickett

Controversy on authenticity beats at the heart of General George E. Pickett's letters published by his third wife, LaSalle Corbell Pickett, in the early twentieth century.[55]

General George E. Pickett was born in Richmond, Virginia, in 1825, graduated at the bottom of his West Point class in 1846, and was assigned to the 8th Infantry, Winfield Scott's regiment in Mexico. He had the daring and drive that made him a hero and gave him quick advances through the ranks. By 1862 he was a brigadier general. He married twice before the war.[56] On September 15, 1863, he married a third time—LaSalle Corbell. They were married in Petersburg at St. Paul's Church. Music was called "Pickett's Chimes"—from the chiming in the belfry.

Infamy followed fame after General George Pickett's disastrous action at Gettysburg, an event that destroyed his reputation and his career. A collection of letters, reputedly written by General George Pickett to LaSalle, was edited and published after the war by Seth Moyle with the help of LaSalle Corbell Pickett. The focus of the letters was positive and affirming of a relationship recalled by LaSalle (or Sally as she was called) as a beautiful courtship flowering after a memorable first meeting, in which she recalled "my soldier," and listening to songs he sang to her as he accompanied himself on the guitar. In a romantic reverie she added that three years later, in the "Indian War, he learned Chinook and taught the Chinook his hymns and songs. They taught him theirs and they [the Picketts] sang Chinook songs to their first child after they were married."[57] The collection highlighted Pickett's successes in the San Juan Islands and ended with a positive spin on his career in the Confederate army. LaSalle added testimonials to her husband's conduct and nature from Longstreet, McClellan and even Lincoln and Grant. Much well-known information about Gettysburg was omitted. Pickett's reports were destroyed, according to LaSalle, by direct orders from General Lee. George E. Pickett died in 1875; the edited letters were published between 1908 and 1913.[58]

This compilation of letters was revered as authentic until questions arose about LaSalle's motives and possible revisions. Despite the controversy, the letters, whether edited or not or whether changed to provide a positive political spin, provide LaSalle's view of her husband, his dreams, his ambitions, and his drive. Whether authentic to Pickett's words or to LaSalle's, the letters still speak to the authenticity of the culture of dreaming and the sway a good dream or an unnerving presentiment held in 19th century America.

In a flowery testament to "presentiment" of danger on the field, LaSalle (hereafter "Sally") printed a letter supposedly penned by George the night before he was wounded at Gaine's Mill (Cold Harbor). He wrote that he had felt the spirit of his mother hovering over him all day, a familiar feeling that he had experienced in the same way when she was living. He knew that the feeling, when she was alive, precipitated the receipt of a letter, which would come into his hands at the very moment he sensed her presence. "I wonder if up there she is watching over me, trying to send me some message—some warning. I wish I knew." George's letter continued into a description of a morning brigade move from "its cantonments on the Williamsburg road and by daybreak ... marching along the Mechanicsville turnpike, leading north of Richmond. The destination and character of the expedition ... unknown.... This evening we crossed the Chickahominy and are bivouacked on our guns in the road in front of Mechanicsville." George was wounded that day and was sent home to recuperate. Recovered and returning to his command, he wrote to Sally, "[M]y heart turns to you with a love so great that pain follows in its wake.... Pray for a realization of all our beautiful dreams, sitting beside our own hearthstone in our own home—you and I, you my goddess of devotion, and I your devoted slave."[59]

Less than six months later, George Pickett proposed to Sally, begging her to marry him at once. Inspired by a beautiful morning dream, George proposed "while its glory still overshadows the waking and fills my soul with radiance." They had "no prophets," George pleaded, to share news on the end of "this awful struggle," seeing the worst of possible scenarios where he knew General Grant was the strong contender and where already so many hopes of the Confederacy had been "dashed to the winds." He used these hopeless words to beg angels to guide his pen, to "voice this longing desire of my heart," born from a beautiful morning dream, to intercede for his wish for Sally to be his wife. He added that he had to remain at his post, so she must come to him to fulfill the request. He begged her to throw tradition to the wind (and probably gossip as well) and come immediately: "You know that I love you with a devotion that absorbs all else—a devotion so divine that when in dreams I see you it is as something too pure and sacred for mortal touch. And if you only knew the heavenly life which thrills me through when I make it real to myself that you love me, you would understand. Think, my dear little one, of the uncertainty and dangers of even a day of separation, and don't let the time come when either of us will look back and say, 'It might have been.'"[60] Sally was not swayed by such an outrageous request—or by the dream—to suddenly leave home and run to a wayside camp. She coyly wrote that both of them should wait till a more suitable time.

Though it would be difficult to know if the introspective nature of many of the published letters were typical of George's writing or were embellished later by Sally, the sentiments of the summer 1863 letter reminded a nation of the advantage of stepping back from a war and seeing the humanity of both sides and feeling the potential for soul loss in a struggle so vicious, so destructive of both property and human life, and so destructive of the humanity of men. George's letter spoke to the folly of feeling puffed up as a "Conquering Hero," a confession of the wrongness of "Hurrahism":

> I can fight for a cause I know to be just, can risk my own life and the lives of those in my keeping without a thought of the consequences; but when we've conquered, when we've downed the enemy and won the victory, I don't want to hurrah. I want to go off all by myself and be sorry for them—want to lie down in the grass, away off in the woods somewhere or in some lone valley on the hillside far from all human sound, and rest my soul and put my heart to sleep and get back something—I don't know what—but something subtle and unexplainable—something I never knew I had till I had lost it—till it was gone—gone—gone![61]

George contrasted the woeful "ravages of war" and devastation of the "land where we lay dreaming" to the beautiful prosperous country with thriving fields where strong healthy horses, oxen, cows and crops thrived, where war was coming with its destructive force but where nature rebuilt with a more generous forgiveness than mankind. He wrote again and again, "I love you—love you—love you, and oh, little one, I want to see you so!" He promised Sally the day would come when the war would end and all the pretty things of the world would be hers, peppering letters with either his words—or Sally's: "Can my pretty do patchwork? If she can, she must piece together these penciled scraps of soiled paper and make out of them, not a log-cabin quilt, but a wren's nest, cement it with love and fill it with blue and golden and speckled eggs of faith and hope, to hatch out greater love yet for us."[62] These letters were written just before the battle at Gettysburg was lost, the only words on that battle included in Sally's publication of George Pickett's letters: "Well, it is all over now. The battle is lost and many of us are prisoners, many are dead, many wounded, bleeding and dying. Your Soldier lives and mourns and but for you, my darling, he would rather, a million times rather, be back there with his dead, to sleep for all time in an unknown grave."[63]

In the Wilderness before Cold Harbor in 1864, George, now married, clung to love and a vision of home with his beloved, turning to lines of favorite songs, "lying in my tent all alone, thinking of you, and while I built wonderful castles I was serenading you with the songs I love." He wrote that he sang them all and then his mind wandered to the "Salmon-Illahie" where he sang Anne Boleyn's sad song, "Oh Death, Rock Me Asleep." A camp mate, "Baird," reportedly heard Pickett singing this song and begged him to stop: "[W]hen you sing that song I haven't got a friend in the world. I'm lonesome and feel creeps and see spooks and, what's worse, I don't know whether I am Anne Boleyn herself, or am myself responsible for all poor Anne's sorrows and death." George continued: "War and its horrors, and yet I sing and whistle...."[64]

Subsequent letters claimed music as a soul-bond between George and Sally. At Cold Harbor he recalled reading to Sally from Moore's melodies, comparing them to the music of her voice and watching her "dark lashes caressing the words." Again, a few days later, he wrote that the "band has been playing the songs that we love, and inside I have been softly singing them all to you, to your spirit far away. Now they have wound up with 'Alice, Where Art Thou?' which might have set me wondering if it had not been the hour we each seek to be alone that we may bring our souls in touch. So I knew that thou wert with me...."[65]

Horror, sadness, and ecstasy came close one upon the other as George received word that his beloved 18th century family home, Turkey Hill, had been wantonly destroyed by Butler, whose ravages and destruction were well known by those clinging to the Confederacy. Ecstasy came with the successful birth of his son—July 17, 1864—and the good health of Sally after that birth. George was granted the privilege of visiting his wife and child and wrote about the "mystic power of the grasp of its tiny rose leaf fingers clutched around my own." In a defeat after the Battle of Five Forks, more agony came, written again in the words of song: "Then in the midst of these calls and silencing them, rose loud and clear dear old Gentry's voice, singing the old hymn which they all knew I loved: 'Guide me, oh, thou great Jehovah, Pilgrim through this barren land.'"[66]

"It is finished," General George Pickett wrote, "...the suffering, the horrors, the anguish of these last hours of struggle. The glorious gift of your love will help me to bear the memory of them.... Peace is born."[67]

Exiled to Canada, George and Sally Pickett remained close to one another. He was offered, and refused, command of the Egyptian army. Back in America, the Picketts built a cottage on the site of George's 1771 family home, Turkey Hill. In a rare moment of separation from Sally, George reported on the progress of the cottage and blessed Sally with dreams and guardian angels:

> The old colonial home of my forefathers, with its rare old mahoganies and paintings, which Butler sacked and desecrated and then burned, has been replaced by a sweet little cottage home built by ourselves, all our very own, and consecrated to love and contentment, with furnishings so simple and plain that we are not afraid of using them.... We must build one of hope and faith and peace and mercy and joy, the foundation of which is already laid in our hearts.... Good night—sweet dreams. Angels guard you while I hear of Lafayette and Nelson and Marshall, through the clouds of old Sims' tobacco smoke for the hundredth, yes, thousandth time.[68]

Whether these letters were written to preserve a reputation, to make a political statement, or to remind the reader of love among the ruins, they were effective and survived through the years to make a statement and to tell a story to generations following the lives and deaths of General and Mrs. George Pickett.

Dreamed She Was Riding in a Hearse: General William Dorsey Pender

William Dorsey Pender, from Edgecombe County, North Carolina, was a West Point graduate and U.S. Army career officer, devoted to responsibility, duty, and the honor of his men. In 1860 he served with the U.S. Army in Oregon and parts of the Western Territory. In March 1861 he wrote to his wife that, "bred to the profession," he could not have stood by and not taken a hand. In that same month he joined the Confederacy, serving briefly as colonel of the 3rd North Carolina Infantry Regiment and as a colonel of the 6th North Carolina Infantry Regiment before transferring to A.P. Hill's division, where he was promoted to major general. William Dorsey Pender died in July 1863 as the result of wounds received at Gettysburg. Only one letter survived from his wife, Mary Francis Sheppard Pender (called Fanny), daughter of former congressman Augustine H. Sheppard of Forsyth County, North Carolina. William and Fanny had three children, Samuel Turner, called "Turner," born November 28, 1859; William Dorsey, Jr., born April 28, 1861; and Stephen, born after William's death.[69]

William's letters to Fanny were straightforward and honest, sometimes to the point of saying too much. He was a popular and brilliant general, much admired by both the officers he served with and the men who served with him, but also, by his own self-acknowledgement, vain, attractive to women, and not complimentary enough to Fanny. He adored her but had no idea how to address the woman of his heart. This omission in his manners, if not in his soul, often left William contrite by his own admissions and omissions in letters, forced to apologize far too often because he didn't quite know when to stop writing! For example, when Fanny expressed a desire to make a flag, William replied that she could and that he would admire her for it but he found the task useless because the regiments could get as many flags as they wanted and that he was "sick" of flags, or, even worse, telling her he had been riding and thinking of her but that usually he didn't think of her at all![70]

Fanny always forgave him but never hesitated, as evidenced by her one surviving letter, to let him know how insensitive he could be. In the surviving letter, William would have known he had crossed the line before reading the letter because she penned at the top, "Read to end." He had crassly written to her about a nice time "dancing and flirting with a very nice girl." William had asked the girl to knit a sac for Fanny's hair; the girl's response was that she would not work for his wife but would do anything for him. Not letting this thread alone, he continued in the next letter, sharing that he was a favorite with "some of the ladies" and that one of them had two peaches and had given him the larger of the two. Then he had the audacity to tell Fanny the "ladies" were curious to see her. In response, Fanny admitted that she had been so angry at first she could not respond. In the letter she finally sent, she enumerated her many duties to their children, reminding him that not all her time was spent thinking of him either or writing to him. She further reminded him that she had done nothing in her life to pain him. She quoted his paragraph about his flirting with a "nice girl" and continued:

> Now, I ask you candidly, in your sober senses, why you wrote me such a thing as that? Was it to gratify your vanity by making me jealous, or to make me appreciate your love still more? You are very much mistaken. I feel indignant that any woman should have dared to make such loose speeches to my husband and that he should have encouraged it by his attentions, for you must have gone pretty far for a woman to attempt such a liberty.... [D]o you think the lady would have made such a remark in my presence? ... What would you think to hear me use such an expression? And would it be more immoral in me than in you? ...
>
> I know you love me, my dear Husband ... [and] you ask me to look over it and forget it—I have forgotten all the anger I felt at first—but I can never forget that letter—nothing you have ever said this whole of our married life—ever pained me so acutely or grieved me so deeply. I know you are sorry for it now, for you must feel it to be unjust, but it is enough to know that you could in any mood say so much to pain me.

She ended the letter with "Your faithful Wife."[71] William, properly chagrined, apologized in several letters and bought Fanny a sewing machine with a polished wooden case!

Although he never gushed in his letters (that is, when he didn't have his foot in his mouth), William sincerely expressed again and again his love for Fanny and their children and his joy in receiving letters from Fanny: "You can judge of the pleasure I enjoy in your letters by that you have in mine. They are the only bright spots in my existence. I look forward for them with feelings in accordance." He responded to a message from her, saying that she was right that he always tried to do right "for others' sake," but, recognizing his own faults, "I fear I love too much the applause of men." He wrote to Fanny almost every day.[72]

Feeling the need for a defining religious experience in his life, William frequently wrote of reading the Bible, thinking and discoursing on sin and his life and seeking a direct path to Heaven so that he and Fanny would never be parted. He expressed disappointment in himself and his inability to fully accept religious principles in his life but he worked hard toward an experience that would be as blessed and wonderful as he read about in others and as exquisite as an experience of happiness he consistently referenced under a tree near the gate at Fanny's home, Good Spring.

William wrote Fanny in May of 1861, recalling that event in a memory with Fanny in Vancouver in the spring of 1860 when they walked to church together. He recalled his joy in her as his wife and of her gift of music, even reminding her of the beauties of her voice "with that old melodeon." He remembered the anticipation of seeing their baby when they returned home. He reveled in the happiness he had with Fanny and told her he was not nearly so cold and matter-of-fact as she might think. Then he reminded her of that particular tree and gate. This event surfaced at least twice in his letters, a bit of a puzzle because it seemed to be a description of a simple, quiet moment of repose and reflection but, in William's mind, it had greater visionary import he never fully explained.

Fanny knew and appreciated the reference: "As soon as I begin to think of Good Spring I go back under that shade tree as the most perfectly happy time I ever spent—Oh! How I should like to be with you even this short day, but as it is otherwise, we will not complain." Again in June of the same year, he wrote, "It is no use for me to dream of home and quiet as long as the war lasts. But that shade tree will rear itself in my memory and oh! That happy day. Darling, I should like to know that you were well enough to enjoy it in my absence. It was the happiest moment of my life. You may think it foolish to always be talking about the tree near the garden gate." Lying on the grass beneath that tree on a summer day, surrounded by people he loved, Pender experienced something so extraordinary, perhaps a fullness of heart and life never experienced before or after that day. Whatever it was he felt—or envisioned—under that tree near that gate at Good Spring he always referenced it as "the happiest day of my life."[73]

In April 1862 William was quite taken with a dream—published in the *Richmond Daily Dispatch* of April 11, 1862—dreamt by a Pensacola soldier who "fell into a long and profound sleep" from which he could not be roused. Finally, awakening himself, the soldier said that he would die the next afternoon at four o'clock, "for so it was revealed to him in a dream." He said the dream confirmed that in the last week of the month of April would be fought the greatest and bloodiest battle of modern times "and that early in May peace would break upon the land more suddenly and unexpected than the war had done in the beginning." The Pensacola soldier died as predicted in his dream—four days later. William Pender had wished Fanny "good night and pleasant dreams to you" in his letter of April 26, 1862, and had included a message about the Pensacola soldier, asking Fanny if she had seen the account. He wrote:

> We were to have a big and severe fight the last week in April, in the first week of May peace was to ensue, and that the day after his dream at a certain hour he was to die. The latter part of his dream was fulfilled and I cannot help from being superstitious enough to think a part at least of the remainder is to come true. May the Lord, if it be his good pleasure, protect me from harm. I cannot contemplate leaving you with any degree of composure. My dear, excuse this laborious strain I am in tonight and set it down as worth nothing, but you know how impossible it is to prevent ourselves sometimes from indulging ourselves far enough to communicate our feelings to others.[74]

Sometime later William shared a dream about a soldier in camp, "Mr. Williams," who had married and had pressed William for a furlough, which he could not grant under any circumstance in that time in the war. In the dream, he, not Mr. Williams, had married, but it was to a woman not known by him in waking. He was also still married to Fanny and was "bashful" and had a hard time preventing jealousy arising between the two. Then he dreamed the next night that "Mr. Williams had got his leave and snapped his fingers in my face." The dreams seemed to mirror his own duality of passion and feelings, his unfortunate propensity for saying things hurtful to his beloved wife to consciously or unconsciously create feelings of jealousy, at the same time addressing the literal desires of young Mr. Williams, who probably would have liked to have disobeyed orders, snapped his fingers, and gone off to a new bride.[75]

Apparently not remembering his fascination with the Pensacola soldier's precognitive dream the year before, or perhaps remembering it too well, on April 1, 1863, Pender responded to a dream shared by his wife—that she was riding in a hearse and "it was a bad sign"—by telling her that he always heard dreams were interpreted by "contraries" and that "hearses indicated a wedding or something of that sort." His language, usually precise and pointed, was off-handed and turned abruptly to another subject: "We are now eating nice shad. I wish you had some." William obviously was shaken by the dream.[76] (William Pender died from wounds at Gettysburg just three short months later. Dreams by contraries rarely proved to be the case.)

William Pender had written to Fanny that "danger always looks more dangerous in the imagination than in reality."[77] Was the dream of the hearse still with him when he wrote his last letter to Fanny? In it he said, "Now darling, may our Good Father protect us and preserve us to each other to a good old age"?[78]

At Gettysburg on July 2, 1863, William Pender, brilliant in his decisions as always, was exhausted from the field. He met his friend Lt. Colonel William G. Lewis of the 43rd North Carolina and suggested that they sit on a large granite boulder at Seminary Ridge and chat while awaiting orders. Shells crashed around them, tearing apart portions of the boulder and exploding near them. William Pender suffered a terrible gash in his leg and could not mount his horse. He was placed in a wagon and his wound was bandaged. The pain was excruciating, but the wound appeared to heal as the wagon lumbered and rolled toward Staunton. Complications arose. The wound began to bleed profusely, and William improvised a tourniquet that held until a surgeon reached him. The surgeon attempted to work with the wound but an artery was damaged and continued to break apart, forcing the surgeon to do the most common and deadly surgery in the Civil War—amputation of the leg. The patient, comforted by the presence of his favorite older brother, David, lingered long enough to hear that the Army of Northern Virginia was once again on Southern soil. His last words were said to be, "My only regret is to leave her and our children," followed by a fitting valedictory for his short life and career: "I have always tried to do my duty in every sphere of life in which Providence has placed me." In a matter of hours, on July 18, 1863, William Dorsey Pender was gone.[79]

A.P. Hill mourned the "irreparable loss" of his favorite subaltern, whom he considered the best officer of his grade he had ever known, and his men also missed William Pender, "with all our hearts" and "credibly gave wide currency to the rumor 'that General Lee had said that General Pender was the only officer in his army that could completely fill the place of 'Stonewall' Jackson.'" Although such a statement was more than likely apocryphal, there is documented evidence that the commanding general definitely felt that William Pender's mortal wound had deprived the army of victory at Gettysburg."[80] Fanny supported her boys by running a school and working as postmistress of Tarboro. She never remarried. She died in 1922 at the age of 82 and was buried beside her beloved general.

CHAPTER 2

Art and Music, Artists and Illustrators: Embedded Dreamers

"...blood, carnage, and death among the sweet shrubbery and roses..."
—David Strother, Artist and Topographer

David Hunter Strother (1816–1888) wrote humorous travelogues for a variety of magazines under the pen name Porte Crayon and wrote and illustrated stories and personal reminiscences of his war experiences for *Harper's New Monthly Magazine*. He supported the Union army, and his Civil War stories, most of them published between 1866 and 1868, were prized for their objective viewpoint.

Born and raised in Martinsburg, Virginia (now West Virginia), David Strother married Ann Doyne Wolff, a Martinsburg girl, in 1849 and had a daughter, Emily. After Ann's death (1859) he married Mary Hunter of Charles Town in 1861. They moved to Berkeley Springs, (West) Virginia, and he accepted a commission in the Army of the Potomac under the command of General David Birney. David Strother was assigned to General Nathaniel Banks's staff during the 1862 Valley of Virginia campaign. When John Pope arrived in Washington to command the Army of Virginia, Strother was called in as General Pope's topographical expert because of his detailed knowledge of the Shenandoah Valley. He was promoted to lieutenant colonel of the 3rd West Virginia Cavalry, later joining McClellan's staff in time for the campaigns at South Mountain and Antietam. McClellan was replaced, and David joined Banks's staff in Louisiana for the Port Hudson and Teche campaigns. He returned to Washington in 1863, was promoted to colonel of his regiment and joined General Benjamin Kelley during the winter of 1863–64. In 1864 he served General Franz Sigel as a staff officer and then served as chief of staff under his cousin, General David Hunter, during the Lynchburg Raid. Hunter was replaced by General Sheridan, and David Strother resigned.[1] Increasingly disillusioned by the war, Sigel and Hunter, he felt, were the last straw in his long experience of a collection of officers whose faults were more outstanding than their work in the field: "What are all our popular great men but fetishes compounded of mud, sticks, and feathers, furnished by our passion-led fancies, worshipped for the nonce, and when the furor which created them is over, cast into the fire and trampled under foot with the ashes of the past."[2]

With disgust and realism, David recorded the charred ruins of war, both human and environmental, but was occasionally surprised by a spontaneous generosity of spirit that gave him perspective and hope. In one such story, anticipated destruction by "rugged looking fellows" fumbling among books around a church organ turned into a tugging-at-the-heartstrings story of those same soldiers opening hymn books and "fifty accordant voices" rising in an anthem.[3]

Juxtaposing life and metaphor, he wrote about magnificent houses turned into hospitals, the amputation tables sitting side by side to the piano—or the piano itself serving in the purpose of amputation: a "gentleman's dwelling" rendered a "butchers' shambles," there was "blood, carnage, and death among the sweet shrubbery and roses."[4] In another house, owned by the one Reverend Slaughter, David witnessed the complete destruction of a rare library when the Rebels found some correspondence by Northern men on colonization. He saw blowing in the wind "fragments of an illustrated Italian work of *Il Vaticano*. The furniture was equally destroyed."[5]

After citizens were arrested for singing "Bonnie Blue Flag" David wrote, "We are a small people and delight in small things."[6] In this constant uproar of destruction, much of it senseless, men slept and dreamed in spite of conditions that would ordinarily deny sleep. Exhausted during a ride that allowed only brief pauses, David held the reins of his horse and attempted to sleep behind some bushes. The whistle of balls and musketry aroused him and he moved behind the front lines till daylight: "Here I found a sheaf or two of wheat, and lying down upon it with the bridle rein in my hand I slept and dozed for an hour or two while my mare amused herself eating my bed. The moon sailed grandly through the heavens, edging with silver some picturesque banks of clouds to the west. At each moment a shooting star would mark the blue firmament. The red planet Mars was in the ascendant. Tomorrow was Sunday, the great battle day."[7]

A few nights later, amidst the chaos of Bull Run and still suffering from sleep deprivation, he later wrote, "I delivered my orders and went into the vestibule of the courthouse to sleep. Lying upon a long box I was told by a guard that there was a dead man in that box. I replied that my lying there would not disturb his rest. So I stretched out to sleep, but presently a man came with hammer and nails to close the lid, so I sought a place in the tavern. It was filled with wounded. Amputations and dressings were going on and the floors were clothed with blood. There were no groans or outcries, however. In a vacant pantry I found a board upon two barrels and upon this I slept for two hours."[8] Slightly more tolerable opportunities arose for sleep as the year dwindled to its end. In December he was grateful for respite on the steamer *North Star* in New York. He found a dirty mattress in an upper bunk, "there being no other cover," and slept, to dream "of being hunted by Confederates and making desperate defense from houses and log cabins," a dream suggestive of his waking condition.[9]

David's dreams, he said, all had a "rehearsal," or precognitive, quality. He dreamed of grand "panoramas" of scenes unfolding before him and smaller dreams of "my sweet friends at home."[10] An important precognitive dream visited him in the winter of 1864 in the New Market area: "At night I dreamed that I was in Richmond with the Federal forces, having approached that city from the west. Our force was small and our mission to destroy all public stores, mills, factories, and railways. Met some friendly people there and some indifferent ones, all poor and ruined. I rode among the manufactories and was anxious for the burning to begin, but waked up before it began."[11]

Following this dream report were pages of entries recording destruction of property, confusion, burning of houses and towns, plundering, and the destruction of Virginia Military Institute (VMI) in the summer of 1864. In disgust, David Strother debated the benefits of the imagination and penned a diatribe on its being the "greatest cause of cowardice," arguing that men will only nobly face danger when it is visible but stampede like wild animals when there is "fancied terror." Fully in contempt of the war by the late summer of 1864, he ranted against an army "petted by friends of humanity, demagogues, and sanitary commissions."[12] Just days later, David Strother had had enough of war, took six months' pay, went to a saloon and drank four large glasses of "abominable" beer, stating, also in contempt, "This great nation of thirty millions cannot be governed by a faction of extremists."[13]

Imagination Is More Than One-half of Realization: Embedded Artist Henry Mosler

Henry Mosler (1841–1920) worked as an "embedded" illustrator and correspondent for *Harper's Weekly* between June 1861 and November 1862. His family moved to New York from Poland in 1849, when Henry was eight years old, and then to Cincinnati, Ohio, in 1851, where Henry was apprenticed as a teenager to a wood engraver. After studying drawing and working as a draughtsman for a comic paper, the *Omnibus* in Cincinnati, in 1855 he moved on to study under James Henry Beard and obtained work with *Harper's Weekly* in 1861. Henry kept a diary in 1862, in which he recorded impressions, observations, and stories in his service as aide-de-camp to General R.W. Johnson of the Ninth Indiana Volunteer Regiment. In a separate sketchbook Mosler discussed a method he was perfecting for lightening the background and brightening features of faces so that they stood out more clearly. He headed his note with a quote: "Imagination is more than one half of Realization." A news clipping from the *Chicago Herald* of May 22, 1892, read, "Henry Mosler's pictures. There is a soul and human sympathy in them."[14]

The illustrated notebook/sketchbook included sketches of dreams, like fathom thoughts, scattered here and there among the pencil sketches. One of the dreams was precognitive of the end of the war, a dream conversation between Mosler's mother, Sophia, and Abe Lincoln: "[1] Dec. 1862 I dreamed that Old 'Abe' was sitting in our room talking with my mother Mother asked him how soon he thought the war would be over, he answered—*not before I'm out*—meaning the Presidency—Also dreamed about J.L. (I afterwards found that she the same night dreamed of me)."[15] The Abe Lincoln dream was interesting because most people in the early years of the war believed that the war could not last more than a few months and certainly not more than a year. Abe Lincoln died three years later, thus ending his presidency. The war ended in the same few months in 1865. Mosler sketched a quick line drawing of a common bed style, possibly mislabeled in editor's notes as a draft for Mosler's *The Assassination of General Nelson by General Jefferson C. Davis*. The drawing was included in the sketchbook in 1862, the same period as Mosler's recording of his mother's dream conversation with Lincoln. The sketch may have been Mosler's drawing of someone (Mosler) lying in bed dreaming of Lincoln, and his mother, Sophia, sketched lightly behind the bearded head [Lincoln?] that is sketched near the bed. If so, this sketch of Mosler dreaming of a conversation between Lincoln and his mother would be an eerie presaging of Lincoln's 1865 assassination dream, pictured in a similar bed.

Mosler scribed two more dreams in the same grouping with his Lincoln dream, much like his incomplete draft sketches, offering a simple record with no additional commentary.

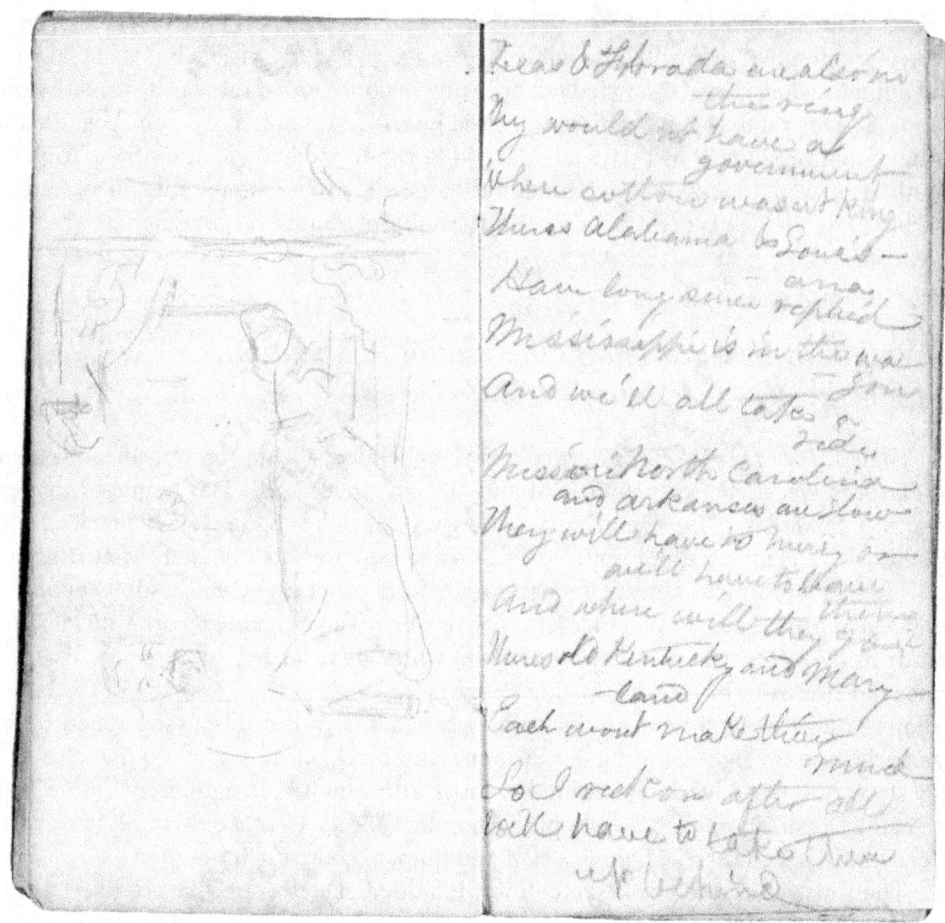

Henry Mosler Civil War diary, 1862 (Archives of American Art, Smithsonian Institution. Series 3: box 2, folder 16, Image 21).

"[2] I dreamed my brother had come home but was very sick—but not dangerous He also told us that the Doctor had given 52 kinds of Medicines—I also dreamed some fellows where going to knock down my father when I immediately started in the store room in which my father was rushed for a hatchet and was ready to defend him but he as it appears heard them talk what they where going to do and when I entered he asked me what those fellows had said, and I told him, he answered bold, let them come."[16] No explanation followed.

Setting the Taste of Patriotism: Currier and Ives

Nathaniel Currier and James Ives identified themselves with the creators of "things Americana" in the sentimental age of the Civil War. They advertised "cheap and popular prints," ultimately producing more than seven thousand prints that sold millions of copies. They were not aspiring to great art but to have their lithographs hanging in every home, store, barroom, firehouse, and barn in America.[17]

Nathaniel Currier began his business in the 1830s when lithography was a new challenge. In 1840 he produced the first of his series of disaster prints, depicting the sinking of the steamboat *Lexington* in Long Island Sound, which took the lives of over one hundred people. A reproduction of the print in the *New York Sun* made him famous. In the 1850s, James Merritt Ives married into the Currier family and became a bookkeeper for the company. He proposed the idea of marketing prints that "presented the plain daily experiences and pleasures of American life"—the prints familiar to everyone today. The Civil War provided endless opportunities for what became more than two hundred prints. Most illustrated battles and disasters. The two men honed their marketing skills by researching the attitudes of their primarily Northern consumers, focusing on the Republican party and Abraham Lincoln, whose dreams and created visions were sold in both serious and cartoon-like productions.[18]

In researching the attitudes of the American public, the sentimental image of home and the connection of home and the dreams of the soldier sleeping on the battlefield and the family sleeping at home dreaming of the soldier did not escape Currier and Ives. They exploited both home and patriotism in lithographs such as *The Union Volunteer* (1861), *The Flag of Our Union* (1861), *The Spirit of 61/God, Our Country and Liberty* (1861), *The Brave Wife* (undated) and *The Soldier's Dream of Home* (1862) and the companion print, *The Soldier's Home, The Vision* (1862). Most Americans had never traveled far beyond their home, and now their sons, husbands, brothers, and friends were going far away from home to fight a war with an impact not envisioned.

The Soldier's Dream of Home, 1862, imagined the soldier's dream as the link between the soldier and home. The soldier [Union] is asleep on the ground, a letter from home beside him. Above him is the "dream," being at home with his wife and child. In *The Soldier's Home, The Vision*, the soldier as a patriotic hero and a savior of the nation appears while the loyal soldier's wife dreams of her gallant, brave husband leading his fellow soldiers into battle. He carries the American flag, a symbol of the Union. The lithograph of the soldier's dream influenced letterhead and envelopes, one depicting a Zouave soldier asleep on the ground dreaming of home.

Currier and Ives added romanticized battle scenes such as *Bombardment of Fort Sumter* (1861), which showed the American flag flying high above the fray and smoke. They blamed the seceding states for the nation's troubles and placed emphasis on Northern righteousness. In support of abolition they published *Freedom to the Slaves* and, in *The True Issue, or That's What's the Matter* (1864), they pictured Lincoln and Jefferson Davis having a tug-of-war over a map of the United States. Lincoln proclaimed, "No peace without abolition." Davis responded with, "No peace without separation." McClellan stands between them, holding each by the lapel and preventing their further tearing the map. McClellan proclaimed, "The Union must be preserved at all hazards."

Emancipation remained a divisive issue for the duration of the war, especially in Currier and Ives' New York City, where news of the proclamation and the draft ignited riots during the summer of 1863. That it remained a campaign issue the next year is seen in Currier and Ives' *Abraham's Dream: "Coming Events Cast Their Shadows Before"* (1864), described in the dreams of Lincoln. LeBeau suggested this lithograph might be better titled *Lincoln's Nightmare*; the president "is shown sleeping on a bare mattress under a starred sheet, dreaming that he has been defeated in the 1864 election.... The disguised Lincoln carries a suitcase and the Emancipation Proclamation and exclaims, 'This don't remind me of any joke,'" another reference to Lincoln's tendency to make untimely jokes.

"*The Soldier's Home, the Vision*" (New York, Currier & Ives, c. 1862, Library of Congress Prints and Photographs Division Washington, D.C., 20540 USA, Call number: DSO-3598-4506).

George McClellan, suitcase in hand, climbs the steps to the White House. After Lincoln's victory in 1864, the successful conclusion to the war a year later, and, of course, his assassination, Currier and Ives pictured the Emancipation Proclamation more favorably. Lee's surrender to Grant at Appomattox Court House on April 9, 1865, prompted a surge of Union patriotism but, attempting a nonjudgmental attitude, Currier and Ives pictured the now deceased Lincoln with George Washington—one as founder of the nation, the other as its savior.[19]

After the war, Currier and Ives followed a confusing path, vilifying Southern resistance to Reconstruction but also critical of the Republicans for their harsh policies against the South. Le Beau noted that the lithograph team seemed to forget why the war was fought and even sampled the fare of Jim Crow by issuing the *Darktown* series, vicious "race prints" of over one hundred individual "comics," which the company insisted were intended as humor. Currier and Ives lost momentum in new technologies and changes in American taste and closed their doors in 1907.[20]

"*Conscripts—seen in a Soldier's dream*"—*Laura Leupp*

Laura Leupp moved easily between the social life of New York City and South Carolina, enjoying travel and friendship with such notable personalities as William Cullen Bryant. Laura's father, Charles M. Leupp, made and lost a fortune and became headline fare when debts and his declining fortune led him to suicide at the conclusion of the Civil War.

Laura continued to travel, in company with her mother and sisters as well as with Bryant and his daughter, Julia, enjoying the art and landscapes of great European cities. During the Civil War, Laura dabbled in political cartooning, one of her most peopled cartoons displaying a crowded scene of "conscripts" as "seen in a Soldier's dream." The motley crew, all in civilian clothing, all rounded up for service and entering camp, walk grudgingly behind a Union officer riding on horseback. Comments by three of them appear in the conversation bubbles: a black man, in slouch hat, thinks to himself, *I's in pretty company, I es*; a large gentleman, wearing a silk hat and smoking a cigarette as he ponders his options, settles on finding a way out of the dilemma—"Double Quick! That is, No! Yes! Damn Me! No!"; and a clergyman cries, "Oh Lud! Oh Lud!" Other stereotypical characters include an Indian wrapped in a blanket; a Chinese man with a long pony tail; a Lincoln look-alike; a young man holding his belly; an eager man leaping into the procession as his wife pulls him back by his coattails; and many others. In the background, a soldier stands by a cannon on an overlook, projecting their futures in combat.

Music in the Midst of Madness

In a dreaming culture such as that shared by soldiers in America's Civil War, dreams permeated all parts of the culture; art, music, literature, theater, and daily entertainments picked up the theme of the soldier dreaming of home on the battlefield or of families dreaming of their loved ones. Music of all kinds, played on a variety of instruments, was part of camp life and helped pass lonely and longing nights. Everyone sang; many had instruments and played. Almost every soldier's letter to home and almost every letter to him from home described a musical instrument, a song, or the effect of music on the battlefield or in the parlor. Dreams of home inspired hundreds of poems and songs. Titles of songs drifted into ordinary language in letters and memoirs—references to the "soldier's dream of home," to someone dying and going to their "long home" and many references in camp near the Potomac to all being quiet on the Potomac that night. Sentimental language and stories inspired songs. George Cooper (lyrics) and J.R. Thomas's (music) song "Mother Kissed Me in My Dream," was published by William A. Pond in New York City. The cover noted that the song was "founded on an incident of the Battle of Antietam." The story continued on the opening page: "A young soldier who was severely wounded at the Battle of Antietam, lay in one of the hospitals at Frederick. A surgeon, passing by his bed-side, and seeing his boyish face lighted up with a peaceful smile, asked him how he felt. 'Oh! I am happy and contented now,' the soldier replied, 'Last night, Mother kissed me in my dream.'"

An anonymous fragment of a letter dated May 3, 1862, found among those written by soldiers of the 8th Illinois Cavalry, Shipping Point, referenced a quiet evening spent eight miles from Yorktown, with an occasional whistle of a ball or bursting of a shell fired at Yorktown, and the sounds of the infantry brass bands playing a favorite of both sides— at least a favorite theme. There were many versions of this song and all of them found their way into soldiers' letters and into the family parlor: "The Soldier's Dream of Home."[21]

An anonymous letter painted an evocative image of a wounded soldier on a battlefield who said, "I could not help singing, 'When I can read my title clear.' And there was a Christian brother in the brush near me; I could not see him, but I could hear him. He took up the strain, and beyond him another and another caught it up, all over the terrible battle-field of Shiloh! That night the echo was resounding, and we made the field of battle ring with hymns of praise to God!"[22]

Music in the Civil War could easily take up many chapters here. It was *the* entertainment, and music commands were the calls for the regiments. Robert E. Lee remarked that without music there would have been no army. For in-camp entertainments—in today's time no longer appropriate, correct, or acceptable—the typical soldier enjoyed minstrel music. Enactments of black-face entertainment were recorded in letters and journals on both sides of the war. The fiddler and the banjo player were not only popular in the field they were also illustrated and popularized in newspapers and cartoons. Jaw harps, harmonicas, and even an occasional piano dragged out into the field from a ravaged

Sheet music for "The Soldier's Dream of Home." This song was written in 1862 by S.T. Gordon, C. Hatch Smith (composers) and E.O. Perrin (lyricist). The song was associated with the Union side of the conflict (Library of Congress, LC-M1640.S).

home and then left behind to molder in the woods would turn up. Bagpipes both cheered and annoyed the field camp. Patriotic songs and parodies filled letters and songbooks; sophisticated music passed back and forth between home and camp; and romantic songs of missing mother and other loved ones, of dead and dying loved ones and heart-wrenching songs of home and loss were heard everywhere and passed from person to person. Regimental officers tried to ban "Lorena" and "Tenting Tonight" from the camps because they stirred such nostalgic homesickness that they feared it would cause desertion. They failed to banish them and the songs continued to be played and sung.

Federal corps commander Samuel Heintzelman joined in a desperate struggle to close his broken ranks in the field and tried to rally them with music. He ordered them to take up their instruments. "Play! Play! It's all you're good for," he shouted. "Play, damn it! Play some marching tune! Play 'Yankee Doodle,' or any doodle you can think of, only

Sheet music for "I Dream of Thee or By the Camp-fire's Lonely Watch." Composed in 1864 by E.O. Eaton, this song was associated with the Confederate States of America (Library of Congress, Music Division, LC-M1642.E).

play something!" Before long, over the roar of the guns, came the incongruous sound of "Yankee Doodle" and then "Three Cheers for the Red, White, and Blue." One of General Joseph Hooker's men thought the music was worth a thousand men. "It saved the battle," he wrote. "Survivors of General George Pickett's disastrous charge at the Battle of Gettysburg (July 3, 1863) remembered in later years that Confederate regimental bands stationed in the trees played stirring martial airs as they started off across the mile-long field that separated them from George Meade's Army of the Potomac. Those same bands greeted them with 'Nearer, My God, To Thee' as they streamed back to the safety of their own lines after being repulsed at the stone wall." At the Battle of Franklin, Tennessee, in 1864 the Confederates charged the Union troops to strains from regimental bands playing "Bonnie Blue Flag" and "Dixie."[23] John Dooley (First Virginia Regiment, enlistment out of Gordonsville) was taken prisoner in 1863. Music kept him sane as he wrote of those around him going insane. In his prison notes he spoke of the long weary days:

> Burchardt plays chess with me and Cronin talks to me—and nothing else. Yes we agree to eat the greasy bacon now, surrendering at *discretion* and we *moan* during the day and *sing* nightfall. It is a strange thing to see a lot of wounded, miserable, half starved, & melancholic wretches gathering in a social knot and forming a *glee* club to frighten off the more gloomy shadows of our prison walls. Imagination can do wonders in making us miserable or happy—"We're saddest when we sing." Cronin sings and McGimpsey is singing and both have *holes* through their *lungs*—this is certainly miserably gay.[24]

John Lockwood of the 23rd Regiment New York State National Guard of Pennsylvania, writing a memoir on the Pennsylvania and Maryland campaign, described the June–July 1863 activities leading up to and onto the Gettysburg battlefield. As Longstreet and Hill proceeded from Chambersburg, the Federal army crossing the Potomac and Lockwood's regiment preparing to march from Harrisburg, John penned a scene set against the lyrics of "Let Me Kiss Him for His Mother." The words and melody, he lamented, "harmonized with our feelings and lent them a deeper tone as our united voices floated out upon the soft, still air." He described these words, as well as the general tones of songs sung: the "songs of pathos, of love and of home" mingled with "strong patriotic airs" dulled the sharp, coarse edges of battle, horror and fatigue. "And in this way an hour passed into oblivion as softly as if we had been asleep dreaming of home which then was heaven, or near it. The bridge had become shadowy in the gathered darkness, the curve line of the bivouac was invisible except as it was dotted out by the blazing fires, the water gleamed with the dancing images of flame, and overhead thousands of stars had come out to be witness of our flow of soul. And now as the spirit of stillness was creeping over the enchanted valley, we spread our rubber blankets under the trees or the open sky, drew on our overcoats, and lay down to sleep."[25]

On July 3, nerves on edge, so many men marching to certain death, John's regiment camped in a rough field a mile from Boonesboro. In the bustle of preparing for camp—tearing down fences for shelter and fires, preparing bedding, and preparing food—a great change came over the spirit of their dreams. They saw the lights of campfires far away on South Mountain and recognized in that "spot of fire" a "Cyclops" of the vastness of an army that their imaginations had not yet taken in. Such a vision played havoc with the soldiers' beguiling dreams of home and cheated them out of the dream that they might any moment be homeward bound. But dreams of home and the music of home were still their hope and comfort in the terrifying specter of battle and its certain aftermath of death and wounded.

Thus is the nocturnal potion to soothe the soul: music and dreaming of home.[26]

CHAPTER 3

Homesickness—
"like fire in my bones"

Soldiers from both the North and South, away from their families and often denied furloughs, all suffered from homesickness—as the days turned to weeks, months, and years—separated from family, suffering almost unbearable physical hardships, risking their lives and having no news from home other than an occasional letter that caught up with them.

Georgia volunteer Malcolm Gillis called homesickness "the most prevalent disease of the camps." John Swann wrote his wife in June 1862 from South Carolina: "Home is the best thing I can think of." He would lie in bed at night, thinking of home, weeping "until the tears would run down my cheeks on my bedclothes, but alas that did no good. It would relieve me for awhile. Nothing but the sight of your beautiful face will do any good and a sweet kiss from them soft little lips." In January 1864 he wrote again of homesickness: "If I could just be at home to stay! For I am tired of this horrible war and living like dogs!" This homesickness was aggravated by anxiety, as Federal troops were being readied to invade Georgia, occupy homes, and cut off communications with the families there.

Frances Clarke of the University of Sydney compared the homesickness of longing for hearth, home, and the good old days, which kept men's spirits up, to "dwelling" on home, which could bring deep sadness and mental instability rather than comfort and solace. It was believed that when nostalgia for home became "melancholia" and was allowed to run amok it could literally slay a man or certainly prey on mental and physical illness already sapping the energy of poorly nourished soldiers on the Civil War battlefields.[1]

John Tilley wrote his wife in October 1861: "I am not one of those unmanly, babyish men that will sit down and mope about going home, but still I long to be at home with my dear wife and children. I didn't leave you all because I had wearied of you, but because a stern necessity required it. I know that I have as good if not the best wife in this world. This is a kind of strong, deep-rooted feeling with me, and I long to take you in my arms, to hug and kiss you." In July 1862 William Stillwell paced in the golden moonlight through tall pine trees, thinking of his family and distant home: "The tears would run down my face while I would turn it up to look at the moon and pray God to preserve my little family."

William Stanley wrote his family from Petersburg in July 1862: "My dear wife, when I think of our parting day and our absence now, my heart often overflows and fills my eyes with tears. To think of your beautiful charms when we did part, it is nearly enough to break my heart. It is bad enough to part with mothers and fathers and brothers and sisters, but when man and wife has to part it looks like it is enough to break their poor hearts." Theodore Montfort wrote to his family after a day of rifle shelling whistling through the air: "I find that men will soon become accustomed to danger as they will to any and everything else ... yet in the dead hours of night, when all is silent, when we feel alone in the presence and care of our Maker, then home with all its endearments come[s] crowding upon our memory. Then men who face and smile at danger, weep and pray for those dear ones at home."[2]

Guy Taylor asked his wife not to worry about him and assured her he was in a place where he could take care of himself. He wanted her to "go to work about something to draw your mind away" because "if I should sit down and let my mind run on things at home I should bin dead long ago. There is nothing that will make a purson sick as soon as to be homesick. Their have bin good many sent to the hospital and the Dockes say that it is on the count of their being homesick, and there is a man in Co. G. that has soured so much about home he has become foolish and sick too and they are trying to get his discharge. You must gust make up your mind that you are agoine to injoy yourself let what will com, and let folks say what they will."[3]

James K. Newton of Company F, 14th Wisconsin Volunteers, was unmarried at the time of his enlistment but was devoted to his parents. He wrote constant letters, often apologizing for writing so frequently but excused himself by saying that he feared homesickness because it was "the worst kind of sickness a person could have down here." In another letter he astutely noted that keeping in good spirits was the best way to retain good health: "As sure as one of the men get a little homesick and down-hearted they are sure to be sick."[4]

"But I want to impress upon your mind the importance of writing often. For it seams almost like clasping an old friend by the hand to get a letter in this dreary country 'forsaken alike by God and man,'" wrote Captain George Turnbull, whose nerves had been tested by the horrific scenes on the battlefield: carcasses of horses strewn along the road and over the field, arms and legs of men sticking up out of the ground or "ruted out by hogs.... I saw a boot in which was the foot ... in another an arm as far up as the elbow in still another a skull which the boys were kicking around like a football ... [and] the contemplation is sickening."[5]

J. M. Davis of Atlanta wrote that homesickness was "like fire in my bones," a feeling that followed soldiers' into the night. Their dreams, often shared in evocative letters, brought them relief, easing the boundaries between dreaming and ordinary reality, blurring the harsh waking and sleeping conditions of their lives. Jack Felder wrote his sister from Virginia in April 1862: "I have just come off of guard and am relieved from all duty until 2 o'clock. Everybody seems to have the blues. I don't think I ever had them as bad in my life. It seems to me if I don't see home soon I will certainly kick the bucket or, in other words, die." Still alive in 1863, he again wrote: "I never in all my life have had the blues as bad as I have since my return to camps. Oh, that I could return home and live a thousand years! It seems to me I would be the happiest mortal that ever lived." To his father he wrote this: "I want to see home worse than anybody. Home is the sweetest place on earth to me. There is no place like home."[6]

Confederate soldier Carlton McCarthy, a private in the 2nd Co., Richmond Howitzers, Cutshaw's Battalion Artillery, Second Corps, memorialized his brother Edward

McCarthy in a conscious choice of recalling not the horrors and blood of the battlefield but the cheerful scenes around the campfire, a forgiving homesickness. He compared those memories to a dream "of happy, careless days and nights," where memories of the soldier's life could be crystallized. This scene, for a very long time, was the soldier's home, where he made and met friends, where the soldier could forget the "long, weary march." The coals of the campfire warmed the body and fired the imagination, which "seemed to feed on the glowing coals and surrounding gloom" and bring to mind peace "liberty, home, strolls in the woods and streets with friends, the church, the school, playmates, and sweethearts ... and even the dead." Here he might also think of an uncertain future, the possibility of his own death, prison, and grief at home, all of which would stir his heart. He might in those moments toy with little gifts from home—the little pin-cushion, the needle-case with thread and buttons, the embroidered tobacco bag, and the knitted gloves. Then it would be "the time to gaze on photographs, and to read and re-read the letter telling of the struggles at home, and the coming box of good things,—butter and bread, toasted and ground coffee, sugar cakes and pies, and other comfortable things" Then the soldier would call on God for protection for himself and for those at home. Then in this frame of mind he would sleep and "dream ... as the trees, swept by the wintry winds, moaned around him ... of home, sweet home."[7]

On Sunday morning, April 26, 1863, John Tidd wrote to his "Dear Friend Amelia" that the homesick soldier often thought and meditated on the "past pleasures of home" and even thought he was actually "enjoying the pleasures of the home circle" only to discover he was in a "midnight dream."[8] He told Amelia she could not imagine the reality of being a soldier: "Hard as it is, we are all willing to endure the hardships and privations of a soldier's life[:] I to, leave home, friends and all the comforts with which we were surrounded and go forth and fight the enemys of our country." John's regiment, the 109th New York Volunteers, was assigned guard duty for the railroads, bridges and telegraph lines from Baltimore to Washington, D.C. The 109th became part of the 1st Brigade, 3rd Division, 9th Army, and moved South toward Richmond. John Tidd fell ill during the last days of the war. He was discharged and taken home to a hospital, where he died on October 17, 1865.[9]

John W. Cotton survived the war but only by months. He and his wife, Mariah Hindsman Cotton, were born in Coweta County, Georgia, in 1831 and 1833 respectively and moved to Coosa County, Alabama, in 1853 or 1854. They already had seven children when John joined the army. He enlisted on April 1, 1862, at Pinckneyville, first serving in Company C of Captain M.G. Slaughter's company, and then in the 5th Battalion, Hilliard's Legion, Alabama Cavalry, which was consolidated into the 19th Regiment, Confederate Cavalry. He came home in the rain, sick with measles, and lived only until December 1865. He wrote, in words similar to most lonely people in war, of not understanding the pleasures of home until he was away from home; but he stood by his country and his family and defended his patriotism despite his longing for home: "I have as much to fight for as anybody else." Furloughs not forthcoming and news of the death of his child coming too late for John to express anything more than his extreme grief, the rumor circulated that the army planned to prohibit the receipt of letters (believing news from home contributed to homesickness). This ill-conceived order was quickly rescinded, but the initial "decision" contributed to feelings of anxiety and more extreme homesickness. News and loving messages from home provided sustenance to soldiers whose only contact with home were dreams and the written word. John wrote, "I am not satisfied about my looseing my furlough yet if I had got my furlough I mite have missed this fite but I hope I will come out unhurt and live to see the war ended and get home to enjoy the fruits of any labor here in this unjust and unholy mess I don't know what I would give to bee at home with you and our little ones but I cant bee with you now."[10]

Editor Neil Kagan wrote of another John Cotton of Alabama being paroled after a long confinement as a prisoner of war: "Love of home and family had made him a soldier. Dreams of home and family sustained him in the field. Returning home safely was his ultimate reward."[11]

Reading the letters compiled by Kagan and Robertson, one can quickly understand the pervasive loneliness and homesickness in the camps of both the Union and the Confederate soldiers, an ache that could not be assuaged on the battlefield. A New York hospital steward told his wife shortly after reaching the front lines in Virginia, "My health is good with the exception of 'homesickness,' a disease, I am thinking will never be cured, though in my case, I hope it will not assume that malignant type that will unfit me for duty." Valerius Giles of the Fourth Texas recalled, "I honestly believe that genuine homesickness killed more soldiers in the army than died from measles."[12] A Tennessee private confessed, "When I think of my native home, in a moment I seem to be there. But, alas! Recollection soon hurries me back to despair. Oh! Tell me I yet have a home."[13]

The younger the soldier the more likely this was his first time away from home. Idle time in between battles increased homesickness. Nostalgia destroyed morale: "A Union captain told his wife of meeting a homesick private in camp, 'I found one crying this morning. I tried to comfort him but had hard work to keep from joining him.'"[14] During the war's last autumn, a lonely Confederate told his sweetheart that only a letter from her would heal his aching heart. "If I was where I could not hear from you," he added, "it don't seem to me like I could stand it, for you are my daily study." J.B. Crawford of the 38th Mississippi informed his wife, "I wood give the Confederacy to the yankeys if it was mine to see you and the little ones." An Illinois volunteer expressed similar sentiments. "One does not know how sweet home is till he goes through the roughs of a soldiers life," he wrote his wife. "You must not think I am despondent for I aint, but I would take a discharge if one was given to me."[15]

Loneliness became deeper and more painful during the Christmas season. Near Yuletide in 1862, Lt. Jonathan Evans of the Fourth Virginia wrote: "I anticipate you will have a nice time at your proposed dinner. I would like to be one of the pertisipants but alas I am doomed to war away the time in dull camp." A man in his position, he added, could not help thinking of "friends far away with the faint hope that one day he may be spared to see them again." Evans was killed in action the following year.[16]

Dreaming of home increased the longing, the aching, the nostalgia, and often the pain of homesickness: "I sit and study ten thousand things to make me miserable and unhappy and when I sleep I sometimes see you coming home and wake myself jumping up to meet you but when I wake you are gone and I lye down and cry myself to sleep again."[17]

Amanda Shelton, a Union nurse and an advocate for both the nursing profession and the wounded soldier, quickly learned that the best medicine for those under her care was visiting them, talking to them, reading to them, and writing letters for them, bringing writing paper and pens as well as magazines. Seeing the war drag on for so many years, she recognized homesickness as being as dangerous as a wound and more difficult to heal:

Poor fellows! There was no remedy for this malady so many, many of them died. Perhaps no part of our service was more beneficial than that rendered to these men. We encouraged them to talk of loved ones at home, wrote letters for them, fed them, if they would eat, and in many cases bade them good cheer when they recovered sufficiently to join their regiments and try again.

We soon learned that wounded men were much easier to care for than those sick with disease. The latter were often fretful and querulous, but a wounded man rarely complained.[18]

"When I lie down to sleep": "Gemütlichkeit" and the German Soldier

When the day had been too harsh for expressing tender lines scratched with bad ink on rumpled paper, men turned to poetry and simple songs, an easy way to express emotions when writing them in prose seemed too close to the bone. Christian Nix, a German immigrant born in Eberbach, Baden, renounced all foreign loyalties, became a citizen of the United States, and enlisted in the Union army June 6, 1861, to fight for his adopted homeland—just two days after he married Maria Kasper. He joined the 6th Regiment of the Wisconsin Volunteers, which brought him to the Battle of Stones River. He wrote a letter to his wife from Murfreesboro, which included this poem:

The Soldier's Dream of Home

The Earth lies peacefully in the dark night.
The stars shine in the sky.
I stand on my watch far away from you.
When the Fatherland called,
I, too, grasped the musket.
In a rush, I hugged my crying fiancee.
Who knows if ever my eye again sees whom I loved
And when I stand so alone
Away from you in a far distance
During the quiet night and moonshine,
Then I think of you with pleasure.
When I lie down to sleep
Tired from the day's burden and misery,
A dream comes up to me—
A picture from my home valley.
There I dreamed I returned back to my love.
Gladly I embraced my wife,
And was glad that I had not stayed.
But, the drum beats and I awake.
Gone are the dreams,
Which in a quiet summer's night
Brought delight to my heart,
While the moon was shining."

Christian signed this letter, "From the one who loves you very much."[19]

Christian was "shot through the body" at the Battle of Stones River on December 31, 1862, and died in a camp hospital on January 5, 1863.

Homesickness posed a particular problem for German immigrants. In a study on Germans and the Civil War, Joseph Foster wrote that the intense longing for home on the battlefield was twofold: soldiers longing for their wives and children in their new home and a longing for their land of birth, a cultural longing and nostalgia that increased their despair and loneliness on battlefields where they were fighting for ideals and politics that had little connection to their normal lives. However, once German soldiers took a stand and a loyalty, they abided by that stand, considering it to be as binding as their loyalty to their old homeland. In his poetic dream of home, Christian Nix wrote of home, where his new wife lived (Wisconsin), embracing her and longing for his home valley, which could, emotionally, have been both his new home and his native home, even though he wrote that he 'was glad" that he had not stayed in Germany, a conflict of emotions identified by Joseph Foster in German soldiers' letters home.

Marcus Spiegel was an example of a German soldier who took a stand and a loyalty. He was born in a German village in 1829 and moved to America after the failure of republican revolution in Germany in 1848. He became first a peddler, then a shopkeeper in Ohio, married a Quaker girl, Caroline Hamlin, in August 1853, and had settled in Akron, Ohio, by 1860 after their third child was born. Caroline studied Judaism in Chicago and converted to it. Marcus joined the 67th Ohio Volunteer Infantry in 1861 and quickly rose from second lieutenant to colonel of the 120th Ohio Infantry. He held firm to his religious upbringing, his love of German culture and food, but completely embraced his patriotic devotion to America and the Union cause. Equally devoted to his wife and children, he dreamed "sweet" dreams of them, exulting when he received a letter, which always "had an electrifying influence" over him and made him feel "bully."[20] Dreaming all night of Caroline and the children on March 13, 1862, Marcus saw "himself sitting in our big black rocking chair and you on that little willow chair. Oncle Josey laying down leaning his elbow on that square carpet covered stool and the children all around us and I was telling you all how I was the 2nd on the Ramparts planting the Colors and how old General Shields complimented me and you said when Jo brought the paper home where you read it how I was praised by everybody you danced for joy and then I said, come on woman, let us dance now and we danced and the children all laughed and just as I was going to jump and cut up, we were called fall in. it was not yet day light. I woke, dit [did] jump up and told Chapman all will be right this day."[21] This dream was indicative, in waking, of Marcus's rapid rise in both rank and respect among the officers and men in the regiment. Compliments came fast and promotions equally fast.

When Marcus had a disturbing dream about the children and "Oncle Joseph" in May 1862, he recognized its reflection of his own homesickness. His appetite and health, he said, were good, but "pictures" of his family and longing for them were constantly before him. He felt that they too wanted to see him. A few months later, as he was sitting on the ground cross-legged eating his meal and thinking of how much that posture would make Caroline laugh, he looked up and "really saw" her standing before him laughing. This physical pairing of thought and action was common between Marcus and Caroline. Marcus wrote, "[T]hese very pretty moonlight nights I sit before my tent most every night and look at the moon wondering whether you think of me, what you might be doing and really I do sometimes forget myself and feel at home. I think sometimes our Spirits in their wanderings meet. Don't you think so dear? After I get through I get up, go in my tent, take a long long look at the 'dear faces,' then go to sleep and often dream of you."[22] Marcus left Baton Rouge on April 30, 1864, on the steamboat *City Belle*. He received news that his son Hamlin had lost a forefinger in a printing accident and Marcus became despondent. He wanted to be home and confided the war would be the death of him yet. His regiment was ambushed on May 3, and Marcus was mortally wounded. His death prevented his long wish of reuniting with his beloved family. "Some of the aging boys of the 120th Ohio did remember him as 'one of the noblest of men' and saw to it that his name was given the most prominent place on the monument of their charge at Vicksburg." Caroline carried on the culture and memory of both Marcus and his Jewish/German heritage, a proud commendation of German patriotism in America.[23]

Foster quoted examples of the intensity of feelings of German soldiers longing for home, whether it be their new home, nostalgia for their homeland, or both, which revealed the reality of loneliness. "Not having heard from you, my dearest ones, for such a long time—not even the slightest news—plunged me into a mood that sometimes bordered on melancholy," wrote Carl Anton Ruff. Valentin Bechler wrote to his wife that "on Sunday I wanted to see my Hildegard," and "I got tears in my eyes and I thought of my children…. And I wished I had the two of them for just a half hour." "Not a minute goes by in a day or night," Joseph Hotz wrote to his wife, "that I don't think about you lonely human being, and also about my child." Hotz's conscious desires to return to his family in Indiana manifested themselves in vivid dreams of returning home. On such occasions, Foster wrote, Hotz's dreams centered on being a father and husband, putting his child to sleep for the night or witnessing his wife's joy at the news that the war was over and he could remain at home with her.[24]

Friedrich Martens noticed that whenever he wrote letters to his parents in Germany, he felt like singing Heinrich Heine's poem "Die Heimkehr" (The Homecoming), and was unable to "determine the sorrow that fills my breast," a stanza from a portion of the poem referred to as "Die Lorelei." "Sometimes I think it is homesickness, although," he believed, "I am too old for that." Foster wrote that from "Martens's perspective, letters to his parents in Germany could trigger feelings of homesickness, an emotion he felt beneath his maturity level, and cause him to reflect on his Germanic identity. A letter was an emotional double-edged sword. Without letters from home, men felt cut-off and isolated, even though the letters and news from home they received sometimes made the men realize how far away from home they were and what they were missing. In the case of Friedrich Martens, letters served as a reminder of the distance separating him from his European homeland as well as a withdrawal from his familiar Germanic culture."[25]

Whether serving among fellow German migrants or not, German-speaking soldiers yearned for a sense of *Gemütlichkeit*. Loosely translated, the word meant "comfort" or "camaraderie." Wilhelm Francksen described the United States as a place where "there's no feeling of being at home, no matter how long you live here, because here there's no Gemütlichkeit, without which," he felt, "Germans can't even imagine feeling at home." Francksen likely felt lonesome and isolated from the culture and familiar aspects of his native homeland.[26]

In August 1864, Wilhelm Albrecht wrote to his family explaining that on December 10 he would fulfill his three years of service. He looked forward to the day he would be released and his "suffering would soon be over." "I hope that on that day I will go home," he continued, "and then by Christmas I'll be a human again, which we can't be as soldiers."[27] Historian Susan Matt wrote that homesickness was a "yearning for a particular home," while nostalgia was "a yearning for home, but it is a home faraway in time rather than space."[28] In this case Wilhelm Albrecht yearned for his particular home. Imagining that place called home was a way for soldiers to have a "stable source of identity" and to "maintain a sense of their 'true' selves" during a time of such great destruction of life and property.[29]

Confronted with the stressful, dangerous, and terrifying situations soldiers encountered fighting in a war, men looked for an environment different from their grim reality and imagined a safe place, a happier time absent hardships and pain. The image of their civilian life was at odds with their field environment and duties as soldiers. "For some men," Joseph Foster wrote, "the distinction between the two lifestyles made all the difference."[30]

Chapter 4

Tenting Tonight: Dreaming of Home on the Old Campground

I will to my Bunk; to sleep "perchance to dream" of Home![1]

An Angel of Mercy: The Night Dream

Henry Lea Graves was a private in the Macon [Georgia] Volunteers during 1861–1862 and a lieutenant in the Confederate marines after October 1862. Physically exhausted from walking, fighting, and four days' detail digging trenches under an unbearable Petersburg, Virginia, sun with "not a breath of air stirring," Henry wrote to his aunt on August 7, 1862, that it was "hot as it ever gets to be in central Ethiopia." Paying homage to both the imagination and the night dream, both necessary to a soldier's survival, he described a dream in which he saw himself standing not with a spade in hand but in the midst of people from home, with his coat off, moving across the piazza, enjoying the cool breeze "that almost always is blowing fresh through there with a basket of peaches at my side and all the homefolk around." He told her that he often went into this place in his imagination to pass time swiftly and he said "soldier mortals" would not survive if they were not "blessed with the gift of imagination and the pictures of hope." The second "angel of mercy," he said, was the night dream, which presented him even more vivid pictures of hope than any daydream: "This is the way I employ myself when I get into an unpleasant place, and, by this means, the time passes much more swiftly and pleasantly." He wrote on:

> Night dreams are as a general thing much more vivid than day dreams. The sweetest dream I have had for many a day past I had the other night, sleeping on the top of a fence with a rail, not remarkably flat or broad, for my couch and my gun barrel for my pillow (an iron pillow can hardly be called a "downy" one, do you think?). My dream, of course, had a "goddess," a sweet little, hazel-eyed girl who lives away down in Georgia and for whom I feel a "very tender feeling" was by my side, my arm was around her waist and her head on my shoulder, and her soft cheek laid most lovingly against mine (the idea of a soft girl cheek laid against my rough, sun burnt, bearded jaw!) and tender words of love were coming from hearts full of love, when alas! alas! The cracking of a stick near by, by an approaching foot, caused me to spring from the embrace of my darling to grasp the cold steel of my gun barrel and from the gentle accents of love to cry out the rough challenge, "Who goes there?" and, instead of the warm breath of the little girl which I had felt on my cheek but a moment before, I wiped from my face the cold night dew and with half a groan I turned me to my rail again.[2]

Just over a month later, the Confederate troops captured Harpers Ferry but with terrible losses on both sides, almost 24,000 dead between the two sides. The Confederates withdrew across the Potomac into Virginia on September 18–19. Henry Graves survived.

Almost two years later conditions had worsened, and homesickness and longing for loved ones at home, or those at home longing for a soldier on the battlefield, were constant themes in letters. Desertion became more common as men sought their way back home. The soldiers of both North and South described conflicting emotions of loyalty to their individual causes, but letters describing a dramatic shift in consciousness when the soldier entered the battlefield and the immense longing for "home," however home was defined in individual experience, were universal.

Occasionally there was a derisive voice about a "longing" letter—or perhaps that voice was a soldier hoping his beloved would disagree with him and tell him how important a letter *to her* expressing longing for home might be. Such a one, a Union soldier, wrote snidely of a Confederate soldier's letter found on the battlefield. He said in his own letter home that he did not believe it possible for a Northern lady "to write such foolish letters" as the one he found. He told her she would be amused "beyond expression—so ardent, so impassioned, commencing, 'Mi tru luv,' &c. the ladies were so gallant, so affectionate, that some even wished to don 'male attire' and go into the army, not to fight for Secessia, but separation was too terrible to endure." One might venture to guess that instead of being amused his lady wished her soldier had a little more Romance in his soul![3]

More common was a longing for home like that written in a letter by Thomas D. Newton, a private in Co. H., 8th Regiment, Louisiana Infantry. He had enlisted in June 1861. Writing to his sister Mary from Madison County, Virginia, on May 28, 1862, he expressed his feelings about the word "home":

> How much pleasure there is in that word…. There is more than tongue can express. How oft have I thought of home. That place that I formerly so little appreciated. And to think of those that are there. The kind Father, the indulgent Mother to which I have been so disrespectful in days gone by. The fond sisters that I have so oft mistreated. Oh, that I could have my time over again how different I would live. One may imagine something as to the ties that home has. Though, it is nothing compared to realizing the true state of things. I will tell you how much I think of home. That delightful home I have so often thought of the greater portion of my day in quietude enjoying the pleasures and comforts of life, and those that are dear to me. I think just enough of home to spend the remnant of my days, though they may be long, or short, in difference. There is of home a delightful place where one can have peace, and just rights with it. But, without those two items death is far preferable.[4]

Thomas believed that in order to come back home honorably and enjoy all the rights and peace of home he also had to follow his heart and duty and endure the hardship of field, camp, and battle. Thomas died at the "Wayside Home," Augusta, Georgia, on April 6, 1864, at age 24. He had been wounded at Antietam and then wounded again at the Mine Run Campaign. He had remained in a hospital in Lynchburg, Virginia, partially recovered and requested a furlough. He was on his way home when he suffered a relapse and died.

Thomas B. Booth of the 3rd Virginia Cavalry wrote one surviving letter from Cockletown to "My Little Darling." This loving letter was written to his cousin, Thomas apparently being interested in a deeper relationship. He wrote of a skirmish, his admiration for Major Hood—and meeting a large force at Messicks Point, which turned out to be a false alarm. More personally he ended the letter with a blessing for the "sweet bouquet you sent in your letter," which Thomas placed in the back of his cousin's daguerreotype. He said it would be some time before he could come home and that he was "sorry your dream of me was not a reality. It would make me very happy to take a ride with my darling. I often think of the many pleasant ones we have taken together and how happy I used to be."[5] He concluded by saying that she could never write letters that were too long—all her letters gave him joy.

Brothers James and Charles Tyrel joined separate regiments, James the 118th Regiment, NYSV, Co. D, and Charles the 22nd NYSV, Co. E., both enlisting at Chester, New York, where Charles lived out his life after the war. James died of gangrene in 1864. Charles wrote to a brother, Mortimer, on September 1, 1861, from a location unknown, that he dreamed of their mother "most every night"; he wrote again in November to give their mother love and to tell her "that I dream of seeing her most every night."[6]

Brothers Captain Francis Donaldson and John Donaldson not only joined separate regiments but also fought on separate sides. Francis, with the Army of the Potomac, dreamed anxiously that his brother John, Captain of Company H of the Confederate 22nd Virginia, was standing "so natural" in front of him but beside a man under "sentence of death." Francis awoke in agony, trying to speak to John and not being able to do so. With relief he heard from another brother, Jacob, that John was in good health and was still among the living. "Indeed," Jacob, John wrote, "I dearly love my rebel brother."[7] Both Francis and John survived the war.

Richard T. Van Wyck of the 150th New York Volunteer Infantry wrote to his cousin, Sarah Van Vechten, after an 1863 visit home and said that "home" had reversed itself in his dreaming life. He found it strange upon his return to camp that it was the noise of the drum and the men "hurrying to and fro" that were so "ingrafted" impressionably in his mind and it was the trip from home to camp that seemed "but a dream." His usual dreams while wrapped in a blanket "in sleep, and dreaming that I saw you all well at home" were simply played out in waking reality in his visit home. Everything, he said, was "in reverse," including the beautiful countryside and balmy air that seemed so inconsistent with the unpleasant event of war. This wise young man returned to family farming in Dutchess County, New York, after the war and married his cousin, Sarah Van Vechten, on October 3, 1867.[8]

Private William Whitlock of the 188th New York Volunteers wrote to his wife: "I dreamed last night after reading your letters of going home and shaking hands with and kissing you. I dreamed of shaking hands with a number of people that I knot know am I ever saw befour. I thought I was home on a furlough but awoke and it was a dream."[9]

Twenty-year-old Edwin Weller had been clerking in a dry-goods store when the war began. He wrote to Antoinette "Nettie" Watkins, "Friend Nett," letters that steadily built affection that led to a proposal of marriage. Nettie asked Edwin what it felt like to go onto the battlefield. His response was one critical to survival on the battlefield and one described again and again by soldiers on both sides of the blue/gray line: "I can not Speak for others but I can tell you how I felt. When we first Started from our position as a reserve to the Woods near where the Rebels were, I thought of Home, friends, and most everything else, but as Soon as we Entered the Woods where the Shells and Balls were flying thick and fast I lost all fear and thought of Home and friends, and a Reckless don't care disposition Seemed to take possession of me. Then was two of our Company Shot down near me and Even their Shrieks and yells did not affect me in the least. This is the way I felt and I have heard other Soldiers Say the Same." Some of the soldiers gave this mind shift a time—five minutes between longing for home and hearth and complete fearlessness on the battlefield."[10]

Guy Taylor of the 36th Wisconsin Volunteers spent his entire service being ill but certainly not out of harm's way from shot and shell. He shared stories and dreams with his wife but he never told her the extent of his personal danger until the last few letters written before he returned home. Because of physical limitations due to illness, he cooked for the regiment, worked in the hospitals, and took care of the horses; but he was often near the battlefields and understood the reckless disposition described by Edwin Weller. In a letter to his wife describing sharp firing and cannonading, Guy explained: "[W]eknow that [the firing] means *death* but then the soldiers do not think about death as a purson dos at home. They are exposed so much that they get so they think if they get hit it is allrite and if not they think they are vary luckey and that is all they think about dien, all they want is what they want to eat and drink, and then they are redy to fite, and they do fite in good earnest, and they are redy to go rite into the mouth of the rebs canons. It looks as though men was crazy to see them in a fite but the thing of it is that men do not have any fear after they wonce commence to fire. The noise drives away all fear and then let anyone breath the smoke of gun powder they get reckless so they are redy for any kind of work that is call on to be don."[11]

Similarly, Colonel William Thomas Poague, a gunner with Stonewall Jackson, described his feelings in his first battle [Bull Run]: "You may want to know how I felt in this my first battle. I was at no time frightened, nor was I excited after we reached the battle line. I was conscious of being in danger, but right there I felt was the place where I ought to be. The thought repeatedly came to me that I was in the hands of a kind heavenly Father, and that His merciful care and protection were over me. With all this was a most novel sensation, hard to describe, a sort of warm, pleasing glow enveloping the chest and head with an effect something like entrancing music in a dream. My observing, thinking and reasoning faculties were normal."[12] The feeling was very different after he survived four years of horrific fighting, loss, and devastation of his home landscape. At the call of "surrender," Poague was stunned. The guns stopped and the silence was deafening. A religious man, he recalled an expression from the Book of Revelation: "there was silence in heaven for about the space of half an hour," only, he noted, one should substitute a very different word for heaven.[13]

Commenting on the common occurrence of the soldier's dream of home, Mississippi soldier Frank Montgomery wrote in his diary that he had a "real soldier's dream" of wife and children and home, but, "like the soldier in the song ["The Soldier's Dream"], 'Sorrow returned with the dawning of morn And the voice in my dreaming ear melted away.... I firmly believe, that if we continue successful a few months longer, the war will close this year, and, as God has hitherto protected me so long amid so many dangers, I trust it is not presumption in me to hope for his protection to the end." This dream came in the final long year of the war, and Frank, like many Confederate soldiers, reflected on their belief till near the end of the war that their cause, in their perceived justness, would end in victory. Like all soldiers in the Civil War, he also believed it would be a short war and noted that he always tried to write home cheerfully because the scenes of war were bad enough "without the apprehension of defeat."[14]

Literate and even sometimes eloquent, Private Roysdon Etter, a Virginia farmer, wrote letters in a country slang and spelling that made their way to his beloved wife, Sarah, who had never traveled out of Warren County, Tennessee, where she had been born. Roysdon described landscapes Sarah had never seen, the deep crags and mountains of Virginia and scenes along the paths he marched. These opened a new world for Sarah, but Roysdon missed home. Just months into his enlistment, he longed for home and begged a dream of Sarah to come in the night: "Tho I am in a fureen land … If not granted that blessing I hope in heaven to dwel Where there no more distresses Fare from the torments of hell."[15]

Two Days and Two Nights in a Tavern

John Black married his sweetheart Jennie during a furlough and made it safely through the war until March 21, 1865, when he received a debilitating bullet in the spine. He lived sixty more years but as an invalid under his wife's care. John was with Company G, 12th Pennsylvania Cavalry. He loved exploring his country and fighting for his cause but recognized the power of homesickness. He wrote that men who thought too much of home would become so overtaken with the thought of it that they would fall sick. He prided himself on his ability to control his life and his thoughts and sought, mostly unsuccessfully, to drive thoughts of home from his mind so that he would not become ill.[16]

John did not drink, in an environment of drinking, but he did imbibe a bit in a camp Christmas celebration in 1864. After a meal of roasted fowl and other good things, he had a "slight sprinkling of something good to drink in the shape of whiskey. It being the first I'd drank since the 21st of September last, I did not take an overdose, but had enough in me last night to make me feel a little 'boozy.' He shared this information with his dear wife, Jennie, because he said he could do nothing else but always tell her the truth.[17]

He went on to comment on Jennie's having her fortune told and assured her he would have done the same thing. He enjoyed an apparent prediction of children and assured her that would probably come to pass and that he would have no objections to children. Then he addressed Jennie's notions of discontent with his lengthy stay in the war, which had created tension between them by 1864. She wanted him home with her and reminded him he had passed on opportunities for furloughs and had even reenlisted! He defended himself by rehashing promotions he had received and promising the war couldn't last much longer.[18] Referencing John's pride in his control of situations, Jennie insisted that coming home was certainly within his control but possibly not his desire.

These exchanges played a defining role in a dream John shared with Jennie just two days after he had imbibed too much Christmas booze. He described the dream as "odd and also laughable" and disturbing. In the dream, he had been given a three-day furlough and he was on his way to see Jennie, but, instead of home, he found himself at "Vaughns old tavern," where he got drunk and remained for two days and two nights: "[T]hen I took a notion I would take a walk down the road and see you. I did so, and found you scrubbing and spoke to you. I thought you turned around to me and told me coolly to go and spend that day & night where I had spent the last two. Without a word I turned around, went back to the tavern, took a meal, and left for camp by next train, and arrived safe in Camp, and then I awakened and found myself in Camp in bed." John surely understood this dream. He was aware of the strain and coolness increasingly evident in letters from Jennie, who had written, as she had spoken in the dream tavern, that she thought he was much more suited to staying where he was rather than coming home and finding comfort by her side. John had made no secret of his enjoyment of being a soldier and advancing through the ranks. The pull of serving in the war, although a detriment to his newlywed relationship with Jennie, was ably served in the metaphor of the tavern, representative of a familiar part of the nineteenth century landscape, a place that served as bed and board but only in a temporary capacity, like a camp in the field. Jennie had been stoic, but, like the dream Jennie, she was growing "cool" to the idea of being second choice in the tug of war between John's domestic life and his camp life and which master he would serve.[19]

Understanding the message in his dream, a few days later John acknowledged Jennie's discontent but lamented that leaving was no longer in his power. He also acknowledged the new feelings in his life of having a wife and joining the ranks of those who missed home and longed for a beloved: "While so studying often do the tears come unbidden. I like the service, and were it not for you ... I would always be a soldier, but no, I will not always be a soldier." He promised that he would come home honorably at the first opportunity but never dishonorably, "for the latter would break my heart."[20]

On March 21, 1865, John was wounded in hand-to-hand combat with Charles Wiltshire of Mosby's command. He was felled from his horse by a pistol ball that "entered the small of his back above the right hip ... paralyzing his legs." A Union family cared for him until he could be moved. Jennie was notified, relieved that John was alive, but she was left with John's care for the rest of his life. John and Jennie did, as predicted by the fortune teller, have children, but they were adopted—Carrie and Lillian.[21]

"Soul on paper": Singular Dreams of Home

Sergeant Charles T. Bowen enlisted in Company G of the Twelfth U.S. Infantry, First Battalion, Ogden, New York. Just prior to enlisting, he married Catherine [Kate] Hammond. Their daughter was born before he enlisted. Charles, a farmer, probably enlisted for money and opportunity to "rise" above his station, neither of those goals proving to be fruitful. He and his new mother-in-law were at cross purposes, and he hated her influence over his new wife and child. Kate and Charles experienced discord in the fall of 1862, which seemed to become fully resolved by 1864. His letters were long and eloquent, expressing his "soul on paper." His dreams were equally long and longing for the dear young wife and a marriage he had barely experienced before leaving for war. He dreamed of his wife and baby "most every night," and in the fall of 1861 he had a "singular dream" in which he was home on a pass. Kate was the first one to meet him. She sat on his knees, "your arms around my neck, mine around yours & *such a time we had*. I thought while all our folks were around me, *I could talk to no one but Katie* for a long *long time*, oh, such a *good time* as we had there. It seemed so *real* that it even makes me feel now as though I had seen you." Kate had dreamed Charles loved and married another girl, probably a reflection of the emotional turmoil between Charles and her mother. Charles honored his dream as proof of their love: "don't dream so no more [about me] for there is no other in this wide world I would love or think of loving."[22]

Near the end of December 1862, Charles dreamed he was home and held "Birdie [his baby] & Katie in my arms & kissed them over and over again." The dream was so real he kicked the blankets off himself and his camp-mate. His camp-mate's temper cooled when Charles shared the dream. He told Charles he did not blame him for kicking, that if he had dreamed a dream like that of his young wife and babe he would have kicked "the infernal shanty down."[23]

Mother-in-law problems and discord over money never dampened Kate and Charles's love-letters, dreams, or nostalgia and longing for one another. Charles often evoked the "love fire" between them and, in one of many references to Kate's appearing in his dreams, he told her that this had been true even when they were courting. That "same dear girl" continued to "trouble [his] midnight visions" in the war down in Virginia. He wrote to Kate of a dream in which he experienced having his leg shot off and he could not move. He awoke joyfully. He read in this dream not a warning but evidence of the power of his love and his connection to a greater authority. Someone in the dream, a "friend" and stranger whose face he could not see, lifted him out of that scene and carried him high above the battle, swiftly away, and carefully sat him "down in a room & on a bed & how happy I can not tell for my arms were around you & your cheek was against mine. The remembrance of that dream made me happy most for it seemed for some days that I had seen you." The smoke in the dream scene was too thick for him to see the face of the benevolent and life-saving stranger.[24]

Finally—"heartsick, homesick, disgusted & tired of the rambling roving & dangerous life of a soldier, & it seems to me that I can just take any amount of regular down-right home comfort for the remainder of my time on earth," Charles was discharged in 1864 and went home to Kate and his baby.[25]

"Some magnetic chain between us": Richard and Mary Watkins

"Oh yes: Miss Purnall you can talk very large when you know I am away off here and my hands are tied by military discipline. Never mind Madam just wait till I get home and call me a 'grand rascal' if you dare.... Oh you are too good, I love you too much." Richard H. Watkins, Company K (the Prince Edward Dragoons), 3rd Virginia Cavalry, teased Mary Purnall Watkins, his wife, with these words on August 21, 1861, from "Camp Ashland." He and a camp-mate, Charley Redd, were "hiding" in the forage room writing on boards, with the paper lit by a piece of candle. Richard told Mary that he thought Charley loved his wife best of all the men in camp except himself. Both of them, he said, read letters from home with tears near to overflowing. He bid Mary good night and wished her "sweet sleep and pleasant dreams."[26]

Richard Watkins and Mary Purnell Dupuy were born in Prince Edward County, Virginia. They married on August 24, 1858, when Richard was 33 and Mary was 19. Richard was listed as a lawyer/farmer on the 1860 census. They lived in the Moore's Ordinary Post Office district and had real estate valued at $10,000 and personal property (mostly slaves) valued at $25,000. They had a daughter, Emily, at the time Richard enlisted in Company K (which would become the 3rd Virginia Cavalry) and later, after a furlough, a daughter, Minnie. Richard became quartermaster in the Commissary Department, first for his regiment and then for the company. In April 1862, he was promoted to lieutenant. In October 1862 he was promoted to captain, after Sharpsburg. He was wounded in 1862 near Aldie, Virginia, and again in late 1864 at Tom's Brook in the Shenandoah Valley of Virginia.

Like most soldiers, his letters spoke of camp life, disease, weather, food, boredom, picket duty, the lack of forage for the horses, a longing to see his wife, and a continuing hope that the war would soon end and that they could be together. He sought information from Mary on the farm and their little girls. Mary wrote about planting, harvesting, making clothing for soldiers, the impressment of crops, raids by Union cavalry, stories about the girls, the challenges of playing the role of manager of a farm and household, the difficulty of procuring cotton and wool cards and household necessities, paying taxes, and hoping constantly that Richard would have a furlough. Disease was rampant in the countryside; Mary wrote about typhoid, typhus, measles, and whooping cough. Friends and neighbors—and their children—died on the battlefield and at home.[27]

Richard's first letter home addressed Mary as "my darling child." Mary's imagination envisioned Richard nearby as she longed for him late at night, longed for him to talk to her and "pet" her: "It hardly seems like home over here without you, I am all the time listening for your step and hoping that you will come in after while.... I wonder what you are doing now, sleeping soundly and sweetly I hope." In others she wrote, "Good night and pleasant dreams to you." Richard wrote of his delight at receiving Mary's letters, and he wondered how his Mary was, how she felt, how she looked, what she was thinking and what she was doing or going to do. He shared a bit of humor to illustrate his longing for her, a story about "old Cyrus Chambers, a lunatic, who lived near Farmville that he wished one day for a million of dollars and on being asked what he wanted with so much he said that he wanted to take one half of it and buy whiskey. And what with the other Cyrus? 'Well, I think I would buy more whiskey.' Thus with me darling, I wish I could get a million letters."[28]

In the days between battles and marching, when there were thoughtful moments when the soldier in camp could take the time to look around him and take in the beauty in nature, he would find the exquisite surprises of the landscape in ways not always familiar from his own home. Many were struck by the forgiveness of nature and its limitless message about the ability to surprise, delight, and to ultimately recover from destruction. Richard felt one of those moments on a bitter damp cold January night in 1862 when he found refuge in his thoughts, first in the glow of a signal light and then in a surprising show of nature's magnificence on a point of the York River. It was phosphorescent lights on the sea that captured Richard's imagination and he penned the experience. He and a soldier named Charley Redd were sent as videttes to a point of the York River about eight miles from their camp. Richard explained to Mary that the York River was almost as large as the Potomac. They were assigned the task of watching the river for any fleets approaching. Their vantage point was good, and they could see for about fourteen miles: "YorkTown & Gloucester Pont were in plain view ... [and signal lights] did not compare in beauty to another that we saw which was the phosphorescent lights of the sea water. This was something which I heard of before but had never witnessed. The River seemed to have hundreds & thousands of lightning bugs & glow worms down under the water and along the beach were streams and balls of fire. It was indeed beautiful. The night was very mild so that we could enjoy the night.... I love you with all of my heart."[29]

Homesickness intensified as the summer of 1862 approached. Shortly after his beautiful description of the phosphorescent lights, Richard was gifted with a furlough; but when he returned to camp the furlough served to intensely remind him of Mary, of his love for his home, and of his "sweet and interesting" children, who loved Mary and therefore were even more precious to Richard: "I love them more for that." "I love you, I love you, I love you, love you, *love you*," he wrote, the words tumbling from his pen in this and subsequent letters, he promising in each of them to write at every available opportunity, even when letters had little chance of getting through in a timely manner.[30]

In this time of such intense longing for one another, Mary realized that there was something greater between Richard and her than their letters; there was a connecting force that tuned and enhanced dreams and intuition. "I dreamed Wednesday night you were in a battle that day and it seems you were sure enough," she wrote on September 24, 1862. "I believe there is some magnetic chain between us and I can almost always tell by my feeling when you are in danger or when you are coming home or the day that I am going to receive a letter from you."[31]

Family members shared news and dreams with Mary and Richard and among themselves in both visits and letters. Richard's brother, Nathaniel, missing his own family, reported simple dreams of home. He described a night reconnaissance maneuver to observe enemy activity on the James River and shared a dream he had while sleeping out in the clover, which reminded him of home. He begged his wife, Nannie, to write to him about their children, and the farm, and told her about the condition, illnesses, and wounds of others, wishing fervently that he could be at home with her.[32]

Pattie Watkins wrote to her sister Nannie that she dreamed about Nathaniel and Nannie's child, Charley: "Kiss the little ones for me tell Charley I dreamed about him last night dreamed I was putting shoes on his feet." Charley was Richard's nephew, and the dream disturbed Pattie Watkins but she didn't understand why. A letter from Mary to Richard on May 1, 1863, revealed Charley had become ill with diphtheria and died suddenly and that his sister Minnie was expected to die from the same disease. Dressing Charley for his burial may well have been the message in this dream of placing shoes on Charley's feet.[33]

Richard sent Mary a likeness of himself during this difficult period of community tragedy, which daily counted deaths from epidemics of typhus, diphtheria, and fevers. Mary wrote back that at first she thought the daguerreotype likeness was "savage." However, when their daughter Emmie recognized it, Mary was then more content with the image. The deaths of children in the neighborhood were harsh and rapid. Both Mary and Charley were deeply affected by Charley's death. The child had become ill on a Friday and died on a Saturday. Mary wrote that Emmie was the only one left of three who were baptized together in the community. Then, closely following, a deep gloom was cast over Richard's regiment by the death of Stonewall Jackson: "His life will ever be regarded as one of the most brilliant on record, as well by other nations, as our own."[34]

Richard, now a captain, wrote his "darling" Mary on February 19, 1863, sharing news of being "snowed up" with six to eight inches of snow, the "roads without bottoms, our horses standing in mortar. Ourselves in soak, surrounded by melting snow." In between the snow was rain pouring in torrents, causing smoking fires and difficult writing. Richard had constructed a desk from piles of wet straw on saddlebags, surrounded by damp blankets and wet saddles. Richard assured Mary he was gaining, not losing, weight and was sleeping soundly, dreaming of her "as sweetly as ever in ... life." He longed for another furlough to see Mary but was rebuffed at every turn. He reported that he even dreamed of asking for a furlough by going to the top for his request: "Last night I dreamed that I applied for a furlough & wrote to old Genl Rob E Lee that I had not been blessed with a furlough or indulgence since last February but that old Genl sent it back with a note that he had not had one since *the war commenced*. Ha Ha Ha! Twas all but a dream." Richard laughed but also took the dream to heart. He told Mary he had not told her everything concerning the dream. He had inquired among those in camp what they thought of such a dream and was told that dreams were often to "be taken by contraries," a dream dictionary-style approach. Feeling confident that was true, Richard took courage. On the morning after the dream he completed an application for a furlough and attached a message describing his dream as an endorsement. He was so confident in this approach that he told Mary he hoped for a positive response from the request even though it might be a few weeks before he would hear. "If the old fellow grants it you may 'bet your bottom dollar' as the boys say that I will come right straight home to see you." It appeared from the subsequent letters that Richard did not receive his furlough and that at least in this case dreams did not come in "contraries."[35]

It was likely that neither Mary nor Richard expected a furlough in the spring of 1863. Furloughs were being denied to all the men, and the need for every able body was evident across the battlefields. Mary accepted that Richard was not coming home on a furlough and responded to his dream with a vision of peace and warmth. She told him she was sitting by a cozy fire in "the old room," thinking about "someone who is away off in the army somewhere and imagining him sitting on the floor of his tent before a good warm fire with his head reposing comfortably on his saddle or roll of blankets taking an evening nap." Not a likely picture of comfort for Richard's actual circumstances, but Mary's imaginative journey continued with a vision of Richard looking into the fire, thinking about home, his children and his wife. When the firelight, in her imagination, grew dim, she envisioned sleep stealing softly over his body, his forgetting about the war "and every other unpleasant thing in his dreams." Mary wished she "had a pair of wings and could fly down close by without anybody's seeing me. I [could] comb your hair whilst you are asleep." Not to be denied the realization of her dream, Mary, in her longing to see Richard, continued: "I mean to borrow some [wings] tonight and go to see you in my dreams any how."[36] His discontent rising, Richard wrote back: "I want to see you so bad … I almost feel like running away from the army or getting out of it any way that I can, and going home to stay with you…. I believe my last visit home has unfitted me all together for camp life. There is nothing here to interest me. I think of you and of our dear little ones all the time."[37]

Carding wool, making clothing, sending anecdotes, and recounting the antics of their children, Emmie, baby Mary, and Minnie, brought flashes of normalcy to life. Minnie had spoken an oration to the moon when she saw it for the first time when it was not full: "somebody had broke the moon right in two." Richard would have cherished that image but would have been heartbroken over the meager Christmas for the children in 1863 she described. They hung their stockings and all of them slept with Mary on her bed. They felt blessed with stockings filled with apples, peanuts, cakes and some candy, although Emmie was expecting a china doll. Mary told her the Yankees would not let Santa Claus bring such things at that time. Richard's own letters relentlessly shared news of harsh marches, little food, and horrible camp conditions. He marched thirty consecutive days through dangerous mountains in severe weather, over 600 miles back and forth through the Alleghany Mountains through snow and ice and sleet, "the ice so smooth & glassy that often nearly the whole march of the day … had to be made on foot." He slept on and under the snow, lived on hard bread and pork, "making the most fearful march that I have ever conceived of. We had ascended … one of the highest peaks along a narrow path used by scouts alone and never by citizens at all in the winter. Night overtook us on the top, the road on the North side was almost perpendicular & covered with ice & snow. Our horses could not be rode or even led but had to be turned loose and driven whilst we were slipping & falling & tumbling & grasping at trees & bushes & at men & horses. We reached the foot of the mountain. I hardly know how, my head swam & I felt like a drowning man…. Well, what did we accomplish. I fear very little for the sacrifice of men & horses and as many cattle.... The counties of Hardy & Hampshire are under Yankee rule.... The secessionists ... are plundered by the Yankees and the union men by the rebels ... [and] a large formidable band of robbers who style themselves Swamp Dragoons [plunder]" both sides. "One old gentleman told me that they had robbed his house three times before his eyes of everything valuable."[38]

Mary reported a dream and a death in June 1864. Her cousin, Ann, received news that her brother, Willie, was wounded on May 27 and died two days later. Ann had been awaiting such tidings. She knew "Johnston had been fighting" and she looked anxiously in the papers for Clebourne's Division, Willie's regiment. She had come awake with a dream in which Willie had been wounded, lost a leg, and was in danger. She had received a letter from Willie the day after the dream and hoped that it had driven away the bad news in the dream. It had not—the dream had been realized.[39]

In a premonition a week later, Mary knew that all the possessions in her house had been destroyed by the Yankees. When she heard they were nearby in Meherrin, she sent word for a neighbor to take care of the horses and then began hiding paper, jewelry and small articles of value. Mary was in the woods burying papers when she had a strong sense that the Yankees were in her house destroying everything. She was right:

> Toby got there just in time to find the house full of Yankees and all of our horses and mules and a good many of the negroes in their possession [she goes on to name all the stolen colts and negroes and plow gear].... They seemed to be in a desperate hurry.... The officer in command then went to the house burst the doors open also the drawers and your book cases and searched about in every place for gold and silver and papers.... Others stood guard over the negroes.... Mrs. Owen ... ran away from home whereupon the wretches took all of her and her childrens ... clothes, ripped up all of her beds, broke up her earthenware and furniture, even destroyed her kitchen furniture, brought in negroe women and made them dress up in Mrs. Owens clothes ... and then shot two of their broken down horses in her porch leaving them lying dead with their heads in her door. Some few fared better and some worse.

Taking this news the best she could, Mary wrote, "Well! There will be so many less to clothe and feed that is the straining point with me this year."[40]

Captain Richard Watkins and Mary both grew more and more weary of the war. On another endless picket in the summer of 1864, Richard entered a dark forest where he planned to stay for the night. The wind was cold: "[A]s I threw my blanket down upon the damp ground many thoughts of the comforts of home came stealing ore me," Richard was still nine months from his parole from his regiment in Danville, Virginia, on May 21, 1865.[41]

Finally receiving his parole, Richard returned to Prince Edward County and he and Mary moved back to their farm and began the long years of rebuilding. Reconstruction was difficult. They, like many others, had little livestock. The slaves had been freed, but, seeing this as something of a blessing, they needed to decide who would be willing to return for hire as farm employees and how they would pay them in the tough years of Reconstruction. Richard resumed a law practice and had enough cases to assist the farm's survival until finally, with several years of bad crops alternating with good ones, they sold the farm in 1866. The sale resolved many financial problems for the Watkins family, and they continued to thrive through Reconstruction. However, Richard's sad words rang strong in a summer letter to his brother in 1866, the year he sold the farm:

> Mary & I moved home immediately on my return and considering all things have gotten along admirably. The Yanks had taken all of our meat excepting four pieces and all of our fowls except a goose

and a peacock & they wouldn't mate.... We planted vegetables and soon had enough to furnish a much better table than I ever sat down to in camp. Now we are really at home.... Corn crop ... promising at least 200 bushels with 25 stacks of oats. My wheat was an entire failure ... have had a prime fruit crop and Mary has quite a bountiful supply of dried peaches & pears laid up.... The Yanks have us completely subjugated. All of our public places garrisoned with negro troops. And our people willing to submit to any degree of debasement & degradation."[42]

A Dose of "Morphine": Dreaming with Octavia and Winston Stephens

Winston Stephens, a 26-year-old planter from Welaka, Florida—and a man who, by his own admission, had already courted ladies and experienced adult relationships—relentlessly courted Octavia "Tivie" Bryant for three years, beginning in the summer of 1856. Octavia was fifteen years old. Her parents, James and Rebecca Bryant, from the founding family of Welaka, opposed the courtship because of Octavia's age and sent her away to a school for young ladies, where she promised to remain and to resist Winston's proposals until she was eighteen. Octavia kept her promise but was still allowed to see Winston.

Octavia's vivid journal and letters began in her courtship, and extended into her marriage, delivering news of the births of her children, her heartaches, and her devotion to Winston, including her doubts about his faithfulness when she missed him and her devotion to his faithfulness when their emotions overflowed with love for one another. Octavia married Winston on November 1, 1859. When the war took him away from her, Tivie wrote long letters to him, recording news of their family, the great and beautiful events of their lives and the heart-wrenching torment of Winston's enlisting in the war and being away from her and their new baby, Rosa, born October 17, 1860. Tragedy haunted the last years of Tivie's life. The details are revealed in the progression of letters: the death of a new baby (Isabella) and the building momentum that characterized the last days of February and the first days of March 1864. In that short span of time her mother, Rebecca, died; Winston was shot and killed; and Tivie's new baby, Winston, Jr., was born without his father.[43]

In the early written record of their courtship and engagement, Octavia Bryant blessed Winston Stephens with "pleasant dreams" and guardian angels in her letters and they chatted happily about planning and building their first home together, a cabin called "Rose Cottage." Playing with words, Winston called Tivie his "Rose Bud" and even more playfully addressed his courting words to a photograph of Tivie, referring to himself as "the Old Bachelor" and begging Tivie to allow him to keep the image so that he could "keep her next to my heart while I am gone." He signed off with a variation on an ending that would characterize each of their courtship letters, through the war and to the end of Winston's life: "Good bye and may heaven protect you ... pleasant dreams."[44]

Less than two years after their November 1859 marriage, Florida seceded from the Union and Winston signed as a first lieutenant with the "St. John's Rangers," a company organized by General Hopkins. The company was designed to be a "home company" to protect the home coast, from the Indian River to St. Augustine, from invasion. Winston was stationed in and around the St. Johns River in several camps, such as Camp Beauregard and Camp Finegan.

In her first war-time letter, Tivie used home images similar to Winston's reverie on Tivie's photograph. She asked Winston:

> Look in upon us to night and see how we do without you? And what we are doing? ... Mother sitting opposite me writing. Henry and George sitting a little to one side studying, poor Ben in bed where he has had fever this afternoon. Rosa asleep, now if you were only here our picture would be complete.... As for getting along, we do that pretty well but I assure you I miss you sadly, but I cannot help thinking that you will be home soon *to stay*. I can not realize that this is only the beginning of *worse*. Rosa has not yet forgotten how to say Pa Pa, though she is too often reminded to forget how to say it, if she does not forget to whom it applies. The first night you were away when I took her into bed Mother had not yet got in and she looked all around and kept calling for Pa Pa and made me feel right sad.[45]

Winston responded with the report of "a regular soldiers dream.... I thought I had returned and after saluting you Rosa called Pa Pa and smacked her lips for a kiss, but alas I awoke and had a soldiers bed and bedfellow." He asked Tivie if she thought he loved camp life better than his home and family, then replying to his own question that she was wrong, that his love for both induced him to duty to his country and duty to his family so that he could keep the enemy from invading the peace of both.[46]

Christmas 1861 brought letters of missing one another and wishes for pleasant dreams between Tivie and Winston. Letters in the new year—1862—brought assurances from Winston that he was always faithful and constantly thinking of Tivie, in fact wishing so to be with her that he often took "her" (an ambrotype, unidentified) "out of my trunk and imagine you are before me and reality." This assurance of fidelity, coupled with loneliness and recalling the time before their marriage when Winston had known other women, invited Tivie's mind to jealousy and allowed her temporarily to focus away from her real fear on the presence of the Union army, which had moved into the area where she lived. She would write jealous words and then repent. Then, naming her real fear, she assured Winston she was prepared to see the Yankees even if she was not fully prepared *for* them. Her bravery turned to "tolerably skeered" after dreams of them at her doorstep caused her to awaken "shaking dreadfully."[47]

In the spring of 1862, Tivie wrote that she wished better dreams for Winston than those of her own. She had dreamed that Winston was "going off somewhere," meaning a battle. She hoped it was not true. She sent Winston a kiss from Rosa, a habitual ending for most of Tivie's letters, with imaginary loving theatrical kisses given and received between Rosa and her father.

Both Tivie and Rosa experienced frequent complaints of fevers and chills. In the fall of 1862 Rosa, two years old, took a tumble down the steps in an attempt to throw a recalcitrant chicken off the steps. She fell on "a puppy" and cut her lip. While trying to handle these daily illnesses and skirmishes in Rosa's world, Tivie dreamed of Winston's more threatening skirmishes and reported dreams of Winston having a "chill" in his camp as the weather began to turn. She wondered if he ever dreamed "of your poor little wifey? I dream of you every night and I think Rosa dreamed up and said in the same whining tone she used to when you went out 'Ma Ma Pa Pas done,'"—meaning "home." Winston surprised them with a visit that evening. After he returned to camp, Tivie pressed again, asking if Winston ever dreamed of her, and wrote that she hoped he was having a "pleasant dream" of her: "I still continue to dream of you, it is so pleasant to see you in my dreams, if I can not in reality. I want to see you very much. I get dreadfully homesick lovesick or something.... Oh if this war would only end."[48] Winston responded that he did not often dream of Tivie but that he thought of her constantly.

Tivie's "lovesickness" and longing for Winston deepened with the birth of a daughter, Isabella, at 3:00 a.m. on December 14, 1862. Joy at the new birth and loneliness for Winston quickly turned to sorrow as fever and rashes engulfed the small new body, mounted in intensity and ended disastrously in the new baby's death just weeks later. Tivie missed Winston even more; life at Rose Cottage was more difficult with no husband present to share her grief. She tidied the house, planted gardens and busied herself with home tasks, "but no matter what I do there still seems to be a great void in my heart."[49] Winston responded with humor and passion: "I want to see you mighty bad. How do you feel on the subject? Golly I would give lots just to have one pouting smack, and I would give any thing I've got to have you serve me as you did you know when and you sayed you would kiss me din't you, that was a kind act and duly appreciated by your old Man."[50]

Humor moved to less solid ground when Winston crassly revealed that he had been invited to stay in a house with "an old Lady" and her daughters. He teased, inconsiderately, that the "old Lady," Mrs. Thomas, talked " pritty plainly" to him. Tivie fired back that she hoped Mrs. Thomas's "plain talk" did not disturb his rest too much and that he did not have to take a dose of "'*Morphine*' to make [him] sleep." Morphine was Tivie and Winston's secret word for sexual intercourse. Tivie went on to say that obviously she wanted to see Winston more than he wanted to see her and then she lapsed into a dissection of her own emotional life, sharing her personal conflict between longing and showing overt affection like "some folks, but the affection is abundant but stays shut up in my heart, will not flow out feely but I often wish that I could show more affection." Then the tone of her letter changed direction again and she warned him to have a cooling drink or cold water: "You said that was a good remedy."[51] Not to be outwitted by Tivie or by his own careless words, Winston replied with a self-congratulatory story of passing in review before his general, turning the story first into compliments from ladies seeing the review and then into an attempt at an apology: "You ought to know I did not mean really to ask any one for *Morphine* but was only jesting, though I really wanted some *very* much, but I don't intend taking any from any one but you, I was well attended to when at home!" Another well-timed visit brought "Morphine" and then baby dreams to Winston. "I feel" he wrote, "like a woman in family way. I had a dream a few nights ago of getting a *representative* and you were the mother, that is the first time I have ever had such a dream with or about you and I hope you will *appreciate* it. I wish I could hear from you oftener."[52]

The letter about the dream of a "representative" lightened Tivie's heart. Winston's expressions, she wrote, "seemed to come from your heart, you have never before spoken quite so plainly of your fidelity to me, that makes me happier than all else." Being alone and "blue," she confessed, brought thoughts that he might be tempted. She prayed, she said, for him to have strength to resist and she confessed she thought he was the best husband in the world. She admitted that the death of their baby Isabella had brought destructive thoughts to her mind. She responded to the interesting dream (dreamt before she knew she was pregnant again) that she did appreciate the dream but selfishly wanted his dreams to be all about her with no one else, not even a "representative," intruding. Then she lapsed into an emotional trigger, hardly realizing what she had done: "I can not forget your actions before we were married, but I do not feel about it as I used to, especially since you have been tried so well and proved faithful."[53]

Winston dreamed vivid dreams of Tivie after the one of a "representative." Speaking to the power of the imagination and dreaming in the summer of 1863 Winston wrote of efforts to supply the camp with milk, butter, meat, and peaches. Peaches were actually plentiful, and their image called up Tivie and Rosa in his mind: "I often wish for you and can bring Rosa before me in my imagination waiting for the peach to be pealed and then hear her say tarta PaPa. I wish it could be real and not imaginary. I can see you sitting down now writing to me ... hope it will be a better and longer one than this.... Good night my love! Pleasant dreams. I finish in the morning." The next morning Winston reported a "Morphine" dream of Tivie: "Good morning Mother Stephens.... I had a dream last night and thought I was taking some *morphine* but some how I failed and woke up disappointed.... I will be able to come once in two months and will be home that last of Sept or the first of Oct."[54]

"Well my darling," Tivie returned in November, "I must go to bed but hope my dreams of you to night may be pleasant, for I love to dream pleasantly of you when I can not have you with me, for I love my husband although I do not show it, and I think he must love me or he would not put up so well with my badness, I often think what a blessed thing it is I have such a good husband, and pray that we may never be any less happy." Winston made one of his favorite "surprise" visits to Tivie at 8:00 p.m. on November 12, 1863.[55]

More difficulties and the advance of Union soldiers into the Jacksonville area forced Tivie and her family out of Rose Cottage and on a search for another home. Letters of advice came from Winston. Failed attempts to rent houses depressed Tivie, and finally she found a house that suited all of them. She headed her letters "At Home," a magical blessing for Winston, who worried about his wandering family. They wished each other "pleasant dreams" in new locations, and Tivie sent blessings for the "King of Kings" to watch over and protect Winston.[56]

Then again carelessly—or was it intentionally ("Morphine" often followed a visit after he riled her)—Winston wrote what he claimed was a letter showing Tivie he had some joy in his life. He reported attending holiday parties on Christmas Eve of 1864. He took tea with Tivie's brother and several lieutenants at the home of a woman named Mrs. Capp. There was a dance, lots of good food—including a large roast, ham, chicken pie, pound cake, potato pies and other good things—several dances, and a "play" after dinner that involved kissing one of the invited guests, a woman. Winston wrote that he and Davis kept their dignity and that it was a great joke. It was *not* a great joke for Tivie. Her temper flared and she did not hold back. She was "sorry," she replied, that her husband could not spend Christmas without indulging in such company. She attacked his use of the word "dignity" and his good sense when the games commenced. All her pent up anger triggered a dream she reported to Winston with much ire: "I dreamed last night of being in some such company and it was a relief to me to wake, but enough, I hope you will not have any more invitations of that kind, if so that you will have dignity and respect enough for my feelings (if you should think them foolish) to refuse, I love my husband too well to want the least spot or suspicion to rest on his name, and his kisses are too precious to me to be thrown away, I expect you will be angry with me for writing this."[57]

Letters crossed in unfortunate timing in this crossfire of emotions. Winston responded with joy at seeing "At Home" firmly heading Tivie's letters: "What a magic there is in those two little words!—I have so longed to be with you and hug you up these cold nights to keep me warm. I think of you and dream of you. I fear if they don't let me come I will be induced to come against orders, sometimes I feel like I would be willing to give up everything on earth to be assured the privilege of living with you as we used to. I think if this War lasts much longer I will go crazy and desert." Tivie's new pregnancy was going well but she feared Winston would not be present for the delivery, the time referred to as being "sick." She begged him to come "now" because she wanted and needed to see him. She feared furloughs would be curtailed, but she begged him not to "go crazy and desert." She apologized for her hasty letter accusing Winston of losing his dignity and begged him not to have hurt feelings. She wrote too strongly, she said, about his frolic and acknowledged her jealousy. Then she revealed her real fears. In the anticipation of a new birth, she had relived her old grief in a dream about the death of Isabella. She woke up frightened of losing the new baby in the same way she had lost Isabella. Also weighing on Tivie and Winston's minds was the death of a child in their extended family. Winston had sent his condolences on the death but was really thinking of the death of his own child and his own sadness at not being present for Tivie's grief. His subsequent message to Tivie rekindled her own grief and possibly her dream of loss.[58]

Winston received Tivie's first letter correcting his behavior at the time Tivie was penning and mailing her letter of heartfelt remorse and her dream of reliving Isabella's death. The dated letters followed in a crazy mix of slow and infrequent and sometimes schizophrenic mail delivery. Winston defended his actions and defended his maturity, self-respect and pride and assured Tivie he had no thoughts of roaming sexually. Not to allow Winston the last word, Tivie then replied she thought she *was* "considerate" in not writing what she wanted to write and reminded Winston she was simply expressing a "wish ... that such a thing would not occur again." The two finally stepped away from the issue. Winston would have received Tivie's more "considerate" letters and heart-wrenching dream by the time he responded with his irate defense in February 1864.

Winston then sent a letter from his heart, apologizing for his despondent letters, acknowledging they were often veiled in humor and sarcasm: "[S]ometimes I am blue for true and I can't see our way through this War ... then I feel cheerful and write good letters." But then he joked again, this time about getting fat and the men vulgarly joking that he had breasts. That image reminded him that he missed Tivie and could not bear to be separated from her and wished he "could feel some ones breasts tonight." The surviving letter showed that Tivie tried hard to cross out these embarrassing sentences.[59]

Finally, a letter-truce. In Winston's letter about "breasts," he had declared his determination to be home in March when the birth of their new baby was anticipated. Tivie humorously responded that she didn't know what to say about his last letter and that she would rather have him fat than too thin and wrote he should "tell those 'vulgar fellows' to stop making remarks on my husband."[60]

The next set of letters flowed like a slow dirge to disaster. Winston wrote Tivie from Lake City, where the squadron was forming to go to the front. He wrote, "God grant I may be spared to you. If not, grieve as little as you can for your lost husband and take consolation that I died a soldier defending a just cause. Davis is with me ... and goes with me to the front."

Tivie's mother was "taken with a kind of congestive chill" on Sunday, February 28. On Friday, March 4, 1864, Davis delivered the news of Winston's death. Winston had survived the fierce fighting in the battle of Olustee but was brought down by a single sniper's shot on a routine patrol. Tivie's brother Willie, a devoted free spirit and fighting in a nearby Confederate regiment, wrote to their brother Davis: "Mine is not a grief that can relieve itself in words." Tivie recorded the following in her journal:

> With what a sad, sad heart I begin another journal. On Sunday Feb 28th, dear Mother was taken with a congestive chill. On Friday March 4th, Davis came with the news of the death of my dear dear husband, he was killed in battle near Jacksonville on the 1st. of March. Mother grew worse and on Sunday, Mar 6th, she too was taken from us, between 12 and 1 o'clk she passed quietly away from Typhoid Pneumonia. At 7 o'clk p.m. I gave birth to a dear little baby boy, which although three or four weeks

before the time, the Lord still spares to me. Mother was buried on the 7th, and Rosa was taken with fever, but recovered after two days. Davis returned to Lake City on the 10th, and Willie arrived here on the 12th, and he and Henry left to day for Monticello.... I have named my baby Winston, the sweet name of that dear lost one my husband, almost my life. God grant that his son whom he longed for but was not spared to see may be like him. I now begin as it were a new life and I pray that the Lord will give me strength to bear up und[er] this great affliction ... and be prepared when the Lord calls to meet them in that "better world" where there will be no more parting and no more sorrow.

Winston's brother, Swepston, also with Davis and Winston, wrote to Tivie about the anguish in his own heart: "[T]ho' I was not looking at him when the fatal ball pierced him I heard it and turned and asked him if he was hurt. He turned and looked the reply but could not speak.... That look, the last look was full of love. His lips moved but no word escaped. I see that look now and ever will."[61]

For the rest of her life Tivie looked back to what could have been rather than ahead to the future. Like other widows of that war, she could never come to terms with her loss.

Dreaming of Home—with a Sharp Edge

Dreaming of home reflected realities that were often painful on the battlefield. If "home" was not the perfect place with a perfect marriage or perfect relationship, dreams of home could bring stress and anxiety. Men dreamed of those painful relationships, which added to the stress of battle, alongside disease, poor diet, and often horrific weather and less than ideal camp life. Some men went crazy with worry and the distraction of not being home to monitor already shrinking relationships with sweethearts or deteriorating relationships with wives left to run farms and raise children on little or no income and having to pick up the male responsibilities of running a farm or business while looking for extra work to bring in money.

Captain Thomas J. Hyatt of the 126th Ohio Volunteer Infantry struggled with the uncertainty of the feelings of his wife and the loss of his impact on the lives of Edward and Harry, his two young sons. His wife, Mary, was lonely, facing debts, not receiving promised support from the government and did not hide her distress at having Thomas far away and inaccessible. Although we have no reference to Mary's dreams, if she remembered them, they might have expressed her equally stressed and anxious life. Many of those writing from home attempted to provide a façade of hope, joy, and support. Even those women sometimes broke down and confessed in moments of stress that their difficulties were mounting—dealing with rampant home-front disease, physical limitations, and having to do the jobs of two people.

When the omniscient reader looks into Mary's life and reads her life through the words of her husband, one might wonder if she suffered from manic-depression, certainly severe depression on the days of downward spirals. This condition of exhibiting dramatic patterns of highs and lows would not have been diagnosed as a mind/body problem in the mid-nineteenth century. Unsympathetic to the distress in Mary's letters, Thomas saw instead stubbornness in her not accepting help offered by her community. He upbraided her for attempting to portray herself as a woman of "pure grit" and then chided her for sentiments he found appalling. Apparently in letters that did not survive but hinted at in Thomas's responses, Mary had wished herself "under the ground." Thomas charged back that her silly household dilemmas (failing to get a "little lard") were "wicked." He reminded her that she had good health and that her children were intelligent and agreeable. He tried humor, saying he was having difficulty raising *her*; but then he would look back in reverie on his marriage with conflicting views. "One day" he complained, he would see a wife in a ragged dress, hair pulled back over her ears and "a spell on." There would be no sunshine at home on those days when she provoked him with her dowdy and sullen appearance. On another day she would fix herself up, comb her hair and have a "pleasant and affectionate" appearance. This is how it had been, he plainly stated, for eight years. Thomas ended this unpleasant letter with an even more unpleasant didactic "lesson" for her to read to their sons, a rather formidable but typically nineteenth moral tale in which a child inadvertently kills the dog it loves.[62]

It was little wonder that only three months later, Thomas dreamed "queer dreams." He dreamed they had been married some years, as they had been, but that the time had "run out and we were about arranging for another term." That was the first dream. In the second Thomas dreamed that Mary had abandoned him and was forming "an alliance with Lt. Watson of this Regt." This thought, in the dream, was not at all disagreeable to him. It allowed him to consider the sullen unaffectionate wife that provoked him, allowing him, inside the dream, the freedom to go and do as he chose. But then in the same dream "we were thrown together soon after, and I began to feel very badly, and could not think of the separation." This was the Mary he loved and cherished, the Mary whose letters he longed for and felt disappointed if they did not come to cheer him. When, in the dream, he realized he had no desire for separation, then the dream Mary "seemed quite offish, and looked toward Lt. Watson with a good deal more favor than you did me, but finally you began, I thought, to regret the steps you had taken and began to think I was a *little* better than your second choice." Thomas awoke from this dream relieved that it was a dream and that his relationship with Mary was still intact. The dream permitted Thomas a review of his conflicted marriage. Seeing Mary with someone else—and enjoying the new relationship—solidified Thomas's preference and love for Mary.

The reader does not know Mary's reaction to Thomas's dreams. His responses to her letters showed a return to his wishing and hoping to have letters from her and a return to exchanges about debts, buying out a neighbor who had property for sale, household duties and responsibilities, progress of the children's lives, and comments on the discomforts, comforts and vicissitudes of life.[63]

Captain Thomas J. Hyatt was killed September 19, 1864, near Winchester, Virginia. He had participated in battles at Cold Harbor, Petersburg, Monocacy, and finally Winchester, where he was buried. He may have had a sense of presentiment when he wrote Mary a letter just days before about "Religion" and his sense of Christ being his "Balm in Gilead": "When I am in the midst of danger I am able to look death in the face without fear, for I have a firm faith that nothing will happen to me that will not be for my good. Sometimes when I think how you will miss me at home it is hard to be entirely willing to never see you and the boys again, but I know all will be for the best." He sent Mary his love and asked her to lean on God if he did not come home.[64] Mary was sent Thomas's valise along with a promise to try to find his sword.[65]

Blessed with the Gift of Dreams

Hiram Camp dreamed he was at home in Virginia and "thought that I was eating roasten ears and hoecake and butter, but when I awoke I was lying in my old tent."[66] Azra

Bartholomew wrote to his wife, "Frank," that he dreamed of her and their newborn baby every night. Most soldiers' letters to home or family letters from home contained similar sentiments, often followed by "these dreams were so real that I thought you were there." Grant Carter told his sister that he was sorry "Florine was disappointed in her dream," which placed him at home on furlough to see her. Blanton Fortson told his mother that he was fighting hard and, at the moment, had no opportunity of dreaming. Bolton Thurmond wrote to Frances Porterfield in 1864, speaking of the war ending, in his opinion, because the men passed their homes and simply stopped and went back to them. He enclosed in his letter a Confederate tortoise shell ring, "very fine," for remembrance, but his real remembrance, he said, came in the night when he could simply close his eyes and the two of them were together. She was always on his mind, day and night; but in the night, "I met up with you and hugged you and you are beautiful, courteous and charming, and I awoke and oh, how sad I felt!" "I am yours forever," he ended, "till death."[67]

"I thank God for dreams"—William Stilwell

William Stilwell joined Company F of the 53rd Regiment, Georgia Volunteer Infantry, in James Longstreet's Corps in May 1862. He wrote over 200 letters to his wife, Mary Fletcher Speer (Molly). The first letter that recorded a dream was written from Antietam, ten miles above Harpers Ferry on the Potomac, only five months after William's enlistment. He was pining for home but feeling blessed with a pleasant dream of both Molly and his son Tommy:

> I thought I was at home and I could see you and Tommy so plain. Oh how I would like to feel of their little golden curls and see their little bright teeth shine and little plump feet paddle around the house. I reckon he can talk plain now and is most large enough to carry wood for his ma. I hope to see him soon yet. Surely this war won't last much longer but if it does let us do the best we can and trust to God for the rest.... Molly, I think [of] you while the cannon roar and the muskets flash. Never have I been so much excited yet but what I could compose myself enough to think of you, and I have often thought if I have to die on the battlefield, if some kind friend would just lay my Bible under my head and your likeness on my breast with the golden curls of hair in it, that it would be enough. Molly, I shall have to close, for my eyes is bathed in tears, 'till I can't write.... [P.S.] Good by, Tommy, my son."[68]

Stilwell escaped injury in what was considered the bloodiest single day of the war, with over 23,000 dead and wounded from both armies on the Antietam battlefield. Dreams and Stilwell's vivid imagination helped him survive numbing homesickness in camp and kept his spirit alive on the battlefield. He wrote that "some time" he could "see" Molly, his pa, and Tommy sitting up on his box near the table eating dinner and he could vividly see little Tommy with his head on Molly's arm in bed at night: "[A]nd when I lie down on my blanket in the broad moonlight and the dew of heaven is far down in my face ... I lay there while tears would run down my cheek but I would get up with my voice ringing through the camp, 'on Jordan's stormy banks I stand and cast a wishful eye!' and thus I go along through life. I like Paul, have learned how to be cast down and how to be exalted."[69]

A beautiful landscape, an enchanting night that showed its splendor across a landscape of agony and destruction, all of these reminded William how far away he was from those he loved and those who loved him: "I was on guard and the moon was throwing its golden light down through the tall trees around me and the gentle breeze was blowing its whistling sound through the leaves of autumn ... and I was thinking of my family in the distant land.... The tears would run down my face while I would turn it up to look at the moon and pray God to preserve my little family."[70]

In March 1863 William wrote that in his little cottage, while all others were sleeping, dead to care, and perhaps "having pleasant dreams of loved ones far, far, away, here I sit all alone writing to my Molly. Oh, who can tell the worth of pen, ink and paper. It is the telegraph which carries the prayers, pleasures and sorrows from an absent husband to an affectionate wife who dwells in distant lands." From Sweetwater, Tennessee he wrote, "I had one of the most delightful dreams I ever had in my life. I met you and Tommy and kissed each one and had a few pleasant hours in conversation. Oh, how happy I was! But, alas for me, I awoke and found it only a dream. I would to God it had have been a reality."[71] In a camp near Hagerstown, Maryland, he wrote, "I lay down night before last very wet and tired. I dreamt that I was at home and oh how glad I was but when I woke I found that I was still lying in mud and water, I was greatly disappointed."[72]

In mid-summer 1863 William penned the words of a popular song, "I Watch for Thee," to Molly, all three stanzas carefully written beneath an exquisite word portrait of a stunning July evening, the magnificence of the woods and the stars glowing as brightly inside his soul as in the sky as he walked to the top of a ridge on that warm gentle night. He took with him a small black box that contained, imaginatively, the "moments of my soul":

> When it rains they let me go in the house and when the moon is up in the heavens and the gentle wind from the mountains sends forth its still rustlings among the aspen tree under which I stand while the thousands of rattles of the drums are all still and the frogs that sing in the swamp all around are sending forth their beautiful melody while I go from post to post with a little black box in my hand containing the moments of my soul with a little lock of golden braid.

Clutching these moments of his soul, William's dream agony continued: "I often times dreamed of being at home but when I would wake up I would find it a mistake."[73]

Late in the war—in 1864—William wrote of the beautiful spring flowers in the Virginia vales and how much more constant they were than the fleeting nature of the dreams he dreamed of his Molly, the flower of his heart. He awoke each morning and the flowers still greeted him. Each evening he dreamed of Molly, reached for her time and again, and each morning she vanished just as he was near enough to touch her: "They always remain in my presence but you, whenever you appear to me in my dreams, vanish from me whenever I awake and I see you no more until I again fall asleep. The flowers are not so, when I dream of them in sleep, I awake to find them present with me, nevertheless you are the flower of my heart, the darling of my life, the queen of the flowers."[74] A month earlier, writing from Greenville, Tennessee, William had plucked a flower and held it to his heart, groaning that his one flower, Molly, would not stay upon his waking from a remarkable dream:

> I dreamed a most delightful dream last night. I went to sleep after commending you and our sweet children to God. I was thinking how sweetly you were lying in bed, perhaps not asleep but resting your weary body and thinking of the one on earth most dear, with one [child] on each side. Oh, how sweet thus I was thinking when I fell asleep. I thought we were together and had walked into a garden of flowers oh, it was so beautiful, we had been walking hand in hand, we came to a pretty bunch of

flowers and stopped to look at them, one on either side. I thought you raised your head up to see what I was doing. I looked at you and you smiled. It pleased me to the heart, I sprang over the flowers to catch you around the waist and just as I caught at you, someone called my name and you vanished from my sight and was gone. I awoke, someone was calling me, oh, to think that you would treat me so. If you had just stayed until I could have kissed you once more. I would not take anything for my dream, your spirits must have been hovering around me here. Yet it was so lovely and sweet. I was so much delighted and happy but to think that you would leave me thus without allowing me to embrace you or to kiss your hand, say what made you do me so, you loving creature. I would have been happy all day if you had just given me one kiss. Oh, don't do me so no more, my dearest wife, leave me not thus in anguish and pain but again when we walk among the flowers, let me embrace thee and kiss thy loving brow and be not scared off by anyone that calls my name. I wish they had been somewhere else and then I could have kissed you and been happy once more. I thank God for dreams for thus making me happy once and hope he will give me another visit soon and if so, I hope no one will interfere with my happiness for I don't have those blessed opportunities often. Still, I am happy today to think that I once more was by thy side amidst flowers and did see thee smile once more, one of those bewitching smiles which only those that love can give. Oh, my dearest, do smile once more upon your unworthy Husband, one of those sweet smiles that only you can give. Forgive me, my dear if I cause you to shed a tear, if I do I know it will be a tear of love and not of grief. Oh, Molly I have loved as never man could almost. Come tonight and let me kiss you, dear![75]

William's biographer wrote that William Stilwell was uneducated. His language was not. What stirred in his imagination to produce such magnificent letters? Was it the Celtic soul in the Southern mountains? Soul and Spirit—when nurtured by the Imagination—and a special spark of genius? William Stilwell's dreams were a remarkable miracle of communication and survival. Their reality was heartbreaking when William awoke to find his embrace and his love drifting away into the mist of morning; but the dreams sustained him through the harshest fighting and the most deadly battlefields of the Civil War—Antietam, Chancellorsville, Gettysburg, the Wilderness and Cedar Creek. The confluence of synchronistic events, perhaps in a nod from the Universe, was the final miracle in Stilwell's military career.

The last letter on record was written just days before he returned home. He had lost his foot in the battle of Cedar Creek on October 19 at Strassburg, Valley of Virginia, and was captured the same day. Suffering badly from his wound, he endured a twenty-day trip on water and land to Savannah and would have died but for a fated moment of coincidence. A Virginian, a woman named Mrs. William A. Davis, came to the place where William was being held as a prisoner. She asked those in charge to allow her to take two or more prisoners "that were in the most desperate condition" home with her so that she could care for them. She walked over to William, asked him about his wound ("I told her I would surely die unless something was done") and chose him as one of those she would care for. "She had me placed in her carriage and I was carried to her home. She prepared food that I could eat and nursed me as she would her own son until I was able to travel." She wrote to Mollie from her home in Newtown, Virginia, describing William's condition and saying that he had been taken prisoner. William Stilwell, when well, made his way home. He credited extreme providence for this unaccountable twist of fate that Mrs. Davis chose him among the hundreds and hundreds of bodies lying on the straw, bleeding and dying.[76]

In the almost 200 letters to his family, William penned eloquent passages, describing unimaginable contrasts: the magnificent beauty of the mountains, battle sights and sounds and the inevitable "day after" when beauty was marred by streams running with blood and so many body parts estranged from bodies that one ceased to even see them as

Crossroads at Newtown, Virginia, 2012.

human. His dreams kept him hinged and in touch with a personal vision of beauty, life, and home, where Molly and his small family awaited his return.

"You come very near to me in my dreams"—Frank Griffith

Frank Griffith's wife was present almost nightly in his dreams. He astutely and quickly determined that dreaming of home was not only his life-line to a loving, familiar place and a refuge from intense loneliness but also a "forerunner" of what lay before him—ultimately giving him confidence in his survival and return home, his happiness place.

He enlisted in Company K of the 116th New York Volunteer Infantry on September 2, 1862. In October, only a month later, he wrote his wife, Thankful, that he would never forget home because her "dear face" was in his waking and sleeping: "in my dreams your dear face is ever present with me."[77]

Strains of "Do They Miss Me at Home?" rang through the camp at Fort Monroe in early December and set Frank to thinking about whether or not he was missed at home and whether those he loved even thought about him in their daily lives among their individual pleasures and easy comforts. In this dreadful homesick reverie—made more palpable because the song was one his wife played on the harp when he was home—his mind wandered to the sacrifices a soldier makes to keep those at home safe and secure, and then his thoughts wandered to the "One" most dear to him who would welcome him back no matter what the condition of his body when he returned.[78] A supply of fresh letters lifted his spirit but then he drifted again into an abyss where no one there (in camp) sympathized with him or greeted him with a smile and kiss after the day's work. But loneliness had a savior in the night, he confided, "[Y]ou come to me as of old with the same fond caress and [I] feel your warm kiss upon my brow, and I live out those blissful hours again. Oh dear wife, if God in his great mercy should permit me to come to you again may I know better how to value the great blessings he has given me in our own dear self and those darling children He has given to us."[79]

Foretelling and "presentiment" played a role in Frank's letters, though not as profound a role as those who experienced presentiment of death or safety that could lead to reckless risks in battle. His presentiment was more of a longing, with a sense that he would be home again to share future joy with his wife and family. He claimed such presentiment cured his impatience. Each time he drifted into self-pity and what he called "pettishness," the quick fix came in a "real" dream. On a clear night, just after word of Union victories at Vicksburg and Port Hudson, Frank was particularly hopeful that the war would end soon. "Hope [brought his wife] near to me last night in my dreams. I thought that we were at home again in our room and you came and put your arms around my neck just as you used to, and I was so happy. Then it seemed as though my troubles were over and I should not start at the sound of the drum. And then I woke and found that it was all a dream. But I believe it is only a forerunner of the happy times that are in store for us in the future. Don't you think so dear?" A few days later one of Thankful's letters asked if *he* thought of *her*, although his letters should have left no doubt of that. He responded that he thought of her every day and every night, assuring her that his life was blessed by her love and that he loved her "even as my own life ... and in my dreams you come very near to me and I seem to live over again the happy days gone bye."[80]

A similar exchange of letters occurred in the spring. Thankful, looking for a predictable and loving response, asked if Frank ever dreamed of her, and Frank assured her he did—often—and described as an example a dream that broadened home to include a dream visit by Nettie, one of his children: "You want to know if I ever dream of you. Yes dear, very often in my sleep and you are by my side and I live over the happy hours of other days. And darling Nettie, how often I hear her dear voice saying *pa come pa come* and I feel the little arms around my neck and the pure innocent kiss upon my lips. And how often I have held her in my arms in my sleep as of old. And when I have waked it seemed so much like reality that I was sorry to wake up, it made me feel so lonesome." He described thinking of his mother when he was on picket duty, writing in lonesome detail of her care and love for him and how undutiful a son he had been in not recognizing her devotion until he was away.[81]

Soldiers journaled not only news about battles, camp life, friends, and family at home but also descriptions of the architecture and landscape of areas till then unfamiliar to them. They offered detailed descriptions of places such as Mount Vernon and Arlington and described plantation houses (many of them before and after their destruction), and other places that fell within their paths. The 116th camped in the area of Baton Rouge in the spring and summer of 1863. The city had been burned and Frank must have seen on countless occasions the destruction of a once beautiful landscape and built environment. The Louisiana State House had been burned the night of December 28, 1862. Frank's journal became a witness to the destruction, and Frank, thinking constantly of his own home, family, and longed-for "place," expressed a generosity of feelings toward the South when he pondered their sacrifice of people, landscape and built environment, which forever changed, for some, the sense of what had been "place."[82]

Frank lapsed again into homesickness and longing for his own special place, still intact, this time attributing his feelings to the intensity of the imaginable presence of those from home when he was most lonely, particularly during picket duty when danger and death were ever present, or in the night when the pain of separation brought most closely the faces of "dear ones at home, and in the feverish dreams of sleep I have felt your dear presence, and I have thought of your dear love and kindness always to me." He promised again and again that if he were allowed to come home safely, as he did each night in his dreams, that he would spend his remaining days making up for any lack of devotion he had shown before he became a soldier. This was the "secret influence" of having someone at home who cared as much for him as he did for them.[83]

In an autumn letter, from the aptly named location "Camp Misery," Frank dreamed again of Thankful, but this time he said, teasing, that he would not write this dream "for it might not please you to see it on paper, and I had rather tell it to you by word of mouth." More than likely it was a dream too sensual for a letter.[84] In a thoughtful vein, he wrote of the power of the letter from a loving home, especially *long*, loving letters from those far away, and their influence on the soldier in the field. Survival, he said, depended on "good spirits" and on states of mind:

> And there is many brave boys died whose death was hastened by the neglect of the dear ones at home to write often such long, loving letters and encourage him to hope for the best. For when we do not get any letters from home ... we get lonesome and melancholy, and then is the time that we get sick.... And if one is sick he bears to suffer in silence till he gets so that he cant help himself any longer. Then he is sent off to the hospital to die. Oh, if those that we have left at home ... wish to see their sons, Fathers, and brothers, husbands come home to them men and not brutes write to them such good long loving letters as you write to your own unworthy Frank.

He ended his letter as usual: "Do you ever dream about me?" He dreamed of *her* three days later. This time he dreamed not only that he was home but that the war was over! Promising to continue to share dreams of her, he asked for a new likeness of her, this time with a looking glass opposite the likeness so that they would be side by side.[85]

Still at Camp Emory, Frank tried the common visionary diversion of imagining his beloved in his presence, but he mixed it up a bit, proposing that Thankful might be jealous of this presence of herself. There was, he said, a woman every morning at the head of his bunk and she looked down and smiled at him just as Thankful once did. This comforted him, he confided, "and ... she looks just like *you*. And there is a little one to[o] that sometimes comes too and looks on with big bright laughing eyes, like one that I left at home." Bawdily teasing Thankful, he supposed he would make a "clean *bosom*, or breast, of it" and promised no more secrets. He "supposed" she would accuse him of "making *love* to her and all that, but I tell you it is no such thing for when I talk love to her she says *never a word* and makes [as] if she did not hear me. So you will hold her guiltless[s] of any wrong. Well now, I suppose that you will want to know her name, but I think that I will wait a while and see how you feel about it. Just Please to write and tell me if I have done right."[86]

Frank's regiment moved toward New Orleans and then into Washington, D.C., during the final days of the war. Frank continued to write longing letters home and wept in May 1865 at a Groves Theatre production of *Uncle Tom's Cabin* because the little girl playing the role of Little Eva reminded him of his daughter Nettie. While there, a dispatch arrived regarding the capture of Jeff Davis. People went wild with excitement; "The Star Spangled Banner" was played and Frank looked toward home. Near the same time, he received news that his father was dying from lip cancer, which had been discovered in the last months of Frank's enlistment. Frank may or may not have seen his father alive again. He was heading home at the end of the war and his father died either before he arrived or shortly after he returned home.[87] But, as Frank had promised Thankful, he survived the war and came home safely.

Somewhere Out There: Dreaming Under the Same Moon

Captain Jacob B. Ritner, 1st Iowa Infantry; 25th Iowa Infantry; 15th Army Corps, Army of the Tennessee, served the entire length of the Civil War away from his beloved wife and their four children. Jacob's wife, Emeline Bereman, was born in Kentucky in 1831, but her father moved the family to Indiana because of his opposition to slavery. In 1845 the Beremans moved again, this time to Mt. Pleasant, Iowa, where Jacob and Emeline met at Howe's Academy, a school run by a former high school teacher of William Tecumseh Sherman. They married in 1851 and Jacob became a teacher in southeast Iowa. Emeline lived with her mother during their long war-time separation, writing and receiving longing letters, at times exquisitely beautiful ones, expressing melancholy and devotion: "Where are you tonight, and what are you doing? Oh I would so like to know. I have got the blues most horribly tonight and the wind is blowing a perfect streak. Your old canteen is bumping & banging against the wall in the porch, trying to keep time with the howling of the wind, and the dismal patter of the rain. Oh how gloomy everything seems tonight! How I wish you were with us to chase away the melancholys, but where are you tonight and what are you doing?"[88]

Jacob wrote that he was seeing the same moon Emeline saw and wondered if she was looking with him at the same moon and the same stars: "And then I think that maybe you are sitting in the door at the same time and looking at the same objects, or perhaps the same stars I am looking at are shining through the window into your nice room where you are sleeping in your snug bed, and then I feel very near to you and love you, Oh! so much! And then I think again that however this may be, there is one thing certain, we have the same kind Providence to watch over and protect us both, and the same Heavenly Father to call upon for help in time of need. I feel very grateful that I have a dear wife and kind friends at home who remember me in their prayers." He lovingly addressed

Emeline in the first person, inviting her gently into his camp to share his company, to sit in his lap and give him a hug and kiss: "Come and sit down on my lap and let us have a talk—come right along now. I want to tell you something. There now, ain't you sweet? If I had you in my arms again I would kiss you a thousand times. I have just been looking at your picture and I just know it is the prettiest thing that ever was. Be still now!! You ain't going to get away yet. If you wasn't such good stuff I believe I would scold you a little. But you are my own sweet dear." In the same way, Jacob invited Emeline to see his tent and an addition the men had created. He would kiss her quick, he wrote in first person, and then he gave her a visual tour of the stools, the fireplace, bench, racks for personal items, trunks, and shelves and invited her to "*come right in* and sit down by me. You may have the captain's stool, as he is gone foraging. Oh, that won't do? Well, you may sit on my lap! I know that is what you want." Again, he wrote, "Well, now, dear, just come and sit down by me and I will try to tell you all about it. You must be careful, though, how you go to hugging me, if you touch my sore hand I will squeal. Now I wish I had you here to growl and complain to. There is nobody to pity me at all, and I feel quite lonesome away from the company. You are the dearest, sweetest wife in the world, and I know it."[89]

In exchanges of dreaming, each dream "seeing" Jacob at home, sometimes teasing one another with an edge sharpened by long separation, Emeline trusted that these dreams foretold Jacob's eventual safe return. One concerned her: (January 5, 1863) "Now mind! If you are wounded and can't do anything for a while you must be sure and come home. I can't help but feel that you are safe, but I dreamed the other night that you were at home sick, and that you had gone crazy and come very near killing me in one of your crazy spells, but that is all nonsense."[90] This dream triggered a pensive return from Jacob, who described his heartfelt desire for the war to be over and all of them home again, at the same time reminding both her and himself that he enlisted for a reason and would see the war through. He shared some of the horror of what he daily faced, of walking over the battlefield strewn with the dead and dying, some "lying almost in heaps and some scattered round in almost all kinds of shapes, limbs torn off and bodies mangled in almost every manner."[91]

Emeline's dream of Jake was more than likely precognitive of the condition of Jake's brother, Judson. Judson, also in the army, had fallen ill at the time of Emeline's dream and died on April 16, 1863. In her vision of a "crazy spell," it is probable that Emeline looked in on Judson's condition near his death in an inhospitable environment of disease and delirium. Jacob shared the news of his brother's death and, in recognition of the dream that came at the same time, lightened the mood by writing he was not home "the other night when you dreamed I was, But I have often dreamed I was at home." Jacob hoped to gain a short leave of absence. He consoled himself that the dream of home would eventually come to pass and that it was a great comfort to think he had a wife and loving family at home thinking of him and sharing in a dream of all of them being at home.[92]

Jake teased Emeline that she would not recognize him on his return home, setting off her fears for his long-term health after such a war, but he assured her she would know him no matter how poor or sunburned or dried up or bald, that she would know "the crook of his nose anyhow." She said she had worn his picture for so long she had broken the pin from the back and "dreamed last night you were home."[93]

Emeline's father died in June 1864, and the pain of a family death without the presence of her beloved Jacob hurt her. Jacob sat on a hill in the moonlight and considered the war and the difference it had made in his family life, how they were once at home together and now were scattered and some no longer there. He wished Emeline pleasant dreams and begged that she would share them with him.[94]

Dreams of home and of Emeline intensified in the fall of 1864, almost every letter speaking of reading Emeline's letters "by the light of a fire," dreaming about her "all night" and dreaming of home. Emeline was dreaming with Jacob, dreaming that he was home with her, a beacon of hope that he would survive the war and return to her and their children. "I am very anxious to hear from you again. Hope you have got through with that campaign and are now ready to go into camp and as soon as that is accomplished, I expect to see you at home. I dreamed last night that you were here. Hope I shall soon get a letter from you again." Jacob returned the hope with a "good night" and a wish that "you may have sweet dreams," followed by a letter of longing and thinking about Emeline—"Then I shall be thinking about you—perhaps you will be asleep in your warm bed, dreaming about me. Only think how far we are apart!" Jacob dreamed again of home but, possibly accurately, dreamed of the stress of the long parting on his wife's health and chided her about a cough she possibly had written about: "[I] dreamed about you several times lately. I dreamed the other night that I had you in my arms and was kissing you. I thought you were just as pretty and sweet as ever, but that you looked pale and thin, like you had been sick for a long time." His dream accurately saw Emeline sick with a cough. "I hope you have taken medicine and got over that bad cough."[95]

Jacob survived, returned home to his family in Mount Pleasant, where he assisted Emeline's brother Thomas at the *Mount Pleasant Home Journal*, and worked in the local school district. His health was impaired by the war, however, and he never fully recovered. He died eight years later on January 17, 1873.[96]

My Dream Pictures: James and Elizabeth Bowler

James Madison and Elizabeth Bowler lived what must have seemed to them an entire lifetime during the Civil War. They courted, married, had children, and bought a farm. Elizabeth went to dances, circuses, expressed her opinion on war and politics, shared an abiding love of music and confided her deepest feelings to James. Madison gave advice on farming and suggested remedies for Elizabeth's dying sister while he was serving in the Third Minnesota Volunteer Regiment and in the 113th U.S. Colored Infantry. Elizabeth, called "Lizzie," remained in Nininger, Minnesota, longing for Madison's furloughs, which were brief and far apart. Emotions ranged from her support of Madison's enlistment at the beginning of the war to annoyance with his dogged sense of duty after he joined. His patriotic fervor got in the way of her perception of him as a devoted husband and father. In September 1864, she wrote, "I want you to really think the matter over whether it is your duty to spend all the best of your life away from those who love you best and sighs for your presence every moment of her life time."[97]

Throughout their correspondence the Bowlers wheedled and cajoled and argued over whose notion of duty would prevail. Their arguments, however, did not dampen their romantic notions of one another. They accessed their vivid imaginations and took every opportunity to describe their images of one another. Madison found a pretty flower for Lizzie but wrote that there was always one flower he preferred above all others—"But

I have a *picture* of it—a great consolation to me. If you knew how my friends complement that picture, you would think yourself handsome. But I must close, for supper is ready."[98] A few months later Lizzie recalled their last Christmas together before Madison left. He had shared his intentions of becoming a soldier, and she recalled the carelessness with which she listened because she neither considered herself in a relationship with him nor her country in a relationship with war.

Madison shared a story about "a dog that isn't a dog," a young raccoon adopted by Company F. Civil War soldiers had an interesting menagerie to keep them company. Some horses and dogs became battle companions and heroes. Soldiers wrote of pet bears, sheep, raccoons, birds, and other animals. Madison teased Lizzie about the pet raccoon turning over his ink and walking across his letter and left the paw print intact. Lizzie received the coon's paw. Her responding letter noted that she had dreamed three times of Madison, a notion that greatly disturbed him. He viewed the dreams as warning dreams, content unknown to the reader but presumably precognitive of an event that began to play out as a dangerous prank, leading to Madison's arrest, a court-martial and, thankfully for Madison, an honorable acquittal.[99]

The Third Minnesota was diverted to the Dakota War in the fall of 1862 and then returned to Fort Snelling in the winter. Lizzie and Madison had a few weeks in which they settled their relationship and married on November 30.[100] Emotional intensity increased in their letters, each expressing a deep sense of the vacancy left by the other's absence. Darkness, Lizzie said, helped her to think and she wondered if he thought, as she did, of the other "occupying some vacant spot in some place that you are familiar with." She explored the notion of the imagination and where it led, sometimes to dark places, seeing him no longer in the land of the living. Only sleep, "the arms of Morpheus," brought her peace.[101] Madison responded with a letter about soldiers dreaming of home, oblivious in those moments of the trials that lay before them. He blessed her with "sweet sleep" and pleasant dreams, reminding her of the need for frequent letters from one he loved so much. Lizzie was pregnant at that time.[102]

Stationed in Little Rock, Arkansas, in late 1863, Madison took an imaginable journey home to Lizzie, ill after childbirth, seeing her and her "little birdie" (their new child]), seeing the house, "the same objects, the fences, the same house standing out on the familiar prairie, and the plainest of all, I could see my poor, sick Lizzie, with her little birdie by her side, lying in bed and writing those sober lines to me." In his imagination, Madison felt his heart close to her, drawn by "chords of deep, pure love." He longed to see her, to press her close, "to rest my rough cheek once more against yours, and to rest my head once more beside yours on the pillow where I can tell you in words the love I cannot express in writing. The only regret I have is that I am not worthy [of] the love of one so pure and so good as you. I am too rough, too wicked for you. Yet I do not know what I should do without you.[103]

Accessing her own imagination and dreams after a lengthy separation from Madison, Lizzie expressed displeasure with the situation. She had dreamed a horrible dream that she interpreted as indicating Madison did not wish to see their new daughter. Madison quickly responded that he most certainly wished to see her "little birdie" and her as well. He commiserated on the sickness and pain she endured alone in bringing their child into the world and told her he could do nothing at present but love the child. He tried to soothe her with a story of imagining her in her suffering "and wishing that Mad were there to help beguile those weary hours, to give assurance of his deep sympathy, to look with a father's eyes upon the little 'prize' you have given him, to thank you for what you have endured in his behalf, to rest his head upon your pillow and tell anew the story of his love." He went on, desperate to favorably survive her dream image of him. He painted a picture of his surroundings, not unpleasant in their appearance, in fact fairly nice for a war camp—lots of noise, military pomp, an elegant building for headquarters, food to eat, clothing to wear, warm blankets, and even a fancy bedstead with two mattresses: "But *here's the rub*. I sleep on the back side and on the foreside is my unwelcome bedfellow, 'Miss Painful Vacancy.' I can hardly bear her. She does not lie up so close, put her arms around my neck, and kiss me like Lizzie used to." He suggested maybe Lizzie should buy the baby its own bedstead, because he would not want anyone to come between them when he came home. That message possibly destroyed his intent at imaginable reconciliation![104]

"Mad" not being off the hook yet, Lizzie reported a second dream that did not sit well with her image of Madison as a caring father. She carelessly wrote that she would go and dream of her "absent hubbie," offhandedly noting: "By the way, I must tell you what I dreamed the other night. I thought you came. When you came in, baby was lying in the cradle. You passed right by her and never looked at her. That made me sort of spunky & I would not show her to you. Then baby cried and spoiled the rest of my dream." Lizzie refused to place the baby in a cradle of her own, seeing no need to accommodate the wishes of someone who wasn't even there![105]

All "little birdie" issues were forgiven, and Lizzie and Madison's letters sparred over location and the end of the war rather than their child. Madison settled more firmly into what could become a permanent job working with the U.S. Colored Infantry in Little Rock, Arkansas. Lizzie at first refused to leave her home but finally relented, realizing Madison had no plans for returning to Minnesota. In early 1865 she had written of looking out the window expecting to see Madison coming home, but all that came to pass was time: "Sometimes I feel that the last five years of my life have been a blank. There is one subject that I dwell on night & day when the subject that ought to be constantly before me is forgotten. All night after retiring, before I can close my eyes to sleep, [I think of] every unpleasant word ever spoken between us (if ever there were any) and every unkind act & I drop to sleep wondering how I could do any thing unkind to one I love as I do you & dream of having you with me but wake up to find it all a dream. Thus pass the days, weeks & years." Unrelenting dreams of seeing each other had passed back and forth between them; but Lizzie intentionally, Madison felt, denied them the waking reality of those dreams. Madison wrote that he thought of them both constantly, "the light whose memory brightens" the humble camp and "lingers in dreams around his lonely pillow by night." He wished her pleasant dreams but again and again begged her to come to him. They both stood their ground, each responding that they were dreaming "of seeing you," sharing that they asked for sleep dreams that would allow them to see each other. The question was *where* those dreams might ultimately place them in fulfillment. A soft ultimatum came from Madison in words appearing to offer Lizzie a choice. He used the motif most familiar to both of them, dreams and the imagination: "I speak in sober earnestness; and if I leave the army on your account it must be at your plain say so. I shall not allow you to flatter yourself that you can 'wheedle' me to do so, by making light of my schemes—my dream-pictures." It worked. Lizzie packed her belongings, her child, and her own dreams of Madison coming home to Minnesota and headed south to Little Rock, Arkansas.[106]

An Invitation: Come See Me in a Dream

William E. Stoker served with Company H, 18th Texas Volunteer Infantry, in Arkansas until his death at Jenkins' Ferry in April 1864. He had been a property owner in the Coffeeville community of Upshur County, east of Gilmer, Texas, when he enlisted for three years in a "duration" volunteer regiment, serving not of his own volition. He hated the war and wrote constantly of home. Soon after he left Texas, he began dreaming about his wife, Elizabeth, or "Betty," and their little daughter Priscilla, their son William and little "Net."

On August 27, 1862, he wrote to his wife: "I dream of seeing you often. It appears to me just as natural to be talking to you & Priscilla. When I wake, it nearly kills me for to think it aint so. I think of you all the time nearly." On September 7, writing from Prairie County, Arkansas, William said, "I am constantly dreaming about home." He made a suggestion that might astonish the dreamer who does not understand the intense reality of the dream of home: "I dremp about Net the other night and I dream of being with you often. I wrote to you to see William [his son] and see if he would come with you to see me in a dream or not. Write what he says about it."[107]

On November 4, 1862, William asked Betty to receive all the affection "a heart could imagine for your self. Kiss Priscilla for me.... I don't know what I would give to be with you & her to night. I dremp of being with you last night. I would give any thing in this world if my dream would come to pass, but I can't take time to write it to night. Tongue cant express nor I cant write how bad I want to see you."[108]

William received a furlough in January 1864. He returned to his unit and fought in battles at Mansfield and Pleasant Hill, Louisiana, and then marched to Camden, Arkansas. He was shot and died on April 30 at Jenkin's Ferry. A relative wrote a last letter.[109]

I dream of you often; come close to me in my dreams; dreams so real that I thought you were here. There are thousands of soldiers' letters home and thousands of letters from family members back to their soldiers, in which they write of dreaming dreams, longing for home, sometimes waking in joy, often waking in the disappointment of an unrealized dream. Some taunt, some tease, some are angry, but these dreams and imaginative journeys into each other's lives remind them of their humanity and provide an escape from the loneliness and terror of war.

CHAPTER 5

Dreaming of Children

Fathers dreamed of soft kisses from their children or saw their sweet faces and wrote from a reality that touched all the senses. Tullius Rice, a surgeon from Macon, Georgia, wrote from Virginia in July 1861: "I dreamed of Mary and our little one this day while asleep. I thought that my daughter was afraid of me on account of my whiskers." W.H. Mangham wrote his mother from Fredericksburg in January 1862: "I have not seen no little children since I left. It is nothing here but big guns and big men, and I am getting tired of it and every once and a while march out and face the cannon balls."

The grief and longing of the soldiers for their families, including heart-felt and heart-wrenching messages of love for their children, haunted the men in the battlefields and stood in firm contrast to modern perception that nineteenth century fathers stood back and did not participate in the lives of their children.[1]

Benjamin Moody whispered in his dreams, in 1861: "Wife, sleep with your children in your bosom in place of me."[2]

In an intriguing letter dated June 12, 1864, from First Lieutenant George Howe of Shoreham, Company B, 11th Vermont Infantry, to Lorette Wolcott, his sweetheart, George asked how "Julia" (a young girl) was getting along in school and "why don't she make up a dream if she is going to and write it to me. Ask her if she can't, dream it over again." It must be she dreamed about him or something she wanted to share with him but couldn't remember the dream; such was his confidence in her ability to return to the dream or its theme that he asked her to either make it up and send it to him or just dream it again.[3]

Richard Richards, born in England, immigrated to New York and married his sweetheart, Sarah Walford, in 1856 in Peoria, Illinois. He enlisted in the army in 1862 and served with Company C, 125th Illinois Volunteer Infantry. He survived the war but suffered from a wounded left knee and right heel and gangrene after being bumped around among several hospitals in 1864 and 1865. Surviving letters to his wife began in December 1862, with "kisses" sent to his "dear little Boys." He first mentioned the boys by name, Freddy and Eddy, in June 1863 and again in a letter from March 1864. Extremely anxious about Freddy, Richard wrote that he "dreamed last night that my dear little Freddy was dead." He looked anxiously for a response, adding, "God grant that it may not be and I hope he is well."[4]

This kind of reference, if not proven precognitive, was generally born from anxiety and distance from those loved ones so dear to the soldier. That dearness increased, as Richard noted, like the truth of the line from an old song that "absence makes the heart grow fonder." Richard reminisced in his letters about his unworthiness for the affection flowing from home, revisiting memories of the days he and his wife met and married, the trials they had endured and the love after the storm of each learning the faults and delights of the other: "No freezing wind can chill that warmth of mutual love. No dashing snow or pitting rain can drown even one spark ... [and] we are together in spirit and enjoy a sympathy of soul which neither time nor space can deprive us of." Perhaps he was not as eloquent as some, but his words were just as longing, and Richard vowed they would be together in Heaven if war separated them on "this terrestrial ball."[5]

Freddy was still among the living in late 1864 when Richard was treated for his wounds and gangrene, both dangerous to his survival. Richard wrote to both his boys and asked that they keep his letters. He shared some of his hardships on a long cold march and relayed how important their home and warmth was in his mind as he imagined them safe and snug in their beds. With a final nod to a wish for their preservation, no other letters survived.[6]

Dreaming of Willie

Willie McLaws, the young son of Major General Lafayette McLaws, CSA, was described as being gentle with a loving heart. His unnamed health problems left him weak but minimally thriving, like a hothouse flower. His father adored him; his mother, Emily, guided and protected him. Letters home from General McLaws included suggestions for outdoor exercise—fishing, opossum hunting, learning to swim and hunt.

McLaws served alongside important figures in the Confederate conflict—Robert E. Lee, Joseph E. Johnston, John Hood and a controversial childhood friend, James Longstreet. He adored his family but honored his career as a soldier with responsibility and duty, ultimately fighting and winning restoration of that honor in a court-martial against charges by the dishonest and inept Longstreet. McLaws loved his wife and family but his career was foremost in his life and necessitated long absences from home. He asked them all to write letters and pretend contentment " although their hearts may be heavy in the effort."[7] Shortly after his promotion to general, Lafayette McLaws looked for a congratulatory letter from Emily. None came, and he sought news of what might have prevented letters from reaching him. His anxiety spilled over into his nights, one of his dreams alarming him. He dreamed Willie was missing from home and no one knew where he was: "The dream awoke me and I lay a long time thinking about it, and wondering why you were so long silent— ... I have written also to Willie." The day of his dream had been grueling and tense. Twenty-seven hundred men were in the field with no fight, and mud and rain wreaked havoc with plans for a defensive position. His dream of Willie placed unspeakable anxiety front and center in his mind.[8] Finally he received a letter, quite funny, from his daughters and his wife, announcing a new baby, with some of its hair enclosed, mixed with hair from several heads, and revealing a name for the baby not entirely suitable to the general: Uldrick Huguenin. Many letters followed with pronouncements of love, tempered with an explanation that his emotions, as a general, must be suppressed even though he longed to be with his wife and children.[9]

Confusion followed when Lafayette received incomplete letters about Willie. He asked that Willie be sent into the country if he was unhealthy. He thought the country air and country play would restore his son's health. He pleaded again for understanding of his situation and asked Emily to try to find happiness for inspiration for both of them: "[Y]ou are my thermometer & must be careful, as to the variations of your temperature."

A visit home revived them both. He wrote that his visit was like a dream, his only regret not showing more "how *much* I love you & the children."[10]

A new depth of feeling revived between Emily and Lafayette. He declared they were still lovers and could see things through a silver veil and not "a darkened glass."[11] War was at their doorstep, and Lafayette had suggested a move to Sparta but had heard nothing from Emily on whether or not she thought that might be a good idea. He purchased a house and wrote to her that he "dreamed one night that you had [heard about the purchase], and were pleased with it." Practicality made this dream a reality. There was less danger—and fewer Yankees—in Sparta, where the house was located.[12]

Emily's focus on Willie's health and her fears of the war increased; she wanted to send Willie away. Lafayette reacted swiftly, chiding her for proposing to send her most helpless child away, the one who was far less capable of bearing the loss of his mother than the others were. He suggested Willie's personal nature and "peculiarities" would not endear him to strangers and would make all of them unhappy. Following this admonition were letters of strength and endurance as the family moved into Sparta and prepared to survive the worst. In an unprecedented declaration of love near the end of the war, perhaps generated by less constriction to duty and more freedom to express emotion as all around him began to crumble in defeat, Lafayette recalled a past memory of being in Savannah with Emily and her hand in his, the two of them surrounded by love and contentment:

> How little do we prize the blessings which are dayly showered upon us and around us, until we are deprived of them and have their opposites to contend against—the sweet welcome of my wife and her sweeter kiss of love, and the unaffected welcome of my children, now so highly appreciated were once regarded as too much a matter of course.... But now what price could buy them, how much would I sacrifice to obtain them? And what have I to compensate for or replace them? My time is occupied with caring for others who do not care for me, who give me no smile of welcome but seldom—and the feeling or expectation of gaining love is never thought of— ... even we laugh because it is our duty, and from half recklessness—but my dear darling ... write me a long sweet letter.[13]

General Lafayette's dream of Willie's being lost, probably in tune with the child's unidentified health problems, became a gradual truth. Willie, nine at the time of that dream, died in 1870 at the age of 18. More grief was in store for this family. Although three additional daughters were born after the war—Annie Lee, Virginia, and Elizabeth—another daughter, Laura, contracted typhoid fever while away at school in Virginia and returned home, where she died in 1877 at the age of 21. Both Annie Lee and her mother, Emily, died of typhoid fever the same year—1890, in April and May. General Lafayette had two sons remaining, Johnnie, who was born in 1853, and Uldrick, who was born after the wartime visit in 1861, in addition to his two daughters, Virginia and Elizabeth.

Awakened by "emotions of gladness"

Harvey Luttrell, an Alabama merchant, joined the 10th Alabama Infantry in April 1863. Unfit for regular duty due to asthma and rheumatism, he served as a hospital nurse in various locations in the Richmond, Virginia, area. He spared his wife, Sue, the more morbid details of working in the hospitals and reserved his comments to personal thoughts on general conditions around him. A letter written to his father in 1861, before he joined the infantry, confirmed a prediction he heard, as a child, his father make—that civil war would come and tear the country apart. Harvey hated the discord and never ceased longing for home after he enlisted, but he hated even more the destruction of values he held dear and what he called "northern aggression" for the sake of politics and office.[14]

Harvey's first letter after he joined the 10th Alabama opened with both gratitude for a good situation and sadness at seeing so many men "shot to pieces"—and his first dream of longing for his wife and children, the only place in his heart where he found happiness: "It is 9 o clock at night I am very tired—will go to bed and see if I cant dream about you and our baby, and be happy, at least in my sleep."[15]

In every letter he wrote Harvey asked Sue to send his kisses to his beloved children and to receive kisses and endearments as a token of his love for her and his family. A year later, in May 1864, he dreamed of a sweet embrace from Sue. He wrote in his letter, again, how much he loved his children. Seeing his small daughter reminded him that she was "an angel":

> Well Dearest, last night I dreamed of meeting you at home and after a sweet embrace I hurried to the bed with you, to see our four cherubs, who were all sleeping not knowing that I was present. The emotions of gladness were so great as to awaken me almost immediately. Oh Surely, our meeting will be a happy one.... Yes Love, that Daughter of ours is an angel, oh how I could enjoy the company of our babes and I would not have one less for anything.... Dollie, Oscar, Elston and Chester, my sweet little Children how badly I do want to see you. Your mother only knows. Oh Sue is it not hard? but I have witnessed things recently that were as trying to others as this to us. I can tell you a great many distressing circumstances that have happened, when I see you.[16]

The reader feels Harvey's heartbreak as he saw his children so very close in his dream, realizing they did not see or hear him. With difficulty he tore himself away from the dream and from their presence. Harvey dreamed often of his wife and children, always blessing them with adjectives of sweetness and joy and often describing them in angelic terms and with a heart filled with longing for home: "I often dream of thee + our Sweetest children."[17] Tokens of love passed back and forth between Harvey and his family—ribbons, lockets, combs, snippets of hair, which he protected and cherished.

Harvey's unit was heavily engaged at Petersburg. There they participated with General A.P. Hill's 3rd Army Corps and were part of the Confederate line along the Boylton Plank Road south of the town. On October 27, 1864, Harvey tended the terrible wounds of those who participated in the fight at Hatcher's Run. On October 14, Harvey had dreamed he " saw "the most Angelic woman ... I ever beheld. She was draped in plain white. I was only ten feet from her, but I did not go to her. Her name was Sue Luttrell." He feared his vision of Sue would vanish if he reached for her; how his heart broke, but "oh how happy I was for a moment!"[18]

Harvey returned to his home seven months later, in May 1865, in decent health, and united with his family. He found the farm in terrible shape. Still, he was lucky—his property, though in poor condition, was intact and his family was alive.

"I heard their sweet little voices"

John Yates, Company K, 38th Indiana Infantry Volunteers, wrote letters to his wife, Elizabeth Robertson Yates, between 1861 and 1864. A last letter was written by John's brother-in-law, George W. Riggle, a private in the same company. Written to Elizabeth, its sad notification was of John's death on July 15, 1864, not in battle but by accident: a tree fell on him, and George said he never knew where the "hurt" came from.

In the summer of 1862 John had written a longing letter home, telling his wife that he was well and hardy except for an injured knee, which was already healing. He feared that the injury might produce permanent stiffness, but he assured Elizabeth that he was in a good place and that he even had a straw bed and plenty of good food to eat. He shared a heart-wrenching dream of longing for his twins. His feelings were so present both in the dream and upon waking that he could not forget them. In the dream he had returned home during the night and had gone to the bed where the twins, Jony and Emmie, were sleeping: "They awoke and both fetched me around the neck and I heard their sweet little voices saying 'My Pap!' 'My Pap!.' When I awoke with my arms hugged up as if I had their sweet little bodies I then cried and went back to sleep again."[19]

"Keep her in good health & cheerful before going to bed"

An English immigrant to America, William Bradbury was a Union soldier, land speculator and devoted husband and father who took an active role in his family's affairs even from the battlefield. His landed wealth continued to increase under the astute management of his wife, Mary. Although he was only a private in Company B, 129th Illinois Infantry Volunteer Regiment, William's role as clerk gave him intriguing access to powerful figures in the Union army. He had learned "phonography," a sort of Civil War shorthand, and this skill kept him out of battle and actively engaged in letter writing to his family, for whom he longed.

William worried about the constant dreams of his daughter, Jane, writing that he was sorry she dreamed so much. In a letter in 1862 he made an obscure connection to his daughter's prolific dreaming to a dream he had in which he was wading through "deep water the night before I got the letter." Concerned about Jane's dreams (the subjects were not revealed), he asked his wife to keep her in good health "and cheerful before going to bed." A few nights later he dreamed he was kissing his little son, Willie. William's particular concern about Jane's dreams may have stemmed from published articles on children's dreams indicating unhappiness or poor health, particularly mental health. Articles in *Harper's* published in 1851 and 1864 proposed that girls were prone to nightmares and were more easily disturbed in their mental and physical health.[20]

Chapter 6

"Just So" Dreams

The Sentinel's Dream of Home
by Colonel A.M. Hobby

'Tis dead of night, nor voice, nor sound, breaks on the stillness of the air,
The waning moon goes coldly down on frozen fields and forests bare:
The solemn stars are glittering high, while here my lonely watch I keep,
To guard the brave with anxious eye, who sweetly dream and sweetly sleep.

Perchance of home these sleepers dream, of sainted ones no longer here,
Whose mystic forms low bend unseen, and breathe soft whispers in their ear:
Sleep on, sleep on, my comrades brave, quaff deep to-night of pleasure's cup,
Ere morning's crimson banners wave, and reveille shall rouse thee up....

To softer scenes my spirit yields—to-night a sweeter vision comes....
The moon has waxed and waned away; the morning star rides pale and high—
Fond dreams of home no longer stay, but fade like stars on mornings sky.

Galveston, Texas, February 1, 1864.[1]

Many dreams of home had the quality of "just so" experience that many of our dreams have when we dream into the waking reality of our normal days and normal events. William Elliott, known as "Billy," wrote to his father, Dick Elliott, on September 11, a few months after his enlistment in the 11th Regiment, Company A, of the North Carolina Confederate Troops (July 7, 1862). Billy said he would like for a neighbor coming his way to bring some butter for him, and also said he dreamed "the other night that I had just got the fulest poke of aples from home. I just thought then I was all right."[2] In the same "just so" manner, Billy was said to have given his pocket comb and a copy of the New Testament to Cyrus, his cousin, telling Cyrus on June 30, 1863, to give "these to Ma because I'll die tomorrow."[3] Billy died on the Gettysburg battlefield on July 1, 1863.

Harriet Dada, a Union army nurse born in Hannibal, New York, was tending a young man who was sick with measles near the final days of the war. She wrote that on March 19, 1865, she came in after supper to check on him because she had been unable to get to his ward until late in the day. He told her he was afraid she had left. He had dreamed that she had come and had given him two lemons. "Oh," she said, "you want some lemonade, do you?" She told him she could not get lemons but would do the best she could in making him a special drink. She did that and brought it back to him. This "just so" dream also highlighted Harriet's largest disappointment in being a nurse. She had to fight for any delicacies for those who were wounded and sick; even the most basic supplies, such as chicken, eggs, potatoes, and milk were either difficult to come by or outrageously expensive or both. She wrote that the men were given bread, applesauce and tea. She fought for her own kitchen and finally won the right to a stove and a girl to help with the cooking; a generous ward surgeon helped her find chickens, eggs, milk, and other supplies. Harriet was remembered for her nurturing spirit and her insistence that patients needed hope to survive. One young man recalled after the war that he was told he would die and was quite indifferent about it until Harriet stopped by his bed and told him to choose life. He was grateful for the strength and happiness that followed in his days and life when he took her advice. "If a patient gave up all hope he was almost sure to die; therefore it was necessary to inspire courage."[4] Harriet wrote.

"I dreamed last night about the cheese which you wrote about in the letter I got three days ago. Sure I would like a taste of it," wrote Chauncey Cooke of the 25th Infantry, Wisconsin in a letter to his mother; but he asked her to stop making cheese with all her other work. Having grown up in war-torn lands, Chauncey promised her he would come home some day and that when he did he would help in "so many ways that I never thought of before."[5]

John H. Worsham of Company F, General Jackson's Foot Cavalry, lucked into some relief after several days of hard marching through the Virginia valley, arriving in Martinsburg on June 28, 1864, where they scattered a regiment of Yankee soldiers guarding an office and depot filled with boxes of supplies sent by family and friends for an upcoming Fourth of July celebration. John volunteered to assist the assigned Confederate guard at the office. In return, he was allowed to sit down in a "sure enough chair" both to eat his fill from the boxes and to carry away a large box for his grateful company. The company box was filled with cakes, oranges, bananas, lemons, a bottle of wine and other items. In a second "gift," this one from the depot, John "confiscated" a plum cake, clothing, which he gave to the quartermaster, and a fine pair of boots that fit his sore bare feet. Once his bruised, bleeding feet healed he put on the boots and wore them till the end of the war. The night of the office/depot "guard" on the delectable boxes (July 3), John dreamed of "little cakes, big cakes, and a mountain made of cake." The next day was July 4. General Early dispensed the rest of the boxes, distributing oranges, lemons, cakes and candy, plus kegs of lager beer. John said the army enjoyed the treat and drank the health of their "hosts," celebrating in their stead as best they could.[6]

Col. Winston of the 45th North Carolina Regiment related a story of one of his soldiers deserting and heading home. On the way, the deserting soldier rested and dreamed that he arrived home where his mother's joy quickly turned to angst when she discovered he had deserted and would be a hunted man. She wept—in his dream—with a broken heart when he told her he had deserted. Then the young man, believing he had seen an accurate picture of his return home, turned around and arrived back with his regiment before the day broke. His colonel wisely believed that he would have no further problems with this young man and probably had a better soldier for the experience of the dream.[7]

"If this man gets a dream at you he'll find you sure"

Dream tracking was a particularly useful "just so" tool that enabled the dreamer to see across time and space. In a dreaming culture such as that of nineteenth century America, a Confederate soldier made the news in the *Richmond (VA) Daily Dispatch* on November 24, 1863, "Hid Away in the Smokehouse." The newspaper reported that one of "Captain Shannon's men fell asleep" and while "in this mood" dreamed of where a deserter could be found. He woke up and told his captain his dream. Because of this soldier's history of accurate dream tracking, the captain had no problem believing the validity of the dream and immediately sent a small detachment of men to the house where the soldier dreamed the deserter was hiding, using the details of the soldier's dream for an exact location within the house: "Well, reader, where do you think he was? He was in a hole or cellar, all hid away, and things such as barrels, boxes, &c., piled up over him, in his smoke house. There was a small space left open through which his wife fed him. When taken by the cavalry, he begged them to let him see his children, that he had not seen them in five weeks.... This is not the only deserter that this same soldier has dreamt of and found. We would here say to the deserters (in the way of parentheses) who are in caves and close places, that you just might as well come along and report, because if this man gets a dream at you he'll find you sure."[8]

In similar fashion, William Turner, reminiscing about his father's stories of his escape from Libby Prison, recalled an oft-repeated dream shared by his father. His father had been on the run after his escape, had returned to his home to have his wounds treated, and had set off again. He tied his horse in the woods and went to the house of a friend, whose name was recalled as "Crump." Mr. Crump helped him find his way to his brother's house, where it was determined the best place to hide was the barn. William's father burrowed a hole deep in the hay and remained there several days until he dreamed a dream with a message to leave at once. His brother thought this imprudent, but Turner's father also dreamed the Yankees had come, gone directly to the barn, come up to the loft and at once went to the hole in the hay and took him out. "My uncle thought it foolish to leave such a good hiding-place; but my father was so much in earnest that he would not try to dissuade him." They went into the woods where the horse was tied, and the father rode away. The next morning the Union soldiers did arrive and went directly to the barn and to the hiding place. A "colored girl had seen my father there" and had told someone and the information had spread to the Union troops.[9]

"Normal" in these "just so" dreams was the harsh environment of war, the cold ground, the protrusions of bones and skulls on marches the men made across fields that were recently battle sites, with hastily dug shallow graves, mud, unbearable summer heat, frost-bite in winter, poor rations, and disease. The soldier's dream often included elements of those extraordinary "ordinary" events.

Marion Hill Fitzpatrick left Crawford County, Georgia, in May 1862 to join the Confederate army in Virginia. He had a wife, Amanda, who was 18, a son less than one year old, a widowed mother, a farm, and a store. Marion joined the 45th Georgia Volunteer Infantry Regiment, Company K. He wrote nonchalantly of dreaming, referring to the wild imagination stirred in his dreams by his first views of the Blue Ridge Mountains. He just as matter-of-factly told his wife that he appreciated her dream of seeing him arriving at home. He hoped, he wrote in the fall of 1864, that dream would be soon. Marion was wounded on April 2, 1865, and died waiting for care during the siege of Richmond. A fellow soldier, William Fields, wrote to Amanda that Marion died asking her to meet him in Heaven.[10]

Rain, Snow, the Bare Ground and When Is a Comet Not a Comet

Dreams of environmental and heavenly events always stirred the imagination and penetrated dreaming with messages of import. Soldiers were often away from home for the first time and experienced natural occurrences in an environment unlike that of their home. John Jones, a Confederate clerk, wrote about an "unannounced" flaming comet in the sky. It took a northwestern course and followed his June 28, 1861, dream of "a great black ball moving in the heavens, and it obscured the moon." This dream was "just so" but shared dual meaning. John understood it was about more than a natural event in the sky. It was a metaphor for the war. In the dream he saw the "stars in motion, visibly, and for a time afforded the only light. Then a brilliant halo illuminated the zenith like the quick-shooting irradiations of the aurora borealis. And men ran in different directions, uttering cries of agony. These cries, I remember distinctly, came from men." As John watched the moon fade and dissolve both in his dream and in reality, he thought about the war and the end of the government. In the dream his family was standing nearby. He noted that none of them was afraid, "alarmed or distressed. I experienced no perturbation; but I awoke. I felt curious to prolong the vision, but sleep had fled. I was gratified, however, to be conscious of the fact that in this illusory view of the end of all things sublunary, I endured no pangs of remorse or misgivings of the new existence it seemed we were about to enter upon." This dream would prepare John Jones for the end of his familiar definition of home and the birth of another and, it was hoped, prepare him to accept the Confederate ending that in the dream left him and his family neither alarmed nor distressed.[11]

John Jones also dreamed, on November 23, 1864, that there had been a meeting of a few men "in my wood and coal-house." In the dream, he had nominated R. Tyler for the Presidency and the nomination was well received. He shared the dream with someone named "Mr. T.," who responded with the offer of a clerkship for his son Thomas; but Thomas was already a clerk in conscription service, making a handsome salary. "But still that dream may be realized. He is the son of President Tyler, deceased." It's unclear what connection "Mr. T" found between his son's already having a clerkship and R. Tyler's being nominated for the presidency, but John made a connection, perhaps one more important. His son did not need the clerkship offered, and Robert Tyler never ran for president.[12]

Jenkin Jones's dreams illustrated waking in the middle of an ordinary situation (his dreams are explored further; see Chapter 8, "Precognitive Dreaming"). Jenkin dreamed "of being buried in snow drifts and surrounded by ice. Awoke to find it nearly a reality."[13]

J. Franklin Dyer, surgeon of the Nineteenth Regiment of Massachusetts Volunteer Infantry, wrote of the "dissimilar" among the odd contradictions of normal business of the day: "We had finished breakfast, one was reading a paper, another writing, others talking. I was enjoying the fragrance of a bouquet of roses; the band of the Eighth New York was playing. The Negroes about the house were gaping and listening to the music, while three hundred yards in front there was pieces of artillery firing and farther in front a sharp skirmish going on, every moment someone being hit—orderlies coming and going—business going on as usual—boys washing dishes and blacking boots, everybody minding his own business. "

He dreamed "last night of being at home" but complained that his surroundings bore little resemblance to home, "for I was sleeping on a bare hillside, one blanket over and one under me, and my coat cape over my head." In a dream more to the point, the next year he dreamed he was conversing with a rebel soldier and told him "if we could not whip them in two years we would acknowledge their independence, but can't say that I acknowledge that when awake." Dyer dreamed this bit of information on April 23, 1863, just a few weeks shy of the projected two-year dream date of the end of the war. The content of his dream undoubtedly came into his sleep from his daily experience.

Only ten days before that, he had written in his journal "thirteen thousand cavalry moved somewhere today, and this evening we are under orders to march with eight days' rations, the men to carry rations in their haversacks and knapsacks, leaving their clothes out. This indicates a rapid march. This will give some of the nine months' men a chance to fight before they go out. A good many must be killed and wounded, both friend and foe. When will the Rebels learn that we will never give up the contest until they lay down their arms." Rebel soldiers, the war's end, and, in his perception, the Confederacy's obstinate refusal to end their fight were on Dyer's mind and in his journal writing. He dreamed of them all.[14]

With a similar reaction to the contradiction of his surroundings to the tenor of his dreams, George Lawrence, a British novelist, came to America. Intending to join the Confederate army as a staff aide with the army of Virginia, he was instead taken prisoner by a Union regiment and released on his promise to return to England. His original plans had been to witness a war "the like of which this world has never known" and to experience materials for a book.

His beginnings, scribed in his journal, were "foul" and got no better. He complained that the food, such as it was, was "dioramic," mutton and beef "of mature age, leaping about with a playfulness only becoming living lambs and calves." He further complained that the reality between life and dreaming was equally discomforting "after falling into an uncertain doze, to feel dampness mingling strangely with your dreams, and to awake to find yourself, as it were, an island in a little salt lake formed by distillation through invisible crevices." Disillusioned with his project even before becoming a prisoner, George determined such dreaming and waking was unacceptable: "I suppose, it is nothing 'unbecoming the character of an officer and a gentleman' to hold such midnight irrigation in utter abhorrence."[15]

The Drum Roll

J.M. Addeman, captain, 14th Rhode Island Heavy Artillery, Colored Troops, recalled a dream that came in the scurry of orders when his troops were within a mile or two of Baton Rouge. There had been a change of commanders and everyone was quickly getting into fighting "trim," with the rebel army close behind after a victory. There was no transportation across the Atchafalaya River. Everyone in the 14th was on high alert, expecting a raid just twenty-five miles below them at a post at Donaldsonville, the area of principal defense on the river above New Orleans. The beating of the "long roll" was a nightly occurrence. Addeman fell asleep in this turmoil and dreamed that he had been ordered home and to proceed immediately to some point on the border. All the movements regarding his departure and his troop's arrival "at Providence, were before me. As we were halting in Exchange Place, with arms stacked and men at ease, I obtained permission to go home for a few minutes to see my family, to whom our arrival was unknown, when the roll sounded and we were ordered to fall in at once to take the train. Of course my momentary disappointment was great, but awaking at once, I heard the drums beating in reality, and jumping into my outer clothing and equipments in a hurry, was shortly at the head of my company." When fully awake, Addeman realized he had moved into the dream on the first beat of the drum and that sound had begun the "long train of the incidents of my dream."[16]

Thunder Snow

In the winter of 1862 in Virginia, Sam Watkins of the "Maury Grays," First Tennessee Regiment, described the phenomenon of "thunder snow," beginning the experience awake at the first appearance of the storm, falling asleep in the midst of its magnificent energy, thence into a dream, and back to ordinary reality amid a flurry of live ammunition:

> When we had crossed the bridge and taken our station for the night, I saw another snow storm was coming. The zigzag lightnings began to flare and flash, and sheet after sheet of wild flames seemed to burst right over our heads and were hissing around us. The very elements seemed to be one aurora borealis with continued lightning. Streak after streak of lightning seemed to be piercing each the other, the one from the north and the other from the south. The white clouds would roll up, looking like huge snow balls, encircled with living fires. The earth and hills and trees were covered with snow, and the lightnings seemed to be playing "King, King Canico" along its crusted surface. If it thundered at all, it seemed to be between a groaning and a rumbling sound. The trees and hills seemed white with livid fire. I can remember that storm now as the grandest picture that has ever made any impression on my memory. As soon as it quit lightning, the most blinding snowstorm fell that I ever saw. It fell so thick and fast that I got hot. I felt like pulling off my coat. I was freezing. The winds sounded like sweet music. I felt grand, glorious, peculiar; beautiful things began to play and dance around my head, and I supposed I must have dropped to sleep or something, when I felt Schwartz grab me, and give me a shake, and at the same time raised his gun and fired, and yelled out at the top of his voice, "Here is your mule." In the next moment Sam was dodging a storm of mini balls, stiff and frozen from the snow and howling winds.[17]

Sid Champion, already 38 years old when he enlisted in the Confederate army with the 28th Mississippi Cavalry, thought, like most, that the war would be short and victorious for his side. Sid's regiment was assigned to the Vicksburg area and charged with orders to guard the Mississippi River against Union naval operations. Sid, practical and bound to do his duty but lonely for his family, shared letters with his "precious" wife, Matilda, and their four children, who remained on their plantation, Champion Hill, located between Jackson and Vicksburg. Matilda's letters chronicled life on a farm, raising four children, and trying not to lose her home and farm. Sid sometimes reacted with annoyance, telling her to "bear up and be a woman." In these heartless moments, fortunately few, he would counter her sufferings with examples of how much more he was suffering. She never complained about *his* letters.

Champion Hill was a two-story white plank house sited on land that became the bloody battle site for Grant's siege of Vicksburg. The house was first occupied and used as a hospital by the Union army after a victory gained at great human cost and horrendous casualties on both sides. Amputations were carried out on Matilda's dining room table; a few weeks after the Union soldiers left, the house was burned when Union soldiers passed by a second time. In each their own way, both Sid and Matilda grieved the loss of their home, and Matilda the loss of her beautiful gardens, as though the roses, flowers, furniture, and buildings were their children; but they pulled themselves together and moved on.

In 1864 Sid reminisced about his beautiful home while passing through Georgia, referring to MacBeth's "Banquo's Ghost" as a metaphor for this unbidden memory and to "a sorrow's crown" from Alfred Lord Tennyson: "I am often reminded of our once happy but devastated home by the ruthless vandals of the North. It is seldom I ever mention it in my letters but it will force its self upon my mind like 'Banquo's Ghost'—unbidden—and the contemplation of the past forces me to the realization of the fact—'That a sorrow's crown of sorrow is remembering happier days.' And this will find an echo in your lacerated feelings but cheer up my precious. We have drunk the bitter dregs and now we have hope—the blessed hope 'that a joy's crown of joy is the assurance of happier days.'"[18]

In spite of a few comments made without thinking, Sid's longing was for home and family. He chastised himself for his terrible homesickness and for forgetting God in "this disgusting" war and begged his wife to pray for his life and safe return.[19] Patriotism, Sid wrote, was taking a backseat to home and "its treasures. Its enjoyments and its endearments all seem to cluster around my memory—aye—my heart also—where I am no soldier—and I am not one as I was last year. My dear; let your deep, fervent heartfelt prayers go up to almighty God thrice a day that I may be spared to you and the children. And whatever may befall me or you and the children look to God always."[20] He hoped that "your home be spared in the Eden of all my thoughts. I see you still in my dreams, amid the flowers, may it long be your sweet home.... Ever your devoted husband."[21]

While her heart was "wandering about after [Sid] so much now that I cannot say I have any home," Matilda was struggling with a temporary "refuge" home near her parents a few miles from Champion Hill, lamenting that the war had taken all that was dear to them except each other, and that her spirits rose and fell "like a thermometer in a southern climate." One person might cheer her; another might leave her feeling dark and gloomy. Her thoughts and her dreams, like the needs of her everyday life, turned equally practical, brought focus to her daily activities and reminded her of her husband's needs and his own depressing realties: "[A] few nights since [I] had a sweet long dream and conversed along with you asking you questions that I know that I should ask if I could see you. You replied Just as I expect you would if I were to ask about the pants I sent by Jim Clark. I thought I asked you what you had done with them and you said they have been wet so much they were spoiled and you gave them away. Soon I expect this is what will become of them for the weather was so bad that I have apprehensions of their being ruined as they would be wet so long."[22] Worn pants, all too real in fact, seemed a common theme in Civil War dreaming!

Sid came home at the war's end with a physical wound. They built a new house at Champion Hill, but Sid never recovered his health. "He had drawn too heavily on his spiritual strength and his physical energy. He now knew that he had believed in too many things that were not so. He had no will to live and so an attack of fever carried him away in 1868. A broken old man at 45 years of age." Sid was buried in the grove next to the house that he and Matilda built after the war, located several miles from the site of the house that was burned.[23]

God's Dealings Suggest a Cold Bath

Mary Jeffreys Bethell journaled on the weather, family illness, and religious camp meetings that were "heaven on earth," and prayed as the Union dissolved, South Carolina seceded, and fears mounted in her household. She begged God to be with her and dissolve her troubles, her fervent prayers mounting on every page, sentiments of love and adoration for her Savior pouring forth line after line. "The Lord has been with me in every trouble and comforted and blessed me and brought me out of many troubles, therefore I will continue to look to him with strong confidence and faith, he is my best friend," she wrote on November 16, 1863.

Undefined illness plagued Mary's body and she begged intervention from God. With this intention set in her mind, Mary received a practical dream from a guiding voice: "Take a cold bath." Such an action, her dream guide stated, would be beneficial to a "weakly person." She did just that and journaled that she had been trying the cold bath remedy and was indeed "strengthened, and my health is restored. I bathe all over in cold water every morning, I have had some remarkable dreams, some of them have been the means of comforting me. I receive them as from God, who does all things for my good. I have had great temptations and trials lately, but Jesus is my Saviour, he has kept me from sinking.... I will say glory to God for his goodness and love to me, a poor sinful unworthy creature.... I give myself to Jesus Christ, and pray him to guide and lead me into the right way."

Mary's dream guidance was aligned with that of the Greco-Roman gods, one of whom advised Aelius Aristides in dreams to take cold baths (in wintry rivers) when sick and weak.[24]

"These terrible times haunt me"—Elizabeth Blair Lee

Elizabeth Blair Lee, the wife of Samuel Phillips Lee (both of them born into politically and socially powerful families), an officer in the U.S. Navy, kept a stream-of-consciousness diary, some thoughts seeming lightly breathed words still forming in her mind. Apparently chided by her husband, "My Dear Phil," for her half-expressed thoughts, she reminded him that he once told her to not look back and correct her sentences but to keep writing. She took that advice to heart.

Practical to the core, Elizabeth, signed "Lizzie" in her letters, rarely flinched—even in her bouts of loneliness. She supported her husband's political and military career *and* kept abreast of daily news and world news, making sure that any negative or positive spin would benefit her family, most particularly her husband. Her nature reflected the practicality of her father, Francis, who was a circuit court clerk, land speculator and newspaperman, and of her mother, Eliza, whose equal partnership of intellect and perseverance earned her the nickname "Lioness." Elizabeth and Phillips moved back and forth with the seasons between a farm in Silver Spring, Maryland—in spring and summer—and the city of Washington, D.C., in fall and winter.

Phillips' ("Dear Phil" in "Lizzie's" letters) military career did not end with the war. As a naval officer, he had the complicated task of deactivating a wartime fleet. Promoted to rear admiral in 1870, he continued his career as commander of the Atlantic Fleet for two more years. After February 1873 he settled in as a "gentleman farmer" at the Lee farm in Silver Spring for twenty-four more years.[25]

The Lees' public political life created an immediate need for additional security during the Civil War. While Elizabeth's husband was away from home as few as four and as many as eight soldiers slept in Elizabeth's house, and she dutifully confined her travel to her "own garden and hen house," a space she described as "my chief out door resorts." Her father and her coachman armed themselves, and scouts followed her small entourage if she ventured outside the house. The Lees had one child, a son named Blair, on whom Elizabeth doted. She spoiled and reveled in him for solace and comfort during the long war and long absences of her husband.

Innocent words, picked up from soldiers, family, neighbors, and political acquaintances, repeated by Blair, could send Lizzie into instant depression. Elizabeth wrote to her Phil that the child was heard to say his papa was away so long that he feared "the Secessioners" had caught him. When asked why he said such a thing, Blair answered, "A little Secession told me so." Whether this was imaginary or otherwise, Elizabeth became frenzied.[26]

The "realness" of her dreams haunted Lizzie. In September 1861 she wrote of the armies of the Potomac "looking each other in the face," each trying to circumvent the other, while she pondered a dream that the rebels "had taken one of our Forts, & that I was on the Avenue in a scene of great anguish & trouble— ... [and] these terrible times haunt me." Elizabeth struggled to keep a cheerful spirit so as not to "chill" her child's young years with trouble.[27] But her anxiety, accompanied by horrible "sick" headaches, increased as the war wore on and Phil's absence became a normal part of her life and her son's. "Superstitions & nervous anxieties ... plays upon one," she wrote upon hearing that her husband had run the gauntlet of rebel defenses. "All joy" was knocked from her heart and "fears haunt me waking and sleeping."[28] Anxiety increased with a situation that mirrored Elizabeth's dream of September 1861. In the naval campaign to capture New Orleans, McClellan's activity at Yorktown was eclipsed, at least in Elizabeth's household, by four days of Farragut's bombardment of Forts Jackson and St. Philip. Phillips Lee's ship, *Oneida*, was under heavy fire. Elizabeth was in a high state of anxiety. Her family went to the city and reported back on the numbers and names of the killed and wounded. Phil was safe. Elizabeth did not recover until the end of May 1862.[29]

Seeking solace, Elizabeth cradled Blair in her arms, warming his feet by the fire and singing her favorite ballad, "Billy Barlow." Blair wept and she asked why: "Mama, you sing so sorrowful it makes me cry." Phil once told her he thought she was "saddest" when she sang. She vowed to sing only when alone, "then I confess I have either to sing or weep."[30] Her nannie, Betty, accused Elizabeth of tramping "around like a troubled spirit."[31]

Elizabeth dreamed in early January 1864 that Phil was ill. During the day she felt it in her bones and "it stuck in [her] thoughts many days." Hearing that her dream had been true—but only after Phil was well again—Elizabeth rejoiced.[32]

Taken to bed with one of her debilitating migraines in August 1864, Elizabeth dreamed of her husband. She did not describe the details but noted that the more she dwelled on them the more important she felt they were. She mined information from those dreams and wrote a letter of advice to Phil detailing how his captains should report every noon from each ship individual incidents of blockade runners and save them as an official record. She advised Phil to write this idea, respectfully, into a private report. The reader is not told if Phil followed this dream advice—or to what outcome.[33] In December of that same year, Elizabeth's dreaming meandered through the "Cumberland now with its heavily wooded Banks nervously—as well as of the Savannas of Geo." Elizabeth's disjointed sentence structure referenced dreams of Phil's fleet steaming up the Cumberland River toward Nashville to join General George Thomas in the defense of that city.[34]

Politics interrupted a February dream in which Elizabeth was visibly distressed, speaking loudly and calling "Mr. President" over and over again so loudly her mother heard her in her own bedroom. Elizabeth was sound asleep in the dream but defiantly wrote to her husband that she would do the same awake in the next few days. These tangled political dreams, just on the verge of the signing of the 13th Amendment, were intertwined with her husband's attempts at advancement. Phil urgently requested Elizabeth to keep still and stay quiet.[35]

Rapidly following this frenzied dream of trying to attract President Lincoln's attention, he was assassinated. The news shocked all but the most radical and staggered all but the most defiant. Mary Todd Lincoln turned to Elizabeth for consolation, clinging to her night and day, requesting her to sit and watch through the night. In this same period Elizabeth, still without the comfort of her husband, had to deal with a lump in her breast and surgery and, at the same time, take care of Mary Lincoln. Pushing her own needs aside, Elizabeth truly empathized with Mrs. Lincoln: "She has hysteria & has sometimes been very delirious—I have offered my services to watch & wait upon her." On April 19, Elizabeth wrote, "I agreed to do so most promptly & am now all ready to go but must say a word to you—for I may be detained longer than I now expect to be & will be weary after a night of sad watching & need sleep & rest—tomorrow— The Dr. says she spoke of wishing to have me there as one who had attracted her sympathies & confidence more than almost any one in the City."

Pity for Mary Lincoln won Elizabeth's heart: "—[I]t is a terrible thing to fall from such a height to one of loneliness & poverty— And no woman ever had a more indulgent kind husband Some have thought she had not his affections but tis evident to me she had no doubt about it and that is a point about which women are not often deceived after a long married life like theirs.... A little while afterwards she was talking about going to the country—saying she meant to stay with her husband for he needed her care and she meant to [be] a good wife too.... She then dilated on the havoc which the labors of the last 4 years had made upon Mr Lincolns constitution—." Elizabeth diplomatically said nothing on the wanderings of a mind that still felt comfort could be had for her dead husband in the country. However, Mary Lincoln's constant requests for Elizabeth began to wear on Elizabeth, who wrote on April 20 that she had not left Mary's side until after 6:00 a.m. when her children "returned from the obsequies of their father." Refreshed, Elizabeth tended to Mary on April 22. Mary told Elizabeth her hand was on her husband's arm when he was shot but that he never quivered; the pistol flash made her hold tighter and when she looked at him "the *head had drooped upon his chest— & eyes closed & it looked calm & Thy will be done. His spirit fled then for he was never once moved by my anguish.*" Mary spoke to her husband in her sleep and in her delirium and in a raging fever and was always tender when she spoke to him. Elizabeth was disturbed that Mary acknowledged President Lincoln's religious faith but not her own. However, she vowed to tend Mary as long as she could stand it![36] Mary's grief did not abate. Elizabeth continued her visits until she felt she was of little use then turned to her own household.

Elizabeth awaited her husband's return, which was delayed until August because of the complexity of deactivating a large war fleet. The war was over; the rebuilding of hearts and minds had only just begun.[37]

The "Just So" Dream as a Figure of Speech

William Wrenshall Smith, a Washington, Pennsylvania, businessman and a first cousin to Julia Dent Grant, wanted to "see" the war. To do so he traveled by train to Bridgeport, Alabama, and by steamer up the Tennessee River to Kelley's Ferry, arriving in time for the Battle of Chattanooga in November 1863. General Grant had received orders in October 1863 appointing him commander of the new Military Division of the Mississippi, covering the area from the Allegheny Mountains to the Mississippi River. Grant awaited the arrival of Sherman and four divisions of the Army of the Tennessee in Chattanooga.

William Wrenshall Smith found Grant "telling stories of old army acquaintenses" when he (William) rode back toward the ferry. He wrote that Grant was in high spirits, told a good story and was quite amiable when among friends. William Smith found the camaraderie of war just as amiable at that moment, which was November 16. On November 24, Smith was standing with several captains at the front of Fort Wood when fierce and "tremendeous roars of both cannon and musketry" broke out on the "other side" of Lookout Mountain and on either side of the river. Days later, still protected from the impact of cannon and musketry, William wrote in his journal from a secure place about two-thirds the way up the mountain. From the porch of his quarters he had a spectacular view of Lookout Mountain, watching the view of campfires and "flashes of musketry—till about midnight. The next morning he wrote eloquently, punctuating his notations with poetry, about the men who the morning before had been 'full of life and health and hope ... to-night, lying among the crags and bushes of Lookout, cold in death.'" He slept in a fitful "dream of the roar of cannon the rattle of musketry and the tramp of charging squadrons." He went home, probably still not fully understanding the impact of war, of starvation, of disease, of broken bodies and minds, or of the dream that came to the soldier in the field night after night of a home that lay in ruins or a home that could not be accessed in the morning light.[38]

At the same time—November–December 1863—Wilbur Fisk of the Second Vermont Regiment was "roused from a good sweet dream," a "just so" expression of sleeping and dreaming commonly noted in both the best and worst of sleeping conditions. He had been in a dead sleep after marching for miles into the night, awaking after only a few stolen hours of sleep, shivering with the cold "and trembling like a man of ninety." Marching warmed his still-tired body. His regiment had been on the plank road that led from Culpeper to Fredericksburg when he astutely observed a lack of action, which ordinarily would have led to the regiment's taking possession of "the heights" but instead they fell back. Fisk—and the men of the Second Vermont—recognized a retreat even when no order for retreat was given. He wrote a review of the Sixth Corps for the *Green Mountain Freeman* of November 20, describing activity in the "Mine Run" campaign, which cost the Union 1600 men killed, wounded and missing. The Confederate casualties numbered 600.[39]

The True State of [Russell's] Appearance

In Washington County, Vermont, Russell Silsby enlisted as a sergeant in his local company, the 13th Vermont Volunteers Infantry. He left behind his wife, Marinda, and three daughters, Martha, Mary, and Ellen. Marinda ran the farm with the help of her elderly father-in-law, Asaph, and an occasional hired laborer, who proved unreliable. In November 1862, at a time in the war when morale was low both on and off the battlefield, Marinda wrote that although she had suffered "all this turmoil and trouble" she too was in battle (of a different sort) and had decided to fight. Encouraging her husband to do the same, she wrote, "I have put on the armor and I feel like fighting my way through." Although not unique sentiments, they were statements of trust continually expressed in the handful of letters that survived between Marinda and Russell.[40]

Letters traveled slowly. Marinda had a long walk to the post office in Moretown and often had to contend with poor weather.[41] She continued her usual chores as well—

making butter and cheese, going to market with the surplus, tending to the poultry, drying fruit and making cider. She hired help during maple sugaring.[42]

The emotional loss of Russell in Marinda's family had torn at her heart. In her last surviving letter she had news that Russell was coming home. Joyful, she said she had been counting the months and then the weeks and now the days and had to exercise discretion to "keep [herself] under control." She had hidden her longing in humorous anecdotes, one of those being a dream in which she saw Russell finally coming home, "and while he looked well and clean and tidy, his pants were the worst looking things" she had ever seen, more than likely a "just so" statement of his appearance when she in reality saw him finally back at home.[43]

Chapter 7

Dreaming of Home— with a Smile

John Brown Gordon raised a company of volunteers in Upson County, Georgia, in 1861. His rise from captain to corps commander in the Army of Northern Virginia was unprecedented; he was considered one of the South's most respected generals. He wrote reminiscences about the weary days and nights preceding Confederate battles and the Southern troops who found humor in the most depressing of situations. He told of "yarns" spun by the campfire to invoke laughter: those moments following the sad days of the Chickahominy, standing duty on picket in thick darkness alongside swamps, and fighting at the front in slush and bogs. Finding a few moments of sleep after standing guard duty, a soldier had lain down on a log to catch a nap, dreaming that he was at home in his own bed. He turned over and fell off the log into the water at its side. Not ordinarily a humorous moment, the men all roared with laughter, even the soaked dreamer.[1]

With a touch of humor, James Parrott of the Georgia 28th Consolidated Infantry dreamed of dining with his wife, Mahala. There was a delicious meal ("*you* had a good dinner") of ham and cabbage, chicken and other items. He pined that if it were "soe it would be a great pleasure to me. I long to see the time come when I can et the pleasure of coming home to stay If I could get one kiss from you it would be more pleasure to me than every thing here."

A more frightening dream wakened James after he heard that his children were sick: "I will tell you my dream the 14 night of May. I dream that little John was dead." The dream was so real that it troubled him greatly and he could not "keep still." He remained anxious until he received a letter dated May 15 from Mahala assuring him his boys were ill but out of danger "and on the mend. But I am uneasy yet about you all." He begged her to write again quickly for more assurance. He dreamed again, several months later, of seeing his wife and Lety, a neighbor or family member. In the dream he heard Lety laugh. Mahala and Lety were sitting and spinning and Lety shook hands with James and asked him to come in. He moved forward, in the dream, to hug and kiss his wife but she would not let him. Instead she only shook hands. Both she and Lety were "so fat that you did not look natterile [natural]." James wrote candidly, perhaps humorously, that he was glad to see that Lety and his wife were in good health, particularly since she weighed so much in the dream! As in so many soldiers' letters, he never questioned the waking reality of what he had seen; but, in this case, he hoped the condition of her weight would resolve itself before he saw her! In June James wrote that he thought of Mahala "every hour in the day and dream of you oftener when I sleep."[2]

In 1864 Confederate soldier William Herrick, in total trust of a dream of his wife, Dot, in vibrant slang wondered what to call the daughter or son he dreamed she carried:

> It is with a good deal of pleasure that I begin to write you these few lines after doing so much cooking today. You don't know half of what I think of you all the time. I keeps dreaming of you a good deal.
> Now, my dear Dot, I am a-going to tell you my dream last night. I ain't been myself since. I dreamed I was with you, Dot, and we was on the bed. I had covered you two or three times, and we 'joyed ourselves tarnal [a lot]. Well, now, my dear Dot, I believe I'd got you in a baby way, for I'd puke every morning before breakfast. And if it is so, I'd want you to call it William if it is a boy and, if it is a girl, I'd want you to call it Dot.... I never will forget that night you and I ate them eels, Dot. It made you so slippery I could not hardly find you in the morning. I'm in the cook house now, Dot, [as] head cook, too.... Well now, Dot, I must stop, for thinking o you makes my old thing look me right in the eyes. I'm calculating we must get [re]ligion now we're married. I'm going off now and sing a hymn, "Be thou, O God, exalted high!³

Eating Mussels

"Reader, did you ever eat a mussel?" asked Sam Watkins of Company H ("Company Aytch"). He and several others serving with him with the First Tennessee regiment, decided to try gathering and eating some fresh water mussels in Shelbyville on the bank of the Duck River. They filled their meal sacks, went back to camp and cracked the shells. That part was easy. Cooking them—and digesting them—was not. They had plenty of them, so they tried frying, stewing, boiling and baking them. The mussels were too large to swallow whole, and they were invulnerable to every attempt to soften them. The men even tried cutting them with a hatchet. Finally they considered them cooked after a last attempt to batter, butter, salt, and pepper them. They admitted that ultimately they tasted good; or maybe they were so hungry it didn't matter. Well, private Watkins went to sleep that night. No, he didn't dream of home or family; he dreamed of mussels! "I dreamed that my stomach was four grindstones, and that they turned in four directions, according to the four corners of the earth. I awoke to hear four men yell out, "O, save, O save me from eating any more mussels!"⁴

Not unlike the dream of tough mussels, Southerner James Dickson, assailed by mosquitoes on a boat sailing to Georgia, dreamed of "a bedbug exterminator."⁵

Mad as a Hen "ducked in a tub of water"

A *Richmond Daily Dispatch* story of October 22, 1861, titled "Spicy Letter from a Yankee Girl" was said to be a letter found on the body of George Lucas of Fairfax, Virginia, killed at Manassas. Emma Wilson, George's possible and most recent intended, wrote that she was well and that her heartfelt "passion" for George was raised "to a considerable extent." Emma had some indication George intended to come home and make her his bride, as bargained; she added she was bored with "living single" and her mother was anxious for the match since President Lincoln was going to give them all a farm and laborers to work it. Since they didn't have much to live on, she thought this might seal the deal with George. However, Emma warned George not to disappoint her because if he wanted "Mary Clark—which I understand you asked her to have you—I hope you will be taken prisoner and kept there forever." After the threat came the dream: "I am thinking of you all the time and dreaming at night, but dreams do go by contraries. Sometimes I dream of being at fishing frolics, but, alas! Awake disappointed—though in hope it will not always be so." One wondered which event disappointed her in waking—George's not being there or she not being at the fishing frolic! Fishing frolics were popular in the South—and possibly the North—and generally included picnics, lots of young women bringing baskets of food and plenty of fishing of all kinds! Contraries or not, she could catch another George there!

Poor George—while still alive—was the "contrary" in this relationship. Emma went on to quote from a letter he sent to another young woman: "Disappointment sinks the heart of mankind/But a renewal of hope given consolation." She reminded him that he wrote that to a woman named "White in 1854," when "John Smith" outed George and married Miss White himself, "which made you mad as a hen that wanted to go setting on her own eggs and was ducked in a tub of water for it," a priceless "mad as a wet hen" metaphor. Emma closed her letter as George's "real admirer."[6]

Dreaming of the Other Side

Sam Watkins reminisced about soldiers' tales of religious fervor in the camps, satirically reporting the story of men gathering for a sermon preached by the Rev. John Bolton, chaplain of the 50th Tennessee Regiment. Mourners were called to the "Mourners Bench" to confess their sins and save their souls. No one noticed an old tree that had been set on fire days before was still smoking and burning. It caught full blaze, fell on the ten mourners and killed all of them instantly. Sam figured they had a direct path to Heaven.

In another tale, Sam told the story of Uncle Zack and Aunt Daphne, a black family who lived in a hut and took in soldiers' washing. Sam enjoyed Uncle Zack's stories of 'fessing religion, the best a vision of hell in which Zack claimed the devil himself as escort. The devil strung up Zack on a wire, "jus same like a side of bacon, through the tongue" and then threatened to shoot him, but Zack got away, flying to Heaven. Sam asked if he had wings and what he did there. Zack said, yes, he had wings and when he got there he ate grass like the lambs. Sam teased a bit more, asking what color a lamb he might be and how often he was sheared, but Zack fell asleep, "dreaming no doubt of the beautiful pastures glimmering above the clouds of heaven."[7]

Sam Watkins, on a more serious note, reported a dreamed vision of the Other Side. In 1864 he was taken to a hospital in Atlanta where he abhorred the smells. He ate a bit of thin bread and a bowl of soup and went to bed in a little bunk. His dreaming was unpleasant, sporadic and uneasy in his new surroundings. He was no longer accustomed to a bed that was off the ground or even the new sensation of sleeping inside a building. The room was dark and claustrophobic and real sleep came only at dawn. Then he dreamed—a remarkable, if not humorous, vision of what he believed to be heaven, opening with an image of a pair of stairs with richly carved balusters and wings and golden steps overlaid with silk and golden-colored carpeting that came down from heaven right into his room. Two beautiful women peeped at him from the steps and played traditional harps, singing sweet songs; others passed alongside dressed in the expected shining garments but looking uncharacteristically like schoolgirls.

Two or three times the two women brought Sam fruits and vegetables. He had been deprived of those items for so long they looked like "pure gold." The steps lengthened out and surrounded him and light poured in from everywhere. The women danced, tossing wreaths of flowers. Just as Sam reached out to embrace one of the women and the beautiful vision, he was awakened with this from the soldier in the next bunk: "D__n ye, I wish you would keep your d__n arm off my wound, ye hurt me." Sam's heavenly vision was interrupted, but he attributed the after-effects to the remaining glow. The sun was shining; the food was improved; and he wandered the streets of Atlanta, where business was going forward as though there "was no war." Everyone was smiling and prosperous.[8]

Chapter 8

Precognitive Dreaming

Dreams That Bother the Mind: Dreaming into the Future

Dreams that "pried" into the future were both small and large—a wife dreaming that her soldier husband was wearing tattered pants and, finding that his trunk had never arrived, that he *was* wearing the pants of her dreaming; a soldier dreaming of an important salt-works city burning years before the event; or the simple dream of being impaled by sword-like ice and awaking to find oneself in freezing temperatures and icy conditions. These dreams were not the same as "presentiment," which predicted events or conditions intuitively either alongside or apart from night dreams. These dreams stayed with the dreamers like a mist when they were waking and reminded them that dreams do pry into futures and that paying attention is the better side of caution when the morning comes and the dreams persist.

Buried in Snowdrifts and Prying into the Future

A Wisconsin artilleryman, Jenkin Jones, when he slept at all, had dreams of home and dreams of his mother. Those dreams helped him endure mud, swamps, battle fatigue, and hacking through canebrakes, and they provided a peaceful place for reflection in the still hours around midnight when "all is quiet and minds" were away in the "happy land of dreams." Dreams reminded Jenkin of "better and happier times to come." A "waking dream" in Vicksburg pulled him away from his intense feelings of loneliness thinking of home and bygone days.[1] He wrote his mother that she should not wonder that he dreamed so of home after the weary battle at Vicksburg; there was more marching to "we know not where, but we know it is for war, marching, fatigues, battles and perhaps wounds and suffering, and that, while the anxious heart of an invalid mother, an aged father, sisters and brothers dear, are waiting my return."

Marching from Memphis to Corinth, Tennessee, the regiment paused at Porter's Creek, where the men took on wood and water. From there, fourteen miles from Corinth, they paused again at Pocahontas, fatigued, hungry and cold—rain having fallen all day and a chill remaining in the air. Having no room to lie down, Jenkin sat on the "footboard of the timber," braced himself, fell asleep, and dreamed of a warm room and a "comfortable bed," waking to write that it was a "tantalizing dream."

Christmas Eve on the Nashville road brought intense loneliness for home and the excruciating pain of a toothache. The only relief was sleep, which brought "dreams of home." In those he saw both past scenes and present and found his dreams "pry[ing] into the future."² On the Sabbath in camp in 1864, near Huntsville, Jenkin was in charge of the guardhouse. He walked his beat in "calm twilight and, in sleep, allowed a thousand pleasant dreams and anticipations" to crowd his memory and carry good feelings to his "longing spirit."³ He dreamed of his mother and the "endearments of home on a cold night in March after a warm, beautiful day."⁴

He survived the marches, the hard, disease-ridden camps, bad diet and battlefields, but many of his dreams reminded him of the conditions of battle and the hardships of living in an unforgivingly harsh and dangerous environment. His body was impaired by illness, lack of rations, hard travel, long days, and cold nights when he was compelled to sleep outdoors: "Three of us made our beds together and slept quite warm until midnight, when we awoke to find it sprinkling and the wind driving threatening black clouds over us. Not wishing to get soaked, we pulled out, rolled up our blankets, etc. and sought shelter. The storm passed harmlessly over, but we found but little sleep. I rolled in my blanket on the stoop of the dwelling house, where I slept some. Dreamed of being buried in snow drifts and surrounded by ice. Awoke to find it nearly a reality. Benumbed with cold and clogged throat, I sought the fire to wait for the dawn. Long and anxiously did we watch the coming of the morning."⁵

Jenkin found such safety and blessings from his dreams of home that he asked for those dreams to come, discovering that they cooperatively brought him again and again back to his home and family: "How did they spend to-day at home? Would that I could but have one glance.... Jenkin ... is thinking of you." Dreams that allowed that "prying" glance were his relief from despair and loneliness, and both mail and dreaming of home were welcome confirmations that he was not forgotten: "What kind of a being would I be were it not for these heavenly messengers from home. It is they that give courage in danger, cheerfulness in camp, and [provide the material for the] happy dreams which I expect to-night."⁶

"Dreamed I was forgotten"

Edward O. Guerrant exhibited a talent for precognitive dreaming, rivaling Jenkin's dreams of bitter cold and ice and fearing, like Jenkin, that he would be forgotten by those at home. His dreams surveyed his surroundings present and future, one notable dream bursting into his night on Sunday, March 16, 1862, leaving him distressed and anxious. He dreamed of "fire & destruction, blasted hopes & ruined fortunes." Trying to shake the images, he protested, "*I don't believe in dreams!*" But he went on, noting that his sleep was so disturbed by the dream that everyone noticed his behavior. "Strangely dreamed that Abingdon Va was burning up and some friend of mine was in great danger—which frightened & grieved me beyond degree. Also I saw a drill of a company & a friend of mine from K'y was marker or pivot—tho' a perfect stranger."⁷

Edward Guerrant was a Kentucky staff officer to several Confederate generals in campaigns in eastern Kentucky and southwest Virginia and in the Army of Tennessee between 1861 and 1865. His dream of Abingdon, Virginia, burning down, incomprehensible to him in 1862, did happen, just as the incomprehensible loss of the Confederacy's hopes and fortunes happened in "fire and destruction." Abingdon was a well-established population center of Southwest Virginia, but, more important to the cause of the Civil

War, it was not far from the location of a large and vitally necessary saltworks in Saltville, Virginia. Confederate troops went to great lengths to protect the saltworks. Losing those would have been inconceivable at the time Guerrant dreamed of Abingdon burning.

After Virginia seceded from the union on April 17, 1861, Colonel James F. Preston led the Washington Mounted Riflemen from Abingdon to Saltville to protect Southwest Virginia's valuable salt mines. The Union recognized the South's need for salt to preserve the soldiers' meat and it began to press toward Saltville to blockade the railroad. In December 1864, as the War was nearing its end, Union general Stephen Burbridge invaded Tennessee and moved north to conquer Abingdon. The local Confederate troops, led by General Basil Duke, were defeated and fled into the houses. Burbridge moved on but one Union soldier, Captain James Wyatt, remained in Abingdon to seek revenge for a wrong done him. He set fire to the courthouse and continued up Main Street and to the south side. According to the story, he stopped at the intersection with Court Street, turned his horse around, and prepared to watch the defeated little town go up in flames. Two Confederate soldiers advancing "ahead of units pursuing" General George Stoneman witnessed this horrible event and gave chase. During the pursuit Wyatt's horse fell on him and he was killed. A few months later, the Civil War ended, and Abingdon was left to rebuild, along with the rest of the South. Guerrant's dream had sadly come to pass.

Serving with General Humphrey Marshall in the early part of the war, Guerrant clung to the hope of Federal defeat declaring, tongue-in-cheek that Marshall was a prophet. On Wednesday, March 19, 1862, Guerrant recorded the general's "spirit rapping experiences," led by his daughter "Ella" (a nickname), who was a "medium" and later wrote tracts and novels. The "Spirit" called up the general's mother, who imparted exciting information, foretelling peace in September 1862, which of course proved to be inaccurate. Guerrant humorously noted it must be so because the general "saw a table move." Guerrant tried to "raise a ghost" in company with two other soldiers but failed and thought perhaps the general's departure was "hastened" by his "queer" experiences. More interesting to Guerrant that night was the story of a soldier friend, Easterly, who stole the jailor's daughter and ran off with her in the twilight.[8]

Taking "hope" in large doses to cure a peculiar illness that briefly deprived Guerrant of the use of his limbs and tongue, he sighed to his journal that he lived "as if in a cage" and found "hope" the only medicine for the miserable: "It" [hope] … is mighty slow in its effects."[9] His dreams drifted, one featuring him back in college with a friend, Tom Pickett, in a grammar school and one humorously placing him "in terrorem." The first more than likely reflected his regaining his limbs and tongue and relearning (as in a classroom) their full use again; the second reflected his disastrous track record with women in his life and accurately took him to account. In this dream he found himself married to the "wrong woman," and he lamented, "Made me miserable. Who was ever haunted with such dreams before?! I pity them! To be married to the wrong woman is a consummation of misery on Earth! Do they portend anything? … They dare not face me when I am 'wide awake & duly sober'.… But they do agonize my soul when they persuade its midnight fancy that it is not as I wish it."[10] The lady who was his bride in this "terrorem" dream had been his sweetheart, who married someone else. The news of her betrothal had reached him on the battlefield. Guerrant, popular with the ladies, quickly found another young woman.

His stormy love relationships continued to replay in terrible dreams, one in which he was slighted and killed a man, both accurate in an ordinary way in his not-so-ordinary environment. He had been slighted, from his point of view, in relationship situations more than once, and in his situation on the battlefield he had killed men. The event of being slighted and killing a man did not seem to take place together, although his thoughts might have easily drifted into such thoughts on more than one occasion.

Guerrant dreamed of Yankees and death frequently, finding some peace in the beautiful Virginia landscape, which "appears like an asylum to an orphan child, or like a kind welcome to a homeless refugee, in a strange land. I love its quiet sunshine, & its peaceful shades.... [I] slept quietly without dreaming of Yankees." Guerrant's beautiful writing, evocative of a South fondly remembered by those born there and torturously ravaged by the war, sometimes gave him respite in quiet memories in his journal—the sounds of katydids rising on summer nights into a steady crescendo then falling into soft droning, then rising again: "Grasshoppers & Katydids in full chorus. How I love their melancholy music. I use to hear it at my father's humble door. It's associations are sacred, sad, & mingled with much pleasure."[11]

Sweet memories of home, in a dream late in the war, tortured Guerrant more than any dreams of inconstant sweethearts and Yankees. He hoped and yearned for home as a waking reality. So why was this dream horrible? For Guerrant, at this time, amid such unrelenting battle horror and drama, such a dream was "unnatural": "Unnaturally at home. Ah, me! How the world has turned around." To protect himself from such longings he wrote far into the night, dreamed of more Yankees and asked for better dreams as he piled rails on the fire and wrapped himself in overcoats and blankets.[12]

December brought two longed-for happy dreams of home but the daytime robbed him of his dreams as he marched thirteen miles in wind and mud after the first dream. Before the second, he marched endless miles across the Valley of Virginia, walking most of those miles, riding some, for a total of sixty continuous days.[13]

Beginning December 29, 1864, a seemingly endless battle with fearsome cold and snow began, like the experience of Jenkin, becoming a battle of wits and endurance: "Dreamed last night of fighting a fearful battle with icicles, in which I was transfixed, bayonetted through & through, one was thrust in my eye, one through my knees, & arms, & breast, & back, & sides. I was as full of icicle-bayonetes as the 'fretful porcupine' of quills. Woke up about 4 O'clock almost still with cold, which readily explained my icicle dream." Guerrant rose and stirred the fire and tried again to sleep. The cold was relentless. It snowed four inches on December 31, and he awoke with wet feet. January 1 was so cold Guerrant announced the "Old Year froze to death last night. Tho' many years older than he, I nearly froze myself." Sleeping out of doors was almost unbearable. He and his regiment slept together under piles of blankets but still froze. Their breaths froze in their throats and many of the men were frostbitten. Guerrant longed for the horrible mud from past expeditions as an alternative to the relentless cold and joked about his icicle dream that presaged the icy waking nightmare of "icicle fingers" under his blankets. By January 3 he had found a feather bed, which "revived my old attachment to feathers, which had nearly died out in my new manner of life." The brief respite in a real bed inside a house relieved a severe blinding headache brought on by the near-freezing of his body.[14]

Guerrant survived the war, but one last fearful dream, recorded in 1865, reached far into his anxious mind after so long from home and awoke him with the fearful hope that this dream was "all a dream" and "nothing more.": "Dreamed I was *forgotten*—*— and was miserable. Daylight dissipated all but the unpleasant memory of the dream, the fearful, awful dream when the bright sun was extinguished & the stars did wander to sparkle in eternal space." The asterisk in Guerrant's dreams indicated his sweetheart. This use might have scrolled back to an alternate time with his earlier sweetheart who married someone else. He felt he had moved on from that relationship *and* that dream but subconsciously the experience might have still been with him, or old fears of abandonment might have invaded his night dreams and produced familiar anxiety for his present relationship.[15]

C.C. Burns Dreams: "Shot a pig through the body"

Christopher Columbus Burns joined the 24th Cavalry Regiment, also called the 2nd Texas Lancers, under Franklin C. Wilkes in 1862 and wrote his first letter home to his wife, Georgia, on May 23, from a "camp near Nacogdoches." He complained quickly of illness and on May 27 wrote that the camp was down "in a hollow ... where I could see nor hear nothing but cricketts." He wrote that among his studies were "dreams." He wished he could dream "some pleasant dream" but he did dream about shooting a pig "in the body." He woke that morning hearing someone talking about a dead horse and feared it was his own but found his horse, Betty, still among the living. The pig dream was on his mind and he looked for some kind of verification of what the dream might mean. The truth of it came quickly. Burns heard a soldier passing by his captain's tent shouting, "Dam old hell." The man had been placed under guard the day before for fighting and drinking and was still a prisoner but had gotten away from the guard. By the time he reached his own tent, the man had drawn a knife "on a little boy," telling him if he did not "mark time" he would chop off his head. The captain ordered the man's arrest. The guard approached the man but found himself in a knife match. The soldier who was under arrest began cutting at the guard, the guard backing up and drawing "his six-shooter," still backing up to keep away from the slashing knife. The guard backed against a rope tied between trees and, having nowhere else to go, had to kill the soldier or be killed himself: "The guard shot him about where I dreamed I shot the pig. I saw him fall he lived about half an hour, and was burried like a dog, he had no friends." His name was Miller and he was from Hempstead, C.C. noted. C.C. said nothing more about the dream of the pig but was apparently satisfied that he had discovered its truth in the guard's shooting this "pig" of a soldier in the spot where C.C. saw the dream pig shot and killed.[16]

In the summer of 1862 Burns wrote to Georgia that he had received a gentle loving letter from her. The letter reminded him that he valued her "above all other jewels upon this old world of trials" and he was "filled with new life."[17] Receiving news of the birth of a son brought C.C. joy in September 1862, with humorous comments on a suggested name of Stonewall Jackson Burns. C.C. felt the name was appropriate for the times but might load the child down "with big names," already in evidence in the Burns family naming patterns. Stonewall it was, but the child's life was short. News of his baby boy's death reached C.C. on October 21. His own letter of September 1 had crossed Georgia's in the mail and was written when the child died. He wrote that he wished he were home to comfort Georgia. She had written that she wished she could bite and kiss C.C., and he wrote in return that he longed for the happy day when "we may bite Kiss Kick Romp & wallow over the old house & bed Oh those sweet happy heavenly blissful days.... [T]he pleasure would be twice as great as it use to be."[18]

In the fall of 1863 C.C. wrote that he had "such a bad dream on the night of the 14th, I will tell you my dream some other time." He followed this ominous dream tease with a note hoping nothing was wrong at home: "I am very uneasy about you." With mounting concern, he told Georgia he wished he could get home and would give anything to be able to come to her. Although he did not reveal the content of the dream, there was an obvious connection to his extreme anxiety for his wife. C.C. would have been in prison during this time, waiting to be exchanged. He wrote about the horrible conditions of the men both in the stockade and in the camps and even worse temperaments from shootings, disease, and insufferable heat. He could have been dreaming about the tenor of life closer to him than home. He described himself as bedraggled in subsequent letters, citing horrible rashes and a boil on his knee.[19]

C.C. survived, his final letter a disheartening acknowledgement of Lee's surrender and a brief ending: "We have orders to move from here."[20]

Hearing Voices

A more publicized precognitive vision was recorded in a letter to his wife, Nancy, by Private Charles McDowell of the New York Ninth Heavy Artillery. He described fighting for four days with no sleep at Cold Harbor and shared a story of "young Mrs. Seward [the wife of the Secretary of State, William Seward] having a visionary experience of her husband just as he was going into the battle of Cold Harbor. She had not heard from him for weeks. After dinner on the evening of June 1, while sitting in the twilight, she heard him call 'Jenny.' She jumped up, listened, and heard again, 'Jenny,' so distinctly that I went into the hall, and again came the voice, 'Jenny' so plain I looked over the railing, fully expecting to see him coming up the stairs. There was no one there, and I went back disappointed, thinking how strange it was. Afterwards, I found that this occurrence took place at the very hour that he was in the Battle of Cold Harbor, and came very near losing his life."[21]

Coming Home Safely Through a Field of Briars and Huldah Survives an Accident

Samuel T. Reeves was a farmer from Vigo Township, Knox County, Indiana. From September 1862 to June 1865 he served as a sergeant in Company C of the 80th Indiana Infantry. Most of his letters were written to his wife, Huldah, in the spring of 1865 when he was convalescing in the army hospital at Camp Dennison in Ohio. On March 22 he wrote Huldah that he needed to share a lengthy, detailed dream that "bothers my mind."

In the dream, Samuel saw a large congregation or a big meeting. He noticed many of his old acquaintances in the meeting. He and Huldah were both present and both started home together. Huldah took Samuel by the right hand. This was an important detail: "[Y]ou helpped me considerably altho our way led through a old field that was full of Briars about knee high yet wee got along without being harmed by them (you Seamed liveler and lovelier than I had Seen you for Some time my heart thrilled with Joy at your lively appearance) it Seamed that the war was all over and Several of the Boys of Co. C. was going home with us for dinner."

Among the boys of Company C in the dream were Private Amos Jarvis and "little" James Huleon, who took some water out for the boys to wash up and then called out to Samuel. Samuel went out with James, who shared with him that Amos was drunk. At this moment Amos "commenced some vulgar talk," and Samuel was prepared to speak sternly to him when he " heard a Shriek from you [Huldah] (it Seams that I can almost hear it now) I run in the house you was laying prostrait on the hearth your right elbow under the forestick I caught you and turned you around on my lap but no Simptoms of life I called for James)."

In the dream, Samuel noticed that Huldah's sleeve was not burned but there were drops of sweat on her face. She was breathing. He was terrified that she was near death, but "to my greate Joy you Spoke I don't remember what you Said but my Joy was so greate."[22]

Samuel awoke, exhausted and relieved that he was awake; but he did not forget the dream, even after he recorded it in a letter to Huldah. He insisted that she return to the details of the dream, that she make sure she was careful when she was working at the hearth; he also insisted that she begin a routine of seeing the local doctor so that they would be forewarned of any health problem and would understand how to "do if any thing Should happen" as it did in the dream. Samuel intuitively understood the importance of taking proactive measures to change or work with a dream that troubled him and he wanted Huldah to understand the importance of this dream and the importance of paying attention to the dreamed details.

Most parts of this dream could be an accurate foretelling of possible futures for both Samuel and Huldah. All of the individuals listed in the dream survived the war and came home. Samuel was very involved in evangelical activities, and a large congregation or big meeting would have been a common activity in both Samuel and Huldah's lives. The interesting metaphor of Huldah leading him through the briars could have indicated life situations for both of them as well as the implied significance of Samuel's making it though the war alive. The Reeves letters do not provide a further glimpse into their future daily activities, but both Huldah and Samuel lived to be old, so one can assume Huldah followed Samuel's advice and paid attention to her health and her hearth; or, if such an event took place, that she survived it in the same joyful way she did in Samuel's dream.

First Rate Dreams: The Goldwaites Dream of Home

> *My dearest friend in bonds of love*
> *Our hearts in sweetest union move.*
> *Your love is like a drawing band,*
> *Yet we must take the parting hands.*[23]

Richard Matthew Goldwaite, born in Albany, New York, on May 24, 1825, married a young woman named Ellen Trice Hill, who worked in Albany as a milliner. Ellen, or Ellie as she was known, was born also in Albany, on May 30, 1840. The two married on January 29, 1861, eleven days after shots were fired in the siege of Fort Sumter. Four months after their marriage Richard enlisted in the 3rd Regiment Infantry, New York Volunteers, also known as the First Albany.[24]

Ellie moved into the country (Clifton Park) with Richard's family and immediately became bored and lonely because she was accustomed to the bustle and social life of the city of Albany. Newspapers and friends were inaccessible and she felt cut off from the world and from life with her new husband. With barely any time to get acquainted as a couple, their link to one another was a continual stream of letters and detailed dreams that assured Ellie from the start that her new husband would return healthy and whole to her before the war's end. Both Richard and Ellie dreamed of one another, many of Ellie's dreams being precognitive of Richard's state of being and both of them being convinced of her powers as a "fortune teller" of dreaming.

Ellie's chatter is straightforward and often humorously abrupt. In her first letter she wrote she was so glad to hear from her lieutenant husband she could have "jump[ed] out of" her skin: "I sleep with your picture under my pillow every night and then when I hear from you, it seems as if your picture talks to me."[25] Richard challenged Ellie to keep up her courage, that if God spared his life it would be an honor to him and if he should die that would also be an honor, to fight for the Stars and Stripes. Whichever happened, he always had Ellie "with me upon the Battlefield and [in] my tent at night."[26]

Richard's first serious combat was in the Battle of Big Bethel, and his first experience with Ellie's dreaming was in reference to that same battle. Ellie recorded a church dream, a theme that emerged as a presentiment of battle outcomes. Although Ellie often failed to share the telling details in her church dreams, they always bode well for Richard even though she equated the "church" dreams with trouble or engagement in dangerous activity. Ellie clearly understood Richard's name was not among those names on the "sheet of paper" in this church dream and that he left the church, a good sign. He survived: "I had heard of a Battle and Dick, you may laugh at my foolishness, but by my dream I knew you was in trouble for I dreamt you was in church and I went up to you and handed you a sheet of paper with names on it and I thought you was at fighting, but Dick, I did not think you would get hurt. So now you see I can dream pretty true, for church is trouble, but you left the church, so that was good."[27] Richard acknowledged the importance of Ellie's dreaming: "You had a dream about me and I guess you dreamt about right." At the Battle of Big Bethel Richard survived by "a handful of providence [a terrible shower of grapeshot and] canister shot that flew around me."[28]

Ellie noted casually that she dreamed about the same "as ever." She dreamed that night that Richard was home, but she awoke—and like most dreams in which a loved one was home—found it not so. Not surprised but disappointed, she wished she were a mouse in his tent so that she could see and hear how he lived with other men, chiding him that he probably said everything in his tent except his prayers.[29] Richard replied that he thought of Ellie while he was on the picket guard and the battlefield and that he could not sleep without thinking of her; but, he warned, he was there to fight for his country and must continue to do that even though he longed for home.[30]

"Dick, I dreamed last night that I was with you," Ellie wrote. In two dreams in two nights she dreamed Dick was home and that ordinary activities were proceeding around them—Ellie was with her husband's mother and a neighbor in a store in the first dream. In the second she was ironing in the parlor with Dick's mother. Ellie concluded that they were both good dreams because they were all working in an ordinary environment in the dreams.[31]

In the fall of 1861 Ellie met with a serious accident on her way to Albany. A carriage horse shied and threw her out, causing bodily trauma including a broken collarbone. Just days later, Richard's brother Tom, also serving in the 3rd Regiment, New York Volunteers, fell ill. The double trauma of injury to her body and hearing that Dick's brother was dangerously ill left Ellie's sleep open to a ghostly dream that left her shaken. Her confidence and absolute knowledge that Richard would return home well and unharmed was never shaken—"something tells me so"—but she held less hope that Tom would return home. The dream terrified her so much she had to change bedrooms; she could not sleep in the same room where she had dreamed the dream. In the dream she had heard two hard knocks on the door and saw a "ghost" in the corner. It placed its hands around her body right over her heart "and I thought they was cold like death." Fearing that the ghost would cause more damage to her shoulder injured in the accident, she called her mother for help and "at last she came." One could feel Ellie's terror as she wrote to Dick that she could still see "the white ghost" and feel its cold hands. The next night Ellie slept in the bed where she had last slept with her husband, but, still feeling the nearness of the dream, she wrote "the sweat came on me like rain" and she begged "Mother" to come and sleep with her.

Ellie sent her dream to Richard on September 29, not realizing that Tom, Dick's brother, had died the evening before, disease leaving him in a ghostly state similar to that of Ellie's terrifying dream visitor. Richard returned to Albany with his brother's body, arriving on October 1. Corporal Thomas Goldwaite, 3rd Regiment, New York Volunteers, was buried in Albany Rural Cemetery in the area set aside for fallen soldiers.[32]

Richard dreamed of being home from the battlefield while Ellie dreamed him at home. Since Ellie's first letter, which included the dream of Richard's surviving a battle, he asked her to tell him everything she dreamed and he would do the same, although dreams of home always left him disappointed upon waking: "I dreamed that you was a sleeping with me and I woke up in the morning and feeling for you and you was not to be found, and if you know how disappointed I was, you would come and see me." Both of them grasped the importance of continuing to see Richard being home in their dreams. If he was at home in both their dreams he was not dead on the battlefield. They reminded one another of Ellie's prophecy that she "knew" he would come home whole and well.[33]

Richard and Ellie had discussed starting a family. In late December Richard sent two dreams to Ellie, one of a baby that looked just like Ellie. It had "pretty blue eyes and a nice little face and I was so proud of my pretty little boy that I showed it to all of the soldiers in my Company and the boys all thought it looked just like me. But I thought the little fellow looked more like you and I did not get mad." Like all soldiers, Richard was sure it was a boy! In his second dream on the same night Richard dreamed "that you came here to see me and we were a going to have a good time in my tent when night came and when I woke up in the morning and did not find you, I was mad enough to go over to Baltimore and get drunk." He asked Ellie to send more of her dreams and teased her with one "too long to put in writing." He promised to send it when she sent a dream to him.[34]

The request for more dreams was answered by one of Ellie's church dreams, which as usual she defined as "trouble." In this church dream she was with Richard's mother when three men "gagged her" and took her to prison in a "private house." She awoke crying out for Richard. The dream haunted her because it felt "as if it were a reality." She dreamed that Richard's brother John was living in the same confined place, an environment Ellie failed to identify with her own feelings of boredom and frustration, of being shut away out in the country away from the city and her friends, away from newspapers and sources of information on the war, which was important to her. She often expressed these feelings in letters to Dick and expressed them to his family, but she had not recognized those feelings as "being gagged" and taken "to prison" in her night dreams: "Dick, church is trouble. I do not like to dream about it." She begged Richard to send her all the news he could and to send her his dreams. She concluded with a "first rate dream" of the new moon and "the sky as bright as if it was all afire." Then Ellie dreamed her house was afire, and, through her tears she saw "an old witch" who came toward her but "didn't hurt me." In a later volley of letters about ill will between neighbors the word "witch" would be tossed back and forth between Richard and Ellie, neither of them recalling her dream of their environment being "afire" and a witch that didn't hurt her.[35]

In her "first rate dreams" of a new year, Ellie saw a schoolhouse filled with honeybees, which she dislodged by throwing snowballs at them. At least once, she mentioned having a dream book, or dream dictionary. She commented that the snowball dream meant she would soon see Richard, apparently a meaning found in her dream dictionary. The night before the snowball dream she dreamed "that you was home and that you was so cross that I was afraid to speak to you and I thought that you looked so big and fat and you was going to bed, but I was afraid to go with you because you looked so cross." Blending her dreams, Ellie humorously noted that if Richard were cross when he came home she would "snow ball" him till he got "pleasant again."[36]

Still bitterly complaining about being shut up in the country, bound, gagged and imprisoned by circumstances like those in her earlier "church dream," Ellie wrote that three weeks felt like three months and moaned, "By darn, Dick, I never shall stay in the country another winter. It is enough to kill the devil himself." There were no papers or news of any kind, "nothing to do but sit and think of trouble." Apparently sharing her dreams with the entire family, Ellie wrote that "our folks" told her she was "dreaming all day and night both." She dreamed she tried to get into Albany with "Father," but they could not get any further than the Albany Arsenal on the corner of Eagle and Hudson streets because the city was covered in deep water. Moving from this accurate but frustrating dream of not being able to go into the city where she longed to be, Ellie reported a dream with her usual accuracy: "I dreamed that I got a newspaper from Schenectady and that I was reading how the 3rd Regiment was a going to Western Virginia and I thought that I sat down and would not smile nor speak to anybody." When Ellie heard that the dream was true and that General Dix's division was moving out toward western Virginia she reported that she felt just as she did inside the dream; it gave her "such a pain in my forehead and temples that I did not feel like speaking to anybody."[37]

Tit for tat, Richard dreamed he was home, sitting by the window, looking at the snow banks and simply enjoying the sensation of being home. He considered the dream closely and felt that he had returned from the war in this dream and was sharing with Ellie everything he had been through. In the dream Ellie had responded, "Dick, you shan't go away again." He had agreed with her and told her he would "not go away to the war again." Reflecting his disappointment in not being in this comfortable scene upon waking, Richard wrote that this was "not a good dream" and he thought he "better not come home. But I don't believe in dreams." Of course he believed in dreams—he lived for the comfort of Ellie's dreams of him at home. But this dream brought such longing that he found it depressing rather than comforting, even though it foretold a time when, as Ellie frequently wrote, he would indeed be home again, probably in an identical place sharing his stories with Ellie. He revealed the discomfort and fears generated in this sweet dream of home in the parting words of his letter: "I should like to come home and see you, and nothing would give me more pleasure than to come home and see you before I am ordered to march on the Battlefield. Although I am not afraid nor do I feel that I am cowardly, but I think we will have a desperate fight, and can't tell what might happen. But I will trust to God who Rewards the Brave and I feel that I am one of them, and carry with me your words that I am a going to live to see you again.[38]

Richard's spirits and sense of humor were restored in the next few days. Writing on board the steamer *Adelaide*, Richard evoked Ellie's role as "fortune teller" and told her that when he came home it would be "for good," as in his dream. He also told her he relied on her intuition and dream foretelling, believing that he would not be killed in the war and would come home safely. Ellie had shared a dream in which she was in the South. Both of them realizing it was Richard, not Ellie, who might be in the South, he humorously promised that if she came South to see him he would provide a servant so she could lie around and do nothing "same as the Southern ladies do."[39] Closely following this letter was one revealing gossipy neighbors saying Richard and Ellie had married in a hurry "and I went away in a hurry and I will come home in a hurry." Richard said he would love to come home but found it astonishing that anyone would be "against" Ellie "for what have you done that anyone should be down on you?" Richard vowed to defend Ellie and said they would have nothing to do with these people: "You must not believe everything you hear, nor what that old Devil of a witch says." Both of them should have recalled Ellie's December dream of a witch and a house afire. In that dream she had noted that the witch couldn't hurt her.[40]

Ellie longed for Richard to come home, each letter sharing painful loneliness, wanting him with her and not on a battlefield. Intuition told her he would "soon make a visit home." She reminded Richard that she had dreamed him home "last August" and dreamed him home "last October," so she proclaimed, "I know you are coming home before long." Instead Richard suddenly resigned his commission with the 3rd Regiment and reenlisted with the 99th Regiment, which began as the Naval Brigade and was known both as the 99th Regiment, New York Volunteers, and "Union Coast Guard." They would have ferried Richard's old regiment across Hampton Roads to Bethel when he fought in that battle[41]

In April Ellie dreamed one of her church dreams of trouble. She was so nervous she "could not eat anything today scarcely." These were typically dreamed before Richard went off to battle. Richard coincidentally wrote that 150,000 men were arriving from the Grand Army of the Potomac and that they were off to form siege lines around Yorktown. "You must not worry about me," he wrote. "The Battle has begun." Ellie replied with confidence that he would come home: "You know I am quite a fortune teller." She had dreamed "first class dreams these last few nights." She saw him home out there with her in the country, rocking in the rocking chair, eating "cake and pie, with a good relish." Oh, she wished it was in waking and not just a foretelling.[42]

Letters from Ellie were mysteriously snagged for awhile but finally reached Richard as a group. Richard assured her that when he finally came home it would be for good but that he must be assured of money and a job in an economy and environment that promised little work for anyone not a soldier. Ellie wrote that the war had made her a pitiful crybaby, sitting alone in a room with his picture and crying. She reminded him that they had barely begun a life together when he left for the war. His sister Eliza had met a beau and was making marriage plans. She and Eliza had visited an "old fortune teller" who had predicted Eliza's meeting a man and getting married. The same old fortune-teller had told her Richard would "live many years, that [he] was not going to get killed" and that she would be with Richard in the fall. Since the prediction of Eliza was coming to pass, she thought the prediction that she herself would be seeing Richard home in the fall would also come true. Ellie, the "real" fortune-teller, had many confirming dreams of Richard's return home, a much more reliable source than the predictions of the "old fortune teller."[43]

Still crying and still dreaming Richard home, Ellie reported, "I have dreamed about you three nights *running* and you was home here with me every time. Last night I dreamt you had such long whiskers and I thought you looked so smiling at me and I was crying as hard as I could cry. I wish that the one part of my dream was true, that you was home. But I do not want to be crying if you was home." Ellie's pleas had become desperate![44] Richard was trying for a furlough, but Ellie's constant letters of crying and wanting Richard home must have been draining for a soldier who wanted to be home as much as she wanted him home. His mood began to change from wanting to fight for his flag to feelings that he had done his share in the war. Although Ellie "knew" Richard would not be killed in this war she asked him to be careful because "where there is war, there is danger." She was again dreaming "about you every night" and she was with him "all night in my dreams."[45]

Richard came to Albany on recruiting detail for almost a month at the end of September. He attended his sister's wedding and he moved Ellie to Dove Street in Albany while he was home. When he returned to the war Ellie revealed she was "fat" with the baby dreamed about so many months before. Richard hoped for a boy, a little soldier.[46]

Desperate to see Richard after having him for almost a month and then having him snatched away again, Ellie threatened to kill half of the generals who were "whole sale murderers" and threatened to come where he was and "take a little pleasure with you."[47] Astonished, Richard seriously told her if there "was any pleasure down here for you" he would invite her but since he was in the dismal swamps of Virginia he felt she would not be satisfied!

Ellie's relentless thoughts continued to be of his coming home to her. She dreamed "Albany was full of Colonels and Captains, all had resigned. And I was crying so hard it awoke me. I thought I was getting ready to go off to you to coax you to resign and come home before Fremont got in to be Commander-in-Chief. Oh dear, what don't a person think of in their dreams." It was hardly likely that the ambitious but weak John Fremont would have such an office but she was dreaming true of resignations. Fremont had been relieved of his duty in the last year, and shifts in command were taking place rapidly.

Relatives and neighbors were now sharing their dreams with "fortune teller" Ellie. One of them, Henry, had dreamed that "Katley (Plough, used to be) who is now Lewey Reel's wife that she had a baby and Henry thought he was nursing it, so I was telling our Thomey how Henry and me was both dreaming about nursing babies the same night [apparently Ellie had dreamed of nursing her dreamed baby], so Tom told her in response, 'Well, Lewey's wife has got a baby most two weeks old, so his dream may be true.'" Lewey was married in June 1862.[48]

Ellie dreamed Richard was home, walking with her in Albany, and a "policeman wanted to take you to the station house. And I thought that I got you around the neck and told the policeman that he would have to take me too, so then he let you go home." In this forceful dream of bringing Richard home, Ellie looked up dreams of police in her dream book and found that they were dreams of "distinguished honor." If she looked closely at her increasingly frantic desire to have Richard home and at her increasingly frantic crying bouts, she would have discovered the spot-on waking reality in her dream (getting Richard "around the neck") of her obsession with forcing a situation that brought both of them home together.⁴⁹ Richard's response, no longer a surprise, was a determination to leave the army in the spring if he could find a way to honorably resign his commission. On January 1, 1863, President Lincoln had signed the Emancipation Proclamation. Many Federal soldiers, such as Richard, had joined the war to fight for their flag and for the union, not for banning slavery. This was the final disillusionment in Richard's war experience. He had no interest in fighting to free slaves. He was now ready to go home.⁵⁰

Richard wrote to Ellie: "Sometimes you … dream what will come to pass." Then, probably wondering about his own ability to dream of the future, he shared his dream that brought him into the presence of the dead—he saw dead relations and dead brothers and his dead father. When he awoke he thought maybe he was dead himself so he quickly shared the dream with his regimental friends, who said it was a sign of life, a sign of the birth of his baby. He went with that with gusto. He did not reveal any additional anxiety about the dream; it appeared to be a simple visit with all his dead relations with no dire consequence in his waking life. He asked Ellie what she thought of the dream. We do not have her reply,⁵¹ except in response Ellie wisely reminded him of a dream she liked. She was so taken with it she wrote that if she had not been dreaming nonstop both day and night about Richard she could not have dreamed anything more clear and real than what she "dreamt that night." She had dreamed it earlier and then dreamed it again "night before last": "I was standing in George Van Vechten's store door and you came along walking on the sidewalk, eating a piece of pie and you looked as independent. I thought everybody was looking at you eating pie in the streets, but you did not seem to care for anyone. I thought I said to myself, 'Dick has been drinking a little too much brandy. He feels good, in spirits anyway.'" Ellie loved the dream; it lifted her spirits and brought Richard home and into the city where she longed for both of them to be.⁵²

Richard wrote a sweet spring letter while on guard duty, saying he hoped Ellie was well and "lying asleep in bed wrapped up in sweet dreams." He also asked her not to dream any bad dreams, for he knew she dreamed "too true." He was looking for a clear path out of his commission and relied on Ellie's safe dreams of home as true dreams.

Both Richard and Ellie's two years of dreaming Richard home finally came to pass when Lt. Richard Matthew Goldwaite was honorably discharged from the U.S. Army on June 5, 1863. He moved with Ellie to Albany, where they lived on Central Avenue. Richard worked as a tobacconist, in business with his cousin George Van Vechten, as predicted in Ellie's "true" store-front dream just months before. Richard, as a young businessman, would have every reason to eat pie and feel independent, just as Ellie had dreamed him. Their first child was a girl, not a boy; but she was a pretty baby, as dreamed by both Ellie and Richard.⁵³

"I … dream of you by night": The Caldwell Family Dreaming Together

The daughter of a sailmaker and born in Charleston, South Carolina, Susan Emeline Jeffords Caldwell lived in the town of Warrenton, Virginia, with her husband, Lycurgus Washington Caldwell, and their children, Jessie, Frank, Willie, and a baby, Lucy Lee. Emeline was Mrs. Caldwell's favored name.

Lycurgus had worked in a printing office before the war and had left home as a young man to work for Samuel F.B. Morse, learning a valuable trade in telegraphy. After he married Emeline in 1851 he worked for a time with the U.S. Treasury Department in Washington, D.C., taking the Confederate post at the beginning of the war. Emotionally, Emeline's letters to Lycurgus ranged from a belief early in the war in the glorious cause to the eventual realization of the hardship, horror, and intense personal and family suffering the war created on both the home front and in the loss of lives among the families in the North. One of her daughters died during the war. That loss, suffered apart from her husband, created an even greater sense of the suffering of the innocent in a war fought sometimes outside her door (in Warrenton and Fauquier), where she witnessed both the best and worst behaviors of Federal troops, and inside her house in a heartbreaking scene of plundering. Both Emeline and Lycurgus yearned for peace, each in their own way, and each believed that God watched over them and would allow them a life together beyond the war.[54]

Emeline, as a mother, used an old term of endearment in her letters to Lycurgus, addressing him as "Dearest Papa," and he often addressed her as "Daughter," probably a term used from his days of courtship in her family home or from a term used by her family when speaking to her. She shared simple dreams of Lycurgus being away from her, most of them making her heart "heavy and sad." The dreams were not nightmares, but missing Lycurgus and dreaming of him brought weariness and sadness to her waking moments. She understood, she said, "[I]t must be your being away—and the sad state of the time." Emeline begged Lycurgus to tell her all his feelings so that she would understand more fully the nature of her dreams: "I dream of you often times and sometimes I feel unhappy and low spirited from my dreams fearing you may be again suffering from sickness. You must always write me if you are sick, would much rather know all about you at all times. Be sure you do it always."

Lycurgus had suffered illness in the past. Emeline knew as well that he was not forthcoming about personal news, and gentlemen who knew the Caldwells had reported that Lycurgus seemed discontented. Emeline insisted that he find reasons for contentment of mind and that he needed to be candid with her about his physical and emotional state. She reported that the children were well and near enough that if one of them were sick they could send word quickly. Lycurgus, she reminded him, had a good safe position and was "pleasantly situated in a nice boarding house, pleasant friends, and a good situation yielding a sufficiency of business from Washington." Emeline exhorted him to take "all these things in consideration—you should be cheerful and happy and spend your spare time pleasantly.... [W]e feel assured that Lincoln and his troops will never trouble Warrenton—we feel happy and secure in our own home.... Now write on the receipt of this, if the gentlemen only imagine this of you or if you are really dissatisfied in mind in regard to your absence from us all. I feel very anxious to know the state of your mind."[55] With a strong belief that a soldier must be contented or he would be susceptible to death and disease, Emeline begged again that Lycurgus make himself "perfectly happy during your stay from us in Richmond." She reproved herself, saying that she had everything she needed to make herself happy but that she still missed him and longed for him.[56]

The number of dreams recorded by Emeline and reported dreamed by her children and possibly her husband were astonishing in themselves, but a large percentage of those dreams were precognitive. Emeline's children, especially a young daughter named Jessie, played an important role in the dreaming. Emeline wrote that her children dreamed of Lycurgus almost nightly and shared the dreams in conversation the next morning. Jessie was just barely old enough to talk, but each time Emeline mentioned a dream she wrote of Jessie's coming awake with an announcement of her papa's activities, which exactly mirrored Emeline's night dreams. Consciously or subconsciously Emeline was aware that Jessie was either intuitively picking up on the same information or dreaming the same dreams. Each time, Emeline sent both messages to Lycurgus—the night dream and the corresponding words from little Jessie: "Dearest Papa ... I spent an unhappy night, dreaming and thinking of you while asleep and when awake troubled—on awaking this morning, Jessie awoke and after asking for a piece of bread she says Mama, Papa sick—me sorry, Papa sick. And then in an instant she turned towards Frank and said Fanky—Papa dead—and continued to repeat."

With such a heavy dream, confirmed by Jessie's words upon waking, Emeline sent a letter by a friend, begging that Lycurgus confirm he was well "and able to be out and at your business." Knowing his reluctance to reveal the state of his health, she asked again for just one line sent back in return and even asked "Mr F," the bearer of the letter, to bring Lycurgus home to mend if he were ill. At the same time, she sent up a trunk of clothing that would play a role in a future shared dream and intuitive experience between she and Jessie. Emeline did not hear from Lycurgus in a return letter but instead experienced additional dreams and intuitive statements from both Jessie and her young son Frank that their papa was sick. Mr. F (Mr. Finks, Lycurgus's business partner) waited for a return letter "on the arrival of the cars." None came, but word came from another friend, a gentleman named John Spillman, that Lycurgus had indeed been very ill but was now recovering. A packet of letters from Lycurgus confirmed he had suffered from the return of an old illness, its type not revealed in the letters. Emeline calmed a bit and suggested some home remedies, including red oak bark tea.[57]

"Willie and Frank often dream about you and it is quite amusing to hear them tell their dreams," Emeline wrote on April 27, 1862. A few days later, Emeline heard Lycurgus's voice "in the passage. It gave me the heartache—I feared you may be sick." Letters received from him dated April 30 and May 1 quickly relieved her mind. Emeline was also dreaming of her parents, who lived a distance from her, and awoke sad and wishing she had letters from them. It had been many years since she had seen them, and the difficult war years made a visit impossible.[58]

The year 1862 brought more destruction by Federal troops. Houses were plundered in the area where Emeline lived; crops and gardens needlessly and intentionally destroyed; mules and other animals turned into gardens; and cropland destroyed. A mill dam was opened to allow water to run in, and buildings were burned. Through it all Emeline, sick with migraines and depressed in spirit, still rallied the best she could and wrote, "We never allow our minds to dwell on the dark side of the picture that is now turned towards us—the cloud will soon disperse and the bright sun shine will be ours again—It may be we will have to endure the burthen for months, but help will come if we trust in Almighty God—We are now in their power and God grant it may be short lived—oh! May we be freed."[59]

A neighbor sent the children candy imprinted with the motto, "Hope on, Hope ever" and Willie wanted to send a piece to his papa, thinking the sentiment would cheer him. "God grant I may hear from you soon—I think of you by day and dream of you by night," Emeline wrote. Her dreams, she wrote, "have generally been pleasant and I have fervently prayed that your life may be spared to be once again united to your family."[60]

Captain Richard Watkins, in camp with Lycugus, dreamed of a furlough, but the dream ended with his not receiving one. Wishing for a different ending to the dream, he asked Emeline what she thought of dreams being interpreted "by contraries." Emeline had heard old wives tale of dreaming by contraries—and even teased that she hoped disturbing dreams were "by contraries"—but she held no hope for a different outcome for the furlough dream.[61]

A brief subsequent visit by Lycurgus on furlough seemed "like a dream" to Emeline. The next reported dream was another shared dream/intuitive experience between Emeline and Jessie, reflecting the ill-fated whereabouts of the trunk of clothing sent to Lycurgus. The day—Christmas morning—began with the children receiving stockings filled with candy, cake and apples and being somewhat disappointed until they were told "Old Chriss" was a "yankee and our pickets would not permit him to pass through our lines." Emeline wrote about the children's Christmas and wrote that she had been dreaming "your pants are out at the knees, or you are ragged. I hope dreams go by contraries and you are in a good condition." Emeline ended the letter with cute notes about their newest baby, Lucy Lee. Jessie announced days later that papa was a bum and that his clothes were ragged.[62] An undated letter from the new year received just days after the dream of ragged pants confirmed that Lycurgus had been forced to buy a "common pair pants" at an exorbitant price because he had been unable to access his trunk and his clothing sent by Emeline. Lycurgus was indeed wearing ragged pants in "dilapidated" condition and had been for quite some time.[63]

News came that clerks working for the Confederate government and laborers in the Richmond defense mills were being mustered into battle service. This applied to Lycurgus, and now he was in the same battle arena and subject to the same risks of death and disease as all those whom Emeline had pitied. Lycurgus wrote that he was in Company F, 3rd Virginia Infantry, Local Defense, also known as Departmental, Henley's and McAnerney's Battalion, mustered in on June 20, 1863. Lycurgus was a sergeant. The news filled her mind with apprehension, and she came near a personal breaking point. She wrote that she had tried for years to put on a cheerful countenance under the most trying of circumstances and had suffered separation and the destruction of her homeland, hoping each year would renew the hope of peace. "Your being arrayed in *Uniform* and ready at a moments call to withstand an enemy outnumbering you has come upon me like a thunderbolt and I feel as if I cannot rally my spirits again while you are in such an exposed situation." Emeline wrote a few days later that she was truly "miserable about you—I dream about you and always in trouble about you—" A few months later her dreams were good: "I dream of you and you are always well and happy." Although she appreciated the tenor of her dreams, homesickness brought terrible headaches, and the subsequent death of Lycurgus's mother "pervade[d] the house."[64]

A letter from Lycurgus cheered Emeline's heart and relieved her dreadful feelings of hopelessness after "dreams" that made her "miserable during the day." "Frank wants to see you," Emeline also wrote, "he dreams oftentimes of you and is trying to learn but he is rather too fond of playing out doors." In the same time period, in a rare surviving dream report in a letter from Lycurgus, he noted that he had written "the dream for fun." The dream was apparently reported in an earlier letter that no longer survives; but it seems to have been a "just so" dream about the state of home life in the Richmond area. Lycurgus said that the dream was "literally true of Clerks here with families—Few of them have meat for their little ones and most of them look seedy.—Indeed some of them actually suffer."[65]

Lycurgus wrote in August 1864 that he could not continue to be separated from

Emeline and suggested that they would find a way to survive if he found a small place for them to be together. He imagined the individual antics of his children: Lucy Lee munching apples, Jessie singing a lullaby, Frank counting goodies in his "saving box," and Willie "bridling the colt ... preparatory to riding them to water." He imagined Emeline running tucks in Willie's pants—and himself popping in:

> [U]nawares and kiss right and left, and spend a month, yes a lifetime with you all.—There is a misty rain falling and such days there is racket at home I know, but to me now it would be sweet music.—How much I would enjoy a wild romp with the little ones.—How many anxious thoughts they give you! Well daughter, imagine what you would have them be, and live yourself precisely that character perpetually before them; and they will always be good children....—The little things are continually aping and copying the manners of those they love. Being so much away from home you will have had more influence in fashioning and moulding their characters and conduct than I; but this does not relieve me of my responsibility to them and God. Dear little souls—Heaven's choicest blessings rest upon their heads![66]

As summer moved to fall, Lycurgus received devastating news. His youngest daughter, Lucy Lee, whom he had imagined munching apples only a month earlier, had died of scarlet fever on September 10, 1864. "I know that heavy sighs well up from the very depths of your bereaved heart every hour of the day, and that you crave my presence to beguile and cheer you," Lycurgus wrote. For economic reasons and because Emeline had "too many things already to remind [her] of [her] bereavement and oppress [her] spirits," Lycurgus asked Emeline not to wear black, an added expense of fabric and sewing that would stress their finances: "Little Lee is now clad in raiment white as snow ... [so] do not you put on black."[67]

October 2 marked both the anniversary of Lycurgus and Emeline's wedding and Lucy Lee's birthday. Anticipating pleasure, Emeline instead experienced deep sadness and sorrow, reminiscing about "no loved baby to nestle in my lap and with loving arms to encircle my neck and whisper words of love." She complied with the request not to wear black, although she protested lack of correspondence between her mourning heart and her outward appearance of dress. Emeline's dreams were "distressingly painful": "I awake and start not knowing where or scarcely who I am— This cruel war, the sorrow and anguish of heart it costs the many thousands of beings. Would that I could hear from you *daily*, it would comfort my aching heart. Oh! Papa you don't know how much I suffer—I feel at times that God will punish me yet more severely because I cannot gain power over my own rebellious heart to say *God's will be done*." Emeline's mother wrote about her own dreams of Lycurgus, that she had seen him and had to help him because he was faltering.[68]

To add further insult and powerlessness, the Federal troops raided Emeline's house, taking cloaks, hats, frockcoats, and money, looking for arms (there were none), going through trunks and creating turmoil. Emeline and her sister hid some items "and I feel tired out, I have but little fortitude. I cannot stand a great deal more. I long for quiet—my mind is in a miserable state, I am tired of living such a life—but oh! why should I complain when thousands are faring worse than I— God help me to be resigned. I long to be a true pious Christian—to live for Heaven— ... but I find it hard. My heart is so *rebellious*." Rallying her humor, Emeline concluded with a story about the stolen hats, worthy, she said, of a notice in the newspaper:

> After stealing the 4 hats out of my wardrobe Mr. F. anxious to get them back offered the rascal $5 for them. He agreed to the bargain but held on to the hats till he made sure of the Greenbacks—Mr. F.

was afraid to trust him. A "*Sargant*" was near and offered Mr F. to see he got his hats if he gave him the $5 in his hand. Mr. F. did so. The Sargant held the money to the man, the man held the hats to Mr. F. and before Mr. F. could take hold on the hats, the Sargant let go the $5 to the man, the man cut his horse & galloped off with hats and $5 to boot. The sargant said 'tis too bad for him to have acted so and promised to pursue him and get them. In about half an hour the sargant returned (much intoxicated) and met Mr F. by the gate—told he had tried to get the *hats*—but did not succeed. Mr F. says strange you should say so—when you have one of the hats on your head. 'Tis too bad he should act so.[69]

After the burning of Richmond, Custis Lee's men moved toward Appomattox with the remainder of the Army of Northern Virginia, surrendering on April 6. Lycurgus Caldwell was probably among them. He made his way home and, on Saturday morning, November 11, 1865, a new weekly newspaper for Fauquier County—published and edited by John W. Finks and Lycurgus W. Caldwell—made its appearance and its first statement on the South's postwar predicament: "We see no path open to our people but that of honest, sincere, and persistent effort to repair as far as possible the damages already sustained, and to avert those which a senseless adherence to exploded theories will most surely entail upon us."[70]

CHAPTER 9

"Sacred Soil is adhesive"

David Lane, Company G, of the Seventeenth regiment of Michigan Volunteer Infantry, wrote, "Sacred Soil is adhesive."[1]

A sense of *Place* in Civil War letters sent home figured strongly in who these men were, what they fought for and where they found solace for heart and soul. Despite war's powerful damage to mind, spirit, and body, those men who survived went home to Northern families in 1865 feeling their part in the Civil War was justified because they preserved the Union and destroyed an evil institution. Southern soldiers went home beaten but forever wedded to the soil that gave them birth, struggling to rebuild and find that sense of *Place* again in a torn and weary landscape. The tie that bound them together was family, a home landscape, and the night dream of home as a place so real they could survive battle landscapes more horrific than any nightmare conceived by any one of them.

Southern writer Eudora Welty echoed that sentiment in her opening lines in *Some Notes on River Country*: "A place that ever was lived in is like a fire that never goes out. It flares up, it smolders for a time, it is fanned or smothered by circumstance, but its being is intact, forever fluttering within it, the result of some original ignition. Sometimes it gives out glory, sometimes its little light must be sought out to be seen, small and tender as a candle flame, but as certain."[2]

Annihilating Space, Astral Flight Home, David Lane

David Lane enlisted on August 12, 1862, was mustered into the service of the United States on the 18th, and was assigned to Company G of the Seventeenth Regiment, Michigan Volunteer Infantry, then in barracks at Detroit, Michigan. He noted at the time of his enlistment that ninety-three men enlisted and "sixty-five were farmers, ten laborers, five carpenters, six shoemakers, three clerks, one baker, one miller, one tinner, and only one professional soldier." In letters home to his wife and children David wrote about his reliance on hope and the right mix of coincidence and good planning to help him survive. But he chiefly relied on his dreams to help him through. He was more adept than most soldiers at moving across time and space and more willing than most to write about the process of crossing those boundaries. He wrote in 1864, "The most potent reason, or excuse, for playing cards, and one that seems to satisfy men is, 'it serves to pass away the time.' To most soldiers, when not on duty, time passes heavily.... My pastime is to dream of home and loved ones. From early morn until late at night I am busy—yes, doubly busy—for, while I do not neglect my duties, my mind is hard at work far from this cumbrous body. Annihilating space, it leaps all barriers and pauses not until by my loved one's side."[3]

In his earliest journal entries, David pondered the nature of the imagination and explored the powers men have for mental telepathy, which he defined as "occult," a "mysterious power" that "enables us to divine the most secret thoughts of men." That power manifested quickly in 1862 in what David described as a sense of knowing that the 17th Regiment would be involved in a mass meeting to "discuss secession" (a clever metaphor for going into an unexpected skirmish). David—on picket duty on the evening of victory in that "sensed skirmish" in an area near Maryland Heights, Virginia—stood in contemplative silence among sleeping comrades in a dark, still landscape, which just hours before had been shattered by the fury of bursting shells. He asked himself about the reality of a vision that flashed before him during his solitary duty in that dark and silent night. His mind—or a double—had raced home where "the most vivid pictures arose before me—so real—could they be imagination? And as I gazed upon these fancied visions and pressed them to my soul as a living reality, I asked myself the question, 'Can this be homesickness?' The answer came, quick and decisive: No; I have never seen the time—even for one short moment—that I could say to myself, *If I had not enlisted, I would not*. On the contrary, if, after the little experience I have had, and the little knowledge I have gained, I had not enlisted, I would do so within the hour."[4] His "double" had visited home and it was as real to him as though he were there in living flesh. He determined that he was home and on picket duty at the same time.

Like many other soldiers, David's decision of enlisting in the service of his country had not grown weak in the absence of his beloved home, nor had it dampened his love for his family or his intense longing to be with them. In one of his many beautiful tributes to his family, to his longing for them, and to the intense connectedness between the mind and the written word, David addressed his journal familiarly as his "confidante." Using his "silent friend" as a conduit to his Northern home and to Jane, his wife, and his children, "loving and beloved," he asked his words to "whisper in your ear the sacred secret":

> Then listen.... I have a wife and four small children far off in Michigan. I love them with all the intensity and devotion of my nature. The thought of them is ever uppermost in my mind. In the daily, monotonous rounds of duty; in the long, dreary evenings, when folly reigns, in the stillness of the night; on the rugged, toilsome march, or in the tumult of battle, thoughts of the dear ones at home are ever present, inspiring me with hope, encouraging me to duty, a shield against temptation, a beacon light, shining out upon the stormy sea of strife on which my frail bark is launched, enabling me thus far, to shun the rocks and quicksands that surround me.[5]

Five weeks later, having survived forced marches, exposure, insufficient food, pouring rain and then continuous snow, the regiment paused, the men too exhausted even to pitch their tents. David fell asleep outside on the wet ground but awoke intermittently, starving, weak, and suffering from a fever, lying in a pool of water from the incessant rain and snow. He moved in and out of a vision of a presence that transported him to a place where he was "cared for by somebody, somewhere. I had no cares, no anxious doubts or perplexing fears. If in pain, I had not sense to realize it." When he became mostly conscious, he saw and felt Jane's presence. He heard a "well-remembered step tripping across the floor and stop at my bedside, a soft, cool hand was pressed upon my brow; a sweet, familiar voice whispered in my ear: 'You are better, dear; you will get well now.' Nay, do not smile, thou unbelieving cynic, for from that hour—yes, from that instant—I began to mend."[6] A few days later he received a letter from home, the perfect final dose of healing medicine: "[A]fter perusing the welcome contents over and over again, I went to bed and dreamed of home."[7]

David became a frequent dream flyer, racing to visit home, gauging his visionary experience to help him understand how to respond to Jane's emotional response to his being far away from home. On January 15, 1863, he shared that they had between them "a bond of sympathy ... that knows no bounds—is not confined by space." He told Jane that many times he visited her—or received visits from her—"and the impression left was that of reality. Last night, after I retired to rest—before I went to sleep ... I held your hands in both of mine, trying to comfort and console you, and it was real as reality itself."[8]

In June, Jane shared a traveler's dream not unlike those of David's visits to her. He had already professed a bond between them that was not confined by space and wrote back confirming her dream visit and apparently confirming details that she had dreamed in her visit. He assured her that his "darling's dream" was not all a dream:

> On that same day, the 9th of June, I was on my way from Louisville to Cairo. We went directly north to Seymour, Indiana. Almost home, it seemed to me, where we changed cars for the southwest. I was cast down, discouraged, more so than at any other period of my life. My thoughts and affections were drawn out to my sorrowing wife with an intensity that was agonizing. I had given up hope of her ever becoming reconciled to our fate, and believed she would mourn her life away for him who would gladly have given his own to save his wife. I felt I could do no more. Under the circumstances was I not permitted to visit her, that my spiritual presence might cheer, comfort and encourage her by the assurance that she was not forsaken; that, though far away, her husband was still present, even to her outward senses. I believe my darling has often visited me, and I love to cherish the fond thought. Every nerve and fiber of my soul has thrilled with joy unspeakable at the familiar touch of her dear hand upon my brow.[9]

He noted in his journal that he read this letter over and over again, a mutual visitation that cheered both of them, so far away in waking reality from one another, so close in time and space unbound by obstacles of normal reality.

As the war progressed, David struggled with the difference in views between his "visits" home and Jane's "visits" to his surroundings, which were far less comforting than his view of home and family. Considering those differences caused him anxiety. When he became depressed or anxious, his mind filled with dark thoughts, then, he said, his flights home were a "ray of light." He could see his Northern home flash across his vision and in that moment "the whole current of my thought is changed, and thankfulness takes the place of my repining." In his imaginable visits home, he said, "I am in ... a pleasant, shady grove, enjoying a season of welcome quiet and repose, soft bread to eat, plenty of pure, cold water to drink." He confessed that he understood her visits to him brought burdensome thoughts: "For instance, my beloved wife's imagination pictures me on my weary way back to old Virginia's blood-stained fields, subject to every hardship, exposed to every danger ... [and] her suffering could be no greater if it were so." He tried to comfort her and change this picture in her mind: "Oh, that I could remove every burden, and make their pathway smooth and flowery. I find most of our trials are imaginary, but none the less real for being so."[10]

Soldiers' emotions soared when letters from home arrived in camp. David cursed the souls of those who did not speed along letter delivery, claiming they had no notion of "hope." Hope was hearing from those one loved. Without hope, the heart broke in sorrow. With a letter from home, hope, confidence, and trust revived.[11] When a letter arrived in October 1864, filled with gloomy forebodings from Jane, he knew he needed to act. He feared his own gloomy thoughts that crept in when he gave way to despair had made their way home, where Jane had breathed "the tainted air from the 'slough of despondency.'"

He realized he had to do something for both of them, so he dove deep "where hope lies buried" and invited his wife to come up with him, the two of them together, and climb the "mountain of hope": "Lean fearlessly on your husband, for he is strong in faith and will lead you gently up, above the dark, murky clouds of doubt, to bask in the bright sunshine of trust and confidence." He took an imaginable deep breath, inviting her to do the same: "Viewed from this height, how bright the prospect."[12] Each one understanding the power of the imagination, they moved boldly into a more positive view of David's situation, and the magic of receiving letters once again restored hope to David and confidence in his return home.

Continued survival into 1865 and the promise of home became such a fevered wish he could barely tolerate the last days. Finally discharged at Delaney House, D.C., on June 3, David wrote a last letter home, dated June 8. He announced that he was taking the "cars" for Detroit, and he wrote in his journal that he was on the midnight train for Jackson, where he arrived at 5:00 a.m. His last remarkable entry, in keeping with his imaginable journeys home, described every detail of his approach, his anticipation and expectation of the first vision of his house, of Jane's first catching sight of him, of his children, and how they would greet them. He recorded details like one speaking into a microphone as he approached:

> It is now five miles to my country home. I lost no time in friendly greetings by the way, but leaped from the cars before they fairly stopped; passed swiftly up the track to the first street crossing: up "Moody Hill" and along the "Gravel"; turned to the left; on down the "Marvin Hill" to the old "Clinton House"; again to the left, past "Markham's" and "Shipman's," to the little school house on the corner. I am now one mile from home. What a beautiful world it is, this bright June morning; and how familiar the sights and sounds that greet my senses.
>
> The trees, dressed in their robes of darkest green, wave me a welcome. The wayside thorn, arrayed in spotless white, doth waft to me its richest perfume. The feathered songsters, their bright plumage flashing in the sunlight, attune for me their sweetest melody, and every nerve and fiber of my being responds to these kindly greetings.
>
> I am almost home; just around the corner. I see the cottage now, set in a grove I planted many years ago, when first my mate and I did build our humble nest. I wrote them yesterday I would break my fast with them this morning. I wonder, did they get it? Yes, they are on the lookout. In the east door, that commands this angle of the road, stands my darling, waving her handkerchief, her dear face transfigured with joy and happiness. In the south door is my eldest daughter, clapping her hands in unaffected delight. Another daughter and my son have climbed the road fence, and are giving vent to their joy in childish boisterousness, while "pet," the little lass, is running down the street, fast as her little feet can carry her, to leap into her father's arms and bid him Welcome Home.[13]

David was home!

Sending Flowers from the Battlefields of War

Levi Duff of the Army of the Potomac, Company A, 58th Regiment, Pennsylvania Volunteers, was a highly educated writer studying for the law when he entered the military in 1861. Levi's initial enlistment was in the Pittsburgh Rifles for three months' service in the early days of the war. He wrote to his friend Harriet Nixon, a young schoolteacher he had met in Allegheny City, Pennsylvania.

Eight days after his enlistment, Harriet wrote about watching Levi drill and reported that she liked it "very much." She had visited Camp Williams, where Levi was stationed in those first days, on May 9 for the drill event. Two days later she questioned the rightness of such an educated mind as Levi's being lost, let alone his life: "Oh how hard it is to look forward with calmness to the approaching conflict, it will be a sanguinary contest. Thousands must die, whose precious ones will they be? Suffered from nervous headache the rest of the day." Harriet wrestled not only with the conflict of war and religious justification—and headaches—but often was seized with fear that Levi would not return. She noted more than once that she needed to "school myself to bid "good bye" as though it were for an hour." Fortunately this fear was less of a presentiment than a frightened reaction to Levi's service in a horrible war.[14]

Philosophical religious differences between Levi and Harriet emerged in letters and divided their opinions but not their growing love and devotion to one another. Except in fearful episodes of realization of the deadly war and the possibility always before her that Levi might die in battle or from disease, the two set aside their differences or they surfaced only in Harriet's belief that God had a greater purpose in what seemed to be an endless war.

Levi rarely returned comment on Harriet's fears and, in fact, commented only briefly on death, disease, and the horrible scenes he encountered on the battlefield: "You say that the sight of those wounded at Shiloh has given an idea of war; but allow me to say that you have seen nothing ... approaching the horrors of war. I should be afraid to tell you what I have seen. It is best to leave it unwritten at least." Harriet wrote back: You always write to me of the bright side but I can clearly picture to myself the dismal, cheerless days and nights.... What would the happiness be if this night I could *talk* to you."[15]

Levi's letters to Harriet deepened into love, and love softened his heart and changed his view of women. On March 16, 1862, Levi wrote to Harriet that he had spent his life being selfish, thinking only of his own ambition and thinking of women as "pests" and "useless objects." In fact, in his daydreams he saw his life "*finished* gloriously without the smile or blessings of a woman" until, Levi romantically penned, he "looked into your face." Harriet's "face" followed him first into places of seclusion in his room and then into those previously vacant daydreams where he had to acknowledge—at first reluctantly—she was everywhere in his mind and heart and could not be displaced. This letter was a proposal of marriage. His proposal was accepted by Harriet with an eloquence Levi had only just begun to explore in his devoted writing to Harriet and in hers, even when frantic with fear, to him.[16]

The fear escalated when Levi came home on a furlough, but this furlough was one generated by a serious wound suffered in battle in June 1862. He was shot in the right breast, the "ball coming out of the back below the shoulder blade." Harriet was beside herself with fear, her constantly fragile nerves torn. She went to bed with an already chronic throat condition made worse by the news. When Levi arrived home, Harriet could barely speak, but the intensity of their growing love defeated whispers and wounds and they were married. Levi recovered sufficiently to return to his regiment.[17]

Levi's ritual each night was to settle in at camp with a candle and write his letters to Harriet after his long days. He would awake before dawn, lying in his bunk imagining Harriet close by, her head on the pillow next to him or her head on his chest, each of them offering the other soft kisses: "I am content. Henceforth let it be known—*just* to *you* and *me—I love you—you love me*. Now kiss me and let me kiss you & look into those beautiful eyes where I first met my doom & where I see reflected all the virtues that a husband's pride can name.—my harp to-day would sing only of love. I must turn it to something else. I can think of nothing but my home—no one but my good Harriet." Even patriotism suffered as the months wore on, but Levi performed his duties well, bound by a sacred oath to his country: "I have ceased to talk and ceased to think of our country. My patriotism is about extinct and I am beginning to think of personal safety and comfort.... In this country a patriot is a fool, and he needs only serve in the army a short time to be cured of his folly."[18]

Levi assiduously avoided tobacco, liquor, and profane language, habits that distanced him from all but a few camp-mates but kept him strong and close to Harriet. Harriet was his safety net and his solace. From each battlefield Levi sent Harriet a flower or a twig that commemorated the progress of the war and marked his deepening love for her as well as marking his survival and his hope for a future in a world he knew would be changed forever.

One of the first flower gifts was sent in December 1861 from Drainsville, a battle that made the newspapers. Certain that Harriet had seen the reports, Levi wrote that he had been in the hottest part of the fight but was uninjured; he noted the wounded and those who had died or might die, quickly assuring her he was safe and well. In return, Harriet wrote that she had read the news and had shut herself away with a headache, consciously driving away the thought that her dearest "Bird" was in the fight. She cherished the flower from Drainsville and began a collection, pressed in a history book published by "J & H Miller," that would become a growing bouquet of taped flowers, leaves, and twigs, all mementoes of Levi's thoughts and love.[19]

In 1863 Levi sent a rosebud from the Gettysburg battlefield. Harriet had not heard from him and feared he was dead. The receipt of the rose was magic, and she understood its significance. A few days before, Levi had addressed Harriet in the motif she had come to expect—from a dream of her or, more often, from his keen imagination. He kissed her on his pillow and conversed with her in loving language: "My good good wife how I would like to sit down beside you this pleasant morning & talk to you.... This morning when I first awoke I beheld your bright face and received your warm kiss. Take one in return."[20] On July 9, 1863, Harriet held the rosebud in her hand:

> The sad anxiety is past—forgotten in the joy of the present.... How more than terrible the reality must be to those whose dear ones *are* the dead upon that battlefield? There was no strength left within me— and I had hope to buoy me above despair. You cannot measure the change which came to us in a moment's time.... *Levi* was safe, *was safe*. The rose bud is a curiosity to all—not to me. To me it is magic itself—looking at the silent, faded thing I see pictures of the fray—the hot breath of the wide-mouthed cannon flushes my face—the sulphurous air stifles me. I hear the shouts. I see the unequaled valor of my countrymen. I am very near to you, my husband.... I dare not look back to the blank world I saw last night. Thanks be to God for life.[21]

The gifts of flowers continued throughout the war. On July 26, Levi sent flowers from the garden of Chief Justice John Marshall, a celebrated jurist whose home Levi admired. Marshall's grandson was killed, Levi believed, at Gettysburg and he noted that the home, called Oak Hill, had once been beautiful but was now neglected.[22] This travelogue of flowers was punctuated with expressions of loneliness as Levi reached out for Harriet and this new force of love in his life. An apple bud came from Brandy Station, sealed with a kiss. A deserted garden where "an old house stood once," near the same area, reminded Levi of Harriet and provided a lone flower.[23]

Three miles outside of Chancellorsville, a year after the fierce battle there, Levi's regiment set up headquarters at the graveyard near "the Fairview House." The house had been burned; the Union dead had been buried in unmarked graves. Writing to Harriet that he hoped someday the bones of the dead would be collected in a memorial to their memory, he rode over the field to a spot where a colonel familiar to him had fallen and died. There he picked "these small purple (4 leaf) flowers which I enclose." He included them in a letter along with "other flowers which I enclose we collected on the hottest part of the field & are sent to represent the battleground of Chancellorville in your collection. The velvet flowers are very pretty I think."[24] Just three miles down the road he chose a rosebud from "the residence of Dr. Fox south of the Anna. It was a beautiful place. But being on the battlefield [it] was destroyed."[25]

Receiving and pressing each flower in the Miller book and among the cherished letters from Levi, Harriet was buoyed by hope and a different kind of presentiment in the long days of fighting at Petersburg. She had been thinking that in all the horrific news of Petersburg there could be no way that Levi was still among the living or unharmed in some way when, like a moment of inspiration, "came the sure *belief* that you were unharmed. I could not help rising up to my feet with the impetus the feeling gave me. And now I am seated to tell you—or rather to talk with you, so sure am I that you will hear.... I have nothing of moment to say, now that I *am near you.*" This feeling was only partially true. A telegraph arrived from Levi stating that his right leg had been amputated above the knee and asking Harriet to come to Washington without delay. She did and found that Levi was doing well even though the sight of his wound and missing leg was terrible.[26]

The presentiment was more likely intuitive visioning of an amazing recovery in a time when most people died from amputations. Levi and Harriet spent their remaining years in Pittsburg, Pennsylvania, with Levi striding about town on a wooden prosthesis with articulated joints controlled by springs and held in place with straps. He manipulated his body into buggies and streetcars, used canes, and held firm in his devotion to honesty and duty while serving in offices that required a firm will to resist political favors and influence. He and Harriet had mixed success in producing healthy children. Harriet's headaches proved to be serious, and she died of "congestion of the brain" in 1874.[27]

Chapter 10

Families Dreaming at Home

Young women with their lives on hold dreamed of their Southern homes in danger, their lives in turmoil, the deaths and lives of brothers, fathers, and husbands. Northern women dreamed of their loved ones far away or in situations of families on both sides of the war and of seeking a new home when a beloved one was lost. Julia Johnson Fisher of Camden County, Georgia, wrote in her diary on a Sabbath morning in 1864 that she now dreaded Sundays. Her Georgia family had additional family in the North and she wanted desperately to hear from them. She envied them: "Everybody there seems flourishing." Her family in the South had applied for passports to the North but the process was slow: "Had I a home how eager I would be to fly. I want to go North and have some enjoyment of life once more. I am there almost every night in my dreams, but the home is always lacking. If we go North, where shall we go."[1]

Wives and children recorded dreams of people and events reminding them that they still had normal things to think about, such as a future husband or, in a "just so" way, a future without war. Some dreams predicted not only a future event but also a course to take in that event or a glimpse of a small, hopeful outcome such as the few items saved "in trunks" in Sarah Morgan's dream of her destroyed home.

These dreams provided hope to the family left on the home front and if the family included a soldier in battle to that soldier receiving the inspiration of a family dream.

Naming the Bedposts: Sarah Morgan

In 1862, Sarah Morgan Dawson, age 20, a wealthy young woman from Baton Rouge, thought she had already lost everything. She endured the unforeseen death of her father, Thomas Morgan, preceded by the death of her beloved brother, Henry, in a duel. Then the Civil War brought physical destruction to her doorstep, first in Charleston, then in Baton Rouge, where her family's house and possessions were destroyed.

Sarah Morgan began a diary, recording her frustration, anxieties, hopes, and dreams. Her first journaled dream was May 10, 1862. She dreamed that her mother and sister, Miriam, had come home from a trip. Sarah hugged Miriam in her dream and then came fully awake to discover they were close by, waiting at a wharf, on their way home. She dreamed accurately of "rifle shells and battles" while trying to knit together the threads of her torn life and face her present, in preparation for whatever the future might hold. In June she "packed up a few articles to satisfy my conscience":

> I'm afraid I was partly influenced by my dream last night of being shelled out unexpectedly and flying without saving an article. It was the same dream I had a night or two before we fled so ingloriously

from Baton Rouge, when I dreamed of meeting Will Pinckney suddenly, who greeted me ... and told me that Vicksburg had fallen, he said he had been chiefly to blame, and the Southerners were so incensed at his losing ... he was running for his life. He took me to a hill from which I could see the Garrison, and the American flag flying over it. I looked, and saw we were standing in blood up to our knees, while here and there ghastly white bones shone above the red surface. Just then, below me I saw crowds of people running. "What is it?" I asked. "It means that in another instant they will commence to shell the town. Save yourself." "But Will—I must save some clothes, too! How can I go among strangers with a single dress? I _will_ get some!" I cried. He smiled and said, "You will run with only what articles you happen to have on." Bang! went the first shell, the people rushed by with screams, and I awakened to tell Miriam what an absurd dream I had had. It happened as Will had said, either that same day or the day after; for the change of clothes we saved apiece were given to Tiche, who lost sight of us and quietly came home when all was over, and the two dirty skirts and old cloak mother saved, after carrying them a mile and a half, I put in the buggy that took her up; so I saved nothing except the bag that was tied under my hoops. Will was right. I saved not even my powder-bag. (Tiche had it in the bundle.) My handkerchief I gave mother before we had walked three squares, and throughout that long fearfully warm day, riding and walking through the fiery sunshine and stifling dust, I had neither to cool or comfort me.[2]

On July 20 Sarah moved with her mother and sisters from Baton Rouge to Linwood, the plantation of a family friend, going back again to occupied Charleston, recording houses and plantations that allowed refuge in a vast network of friendships and family. Sarah looked on a burned southern landscape with hope from her dreaming: "Miriam and mother are going to Baton Rouge in a few hours, to see if anything can be saved from the general wreck. From the reports of the removal of the Penitentiary machinery, State Library, Washington Statue, etc., we presume that that part of the town yet standing is to be burnt like the rest. I think, though, that mother has delayed too long. However, I dreamed last night that we had saved a great deal, in trunks; and my dreams sometimes come true."[3]

The house was totally destroyed, paintings ripped from their frames and slashed repeatedly, dresses and textiles ripped to shreds, furniture broken and burned, books ripped and burned, china smashed. But in the end, as in the dream, "Forgot to say ... Miriam recovered my guitar from the Asylum, our large trunk and father's papers (untouched) from Dr. Enders's, and with her piano, the two portraits, a few mattresses ... and father's law books, carried them out of town. For which I say in all humility, Blessed be God who has spared us so much."[4]

Dreams poured through her diary, pleasant dreams, confusing dreams, touching dreams of visits with family and friends, sometimes a confused medley of dreams of family acquaintances. In her move to Linwood she recalled having a sense of dreaming something "very pleasant" but could recall only confusion and a sense of being alive.[5] She wrote of another dream: "The first dream in a strange house comes true; but I tried in vain to recall it. Sometimes it was all before me, but the same instant it was gone. I only remembered writing a letter to Howell, in which I wished to tell him something that I did not wish to be seen by someone else who must first read it, and that Mr. Talbot's name stood out in most extraordinary relief on the page; but what connection it had with the rest, I could not remember."[6]

In September, at a house called Beech Grove, Sarah dreamed of her two brothers coming home: "I wanted to have a splendid dream last night, but failed. It was pleasant, though, to dream of welcoming George and Gibbes back. Jimmy I could not see; and George was in deep mourning. I dreamed of fainting when I saw him (a novel sensation, since I never experienced it awake), but I speedily came to, and insisted on his "pulling

Henry Walsh's red hair for his insolence," which he promised to do instantly. How absurd!"[7] Not "seeing" Jimmy and George being in "mourning" may have been a first glimpse presaging both Gibbes' and George's deaths in the war.

Sarah was once asked, "Miss Sarah, do you ever dream?" Sarah replied with an astounding statement of affirmation: "Dream? Don't I! Not the dreams he meant; but royal, purple dreams, that DeQuincey could not purchase with his opium; dreams that I would not forego for all the inducements that could be offered." In her dreams she could visit heaven or a fairy land. In one she had white wings and could float "in rosy clouds, and look down on the moving world"; in another she had "the power to raise myself in the air without wings and silently float wherever I will." She heard Paul preach to the people, visited strange lands and great cities, talked with people she had never met, including spending a week with Charlotte Bronte hearing details of her "sad life." Shakespeare discussed his work in her dreams "tete-a-tete over a small table," pointing out the characters "of his heroines, explaining what I could not understand when awake," closing his private lecture with, "you have the tenderest heart I have ever read, or sung of," which compliment, "considering it as original with him, rather than myself, waked me up with surprise."[8]

On September 28 Lydia, the daughter of General Carter and the wife of Captain Gibbes Morgan, arrived with another friend, Eugene Carter, the eldest son of General Carter. News of who was alive and who was dead was shared as well as catching up on the plundering of Sarah's house. They shared stories of homesickness. Lydia had seen "Mr. McG__" at Lynchburg, who sent Sarah his regards and said he still dreamed of her. He had told Lydia his dreams and Lydia shared them with Sarah—a dream of meeting her at a ball where she had "treated him with the most freezing coldness. The same old nightmare." Sarah huffed that he always shared that old dream that had "haunted" him for at least eighteen months. She scornfully said that he always sent thoughts of her and dreams of her; and she unconvincingly and even more scornfully of his "dream" advances replied, "Dreams are baseless fabrics whose timbers are mere moonbeams. Apply your own proverb!" Sarah was not pleased with this report of a young man's dreaming heart.

A clamorous beginning to the day of Wednesday, March 25, 1863, ended in delightful dreaming. Captain Bradford, a family friend, arrived with clattering sword to say goodbye. The Union army was threatening Ponchatoula, and his battery, with an infantry regiment, was on its way there to drive them back. He promised to take care of "her John" when John himself arrived. John agreed, amidst a chorus of admiring ladies, to stay the night and leave in the morning. Brimming with romance, Sarah awoke the next morning just after sunrise, "the most delightful dreams" floating in her memory, the voice of little Gibbes shouting, "Sady! Sady! John Hawsey say so! Say give Sady!" Sarah accepted the gift of half-opened rosebuds and a piece of arbor vitae, a special bouquet from John Halsey, who had sent the flowers as his final good-bye. Sarah wept.[9]

As time passed a thoughtful Sarah wrote, "I see father and Harry in dreams." Hal invited her through a portal and into his "Paradise," giving her a beautiful glimpse of the Other Side. "Once I walked with Hal through a garden of Paradise. Fountains, statues, flowers surrounded us, as we wandered hand in hand. We stopped before a statue that held a finger to its lips, when he said 'Did you ever see Fitch's celebrated picture of Eternity? No? Well let me show it to you. Nothing but that picture can give you an idea of the vastness of this eternity. Come!'" Sarah followed until they arrived at an immense crystal wall where she saw moving figures she could not define. Fascinated, she wrote passionately that she watched these "otherside" figures, knowing they were real and always moving, above all of them hovering "a Something" too mysterious for her comprehension: "Dreams! Who would give up the blessing? I would not care to sleep, if I could not dream."[10]

Servants believed Sarah spoke to the spirits because she talked to them. She admitted to her journal, if not to the servants, that "every morning and evening I walked to the graveyard with a basket of flowers, and would sit by father's and Harry's graves and call their spirits to me; and they would all fly to me, and talk and sing with me for hours until I would tell them good-bye and go home, when they would go away too." In a sweet final dream of her brother, Sarah dreamed she was sitting by Hal's grave, only he was buried in the earth, "instead of that close vault; and that as I plucked the weeds that covered it, gradually I unburied him. O how distinctly I saw him! I dreamed he opened his eyes." He told Sarah he was lonely and asked her to hold him. She held him and rubbed his wounds until he was warm. She wept that she could not warm life back into his body; but he did not want her to stay. He asked her to lay him down, watch him sleep and then leave him to rest. Sadly she complied.[11]

Sarah loved her "royal purple" dreams where romance survived when family were dying and the land outside was torn and bleeding. She dreamed of marriage, once with someone she did not care for. She awoke in a torrent of emotions, begging the opportunity to change such a dream. In the lengthy dream she first begged help from her mother, who returned to her toilet, ignoring her, and then her sister, who at first ignored her and then complied: "If you really feel so—" Miriam began; but I stopped further remark ... while I pushed her towards the stairs. I heard her as she reached the parlor, heard her voice first in astonishment, then in anger, and hugged myself for joy crying 'Saved! Saved!' His voice ceased. I suddenly found myself near a corps[e]. Whose, I do not know. I kept repeating 'First I dreamed of a wedding, then of a funeral. One destroys the other; neither will follow. Thank heaven I am saved! Blessed be heaven, I am not married.... And his name was John! Bah!'"

With the dream help of her sister, and a little superstitious magic in which the disturbing corpse was invalidated, she escaped the marriage: "A tame ending, but my horror at the thought of marrying that man has not yet deserted me. I am glad I did not, even in my dreams." John Halsey? How quickly rosebuds had turned to scorn in this wedding that was also a funeral of emotions.

A few pages further in her journal she expressed disgust when she reported that "John" had been dreaming of her as well. She decided, briefly, that maybe dreams weren't all she thought they were. Then she was awarded with another romantic dream. She saw a marriage with a foreigner, swearing that if the dream meant he was a Federal soldier she would still follow her heart and marry him. Sarah married not a Federal soldier but someone equally foreign to her life: an Englishman, Frank Dawson, in 1874, more than ten years after that journal entry.

From Linwood Plantation she had written she was not conscious of being "alive until I awake abruptly in the early morning, with a confused sense of having dreamed something very pleasant." In the war-torn South, a girl's pleasant dreams were a gift rather than an expected evening offering. In a possibly prophetic dream (July 27, 1863) of the destruction of the South, terror replaced anticipated dreaming delight. Sarah awoke sick, trembling, apprehensive, unhappy, and out of breath: "Trouble will follow, I feel. O my prophetic soul! I do believe in dreams!" Sarah noted that "as usual" she named the bedposts, a habit she adopted to remember her dreams.[12] She dreamed of three letters, one from a man familiar to her, Col. Steadman, a second in which she saw herself speaking to a Yankee officer who described the loss of their possessions, and a third with a horrible ending, in which she saw herself carrying a baby that grew larger and heavier and finally turned into a great bloody ball that burst. She awoke saying aloud, "Bless that baby; my unfailing prophecy of trouble!" The smaller details of her prophetic dream unfolded the next day when her sister held out to her three letters, one from Col. Steadman. Next she was placed in contact with the Yankee officer in charge of Confederate prisoners she knew. She did not understand the bloody baby but felt it was a dreadful prophecy. Still believing the South would find its way to victory, she could not conceive of a dream that foretold the end of a way of life she had known her entire life.[13]

In an 1864 note, after hearing of the deaths of her brothers George and Gibbes, Sarah scribed, "How will the world seem to us now? What will life be without the boys? When this terrible strife is over, and so many thousands return to their homes, what will peace bring us of all we hoped?" Her final diary entry acknowledged the sad end of her beloved South as she knew it and what she could not face in that disturbing dream of the bloody baby: "Our Confederacy has gone with one crash—the report of the pistol fired at Lincoln."[14]

A Message in the Stars: Sarah Lois Wadley

Sarah Morgan began her diary in 1862 at age 20 when she was just a year older than Sarah Lois Wadley, whose dreams, "vivid as reality," graced her own journal in Georgia. Her father worked for the Vicksburg, Shreveport and Texas Railroad, appointed in 1864 superintendent of the Confederate railroad system. Both Sarah's dreams and her observations about her family and her life in the Civil War in the South collaborated in exacting truth.

A dream dated Thursday, August 6, 1863, Oakland, Georgia, misunderstood in its revelation, remained in her memory her entire life. Although family members were in the garden, Sarah was alone inside the house on the evening of the dream. Intuitively she felt and recorded that something was going to happen. The manifestation of that premonition was her "vivid" dream, more like a vision, made more real in its introduction—her mother standing in the hall of their home, calling her from her hall seat in the east window and pointing into the evening sky where a star with the brilliance of Jupiter shown: "I gazed in a thrill of awe and wonder at the sight before me, a few degrees above the belt of trees there shone a star, the size and brilliancy of Jupiter, but not him, because he was lower at that time, this beautiful star gradually yet quickly grew as large and round as the full moon, sparkling all over its surface at brilliant points like diamonds, while below it many other stars of the same shape and brilliancy but smaller, formed out of space." The stars formed themselves first as the word "Nebraska," clear and distinct against the dark blue sky, the letters as perfect as if printed. Sarah felt both awe and terror, feeling that she was witnessing something to do with the destiny of her country. Those stars grew dim and faded into the blue of the sky, but other stars grew more brilliant and formed the word "Massachusetts." The young Confederate woman reacted with horror and disappointment on seeing this word and believing it spelled complete doom, then she felt terrible grief and agony for her country.

A more gentle hand touched her shoulder and she heard the word "look." Sarah looked and she saw the word "epouvantee." Not understanding why, she felt joy and relief, perfect peace instead of the bitterness and terror that she recognized as the word's meaning. The words disappeared from the sky and in their place, rising from the east, was a glorious sun with beams of crimson and gold and amber light shooting through the sky like fireworks. Outside, as dawn broke, the lawn was "crowded with negroes gazing awestruck, but they began to disperse" and Mr. Kern, her grandmother's pastor in Savannah, drove up. In the dream she took his arm and walked with him. While sharing with him the dream and talking to him, Rose, a servant, woke her. She told Rose she could not get up yet because she had been up all night. She asked Rose if she had seen the stars last night. Rose was puzzled at her strange responses.

When she did come fully awake, Sarah found her French dictionary. She found the word "epouvantee" but was puzzled. She had felt such joy and peace but the word's meaning was of terror: "Can it be that this is a vision, and this french word ... is ... that France has recognized the Confederacy and has a fleet in the Mississippi, but I must not trust to these rumours and to confirm a dream. Yet this vision gives me new confidence, it seems to me that God has revealed to me that we will prevail through his mercy helping us, oh that this might be. It was so real to me, even now I can see the glorious dazzling vision of stars and suns, it has been present to me all day."[15]

In sharing her dream with her family, Sarah mistakenly presumed that her joy in the dream foretold Confederate victory. More likely she dreamed terror, horror, a glorious resolution—the end of slavery—a declaration of emancipation—that would be hard fought and won with much bloodshed, the dual meaning of the word in her dream ultimately leading to a more enlightened solution in a country ripped apart by death, hatred, and terrible suffering on both sides.

Thomas Nast's *Emancipation,* circa 1865 (Library of Congress, LC-DIG-pga-03898).

In comparison, Tally Simpson, a South Carolina soldier, imagined an astonishingly similar image of "grand result," a personal vision of God's plan, which he too misunderstood to mean Southern victory: "He will roll the sun of peace up ... and cause its rays to shine over our whole land."[16]

Sarah's dreams shifted to more simple but no less accurate images and visions of life events: moving around from place to place; seeking shelter and refuge with friends and relatives in the same manner described by Sarah Morgan. Sarah Wadley wrote on September 26 that her family was staying at the house of an old gentleman named "Cole." Her father had napped on the piazza and had come awake from his own "just so" dream, asking her brother, Willie, "which wagon broke down." Willie, not even thinking this a strange question, replied that the wagon had not broken down but that he had simply needed to replace a broken bolt.[17]

Sarah spoke of her favorite song, "Sleeping I Dream'd Love," and dreamily recorded her girlhood thoughts. She reported family excitement and an accident on Friday, February 26, 1864, which somehow reminded her that she had dreamed that morning of her good friend Valeria and had been thinking about her all day. She had not seen her friend in three years, but in the dream she saw a long narrow vista open and her friend's form in that vista "as clear and full as when I last saw her.... [H]ow vivid my imagination is, sometimes these impressions are so powerful that I feel like ascribing to them a kind of spiritual reality."[18]

Visions such as these remained with her. The vision of the words in the sky was so dazzling that she never forgot it, and she eventually shifted her interpretation to feeling that the unseen hand was that of a greater power whose mercy and wisdom prevailed in spite of her wishes for a different outcome. Sarah's family survived the war. They moved to a plantation, "Great Hill Place," near Bolingbroke, Monroe County, Georgia. Sarah tended her parents there in their elderly years and died there in 1920.

Love Lost: Tavey's "dark Image sadness"

Mary Octavia Smith, known by her nickname, Tavey, was born on March 18, 1845, in Smithville, between Yorktown and Hampton, Virginia. Tavey began a diary the first day of 1863 when she was seventeen years old, eighteen months after the Battle of Big Bethel, which took place on June 10, 1861, near her York County home in southeastern Virginia.

From the start of her diary, Tavey spoke of her grief for a young man whose heart and soul had touched her own. He had been killed early in the war, at Big Bethel. She never revealed his name but revealed her love for him, and her even greater grief. Today we would call Tavey's condition, revealed first in 1861 in her diaries and extending through 1868, chronic depression. Her grief disturbed her daily activities to such an extent that it interrupted her life and her dreams. She was lonely, and, although she had siblings, she confided only in the invisible reader of her diary—"I, having no Confidante into whose ears to breath[e] my feelings with the exception of this little book."[19] Every entry, even those spiked with notes of daily activities, began and ended with her grief and despair. Particularly desperate grief exploded each January, the month commemorating her love's death: "Why does the sigh escape so heavily from my heart? Although 'my face still wears its wonty [sic] glee.'" Yet that dark Image sadness still lives within my heart and how little does the observer know the many feelings too deep for utterance that are its constant inmates. When I come to read those feelings deeply, it is with reluctance to know its fondest hopes have fled."[20]

She shared again and again with her diary the desire for pleasant dreams but wilted into depression and endless self-reminders of the day "he" died or the day that would have been "his" birthday "had he lived to see it, but he like the brave and true lost his life on the far off battle plain.... Does he tonight think of those who loved, and gaze upon them from his home above?"[21] She attracted a few suitors in those five years, but they were quickly confused and discouraged by her grief. After this grief-gushing sentiment of March 1868, she confided that she "thinks" she has a new suitor. He was warmhearted, but like others before him he departed, confounded by her grief and by her five years of night dreams of her long-dead friend, whom she perceived as her one and only real love. On Friday, July 3, 1868, she dreamed "visions of past years," and in language even old-fashioned for her overwrought grieving, "ere the first cloud had marred my life's young sky," confessed that while she was still seeking him in her dreams he was not dreaming of her. Tavey found him instead, even in her dreams, reserved and standoffish. She sadly wondered in one diary entry whether in his "bright home" on the other side that he might love her less because she was still trapped as a "sojourner" on earth and he was free and in a greater dimension.[22]

Tavey finally gave up or gave in. Once she abandoned her obsessive grief, she dreamed that she was married. In the dream her husband's name was Herbert and she wondered who he might be. She wrote in her diary that her dream mate needed to be "something more than ordinarily attractive to win my love," because she would not freely bestow her love on any but the most worthy. Two years later she *was* married. His name was not Herbert, but Alexander Tabb. They wed on April 4, 1871. In the "Herbert" diary entry she had speculated "Herbert could be a place name" for someone who would finally become her partner.[23]

Letitia Burwell: Astral Travel from Otterburn

Letitia Burwell was born on a plantation in Virginia and spent most of her life in the rural regions of that state. In 1865 she published her recorded memories of the antebellum South, romantically describing everyday pastoral scenes of her wealthy Virginia family. Letitia included tales and stories passed down from neighbors and family members, scenes of social dances, food, the relationships her family had with their slaves and life among family members: "Confined exclusively to a Virginia plantation during my earliest childhood, I believed the world one vast plantation bounded by Negro quarters. Rows of white cabins with gardens attached; Negro men in the fields; Negro women sewing, knitting, spinning, weaving, housekeeping in the cabins; with Negro children dancing, romping, singing, jumping, playing around the doors,—these formed the only pictures familiar to my childhood."

Of especial interest, she related an account of a "travel" journey on the astral plane, dreamed by a family friend, Benjamin McDonald from Scotland, who lived at Otterburn, the Virginia plantation where the dream occurred.[24] The dream had impressed Letitia and she noted that she asked him to write it for her before he died. In her recollections, she copied from his original handwritten letter.

McDonald had "returned" to Virginia to settle his father's estate and three years from that event he received a letter from his sister informing him of her coming marriage and insisting that he return to Scotland for that event. McDonald had no wish to leave Virginia for the wedding and went to bed thinking about the dilemma. He dreamed he had landed in Greenock in the night and had headed for home, thinking to take his aunt and sister by surprise:

> When I arrived at the door, I found all still and quiet, and the out-door locked. I thought, however, that I had in my pocket my check-key, with which I quietly opened the door and groped my way into the sitting room, but, finding no one there, I concluded they had gone to bed. I then went upstairs to their bedroom, and found that unoccupied. I then concluded they had taken possession of my bedroom in my absence, but, not finding them there, became very uneasy about them. Then it struck me they might be in the guest's chamber, a room downstairs kept exclusively for company. Upon going there I found the door partially open; I saw my aunt removing the burning coals from the top of the grate preparatory to going to bed. My sister was sitting up in bed, and as I entered the room she fixed her eyes upon me, but did not seem to recognize me. I approached toward her, and, in the effort to make myself known, awoke and found it all a dream.

McDonald was disturbed by this dream visit, particularly its realness, and shared the dream at breakfast the next morning.

Still focused on the dream, he decided to attend the wedding and prepared to go to Scotland. He attended the wedding and watched his sister and her husband set off for their wedding journey. They returned a month later, and McDonald shared the dream with them at dinner. He looked up and saw them staring at him, his brother-in-law seriously asking him to continue the story. They asked the time of the dream. McDonald had been stressed enough by the dream that he had jotted down the date and time and he showed them his notebook: May 14. The two took McDonald into the bedroom and showed him a penciled note on the white mantelpiece: May 14. He asked them to explain. According to McDonald, he was told that on that night, the only night they ever occupied that room during McDonald's absence, "my aunt was taking the coals off of the fire, when my sister screamed out: 'Brother has come!' My aunt scolded her, and said she was dreaming; but she said she had not been to sleep, was sitting up in bed, and saw me enter the room, and run out when she screamed. So confident was she that she had seen me, and that I had gone off and hidden, that the whole house was thoroughly searched for me, and as soon as day dawned a messenger was sent to inquire if any vessel had arrived from America, or if I had been seen by any of my friends."

Letitia observed, prior to sharing this story, that she had noticed that those of Scots descent had the "place of their birth written on their soul ... [and] impressions made on the retina are really made on the soul, and the mind becomes what it contemplates.... The noble old Highlander has mountains in his soul, whose towering peaks point heavenward; and lakes in his bosom, whose glassy surfaces reflect the skies; and foaming cataracts in his heart to beautify the mountain side and irrigate the vale; and evergreen firs and mountain pines that show life and verdure even under winter skies."[25]

"Last night I dreamed I was in a commotion"
—Keziah Goodwyn Hopkins Brevard

This phrase, the beginning of a dream record, could sum up the tenor of Keziah's days as a fifty-seven year-old widowed plantation mistress in charge of four homes, three plantations, a grist mill, and over two hundred slaves, running all of them in a hectic, practical, sharp-witted manner with the Civil War at her doorstep. Her diary was brief, written between July 22, 1860, and April 15, 1861; but it painted a portrait of a determined and self-sufficient woman who doubled her land holdings between 1844 and the time of her death in 1886. She cooked for herself and others, although she complained bitterly that nothing she cooked was "fit to eat": "What is the use of so much property when I can't get one thing cooked fit to eat—such a dinner."[26] She preserved fruit and vegetables, made wine, kept up with neighbors and bemoaned almost every day her unworthiness before man and most especially before God: "Oh my God help me to bear all of these crosses with more patience & Oh God fit me to leave them & take me to *Heaven*—there is nothing on *earth* worth staying *one moment* for if we can only get to a better home."[27]

Keziah's journal became her sounding board for her fears for her land and home and her political anger regarding the secession of her state. In one moment she would pray to God to save her and in the next wish that Lincoln had died before he was elected: "Oh God I am sad now—we have nothing before us to hope for … but God can spare us—I wish I was a cheerful Christian, one whose faith could carry them through. My God spare me from witnessing war & murder—*My God save our Country*.… We are all to see trouble, I fear—God spare us—I expect nothing from man—all good must come from *God*—sometimes I hope our dear country is not to be torn asunder …—be still. Oh my God save this pleasant land & make all thy creatures to bow to thee alone. (God's ways are not ours—Oh how thankful they are not.)."[28]

In the midst of her political and spiritual angst, Keziah recorded her dreams, many of them indicative, if not precognitive, of the turmoil in her landscape and in her mind. On a hot July night she recorded she had sowed turnip seed and then dreamed there was to be a commotion in Columbia, her town. She specifically dreamed that it would be that night, so she begged harder for God to grant her strength and to grant additional strength through Jesus so that she could bear such a dream.[29]

More dreams of turmoil were softened by a hopeful dream for her nephew James Hopkins Adams, the only son of her half sister. He had been diagnosed with cancer and was away in Europe consulting with specialists. Keziah dreamed, between midnight and dawn on August 5, that he had returned. Keziah saw herself at the top of a stairs in this dream. James had a "complexion of death" and looked wearied but he was returning slowly to his wife and family. Keziah, in the dream, clasped his hands in hers and shouted, "My God! My God!" and James turned to his wife to tell her how she cheered him.[30] Keziah dreamed again near the end of August that James experienced both a physical return to the area and a return to health: "Last night I dreamed James H. Adams & family had returned, all well—I only hope they may.… I hope they may all & every one of them be blessed here & here after."[31] James returned home, wife and daughter with him, on September 19, 1860. Although no details survived, James continued to live with no additional mention of cancer.[32]

Keziah turned again to God and her worthiness or unworthiness as she wrestled with thoughts of abolition and what might be right or wrong, begging God to show her the right actions each day. She described her fall and early winter dreams as "unpleasant" but then busied herself with making butter for the winter and speculating on how much better a large house looked with a large lawn at the front and sides. She noted that James still did not look well but that he seemed to have been spared, this comment juxtaposed against her plaint that nothing she read or heard "comforts me."[33]

In the spring of 1861 Keziah recorded a lengthy dream. Although there was much that was unexplained in the dream, there was a tenor, seemingly precognitive, that spoke to her concerns about abolition, about her personal landscape and the country's political and physical landscape in the coming years of war:

> Last night I dreamed I was in the Presbyterian church in Col[umbia], sitting either in or near Mrs. C. Bryce's pew[34]—I thought Old Mrs. Bell sat at my right & young ladies at my left—I soon missed Mrs. Bell—I turned to the left & saw Mrs. B.M. Palmer going from the pulpit up the aisle to the door—she was dressed in deep black with a black bonnet trimed very much—some one told me she had been up to the pulpit taking some bandages from Mr. P__ ['s] face[35]—his health was feeble & he had to use them—I thought Mr. P__ looked sunken near the eyes—then immediately I found myself alone—looking around, every one had left the church & gone out doors to hear the preaching—on my way out I saw Mother's old neighbor (long since dead), Mrs. Staunton, sitting on a chair looking very cheerful & happy—I proposed to go to the stand with her—she said not while Mr. P__ was there—I do not recollect her reasons, if any, for not doing so—is there any thing in dreams?"

Mr. "P" was an ardent secessionist, probably an important element in this dream. After dinner Keziah sent Tom to the field to get John to go with her to "Sister's—he came running back with drops of sweat on his face saying the fence at the field was all on fire—I called to the servants—in a few minutes all left the yard"—and they vacated the church that was in Keziah's dream, leaving her with only Tom in the yard and Sylvia and an invalid mother in an outbuilding: "So I hope the dream is out—since writing this, Rosanna returns saying about sixty pannels of fence got burnt, they think they have subdued the fire—O Lord how uncertain is every thing in this world. It seems John alarmed the near neighbours who went to their assistance—while not one here either heard the noise or saw the smoke, there were eleven here & no one saw the smoke—I was thinking of riding to see my Sister, was in my bed room part of the time preparing to go."[36]

Keziah hoped the "dream was out" or had been fulfilled in the burning of the fence, but her life and her surroundings were just beginning to change. In a matter of only days she sat and comforted neighbors whose sons had left for Charleston to join the 6th Regiment. Another neighbor fired shots at Fort Sumter. She begged her God for no more blood and begged that her life end before more misery. Her wish was not granted. Rain fell and she felt a darkness coming over the land. Before the war ended, Sherman's men burned at least two of her homes; it was unclear what became of some of her other properties. Her slaves were set free; railroad stock she held became worthless. Her sister Sarah went insane after Yankee troops burned her home, Bellewood; but God did not allow Keziah to die, although she begged for that release. She survived the war and survived Reconstruction, carrying on in her usual determined fashion, rebuilding, leasing her lands to tenants, and using the income to pay her taxes![37] Ultimately, as Keziah said, "the dream was out!"

"Troublesome Dreams" of the Existence of the Soul: A Schoolteacher's Journal

Jennie Lines, a young Georgia schoolteacher, was born Amelia Akehurst in England but lived her adult life in various locations in Georgia. She grew up in Clinton, New York, with her father, a tanner, and her mother. Her mother died of consumption when Jennie was eleven, and Jennie was sent to live with a family friend who headed west. In

1843 Jennie returned to her father's home and lived with a stepfamily. Two of her sisters, a brother, and a half sister died of consumption and other illnesses; and Jennie, qualified to teach school, left for Atlanta, Georgia. Over the next few years she moved frequently from one rural school to the next due to a lack of enrollment and agricultural responsibilities of the families of the schoolchildren that took precedence over school attendance. In at least one instance she left her teaching position because of a disagreement over her instruction methods. She then advertised and received a position as a tutor for a plantation owner near Stilesboro, a few miles from Euharlee in Bartow County. Unhappy in this position also, Jennie complained because she was expected to take care of the children as well as teach them. Economically strapped, she became more and more disgruntled with her lot in life. She wanted to work, be independent and have her own pleasant place to call her own, one that had grown in her imagination and in her dreams; but she was stymied by low enrollments in school and complex feelings about society. She admired intelligence and diligence but hated the lower classes she met in the rural South and hated sloth and privilege without responsibility. She hated slavery, but she also despised abolitionists and the slaves she met. She left the plantation and took another rural teaching position in Walton County, fifty miles east of Atlanta, near the Sardis Church community. A chance encounter led Jennie to an opportunity for a position as an instructor in the preparatory division of the Southern Female Masonic College in Covington, Georgia. The focus was on the social graces and the arts. While staying at a hotel in Marietta, Jennie wrote, "We have a crowd here from Augusta ... [and] they seem oblivious to every thing but their own comfort and amusement." This "promiscuous crowd" slept "half the day and then are prepared to sit up until midnight, singing opera music, dancing, talking and laughing in the highest key.... [W]ealth can-not and does not make them, either intelligent or agreeable." She hated northeast Georgia residents even more. She called them shiftless, irresponsible "common crackers."[38]

Jennie resolutely believed the South should be left alone to work out its problems, but oddly she wrote almost nothing about the war until her family was forced to leave Atlanta in 1864. During many of her moves she corresponded with Sylvanus Lines, who wrote to his "friend Jennie," and Jennie relayed thoughts about marriage, courtship and her complex views of society to her "sister" Maria. Jennie married Sylvanus in August 1859. A child, Forrest Lillie, the apple of her eye, was born in 1862 and died in 1863. Again, there were never entries on the war, which would have been on her doorstep during these years.

When Lillie died Jennie ceased writing in her diary until the war's end. She resumed writing during Reconstruction when she and her husband left for Connecticut. They had a daughter, Daisy. Neither of them able to find employment, Sylvanus returned to Georgia. Jennie gave birth to a son, Herbert, and she and her children remained in Connecticut. Herbert died in 1869 and eventually Jennie, Sylvanus, and Daisy reunited in Macon, Georgia.

This lengthy background, a tale of hardship, love, determination, and a commitment to finding peace and joy in a disheartening and disheartened landscape, defined Jennie's daily entries in her journal, which she addressed often as "Dear Book," or in her letters to Sylvanus and Maria:

> Dear book, one whole week have I neglected thee; but it is because nothing of sufficient importance has occurred, to not[e] upon thy pages. I feel sad to night, and fly to thee for sympathy. I know of no particular cause for this depression of spirits, it is a feeling which will sometimes steal over me, in

spite of my efforts to feel cheerful, and I can not always throw it of[f] immediately, it often remains an uninvited, and unwelcome, guest in my heart for many days. Sometimes I find myself amid the clouds of despair which for a time hide the bright star of hope from my view, but she soon smiles upon me again and I arise shake off my sadness and plod onward with renewed courage.[39]

Jennie wrestled with religion and slavery, complex contradictions swirling in her mind. She desired a perfect place where she could understand the soul and its position in the universe. Exhausted with daily duties as a schoolteacher and night duties taking care of her small household she found restoration of body and soul in her sleep dreams, "nature's sweet restorer," where fatigue could be forgotten for just a while.[40] In July 1858 she wrote in her "dear" book that she had read a Psalm: "His breath goeth forth, he returneth to his earth; *in that very day his thoughts perish.*"

"What are thoughts but the *soul*?" she asked her journal. "The soul surely can not *die*. What then does the Psalmist mean? Sometimes the thought of annihilation intrudes in my mind and almost forms itself into a belief. I have somewhere seen the idea advanced that the spirit is an emanation from God, and at death it returns to him from whence it came and forms a part of his being. That when the body dies the soul ceases to have a separate and *conscious* existence, but is absorbed into the great Author of its existence." Longing to speak to someone about this theory, she felt helpless and exhausted trying to understand something that seemed to be cloaked in darkness.[41]

These thoughts continued to surface in letters and in her journal. Thoughts of a more interesting life for the soul led to a conversational dream in 1859 in which Jennie visited a dream-space that evoked the preexistence of the soul. It was not a satisfying dream. It seemed to intrude into someone else's past, not her own, but she found a willing stranger inside the dream who was interested in what she had to say. She had to leave before she had the answers she sought. The dream opened with her visually impaired, her eyesight almost completely gone, and closed with her waking with a blinding pain in her eyes and head:

> I dreamed my eye sight was nearly gone and I was groping my way through a strange house in search of water; but every room and article of furniture and even the two persons I met there, seemed familiar to me as if I had once been an inmate there. I thought I had faith in pre-existence of the soul, and remarked to the woman who gave me water that I had met her before in the same place and under similar circumstances in an earlier stage of our existence but that both her soul and mine were then inhabitants of other bodies that had long since mouldered back to dust. She seemed bewildered and unable to comprehend my meaning. In an adjoining room lay a gentleman on a sofa; he seemed interested in the subject of our conversation and began to converse freely with me.

At this moment Jennie woke "with hard pain in my eyes and head, probably the cause of my dream of blindness."[42]

Two years later Jennie experienced an anxiety dream of her sister Maria when she had not heard from her for months during the war. She dreamed Maria was dead and wrote a concerned letter to Maria, telling her the thought of her being dead had "haunted" her ever since the dream. She completed the letter with a description of her new house, which she was delightedly furnishing while Sylvanus hung curtains and made cornices for her.[43] Only two years later Jennie and Sylvanus were forced to leave their little dream house. Atlanta was under siege, cannon were at their door, and employment once again became an issue for both of them.

The word "imagination" occurred more frequently than dreams in both Sylvanus's and Jennie's letters and in Jennie's journal. Jennie mentioned books she read, such as

Bayard Taylor's *Travels* in the "Oriental world" and imagined herself traveling in romantic environments in Germany: "My desire to visit the old world is always renewed by reading the travels of others. From my earliest recollection this has been a day dream with me, and one which can never be realized I fear, certainly not unless fortune play some unexpected freak in my favor. If I was a man, I would start as Taylor did, with a cane in my hand, and knapsack on my shoulder."[44]

After her daughter Lillie died, Jennie went into a deep depression. Even the birth of her second daughter, Daisy, did not bring her out of reveries, in which she would see Lillie's little white hand on the bars of the crib or hear her musical little voice. She would watch Daisy playing or eating and "see" Lillie, only older now, playing alongside Daisy. Sylvanus used the word "imagination" to describe missing Jennie or Daisy when he was away from them rather than envisioning places far away or envisioning the departed. He wrote to Jennie on November 8, 1868, during the hard years of Reconstruction when he worked in Macon, Georgia, while she remained with friends in Connecticut: "[T]he congeniality of your spirit which I imagine is before me while I write; would that my imagination were in truth a *reality*." He also saw Daisy: "How often do I see her smiling face, in imagination, as she would run to meet me."[45]

Sylvanus died in 1875, Jennie in 1886. Her only living child, Daisy, shared the last moments of her mother's life and wrote afterward to Maria: "I could only think how sweetly she was resting after so many weary months of unrest and almost ceaseless pain. Nor can I realize it yet; I feel in a dream…. I can only think it all over and over until my brain refuses to think, and I sleep; only to wake and go over it again."[46]

Kate Plake: A Kentucky Spy for the Union Army, or, a Not-So-Clever Con Artist

Kate Plake wrote her own story, supposedly of spying for the Union army, after the war ended. She announced to the reader that they would hear about her early girlhood, her marriage and her divorce from a man who neglected and abused her. After the war she supported herself and her child by offering her services in the Secret Service Corps on behalf of the Union army. She worked in Kentucky. In her earliest remembrance she envisioned her mother awakening her from a frightening dream in which she was inside "a lion's carcass, and the bees had filled me with honey." Her mother had predicted a fearsome fate for her daughter from that dream, one in which she might be saved by some honeyed grace.

That honeyed grace took strange forms. Tied and bound by her Confederate husband and his mother in their house, Kate relied on a visiting "Indian chief" and her summation of his character to engineer her escape. Playing upon an old "saw" that Indians never betray a trust," she told him she would go to the Miami Mission and sew for Indian children if he would help her. Buoyed by dreams of her maturing plans, she went in and out of consciousness in her peculiar situation of house captivity until she escaped without the Indian's help.[47]

Still relying on Confederate relatives, Kate too freely shared dreams that presented warnings of events, one involving an uncle who was traveling to Owensville to a speech. Kate dreamed "that I could see all around my uncle's house; and in one corner of the yard stood a paw-paw bush, and in the bush I saw a large snake, that looked very sly at me.

It had one blue and black stripe around it. All of a sudden it came to my bed and attempted to slip under my neck. I caught it at the back of the neck and threw it out on the floor." Her uncle picked up a hat and said that was what was in her dream. Kate believed he would say something to a "Union man" for which he would get a beating or, as in her dream, "get choked." Her uncle went to the meeting and got into a political argument. A man grabbed him by the throat and started choking him. He blamed Kate for bringing about the "prophecy" by dreaming the incident. Neighbors threatened Kate's life when she revealed Union sympathies and they made threats, saying she prophesied things that came true and was a dangerous woman.[48]

Kate accused her husband of misrepresenting her character to her children, although her journal might have provided some justification of that character if he had not been portrayed as such an unsavory character himself. Kate reported a dream (asking the reader to forgive her for accepting guidance from a dream)—in which she was walking down a muddy stream, the murky water threatening to sweep over her. Exhausted, she looked at the shore but there were steep "yellow banks on each side." She knew she was to die but then saw golden sunbeams on the bank and asked for their help. Instantly she stood on the bank in the midst of a meadow of flowers "whose fragrance floated on the calm, sweet breeze, and was almost intoxicating." A mirror descended and showed Kate an image of her younger self with an angel standing behind "oiling" her hair and speaking in a language she did not understand. Her hair was so long it touched the ground, and she was dressed as a male with shoulder-straps on each shoulder. She said in the dream, "I am in the good land at last." She awoke disappointed to find herself still in the old world. That dream—and looking out into the woods the next morning—set her resolve to leave the place where she was living, to divorce her husband, and to begin a new life. It was after this dream and leaving home that she offered her services as a spy for the Union army (via Major W.W. Carter, 5th Indiana Cavalry). Kate, with a Union pass in hand, left for Missouri where her daughter lived with relatives and managed to collect her after some opposition.[49]

Kate had such a talent for dreaming true that regimental officers, sharing a joke about their lieutenant outside her hearing, challenged her that if she dreamed the joke that night that she could do anything she wished. She was to tell the joke at the breakfast table the next morning and prove it by the innkeeper, Mrs. Hanah, if she "dreamed right." Mr. Hall, the person responsible for the joke, did not show up at breakfast the next morning for fear she "would dream right" and that he would be in trouble. In fact, Mr. Hall asked for a furlough to see his wife and children—and to leave town. The matter was finally resolved. Kate had not dreamed the joke but Mrs. Hanah told her the joke and she was able to profit from the telling by receiving dollars from various members of the regiment, pay-off money for her to stay quiet. Kate's life went on in this fashion. It would appear that she spent more time in efforts to keep her daughter or in promoting herself with a romanticized book of her travails, titled "Trouble and Romance; or, Real Life of Mrs. Kate Plake," than in efforts for the Union army! In 1888 she wrote *"The Southern Husband." The Husband Outwitted by His Wife*. Plake was probably a pen name.[50] She ultimately abandoned her daughter, who was, fortunately, adopted. Mr. Grifin died in the Civil War.

Chapter 11

Dreaming in Prison: Seven Occupants to Make a Shadow

So within the prison cell,
we are waiting for the day,
that you'll come to open wide the iron door.
And the hollow eye grow bright and the poor heart almost gay,
when we think of seeing home and friends once more
TRAMP, TRAMP, TRAMP[1]

You will recognize the names: The Union prison camps of Camp Chase (Columbus, Ohio), where the capacity was 4,000 men but over 10,000 were ultimately housed; Elmira Prison Camp (Elmira, New York), where almost 3,000 men died before it closed in 1865, its percentages if not its numbers equal to the horror of Andersonville; Johnson's Island (Sandusky, Ohio); Rock Island (Rock Island, Illinois); Camp Douglas, Chicago, where 10 percent of the prisoners died during one cold winter month; and eight other prison camps, all of them equally ill-equipped and over-filled. On the Confederate side were Belle Isle (Richmond); Danville (Virginia); Libby (Richmond); Camp Sumter (near Andersonville), where 28 percent of its "population" died; and the notorious Andersonville Prison in Andersonville, Georgia, joined by eight additional Southern prison camps.[2]

Altogether, an estimated 56,000 men died in Civil War prisons, a casualty rate that accounted for at least 10 percent of all fatalities in the Civil War. Food, clothing, and shelter shortages; poor administration for unprecedented numbers of men; poor and contaminated food; and contaminated water: all led to rampant disease and death. Exchange was a daily dream; survival was miraculous. In Andersonville alone there were over 30,000 men, packed into slightly over twenty-six acres, living on meager rations of salt pork, corn meal and beans (no fruits or fresh vegetables), eating rats when desperate and feeling blessed if they avoided or survived typhoid fever, measles, dysentery, cholera, malaria and gangrene. Northern prisons rivaled the conditions of those in the South. It was propaganda of the victor that created the illusion that conditions were worse in the South.

Andersonville, due to its size, death-rate, and overwhelming conditions of horror, had the well-deserved reputation of being the worst of all the prisons. David Kennedy of the 9th Ohio wrote in his journal on July 9, 1864, from Andersonville: "Wuld that I was an artist & had the material to paint this camp & all its horors or the tongue of some eloquent Statesman and had the privlege of expressing my mind to our hon. rulers in Washington, I should describe this hell on earth where it takes 7 of its ocupants to make a shadow."[3]

11. Dreaming in Prison

Robert Sneden, of the 40th New York Volunteer Infantry Regiment of the Army of the Potomac, was captured by Confederate troops under John Mosby and held first in a tobacco warehouse next to Libby Prison, where he contracted and survived typhoid fever and then was shipped to Georgia and held at Andersonville Prison. Here he made what became the most famous and most evocative clandestine drawings of that "hell on earth." Sneden water-colored his sketches after his exchange. The images, such as *The Dead Line*, graphically depicted Kennedy's "7 of its occupants to make a shadow." Sneden's artistic gift brought the horror of Andersonville to life and memory. His paintings even today transport the viewer inside a place worse than a battle front and tear at the soul when coupled with the words of men more eloquent than they realized.

Sergeant Lyman H. Needham, Company K, 42nd Illinois Infantry, and listed as an artist in Civil War military records, was wounded and taken captive on September 20, 1863, the second day of the fighting at Chickamauga in northwest Georgia. His case was a sad example of what happened to thousands of men who needlessly died because of prison conditions. On September 29 he was processed for confinement in Confederate prisons at Richmond, Virginia. His family first had direct news of his whereabouts in a communication of November 12. They were told he had a minor chin wound, not serious. Lyman wrote to his family, sharing his address in Danville Prison #6, first floor, and expressing his belief that he would soon be exchanged. In April 1864 Lyman was moved to Andersonville and died from scurvy, starvation and horrible conditions in the Andersonville prison hospital.[4]

The Dead Line at Andersonville by Robert Knox Sneden. The "dead line" was the point past which no prisoner was allowed, so that they would have no access to the stockade walls and be in sight at all times. The illustration shows a prisoner being shot by guards for taking part of the dead line as firewood (Virginia Historical Society, Library and Manuscripts Collection, Museum and Photograph Collection Record, Robert Knox Sneden Diary, 1861–1865, Volume 5: 1863 November 9–1864 August 10, Mss5.1.Sn237.1.Vol5_0653).

Robert Knox Sneden's May 10, 1864, sketch of his shanty and surroundings at Andersonville Prison (Virginia Historical Society, Library and Manuscripts Collection, Museum and Photograph Collection Record, Robert Knox Sneden Diary, 1861–1865, Volume 5: 1863 November 9–1864 August 10).

The dreams of those incarcerated in prisons in both the North and the South either glowed with hope—even in the disappointment of awaking starving, weak, and ill in places of such anguish and horror—or drove them crazy. Those dreams of hope spoke eloquently of the power of the dream and of the imagination to negotiate survival of mind and body in situations of living hell.

Inside a Grand Hotel: Planter's House

Henry Graves spoke eloquently of the gifts of dreaming and imagination keeping the soldier alive. Examples of that gift were the men who walked out—or were carried out—of Civil War prisons still able to claim life.

Houses in night dreams are places one can go to experience a moment in time where one is alive in body and soul, nourished and loved, and can expand and contract the environment as needed and find the sustenance of survival. A remarkable example of staying alive inside the landscape of a dream "house" appeared in the prison letters of John McElroy, Illinois 16th Cavalry, who was incarcerated in Andersonville during the

Planter's Hotel, St. Louis, Missouri. John McElroy found sustenance at Andersonville by dreaming of boyhood visits to a banquet at Planter's House, an elegant hotel, filling a whole block on Fourth Street in St. Louis (Library of Congress, LC-DIG-det-4a08634).

last two years of the war. He remained alive by dreaming imaginable visits to a happier place: Planter's House, an elegant hotel filling a whole block on Fourth Street in St. Louis. He had dined there with his father when he was a young boy. Although he awoke into the waking embrace of starvation, his mental excursions brought him relief in the night: "We thought of food all day, and were visited with torturing dreams of it at night. One of the pleasant recollections of my pre-military life was a banquet at the 'Planter's House,' St. Louis, at which I was a boyish guest. It was, doubtless, an ordinary affair, as banquets go, but to me then, with all the keen appreciation of youth and first experience, it was a feast worthy of Lucullus."[5]

McElroy dreamed "hundreds of times" that he was once again at Planter's House. He visited the wide corridors with their dancing mosaics, entered the grand dining room, and savored, on command, all the dainties and delicacies on the menu, making sure he tried everything available. His gourmand guide, a "dream friend" who directed McElroy's adventure through his fabulous mirror-lined Taj Mahal of dreams, permitted him access

Dining room, Planters Hotel, St. Louis Missouri (Library of Congress, LC-USZ62-57688).

to all his senses of smell, taste, touch, and the pleasures of extraordinary visual imagery. The ceilings glowed, bedecked with evergreens, festoons, and scribed mottos; the tables gleamed with cut glass and silver and brimmed with wines and fruit, all served by a gracious army of white-aproned waiters commanded by one with "presence enough for a major General." McElroy reveled "in all the dainties and dishes on the bill-of-fare; calling for everything that I dared to, just to see what each was like, and to be able to say afterwards that I had partaken of it."[6] Then McElroy awoke "to find myself a half-naked, half-starved, vermin-eaten wretch, crouching in a hole in the ground, waiting for my keepers to fling me a chunk of corn bread."[7] But this extraordinary dream was more than compensation for hunger or escapism from the horror of his surroundings. His dream helped him survive; and his "dream friend" was an incomparable guide for nourishment of both the body and the soul!

Even in dreams that helped him forget the stench, the lice, the heat, the maggots, the dead and dying, and "the insulting malignance of our jailors" it was hard work "to banish thoughts and longings for food from our minds. Hundreds became insane from brooding over it.... Their babblings and maunderings about something to eat were painful to hear. One insane inmate imagined he was sitting at the table with his family, who would go through the show of helping them to imaginary viands and delicacies." Some of those men did not survive; others clung to their dreams and survived on crusts of bread. When John McElroy finally fell stumbling from the train that took him away from Andersonville, dropping on his knees to bathe his face in a muddy ditch, he accepted from friendly hands crackers, pickled pork, ground coffee, sugar, fresh bread, "a riot in undreamed-of luxury," barely comprehending that there was more food for the taking." He and his fellows, former prisoners, filled a half-gallon bucket with coffee just so they could collect the delightful fumes in their senses: "I feared that it was one of those tantalizing dreams that had so often haunted my sleep, only to be followed by a wretched awakening."[8]

"A table loaded with good things"

William N. Tyler, a dispatch carrier, enlisted in a cavalry regiment out of Belvidere, Illinois, in 1861 at the age of twenty-three. He was captured in Memphis, Tennessee, and incarcerated in Andersonville. He survived and wrote his memoirs after the war, describing his capture, imprisonment, escape and recapture after being chased by bloodhounds. He shared the stories and dreams of those in his regiment and in Andersonville.

His first story was about "Jim," a young man in his Illinois regiment (using his first name only in his narrative). Jim consistently ran across Confederate lines, foraging for the Union army in Confederate territory, more than once visiting a plantation near the St. Charles, where he had fallen in love with a young Southern woman. She hid him once when Confederate soldiers arrived but he returned more than once, each time teasing his way past her warnings to stay away. Jim finally won her heart, proclaimed his love and asked her to be his wife, telling her that he had thought of her and "dreamed of" her every night and that she would be better off marrying him rather than remaining in a place between two contending armies where she would be burned out. Based on his declaration of dreaming and his dare-devil risks, she struck a deal that allowed him to take both her and her mother across the lines to Illinois, where she agreed to wait for him at his mother's house and marry him after the war.[9]

William Tyler's most moving story was of his own incarceration at Andersonville prison, an experience, he wrote, that could neither be forgiven or forgotten. He had been camped with his regiment in Memphis, Tennessee, in June 1864, fighting General Forrest on the 10th in the area of Forrest's operation in Guntown, Mississippi. William described the battle as "desperate" and described part of his regiment heading toward the main road, where they walked into a trap that led to more than 1800 of their men being captured.[10] They were marched to Meridian and then down the Tombigbee River to Andersonville, where more than 35,000 men occupied sixteen acres of penned stench and filth:

> The stockade was in the form of a square, and made by placing logs in the ground and forming a fence eighteen feet high. Inside of the main fence was a line of posts set twelve feet from the stockade proper, and joined together with slats about as wide as the hand, thus forming a second fence four feet high which ran parallel to the stockade and all around the pen. This was the dead line. A prisoner that came anywhere near the line was shot by the guards. The guards had little sentry boxes built to the outside, and well up to the side of the stockade; were just high enough to allow the guard's head and shoulders to come above the stockade; these were reached from the outside by means of a ladder. They took us from the cars and marched us up before Captain Wirz's headquarters. We were formed into line and counted off; were divided into hundreds, and again into squads of twenty-five. A sergeant was appointed over each department. Captain Wirz came out in front of us and said: "You are a fine looking lot of men. I will fix so you will not want to fight any more."[11]

The ground, Tyler wrote, was covered with maggots, and men's sores were full of maggots. The men had no energy or strength; they were filthy, with lice covering their bodies and their hands rotting off from scurvy. Those who were not dead were dying.

In the midst of this horrible nightmare Tyler attempted to find enough sustenance and shelter to survive. Shortly after his arrival, he managed, with help, to tunnel out and then was chased by bloodhounds and recaptured just seven days after his escape.[12] Most of the men involved in the escape were either shot or torn to pieces by the bloodhounds. He recalled, with some irony, Captain Wirz's telling the few of them who survived they were "lucky" to be alive. Doubting the providence or luck in that statement, Tyler recalled an event that was possibly both luck and providence. Some called it a miracle.

Tyler noted there were "some praying men at Andersonville. They held nightly prayer meetings, and they prayed for water. They prayed like men that meant business, for we were all dying for the want of it." One day after one of the prayer meetings there occurred "the most fearful rains I ever saw." Other accounts described the event as a tornado: "It washed the stockade as clean as a hound's tooth. Right between the dead line and the stockade it washed a ditch about two feet deep and a spring of cold water broke out in a stream large enough to fill a four-inch pipe." The men named the spring "Providence." It was protected on one side from the rebels and the dead-line protected it from prisoners camped on the other side. The men in Tyler's group protected the fountainhead and they "had good water from then on."[13]

Starvation was an hourly possibility. The food, such as it was, was the consistency of mush, distributed in barrels, the men fighting over it "like cats and dogs." All sense and manhood left them, Tyler wrote, and "starvation made them little better than brutes.... I would dream that I was sitting up to a table loaded with good things, but would always wake up before I got them."[14]

Tyler described the horrors of scurvy: "[T]he cords of the victim would be contracted and the limbs drawn up so that the patient could neither walk, stand, nor lie still. Sometimes it would be confined to the bones, and not make any appearance on the outside.

At other times it would be confined to the mouth, and the gums would separate from the teeth and the teeth would drop out."[15] Captain Henry Wirz, Andersonville's commander, had married a Southern woman William described "of the kind called creole." He claimed that Mrs. Wirz, unlike her husband, evidenced humanity toward the soldiers. He also confided, "I cannot sleep nights; my dreams are one continued nightmare."[16]

Writing of his last days at Andersonville, William described confusion when prisoners were marched to flat cars, unsure if they were being freed or transferred to another prison. They were sent to Salem, Alabama, in February 1864, then to Jackson, Mississippi, where they were ordered off the cars. They marched on foot to Vicksburg and through to their own flag "on the other side of Black River.... I never shall forget it. It did seem as if I could fly. I was going home for sure." The men embarked for St. Louis on a boat: "I never will forget how happy I did feel when the big wheels began to revolve, and she made out into the broad Mississippi. I was on my way home, sweet home, where I would have a good bed, and sit up to the table and eat with my family once more." Food would no longer be an unfulfilled dream; it would be a waking reality: "Oh, happy thought! It seemed to me as if the boat only crept along; I wanted to fly; I was sick of war and rumors of war; I did not want any more of it in mine. It was all the officers of the boat could do to keep their prisoners in subjection. They were running from one side of the boat to the other for every trifling thing they saw on the banks of the river. They were free men once more, and were going home; no wonder they were wild."[17]

William Tyler weighed less than 100 pounds, "rotten with the scurvy," his skin blue and drawn over his bones; his mind "shattered as my body, and didn't become sound till I had been home two years; and the fact of the matter is, I never have become sound."[18]

Andersonville Prison, Georgia (Library of Congress, LC-USZ62-149).

William said he had a praying mother whose prayers got him through the long journey home. Leaving the boat and traveling the last leg of his journey from Chicago to Belvidere, William was wild with excitement as he neared home. He took the train to Belvidere, where he lived just four miles south of town. Cheering residents met him and set him in a carriage: "As I came in sight of the old farm house the feelings that came over me I shall never forget. The carriage stopped; I got out and stepped to the gate; my old mother stood in the door; we gave one another a look and I was in her arms. 'Oh, this is my son, who was lost and is found; who was dead and is alive again.' And surely, if ever the fatted calf was killed it was killed for me. Then, oh, how good it did seem to have my wife and little ones around me once more; and sit up to the table and eat like a Christian."[19]

Henry Wirz, a Swiss immigrant and commander of the Andersonville prison, was one of the few men convicted and hung for murder and torture of prisoners and crimes against humanity in the administration of the Civil War prisons. He was executed on November 10, 1865. There is still controversy on how much of the testimony against Wirz was based on fact and how much was contrived because of hatred of him and the desire for a scapegoat to ameliorate feelings surrounding conditions at Andersonville and prisons across both the North and the South.

A Prayer for the Child Saves the Man: A Dream of Being Home Eleven Years Earlier

John Maile of the Eighth Regiment, Michigan Volunteer Infantry, and later a lieutenant in the Twenty-eighth U.S. Colored Troops, was imprisoned first at Lynchburg and then, in succession, Danville and Andersonville, Virginia, Florence, South Carolina, and Salisbury, North Carolina. He wrote at length about a dream, or series of related dreams, in Andersonville, that he attributed to saving his sanity and his life. He included a sketch representing a small part of his dream—a bountiful spread of food, either turkey or chicken on a plate, cruets of salt, pepper and other condiments, plates of vegetables and bowls and specialty dishes of sauces and other small delights. A goblet filled with some delicacy sits near the plate, which resembled a platter more than a plate.

In his journal John offered a simple title, *A Dream*, but he introduced the dream with a story from his boyhood. He was thirteen and had become profoundly involved with religion, belief that followed him into his studies in law. For him, professing religious conviction was embarrassing, so he made a covenant with himself to first become a lawyer and then he would embrace Christianity after success. Instead, John became a soldier. Now, at Andersonville in August 1864, he was near death, praying to the God of his teenage years. John was suffering from a virulent form of scurvy that had manifested as blood-poisoning and "settled in [his] face." His illness, made more wearisome by sleeping outside between tents and experiencing horrible sights and sounds, diminished his strength, blurring time and sensibilities. Memory of his covenant returned in his confused thinking. He determined he could not be a Christian because he had never become a lawyer as promised. What to do now? Who could he beg for his life after drifting into this strange dilemma? What God would believe him to be sincere? In response, John's mind shifted into a dream or vision in which eternity, unfettered by broken promises, opened its portals, where John saw a radiant being enthroned in love. He refused to accept this dream or the almost identical scenes over several additional nights, still believing himself unacceptable to such an inspiring spiritual being. Denial brought a sense of doom, intensified by oppressive heat and the belief that each moment was his last on earth.

Dreams don't let us down, but they might change the set to make themselves more palatable to the denying brain. John's first dream portal had been blocked by his feeling of unworthiness; the next was, for him, more real, more believable, less dependent on philosophy or origins. The second dream recalled a long forgotten memory set in the spring, eleven years earlier, in a village on "old Ridge road" in Niagara County, New York. The area was noted for its orchards, and, in the dream, the flowering trees were in full bloom, filling the air with their aroma, framing the homesteads, the sounds of bees distinctly heard in the dream. He saw, felt, and tasted the once familiar scenes of sharing life in this village, including the plate of tasty food he sketched in his journal. He saw a family he recognized heading for the village church, passing a familiar stone house, and he recognized, in them, the similarity of their concerns to that of his own. The woman had her husband's health in mind, and John realized she was imagining that her husband was in danger, unattended, and facing death, in a situation that mirrored his own. He saw her, in her own great faith in God, arising the prior evening from her bed and begging in prayerful intercession for her beloved. He saw her heart filled with light and her "being" filled with complete assurance that her husband would be well and would be rescued from danger. He saw and felt her intense gratitude for his life. In a confusing genealogy of this assemblage, John saw himself now as a child in this dream, following along to the church (and misbehaving, as children do) and the woman in the dream traveling to the church with the assemblage and praying *now* for the child. She begged a higher being to bestow on little Johnny a full dose of belief and Spirit.

John awakened from this dream, astonished that instead of receiving the anticipated dream of approaching death he had been gifted a vision so vivid and so real that it transformed itself into healing in the "prison pen." Everything had changed. Instead of despair, he felt hope. He had seen and heard the real voices of loved ones, and he felt their concern for "little Johnny," translated into hope and healing for John, the imprisoned soldier. He permitted the woman in the village dream to access portals to a heavenly realm on his behalf, gifting healing to both the teenager and to the soldier in danger. The dream repeated itself a second night, and, like the second dose of a healing drug, it restored normal thought processes to his waking brain and turned what he thought an irreversible path to death into a path to life and health—and to survival.[20]

An Andersonville Hoax or Political Necessity: Ransom Journals

> *Because those imaginary people*
> *are created out of the deepest instinct of man,*
> *to be his measure and his norm,*
> *whatever I can imagine those mouths speaking*
> *may be the nearest I can go to truth.*
> —W.B. Yeats, *Autobiographies*
>
> *The facts are the enemies of the truth.*—Don Quixote

John Ransom wrote that he was captured near Rogersville, in East Tennessee, on November 6, 1863. Only twenty years old, he was a quartermaster sergeant, with the 7th

Ohio and 1st Tennessee Mounted Infantry, when a ruse, carefully orchestrated as a dance for Union officers hosted by the Confederate citizens in the local village, led to capture and imprisonment of the Union officers.

In an introduction to his journal—claimed to have been written and protected against theft and loss through torturous years of imprisonment, first at Belle Isle and then at Andersonville—Ransom wrote that the original diary was destroyed by fire years after his release. He also claimed that the contents had been published in a series of letters to the *Jackson (MI) Citizen* and that the contents of his published work were little changed.[21] Ransom's journal was quoted for decades by historians and researchers as a valuable portrait of life in Confederate prisons and certainly of the hellish existence of soldiers incarcerated at Andersonville. Years later historians questioned these assertions and, in fact, found disturbing discrepancies between Ransom's dates and times and large sections that appeared to be plagiarized from other journals.[22]

Despite overwhelming evidence that the journal was constructed for political purposes and for a personal agenda in obtaining a pension as a wounded survivor of Andersonville, ably described by historian William Marvel, one could argue that even in the mix of dates and times or even in the journal's use for political and personal reasons, Ransom's incarceration in one of the country's most disturbing environments and his survival of that experience might justify any means to the end for recompense for his suffering and for the collected cause of those who suffered with him. His words, whether they were or were not his own words, yet reflected the appalling conditions and the incredible survival of the human spirit that carried Ransom, ill, bent and broken, out of the gates of Andersonville. We may never know Ransom's truth; but other words and other journals have borne out the truth of the conditions of the Civil War prisons. Ransom, or those his journal represented, stared death in the face, was released near the point of death, and ultimately found the care and sustenance that enabled him to recover, just as others had done. The care Ransom described, accurately or inaccurately, was received in the Confederate South in the same area but not in the same environment that almost destroyed his life and the lives of all those his journal represented. Marvel used the word "imagination" to partially describe Ransom's re-creation of his dubiously journaled experience. In this author's mind, imagination was the most truthful testament to Ransom's survival and may be his most truthful and heartfelt words in his published memoir.

Ransom wrote, like most imprisoned Civil War soldiers, that his night dreams were continually "about something good to eat," making the political point that plenty abounded in the North but that he and the other soldiers were starving in the prisons: "A man froze to death last night where I slept"; "The ground is alive with them [ticks, called graybacks], and it requires continual labor to keep from being eaten alive by them. I just saw a man shot." Survival, Ransom often noted, was dependent upon one's imagination, humor, and hope. It was of the utmost importance to keep from being despondent; one must talk and laugh and find lightness in every situation because it was "sure death for a person to give up and lose all ambition."[23] "If it weren't for hope the heart would break, and I am hopeful yet," he wrote in the summer of 1864, just before penning a series of notations about "building air castles" in the hope of being exchanged or being released. He wisely took comfort in his air castles as a better use of his time and energy than "getting blue and worrying myself to death," and they considerably better than the dreams of "hideous sights" that came unbidden after being awakened by the kicks of a dying man.[24]

Equally as believable was the horrible yet humorous dream of "graybacks," the common slang name of the ticks that covered the clothing, bedding, bodies and ground the men slept on. Ransom dreamed the "rebels were so hard up for mules that they hitched up a couple of grayback lice to draw in the bread."[25] These pests were such a common torture, both in the prisons and on the battlefield, that they inspired a parody of "Marching through Georgia," titled "The Graybacks So Tenderly Clinging."[26] Thomas Wentworth Higginson wrote equally disheartening notes about sand flies in the Carolina landscape:

> Such immense and lustrous butterflies I had never seen but in dreams, and not even dreams had prepared me for sand-flies. Almost too small to be seen, they inflicted a bit[e] which appeared larger than themselves—a positive wound, more torturing than that of a mosquito, and leaving more annoyance behind. These tormentors elevated dress-parade into the dignity of a military engagement. I had to stand motionless, with my head a mere nebula of winged atoms, while tears rolled profusely down my face, from mere muscular irritation. Had I stirred a finger, the whole battalion would have been slapping its cheeks. Such enemies were, however, a valuable aid to discipline, on the whole, as they abounded in the guard-house, and made that institution an object of unusual abhorrence among the men.[27]

Enduring the most foul conditions imaginable, Ransom and others survived against incredible odds. He wrote that his physical condition and the "spirit of" his dreams changed almost the moment he was moved from Andersonville to the Marine Hospital in Savannah, where he slowly regained enough health to survive the war.[28]

In the realization that his actual living experience in the two prisons—Belle Isle and Andersonville—was every bit as horrific and more real than the words Ransom claimed were written on site and smuggled out in the lining of his coat, one can accept that the most heartfelt words were those describing the strength, energy, and power of the imagination in surviving. There was possibly more truth in imagination, or certainly as much truth, as in writing diligently every day of the horror of that environment.

Distracting the Mind with Entertainments: The Libby Chronicle and Libby Prisoners

The *Libby Chronicle* was a newsletter written by inmates inside Libby Prison in the summer of 1863. It was read aloud every Friday morning. Irreverent humor filled its pages, and both the reading and writing of it became a lifesaver in that summer of hardship, brutality, and starvation in an environment where one sweet potato a day was considered extravagant. Not so humorously, one inmate wrote, "During the last few months of my experience in Libby rations grew more and more scant. Prisoners would lie down to sleep and dream of home comforts, and awake only to feel that horrible gnawing and craving for food magnified."[29] The messages, many on the subject of food—or the lack thereof—were irreverent, hostile satire and revenge for horrendous conditions and treatment.[30]

Dreams as literary devices were equally irreverent and inventive. In the August 28, 1863, issue, the editor wished officers (names invented to protect them all) "a dream delirious [in which] he'll find his boots are full of snakes. He has an oily tongue and face full of deceit and evil. Should Old Nick miss that scape-goat, there's no need of a devil."[31]

Johnson's Island: An Officer's Prison

Entertainments in Block 8

Johnson's Island Civil War Prison, located on a small island in Sandusky Bay, Lake Erie (just north of Cedar Point), held over 10,000 Confederate officers captured at hundreds of battles during the Civil War. One of the unique aspects of this site was that it held only officers. Block 8 was a general housing block reserved for a number of well-known individuals, but the unique thing about Block 8 was its theatrical performances, particularly those called the "Rebellonians."

Also in Block 8 was William Peel, one of a handful of prisoners who became expert in the production of hard rubber jewelry. Inmates at Johnson's Island formed a YMCA and a debating society and when snow was present, some held snowball fights. There were newspapers and games, especially cards and checkers or chess. Burton Warfield, a Confederate captive from Hampshire, Tennessee, wrote to his wife about Bible classes, concerts, a thespian and debating society, ball and marble playing and "almost anything else you could think of" for men "accustomed to mental and physical exercise … to employ the mind." Yet, he said, the greater portion of men's time "is occupied mentally in day dreams and nocturnal visions of loved ones at home. We lie down to rest at night to visit perhaps the beautiful and magic world of dreamland, which mocks us with its unattainable witcheries."[32]

John Dooley in Block 8

John Dooley left Richmond on August 12, 1862, to join the 1st Virginia, stationed then at Gordonsville. He headed out to find field activity armed with a weapon and a change of clothing wrapped in a blanket and was immediately faced with images of mangled and mutilated bodies from the bloody Battle of Cedar Mountain, Virginia. Nauseated by the scenes of war and confused by the strange faces and sounds of his first night in camp, the glaring fires, neighing horses, and deep "shadows of a dark night overhanging all," John fell on his knees to pray and rose to find a bed and sleep in peace, "for my Guardian Angel was watching by my side, and though I little suspected it then, bore me through many a dreadful peril even to this hour."[33]

Wounded in 1863 during Pickett's charge—and just promoted to captain—John Dooley was captured and incarcerated at Johnson's Island, part of Block 8. His first journaled notes, designated "Prison Notes, Series I," covered July–November 1863. He occupied a space with over fifty others. He hated the endless card games, which he called "gambling hells," and barely tolerated the cottage industries. He filled his time with reading and chess playing, becoming a member of a club whose matches with another club in the room became major events.

On a cold winter evening, he participated in a Spiritualism adventure that yielded a violently shaking table only after some of the bored participants left. Humorously, John noted:

> At first it was supposed that the table was too heavy and if the spirit *was weak* it could not stir a heavy prison table with such a weight of large hand upon it. Then again it was conjectured that there were some objectionable characters around the object, men of little faith, etc. and this idea was confirmed when after several of the circle had retired, the table appeared violently agitated; But the truth of the matter is that one of the Knights of this *enchanting* circle applied his knee underneath to the object

and gave it a rocking motion, which deception he acknowledges *now, altho' when accused* at the time he flatly denied this; his denial with indignation is supposed to have been owing to the direct influence of the spirits; but *I'm* inclined to think that the only *spirits* in that room at that time were very safely and securely *corked up* in the *other bottle* I'm keeping for Christmas.[34]

John spoke of the power of music on the imagination and the power of theatre. There were two thespian troupes, the first simply called the "Thespians." The Thespians were dissolved after performing a play called the *Battle of Gettysburg*, which included material the guards considered offensive: "[There were] many hard hits at the Yankees for which they will have their *revenge*. Nov. 14th We, the Thespians, are ordered by the authorities to pull down our Stage on block 8 (two weeks work it cost to erect it) and 'vamous the Ranche.' 'The Battle of Gettysburg' was too hard on them."[35]

John had been invited to perform with the Thespians on September 22, 1863. He wrote that the purpose of the performances, for which fees were charged, were to help those who were most ill and destitute. He also noted that the Thespians wished to improve on the more common minstrels, abandoning "burnt corks" and striving for plays "worthy of the intelligence and admiration of men of education and enlightenment."[36]

In the spring of 1864 the Rebellonians cautiously took the place of the Thespians. John wrote about the new company and its efforts to more carefully portray their satire, a bit to the detriment of quality in John's opinion: "[A] new company of minstrels, play to day—band not as good as the old one. Farce rather low and even obscure, but represents Yankee life and character, the Northern press, and northern preachers, quite accurately."[37]

John was also part of a prison glee club and an opera club: "July 15th—oh how dull the long weary day drags its slow length along Burchardt plays chess with me and Cronin talks to me—and nothing else ... and we *moan* during the day and *sing* nightfall. It is a strange thing to see a lot of wounded, miserable, half starved, & melancholic wretches gathering in a social knot and forming a *glee* club to frighten off the more gloomy shadows of our prison walls. Imagination can do wonders in making us miserable or happy.... Cronin sings and McGimpsey is singing and both have *holes* through their *lungs*—this is certainly miserably gay." Feeling particularly depressed and fatigued as the spring opened in 1864, with exchange not possible, music was still John's saving angel: "At night we have music and dancing which does much towards driving away fatigue and sorrow and chasing the gloomy shadows from our hearts."[38]

John dwelled on the range of possibilities the imagination could enact or perform in the waking environment. He had already considered that, although music was a vital part of his survival, a sad or even a gay song could be depressing when performed against the backdrop of the prison environment and could indeed wreak havoc with the "miserably gay." Seeing starving men raid the "ashpile" (garbage) for dry bones and tiny scraps of food, he considered further how the energy of imagination, if not consciously directed toward positive results, could play out for either survival or more depressing consequences in the waking reality of men already bowed down by circumstance:

> [T]he ration of bread is about 10 oz and that of meat 7 oz; and actually you may see officers, at least prisoners with officers' coats on, prowling about in rear of the buildings *picking up old dry bones, that a respectable man's dog would disdain* to crunch; and what to do with them? Ask them and they will tell you to make soup of them: do you think this is affectation? Alas it is most melancholy affectation: you may say imagination, but one suffers oftentimes more from the imagination than from realities—and I think if one gives you a blow upon the head, in which the imagination probably resides, you would feel but little consolation in saying to yourself, "pshaw! The pain I seem to feel is only in the imagination: the blow for all that would not be the less severe; and when hunger *seeming or real* gnaws,

as it were, the very vitals, the imagination may increase my suffering, but for all that there is a frightful reality in an empty stomach, & a dismal void out of which a weak and trembling voice articulates '*go gather bones*,'" these prisoners would not surely go from drain to drain in quest of dry bones wherewith to make soup if a terrible necessity did not drive them to it, and one may say what he pleases concerning this or that allowance or quantity being sufficient to sustain and nourish life: this is all very well in the abstract, but when you come to realities a man who has been accustomed all his life to eating certain quantities will in all probability break down if you try to force him to live upon less, and that suddenly, upon compulsion, and when his mind is troubled and in continual agitation: & like the horse which his master had just *begun to accustom* to live upon *one straw* a day, he will die.[39]

John Dooley survived Johnson's Island and the war. In the days between his release and his harrowing journey through the ravaged South, he received news of death in his family and debated on whether or not he would go home. He determined that some secret desire urged him toward home. Music had been his savior in prison. Hearing the Confederate song "The Vacant Chair," John Dooley followed the urge and headed home, completing his last journal entry as he walked into the ruined, burned remains of his hometown, Richmond, Virginia: "I shall not attempt to describe my feelings: the city in ruins and the hated and triumphant army of our malignant foes marching through the ruined city—with a raging headache and swelling heart I reach my home and here the curtain falls."[40]

"Psychal" Flight from Johnson's Island: James Caldwell

My smoke wreaths are curling
Like wind driven clouds
When moonlight our bright world
In silver, enshrouds;
My thoughts, like the silvery clouds
Flits swiftly away
Reminding that life
Is but the dream of a day.[41]

James Parks Caldwell entered the Confederate army as an artillery lieutenant. He fought at Shiloh, Port Hudson and other campaigns before being captured in 1863 and imprisoned on Johnson's Island. He was confined in the customs house along with forty others. He was in ill health when he arrived but was not allowed to "smell fresh air." Meals consisted of sour bread, salt beef, and coffee. James kept a daily diary for eighteen months, describing the prison food and conditions, as well as recording detailed descriptions of his classicist and intellectual interests. He was a prolific reader and devoured books, often one a night. In an environment that was bent on starving his body, he read Kant, Shakespeare, Greek and Roman philosophy, and every novel, good or bad, he could lay his hands on, commenting at length on many of them and creating parodies, some in Latin, on others.

Illness and nausea generated medleys of dreams like those of an "opium eater."[42] One "dark and stormy" evening (a phrase coined by Edward Bulwer-Lytton), after reading Bulwer-Lytton's *A Strange Story*, he dreamed. Attributing his absorption into Bulwer's occult fantasy to the direction of his dream/vision, he recorded a "delightful dream" filled with intellectual pleasure, "thrilling" thoughts, beautiful images, and "powerful phantoms," all of which he described as a "psychal" journey, not unlike those described by Bulwer as trance-like journeying, with the energy and power to transport the soul to places and people both familiar in waking—and unfamiliar.[43]

11. *Dreaming in Prison* 155

A Richmond, Virginia, street in the burned district, 1865 (Library of Congress, LC-DIG-cwpb-02673).

James journaled about his amazing experience: "There was nothing merely physical in my dreams,—it was a vision of the *soul*." Caldwell was ecstatic about this exquisitely visual dream, which gave him pleasure and transport in a way no dream had previously accomplished. He mentioned again in his subsequent journal entries the entree his dream presented for a pleasurable "visit," particularly with "one" familiar face, embracing his freedom in a way reminiscent of George du Maurier's 1891 character Peter Ibbetson, who dreamed himself beyond the bars of his prison cell.

The "one" familiar face was that of Virginia "Ginny" Moon, whose letters to Caldwell gifted him with an additional force of survival. Ginny had an extraordinary life, not the least aspect of which involved her work as "spy" for the Confederate Nathan Bedford Forrest. Caldwell's soul leapt when he received letters from Ginny; he journaled that he denied a brief dream of her as a venerable white-haired old lady. He would always see

Ginny as young and beautiful; he abruptly noted that he would not accept this dream: "*non accepi*" (October 2, 1864).[44]

Surviving Johnson's Island was a challenge, with victory belonging to James's intellectual pursuits, imagined journeys and "air castles,"[45] and his dreams, which offered soul-nourishing food undiminished by confinement and starvation rations.

A Remarkable Exception: Cahaba Federal Prison

Cahaba Federal Prison, located just a few miles southwest of Selma, Alabama, is rarely mentioned in the Civil War prison listings and defies the odds in numbers who died there, a mere 147 of 5,000 prisoners. According to Peter Cozzens, a *New York Times Disunion* blogger, the reason for such a low death rate and such rare mention was an even more rare condition—humanity.[46]

The prison commandant, Colonel Henry A.M. Henderson of Kentucky, a Methodist minister before his assignment to Cahaba, assumed command just one month after the prison opened in July 1863. He pledged to run the prison "with as much compassion as discipline and good order permitted." He kept his promise. The prison, built around a cotton warehouse, had 250 bunks, designed to sleep two men each, an unfinished roof partially exposed to the elements, a stockade, over-crowded conditions, lice and polluted water from body washing, spittoons, hospital waste, animal waste, and other filth. Colonel Henderson enlisted the aide of his surgeon, Dr. R.H. Whitfield, and together they won an uncommon victory with a fulfilled request for the installation of piping to replace

Stockade and prison at Cahawba (aka Cahaba), Alabama (Library of Congress, LC-DIG-ppmsca-33764).

the open ditch. Latrines were moved away from the water supply; dysentery was almost unknown. Those who died at Cahaba were already weakened by other conditions of war and disease before their arrival.

When conditions deteriorated in a severe winter in early 1864, a dramatic lack of rations and supplies, clothing wearing thin, and even more men being placed in the prison, Henderson fought against the only enemy they could control—homesickness and ennui. To distract the men, "Every day on the arrival of the mail, one of them would bring in a late paper, stand up on a box and read the news," recalled Sgt. Melvin Grigsby of Wisconsin. "In many other ways, such as procuring writing material and forwarding letters for us, they manifested such kindly feeling as one honorable soldier will always manifest toward brother soldier, enemy though he may be, in misfortune."

Another "angel of mercy," Amanda Gardner, whose home stood just outside the prison compound, sent her daughter with gifts of food slipped through cracks in the stockade walls with the connivance of friendly guards. When winter came, Amanda cut every carpet in her home into blankets to "relieve the suffering of those poor prisoners." She also sent books, including novels, classics, history, science, and poetry. Life was still not easy. Rations continued to fall and the men, like those in other prison camps, dreamed of food: "The same experience was often repeated," remembered an Illinois cavalryman, Jesse Hawes. "Go to the bed of sand at 9:00 p.m., dream of food till 1:00 or 2:00 a.m., awake, go to the water barrel, drink, and return to sleep again if the rats would permit sleep." Lice were a constant condition. Rain, always a nuisance, became a nightmare when the Cahaba River flooded on March 1, 1865, backing up latrines and creating a fetid horror.

In the final days of the war, Henderson was reassigned and an unsympathetic lieutenant-colonel replaced him; but there was one last tragic moment greater than the loss of a sympathetic commander. Union prisoners had been released and placed on the Union paddle steamer *Sultana*. The *Sultana* left Vicksburg with 2,000 prisoners, over half of them from Cahaba. The boat's capacity was 376; three of its four faulty boilers exploded, killing three-quarters of the men aboard, a sad end to a story of attempted humanity and hope in a difficult environment for either.

Writing and Dreaming of Home

While providing a chilling record of starvation, disease, and death, letters and journals written by prisoners of war in the Civil War were the primary mind-saving and life-saving preoccupation, and many of those who found sleep provided a consistent record of dreams of family and other loved ones.

William Williston Heartsill enlisted in W.P. Lane's Texas Rangers in 1861 and was taken prisoner in 1862 when the Rangers moved into Arkansas as a cavalry unit and were overwhelmed by the Union army. He was transported to a prisoner of war camp near Springfield, Illinois, and moved to City Point, Virginia, where he was exchanged in April 1863. His men joined General Braxton Bragg's army in Tennessee and fought at Chickamauga: "It seemed that if ten thousand earthquakes had been turned loose in all their power," he wrote, "they would not have made so much racket." Heartsill's unit was disbanded in 1865. He kept his journal throughout his military career, "four years, one month, and one day," including his days in prison. He said that he did not claim great things from his journal except a "mirror of ... the trials and pleasures, of a private soldiers life in the army."⁴⁷ Prison life was dreary and depressing and forced body and mind to defend themselves against the cold, bad food, the physical discomfort of close confinement, and disease, which brought record numbers of deaths. Despite these conditions, he would not take the oath of allegiance to gain his freedom.

Heartsill tried to hold onto his dreams for journal recording, but living conditions interrupted even the most hard to come by pleasant sleeps "in my dreaming experience," with rain dropping in his face and sending him into the night crouched down behind a tree with his blanket over his head.⁴⁸ After his exchange, during the Chickamauga campaign, he wrote that the normalcy of dreaming of coming events or of loved ones at home provided the world over "aching hearts." He intimated that no one wished to dream of coming events when those dreams presaged "cruel cruel war and thrice cruel invaders that come to drench our sunny south in blood and drag us to worse than slavery."⁴⁹

A Large Pint of Butter—and Exchange

John McElroy, William Tyler and others, starving in the waking reality of day, survived Andersonville by dreaming of tables laden with food. Prisoners of war frequently recorded dreams of meals shared with loved ones or dreams of abundant nourishment. Dreams of food, in most cases, sustained the soul, and, remarkably for some, generated enough energy to avoid death and the very real possibility of starvation.⁵⁰ Private William Downer dreamed of home, a table laden with food—and exchange!

Private Downer was in the 6th Virginia Cavalry and became a Confederate prisoner. He wrote to his wife on Christmas Day 1863, just months after having been captured and imprisoned at Camp Chase in Columbus, Ohio. He prayed to God for deliverance and wrote poignantly of home and of missing his wife and children. In his dream his wife had prepared a large loaf of bread, and he was sitting at the table admiring a large pint of butter in the middle of the table: "I was seated to the table and, oh; how I enjoyed it. I really thought the best I had ever eaten. My wife sitting at the head of the table looking upon me with delight not eating a mouthful I had been exchanged and reached home in safety. Willie and Towles sitting on my left calling on Pa for something about every moment and my little baby sitting on the floor, when I was awakened, and, oh; what disappointment when I raised up in my bed and realized nothing more than a dream."⁵¹

This dream of home had the "realness" expressed by so many soldiers but included a pivotal moment, a review of Private Downer's future (*"I had been exchanged and reached home in safety"*), a moment he did not consciously recall in the following months but one that revealed itself in a surprise announcement on February 5, 1865: "What a beautiful morning is this, and, what glorious news we have received this morning.... We are fully apprised of the fact this morning that a general exchange of prisoners is agreed upon and the rolls are now being made out for the purpose of transporting prisoners immediately. Oh, what joyful news to us who have not ceased praying to be returned to our homes and families night or day since our imprisonment.... I know my wife will look with an anxious eye for my return and tell my little children that Pa will soon come home."⁵²

Time dragged on for months. The date for Downer's exchange was pushed forward, bringing anxiety when he heard through an unidentified source that his wife had been told he could come home but had chosen not to. He desperately sent letters to assuage her mind, finally receiving news on June 9 that he was leaving for home: "The joy that thrills my heart, tongue or pencil is totally inadequate to express.... I expect to leave for home tomorrow or Monday.... God only knows my heart, and when I reach home and reveal to her those truths. I know it will be hurtful to her feelings to think that she has for a moment harboured the thought within her breast that I could for a moment be untrue to her or those little ones I have left behind me."[53]

The first leg of his trek home was from Bellaire to Wheeling. He left for Baltimore on June 14 and traveled on flat cars in the rain, arriving at Baltimore on June 16 and at Ft. Monroe on the 17th. From there he traveled toward Richmond, where he chatted amicably with Yankee soldiers on the reasons the Confederates lost the war. Downer reached Richmond at dark and went to the capital square and stayed all night before finally arriving home to his wife and family, whom he had thought were forever lost to him.

A Visual Feast: Sausage or Whatever I Like Sitting on the Stove

John Alexander, a prisoner in Elmira Prison Camp in Elmira, New York, survived typhoid fever and starvation. He described dreams that came to him in February 1864, a month when all the normal horrors of prison life became even more damned with the cold. A man could not sleep for the hunger and every half-hour the sentinel cried, "All's well," words that grated on "the souls of the starving." Hunger drove John to take the ration of bread from a sick man who could not eat, realizing he would be required to forego breakfast the next morning as payback. But taking the bread was worth it. The small morsel allowed sleep and "the sweetest dreams mortal man was ever heir to." They sometimes took him "to another climate if he was cold, sometimes home and sometimes Virginia, where there was always plenty to eat." He saw the cook bending over the stove, "the coffee pot full to the brim, and in a trimble with escaping steam and [he could] see the sausage or ham and eggs—or whatever he liked best sitting on the stove. He could also hear the crackle of the fire, the coffee mill, and the rattle of the dishes—and hear the table as the cook dragged it over the floor, all was now ready." The noise of the table dragging over the floor was so distinct that it waked him, back into the cold but with a small fragment of hope that helped him through one more day.

John was released July 12, 1865. He managed to follow Sherman's burned trail, begging for crusts of bread on his way home and lamenting a devastated and starving countryside that offered only slightly more relief than Elmira Prison Camp. But he was on his way home![54]

"In my dreams I would eat and eat"

W.H. Bland recorded his prison memoirs for a larger memoir of the 61st Georgia Regiment written by private G.W. Nichols. Bland had been captured near Morton's Ford on the Rapidan River on January 4, 1864. He was taken first to the city of Washington and imprisoned in the old capitol building, faring pretty well until Mosby made a raid on the railroad near Alexandria. He was then moved to Fort Delaware prison, where "we were perished nearly to death." He would often dream "of being at home at my mother's table, with plenty of good things on it, and in my dreams I would eat and eat, but it seemed that I could never get enough." His rations were one-fourth of a one-half pound loaf of bakers bread twice a day; meat consisting of a very "small, thin slice of salt pork or fresh beef, which made about one good mouthful, with one Irish potato occasionally thrown in extra." When he was paroled ten months later, he weighed less than eighty pounds and had scurvy.[55]

Sojourning in the Land of Dreams: John Whipple

Dreaming frequently appeared as allusions in letter writing and became part of ordinary dialogue; the generic use of dreams and dreaming flowed in longing sentences between husbands and wives, friends and lovers. Such were the letters Lieutenant John Whipple wrote to his wife, first as a soldier in the 92nd (there is no additional information on his regiment's name) on the road at Fort Anderson, Maryland, in April 1863 and then, over a year later, at Elmira Prison Camp (July 1864). His wife appeared to live in the North, but his imprisonment was in a Northern prison camp, throwing some confusion over John's writing; but regardless of that, the letters were eloquent and longing, the first addressing his wife's advice that he come home.

He addressed the generic "dream," the one that flows seamlessly through our conversation when we express wishes and desires. This dream from all-encompassing peace, to love and family, to untroubled nights permeated the letters of soldiers of every rank from both the North and the South. John Whipple wrote that he wished he could act on such advice, "to come home," but honor would not permit him to do something so dishonorable: "For if I could deceive man, I could not deceive my own conscience. I am coming home as honorable as I left it, or not at all. It is not the whole of life to live in this state of being, for when this world's night shall have passed away with all its darkness, its troubled dreams, its baseless visions, and we wake in the light of an eternal day, may we be spared the thought that *our* part in life's great struggle was not well played; therefore let us not be weary in well-doing."[56]

The following year John's larger and smaller dreaming helped him through difficult months and years in Elmira Prison Camp. He found a unity of purpose for mankind and looked to the night sky to see that there was little difference in who slept under the stars and even less difference in the soothing dreaming nights of sleep

> The moon was slowly climbing up the spangled heavens, shedding its silver light upon the earth. It shone equally upon the prisoner and his keeper; and I reflected: "Is not the infinite and abiding love of the Eternal also manifested unto all these men, as unto us? Hath not God made of one blood all nations to dwell upon the earth? And when we stand before him, will not these minor points of difference that now separate us, shrink and vanish away?" Thus meditating, I entered my room, remembering a prayer once offered: "Father, forgive them, they know not what they do"; and, likewise, the injunction: "If thine enemy hunger, feed him; if he thirst, give him drink."
>
> When the drums had beaten "lights out," as in duty bound I locked my door, turned down the kerosene, crept under my blankets, and soon, under the soothing influences of Morpheus, I was sojourning in the land of dreams.[57]

John's words are worth repeating because, in all these dreams behind prison walls, the desire for freedom and peace became louder and more unified: "It is not the whole of life to live in this state of being, for when this world's night shall have passed away with all its darkness, its troubled dreams, its baseless visions, and we wake in the light of an eternal day, may we be spared the thought that *our* part in life's great struggle was not well played; therefore let us not be weary in well-doing."

Chapter 12

Caring for the Wounded

"...he is I think gradualy waisting. So it is the world over..."—Ada Bascot

It is the night before a battle. The enemy, Fredericksburg, and its mighty entrenchments lie before us, the river between—at tomorrow's dawn our troops will assay to cross, and the guns of the enemy will sweep those frail bridges at every breath.

The moon is shining through the soft haze with a brightness almost prophetic. For the last half hour I have stood alone in the awful stillness of its glimmering light gazing upon the strange sad scene around me striving to say, "Thy will Oh God be done."

The camp fires blaze with unwanted brightness, the sentry's tread is still but quick—the acres of little shelter tents are dark and still as death, no wonder for us as I gazed sorrowfully upon them. I thought I could almost hear the slow flap of the grim messenger's wings, as one by one he sought and selected his victims for the morning. Sleep weary one, sleep and rest for tomorrow's toil. Oh! Sleep and visit in dreams once more the loved ones nestling at home. They may yet live to dream of you, cold lifeless and bloody, but this dream soldier is thy last, paint it brightly, dream it well. Oh northern mothers wives and sisters, all unconscious of the hour, would to Heaven that I could bear for you the concentrated woe which is so soon to follow, would that Christ would teach my soul a prayer that would plead to the Father for grace sufficient for you, God pity and strengthen you every one.[1]

Clara Barton's Civil War work began in April 1861 after the Battle of Bull Run when she established an agency to distribute supplies to the wounded soldiers. By the summer of 1862 she had proved her invaluable service off the field and obtained permission to go behind the lines, witnessing some of the most grim scenes in America's history. She was in the field at such well-known scenes as Fredericksburg, Petersburg and Richmond. Not allowing politics to stand in the way of helping the wounded, she delivered her service and empathy to soldiers on both sides. After the war this once shy woman became one of the most respected lecturers in the country, and in 1881 she founded the American Red Cross, for which she served as director until her death. Her memory became an example in the field for all generations to come.

The Woolsey Family: Fountains of Courage and Love of Country[2]

Jane Eliza Woolsey gave birth to eight children, seven girls and one boy. Her husband, Charles, died, leaving Jane to raise a large family; but Charles left them comfortably cloaked in inheritances and the support of a wealthy family in New York City. The family hated slavery, even though their ancestry was as Virginia slaveholders. The children grew up with strong political connections and were well-educated and strong supporters of abolition. They also grew up steeped in a sense of duty and hands-on participation. Georgeanna, Jane, Eliza, Carry, and Hatty served in military hospitals. Abby organized sewing and supply work for the Sanitary Commission. Mary wrote patriotic poems published by her family; and Charles worked with the Sanitary Commission and secured a post with the Army of the Potomac. Other family members served in political and military positions and kept one another informed of important military events. Letters streamed to and from the elegant house at 8 Brevoort Place: politics, hospital issues, and humor volleying back and forth among the sisters, Charles, and their mother, Jane. (Mary died on May 31, 1864, her last words the final phrase of a poem, "Taps," the army bugle call to sleep, to put out the lights: "The notes rising and falling, say as plainly as music can say anything—'Put it out; put it out; put it out!'").[3]

Jane Stuart Woolsey, the second daughter, participated in early meetings of the Women's Central Relief Association, which evolved into the U.S. Sanitary Commission. Undaunted by Dorothea Dix's odd prescriptive qualifications and detestations, Jane became superintendent of nurses at Fairfax Seminary Hospital, near Alexandria, Virginia, and personally advocated for and cared for the maimed, diseased, and dying soldiers, whose stories—and dreams—touched her life and her heart. She remained there, devoted to the Union, until the end of the war. A letter between Abby and Eliza reported a heated 1859 abolition meeting at the Cooper Institute involving speeches that erupted into pandemonium and an effort to challenge Charles to a fight. The effect on Jane was a nightmare that manifested in a sleepwalking adventure, in which she "went into the little room next to ours and locked herself in; barricaded the door with baskets and chairs, throwing one of the latter over and breaking it. She had previously closed the doors between our room and Mother's, so that Mother only heard the sounds indistinctly. Jane lay down on the little bed, without covering, and toward morning the cold awakened her, to her great bewilderment."[4] Concern for her sisters' work in other hospitals also entered Jane's dreams.

Abby wrote to Georgy (Georgeanna) and Eliza that Jane was dreaming a "catalogue of evils" for her: "awful dreams about Georgy, that the other night a message came that she was ill with hasty typhoid fever followed by paralysis from over-exertion." Georgeanna did not contract typhoid, but she was continually reminded by the doctors who worked with her that she needed to take time for herself. For her family's benefit, Georgeanna always wrote that she was "perfectly well, and in the best of spirits." Her family understood the dangers of suppressing anxiety and saw their share of mental as well as physical wounds among the soldiers they tended. They seriously considered Jane's anxiety dreams for Georgy and wrote that Georgy pretended to have no heart: "Tell her, of course she hasn't or won't have soon—it's *ossifying*, that, or something kindred, is what all surgeons die of—suppressed emotion. Tell her we insist on her coming home for a few weeks."[5]

However, the Woolsey girls tended well and faithfully to those under their care. They introduced games, gave out tools, and established rooms for work and play and noted the improvement in the men's health. They wrote and understood the power of the imagery of sympathy and encouragement, which was "sometimes more potent to cure, than brandy or quinine from the hands of the most skillful physician. The kind looks and deeds of our nurses, and their kindlier words go straight to the hearts of the sick men and bring them nearer home by many a weary mile."[6]

In her *Hospital Days* reminiscences of the soldiers at Fairfax Seminary Hospital,

Jane Woolsey wrote about the men being fond of flowers—no surprise in a landscape trampled of all vegetation, stripped of crops, trees blasted apart by shells, gardens destroyed or overgrown with neglect. Time and again a poignant moment occurred in the mention of flowers blooming in some protected glade or a rose bush thriving on battlefields strewn with dead bodies. People sent Jane flowers for the men, some of them seasonal, many of them hothouse blooms. One sergeant especially delighted in hothouse carnations, white and red; he fondled them and attached them to his bedstead over his head. He died with one clutched in his fingers. Jane brought a bunch of lilacs to a sick New England boy: "'Lalocs!'—he whispered, and I laid them on his folded hands;— 'oh, lalocs! How did you know that?' The lilacs outlived him."[7]

"[The letters to soldiers' families]," Jane wrote, "were no common, formal statement of facts. They must be framed with care and conscience. They carried precious things; the note-book leaf, the hymn-card, the lock of hair, the plain gold ring; they carried the last look backward of the parting soul: 'Tell her I kissed her picture and wished I had been a better man,' the little, little gleam of light across the darkness of the invisible country: 'He said some words at last that seemed like prayer.' How difficult such correspondence must often be, the Chaplain's memoranda show:—" Jane sympathized with the chaplain's "hourly watch," which patiently followed the wandering soul "through the perplexed mazes fever," drugs, stimulants, and the "craze of chloroform, to find the one sane moment." She noted some of the ramblings of the dying mind recorded in the memoranda: "Wandering; one minute charging with his regiment and next with his mother at home; Irrational; cried out, 'Mother, you are wanted,' and died. Dying, said: 'The room is growing dark; are they putting out the lights?'"[8]

The Woolsey girls' mother wrote to Jane and Georgeanna asking if one of them might send the "German soldier boy's dream" for inclusion in the "Drum Beat," a piece for *The Fair Companion*, a Sanitary Fair paper with contributions by the Woolseys. The dream was not recorded in Georgeanna's letters but found its place in Jane's reminiscences:

> The blonde, blue-eyed German ... called G. [Georgeana] to his bedside one morning to tell her his dream of her, "Last night I dreamed," he said, "that I was walking by myself in a great city and came to a bridge over a deep river. As I crossed the bridge it broke and I fell into the water and was sinking, when you came and drew me to land. I was all dripping and you took me to your own house and gave me a whole new suit of clothes all dry and warm. Then you said: 'You may go into the garden and take a flower; take any flower you like.' So I took a rose; but as I was picking it I died and went to Heaven. You called aloud to me: 'Don't drop the rose; take it with you and plant it in Heaven for me.' So I went to Heaven and planted it, and it grew and blossomed. And when the blossoms came I sent you down word, and you died and came to Heaven and found there all ready a rose-tree, blooming for you."[9]

His dream was a vivid example of dreams that manifest on both sides of life, with possible unknown kindness repaid on the other side.

The war ended. Two years later Jane returned to New York City and wrote her memoir, *Hospital Days*, desiring to acquaint her readers with the operation of a hospital during the Civil War. The Rev. Henry Hopkins, the hospital chaplain, wrote many years later, "No picture from any scene of my life is more vivid in my recollection than that of Jane ... as I saw her sometimes at Fairfax—her illuminated face with the wonderful eyes, and the wonderful smile, her fragile form wrapped in the ermine-lined cloak she used to wear." She conquered the life of ease with service—without losing the grace of her social standing and her love of a fine wardrobe.

Jane died on July 9, 1891.[10]

Ada Bacot: Disturbed by Dreams

Ada Bacot was an unrepentant slave owner with a large plantation in Darlington County, South Carolina. Her husband died, leaving her alone with two children, who also subsequently died. She was 27 years old, depressed, and looking for something to do when the call for nurses came. She begged help from her father and neighbors for the plantation and left for Virginia to serve in a Charlottesville hotel converted into a hospital. Surgeons, nurses, and medical care were inadequate. Women were hired as cooks and housekeepers, but Ada was finally allowed to have direct contact with the wounded and ill. She dressed their wounds, cheered them, and discussed their spiritual anxieties. During her service she met James E. Henry Clarke, a wounded soldier whom she married in 1864.

Living conditions were unlike those familiar to Ada. She admitted she liked quiet and quiet was no longer part of her environment. Her night dreams rambled, some pleasant, most disturbing and most influenced by her surroundings. Mice scrambled across her room, nibbling at her soap, causing "me to leave one of my most delightful dreams (for I had two or three separate ones during the night) unfinished as I lay awake my last dream was so vividly remembered that I had half a mind to write it out when I arose this morning, but in the mean time I fell asleep again & by the time I arose the dream had almost escaped me, which I regret for 'twas quite a pretty one."[11]

Suffering from depression and unresolved grief, Ada believed she would not live long and admitted that she was simply weary of life. Except for the possibility of the dream recorded in January, she saw nothing bright in her life. She recorded a series of dreams that were nightmares, leaving her gasping for air, feeling suffocated and a desperation she felt was out of her control. The dreams—and the subsequent physical sensations—presaged "events" that "cast their shadow before them," the birth of an unwanted child in her family. She never elaborated but became more depressed after the announcement of the birth.[12]

Most of Ada's dreams reflected daily activities. Reading in bed left her dreaming of the pages she had read and reflecting on a walk in a garden that brought her some degree of happiness. Flowers were the joy that expanded her soul and made her forget the suffering around her. She attempted to dwell on happier times, before the death of her husband and babies, but her dreams were peopled with "strange beaings" and reminded her of what she feared most—the end of her sheltered plantation life and the end of slavery, although that fear was couched in the guise of a Negro woman afraid the Yankees would shoot her: "I wandered in a magnificent building where I could not tell, as I was asending [sic] one of the splendid stair ways a negro woman came to me & implored that I would protect her that the Yankees were going to shoot her." Ada awoke agitated, exhausted, and alarmed at what this dream might mean. Disturbing dreams came again: "I was ... uneasy ... and was much disturbed by dreams ... [and was] dreaming all the time."[13]

Although there were bright moments in Ada's life, her notes and journaled dreams spotlighted her wounded soul, which had seen so much personal grief before and during her nursing experience. Shortly after her disturbed dream of the Negro woman's call for help, her family called her home to dress a child for burial. Left to keep vigil over the child's body, she could hardly bear handling the tiny wasted frame. Midnight found her drifting in and out of exhausted sleep, calling on God for help for all the world's children and for herself. A few days later, suffering from the Southern heat, she fell into a troubled sleep and dreamed more troubling dreams and then, finally, found relief in a small dream of finding a cool spring of water. This moment of respite was quickly over:

> Gloomy, gloomy, the rain pours in torents without the least appearance of clearing up. I feel as withered as a plucked flower this morning I scarcely closed my eyes during the night, & when I did I was not refreshed. The bed was as hard as a board, then there was some young man sleeping just above me, who came in late & made a great fuss, then a mouse began to nible in a corner of the room there was a hundred & one little things to worry me, when I did sleep I was staring & dreaming all the while. I awoke at the first peep of day. I called to Savary to get up, then tried to take a nap but the flys tormented me so I slept no more, so I got up, not long after Savary came to say breakfast was coming in.[14]

Ada may have found some relief and personal healing in nursing others and ministering to their spiritual needs, and in her marriage to James Clarke, the soldier she nursed to health—but the lasting impression of her night dreams were of desolation and hopelessness: "I have been to see poor Campbell [a reference to a trip to Monticello] since my return he is I think graduly waisting. So it is the world over, while some enjoy themselves others are dieing."[15]

"He was my baby again"

Myrta Avary grew up in Norfolk, Virginia, accustomed to Prussian navy officers being among the visitors to her family home. Men in uniform were part of her life, and she expected to marry someone serving in the military. Her marriage happened quickly. A friend told her she should meet Dan Grey, a young man in the Confederate army. She did and they were married four months later. Shortly after their marriage, Myrta offered to help with nursing in the hospital wards in the Norfolk area, where her patient was Dan's command captain, Jeter, who had fallen in a skirmish. Dan asked her to sit beside Jeter until his wife and mother could arrive. Myrta rushed to the hospital and tended to his wound until midnight, when he died. Jeter's mother arrived the next day. Both of them sat shocked and speechless with the lifeless body of Jeter. His mother reminisced on what a sweet baby he was, how pretty he had been and how he followed her around and pulled at her skirts: "Last night I dozed for a minute and I dreamed about him. He was my baby again, and I had him safe in my arms, and there never had been any war." Jeter's mom pulled from a basket delicacies she had made for him, hoping to bring them to him so that he could share them: "little cakes and crackers, wine jellies and blancmange, and other delicacies for the sick." Mryta's heart broke.[16]

Roll Call: Hannah Ropes and Louisa May Alcott

Hannah Chandler, born in New Gloucester, Maine, in 1809, married William Ropes, a teacher from Bangor, when she was twenty-five years old. After she gave birth to four children, William abandoned her. Hannah became interested in abolition through the work of her son, Edward, who homesteaded in Kansas in 1855. Hannah returned to Massachusetts, where she wrote politically motivated novels (*Cranston House, Six Months in Kansas*) and nursed sick friends. Two things then happened. Hannah received a copy of Florence Nightingale's *Notes on Nursing*, and her son enlisted in the Union army. Hannah volunteered her services and was assigned as head matron of the Union Hotel Hospital in Washington, D.C., where she worked with Louisa May Alcott. Both Hannah and Louisa described the appalling conditions, lack of proper sanitation, cruel treatment of the patients, and improper diets. Both wanted to make a difference and often butted heads with the military and the doctors, those institutions resentful of the intrusions of the women into their environment.

Hannah's diary recorded individual last moments of the soldiers: some miracles of survival in the most wretched of conditions, some a desperate clinging to life until the last moment. In the fall of 1862 Hannah wrote to her mother describing a young man who was shot through the lungs but lived several days in torturous pain. Hannah lay down near him so that she could be by his side if he needed her. In his last moments, he reached for, and called out repeatedly for, his mother, and he struggled "to get away from the enemy" just before he died: "I promised him that nobody should touch him, and that in a few moments he would be free from all pain. He believed me and, fixing his beautiful eyes upon my face, he never turned them away; resistance, the resistance of a strong natural will, yielded; his breathing grew more gentle, ending softly as an infant's. He was a brave soldier and a truthful boy."[17]

Louisa May Alcott's Transcendentalist parents moved the Alcott family from Concord, Massachusetts, to Fruitlands, in June 1843, where they remained in a fascinating Utopian experimental environment created at Harvard, fourteen miles from Concord. They moved back to Concord in January 1844 to a house called Hillside. Poverty followed the large family but they were blessed with interesting friends such as Nathanial Hawthorne, Ralph Waldo Emerson, and Henry David Thoreau. Also, Louisa's talents were allowed to bloom in this robust atmosphere. However, what she wanted most in these family moves was a place of her own where she could "dream her dreams and work out her fancies." "Girls," she wrote, "dream and feel before they know life at all."[18]

She charted and journaled her dreams with delight, including intriguing references to writing in her "Imagination Book," which seems not to have survived. With a history of dreaming just-so dreams, she journaled dreams of muffins, dip-toast, waking up "prancing" from an imaginative dream of being an opera dancer. She dreamed of waking up a millionaire, purchasing flannel petticoats for her mother, paper for her father, a new dress for her sister May and sleds for the boys; she dreamed of fine copies of books being presented to her father for his work on an annual school performance. She dreamed often and consistently small vignettes of family and the imaginative life of her penned characters who closely resembled her family; but actual recorded dreams were devoid of detail, she simply noting that she had a "good dream." She reserved detailed discussion for personal sharing or for rejuvenation in one of her novels and not for the journal.[19]

At least one of her novels, *Little Women*, transcended time and has remained a beloved book among succeeding generations of readers. Fiction followed fact in her life, just as suggested by her German tutor/love interest in *Little Women*—her life was her best work. On March 14, 1858, her dear sister, Beth, died after two years of pain and discomfort resulting from typhoid fever, just as "Beth" had in *Little Women*. Louisa wrote that at Beth's last breath, she and her mother saw "a light mist rise from the body, and float up and vanish in the air. Mother's eyes followed mine, and when I said, 'What did you see?' she described the same light mist. Dr. G. said it was the life departing visibly."[20]

Less expected for those close to the imaginative Louisa was her decision to volunteer to nurse, a determination that became six-weeks' work among the wounded and dying in Union Hospital between 1862 and 1863. Her experiences were recorded in letters home, revised and published, first for the *Commonwealth*, and then receiving critical recognition as *Hospital Days*. Louisa used *Hospital Days* as a voice on the mismanagement of hospitals and the callousness of some surgeons encountered in her brief experience, which began in December 1862 when she was invited to fill a place under the matron, Hannah Ropes. Upon her arrival she found herself surrounded by agony:

> I never began the year in a stranger place than this: five hundred miles from home, alone, among strangers, doing painful duties all day long, and leading a life of constant excitement in this great house, surrounded by three or four hundred men in all stages of suffering, disease, and death. Though often homesick, heartsick, and worn out, I like it, find real pleasure in comforting, tending, and cheering these poor souls who seem to love me, to feel my sympathy though unspoken, and acknowledge my hearty good-will, in spite of the ignorance, awkwardness, and bashfulness which I cannot help showing in so new and trying a situation. The men are docile, respectful, and affectionate, with but few exceptions; truly lovable and manly many of them.

Both Hannah Ropes and Louisa were taken with John Sulie, a Virginia blacksmith who was "all I could expect or ask from the first gentleman in the land. Under his plain speech and unpolished manner I seem to see a noble character, a heart as warm and tender as a woman's, a nature fresh and frank as any child's. He is ... mortally wounded, and dying royally without reproach, repining, or remorse." The two women were "indignant that such a man should be so early lost ... for real goodness is never wasted." She heard the men cry out for home and family in their night dreams or found them reliving the horror of the battlefield, charging up from their beds or shouting.[21]

Both Hannah and Louisa became ill in the disease-ridden environment that became their daily lives. They contracted typhoid pneumonia at the hospital. Louisa survived. Hannah died, at age 54. Just before her death, Hannah recorded the parting words of a soldier named Lewie, who was nursed by both Hannah and Louisa: "Thank you madam, I think I must be marching on." There were also words for their last patient with a few words for the inept physicians assigned to his care: "My boy has not closed his eyes, but tried all night to get away, to go to his camp, to answer the roll call, startled, frightened at the possible consequences of his non-appearance at his quarters. Too much brain too little physical power; his ward physician is in his cups all day! And no attention given to this case! The most important ward in the hospital and the guiding spirit walking about among the amputated limbs like a somnambulist!"[22]

Hannah's daughter Alice wrote to her brother Edward a month later, saying no one had realized how ill Hannah had been before she died. Edward learned of his mother's death in Washington, D.C. Arriving too late, his sadness was lightened by a dream, which he shared with Alice: "Mother was near me last night. It seemed as if I was a little boy, playing on the floor, and mother was sitting, as if knitting, and looking at me very thoughtfully. It seemed also as if she was needed somewhere else, for she did not stay long. It does seem as if mother was nearer to me now than ever before."[23]

At the same time, Louisa fell ill and was ordered to "keep my room, being threatened with pneumonia. Sharp pain in the side, cough, fever, and dizziness. A pleasant prospect for a lonely soul five hundred miles from home! Sit and sew on the boys' clothes, write letters, sleep, and read; try to talk and keep merry, but fail decidedly, as day after day goes, and I feel no better. Dream awfully, and wake unrefreshed, think of home, and wonder if I am to die here, as Mrs. R., the matron, is likely to do."[24]

On January 21, Louisa gave up her noble determination to remain at the hospital.

Hannah had died. Those she cared for came to see her off, but Louisa was drifting in and out of hypnogogic dreaming for a day and a half, half conscious, half wandering in sleep, visiting distant locales, marrying a "stout handsome Spaniard, dressed in black velvet, with very soft hands, and a voice that was continually saying, 'Lie still, my dear!'" She thought perhaps he was actually her mother, who was always nearby; but the presence of this Spanish spouse was fearful and energetic. He came after her, popped up out of closets, appeared at windows, or threatened her in other ways. She appealed to the Pope in this drifting vision, speaking in Latin and then she went to heaven "and found it a twilight place, with people darting through the air in a queer way,—all very busy, and dismal, and ordinary. Miss Dix, W.H. Channing, and other people were there; but I thought it dark and 'slow,' and wished I hadn't come. A mob at Baltimore breaking down the door to get me, being hung for a witch, burned, stoned, and otherwise maltreated, were some of my fancies. Also being tempted to join Dr. W. and two of the nurses in worshipping the Devil. Also tending millions of rich men who never died or got well."[25] From this expansive adventure in sleep and from the nightmarish experience at Union Hospital where many men died and few got well, Louisa never truly recovered. Her health was permanently damaged, but her writing exploded into years of creative energy and popularity.

Struggling harder with her health in the 1880s, she tried popular remedies, including "mind cures" in 1885 with Mrs. Newman, a ladies' club hit, who ultimately did not impress Louisa. Louisa experienced some agreeable sensations of "blue clouds & sunshine in my head," floated a bit, couldn't move and desperately wished for a miracle; but it did not come. She recorded lovely dreams of flowers and moved less and less often from her bed. Predicting on September 1, 1887, that the end was not far off, she lingered until February 18, 1888. Her father died less than a month later, on March 6, 1888.[26]

Pleasing the Spirits: "The song of a dead soldier"

Tasting an offering from the Spiritualists' movement, a young nurse, Annie Erving, wandered into a Spiritualists' gathering after the war in Hartford, Connecticut. At the invitation of the medium, who announced that flowers would fall at the feet of someone in the audience, Annie was *aflutter* because flowers dropped at her feet. The medium told her she must sing for the Spirits. She sang a hymn, but the spirits demanded something less "orthodox" because, the medium said, these Spirits were soldiers. She then sang "Marching Through Georgia." This pleased the spirits, and they sang it with her with gusto: "Then the spirit of a soldier sang the old song, 'My Old Cabin Home.' I recognized it at once as the song of a dead soldier I knew. I confess I was frightened and puzzled. I never was in such a place before and have never been in one since. I was a perfect stranger to all present at that meeting, and in fact in the city of Hartford, but I have often thought that when an opportunity afforded, I would go again." Annie had been a young girl when she volunteered to be a nurse, but she served faithfully and well as a field nurse and hospital nurse in Pennsylvania, her home state. She believed in God, omens, and the basic goodness of people. She recorded a terrifying moment just before the war broke out when the sky turned red during a religious camp meeting and she thought Judgment Day had come. Her minister told her it was a sign of war, "which indeed it proved to be."[27]

Florence Nightingale of the South: Mrs. Fannie Beers

An unlikely candidate for this title, Fannie Beers was born in the North and married A.P. Beers. Little is known about her childhood and youth; she wrote in her postwar memoirs that she met him while he was a student at Yale University when she was living with her mother in New Haven, Connecticut. They married and moved to New Orleans. The war began only a few years later and her husband enlisted in Fenner's Louisiana Light Artillery in April 1861. Fannie returned North to give birth to a child. According to her notes, her husband sent her a tiny Confederate flag, which she pasted on her "naked flesh" over her heart. With her young son, Fannie left for Virginia, was reunited with her husband and worked as a nurse in Virginia, Georgia, and Alabama in her adopted South.

Her work began in a private Richmond hospital where she said she was able to fulfill a dream that had haunted her always, one of tending to those in need:

> During every hour of the day, gentle women ministered untiringly to the sick. They woke from fevered dreams to behold kindly faces bending above them, to feel the touch of soft hands, to receive the cooling draught or welcome food. Every evening brought carriage-loads of matrons and young girls laden with flowers or fruit, bringing books, and, better than all, smiles and pleasant words. The sick soldiers were objects of interest to all. All hearts yearned over them, all hands were ready to serve them. As night came on, the ladies who had served during the day were replaced by others. No one ever failed to meet her self-imposed duties. No patient was for a moment neglected.

She wrote that in the monotony of camp, in between the horror of the battlefield, all men dreamed of home. In the hospital, where the men were ill and alone, their dreams became wild and fevered. Fannie tended to the sick without thought for herself until she caught a "nervous fever" and fainted. The ladies of the Richmond hospital watched over her, those women remembered by Fannie as angelic legions "whose sweet faces bent above me day after day, whose voices pervaded my feverish dreams."

Fannie mended in the care of her husband's relatives in Alabama and returned to nursing, becoming matron-in-charge of the Second Alabama Hospital. The sick and wounded poured in daily, and Fannie worked tirelessly on their behalf until a few weeks after the Battle of Shiloh. Her husband was sent to Tennessee in 1862. Fannie heard that a Confederate army surgeon, Dr. William McAllister, was opening a field hospital in Gainesville, Alabama, to treat those wounded at Shiloh. He placed a notice in the newspaper asking for nurses. Dr. McAllister wrote that what Fannie lacked in age was made up for in vigilance and tenderness. She moved from Gainesville to Ringgold, Newnan, and Port Valley, Georgia, over the next three years, often in charge of more than 1,000 beds, constant in her attention and devotion to the care of both Confederate and Federal patients. In the shelling of Atlanta she took supplies into the trenches and nursed Confederate prisoners during an Atlanta smallpox epidemic when everyone else fled.

William Mcallister praised Fannie's work in the hospital and in the field, quoting a soldier who recalled her care with affection: "She was the moving spirit of the hospital."[28]

A Sad State Over the Spirit of My Dreams: Kate Cumming

> O, thy soft-rolling flood, Chickahominy River.
> In thy flowing disturbeth my inmost soul;
> All unlike is thy gliding, so calm, to the horrors
> Of carnage and bloodshed that round thee did roll.

> If thy tale could be told, Chickahominy River;
>   Of the heart-rending pangs of the young and the brave;
>   Of the husband and father, whose soul, in departing,
>   Wrung with agony, prayed for a home in the grave.
>
> And yet this is not all, Chickahominy River;
>   The sad hearts that are breaking are far from thy shore;
>   But their slain they have left thee, in trust, to thy keeping—
>   Chickahominy River, take care of thy store.
>
> Let thy banks guard them well, Chickahominy River;
>   Let the dust of the hero lie calmly at rest,
>   Till the trump of the dead shall awake them to glory,
>   Immortal to live in the realms of the blest.[29]

Kate Cumming was a Confederate Civil War nurse and diarist born in Edinburgh, Scotland, between 1828 and 1835. Sometime in the 1840s her father, David Cumming, moved the family to Montreal, Canada, and then to Mobile, Alabama. The South spoke to Kate's Scots soul; her diary notes reflected a love of her home and her roots. In the spring of 1862, she rode in a carriage with the Reverend Mr. Clute, an Episcopal minister. They traveled to a home where a young woman played Scots songs for her and gave her an opportunity to describe her emotional ties to Scotland: "It is my native land; and although raised in this, and never personally having known any other, I will not forget the country of my forefathers—the land of Wallace and Walter Scott. I have always found that the southern people speak in praise of it, and the noble deeds for which it is famed, and more now than ever, as we are undergoing the same ordeal through which she so nobly passed in her great struggle for independence."

When the war broke out, Kate's mother left for England, but Kate, her brother, and her father remained in the South. Her brother enlisted in the Confederate army, and Kate participated in home front relief efforts, at first gathering supplies for hospitals and then volunteering as a nurse at the front. Ignoring her family's objections, she left for Corinth, Mississippi, after the slaughter at the Battle of Shiloh in the spring of 1862.[30]

Though Kate faced the hostility of civilians and some members of her family who considered hospital nursing inappropriate for women, the needs and gratitude of the soldiers convinced her to continue her service despite the poor conditions and constant death. When she began her career, the Confederate medical system was disorganized and ill supplied. Her first view of a hospital ward filled her with horror but also confirmed her belief that she had a role:

> Nothing that I had ever heard or read had given me the faintest idea of the horrors witnessed here. I do not think that words are in our vocabulary expressive enough to present to the mind the realities of that sad scene. Certainly, none of the glories of the war were presented here.... Gray-haired men—men in the pride of manhood—beardless boys—Federals and all, mutilated in every imaginable way, lying on the floor, just as they were taken from the battle-field; so close together that it was almost impossible to walk without stepping on them. I could not command my feelings enough to speak, but thoughts crowded upon me. O, if the authors of this cruel and unnatural war could but see what I saw there, they would try and put a stop to it! To think, that it is man who is working all this woe upon his fellow man."

Her first bed was a shelf and then stacks of boxes in a clerk's office, but the experience gave her insight into the life of a soldier who slept on the ground or any place or position he could find, accepting any sleep as a blessing as grand as a bed of down. Exhaustion quickly took a toll on Kate's dreams, and sound sleep erased the soothing effects of the dreams she sought.

After an 1862 hospital reorganization that included creating official "matron" positions for particularly efficient nurses such as Kate, the survival rates of the wounded and ill increased. The hospitals, and Kate, who worked with Dr. Samuel Stout, the medical director of the Army of Tennessee, moved with the battles through Tennessee, Alabama, and Georgia. She was remarkable—in charge of her own army of nurses, who cooked, foraged for supplies, cared for the soldiers' physical and emotional needs, sewed, wrote letters, and attended death beds, seeing the soldier home on both sides of reality. In her diary Kate wrote "the vivid recollections of what I have witnessed during years of horror have been so shocking, that I have almost doubted whether the past was not all a fevered dream." Then she referenced a popular poem, "The Lady's Dream":

> The wounds I might have healed—
> The human sorrow and smart;
> And yet it never was in my soul
> To play so ill a part:
> But evil is wrought by want of thought,
> As well as want of heart.[31]

Kate had mastered arrowroot remedies that did not look like arrowroot, doctored with eggs and preserves to make a palatable drink, and tended men with typhoid fever whose fevered indifference erased "home" from their minds, jawless men and men with severed limbs. She understood the importance of the dream of "home" to survival and astutely noticed that when men became so ill or near a fevered death from illnesses such as typhoid, they became indifferent "as to what becomes of them. In this state they seldom speak [or dream] of home." She wondered if this were a blessing or a curse. On one snowy Alabama night, after tending to a man shot through the jaw and another whose jawbone had been removed, she nostalgically conjured her Scots roots and penned words from a Robert Burns song:

> **Up in the Morning Early**
>
> Cauld blaws the wind frae east to west,
> The drift is driving sairly;
> Sae loud and shill's I hear the blast—
> I'm sure it's winter fairly.
>
> Chorus.—Up in the morning's no for me,
> Up in the morning early;
> When a' the hills are covered wi' snaw,
> I'm sure it's winter fairly. &c.[32]

Borrowing a phrase both from a Bible verse (the "long home") and a popular parlor and camp song ("Somebody's Darling"), Kate lamented that dying in field hospitals was not like dying among friends and family, that "somebody's darling" would leave for "his long home" often in terror and alone in a ward dimly lit, "as candles are scarce," in a dark corner, prepared for death, when it came, by a comrade, or someone who found the body the next morning and transported it to the dead-house. Kate saw an analogy in this often repeated scene to the "spirit of my dreams. What ... was a scene of order and comfort, has disappeared, and in [my comfort dream's] place vacancy."[33] Thinking of her lost dreams and lonely places in death, she accepted a relic offered her, a small red book taken from the body of a dead Federal soldier on the Chickamauga battlefield site. It held a popular Victorian religious allegory using a dream motif for a visit to the afterlife, written by Edward Monro, titled *The Journey Home*. *The Journey Home* took the dying traveler on a dream journey through dark places where the traveler had to find proper guidance to move forward. It included gates, angels, devils—the entire Heavenly staff. Kate speculated that some mother placed this volume in the young man's hands to prepare him for his departure from home and for the "journey he has now taken."[34]

Kate's diary often read like a personal allegory, alternating between light and healing, accompanied by a favorite quote, poem, or piece of music, then drifting into descriptions of bleak, stormy nights that sent her thoughts to men, at those moments, on sentinel duty or sleeping on the wet unforgiving ground, alone with their thoughts and dreams or dying on a campground. Elements warred in the same way as emotions and feelings, and Kate wondered if God had shut the door forever on mankind. She borrowed phrases from music such as "All Quiet on the Potomac" and longed for peace and the return of her "comfort" dreams. Nature refreshed her. Walks in the woods and wild flowers reminded her that strife would end, although when it did Kate Cumming found it difficult to forgive a war that destroyed the landscape of her South, which was in her vision intertwined nostalgically to her Scots roots and to woods, trees, balmy spirits and dreams filled with visions of home that were "safety valves to relieve the pressure of excitement, uncertainty, and dread."[35]

Occupy This Moment

Rhoda Amanda Shelton, a 17-year-old volunteer nurse in the Civil War's Union "diet kitchens," was born long before the modern-day Occupy Movement. However, she did understand social inequality and prejudice against working women. In her journal entry of September 11, 1866, she asked, "When God said 'occupy til I come' did he mean *men* to monopolize the intellectual part of the world?"[36]

Amanda, like other women, found a way to become the heart and soul of the most dreadful nursing experience of her world at that time—a sea of blood, severed limbs, and disease. She did this, also like many others, despite Dorothea Dix's mantra on prohibiting young women and attractive women from nursing. Amanda was both young and attractive but she barged right in, recording her experiences in the special diet kitchens developed by Mrs. Annie Wittenmyer and journaling her move to Mount Pleasant, Iowa, and then to Sickles Hospital in Alexandria, Virginia. Dix had not been able to stop these young women because the need was too great. Amanda was devoted and compassionate with the soldiers under her care. In the wards, under the leadership of Dr. Giel, the physician in charge, she treated every man as a hero. A spring visit through the wards brought her close to a young man whose features were so delicate she thought at first he was a woman. Thin, emaciated, and picking at his fingers and lips as she had noted those near death often did, he still smiled and told her he was "pretty near well." Then he drifted into a dream space where he was "in the midst of pleasant scenes. At last he seemed for the first to realize that there were ladies present and with a deathly grin—which I have not forgotten yet—he said pointing to 'Auntie' 'that's one of the gals come in.' The surgeon pointed to the tent where the dead are taken and as the wind blew aside the curtain we could see stiff forms rolled in the coarse blankets lying side by side. My heart said fervently 'God grant that me and mine may be spared from death in a hospital.'" Another young man, just a boy, who had been groaning, now gurgled and in a delirium dream returned home, where he was driving oxen, and muttered, "'Get up there—git up.' His eyes were somewhat glazed—and hour after hour—day and night with every breath came the command to the imaginary animals."[37]

Amanda continued as a nurse after the Civil War, her particular gift of empathy leading her to the hospitals for the "insane," where she recorded her experiences as bookkeeper at the Hospital for the Insane at Mount Pleasant, Iowa. She understood the healing nature of gentle touch, of music, even joining enthusiastically when her patient was pounding away on an imaginary piano, playing in the light of a window. Amanda humorously told her, near the end of their song, that her piano needed a little tuning! She understood the difficult and twisting path into the psyche of those who were living inside nightmares or those who were lost in a moment's story.[38]

In an early spring entry Amanda described the hill where the ruins of a Confederate mansion stood among the ravaged gardens and orchards, and she found delight in the beautiful spring day, the only thing preserved from war's destruction. Looking back over her experiences as a nurse in the last days of the war, she mused to her journal while riding on a train filled with wounded men being moved to a temporary hospital at the south of the Cape Fear River:

> [W]e watched the twilight coming on as we wound in and out among the sunken vessels which the Confederates had placed in the river to prevent Federal soldiers from navigating it. In the darkening woods on each side the fires of the tar-makers were visible. Suddenly, from the deck below us arose the voice of men singing, "Tramp, tramp, tramp, the boys are marching!" We heard it for the first time. The voices were excellent and the words rang out over the water with a meaning they could not have to those who had never heard the tramp, tramp, of soldiers going to battle.
>
> Through all the years that have elapsed since then when I hear this song I see again the darkening river, the smoke stacks and upper parts of the submerged boats, the fires of the tar-makers, and hear again the voices of the soldiers who had helped to conquer this southland, singing of their bright and happy homes so far away.[39]

Amanda deeply understood how to "occupy" her space and how to claim her moment: "The adamantine rock of prejudice is wearing away by the continual dropping of words & deeds &.... Occasionally a woman has come forward & with hammer-shakes marked reverberation throughout the world—the stroke rebounded & may yet crush her—but an unseen crevice was started which was widened by the sledge hammer strokes of such men as [illegible] while all the time the mass of thinkers were keeping up the continued dropping until through the centre of this rock will soon be a ... highway for the women of the world. The way grows easier year by year."[40]

Taking Morphine to Escape Dreams' Reality

Frank Vandiver edited the letters of an army doctor, Edward Pye, who was so distressed over the tenor of his dreams, which took morbid nourishment from the surrounding horror of the battlefield and were filled with such intense longing for home and family that he took morphine in order to find rest from their vivid reality. The pain of dreaming so intensely about home, of an embrace, a kiss, and even hearing the voices of those he loved, almost destroyed him: "I can hardly sleep the half of these long lonesome nights for thinking of *you all*.... I [experience] dreams ... so life-like & natural that I could hardly realize that I was not *at home* when I awoke in the morning. I seemed not only to see *your faces*—loving faces—but I heard & distinguished the *voices*.... I saw & heard you all *so plainly!*"⁴¹

"I think of you and speak of you. Yes and dream of you"
—Dr. Thomas Hawley

Dr. Thomas Hawley, a Union surgeon with the 11th Regiment, Missouri Volunteers, wrote that three hundred sick men "laying around camp," although bad, was still preferable to the hospital in St. Louis, an old brick and stone building north of town and a mile from camp. The hospital was two stories high, "one story under ground, no floor to this. Two rooms below used as kitchen, and officer's quarters. Two rooms above—no mattresses, no bedsteads, no straw—each man had his blanket ... and a fine carpet of dust and dirt, filth, tobacco juice & cuds. Thousands of flies and duch [Dutch] Surgeon and steward."⁴²

Thomas was devoted to his patients and to his service but loneliness and longing for home filled his letters to his parents and siblings. He missed everything—the gravitation of family, the old family clock, the rocking chair with memories of being rocked as a boy, the garden where he played as a child, and kisses from his mother and father: "I can only enjoy them in imagination and this is so strong sometimes it almost amounts to a reality. But such counterfeit reality, only one can enjoy unless both think at once."⁴³ Thomas spoke often of the power of the imagination that took him back home when the scenes of the hospital grew too strong, when images of severed limbs and dying men needed to be replaced by something pleasant that could draw him back to a safe place in his mind. He saw men go crazy with "*mania a potu*"⁴⁴ and looked inside himself for the attractions that "come before the soldier's mental vision, daily, hourly, even in the thickest of the strife or in the still and starry night."⁴⁵ Bidding his sister good night, he wrote that he made his bed on mother earth to "dream of you."⁴⁶

Late in the war Thomas married and his longing for home became even more intense. His imagination drew images from home both day and night in flowery language of journeys to the "land of dreams to dwell in amnesial bower....⁴⁷ [O]ur hearts leap with abounding joy at the idea of going home,"⁴⁸ he wrote on December 22, 1865. The scenes of destruction throughout the South coupled with the thousands of damaged men and scenes of dying he had witnessed through the long war wore on his heart and soul, but he never doubted the rightness of the fight for his flag. He was mustered out on January 16, 1866, after four and a half years of service.

Angel's Glow at the Hornet's Nest

On the morning of April 6, 1862, there were 40,000 Confederate soldiers under the command of General Albert Sidney Johnston, and they struck a line of Union soldiers occupying ground near Pittsburg Landing on the Tennessee River. The Confederate offensive drove the Federal forces from their camps and threatened to overwhelm Ulysses S. Grant's entire command. By afternoon they had established a battle line at the sunken road known as the "Hornet's Nest." During the first day's attacks, General Johnston was mortally wounded and was replaced by P.G.T. Beauregard. By the next morning, the reinforced Federal army numbered about 40,000, outnumbering Beauregard's army of less than 30,000. Grant's April 7 counteroffensive overpowered the Confederate forces and Beauregard's army retired from the field. The two-day battle at Shiloh produced more than 23,000 casualties and was the bloodiest battle in American history at its time.

An equally deadly post-battle killer was infections from wounds contaminated by shrapnel and dirt, which became refuge for bacteria. Soldiers' immune systems—already weakened by bad diet, spoiled food, contaminated water, fevers and disease, and sleeping, marching and eating in rain, snow, and mud—could not fight even the slightest infection. Bacteria and antibiotics were not yet part of disease knowledge, and the death toll rose both on and off the battlefield in staggering numbers.

At Shiloh soldiers sat in rain and mud for two days and two nights waiting for the field medics to reach them. By dusk a glow different from that seen on any battlefield startled those awaiting medical attention; their wounds glowed so brightly they actually cast a faint but visible light. Even stranger, when the troops were eventually moved to field hospitals, those whose wounds glowed had a better survival rate. Their wounds healed quicker and cleaner than those who had not experienced this strange luminescence. The seemingly protective effect of the mysterious light earned it the nickname "Angel's Glow."

In 2001, almost one hundred and forty years after the battle, a seventeen-year-old boy named Bill Martin asked his microbiologist mom about research she was doing with glowing bacteria. The teen and a friend, Jon Curtis, were challenged to help with the research on bacteria that live in parasitic worms called nematodes.

The strange life-cycle of nematodes—soil, plant surfaces, and odd residence cycles—produce the *Photorhabdus luminescens* that glow a soft blue and produce chemicals that kill the host and either kill or suppress the other microorganisms inside it. Then the *P. luminescens* feed, grow, and multiply without interruption. Eventually the nematodes eat the bacteria. The weather and soil conditions at Shiloh were perfect for this phenomenon. However, *P. luminescens* usually cannot live at human temperature, which would have made a wound an inhospitable environment. But there was one more piece to this puzzle: The wounded men sat for two days and two nights, unable to move, in the raw April cold of Tennessee. This situation would have lowered the body temperature of the soldiers, causing conditions of hypothermia, and would have given *P. luminescens* the perfect home environment. Since these nematodes are not infectious to humans, even the soldiers' suppressed immune systems would have easily eliminated them, like a modern bacteria-based medication—after the nematodes worked their magic. Although the soft angel glow might not have been a heavenly miracle, the peculiar life cycle of these strange residents of damp cold soil saved the lives of the wounded on the Tennessee battlefield.[49]

Phantom-Limb Syndrome: A Dream and Dr. S. Weir Mitchell

The Mütter Museum of the College of Physicians of Philadelphia's exhibit, "Broken Bodies, Suffering Spirits," featured Civil War medical tools and documents. The exhibit included a letter written by Henry S. Huidekoper, a lieutenant colonel in the Union army who found himself reaching for things or trying to write with his missing hand long after his right arm was lost in battle. In the letter, dated 1906, Henry wrote, "In my dreams, I always have the use of both my hands ... [and] last night ... I was holding a paper up with my two hands." In his dreams he had two arms—a "perfect frame"—but pain from the phantom limb often woke him in the middle of the night. Even more interesting, the phantom pain was caused by Henry's continuing to write in his dreams with his missing hand. He had developed a particular fondness for writing with a pen and enjoyed the mechanical skill required, even though he now wrote with his left hand. This skill transferred to his dreams as well but there he wrote with the missing right hand, using phantom tendons to guide and control the pen. The resulting tightening causing terrible pain in the missing finger tendons and would wake Henry from the most "profound sleep."[50]

Henry wrote his letter to Dr. S. Weir Mitchell, a Philadelphia surgeon who was interested in, and followed, the cases of amputee patients long after the war. Dr. Mitchell was among the first to recognize "phantom-limb" syndrome and to coin the term. He wrote that "thousands of spirit limbs were haunting as many good soldiers, every now and then tormenting them."[51] Dr. Mitchell made the important connection between the missing limb and injured nerves. His work in epidemiology established his career in nerve injury.

Chapter 13

Caring for Souls on the Battlefield

Closely related to ministering to the physical body was the ministry to the soul. Chaplains listened to the soldiers' stories, spoke to the soldiers about immortal life and helped the nurses and physicians, who dreamed their own dreams of life, death, and survival and even found themselves in harm's way on the battlefield.

Faith, Valor, Devotion—and the Imagination

William DuBose was described as brilliant and devout, an intellectual man capable of action. He served as a Confederate officer in South Carolina's Holcombe Legion and then as a chaplain in Kershaw's Brigade. He was studying for the Episcopal priesthood when the war broke out and he struggled with questions of spiritual obligation versus going to war; but he eventually became convinced that he needed to fight for his homeland. He was wounded twice in Virginia and was taken prisoner, exchanged and returned to duty. After being wounded a second time, friends arranged his appointment as a chaplain.

All of his letters were written to his fiancée, Anne Barnwell Peronneau, or "Nannie," who became his wife. His French Huguenot descent established his religious conviction; his dreams were consistently and determinedly direct about his love for Nannie, often seeing into his future with her. Seeing physical death and horror inured him to strange scenes, such as one in which he saw a soldier in camp grinding his coffee in a skull picked up from a nearby battlefield. Sentiment for suffering wore thin; but his devotion to Nannie did not. His dreaming record began in 1862 when he wrote that Nannie's birthday had slipped his mind but in compensation he had spent that Sunday night all night "dreaming about you, & very sweet dreams too." He sent Nannie the best wishes of a mutual friend in camp, Dick, who sent his love to his own sweetheart, Miss Annie. Dick wished Annie to know that he thought of her and his family by day and had "dreams of them by night."[1]

On May 25, William wrote a longing letter home, the gloom of the day increasing his particular desire to spend that day with her. He wished for a comfortable room and her company: "Cheerlessness without, like a dark background, brings out in strong relief the peace and comfort within." William's strong imagination pulled her into his imaginable room, which was cozy, with a "fire in the picture … with you, the fire, and a vacant easy chair for me." With the restoration of peace someday soon, he hoped, would come free scope "for the realization of all such happy dreams.... By the by, I had a sweet dream about you last night."[2] Just three months later, William "had the sweetest dream ... about being married," a subject he attempted to put aside in the uncertainty of war; but it came in the night when his guard was down. This dream impressed him in its realness. It was, he said, not "marred by some ridiculous inconsistency; but this was a complete & charming little tableau of a scene after the wedding, the next day probably, the impression of which has clung to me through all the heat and distractions of the past two days...."[3]

William continued his religious and intellectual studies in camp as best he could, reading voraciously and at the same time commenting on the strange calm that accompanied men on the battlefield when they could be so agitated in camp. He wrote commentary to Nannie discussing spiritual perceptions of lectures, such as one by "Robertson" on Wordsworth, Shakespeare's plays and poetry, and novels. Such letters gave him freedom to compare writers' views on spiritual matters and to use Nannie as a sounding board on his own views on the close alliance of poetic and religious faculties. "I do not think the religion of Christ is meant to exclude the religion of Nature," he wrote. "On the contrary it should interpret & elevate it." He found, in his own philosophy, that all faculties deserved cultivation, particularly that of the imagination, which was equal in his mind to "reason & faith."[4]

Nannie's birthday one year later, this one not forgotten, found William exercising the power of his imagination in what he called a test of salvation in the midst of the circumstance of war. His self-assignment was to embrace Nannie's birthday in his imagination. The day was beautiful. He took Nannie on a mental walk beside him. He settled a bit by reading a Shakespeare favorite, *The Tempest*, and found he enjoyed it even more because it was a birthday pleasure: "It is a wonderful creation of imagination, an exquisite blending of the natural & supernatural." He decided to read *Midsummer Night's Dream* next but in a different way, one that would suit his new excursions into the pleasures of the imagination.[5]

After that indulgent excursion, William wrote about music, his favorite pastime. Nannie wrote that she did not have the capacity for music that he had and she felt sad when she read books by musicians or notes on their lives and realized the passion and depth of feeling that came through music. William replied that he did not love her any less, in fact more, because he could share his gift with her, rather than chastise her for the lack of it in herself.

In the summer of 1863 William described an excellent band from a neighboring brigade. Their playing touched William's heart and brought him close to Nannie:

> At this moment they are playing 'Sleeping I dream Love, dream Love of thee' & under its transforming power the realities around me do seem to fade away, & leave in their stead a bright & soothing dream of which you are the *centre* & the charm. Now they have suddenly changed to the Fishers Hornpipe, & my mind runs off to Willie, for whom I used to whistle it, & who had a variety of names for it, such as the "Fish Horn," "Horn Fish," "Fish Pipe." &c &c. And now they have stopped, & my dreams are dispelled & the grave reality resumes its place & its sway. But you need not complain, my Love [for] I think of you, waking.... I dream of you, sleeping. Day dreams are very sweet ... amid these remorseless realities, & the imagination, when it does escape its fetters, bring home sweet joys.[6]

William's dreams comforted him throughout the war. Lying in camp on his bunk, he would do "power of thinking ... like the Hindoos who lie on their back & 'contemplate,'" but he assured Nannie that his reflections, or dreams, turned solely to her.[7] William survived and discovered, gratefully, on March 25, 1865, that his home had survived as well.

He returned home to Nannie and fulfilled the dream of so many journaled years before. He and Nannie were married.[8]

Chaplain Joseph Hopkins Twichell: Which Is the Dream?

Just two years out of Yale University where he was studying for the clergy, Connecticut-born Joseph Hopkins Twichell enlisted in 1861 as chaplain in the Jackson Regiment of Daniel Sickles's Excelsior Brigade in Lower Manhattan. Anticipating a reaction to choosing to serve an Irish Catholic regiment that was made up of men from the brickyards and tanneries of New York City, Joseph quickly wrote his father: "If you ask why I fixed upon this particular regiment, composed as it is of rough, wicked men, I answer, that was the very reason. I saw that the companies of the better class of citizens were all attended by Chaplains, but nothing was said about these. *There*, I thought, is a place for me.... I should not expect a revival, but I should expect to make some good impressions, by treating with kindness a class of men who are little used to it." He served for his contracted three years, often in harm's way himself, and witnessed through the eyes of his regiment bloodshed and horrendous battles: the Peninsula Campaign, Second Bull Run, Fredericksburg, Chancellorsville, Gettysburg, Spotsylvania, and the Wilderness.[9]

Joseph's personality, devotion to his service, and proclivity to self-reflection combined to produce a uniquely sympathetic and empathetic chaplain in tune with the physical as well as the spiritual needs of his regiment. Joseph's mother had died early in his life, and he was devoted to his father. Most of his letters were addressed to his father. One of the early ones set the tone for the kind of interaction he practiced daily. He wrote to his father about a march in which he had taken the rear, where he could carry the knapsacks and muskets of the men who grew faint and fell out of the ranks. Joseph explained that these were men who had become weak from diarrhea, chills and fever, which were so prevalent in the camps. He bragged about his own strength, which enabled him to carry "two or three men's burdens and march without much discomfort." He acknowledged this placed him at a spiritual advantage in camp and reported that he had even heard men say he was the "sort of a Chaplain to have." He encouraged singing, jokes, and stories along the way, understanding that "something outside the present, will slip a quarter mile from under the feet wonderfully."[10]

The following year, Joseph wrote to his father from the hospital near Richmond, where he tried to reconcile a quiet scene inside the hospital while outside there were green fields under a fair sky and just a short distance away the field was "sown thick with slaughtered corpses" and the sound of artillery that "revealed the neighborhood of the hostile lines." He liked to be at the hospital, he wrote, explaining that it was his "place." In the field, in the front lines, with the enemy within sight, with the aspect of an attack or skirmish always imminent, "men are excited—their blood is continually hot, and the gospel of love and peace and charity finds little soil to take root and grow in. Religion there seems to go back to the spirit and expression of the old Dispensation."

The next day Joseph went deep into a reverie that would repeat itself again during his service. The 16th Massachusetts had arrived from Fort Monroe and attached itself to his division. The men were sent to help drive back pickets. As Joseph rode into camp he met up with "Dale Hannahs with his fine squadron pushing back in search of guerillas." Hannahs had been a classmate of his at Yale. Joseph rode about a mile with him and drifted into a waking dream state in which his mind wandered to the "peace and happiness of our golden life at Yale." The present war seemed like a dream and he questioned its reality: "Can it be," I mentally exclaimed, "that these things are real? Here I am going to my tent pitched among the bloody graves of countrymen slain in civil war, and here is my old comrade, with whom when we were boys I lay warm summer afternoons like this stretched out under the cool elms, talking of life ahead and reading the book—a career just opening for each of which we could not imagine a page like this, now galloping with his hundred sabres to the rear on a perilous business? ... Which is the dream, this or that?"[11]

A few days later, Joseph stood near soldiers from the 2nd New Hampshire who were burying their fallen comrades. Nearby, one of the men from Company D in his own regiment, a man named Rednor, lay in his tent "with a shot through the leg—a severe wound." Joseph was bringing him water and "tucking him up." The two scenes, the bloody corpses on the field and his wounded comrade, left Joseph heavy-hearted and he began to think about death and mutilation: "While I mused, I was startled by the sound of a fiddle discoursing a lively air in my immediate neighborhood. It struck me harshly. 'A funeral, a fiddle and a wounded man,' thought I, 'do not fit each other. I will stop the fiddle.' I stepped to the tent door and looked around. One look sufficed to soften my indignation. It was Rednor himself, where he sat propped up, his bandaged leg on a blanket, drawing the bow as cheerily as if at a ball. The contrasts of war are one of its most notable features and often irresistibly funny." He continued, in this letter, describing how he was becoming "not hardened, but accustomed" to amputation—and how that disturbed him. He outlined his progression from being a youth horrified of blood to his joining the regiment and still shrinking from watching operations to finally obtaining enough skill to assist in amputations. On one hand, he felt being able to amputate limbs and not shrink away gave him personal access to the souls of men. If he could remove a soldier from the ambulance, take the trousers off a shattered limb, take a firm hold of the soldier's hand and cheer the man, helping "him grin and bear it, then administer the Chloroform ... and keep my finger on his pulse while his leg is being cut off, and be the first to speak to him when he wakes, and assure him that it is all over, I have the way prepared to say a word *for God* in behalf of his soul. He will at least give me his attention." Joseph retreated into his self-query on which was the dream-state, as he often did when questioning the rationality between what he saw and what he felt: "I cannot feel what is going on—what a page of history is here filling. I cannot realize that I am before Richmond, unless I argue the case with myself. Do you wonder at it? If I can only hold on to God and feel that He and his mercy are real and that my eternal soul is real, and the souls about me, I can let the rest go shadowy."[12]

Yet, he questioned whether or not any of this war would ever go shadowy. "Time would fail me," he wrote to tell all he had seen, but he was sure it would never leave and his "dreams" would "bring it back," "it" being what he believed would be the most memorable time of suffering in his life. Misery experienced earlier in his life would be viewed in the future as comfort: "All [that] weak, deserted, helpless, pain-pierced, despairing men can endure, I have seen borne and patiently confronted.... I have seen a man reeling mile after mile in half-delirium through weakness, and could do nothing for him. I have heard men call on God for mercy, when their comrades had no help for them. I have seen a man walk twenty miles, with a shot through both thighs. I have seen a man walking erect ... while a shattered arm swung on its fractures by his side, yet buoyed up by a will of iron." All this he said would return to him in dreams.[13]

A snowy winter and frozen water pails in camp near Falmouth, Virginia, set Joseph to dreaming at night of home and daydreaming of his childhood. The pine-covered Virginia hills loaded down with snow looked not so different from his Northern home. He joked about the "suffering patriots," comparing his ill-prepared camp with Valley Forge. The men had bad shoes—or no shoes, tents that were ill equipped for snow and cold, and no stoves. On the agenda was building a log house, which consigned to memory any recollections of sleigh bells and shouting, happy boys romping in the snow.[14] The snow continued into "elemental wrath ... [and] the sky put on sackcloth." It piled to a foot deep and the storm continued, "a real northern affair" that sent Joseph again into his boyhood. The image was vivid and intense and arose when he waded into a drift, "leaning against the blast":

> I fancied that I was again struggling my way over the hill toward Lewis Academy.... The old-time exhilaration revived and, forgetting that I was a man and minister, I was invaded by the juvenile instinct of snow bathing. The dive, the somersault, the labors of mine-digging, were only prevented by my awaking to present realities—to the fact that my free mittened and tippered period is left behind and that my way now and henceforth lies through a sober land. My early life was so exceeding happy that my visions of memory are always sweet, and I sigh when they vanish. Occasionally I get back so far that I happen upon Innocence, and then a pang of regret closes the retrospect.[15]

Joseph received an unexpected camp visit from his beloved father in March 1863. Less than a month later his father was dead and Joseph intensely felt the loss. Writing to his stepmother on April 26, he "shouted" in the letter, "Oh, my Father! My Father, where art thou? Is it I, or is it he that is lost? I'm very lonesome here to-night.... Now with unutterable yearning I grope round the shadowed world after him, and find nothing but the fresh grave. I shall never write 'Dear Father' again—never."

A few months later Joseph left the quarters where his father visited. He reminisced about the tent, with curtains that had been created so they hooked up on the sides, cedar boughs and an arbor over the door, "so that I lived in a cool, green bower. My bed was delightful and my chair a luxury. I am enjoying the table for the last time. The place is precious for the reason, above all, that Father has been here. I found an old letter of his today in my valise.... I laid it aside with a moist eye."[16]

That letter was addressed to his stepmother. A more gloomy letter, written in November, near the close of the year, painted a domestic scene of his major reading the paper, potatoes boiling near his toes and nothing, seemingly, to keep him from being happy. But his spirit was oppressed because a march to battle was anticipated and with that anticipation the accompanying scenes of death and mutilation, burials and graves: "I cannot look at my beloved parish—without gloomy forebodings ... [and] a dread comes over me more profound and disturbing than any personal apprehensions could possibly inspire. The great Reaper seems to lead us on with exultation at the food soon to be furnished for his ready scythe. Once it was hard for me to realize, as we gaily advanced, that it was to such fearful places, but now I seem to see them all portrayed before they are reached."[17]

A New Year's Eve letter to his sister was even more gloomy and sinister. Joseph pondered that the night was as dreary "a night for dying as ever brooded over the earth.... Poor old 1863 is going out in a tempest fitful as his own expiring pulse.... I pity thee, Old Year! Hard as thy yoke has been and heavy thy burdens laid on me and mine, I wish thee no ill, and had rather peaceful starlight and the gentle moon should cheer thy exit this rude storm add to its bitterness." Continuing this frightful reverie, Joseph wrote that a "weird, unearthly feeling" begin to creep over him, "as if there was a corpse in the tent, and I craved company—yours, Sis.... Not so much the happiness that finds utterance in merry words and songs and laughter ... but chiefly that blessed inner calm—that peace of God which is our divinest earthly joy."[18]

The deadly marches continued. Joseph witnessed the Wilderness fighting in May when General Grant took 120,000 men over the Rapidan River in an attempt to get through the swampy forest area before Lee could retaliate. The fighting was intense and confused and became hand-to-hand amidst thick smoke from forest fires that consumed acres of woods and acres of stranded soldiers. The Union lost 18,000 out of 100,000 men, killed, wounded and missing; the Confederates lost 7,500 of 60,000 men. Joseph wrote home to the mother of one young man, Vermont private Joseph H. Eaton, killed in battle: "I think, Mrs. Eaton, that he received mercy, for I believe he sought rightly. I prayed with him and repeated to him the invitation and promises of our Lord ... [and] even while I kissed him, he went off into dreams and raved about his comrades and the battle."[19]

Joseph mustered out on July 30, 1864, his three-year contract at an end, and enrolled at Andover Theological Seminary. In 1865 he graduated from Andover, married in November, and in December began his lifelong pastorate at Asylum Hill Congregational Church in Hartford, Connecticut. It was here, in October 1868, he met Samuel Clemens (Mark Twain), while Clemens was visiting his publisher in Hartford. They struck up a friendship that lasted the rest of their lives. Joseph provided Mark Twain with spiritual guidance in a nonjudgmental environment. The two travelled together, and Joseph's stories were reshaped as the character "Harris" in *A Tramp Abroad*, as well as a character in several short stories.[20]

More striking was Joseph's reveries on "Which is the dream?," a question not foreign to Mark Twain and one he explored in his letters and fiction, inspired by events in his own life and in his personal exploration into one's existence in the "multi-verse," the thin boundary between reality and dream, a wavering line. In the war Joseph clawed at that shadowy world between layers of waking reality, and his expression of this experience possibly inspired Twain. Where are we? What is left of us and on which side of the borderless line? Which reality is one living and how does one respond to those realities—both grim and innocent—lying in wait in the shadowy realms? Gettysburg, Fredericksburg, Chancellorsville, the Wilderness. "Half the time," Joseph wrote, "I move through the fields of the wounded 'like one in a dream.'" He found the two realities—the battlefield and his dream vision of another life—sandwiched together, blurring against one another as he moved from battlefield to battlefield. "Do you wonder at it?" he wrote. As a minister and a caregiver he tried to hold God's hand in the midst of such horror and felt that he must not let his soul go, must not let the souls of those around him slip away without some understanding of a page of history "here filling."

Chaplain Charles Hagar: "You will dream of your sweetheart tonight"

Charles Hagar also tested the boundaries of the imagination in the moments he had to himself in the day and in the exquisite opportunities offered to him in night dreams. Charles was a chaplain with the 118th New York Infantry, known as the "Adirondack" Regiment. He was born June 29, 1819, in Vermont and eventually lived in Plattsburgh, New York, with his wife Elizabeth (1820–1888), whom he married November 20, 1839, in Saratoga. He enlisted as a chaplain on August 21, 1862, in New York City, commissioned as an officer on September 2, 1862, and mustered out on June 13, 1865, in Richmond, Virginia. He died on August 28, 1890, in Essex County at the age of 71.

Charles possibly had a better chance at surviving the war than those who were in the thick of the battles, but he witnessed the horror of severed limbs, crushed spirits and demoralized souls. His spiritual counseling placed him in a position of empathy but also burdened him with the sadness, anxiety and depression of his own place in the war—and his need to understand it—as well as experiencing the burden of the spiritual and physical wounds of those entrusted to his care.

His letters bloomed with love for his children, wife, and home. Dreams, music, and poetic sentiments punctuated the harsh environment of his ministry to the sick and wounded. Through all of it, he wrote, "the home voices speak louder than the drums." Charles's dreams of home were the most common communication thread between his family and the battlefield camp. Dreams of home offered him solace and presented a possible future return to a place of comfort and safety, but these dreams were also troubling in the reality of their presence in a place so far from home.

Charles's first recorded dream was penned in 1862 when he was six miles from Petersburg and fifteen miles from Richmond in the area of Suffolk. His regiment was awaiting action from General Meade's army when, anxious and concerned for the well-being of those in his regiment, he dreamed of home. The dream, he said, was "simple" but so vivid he found it "difficult to throw off the impression all day." He was still troubled by its nearness four days after its event. Several weeks later, after writing to his family about the death of a soldier, Charles dreamed of his young son, James, and nostalgically reported his campfire as burning brightly on the hearth. He longed for home.[21]

Early in 1863 Charles awoke from a vivid dream of seeing himself and his wife seated at the breakfast table in an "old-fashioned double chair." The dream cheered him and placed him in a "very pleasant frame of mind." He humorously wrote that he wanted all of it be "so—except the old double-chair." The tone changed a few short letters later.[22]

On February 21, 1863, Charles dreamed that his wife was sitting alone in the "siting room," appearing lonely and lonesome: "I thought I never saw Ma look so lonesome—she looked as she did over twenty years ago. I had a razzy time until I awoke and then—a snowstorm." There were mixed emotions in this dream. He had a "razzy" self-censored time with his wife, who appeared much younger (and probably at her sexiest)! He dreamed of a snowstorm and awoke to the actual event; but, most important, Charles awoke agitated over Elizabeth's missing him so badly. Not questioning the reality of his dream he took action to change it. Determined to create a happy scene of home from this decidedly sad one, he wrote to her that she must have her "image" taken, thinking of how close it would bring them and the smile it would put on her countenance. She must, he wrote, send the image to him and he would do the same, mentioning that he hoped this would cheer her up in future dreams.[23] He followed through. In his next location—Suffolk, Virginia—he passed by a shop that charged $1.50 for a "picture taken." He was appalled at the extravagance but marched in and had his photograph taken and sent to his wife. He reminded her to send one of herself, and he wrote that the blame for the extravagant purchase rested on her sad countenance so vividly brought to life in his dream: "But Ma is accountable for that. I send it to you this day by mail—now Ma send your photograph to me."[24] Charles was then pleased that a dream between the first one and his purchase of the image painted a more pleasing portrait of Elizabeth: "I dreamed of you last night—thought you were well and happy—hope it is so. I can imagine how the old home with its surroundings looks."[25]

Letters over the next few years alternated between descriptions of the wounded, the battles, the dying, the stench of the wounded and dead, the odor permeating the landscape as they marched or camped, to aching expressions of longing for home and family, short descriptions of "dreaming of home" lifting Charles's spirits night after night.

Henry Graves had written from his Georgia regiment that the gift of the imagination was equal to the gift of the night dream. Writing from his work at a Virginia hospital at Point of Rocks, Bermuda Hundred, in 1865, Charles Hagar would undoubtedly have agreed with him: "You are aware that my imagination is very vivid, so I imagine a Kiss to you every night—before I go to sleep."[26] A few days later, March 25, 1865, following a short dream of home, he wrote about a charming moment, designed to please Elizabeth: "Coming up the stairs from the river this afternoon I stumbled and fell up stairs. Some of the surgeon's wives laughing said, chaplain that is a sign that you will dream of your sweetheart tonight—I put my hand on my heart—saying O Ladies, I have dreamed of her every night for a week past."[27]

Charles Hagar dreamed a possibly small precognitive dream of a horse named Tim "running away and smashing up wagons" but he did not follow up with an additional account.[28] What did follow was a poem comparing the anguish of dreaming of home and waking—"Ah, but I am dreaming"—to the reality of the battlefield. He apologized for his poem's rhyme and humorously noted that "one" of his children wrote poetry like his:

> In my tent alone
> Sad the winds are sighing
> Far away at home
> Swift my thoughts are flying
>
> When the war is over
> Gentle peace returning
> Then for home once more
> Then my march ending.
>
> Loved ones gather round
> Happy faces gleaming
> Sweet the voices sound
> Ah, but I am dreaming
>
> Months must pass away
> Frought with many dangers
> Many a weary day
> Dwelling among strangers
>
> Een these visions bright
> Pleasing to my fancy
> Scenes of wounds and slaughter
> Rather than the sight of my
> Wife and daughter
>
> I shall think of wife
> Maria and of Emma
> Charlie dear—of life
> And of faithful Jenni
>
> Thoughts of them will cheer me
> In the hour of battle
> When the foe is near me
> And the ugly rattle.[29]

CHAPTER 14

Dying Tonight on the Old Campground

Recounting the Dead

So much has been written about the numbers of dead in the Civil War and the appalling toll of disease and loss of limbs in long-term survival that it was inevitable the numbers of the dead would be questioned. But it was not until later years that an attempt was made to set those records straight. Drawing from a variety of sources, David Hacker summarized the efforts. The old numbers had been an estimate of 618,222 men dead on both sides. Updated Census records indicated numbers between 750,000 and 850,000.

Old records relied on muster-out rolls and battle reports, updated when widows and orphans applied for survivors' benefits. Estimating the Confederate dead was even more problematic. The Confederate army had been destroyed, and records were incomplete. An early report, called the Fry Report, documented only 133,821 deaths. Confederate widows and orphans were ineligible for benefits, so that count remained incorrect for years. There were additional problems. The Union army count of 304,000 was based on men who died in service. It was estimated that an additional 285,000 men discharged with disabilities, disease and wounds died after their return home. Many of those died within months of their discharge and many more died within two years of their return. Francis Walker, in a late 19th century report, estimated that additional losses just among the Union armies could increase the war dead to 500,000.

Hacker maintained that these figures mattered because they change the way we look at this war. The new estimate "suggests that more men died as a result of the Civil War than from all other American wars combined. Approximately 1 in 10 white men of military age in 1860 died from the conflict, a substantial increase from the 1 in 13 implied by the traditional estimate. The death toll is also one of our most important measures of the war's social and economic costs. A higher death toll, for example, implies that more women were widowed and more children were orphaned as a result of the war than has long been suspected." The war touched more lives than ever thought possible and impacted every community in America.[1]

Carnage on a "once happy land"

The Civil War presented a new and personal relationship with death. Battlefield deaths devastated families; community losses represented numbers that would presage the "slaughter of World War I's Western Front and the global carnage of the twentieth century." In a study of death in the Civil War, Drew Gilpin Faust noted that "the number of soldiers who died between 1861 and 1865 is approximately equal to American fatalities in the American Revolution, the War of 1812, the Mexican War, the Spanish American War, World War I, World War II, and the Korean War combined. The Civil War's rate of death, its incidence in comparison with the size of the American population, was six times that of World War II; a similar rate of death, about 2 percent, in the United States today would mean almost five million fatalities. Although mortality rates differed North and South, with the percentage of Confederate men who died in the war three times greater than the proportion of Yankees," death was everywhere. Its stench filled the camps, fields, roadsides, journals, and letters, and persisted into the night dream. Faust, quoting on the omnipresence of death, noted an observation from the *Daily South Carolinian* in 1864: "Carnage floods our once happy land."[2]

On July 14, 1862, William Stilwell, writing from Richmond after a victory over McClellan, spoke of the "dark" of war and used an expression known in the camps: "You may talk about men seeing the monkey and the elephant but if they haven't seen both since we came here I don't know anything about them.... I can assure you that the battle field is not a delightful place to be at."[3] Seeing the monkey and the elephant were slang expressions meaning to experience combat for the first time.

James Branscomb, one of four brothers enlisted in the Third Alabama Infantry, was disgusted with war after his first battle, at Malvern Hill. Unmarried, his letters were to his sister, Lucinda. He asked her to imagine what she could not imagine and even then she would not be able to fancy the horrors of the battlefield: "Think of a battle field three miles long and a mile wide, literally strewn with dead and dieing. It hardens ones heart beyond conception. The day after the fight on 27 June I was not with the regt and had a good chance looking over the battlefield. I think no more of walking over a dead man now than you would a hog.... You know I have often wished a chance at the Yankees.... I don't care now if I never hear another boom or ball."[4]

Lewis, another Branscomb brother, wrote about the vacancy in their hearts that could not be filled until the war was closed and they were home. "Home," he said, was "the sweetest name on earth." They had friends in camp but none became endeared to them like those through the ties "of nature." Both James (Jimmie) and Lewis died on separate battlefields, James at the Battle of Harris Farm near Spotsylvania on May 19, 1864, and Lewis at Harpers Ferry on July 4, 1864. Communication was swift on Lewis's death but not so for the death of James. Lucinda Branscomb, their sister, repeated words from Lewis's last letter, written at Harpers Ferry just moments before he was killed, that he had "nearly lost his mind. Every one of his messmates were severely wounded and he is left alone." Lucinda wrote regarding Jimmie: "One day we would hear he was dead and perhaps the next that he was badly wounded and a prisoner and then he was in the hospital one place and sometimes another. Such suspense is enough to produce insanity." One of the four brothers, William, died early in the fighting, in 1862, in a hospital from a relapse of measles. The last of the four enlisted brothers, John, survived the war. His letters, written to his wife, were filled with angst over the deaths of his brothers and his longing for his children and wife. Still waiting to hear definitive news of James, John did not yet know of Lewis's death when he wrote his wife to kiss the little ones for him: "I dreamed of being with [you] last night and oh how I was disappointed when I awoke to find it all a dream."[5]

Being Invisible

Dreams of death and dying in Civil War letters "saw" conditions of survival and the death of friends or one's own death.

Young James Culbertson of the 14th Regiment, South Carolina Volunteer Infantry, was killed at the battle of Gettysburg, July 2, 1863. Two of his letters were to his parents, one was to his wife, and the last letter was to his wife from her brother, who was with Young James when he was killed: "Dear Sister, you must do the best you can for I know he has gone to a better world. He talked a right smart about dying.... I think he went happy." Sharing an eerily precognitive dream of being "invisible," James wrote to his mother two years before his brother-in-law shared with his wife that he had talked about dying: "Tell Eliza I want you to take good care of yourself and my little children. I will tell you and the rest about my dream the other night. I dreamed I was at home, I went in the house and Eliza and the children would not look at me hardly. I thought I got right mad, but if it had been so I don't think it would have been like my dream."[6]

Dreaming Peaches and a Grave

Lucy Breckinridge was a young Southern woman whose home and family history were tied to the earliest foundations of Virginia's landed heritage. Her family home, Grove Hill, just southwest of the major military operation through the Virginia Valley, survived the war. Lucy's dreams and observations during the war years were journaled in an old ledger. Her pen lingered over visions of her happy childhood and her mind was haunted by dreamy vistas of sad nostalgic ramblings. She had a gift for words and a penchant for melancholy. Her dreams were predictive of small and large events, an example being a dream in which a rat escorted her "about the yard discussing moonlight, music, love, and flowers."[7] That night a rat had run over her bed and had her in a "constant state of terror." The next day two young men arrived for a visit. They were charming but Lucy grew weary of suitors and perhaps felt a metaphor was at work in the guise of wit too devious in its intentions.

In a family of nine children, three brothers had gone to war. Lucy's favorite brother, Johnny, 17 years old, closest to her in age and her best playmate growing up, had died in the Battle of Seven Pines (1862). He was buried at Grove Hill, and Lucy "dreamed the other night of going up there [to the graveyard] and of seeing his grave with the white cross, and I saw him by it, and he put his arms around me and told me to lie down there by him."[8] Lucy walked to the graveyard and then to a peach tree, dwelling on her happy past with Johnny—and his invitation.

Fruit, and particularly peaches and apples, played an interesting and often dominant role in Lucy's journal entries and in at least one dream. Lucy wrote that she refused to give one of her brothers, Cary, an apple, until his captain, "Houston[,] intervened." Afterward, when the captain's name was mentioned, "a vision of peaches and apples float before Cary's mind."[9] Lucy strolled the gardens with various captivated young men, usually ending their strolls near a tree full of ripe peaches. She dreamed of peaches and then lay in bed thinking "of Dolly's [a servant] mournful interpretation: 'to dream of fruit out of season is trouble without reason.'"[10] Lucy tried to shake the trouble from the dream but was uncomfortable. "[If I] can't people the room with sweet fancies and imaginations

"... I ... have recourse to sleeping dreams," she said.[11] But happy sleep dreams were fleeting. Sad nostalgic visions took their place, Lucy wrote, and then she lamented she would be an old maid because she could not escape gloomy wanderings in her mind. The gloomy wanderings and the troubled dream of an unaccountably delicious offering, peaches, came to bear an unwelcome fruit.

Lucy fell in love with a soldier, Thomas Jefferson Bassett. They married in June 1865. Six months later, and just three weeks after the last Confederate troops surrendered, Lucy died of typhoid fever. She was buried beside her brother John, who had beckoned her to lie down beside him near the peach tree.

Death Is a Journey Home: Rufus Robbins

Rufus Robbins joined the Seventh Massachusetts Volunteer Infantry on June 15, 1861, at Camp Old Colony in Taunton, Massachusetts. Most of the men lived in Bristol County, recruited by the regiment's first colonel, Darius Couch, a West Point graduate who became major general of the Second Corps of the Army of the Potomac. Rufus arrived in Washington, D.C., and was quartered the first night in the unfinished Capitol. They marched from there to Kalorama Heights, near Georgetown, called then "Camp Old Colony." Rufus's first letters home referred to the camp's location high above an open plain, its convenient stream for bathing, and its location in a "beautiful place."[12]

Camp life began well. Rufus wrote home to his mother that his health was good, that he was in a "happy frame of mind" and that he appreciated her "hope" there was a God watching over him and taking care of him. However, Rufus had received an odd dream report in his mother's letter. In response, he assured her that it was possible she would see the two of them together again, as in the dream, but that he hoped "you would not find my trousers so ragged as you dreamed." Humorously, he told her that his trousers were in pretty decent condition (after all, he had been gone from home hardly more than two months) with just a little hole no bigger than a pencil below the right knee and just a little rip "at the pocket on the right side": "They are not so clean as I wish but I have no trouble in keeping my drawers and shirt clean. I have been expecting a new suit so long, I think it must come soon. There is but little of the time when I am off duty that I am not washing or reading or writing. Two pairs of my stockings (my best ones) are nearly as good as when I left home."[13] By August, Rufus was already homesick, giving thanks for cheerful letters from home and wishing he could "take a seat at the old table with you." He noted spells of thinking of home and some suffering, with his imagination taking a "turn homeward and [taking] a view of you as you are seated at the breakfast, dinner, or supper table."[14]

The ragged trousers dream seemed ordinary on first reading, but the theme of Rufus wearing ragged clothing was a rehearsal for his appearance as time passed. This, too, was expected, except Rufus's dreams became more troubled and his mother's dream reports to Rufus more revealing of his falling ill, growing thin and more disheveled, representative of his deteriorating appearance. Rufus bragged that going to sleep was not a problem for him as it was for others. He could place himself in a sleeping position and drift to sleep within five minutes; but his dreams were not comforting even when they seemed ordinary.[15]

Rufus reported feeling unwell in letters beginning in February of the following year.

Diarrhea, a deadly condition in the regimental camps, had been a problem for him from the beginning of his enlistment. He updated Henry, his brother, describing a dream in which he saw himself at home. In the dream his mother told him he "looked as lean as a crow": "I could not help looking in the glass this morning to see that it was so. I think she would not say so if she could see me. And it was also a reality to me for a while that our new horse was guilty of running and breaking the carriage." The mention of the horse appeared to be a separate dream that had come true, possibly unnerving Rufus on the possible future view of himself in the "lean as a crow" dream.[16]

March showed no improvement. Rufus was embarrassed by his feelings of discontent and discouragement and by his up-and-down health, which he interpreted as a disappointment to his brother. In June he dreamed again of being at home, believing he was there on furlough. In his dream he had been "dismissed until the first of February." He saw his mother but could not see his father or his brother in the dream. He did see his grandfather, who was apparently still alive, and shook hands with him. In his letter he told his brother he would like to hear from his grandfather.[17] Rufus reported the progression of his illness and his deteriorating condition in letter after letter, but he always referenced his happy frame of mind and his intention to go joyfully either into health or into death, whichever awaited him. He noted his complexion was "a little yellow," and he had "pain and soreness in the lower part of the stomach and bowels and the loss of appetite." He continued to long for, and dream of, home, each dream envisioning his mother in happier times, which always brought him joy even when he was most ill.[18]

A hospital attendant, "Mrs. Thomas," wrote the final letter home to Rufus Robbins' mother. The date was February 16, 1863, the dreamed month of the end of his furlough. Rufus's father and brother had made their way to the hospital in Philadelphia where Rufus had been taken for his last days. They arrived in time for his final words, which Mrs. Thomas had promised to record. Mrs. Thomas told them Rufus was a remarkable young man who experienced a "peculiarly happy death." He had shared his strong faith and an unwavering belief that he was ready to go to a place already familiar to him in his living and dreaming. Rufus recalled Psalm 91, which had coincidentally opened "itself to" his mother. He could not recall verse location in the Bible in his weak state and sometimes failing memory, but said he "had read it very often while down on the peninsula" and had found great comfort in it. He said there was something in it about "God covering him, and he must trust in Him, and He would give His angels charge over him, so that no evil should befall him." Mrs. Thomas had found Psalm 91 and read it to him.

Rufus's final state of mind impressed Mrs. Thomas: "He spoke of death always more as a journey he was about to take to a new and desirable home, rather than a dreaded change." When Mrs. Thomas told him his father and brother were coming to see him, he shared a final dream. "Last night," said he, "I dreamt I was at home and I was out under the trees and they looked so beautiful. When I got awake it was toward morning, and I longed so to be there to walk under the trees and look up into the sky. Just then I opened my eyes and right down through the window the beautiful moon and one bright star was shining for me. I could not keep the tears back when I thought how good God is. It was just as if He had said, 'You cannot come out to see them but they shall come to you.'"

This dream opened a portal for Rufus. He asked Mrs. Thomas to tell his mother that he had no doubts about the future. It was laid out in his beautiful dream, "all bright to me, and no fear of dying, for I feel that God will make it easy for me." Rufus Robbins died February 16, 1863.[19]

"He fell with his face to the foe": Tally Simpson's "Strange" Dream

"We are now in the land of danger," wrote Private Dick Simpson to "Aunt Caroline" back in Pendleton, South Carolina, "far, far from home, fighting for our homes and those near our hearts." It was July 4, 1861, and Dick, his older brother Tally, and the rest of the boys in the Third South Carolina Volunteers had been in Northern Virginia for only a week or so—but already they were homesick. "I never wished to be back [home] as bad in my life," Dick lamented. "How memory recalls every little spot, and how vividly every little scene flashes before my mind. Oh! If there is one place dear to me it is home sweet home ... [and] to join once more our family circle and talk of times gone by would be more to me than all else besides." His homesickness increased almost daily: "How I do wish that peace would be declared and we could be permitted to return home and enjoy all the pleasures of independence and home. Then I would be happy. I long to see you all once more as only one who has been treading the paths of danger far from home can long. I never knew how sweet the name of Carolina sounded until I was far away. There is a charm that clusters around it that will arouse every one of her sons to rush into the thickest of the battle and feel honoured to die in her defense."[20]

Dick's brother Taliaferro Calhoun Simpson was known to all as "Tally." Tally and Dick had both joined Company A, 3rd South Carolina Volunteers, in April 1861, the same day they received their college diplomas. Tally, like Dick, was bright, personable, cultivated, and articulate. He adored his family. He used fine words not only to paint heart-wrenching pictures of destruction and the smell of death on the roads and in the fields but also humorously to plot and scheme for the lady of his dreams, each missive salted with a good dose of home gossip and rumored romance. Floundering romantically in early letters home, Tally giddily professed his love for several young women. He "released" a woman from an early engagement and expressed joy at the announcement of her marriage: "It has caused me no pain, no anguish. I am ready to unfold my wings and fly off in search of—of—of—yes another gal upon whom to bestow my affections. Who shall it be? Can you not suggest some one? I can rely upon your taste implicitly. Pitch in then, be quick and energetic, and let me know the result of your 'looking around.' I have not heard whether Miss Laura Roberts is in Pendleton or not? What kind of gal is she?"[21]

Fancying himself ready for love, Tally entrusted affairs of the heart to his aunt and sister. Both ladies were ready and willing to play matchmaker, creating an intriguing dialogue and romance between Tally and a young woman from his home. Tally's family was prosperous, hers less so; but no one in the distant match saw this as a problem. The two young people played a penned game in which neither knew the other's true identity, but enough clues were strewn in the young woman's way (known only as Miss Fannie to the reader) that she rapidly guessed Tally's identity. Tally was provided a photograph of "Miss Fannie." He fell in love with the game and the photograph. Punctuating his correspondence with heartfelt longing for home and notes to his family on the importance of receiving letters from home, he shared the transcendent sweetness of the soldier reading a "precious letter from home": "It matters not in what he is engaged, what troubles and vexations are harassing him, a letter from home renders him oblivious of all his trials and sends him dreaming such dreams as thoughts of home can alone suggest."[22] Denied a furlough in March 1863 Tally surmised this was best, because the soldier who received a furlough would only find himself more lonely and homesick when he returned to camp.

Dick and Tally showed remarkable and noteworthy courage and gallantry on the battlefield, both of them participating in dangerous fighting. Tally continued cheerfully to look forward to someday meeting "Miss Fannie," whose portrait held visible hope for a fulfilled life and whose image filled his dreams. He received a dream from Miss Fannie in which she saw him still involved with a former love. He denied the relationship: "You seem to think that, on account of my dream concerning Miss Z, my affection still lies in that direction. Tis true I sometimes think of my old scrape, but [I] have not given it a moment's thought in I can't say when. My thoughts are centered upon some more worthy object, especially when I think in a serious manner. The die is cast, and she can never be any thing to me in [the] future."

This dream of a broken romance paled, however, in comparison to a terrible dream that visited Tally. He sent it home in a letter and begged for some feedback on what it might mean:

> I dreamt I was in Pendleton [home] and went solo to call on Miss Fannie. I thought her father lived in Gaillard's blacksmith shop and was employed in making fish baskets. I knocked on the door, pulled the latch and walked in. There sat Mr. Smith [the father], the worst looking piece of mortality I ever beheld. He was very tall and muscular but considerably stooped by old age. His hair was long, shaggy, and grey; his skin dark, terribly wrinkled, and badly sunburnt, and long grey bristles covered his face, neck, and hands. Work had soiled his dress and it appeared as if there had been a want of soap and water for a long time. All of a sudden he was perfectly nude—scabs, scales, and dirt covered his whole body, and in his predicament he ushered me into the presence of his daughter. The room was his workshop. A large cavity was scooped out in the center of the building to collect shavings, trash, etc.
>
> Miss F was seated on this pile of trash, and when her father introduced me she arose and greeted me cordially, tho modestly. I commenced a conversation, but couldn't carry it on because of my utter astonishment. She was in a manner handsome with a fine form and neatly dressed. Her complexion was almost black and her long raven hair and her dazzling black eyes gave her the appearance of an Indian maiden. She laughed and talked gaily but I was too busily employed in contrasting things in general to pay attention to what she said. Finally the scene was transferred to a very genteel parlor, company came in and my dream changed to something else.

This dream was followed by one in which Tally found himself back at home and seeing Fannie dressed "magnificently" and waiting to meet him in his family parlor.[23]

He cunningly turned the tables, he thought, and wrote that the dream would be reversed [by contraries], that Fannie simply would be disappointed in his appearance. He was self-conscious about his ragged appearance and the ravages on his body caused by bad food, bad water and appalling living conditions, and he forced his wretched appearance into a more palatable interpretation of the dream. He then noted he had eaten wild onions that night, thinking such a supper might have brought on such an unpleasant dream. He could not bring himself to face other considerations about the dream.

Tally died in battle, facing the enemy head-on in a charge at Snodgrass Hill at Chickamauga. He never met Miss Fannie. The description of his body at the close of the battle closely resembled the dream body of "scabs, scales, and dirt." If Fannie ever saw Tally it would have been in a family parlor, surrounded by family, viewing Tally's body in a coffin, as was the custom, a scene possibly presaged in Tally's dream of Fannie waiting to meet him in a parlor.

A condolence letter sent to Tally's parents in Pendleton, South Carolina, told of Tally's being felled "on the bloody field ... shot through the heart by a minnie ball" after his left arm was broken. He was well loved and was buried in a marked grave at a house site, named so that his parents could claim his body when war conditions allowed.

Morphine and "Decoherent" Dreaming

William Kenneth McCoy, the son of William McCoy and Sally Anne Kemper McCoy of Charlottesville, Virginia, was a sergeant with Carrington's Charlottesville Artillery Battery, Early's Division, Ewell's Army Corps, in the Army of Northern Virginia. He was wounded and badly burned Sunday, May 3, 1863, at the Battle of Chancellorsville and died in Richmond, Virginia, on May 19, 1863. William's brother wrote to the family on Thursday morning, May 21, 1863, from "University" about William's agonizing days in a Richmond hospital, wounded and burned, his eyes closed from the burns and his face covered with cotton. Ministering to William and describing his last agonizing moments was torturous for William's brother:

> On Monday, by putting simple lerate and linseed oil on his face I was able to move all the cotton & flim and found to my joy that his face would not be at all scarred. His eyes were still closed with matter but during the day he got them partially open and exclaimed with a quick voice and in a pleased manner, "Lord I can see light...." He seemed to be doing well until Friday and Sat. when his left leg, which seemed to be only a little bruised began to pain him very much and indeed he was in an agony as he expressed it all over. [He was given morphine more frequently,] which made him dream a great deal and talk in his sleep. His dreams were decoherent and mostly of the battle field and his company; he drilled them sometimes calling "Halt!" giving orders about taking out his piece; called the men's names very often. Once he said "You must excuse me gentlemen, I can't engage in this game. I forgot I can't see nor use either hand nor walk a step; I am badly wounded." [He called out] "Charley, Charley McCoy" [and when told he wasn't there, he replied he] thought ... your regiment had been ordered back. [When awake he was] perfectly himself, his manner, his language, his gentleness and politeness which he never forgot for a moment. [I created a machine for raising the bed; often during the day and the night ... he would ask for] a drink of water and then pray a short prayer.... He almost always said "Amen" at the close of it. He said in his sleep "I do try from the bottom of my heart." [Mother asked], "What?" He said "to trust in God and in Jesus Christ." Once he said "I do hate to hear you talk so boy; oh how you will repent it some of these days." Mother asked what? He said "Rick is cursing & swearing and I have tried to persuade him to stop it."

The letter continued with a full description of details of William's death and burial.[24]

"Coincidences are queer sometimes": A Visitation

Mary Boykin Miller was married to Col. James Chesnut, Jr., of Camden, South Carolina. James was a planter, lawyer, U.S. senator, and Confederate States Army general, making Mary ideally placed to watch and record the South's ruin. Although she was from an aristocratic, slaveholding family, she abhorred slavery. She was also a superb diarist, noted for her detailed record of events in the South during the Civil War.

In the winter of 1863 Mary and her family lived in the Richmond, Virginia, house of a Mrs. Lyons, occupying one floor—drawing room, dining room, chamber, and two servants' rooms, for Molly and Laurence. Accustomed to rooms being allotted a specific purpose, Mary moaned that the "poor" drawing room also served as a parlor, dining room, and a room where they danced to the music of an old piano. They received distinguished Confederate company in that room, among them the Confederate president, Jefferson Davis, and General Robert E. Lee.

In this house, Mary wrote a story she noted as being "strange." She had read a letter from her sister, Kate, who asked about an "old playmate, friend, lover" named Boykin McCaa. Boykin was an Alabama planter, and Mary's first cousin, born in Camden, South

Carolina. Her sister related that it had been twenty years since she had seen him and that both of them had married other people. In the "dismal, anxious, and disquieting" years of war, she had almost forgotten that Boykin had existed until the night of the story. Mary's sister said he had come to her, "stood by my bedside and spoke to me kindly and affectionately, as if we had just parted. I said, holding out my hand, 'Boykin, you are very pale.' He answered, 'I have come to tell you goodbye.'" He then seized both of her hands, and his own hands were cold as ice, freezing the "marrow" of her bones. She screamed over and over again, bringing the entire household rushing in, including "the negroes from the yard: All had been wakened by my piercing shrieks. This may have been a dream, but it haunts me."

Mary sat at the breakfast table, reading Kate's letter aloud, interrupting her story to say that she had met a friend of Boykin's "last summer" who said that Boykin needed to say something to Kate. Weighing on his mind was the need to ask her pardon because he had pretended to be engaged to her and knew that it was wrong. Mary then went back to Kate's letter, reading that Kate had received an account that Boykin had been wounded but had recovered. She wrote she knew—because of the dream vision—that this was not true and that he was dead.

While Mary was reading this letter at the table, Mr. Chesnut stopped her because, at the same time, he was reading from the day's newspaper, the *Examiner*, the following: "Capt. Burwell Boykin McCaa—found dead upon the battlefield, leading a cavalry charge, at the head of his company. He was shot through the head."

Mary wrote in her diary: "Coincidences are queer sometimes."[25]

"Whose funeral is that?"

Judith McGuire, an unrepentant rebel from a prominent Virginia family, was married to John McGuire, an Episcopalian minister and secessionist. They were forced to flee their Alexandria home in May 1861. They then resided with various families in Richmond and surrounding areas. John lost his pastorate and the family never regained their home. Judith told a sad story of the McIntosh family, some of whom she met passing through Richmond. Mrs. McIntosh, known only as "J. McI." in Judith's journal, told Judith she was in Memphis when Jemmie, her child, fell ill and grew steadily worse. "J. McI." sent for her husband, Brigadier General James McIntosh, who came but went back immediately, summoned away from his ill child by the imminence of a battle at Pea Ridge. The child died. The mother dreamed only a few days later that she was at Fort Smith, "her home before the war; standing on the balcony of her husband's quarter, her attention ... arrested by a procession—an officer's funeral." She asked, in the dream, "Whose funeral is that?" The answer was "General McIntosh's, madam." The dream haunted J. McI., who had just buried her child Jemmie. Only days beyond the dream a servant rode up with a note, and she took the note, already knowing the contents—her husband was dead. General McIntosh was buried in Fort Smith.[26]

"Johnny is drowned in the river"

In a sad state of dreaming, Johnny Adkinson, Company K, 95th Regiment of Infantry, from Boone County, Illinois, dreamed of death but was sure he was dreaming about his mother's death. He wrote to his mother after the dream, wishing he could see "obsen" and "little henry and my 3 Sisters" and wrote that he had to share a dream he had while sleeping all alone on a "dark and raney nite" in a place he had built with some boards. He dreamed his mother was dead and that he was on guard with some of the boys of the regiment, talking about "their folks and I thought I felt very bad a bout it." He told the boys that life was hard and that he thought his mother was dead "and I thought that I [had] no home now." He awakened to thunder and lightning, rain and darkness as in the dream. The outside environment was so much like the dream that it took Johnny a moment to focus and realize he was no longer in the dream. He was relieved to find it was a dream and that his mother was alive and that he had a home. Johnny was probably dreaming his own death on that dark and rainy night on August 20. The weather conditions were similar to those four days later on August 24 when Johnny drowned.

Six days later the Joseph and Mary Adkinson family in Boone County, Illinois, received a letter from their son-in-law, James Vincent, who reported, "[J]ohnny is drowned in the river." Johnny and five or six others were off-loading a boat that had come down from Vicksburg: "[Johnny] came to his diner and was all right and went back again and the boys seen him about three o'clock and then did not see him after that. they hunted all through the boat and could not find him. this was on the 24 aug and I was on picket that day and dident know anny thing about it until the next day and then I hunted all over for him and could not find him and the next morning he was found. he floated ashore and we got him out." Vincent reported that Johnny's pockets had been "picked" of about twenty-four dollars and that they could not tell whether he fell "over board himself or wether some body knocked him over but we buried him the best we could. the boys all feels bad about it and I feel bad." But Vincent advised his mother-in-law to grieve as little as possible because it would not do any good and would, in fact, harm her.[27]

Omens and Signs

Birds of Ill Omen

Sightings of owls, doves, and all manner of other birds foretold death. Birds of ill omen were passed down in stories like old quilts and mantel clocks, a part of life, never doubted, always trusted, and the messages delivered and feared.

John A. Ratliff, an impoverished tenant farmer, was twenty-seven years old, married and the father of two young children when he enlisted with the 54th Virginia in March 1862, one month before Confederate conscription began. In March 1863, twelve months after departing, he wrote home to describe a series of omens that made him "very uneasy" about his "dear wife and sweet little children." He confided to Adeline, his wife, that he saw "too little birds that appeared before me and staid that way for some time." It was the same vision he had seen before the couple's first child died. Near the end of April his father wrote to say that Adeline and the children "had got out of money."

Worried about his family, John deserted, but "five months later, either because he was captured or because he decided to return voluntarily, Ratliff rejoined the 54th Virginia in the trenches around Atlanta." A couple of weeks later Adeline received word that a "mortar shell had landed near John and killed him instantly."[28]

Seeing the Moon through Brush

John Beatty wrote in his journal that his colonel (Ammen) didn't like to see the "moon through brush" and believed in dreams. The colonel was spooked by a dream of his father, who in the dream drowned and then came up from the muddy water trying to stab him with a rusty knife. The colonel awoke trying to escape. He fell asleep again and again met his murderous father. He shared his dream—and his fear—around the campfire. Several days later he heard of two family deaths: his mother and sister were dead of cholera. In a waking experience, Colonel Ammen felt sharp throbbing pains in his neck. He grabbed his neck and told comrades it felt as though he had been shot in the neck. He noted the time of the pain. Soon afterward he had news of his brother, who was fighting in the South, having been shot in the back of the neck in the same place and at the same time as the colonel's own stabbing neck pain.

Dreams of his own death, instead of frightening Colonel Ammen, gave him courage and a fearlessness in battle he had never before experienced. He met his foes at Greenbrier and Shiloh with calm ferocity. After each of those battles he suffered illnesses he was told he would not survive. The dreams of his death, he said, were warnings of the illnesses, but in those dreams he knew he would outwit death—so he survived. Colonel Ammen told John Beatty, the incredulous recorder of these experiences, "[I]f superstition, or a belief in the supernatural, is an indication of weakness, Napoleon and Sir Walter Scott were the weakest of men."[29]

Northern Lights

Captain George Turnbull of the 134th Regiment, New York State Volunteers, wrote to his beloved "Beck" that the "northern lights you saw are ominous and foretell some bloody conflicts to come." There were two more years of "bloody conflicts" ahead,[30] and George had already seen more than his share of carnage before this "ominous" sign. He wrote of the nerve required to endure the war "without shuddering, the carcasses of horses lay strewn all along the road and the field, and in some places you would see an arm or leg of a human being sticking up out of the ground apparently ruted out by the hogs in one place in particular I saw a boot in which was the foot & leg lyin on the ground, in another an arm as far up as the elbow in still another a skull which the boys were kicking around like a football and a little to the south side in a skirt of woods they said that boddies lay entirely exposed, never having been buried, but enough of this, the contemplation is sickening."[31] Surviving the horror of the war, he said, was dependent on letters being received from those one loved and cared about, "for it seams almost like clasping an old friend by the hand to get a letter in this dreary country 'forsaken alike by God and man.'"[32]

Dutch Paper

Not exactly a "sign," Dutch paper was an amulet used by the Pennsylvania Germans as a "cure." John Derr, from Barry Township, Schuylkill County, Pennsylvania, enlisted in the Union army in September 1861 and was assigned to the 48th Pennsylvania Volunteer Infantry, Company D. Wounded in the leg at the 2nd Battle of Bull Run, on August 29, 1862, John was taken prisoner, paroled and transported first to Georgetown College Hospital in Washington, D.C., then transferred to the Cherry and Broad Street Hospital in

Philadelphia. He was furloughed home and died in 1876 at the age of 37 from the long-term effects of his wound. While still in the Georgetown Hospital, John's parents sent him Dutch paper, a brown paper used for wrapping meat. John thanked them and said it would probably be useful: "Further I let you know that I got that Dutch paper in your letter and I was very glad for it as it may do me some good."[33] Dutch paper was a curing ritual. A word was placed on the paper in a particular order, soaked in vinegar, and placed on the affected body part and then a rhyme was chanted.

Dream Cake: Kate Stone at Brokenburn

Kate Stone, an intensely patriotic Southern girl, lived with her widowed mother, five brothers, and a sister at Brokenburn, their large fertile cotton plantation in northeast Louisiana just thirty miles from Vicksburg, Mississippi.

Kate, born Sarah Katherine Stone, began a journal in May 1861 when she was twenty years old and all the eligible young men were leaving for a war that she initially viewed as romantic and splendid. Kate loved to read; she read Sir Walter Scott and other romance novels and poets, magazines, periodicals, and anything she could find. These filled her mind with the idea that the South could never lose and that the dashing young men, inspired by beautiful women, would fix it all within months.

Early entries in Kate's journal were filled with topics such as basting cakes, sewing comforters, knitting socks, and visiting neighbors. On October 7, 1861, she wrote that Dr. Lily had waylaid her and friends as they wandered in the garden. They stayed out until after dark talking about social activities, including the impending marriage of one Dr. Devine. She said Dr. Lily was attending the wedding and would report "on the bride's dress and bring us a piece of dream cake." A few days later Dr. Lily, as promised, brought the wedding cake, and Kate "made him a dream list, and he is to tell me the favored girl when he comes again." He had a piece of dream cake for himself as well as a piece for Kate. The superstition was that a "slice of bride cake … laid under the head of an unmarried man or woman will make them dream of their future wife or husband."[34] After a few more days, Kate reported, "Have slept on my paper and dreamed my best but to no purpose, nobody coming to marry me, nobody coming to woo."[35] There was no mention in Kate's reports of naming bedposts to predict a beau.

Kate matured during the war. Two of her brothers died; young love came and was lost several times; and Kate's ideas of romantic war shriveled in its realities. She detested the Union soldier and his cause. She never gave up hope for the South she loved, but she learned to be a survivor, forced to live a very different life after facing the terror of invasion at her doorstep. On March 15, 1863, Kate spoke for herself and her neighbors: "For the last two days we have been in a quiver of anxiety looking for the Yankees every minute, sitting on the front gallery with our eyes strained in the direction they will come, going to bed late and getting up early so they will not find us asleep."[36]

After Kate's favorite horse, Wonka, was stolen from its hiding place in the swamps, and after Kate and her little sister were forced at gunpoint into a room by a slave while they were visiting a neighbor, the Stone family decided they needed to leave.[37]

Kate's youngest brother, Walter, died seven weeks before the news of it reached the family—on February 15, 1863, at Cotton Gin, Mississippi. Coleman Stone, "Brother Coley," died at Clinton, Mississippi, in May 1863.[38]

In a hazardous flight to Tyler, Texas, seven members of the Stone family set off on horseback through the swamps and flooded lands where the Union army had cut levees. They followed trails barely visible, took a skiff out of a bayou, and rowed for their lives, with pursuing Union soldiers not far behind. They stopped at Delhi, Louisiana, boarded a train for Monroe and then made their way inland from the Mississippi valley; they spent seven weeks in flight before reaching Texas.

On the way to Texas, in a desperate need for normalcy, Kate's indefatigable sense of humor turned to desperate play. Dream cake was not the only magical superstition used to attract a beau. The bedraggled party of refugees reached Monroe about sunset. They crossed the Ouachita on the skiff and stayed the night at "Mrs. Scale's at Trenton": "Some gentlemen called, and we had cards. After they left, Lucy and I tried our fortunes in divers ways as it was 'All Hallowe'en.' We tried all magic arts and had a merry frolic, but no future lord and master came to turn our wet garments hanging before the fire. There were no ghostly footprints in the meal sprinkled behind the door.... No knightly forms of soldiers brave disturbed our dreams after eating the white of an egg half-filled with salt."[39]

Kate's bright spot was the beau of her dreams, Lt. Henry Bry Holmes, who called on her every day for three months. Kate's journal ended where it began—back to face the sad reality of "home" at Brokenburn, only Brokenburn's fields were flooded, weeds grew on the fertile ground, and there would be years of struggle to bring it back to production under a new system of labor: "At home again but so many, many changes in two years. It does not seem the same place. The bare echoing rooms, the neglect and defacement of all though the place is in better repair than most and the stately oaks and the green grass make it look pleasant and cheerful, though gardens, orchards, and fences are mostly swept away.... But never, never, never more echoes back to our hearts like a funeral knell at every thought of the happy past.... Nothing is left but to endure."[40]

Kate's experiences prepared her for this new struggle, and the end of her war entries prepared its reader for the announcement of her marriage in the next year to Henry Bry Holmes. Perhaps she passed on a piece of "dream cake" to the next young belle dreaming of her beau in the postwar South.

CHAPTER 15

Presentiment: I Have a Rendezvous with Death—or Life

Presentiment is that long shadow on the lawn
Indicative that suns go down
—Emily Dickinson, *Complete Poems*, 1924,
Part 2; "Nature," LXVII

Presentiment Before Battle

John Brown Gordon, CSA, in his *Reminiscences*, reported numerous instances of presentiment of death before a battle. Colonel Tennant Lomax of Alabama, in the seven days of fighting at Richmond, turned to John, took his hand, bid him good-bye and said with no hesitation that he would be dead in battle within half an hour. As the colonel predicted, he was dead within a half-hour. A Union officer, General J. Warren Keifer, from Springfield, Ohio, shared a letter in 1898 with John Gordon relating similar presentiments of death made by two of his officers. One was Colonel Aaron W. Ebright of the 126th Ohio Regiment, who was killed at Opequan, Virginia, on September 19, 1864. Colonel Ebright had told General Keifer that he would be killed before a battle of that date ended. He gave directions for his remains and personal effects to be sent home to Lancaster, Ohio, and had a letter written to his wife about property she did not know about. The colonel died on horseback just moments later when a rifle ball hit him. These presentiments, John Gordon noted, were not precipitated by fear. All of these men had fought in battle; all were calm when they made their predictions. Another of General Keifer's officers, Captain William A. Hathaway, announced his death at Monocacy, Maryland, on July 9, 1864, and died moments later.[1]

William Oake of the 26th Iowa Volunteers recalled a story of premonition he witnessed in the battle at Resaca, Georgia, on May 15, 1864. Two men were killed within arm's reach, one of them a soldier, Jeff Leeper, who died standing beside his brother. That morning William Oake had seen Jeff take his personal effects out of his pocket and hand them to another soldier of the 26th, a man named Horace Humeston, and ask him to send them to his folks if he did not survive the battle: "He said that he had a premonition that he would be killed in the coming action. How true the premonition came."[2]

Colonel Warren Akin, a Georgia lawyer and speaker of the Georgia House of Representatives, had a dream vision just before Lee's surrender. On the morning of February 8, 1865, in Richmond, he dreamed or saw his eldest son lying "on his back at the foot of a chinaberry-tree on the sidewalk in front of the home he then occupied in Elberton, Georgia, his head in a pool of blood. He ran to him, found him not dead but speechless and unconscious, raised him up by his left hand, and the blood ran out of his right ear."[3] Two days later his son was thrown from a horse beside that same chinaberry tree, and a neighbor ran to him, lifting him in the same manner as in the dream and saw blood running from his right ear. Colonel Akin's son died on the third day after the dream.

Major General Ramseur of North Carolina was married and had a young son, who was born after Ramseur left for the war. On the night preceding the battle of Cedar Creek, General Ramseur and John Gordon, who was a soldier in his regiment, sat on the bluff overlooking the field. Major Ramseur spoke about his wife and his longing to see his baby boy, intimating that he would not see him on this side of life. Just as he was readying himself to ride into battle, he turned and said calmly that he would receive his "furlough" that day, meaning the bullet that found him at that very moment.[4]

John Gordon's own brother, Augustus Gordon, a captain and later a lieutenant colonel, was twenty-one years old and in command of the Sixth Regiment of Alabama. With the same amazing calm evidenced in all these stories, Augustus said, just before entering the battle of the Wilderness, "My hour has come." John told him not to let such thoughts catch hold of his imagination, but Augustus said he had not, that he knew this death without doubt. "Riding at the head of his regiment, with his sword above him, the fire of battle in his eye and words of cheer for his men on his lips, the fatal grape-shot plunged through his manly heart, and the noble youth slept his last sleep in that woeful Wilderness."[5]

John Gordon wrote that it would require volumes to record the hundreds of presentiments like these from both the Union and the Confederate armies. They did not arise from fear, nor were they promptings of danger or even apprehension of death. They were more profound, more poised, more sublime, and they were always delivered with deadly certainty. John looked for an answer for the origins of these presentiments and determined that presentiment was simply another "argument for immortality": "It was the whispering of the Infinite beyond us to the Infinite within us—a whispering inaudible to the natural ear, but louder than the roar of battle to the spirit that heard it."[6]

John also wrote about the presentiment of "life," occasionally misplaced by those who believed themselves invincible but more often surrounding some with an uncanny appearance of good fate or maybe pure luck. Whichever it was, they were consistently aware of it. He used Lieutenant General D.H. Hill and a particular occasion as an example. At the battle of Malvern Hill John Gordon commanded Rhodes's Brigade where General McClellan made his last stand against General Lee's forces:

> General Hill took his seat at the root of a large tree and began to write his orders. At this point McClellan's batteries from the crest of a high ridge, and his gunboats from the James River, were ploughing up the ground in every direction around us. The long shells from the gunboats, which our men called "McClellan's gate-posts," and the solid shot from his heavy guns on land, were knocking the Confederate batteries to pieces almost as fast as they could be placed in position. The Confederate artillerists fell so rapidly that I was compelled to detail untrained infantry to take their places. And yet there sat that intrepid officer, General D.H. Hill.... He did not place the large tree between himself and the destructive batteries, but sat facing them. I urged him to get on the other side of the tree and avoid such needless and reckless exposure. He replied, "Don't worry about me; look after the men. I am not going to be killed until my time comes." He had scarcely uttered these words when a shell exploded in our immediate presence, severely shocking me for the moment, a portion of it tearing through the breast of his coat and rolling him over in the newly ploughed ground. This seemed to convert him to a more

rational faith; for he rose from the ground, and, shaking the dirt from his uniform, quietly took his seat on the other side of the tree.[7]

John Gordon confessed that he only had one moment of presentiment that proved instead to be a blessed relief. Ordered at Winchester, Virginia, to storm a fortressed Union army led by General Milroy, John planned the assault but felt that if it were carried out death would come to him and many of his men. He wrote to his wife, whom he always felt near him in moments before battle, and then mounted his horse, expecting the moments to come to be his last. He rode at dawn, ascended the long slope in front of the fortress and found, much to his relief, that the Union army had evacuated in the night![8]

"The death angel"

Sam Watkins wrote about that intuitive feeling of foreboding in the particular way it manifests on the battlefield. He said that it was, to him, a mystery. At one moment the soldier is "in good spirits, laughing and talking": "The wing of the death angel touches him. He knows that his time has come." After that "when" is the only unanswered question, but that soldier's days are numbered.

Not to leave one hanging on words only, as an example Sam related a story that happened at Lee and Gordon's Mill. It was night. Rations were being issued, and Sam noticed that a soldier named Bob Stout had refused his. Bob replied, when asked, that he was not ill but that his time had come and he knew when—three days from that date. Bob pulled out a twenty-dollar gold piece he had carried through the war and a silver watch his father had given him and handed those to "Captain Irvine, to give to my father." Bob distributed his clothing and blanket and said he wished to die with his gun and cartridge box.

The next morning the regiment marched to Chickamauga, camping on the banks of the Tennessee River on a Friday night and crossing over on Saturday. General Forrest's cavalry had opened the battle and men were falling as bullets whizzed in every direction. The battle continued the next day, intense and unrelenting. A retreat sounded on Sunday. "Blue coats" were everywhere, a perfect "hornet's nest": "The balls whistled around our ears like the escape valves of ten thousand engines." Sam ran alongside Bob Stout: "The earth jarred and trembled like an earthquake. Deadly missiles were flying in every direction. It was the very incarnation of death itself. I could almost hear the shriek of the death angel passing over the scene. General Smith was killed in ten minutes after I saw him. Bob Stout and myself stopped. Said I, 'Bob, you weren't killed, as you expected.'" At that moment a shot from a Federal gun hit Bob between the waist and the hip, tearing off one leg "and scattering his bowels all over the ground.... His spirit had flown before his body struck the ground." It was the third day of the intuitive precognition of his death.[9]

Elisha Hunt Rhodes, the eldest son of Captain Elisha Hunt and Eliza Ann (Chace) Rhodes, was born in the village of Pawtuxet, Cranston, Rhode Island, on March 21, 1842. Elisha's father drowned in a shipwreck in 1858, and Elisha, aged 16, became sole supporter of his family. On June 5, 1861, he enlisted as a private in Co. D, 2nd R.I. Volunteers, and remained with them, receiving many promotions, including colonel in 1865. He returned home when the company disbanded on July 28, 1865. On June 12, 1866, he married Caroline Pearce Hunt, the daughter of Joshua Hunt of Providence, and had two children. He took over the firm of Frederick Miller and formed Dunham & Rhodes Co., a cotton and woolen mill business.

Near Petersburg, Virginia, in June 1864, Elisha journaled an intriguing story of Sergeant Major George F. Polley, 10th Massachusetts Volunteers. He watched as Polley meticulously carved his own grave headboard. The men had been stationed together for what became the long siege of Petersburg. Polley had reenlisted and was expecting a commission as a lieutenant in the 37th Massachusetts Volunteers. He showed Rhodes the board on which he had carved his name and date of birth, leaving a place for the date of his death. Elisha asked if he expected to be killed, and Polley said, simply, "no," that he had really carved it for fun. Then he told Elisha that he did not wish to be one of the nameless dead tossed in an unmarked grave. The next day he was killed by a shell fired from a Rebel battery. Even Rhodes, accustomed to death on the battlefield, found this event a peculiar one—calm, reliable and certain.[10]

Looking back over his years of war experience, Newton Curtis—captain and, later, general of Company G of the 16th New York Volunteer Infantry made up of men from DePeyster and Macomb in New York's North Country—spoke of the momentary fear of death on the battlefield as something that quickly passed in the heat of the crisis; but he said presentiment was something, for good or ill, that stayed with you until you understood the time of its completion was at hand. In his case, the presentiment was that he would survive the war, but it was more detailed than simply a premonition between life and death. He knew he would not be killed, but he knew just as certainly that his eyesight would suffer permanent injury: "The fear of death is at best but momentary, and is only felt when it appears imminent; as soon as the crisis is past it is the first thing forgotten.... I had no fear of death in battle, for before I was mustered into service, I had a presentiment that I should not be killed in the army, but would have my eyesight injured." To illustrate his premonition, Curtis shared a story of January 15, 1865, when the 16th was serving as the 121st New York Volunteers. They were at Fort Fisher at the mouth of the Cape Fear River just below Wilmington, North Carolina. Fort Fisher, he said, was "the largest and best equipped fortification constructed by the Confederates." The fort's defensive barriers extended out twelve feet and were twelve feet high or more, and the combat that day was "a hand-to-hand contest with swords and bayonets": "We gained possession of the seventh traverse at 4:45 a.m. ... and shortly after 5:15 p.m. ... when the sun was just disappearing ... while the volunteers were assembling, I went further into the fort and had ascended a magazine or sand dune for the purpose of looking into the angle of the bastion I intended to attack, when I was struck and disabled by two fragments of a shell, one destroying the left eye and the other carrying away a portion of the bone at the base of the brain." Curtis had been the first man to pass through the stockade and continued to lead each assault even though he was wounded four times. He was presented the Medal of Honor "for extraordinary heroism."[11]

Brevet Brigadier General Rufus Dawes, U.S. Volunteers, Lemonweir Minute Men, Company K of the Sixth Wisconsin, noted in his journal that his regiment was named for the peaceful river that flowed through the beautiful valley where most of his men resided. He had formed his regiment as its captain but quickly attained his final rank of brevet brigadier general. While forming his regiment he wrote that he inevitably lost four men, one too old, one too young, one really not interested and one who "had a presentiment that he would be killed." Dawes thought hard about the last because the young man was strong and hearty but let him go because the young man had dreamed that he had "seen himself killed." He had "to let him go," Dawes said.[12]

Humorous comments on the 6th Wisconsin's inept regimental band dominated

Dawes' early journal entries. Anyone who was sick or caught "in a trick" or too green or who lacked any skill was placed in the band, which appeared from all comments to be the worst in the war. Dawes said they played so badly and so slowly that they passed reviewing stands at "about forty-seven paces a minute." He wrote in January 1862 that one of the camp singers, Captain Edwin A. Brown, sealed his own fate with a song. He sang his favorite, "Benny Havens, O," with the words "in the land of sun and flowers, his head lies pillowed low." Captain Brown was killed in battle shortly after singing that piece.[13]

The entries grew more serious and contemplative as the men moved out to field and camp. Dawes reported troubled dreams as the years progressed, Fredericksburg invading his sleep and that of his soldiers and then the horrors of the Gettysburg battlefield, where they held Cemetery Hill and forced the "decision for history that the crowning battle of the war should be at Gettysburg" where "troubled and dreamy sleep at best comes to the soldier." The entire regiment was on edge and were ordered to fall in with heavy musketry firing after a man in the Seventh Indiana regiment "cried out so loudly in his sleep that he aroused the troops."[14] "Change over the spirit of" Dawes' dreams saddened him as the men grew weary, some being discharged and some deserting, and substitutes often were "a sorry set."[15] But the war continued and eventually ended, the survival of his regiment confirmation and "the supreme test," in Dawes' mind, of a greater presentiment of a rightful cause.

Dreaming Death, "like sharp pain around my heart"

The Soldier's Dream
by Thomas Campbell, a Scottish poet (1777–1844)[16]

Our bugle sung truce for the night cloud had lower'd
And the sentinel stars fixed their watch in the sky;
And thousands had sunk on the ground overpower'd,
The weary to sleep, and the wounded to die.
When reposing that night on my pallet of straw
By the wolf-scaring faggot that guarded the slain;
At the dead of night a sweet vision I saw,
And thrice ere the morning I dreamt it again.
Methought from the battlefield's dreadful array
Far, far I had roam'd on a desolate track;
'Twas autumn—and sunshine arose on the way
To the home of my fathers that welcom'd me back.
I flew through the pleasant fields, travers'd so oft
In life's morning march, when my bosom was young;
I heard my own mountain goats bleating aloft,
and knew the sweet strain that the corn-reapers sung.
Then pledged we the wine-cup; and fondly I swore,
From my home and my weeping friend—never to part.
My little ones kiss'd me a thousand times o'er,
And my wife sobb'd aloud in her fullness of heart.
Stay, stay with us—rest, thou art weary and worn;
But sorrow return'd with the dawning of morn,
And the voice in my dreaming ear melted away.

Charles Tenney joined the 7th Ohio Volunteer Infantry in 1861 in his hometown of Mecca, Ohio. He did not have strong family bonds but shared a social life with a small group of friends, one of them a young woman, Adelaide [Addie] E. Case. He asked Addie if she would write to him and she agreed. Charles left with the Ohio Volunteers. Addie kept her promise, and both Addie and Charlie wrote consistently and frequently to one another. But Charles, called Charlie, quickly stepped over the line and suggested the two of them could be more than friends. Addie resisted, suggesting that they be like brother and sister, in fact penning her first letter of January 19, 1861, to "Dear Brother." Charlie confided that his biological sister had fallen prey to his family's ill feelings about him, which had led him to seek Addie's friendship before he left for the war. Addie, saddened by this glimpse into his disaffection and estrangement from his family, imagined that it was even more important that she be Charlie's surrogate "sister."

Charlie challenged this idea, asking for an exchange of ambrotypes, which inflamed Addie. She protested that Charlie's flattery and his presumptuous leap into asking for an ambrotype, akin in her mind to an engagement, was insulting and reprehensible. As letters continued to pass between them, each one edging deeper into emotional attachment, Addie's protests dissolved and blossomed, first into deep and genuine affection and then into love. This scenario of love blooming between a young woman and a soldier was, in itself, not unusual; but Addie felt intuitive surges and experienced night dreams about Charlie. These dreams were not sweet dreams of seeing Charlie at home in a loving domestic setting. They were eerie predictions of danger, illness and death, and they quickly and consistently broke into their exchanges of growing love and their waking relationship, which was distant in physical miles but painfully close in Addie's brutal honesty about her anguished feelings of love juxtaposed against her horrific dreams of Charlie's death. Baring her soul in one of the early letters passing between them, dated October 3, 1861, Addie spoke of "presentiment": "Where are you today? Are you engaged in some bloody battle or are you reposing in security in your tent or on some bed of sickness? How often my thoughts have been with you today." She sensed a "presentiment" of "evil" surrounding Charlie; by "evil" she explained that she meant danger. She feared for his life but was confused about the time and place. She questioned Charlie: was he in danger from a Rebel strike? Was it something else she did not understand? She wrote of her need to let go of the feeling of dread and disaster so that it would not impair both of them: "God forbid, I must dispel such thoughts." If she were near him, she pleaded, she would feel more control over the discomforting information hovering around her: "Then I could feel that let come what might I would know all." She led Charlie through her feelings in an effort to understand them, explaining that they first arose "sad and gloomy" while she sat in a sewing bee for the soldiers. It was there that the intuitive surge occurred, "a strange feeling to thrill through me which is hard to dispel."[17]

A few days later Addie wrote again. She had experienced a dream vision that was extraordinarily real and beautiful but she awoke feeling sadness and terror. She asked Charlie what this meant: "I awoke and wept bitter tears at its departing." She could not integrate her waking feelings of terror with a beautiful night vision of Charlie hovering before her "with such dreamy blue eyes." She eagerly reached for him and tried to clasp him "with a vainly-eager longing," but the vision vanished, not in the usual sense of a dream vision disappearing upon waking but in a terrifying manner that defied her understanding, a rapid departure that expelled his "face ... from reality."[18]

Addie shook off the dream but not the lingering feelings of despair. In her next letters she consciously shared hometown stories about community acquaintances, timidly sending Heaven's choicest blessings to her "dear" friend, Charlie, who boldly pushed ahead in calling Addie "dearest," the prettiest of his correspondents, and offering a kiss, quickly crossed out in his letter but not indelibly. He envisioned her sitting and playing her melodeon, asking if it was indeed Addie who held his spirit in her heart: "Your soul giving utterance to its goodness in happy song, the music of which seems to reach me, and enliven my inmost spirit. How glad am I, to know and feel that you are at this moment holding me in kind remembrance. Happiness, is a boon many strive to reach, but few, comparatively, attain, but if happiness exists among soldiers, it is him, who knows that there is a heart which beats in unison with his own, and feels that her spirit is watching over him, that is the fortunate possessor."[19]

The new year (1862) opened with Addie lamenting the extension of a war that everyone thought would be brief. She longed for peace and shuddered in the continued presentiment of some unnamed terror for Charlie: "I sometimes tremble and entertain vague portentions for your safety. But a feeble effort so made to commend you to Him who alone can rescue Life under the most auspicious circumstances is uncertain but how fearfully uncertain it must be when all the destructive powers of warfare are brought against it, but I trust that you will live to return to your friends." Charlie responded that he could no longer call Addie "friend" or "sister." He passed lightly by her wishes for an unlikely peace and declared boldly that he loved her, not with the effervescence of boyhood love but with enduring fervor and passion that had arisen unbidden and grew daily in strength. He begged for her voice in his love, vowing to elevate his position and make a mark in the world for a return of her love.

Addie wrangled with the idea of Charlie as more than a dear friend. He sent her a love poem, but she protested that friendship was the purest kind of love and shared her "wildest dream"—to write poetry: "[P]oetry in the accent of love and friendship." Then she pondered how to translate her feelings "from brother to a love ... no common affair" for her, in the next instant writing "dear Charlie" and "my darling" and ending with an anguished wish that a "guardian angel from Heaven hover round thee." Love me, Charlie, she insisted in the next letter.[20]

A few weeks went by with letters delayed. Addie feared Charlie was ill. Haunting her was an "ugly dream ... I can not drive ... from my mind": "I shudder even now when I think of it. You were lying ill and delirious where I could both see and hear you. You were calling for me and yet I could not go to you. I struggled long earnestly and in vain, but there seemed some great obstacle between us which I could not surmount.... I awoke completely exhausted and ... weeping." Addie tried to ignore the dream with an offhanded excuse of an absence of letters from Charlie: "Be assured, my darling, there was no more rest for me.... [I]t is no wonder that such dreams, as the above come to torture me when you, before, have written so often. Why! I believe the tortures of the rack can be nothing to the imaginings of such dreams."

She did not believe that this dream came as a simple longing for letters. She openly shared that she awoke exhausted and weeping, understanding her feelings were important and extreme danger was in Charlie's future. The "ugly dream" left her with the "blues" so detestable that only a letter from Charlie saying he was well would soothe her. Addie's presentiment for Charlie crept into her days and nights, sometimes subtly, sometimes forcefully, each glimpse more clearly defined.[21]

Addie wrote about "Love." It was a new emotion for her, and one that frightened her, not only because she so longed for someone to love who would return her love but because her fear that loving Charlie with her entire heart and soul would produce the worst kind of anguish if her dreams were a literal glimpse into his death. Not every night brought her dreams of terror. She blessed God for dreams that brought her close to him and brought him home to her where she could see him and feel him. Addie gave into her emotions and professed her love for her dear Charlie. She had addressed him as Friend and Brother for a few months beyond a year, but she now admitted she loved him dearly and completely, giving herself fully to new emotions. Charlie confided that his dreams of Addie were "Angel Visits." Addie teased back, concerned by his Angel Visits and coyly wondering what he thought his to her must be but reminding him that he needed to tell her honestly about his health. The presentiment dreams were never far from her mind and memories of the "ugly dream" lingered even in the new spring of passionate feelings, so fresh and unaccustomed in her life. Dreaming turned to a charming metaphor in a gushing letter of love written in March 1862:

> What can be more lovely than this day, warm as the summer days generally are and the more beautiful because it is March. Can you see me, Charlie sitting here on the root of a maple tree about two feet above the little brook that is south of Auntie's house? Here I have been sitting dreaming and listening to the babbling of the little stream till it sounded like sweet music and then commenced talking … of absent loved ones. occasionally looking at the sun that is peeping through the soft haze which envelopes it. until—well something struck me. the thought that I would go to the house and get my writing desk…. Here I can sit and dream for hours. with no companion but the little birds that are even now singing among the not leafy but leafless boughs above my head. And of what am I dreaming. do you ask? Of what could I be dreaming save my Charlie? It does seem like "fairy land" wonder if I could not see their footprints up on the hill. How I wish I was an artist would not I draw some grand sketches.

Addie was now a teacher, having successfully attained a position in East Clarendon. She joyfully wrote about her students, and Charlie responded with his own imaginable vision, in which he saw Addie reading the Bible to her students. She confirmed his vision, telling him she would not be worthy of the name of teacher "if I could not open my school with a chapter from God's Holy Book. I also have my scholars learn a verse from some portion of the Bible, which they may choose and repeat just before the close of school." In such imaginative conversations with Charlie, invitations for him to visit her kept him alive in a beautiful reality where there was no danger.

Imagination was an antidote to horrific dreams as well as Addie's ally for healing. In a letter from East Clarendon, she described a blinding migraine alleviated in an imaginable trip into the next room where a young student sat at the piano, playing and singing. She told Charlie that this gift of using the imagination for healing was easily accessed. Using a motif common in Civil War letter exchanges, Addie asked Charlie to come with her in his imagination: "Listen to those sweet strains…. How quickly will music draw the heart to its gentle accents. What language is in music…. [I]t is the influence of that gentle music … to have it sound more like the chanting of angels than like the effect of a human being's voice and hands." She embraced the music and allowed it to flow through her mind and body, momentarily clearing her mind from fear for Charlie's life and allowing the sweet sounds to soothe her head. Addie invited Charlie to see the splendid spring days and sunshine, shared pet names that he could call her and asked him to bask in a beautiful day with a grandness that could drive away "Hamlet's ghost" and restore her half-sick soul that embraced sweet dreams but started at horrific ones.[22]

In late April 1862, Charlie caught a severe cold that settled in his lungs. He could not recognize that this was the beginning of his waking manifestation of Addie's nightmares, which still haunted her with urgency and intensity. Addie addressed herself in the third person in a May 26 letter, speaking to "one lonely being" in solitude in her school room, but not peaceful solitude, "alone to those torturing thoughts which cling to her sleeping or waking." Addie's thoughts dwelled on her powerful and disturbing February 19 dream of Charlie's death. She loved him wholly and passionately, and the waking reality of such a dream and the accompanying feelings of the painful truth around her heart of what her nights had so clearly pronounced was almost more than she could bear:

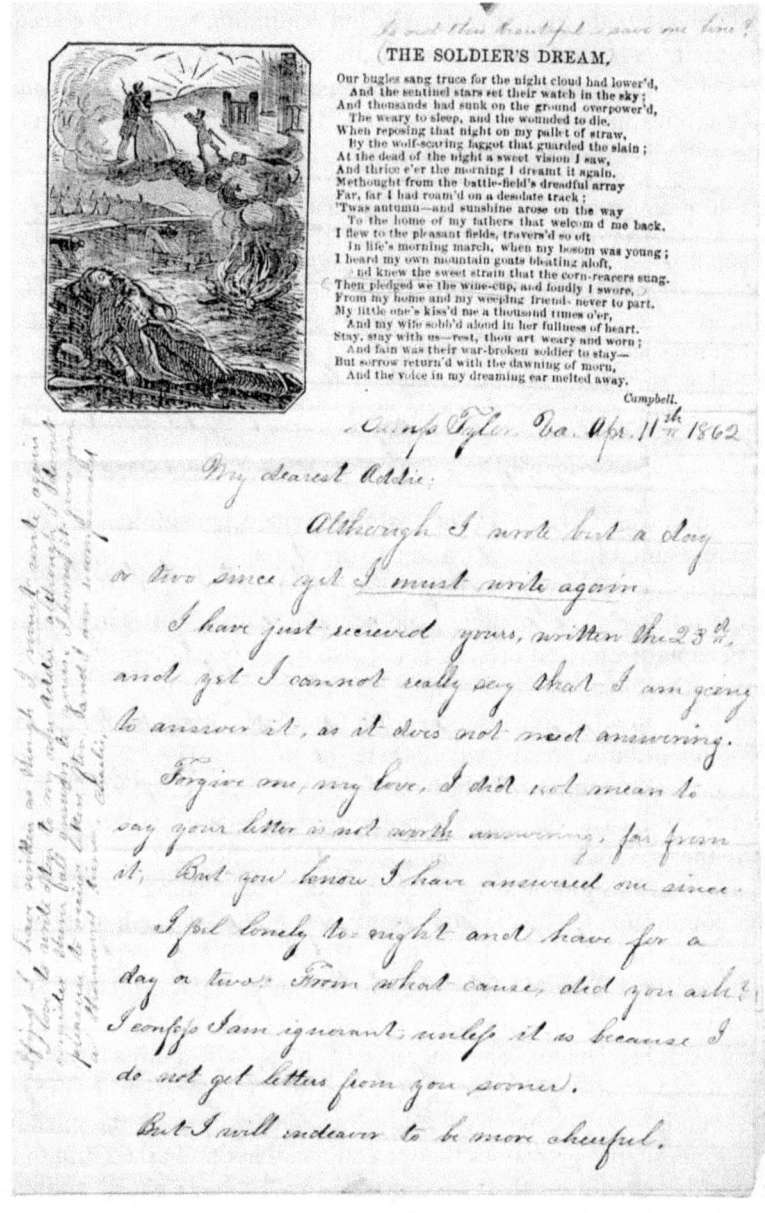

The poem "The Soldier's Dream" was used as letterhead in Charlie Tenney's April 11, 1862, letter to Adelaide Case. Charlie placed parentheses around the title of the poem and wrote above it: "Is not this beautiful—save one line?" The "one line" was "Then pledged we the wine-cup; and fondly I swore…" (Special Collections, University of Virginia Library).

I will never write that thought. If I did I should feel every letter sinking into my heart as if written with a pen of fire.... The thoughts while waking are not enough to torture my poor heart but dreams. frightful dreams! Oh I can not think of them, If the cruel monster *Death*—My God *must* I write it has done his work. why do I not know it for then yes then. I might die. Die! Ah. what is death to this fearful suspense. It is nought.... Here again I am thinking that it must be so. just as my dreams picture to me. and not only thinking but writing it.... Is this madness? or is it caused by that dark yet at times sharp pain around my heart.[23]

Charlie boldly asked Addie's father for her hand. Her father had been enthusiastic. Charlie experienced a brief remission from his illness and a more lasting peace brought through Addie's enthusiastically loving letters. He shared his own dream, asking her if she thought it funny:

Speaking of "kisses" reminds me of my dream last night. My bed was very hard and I was quite restless, and I had just sunk into a troubled sleep when I felt a soft hand upon my forehead. I instantly awoke, the room—it was a pretty chamber—was light, but no one was to be seen. I hastily attired myself, and the light expired. I then lay down upon my bed and closed my eyes in deep thought. Scarcely had I done so, when I felt that same soft, warm hand on my forehead. Upon opening my eyes, the light was again burning, but again no one was to be seen. As I peered around in a sort of dreamy wonder I saw a curtain at the opposite end of the room move slightly, and heard an eager though suppressed breathing. Advancing, I drew the curtain aside, and entered.—I came—I saw—I—threw my arms around your lovely form, and pressed your ruby lips to mine.—and I jumped nearly out of the tent, treading on someone's toes in the operations. I had turned partly over and hit the tent, and a great big bug fell upon my nose—but I feel that loving kiss still—so warm and genial.

Charlie enclosed a flower for Addie. She accepted the flower and teased him about his dream vision of her placing her hand on his forehead, grateful for a dream that felt more passionate than alarming.

It would be difficult to speculate whether Addie recognized this dream as foreboding as her own in his vision of her as a comforting angel in a dreamy light where no one else could be seen, perhaps easily a vision mirroring her dream of his last days in a hospital bed: "Your dream! Oh, how funny! Are you often troubled with such dreadful visions I fear I shall have to prescribe something to make you rest better. I may possibly report you to head quarters. Would not your officers tell you that soldiers had no right to indulge in such dreams?"[24]

Charlie wrote to Addie that he had survived the battlefield. Addie accepted this news with joy, which she admitted was something of a respite from her anxiety, but her dreams of danger for Charlie were not about surviving battle. She felt he was safe on the battlefield. She asked him why he thought it was so easy to feel the angst of dangerous dreams and not the same sensation of joy when there was a presaging of safety. The simple response, she astutely determined, was that the battlefield was not the source of her presentiment of danger; it was of something she did not yet fully understand. She reminded him that, even in joy, she was still gripped with fear for his life: "You will wonder perhaps when I tell you that I had not entertained such ... fears in regard to your safety as formerly specially about the line of the battles.... [S]omething seemed to me so confidently "Your Charlie is safe" that I would not doubt. Indeed dearest Charlie I felt more glad today ... [but] these strange emotions are not caused by the possibility of your being in danger. How strange it is that we are not so willing to listen to the voice of fear as we are to that of safety. I have been trying all day to dispute these dismal thoughts but have not succeeded."[25]

Addie reminded Charlie (in September 1862) that even though she often went into mindless daydreams in which she imagined she and Charlie happily together and was buoyed by his pictures of delightful dreams for their future—and that even though she indulged in "naughty" dreams in which everything in his life except his love for her receded—they were nothing to the heart pain of her feelings of danger concerning his health. She now named "health" as the image of her dire dream prediction, reminding him again that her nightmare had been of illness and not battlefield danger.

In October 1862 Charlie's regiment moved into Harpers Ferry. Charlie felt depressed but expressed a resolve to cheer up with the help of "an hours conversation with my treasure." He carried Addie's portrait as surrogate interlocutor, asking her to sit down on his loving couch beside him. Left behind as his regiment decamped, Charlie was under physician's orders to rest so he could overcome an unspecified ailment. He then invited Addie to a word tour of two hospitals where his injured comrades received treatment, an eerie step into Addie's fearful dreams of Charlie's death:

> Shall we visit the Hospital? Here we are, in the village of Harper's Ferry, and in the Hospital. That laughing chunk of a boy is Billy Bennett ... [and] he is caring for Ambrose Trimmer. He has the fever. Frederick Roberts is here too, not very sick, *but not do*ing duty. Let us go to St. Pauls Church Hosp. Alexandria. Ah! Bob Murray is hopping around on crutches, but will never be fit for duty again. George Moore is here, not very well. He can't keep quiet long enough to get well. He sends love—brotherly love he says, for he is my brother. You do not know the rest, so we will just see that they are doing well, and will walk home. Here we are just at the door, now a parting loving kiss, and "farewell for the present."[26]

Charlie concluded by asking Addie to dream of him, and to write often.

His new appointment, as clerk at the provost marshal's office in Harpers Ferry, kept him away from the battlefield; but he shared that the illness mentioned earlier was more serious than he had revealed. He self diagnosed his illness as a liver complaint and warned Addie that if he could get a furlough she would find him thin and weak. He assured her on November 25 that he was in good health and was "neither dead nor changed" and that there was no "immediate danger of my demise nor consignment to the hospital" (the same hospital revealed in his imaginary invitation). He expressed his deep love and desire to "fold thee to my heart and gaze into those loving eyes—the windows of thy noble soul ... to hear thy gentle voice as it in accents full of love and tenderness, thou sayest "I love you. But the splash of the rain falls upon my ear and I am 'far away.'—the pleasure is denied me. and I still toil on—a soldier in the good cause." He closed the letter with a sentiment of love and a wish for "pleasant dreams ... and happiness."[27]

Addie received letters on December, 15, 18, 19, and 28 on Charlie's deteriorating health and a relapse. She returned letters of wrenching urgency, describing the intensity of her intuitive fears: "And for several days previous to this those same sad thoughts those—I am almost tempted to say unwelcome forebodings have lingered about my heart. at times [I am] so very depressed in spirit as to not care whether life or death were near. and at other times the warm tears would gush forth in torrents, and still I would not know for what I wept."[28]

In anguish she read all his old letters and urgently proclaimed her deep and abiding love—and fear. Her fears were desperate, and her letters answered his every few days. She prayed feverishly that God would provide strangers that would care for him tenderly. On December 31, fearing the worst, she wrote that Charlie's love had sustained her through the year, through her sadness and through her country's sadness. Charlie had repeated his marriage proposal and Addie had accepted, writing of her father's weeping

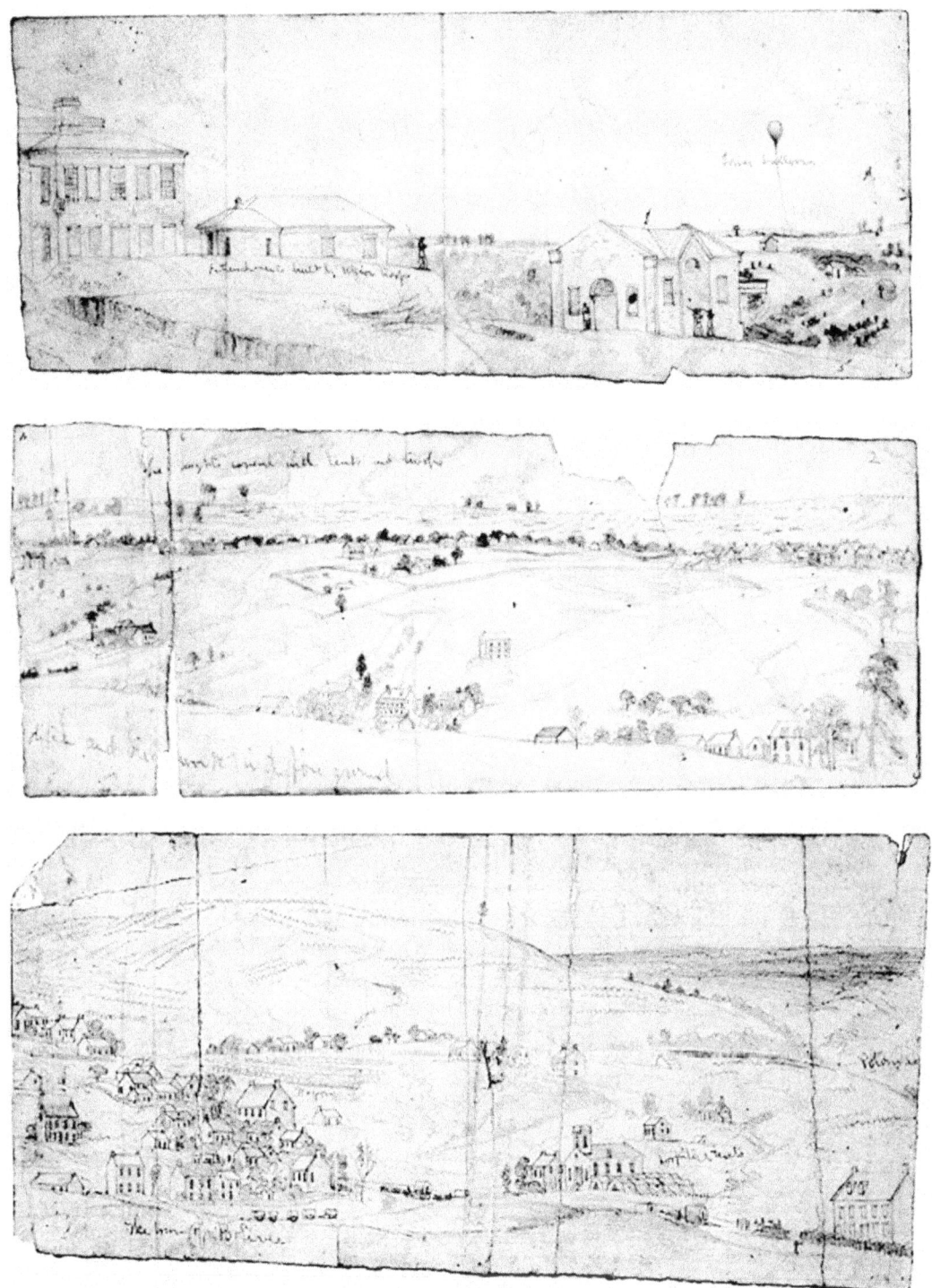

View of the camps of the Army of the Potomac, on Bolivar Heights, near Harper's Ferry, after the battle of Antietam, by Edwin Forbes. The third panel of the three-panel drawing depicted St. John's Church in Harpers Ferry, West Virginia. The church was used as a war hospital during the Civil War fighting in Harpers Ferry, and Charles Tenney died there in the late hours of January 14, 1863. Addie Case's dream report in a letter crossed paths with Charles's death date at the Lutheran church turned hospital (Library of Congress, LC-DIG-ppmsca-22553).

Detail of St. John's Church at Bolivar Heights from *View of the camps of the Army of the Potomac, on Bolivar Heights, near Harper's Ferry, after the battle of Antietam*, by Edwin Forbes (Library of Congress, LC-DIG-ppmsca-22553).

with joy. But her own joy was hostage to her dreams, and she trembled with fear. She hoped for a much-promised furlough that would bring him home to her where she could tend to his health and avert the fate of her fearful dreams.

Addie penned a final letter to Charlie on January 15, 1863:

> In my dreams I was with you last night. I went to sleep wishing that I could fly to you. I had no sooner fallen into a gentle slumber than I was lifted from my bed and wafted far far away, over mountains, hills, rivers, cities and towns, on on till at last I found myself in a dark comfortless room surrounded by men. Some were lying on rough beds, others walking around as if tired of life and wished to walk into eternity. Upon inquiring I was told that I was in a hospital and that those frightful objects were dear brave soldiers. Mentally, I asked if Charlie was there and began searching. Earnestly I gazed in each face hoping to see one familiar glance one *loving* one, but vainly until I looked in one corner and noticed a rude couch of straw accompanied by *my Charlie*. It needed no second glance to convince me, besides over it bent kind Seth Coon, his face animated and his blue-eyes burning with joy as he asked, "Have you come. I flew to thee darling and awoke kissing."

In this, her final dream of Charlie, in dream flight, Addie found herself in the hospital in Bolivar Heights, Harpers Ferry, West Virginia, where Charlie had led her earlier in what he had perceived to be a fanciful visit. She saw the dead and dying soldiers rising from their beds and wandering tired and confused. In searching for Charlie, she was gifted one last glance and a surprised, "Have you come?" Addie's dream visit occurred,

St. John's Church, Bolivar Heights, 2015. Both the church and the building to the left appear in Edwin Forbes' 1862 drawing (courtesy Ronald Burch).

more than likely, near the very moment of his death. Charles Tenney had died at the Lutheran church, which was used as a war hospital in Bolivar Heights above Harpers Ferry in the late hours of January 14, 1863—her dream and his death crossing paths. Addie's letter of January 15 was the fateful conclusion of her year of terrifying "presentiment" and accurate dreaming of his death, not on a battlefield but in a hospital.[29]

Chapter 16

Soldier's Heart

Old War-Dreams
by Walt Whitman

In midnight sleep of many a face of anguish,
Of the look at first of the mortally wounded, (of that indescribable look,)
Of the dead on their backs with arms extended wide,
I dream, I dream, I dream.
Of scenes of Nature, fields and mountains,
Of skies so beauteous after a storm, and at night the moon so
unearthly bright,
Shining sweetly, shining down, where we dig the trenches and
gather the heaps,
I dream, I dream, I dream.
Long have they pass'd, faces and trenches and fields,
Where through the carnage I moved with a callous composure, or away
from the fallen,
Onward I sped at the time—but now of their forms at night,
I dream, I dream, I dream.[1]

J.R.R. Tolkien wrote as follows in *The Lord of the Rings*:

"Do you remember that bit of rabbit, Mr. Frodo?" he said. "And our place under the warm bank in Captain Faramir's country, the day I saw an oliphaunt?"

"No, I am afraid not, Sam," said Frodo. "At least, I know that such things happened, but I cannot see them. No taste of food, no feel of water, no sound of wind, no memory of tree or grass or flower, no image of moon or star are left to me. I am naked in the dark, Sam, and there is no veil between me and the wheel of fire. I begin to see it even with my waking eyes, and all else fades...."

[Frodo] stood stern, untouchable now by pity, a figure robed in white, but at its breast it held a wheel of fire.

As memory of life's simple wonders diminished in Frodo's mind, he also lost the capacity for pity.

Mark Huber, a Vietnam War combat veteran felt that Tolkien, a combat veteran of the "Great War," experienced these feelings himself and saw them at work in others who had experienced war. He said that veterans of all wars come home "naked in the dark." The important piece is whether or not dreams of home do or do not become nightmares after the war and whether or not those dreams help the war veterans manage their lives when they are home again. Mark Huber asked questions difficult to answer about those in the Civil War whose lives became a closed book once the war ended and the letters and diaries were packed away. The genuine love and emotional release of the dreams in the Civil War letters touched Mark's heart and he couldn't help but speculate on whether those soldiers in the South who lost their war had feelings close to his own of having lost *his* war in Vietnam. Did the Confederate soldier whose feelings of a noble cause turned to dust leave him standing alone with nothing left but anger at the human loss "expended in vain" for the wrong cause?[2]

The simple answer would be "yes." Those same emotions were evident in the letters of men writing from the battlefields of the Civil War. The Confederate soldier first believed his war would be over in just days or possibly months and believed his cause to be, as Huber says, "noble." As months wore on, as homesickness burned like "fire in the bones," letters contained more brutal descriptions of lost lives, disease, and comments more jaded about the noble cause. Details on loss of life and maiming became normal and then just daily activity, accompanied by expressions of relief that the writer was either still alive or had escaped being wounded. Seeing lifeless bodies or, worse, scattered limbs on the battlefield, was recorded among mundane sentences describing the weather or the need for better food or clothing.

How to separate the warrior from the war in the return home has been a dilemma since the beginning of time. Posttraumatic stress is not new; its name has simply shifted in terminology and definition through the years. From the first armed conflict when a human picked up the first weapon against another human, when dreams of home became barren and turned into nightmares and when events took on a terrifying life inside the mind, the words describing the resulting desperate mental state changed but the condition did not.

In America's Civil War it was known as Da Costa's syndrome or "soldier's heart," based on symptoms of anxiety and fatigue studied and recorded by Dr. Jacob Da Costa between 1864 and 1868. Soldiers in that war wrote about nostalgia and homesickness that burned through men's souls until they could no longer recognize what was a battlefield and who was their enemy. Other names in more recent wars have been combat fatigue (World War I), shell shock, battle fatigue, gross stress reaction (World War II), post–Vietnam syndrome, and, today, posttraumatic stress (PTS), and military sexual trauma (MST), mainly found among female soldiers. PTS and MST, when symptoms become life-defining, fall within a current term framed as posttraumatic stress disorder (PTSD), a term first used in the American Psychiatric Association's diagnostic manual beginning in 1980 and associated most strongly in America with the wars in Iraq and Afghanistan. More than 20 percent of returning forces suffer from PTSD, the numbers staggering since the Iraq and Afghanistan conflicts. Suicide and homelessness among both male and female soldiers returning from today's wars is three times the numbers among the civilian population. PTSD symptoms include a vast host of terms, to name just a few, from disorientation and depression to nightmares, night-terrors, flashbacks and the weight of unresolved moral dilemmas. If posttraumatic stress becomes life consuming—when the soul loss and self-hatred become daily and even moment-by-moment challenges, when suicide seems a solution, and when the ordinary person on the street looks like an enemy—then it becomes more and more difficult to safely become members of a home community. The soldiers who face good and evil, test the humanity of mind and heart, and experience grief and fear must then live day and night with those emotions in a world that feels strange and ordinary in comparison. In order to heal, the warriors must find a way to place the war in a safe compartment of memory and experience so they can return home with mind, body, and soul intact.

According to a study completed by Judith Pizarro, along with Drs. Roxane Silver and JoAnn Prause, nearly two in five Civil War veterans developed both mental and physical ailments such as those recorded by Da Costa. The study also found that soldiers who enlisted between the ages of nine and seventeen were nearly twice as likely to suffer these ills. Numbers rose for those who witnessed death, handled dead bodies, and lost comrades, likely from their home communities since members of the same communities joined and fought together.

In describing her personal interest in Civil War trauma, Judith responded, "My great-grandfathers on both sides were both Union Veterans." Her mother's grandfather was incarcerated in a Confederate prison camp; her father's grandfather was a seventeen-year-old soldier who was in Sherman's "March to the Sea." Her mother's grandfather became an alcoholic, and, according to Judith, set off three generations ("so far") of alcoholism. Her father's grandfather deserted her great-grandmother as a result of PTSD caused from what he witnessed in Sherman's march. Her great-grandmother raised her family and her sister on her own, and her anger evolved into constant harangues on the worthlessness and untrustworthiness of men. She developed anxiety disorders and migraines that affected the entire family.

Research for their paper was not easy, since the term PTSD is a modern one. Health history was gathered from pension files, and the authors used the *International Classification of Diseases* (9th revision) for the classifications of ailments. To receive a military pension, veterans were required to undergo a physical examination for each illness or disease claim. A veteran, if diagnosed, was classified as having signs of heart disease or some form of nervous disorder. Also classified were ailments such as diarrhea, pain, vomiting blood and other similar conditions—or a general category of digestive problems.

Missing in the study were the personal comments from soldiers' letters, a daunting task since every letter written shared stories of personal loss, death, nightmarish descriptions of battles and human trauma and stories of lives turned upside down when the men came home and were no longer who they were when they left. Many, like those in Judith's ancestral story, abandoned wives and families. Some men shared stories of returned comrades attempting to harm themselves or their families in their sleep or, waking, unable to leave the battlefield.

One of the conclusions of the Pizarro, Silver, and Prause research was that the Civil War was the beginning of the recognition of mental health problems caused by war and was the event that lay the groundwork for modern cardiology. For "soldier's heart" there is now a diagnosis. But a safe place for returning the soldier home is still needed when the dream of hope becomes a violent nightmare of battles and trauma played again and again in the head and heart.[3]

In her thesis, "A Question of Life or Death: Suicide and Survival in the Union Army," Kathleen Logothetis took on the grueling task of looking for the soldiers' own words in Civil War letters and memoirs. The phrases that stood out were "the blues," "lonesome," "disheartened," "downhearted," "discouraged," "demoralized," "nervous," "played out," "used up," "anxious," "worn down," "worn out," "depressed," "rattled," "dispirited," "sad," "melancholy," and "badly blown" to describe what they were feeling, stemming from a variety of causes. "The blues" could result from the boredom of camp, disease, separation from home, inclement weather and sometimes battle. Melancholia, nostalgia, and homesickness were terms used for continuing mental deterioration. Kathleen noted that cavalryman

Henry C. Meyer referred to feeling blue several times in his memoirs: "We all felt rather blue over the loss of comrades in the affair the night before, which had seemed to us so needless." Also, after an engagement at Aldie he said, "That night was rather a blue time for us."

Logothetis found that "demoralized" and "rattled" were most often used when describing the mental collapse of an individual or group, while "badly blown" referred primarily to physical collapse and only sometimes to mental issues. She looked for specific symptoms today associated with posttraumatic stress disorder such as flashbacks and nightmares and found the references that follow. James O. Churchill wrote that he would be haunted by a recurring nightmare about his Civil War service: "I would be in battle and charge to the mouth of a cannon, when it would fire and I would be blown to pieces." Albert Frank, fighting around Bermuda Hundred near Richmond, Virginia, offered the man next to him a drink from the canteen around his neck and the other soldier was decapitated by a shell at that moment: "That night Frank began to act strangely, running over the breastworks toward the enemy where his fellow soldiers found him huddled, and making shell sounds followed by saying 'Frank is killed.'" His comrades had to restrain him and sent him to a hospital in Washington as a case of insanity.

On the battlefield, Kathleen noted, soldiers sometimes "took their removal from combat into their own hands, straggling behind, helping a wounded comrade to the rear, or resorting to the more extreme actions of mutiny or self-mutilation." Desertion was another way of self-removal when the men could no longer manage stress.[4] Elisha Rhodes wrote, "Nothing but drill and guard duty. Even the late battle has become an old story. Some of our men actually became crazy from the excitement. I have recovered my strength and feel that I could make another campaign without much trouble." That journal entry was in 1861. In 1864 he wrote that one of the men had taken "sick and showed some signs of insanity." Some of the men tried to hold him but he broke away from them and tried to tear at Elisha's uniform. Elisha secured him and, in an investigation, found that he had been discharged from the Rhode Island Volunteers for insanity.[5]

John Dooley wrote about those who went insane—using a common Civil War journal term, "mania-potu"[6]—and revealed that opium was Johnson Island Prison's drug of choice to quiet these men. He wrote that one man saw his wife and child dying horrible deaths, the child from drowning and his wife from grief over the loss of the child. This imagined scene may or may not have come from actual news of the wife and child. In his imagination the man placed the bodies in a coffin, held a large funeral, "moaning and roaring ... [and] now he stands up and beats his fist & head against the wall.... They put a straight jacket on him and drug him to sleep." This, at least temporarily, calmed the man. Another was tormented by "innumerable little blue devils and is continually employed in repulsing their legions with the open bible, sometimes he reads a verse or several to them and cries out most fiercely "do ye hear that ye devils?" Another tried to throw himself "from the third story into the yard as a brother soldier of his actually succeeded in doing last week, dying instantly."[7]

In 1864 John related the case of a soldier named Polston who was so starved he had been hanging around the "ash-pile" (garbage heap) taking dry bones and scraps from bowls. John Dooley's group tried to help him by giving him food in return for small services around their tent. In February, the man came inside, sat down and cried, telling the men that everyone, even those who had been his friends, had turned against him. They tried to assure him this was not so. Shortly after that incident John wrote, "Polston is a complete *maniac*, his mind being wrecked by his real and even imaginary sufferings; poor fellow! He is taken to the hospital and cared for, *at least* is not allowed to go at large. This is the only case of mental derangement from want of food that has come under my observation, altho I perceive it is not by any means the only one that has happened."[8]

In a brief stay at the Marine Hospital in New Orleans, Frank Griffith wrote home to his wife, Thankful: "There was a man died here in this ward yesterday of the Typhoid fever. He had worm fits [convulsions] too, I think that he choked to death. There is another one that has got it in here and he is crazy he gets up on his bed and thinks it is a horse and will make some of the funniest speeches, but I do not think he will get well."[9]

Dreams of home offered hope and a touch of normalcy that in waking reality brought some of the soldiers home safely through battles and scenes of trauma intact and even through the worst of prison conditions. But when dreams became nightmares, management of life on either side of sleep became almost unbearable. McElroy described surviving Andersonville by dreaming himself nightly into a childhood scene of tables of food spread before him in an elegant inn in St. Louis. He wrote that his dream was one of survival; he also wrote that other men dreamed of food and went crazy.

A Healing Reflection: Passing in Review and the Long Walk Home

Major General Joshua Chamberlain of the Maine Volunteers was given the honor of commanding the Union troops at the surrender ceremony for the infantry of Robert E. Lee's army as they passed in surrender through the "peaceful gauntlet" in April 1865. Chamberlain offered this opportunity as a challenge to "become as good Americans as any of the Northerners.... Brave men ... may become good friends." The Confederates continued their march down the road to the dissolution of the line, brigade after brigade, Chamberlain naming each one. The surrender was over hours later; 27,000 paroles were passed out; the war was over. But, Chamberlain asked, was it really over? He said, "A strange and somber shadow rose up ghost-like from the haunts of memory or habit, and rested down over the final parting scene. How strong are these ties of habit! How strange the undertone of sadness even at the release from prison and from pain! It seems as if we had put some precious part of ourselves there which we are loath to leave."[10]

If a soldier survived the experience of a Civil War prison, do we know how he came to healing? In many cases we do not because journal entries and letters ceased when the soldier returned home. Home and work must have been the healing path for most of them. Talking about the experience in gatherings of old friends and comrades helped turn the events to memories as it does now. Many might have experienced healing in the long walk home after mustering out of their regiments or being released from prison. Soldiers were exhausted, possibly suffering from disabilities or disease, and had little or no money or resources for traveling home. Some had enough money for trains or water transportation for part of the trip home, but many walked home over the same battlefields where they fought and where others fought and died. Like today's soldiers who make journeys back to fields of war, Civil War veterans might have looked at the landscapes of war and found a sort of forgiveness, tinged with great sadness, and a figurative window to healing. One example of this was William Oake.

William Oake, born in England, was recruited into the 26th Iowa Volunteers in

Clinton County, Iowa, where his family moved in 1852. He miraculously survived the entire war, having participated in skirmishes and battles across the full spectrum of the Civil War playing field. He was wounded, incarcerated in a Vicksburg jail and served time in Libby Prison before being exchanged. He witnessed fellow soldiers go insane, as well as the insanity of citizens driven crazy by the war. An honorable soldier, he abhorred scenes of senseless destruction of property and burning cities and wrote about the horrific scenes he witnessed in the final days of Sherman's march. He wrote a heart-wrenching story of a Southern woman screaming and tearing her hair in the street as shells fell around her city.

William Oake left Washington after being mustered out and began the long trek home, revisiting scenes across the landscape, pausing to reflect and possibly begin the long road to healing. It is possible that healing comes more quickly when the road home is slower. Oake made one last visit to Libby Prison, where he spent "so many days in the summer of 1863." He stood in the empty spaces and "thought if its gloomy walls could talk what tales of suffering and misery it could unfold. As I cast my eyes around the room in which I was confined, I thought I could again see the still and quiet form of some comrade lying with some old rags thrown over him, waiting to be carried to his last resting place."[11] This was sad reflection on a horrible experience, but revisiting the place, the portal to such pain, might have been a step, unconsidered in those times, to healing the mind and the body.

CHAPTER 17

Slavery

*A dream that rests heavy on your mind
is a visitation of the spirit.* —Ophelia Jemison

"A Dream of Deception and Eventually Freedom"

Thousands of pages would be needed to chronicle the experience of slavery in America. Slavery existed, of course, in America long before the Civil War, and the desire of slaves for freedom beat in their hearts from the beginning. The stories of those free people who were kidnapped and sold into slavery before emancipation and the stories of those who escaped from the south into the north after the northern states abolished slavery were told and retold long before the Emancipation Proclamation. One of those was the story of Frederick Douglass.

Frederick Douglass was born into slavery in Talbot County, Maryland, circa the winter of 1818, and named for his mother, Frederick Augustus Washington Bailey. He took the surname Douglass and became a recognized and respected African-American social reformer, orator, writer, and statesman. Frederick escaped slavery in 1838 by a 24-hour route that took him from a train at Havre de Grace, Maryland, to the Susquehanna River by ferry, by train to Wilmington, Delaware, by steamboat to "Quaker City" in Philadelphia, Pennsylvania, and finally to a safe house, the home of David Ruggles in New York. Douglass became a leader of the abolition movement and well known for his speaking and writing, which included several versions of his autobiography. Dreams played a role in Douglass's oratory in the dreamed desire for freedom and respect but they also played a role in the night dreams of escape and freedom.

In his autobiography, *The Life and Times of Frederick Douglass*, he spoke of early planning and dreaming of freedom with the collaboration of a man called "Sandy," whom he called "the root man." Sandy shared with Douglass what he called "distressing" dreams, one of them dreamed on a Friday night:

> "I dreamed last night that I was roused from sleep by strange noises, like the noises of a swarm of angry birds that caused as they passed, a roar which fell upon my ear like a coming gale over the tops of the trees. Looking up to see what it could mean, I saw you, Frederick, in the claws of a huge bird, surrounded by a large number of birds of all colors and sizes. These were all pecking at you, while you, with your arms, seemed to be trying to protect your eyes. Passing over me, the birds flew in a southwesterly direction, and I watched them until they were clean out of sight. Now I saw this as plainly as I now see you; and furder, honey, watch de Friday night dream; dere is sumpon in it shose you born; dere is indeed, honey." Sandy did not like the dream but attributed it to the general excitement over their plan to escape. But he could not shake its effect. "I felt that it boded no good." Sandy was

unusually emphatic and oracular and his manner had much to do with the impression made upon me.[1]

Sandy's dream still in mind, Frederick and five other men tried their escape and found themselves captured and bound together, on their way to prison. Frederick saw this as the fulfillment of Sandy's dream. He was in the hands of "moral vultures and held in their sharp talons" being carried toward Easton. As the day unfolded, Frederick and his companions were taken to St. Michaels to his master's store, where they were questioned. They denied that they had intended flight. There had been the appearance that they were at their work. As the story unfolded Frederick realized someone had betrayed them and that person had to be Sandy. He also realized Sandy had created and used the dream of betrayal both as a covert warning and as a device in the betrayal.[2]

The men were dragged behind horses for fifteen miles and placed in the Easton jail. That was Frederick's first attempt to escape, in 1837. His second was more successful. In his narrative he wrote that his free life began on September 3, 1838. After what seemed an uncannily easy 24-hour journey that took him to freedom, he stood in New York, dazzled: "For the moment the dreams of my youth and the hopes of my manhood were completely fulfilled. The bonds that had held me to 'old master' were broken. No man now had a right to call me his slave or assert mastery over me.... A new world had opened upon me. If life is more than breath, and the 'quick round of blood,' I lived more in one day than in a year of my slave life. It was a time of joyous excitement which words can but tamely describe."[3]

He compared the life dream of freedom to the sleep dreams of his childhood when his "strange dreams of travel" led him to famous places where he heard men speak and saw great sights. In his youthful night dreams, seemingly fantasy, he had traveled to England and France. After his escape he found himself inside the reality of those dreams. He went to Paris, visited art galleries, saw Egypt and stood on the summit of the pyramids, walked among the ruins of ancient Memphis, sailed the Nile, visited the Temple of Wingless Victory, and so many other places he both dreamed and never dreamed.[4]

Frederick Douglass was free. The dreams of his childhood were fulfilled. The dreams of his betrayer crumbled to dust.

"I was again in Saratoga": Solomon Northup

The story—living as a free man but kidnapped, brought to the slave pens (in Solomon Northup's case, those at Washington, D.C.), sold as a slave, secreted into the south to the cotton and cane plantations, buried in obscurity carrying a name forced upon him, which further disguised his true origin as a free man—is familiar to everyone. It predated the Civil War but was an important part of the history of the Civil War. Solomon managed to become free, though, before he died.

Never giving up hope of seeing home and family again, Solomon dreamed dreams of freedom. When sleep came even through deprivation, through torture and pain, through wounds from being beaten and starved, through continual thirst gnawing at his insides, through heartsickness and discouragment, he dreamed: "I was again in Saratoga—[and dreamed] that I could see their faces, and hear their voices calling me. Awakening from the pleasant phantasma of sleep to the bitter realities around me, I could but groan and weep. Still my spirit was not broken. I indulged the anticipation of escape."[5] These dreams were twelve years becoming Solomon's waking reality again; but the homecoming, when it occurred, was the most joyous moment of his life.

Harriet Tubman: Dreams and the Underground Railroad

Harriet Tubman (born in slavery as Araminta Ross and later taking her mother's name, Harriet) has been described as a "Moses" of her people, a "Conductor" on the Underground Railroad and "Moll Pitcher," a reference to her energy and daring. She was a touchstone for those around her and all who came after her, living and dying for the freedom of enslaved people. Dreams guided and restored Harriet. She could fly like a bird in her dreams and gain insight to landscapes that were pivotal maps for the journeys to freedom. Visions and dreams, acting in unison, provided accurate and valuable foresight of situations on the road to freedom. If not heeded, Harriet's work to set men, women, and children free could have been halted, lives would have ended, and the cause of freedom would have been compromised. When Harriet felt danger, her heart would "go flutter flutter," a gift she inherited from her father, who could sense danger, predict weather and "saw" great political events such as the Mexican war.[6]

Suffering a terrible blow to the head at the age of twelve when she was hired out by her master to a cruel overseer, Harriet developed a condition Sarah Bradford, her chosen biographer, called a "state of somnolency," which made waking difficult. In this condition she would see her spirit leave her body and visit other scenes and places, "not only in this world, but also in the world of spirits."[7]

As a relief from terror and pain, Harriet prayed for a change of heart for her master. Failing that, she prayed for his death. *That* prayer was granted, and the result was that all his slaves were sold. Harriet saw a vision of a situation that was even worse for herself. Waking up in terror, she saw the "horsemen coming and heard the screams of terrified women and children," all the time seeing a bright glowing hope: "I seemed to see a line, and on the other side of that line were green fields, and lovely flowers, and beautiful white ladies, who stretched out their arms to me over the line, but ... I always fell before I reached that line."[8]

In a pivotal moment for both Harriet and all those whose freedom she implemented, Harriet walked out of the gate of the plantation singing and just kept walking, looking back only once. Her frightened family did not follow her and she went not knowing where she was going, following the north star to liberty. She crossed her visionary "line" from bondage to freedom, looking at her hands for reassurance that she, in her new state of freedom, was still the same person, still in the same ordinary reality as when she began walking. Bradford recorded her words on crossing the "line": "There was such a glory over everything; the sun came like gold through the trees, and over the fields, and I felt like I was in Heaven [spelling corrected]."[9]

With honey came bitterness. Harriet was free but her family was not. Working for wages, saving money, and using the same unfailing guidance from visions and dreams, she retrieved her brothers and later, in 1857, her parents. She continued to return to free others, never considering the danger to herself. She used her deep, resonant voice in familiar call and response songs to announce her presence to slaves working in the fields. Harriet's dreams and visions never failed her. Mary Bradford wrote that no slave, to her knowledge, placed under Harriet's care was ever arrested.

Harriet had regular stopping places on her route, but one time she changed direction when God, in one of her "somnolent" visions, told her to stop. She asked God what she was supposed to do. God told her she needed to leave the road and turn left, so she did. She came to a small stream where there was no bridge or boat. The slaves in her care were reluctant to follow her into the tidewater stream, fearing they would be swept away. However, God was her guide and, trusting in the voice of that guide, she asked again what she was to do. The answer was that she was to cross. The month was March and the water was frigid. With determined confidence Harriet walked into the water, going deeper and deeper until the water came up under her armpits. The slaves, two men, were afraid to follow until they saw her reach safety on the opposite shore. Then they followed. They had to wade a second stream, and they followed her again. They "came to a cabin of colored people, who took them all in, put them to bed, and dried their clothes, ready to proceed the next night on their journey." Harriet had no money so she paid for their lodging with a gift of her underclothing. As if this part of the story had not been remarkable enough, the master of the two men she was taking to safety had put up a reward advertisement in the vicinity of where she would have originally traveled. By following a different path, as directed by her guide, Harriet led the men to safety.[10]

Harriet continued going back, making journeys of an arguable number that directly brought many to freedom, and indirectly many others, through her work with abolitionists. One of those abolitionists was John Brown, the Bible-wielding zealot of freedom. The two became friends, with an uncommon respect for one another. Because of her manly appearance and fierce disposition, John Brown called Harriet "General Tubman."

Harriet met John Brown first in a dream. She thought she was in a wilderness, full of rocks and bushes, when she "saw a serpent raise it head among the rocks, and as it did so, it became the head of an old man with a long white beard, gazing at her 'wishful like, jes as ef he war gwine to speak to me,' and then two other heads rose up beside him, younger than he." As she stood looking at this scene and wondering who they were and what they wanted, a crowd of men rushed in and killed the younger head and then the older head. Harriet dreamed this dream several times but did not understand it till she met John Brown and recognized him as the "wishful" head and his two sons as the younger heads. She was in New York when the affair at Harpers Ferry occurred, but her heart was fluttering and she knew danger was afoot. She read the events in the next day's news.[11]

Before the end of the Civil War, Harriet grew weary and impatient for a dreamed emancipation. When Lincoln finally signed the Emancipation Proclamation, she did not join in the festivities. Robert Moss wrote: "Lincoln's Emancipation Proclamation was celebrated near Beaufort, South Carolina, on January 1, 1863, with a flashy gathering in a grove of live oaks, with gray moss hanging low over the heads of black women in 'turbans' and black soldiers in wide crimson 'zouave' pants." Harriet said, "'I had my jubilee three years ago. I rejoiced all I could then; I can't rejoice no more.' In her portrait from this time, she is holding a rifle."[12] Harriet Tubman lived out the remainder of her life on a farm in Auburn, New York.

Mr. Sanborn, the secretary of the Massachusetts Board of State Charities, in an 1863 letter requesting reminiscences of Harriet Tubman, wrote: "I found her singularly truthful. Her imagination is warm and rich, and there is a whole region of the marvelous in her nature, which has manifested itself at times remarkably. Her dreams and visions, misgivings and forewarnings, ought not to be omitted in any life of her."[13]

Contraband

Freedom came slowly, even after President Lincoln signed the Emancipation Proclamation. In circumstances peculiar to the politics of slavery and the Civil War, the declaration of slaves as "contraband" brought more people to immediate freedom than any words or actions of abolitionists.

Cornelia Hancock, a nurse in the army hospitals near Gettysburg, Pennsylvania, until early September 1863, recorded the experience of individuals she treated in 1863 in the Contraband Hospital in Washington, D.C. Cornelia had visited family in Philadelphia and New Jersey and had left for Washington in late October, beginning her work at the Contraband Hospital in northwest Washington in November of that year.

She opened a November 1863 letter to an unknown correspondent with a nauseating description of conditions, hoping her words would be used to "affect you to some action." The sick were sent to the hospital from contraband camps in the northern part of Washington. The people "who have been made free by the progress of our Army" were first gathered, she wrote, "in an open, muddy mire': "Sickness is inevitable, and to meet it these rude hospitals, only rough wooden barracks, are in use—a place where there is so much to be done you need not remain idle. We average here one birth per day, and have no baby clothes except as we wrap them up in an old piece of muslin, *that* even being scarce. Now the army is advancing it is not uncommon to see from 40 to 50 arrivals in one day."

Cornelia said there was no clothing for these people. They came first to be vaccinated, but everyone came, the "cripples, diseased, aged, wounded, infirm, from whatsoever cause; all accidents happening to colored people in all employs around Washington are brought here. It is not uncommon for a colored driver to be pounded nearly to death by some of the white soldiers." She described a dreadful hernia case in a woman with three children. The woman was bone tired and had been on the road for a long time. Four of her children were still held in slavery. Her husband was dead. "When I first saw her she laid on the floor, leaning against a bed, her children crying around her. One child died almost immediately, the other two are still sick. She seemed to need most, food and rest, and those two comforts we gave her, but clothes she still wants.... Two little boys, one 3 years old, had his leg amputated above the knee the cause being his mother not being allowed to ride inside, became dizzy and dropped him. The other had his leg broken from the same cause."

Cornelia described a man and a woman without feet, which had been frozen and were amputated. Most of those arriving had terrible scars and weak eyes, and many had been branded. One notable example was a man who, determined to make sure the world knew what was happening, brought all the instruments of torture used on him and others from the plantation he had escaped:

> There were two very fine looking slaves arrived here form Louisiana, one of them had his master's name branded on his forehead, and with him he brought all the instruments of torture that he wore at different times during 39 years of very hard slavery. I will try to send you a Photograph of him he wore an iron collar with 3 prongs standing up so he could not lay down his head; then a contrivance to render one leg entirely stiff and a chain clanking behind him with a bar weighing 50 lbs. This he wore and worked all the time hard. At night they hung a little bell upon the prongs above his head so if he hid in any bushes it would tinkle and tell his whereabouts. The baton that was used to whip them he also had. It is so constructed that a little child could whip them till the blood streamed down their backs. This system of proceeding has been stopped in New Orleans and may God grant that it may

cease all over this boasted free land, but you may readily imagine what development such a system of treatment would bring them to.[14]

Dreams and Visions Recorded in WPA Slave Narratives

Slave narratives were the primary resource for recording personal experiences of antebellum African Americans who escaped from slavery and found their way to safety in the north. Some were autobiographical. Some, such as those written and published by Olaudah Equiano, Frederick Douglass and Solomon Northup, and many less well-known published in book or pamphlet form before 1865, influenced public opinion.[15] Between 1936 and 1938 more than 2,300 first-person accounts of slavery were collected as part of the Federal Writers' Project of the Works Progress Administration (WPA). These were assembled and microfilmed in 1941 in 17 volumes and are now available in an online collection as a joint presentation of the Manuscript and Prints and Photographs divisions of the Library of Congress. All citations listed as WPA interviews are available in that collection.[16]

WPA interviewers used a standardized set of questions designed to mine the childhood or young adult memory of former slaves, most at the time in their 70s and 80s or even older. The questions covered diverse topics ranging from living conditions to "signs" and religious beliefs. When asked specifically about dreams, few responded with specific dreams; but that response may have been more the fault of the interviewer who asked simply if they remembered dreams. The answer was generally "yes." Visions were addressed apart from dreams and would often reflect a memory of a funeral, seeing the dead, or, more often, "getting religion." It became apparent, after reading hundreds of interviews, that "getting religion" required a vision or direct communication or both with "the Lord." Slave owners encouraged Christianity as an antidote to "Hoodoo" and spiritual practices imported from Africa but—from fear of an uprising or a run for freedom—discouraged prayer meetings and large groups gathering for religious purposes.

Seeing the Dead

Oral dialogue between the interviewer and the former slave, sometimes a person without a name given or often with a name associated with the master's slave plantation, brought responses about "signs," spiritual experiences, or evocative imagery used to describe locations or places in time, as in this slave's description of the first train that came to Osceola: "It was built on a prairie, and you could see the reflection of it like the sun shining on it twelve miles away, because when we saw it coming it would be four hours from when we saw it before the train got into Osceola."[17] He told the interviewer he "was a young man when the stars fell ... [and] they just fell and went out before they hit the ground." Seeing death and the dead, not an unusual experience in his everyday life, elicited a calm notation that he waited on his master until the man died, when he "took sick ... inhaled the scent of his brother who was dead, and he took sick and died." That was "after freedom," when the former slave finally ceased to feel responsible for the white family who owned him.[18]

Signs, such as doves and owls or inhaling the "death" of another, were omens of death. Burials incorporated traditional African ritual. Lucinda Davis, of Tulsa, Oklahoma, the slave of a Creek Indian and his white wife, did not know where she was born but recalled that Creek was spoken in their home. She described Creek funerals, dances, and recipes and recalled building a fire when someone became ill and leaving it, even in the summer, until the person either became well or died. Then, at the burial, guns would be shot toward the four directions and the body would be placed in the grave with extra clothing, some food and maybe even a cup of coffee before being covered with strips of elm bark and dirt. When the last dirt was thrown on the grave, everybody clapped, smiled and made sure they did not step on the dirt or they would bring the sickness back to their own house. Then, in the gathering after the burial, Lucinda said the people would always say, "Didn't you hear de … squalling in de night? … is de screech owl, and he suppose to tell when anybody going to die right soon. I hear lots of Creek people say dey hear de screech owl close to de house, and sho' nuff somebody in de family die soon."[19]

An infant funeral recalled by Charles Ball, a slave in western Maryland, incorporated similar traditional African customs:

> [The baby's father placed beside the infant a small box and arrows,] a little bag of parched meal; a miniature canoe, about a foot long, and a little paddle, (with which he said it would cross the ocean to his own country) a small stick, with an iron nail, sharpened and fastened into one end of it; and a piece of white muslim, with several curious and strange figures painted on it in blue and red, by which, he said, his relations and countrymen would know the infant to be his son, and would receive it accordingly, on its arrival amongst them…. He cut a lock of hair from his head, threw it upon the dead infant, and closed the grave with his own hands. He then told us the God of his country was looking at him, and was pleased with what he had done.[20]

Ophelia Jemison dreamed of the dead. The spirits of the dead are with you when you sleep if you dream about them, she said. He (the Spirit) wants to tell you something so, "jes' set youself in mind for somet'ing" that will help you "weather ("wedder de") the storm." She dreamed once about her mother, who had been long dead, dreamed she was sitting right there in the door. Her mother asked if she were happy and then she disappeared. Ophelia "studied" about that dream the entire next day, fearing something was about to happen, and then the next day she dreamed again. This time "death" stood in the same door where her mother stood the night before. "Death" disappeared; someone banged on the door and told her that her husband had been "knocked down dead." Ophelia ended her story with a warning, told originally in the vernacular: "A dream that rests heavy on your mind is a visitation of the spirit. Look on it with concern."[21]

Annie Burton, born in 1858, gained her freedom but remained in Chapel Hill, North Carolina, where she had been "in service."

She dreamed her sweetheart's death. She had been with him for four years and her mother had consented to their marriage. The wedding month was May. The winter before Annie had begun to work for the family of Dr. Drury in Eufaula, and she left Clayton where she had lived before. Invited out to tea the night before she was to leave her current paid service, she told her sweetheart the dream after he told her he had purchased a piece of poplar wood to make a table for their new home. "Don't let that [dream] trouble you, there is nothing in dreams," he said, but one month from that day he died, and his coffin was made from the piece of poplar wood he had bought for the table.[22] [no indent]After his death, Annie remained in Clayton for several weeks and then back to Eufaula where she stayed for two years. Her sweetheart's death profoundly affected her; she began to pray all night on her knees.

Malindy Maxwell was born a slave. She told of dreaming death, of folks on the farm getting "happy" and "shouting" when they "got religion and recalled an often repeated story by her mistress that she had been born 'foot foremost'" with a "veil on my face and down on my body a piece ... a caul." For that reason she would see forms and they would vanish. She was 80 years old and could only see those forms out of one eye, but she had always seen things "like when you are dreaming at night but I see them at times that plain in day."[23]

The "Lord" would visit Maggie Perkins when her "folks were going to die." Just before her grandmother's death, she woke up and told her aunt that "granma was dead." Her aunt accused her of lying but she indeed saw her grandmother's death. Then she saw another aunt lying on the bed with her hand under her jaw, smiling to a house full of people. That aunt died and then they "paid attention" to Maggie's visions when she told them someone was going to die. She and her husband had moved into a house where a man had died, but they moved right out again when they heard sounds "like someone was emptying shelled corn.... When death comes, he comes to your heart. He has your number and knows where to find you. He won't let you off, he has the key. Death comes and unlocks the heart and twists the breath out of that heart and carries it back to God." In a simple belief in the power of her visions, she noted that she couldn't see for eight years without glasses. One morning, forgetting her glasses, she asked for her eyesight to return and the next morning she could see. So, she said, just ask and you'll get what you need.[24]

Hoodoo, Witches, and Casting Spells

Mose Minser recalled that one night he dreamed and that the next morning that dream "come true ... [j]es like ah dreamt."[25] A.J. Mitchell could remember the first dream he ever dreamed—but didn't elaborate—and the first time he whistled. Tom Neal shared information about "hoodoo" and witches. He grew up in the cabin listening to stories about witches and said a witch had to be careful because she would be killed if she was found out. The witches would take on other forms and do "meaness." They could travel through latch holes and they "used buttons and door knobs whittled out of wood, and door latches with strings." Not hesitating to discuss witches, he denied a belief in dreams, except some dreams of the dead that sure meant there was going to be "falling weather." He added that he didn't dream much.[26]

Several former slaves noted that conjuring and "Hoodoo" only worked well if the slaves practiced against each other. It either didn't work against the slave owner or they didn't dare try it. Henry Bibb, however, discussed the use of bitterroot, which was sprinkled around the master's dwellings to prevent flogging. He recalled believing he could do as he pleased if he knew the secrets of conjuring and witchcraft. Talking "saucy" to his master dampened his belief when he was punished with a whip. He tried again, this time for love. He paid for a special bone that was designed to turn the affections of a young woman away from another man and toward him. Henry saw his love and the other man together and, when chance allowed, he rapped her across the neck with the bone as instructed by the conjuror who sold it to him. Instead of glowing with love, she was glowing with anger, so Henry renounced conjuring.[27]

Signs, alongside dreams, were "the way the Lord has of showing you things." Many of those interviewed professed to believe in signs but disavowed using them. They believed using too many signs led to trouble. An anonymous female interviewee said with assurance that if you dreamed of losing a tooth, something was going to happen, some of your "kinfolk" or close friends would get into trouble or die. She recalled that she lay down to sleep, dreamed about losing a tooth and the next morning heard that the lady up the street had died suddenly. She also equated ringing in the ears as being the sign of someone dying. Several former slaves, once again unnamed, recalled dreams being important to their grandmothers, one noting that her "grandma say don't never tell your dream before breakfast, if you do, it won't come true"; but she claimed not to believe in dreams herself because she was too busy working.[28]

Getting Religion

Religious "visions" were reported with more fervor than night dreams. Visions had a palpable presence that awed and inspired, and people—born into acceptance of signs and second sight and accustomed to spiritual trance as a pathway to crossing the thin boundary between waking and ordinary reality—did not hesitate to describe their often labored devotion to visioning as a path to acceptance of Christianity, a refuge from their hard, often brutal life as slaves. A developing hybrid African-American form of Christianity that blended Christian ritual and belief with elements of West African culture resulted in a distinctive worship characterized by singing, dancing, "shouting," and spiritual possession performed in secret prayer meetings held on plantation grounds, where slave owners sent mixed messages, talking of Christianizing the slaves and at the same time living in fear of the freedom inherent in religious expression.

In his elegant narrative, Olaudah Equiano noted that the African people believed there was one Creator of all things, and that he lived in the sun, girded round with a belt, and "that he may never eat or drink; but according to some, he smokes a pipe, which is our own favorite luxury": "They believe he governs events, especially our deaths or captivity ... spirits ... such as their dear friends or relations, they believe always attend them, and guard them from the bad spirits of their foes. For this reason, they always, before eating, as I have observed, put some small portion of the meat, and pour some of their drink, on the ground for them; and they often make oblations of the blood of beasts or fowls at their graves."[29]

The slaves avowed their acceptance of the Christian Lord in acceptable open meetings in grove shelters on the plantations but as much as possible they kept their visions to themselves, sharing the experiences only in secret prayer meetings where "shouts" had to be stifled by a method brought from Africa: a pot was turned down to capture the sound so that their masters and mistresses would not know they were gathering for a praise or prayer meeting. Most of the narratives described in varying detail these religious gatherings, shoutings, and praise meetings, with casual notations of the pot's being turned down to keep out, disguise or drown the sound.

"Mrs. Sutton," reporting the danger in slaves having prayer and singing meetings, talked about turning down the kettle: "[T]hey would get a big ole wash kettle and put it right outside the door, and turn it bottom upwards to get the sound, then they would go in the house and sing and pray, and the kettle would catch the sound. I s'pose they would kinda have it propped up so the sound would get under it." Mr. Reed recalled walking "way out in the woods after getting religion." They would all shout and roll far away from the ears of the owners.

Hearing voices was common—even expected. You really didn't have religion until you had experienced direct communication with the Spirit in some form. One former slave tried to get religion beginning in 1866 but even in a revival he just couldn't do it until he went alone and sat under a peach tree, where he prayed till midnight. Then he heard a voice: "You rise, you rise." He ran into the house and still heard the voice. Realizing he was hearing the voice of a holy spirit, he ran into the woods naked, crying, and happy—religion had come to him "like the wind blows." After that he could talk to all God's creatures, from the ants to the birds. Another man reported seeing things when he got religion but he never heard anything out of the ordinary. He saw the Lord open a cloud and look down on his heart: "He took it out and put it right back in my body. I never have heard nobody say nothing, though. He looked just like you see him in these pictures. Long white robe and long hair and beard."[30]

A woman, a former slave living with her grown children, sought a vision for many years. Finding the shouting and screaming in the meeting house too distracting, she went home by herself and then "the Lord ... called me by my name." She added that she saw him only once: "He was standing on a high hill, on the steps of a great big white house, and He was standing there jest like a preacher was talking. I ain't never saw Him no more on a building like that; looked something like the capital, with them high white steps, you know." She didn't recall any dreams but believed that they were the way the Spirit told you things you should know. A number of reported visions left their recipients light as feathers, feeling as though they had been lifted up or that they had seen a light that came inside them and remained there. Some would be "worried" or bothered by the light until they shared the information with another person. Then the light would become part of them and would be available when they needed to call upon it. Visions of the Lord or voices of the Spirit worked in a similar fashion—the visions or voices would have to be shared or they would become worrisome.[31]

"Vergy" didn't recall seeing the Lord but saw her oldest daughter after she died. When Vergy was sewing on a Saturday afternoon she reported seeing her "just as plain; she had on one of my old bonnets." Vergy thought at first her daughter wasn't dead because she was as visible as "flesh and blood."[32]

"Be ready to receive your prize that is coming"

William Webb, born into slavery in Georgia in 1836, was taught by his mother to believe there was a Supreme Being watching over him and, if William bided his time, what he prayed for would be granted. As he grew older and visited plantations, he saw more cruelty from plantation masters toward slaves than his young mind had imagined. He begged for deliverance and heard a voice say, "I will be with you and your race of people." The voice was so powerful William fell silent. He shared the experience with his mother, who told him he had heard the voice of God and that the time would come for freedom.[33]

When a great sickness fell over the plantation where William lived as a slave he did not get sick. When he was asked why, he replied, "The good man was watching over me and keeping all sickness from me." When asked what he meant, he said, "A voice always followed me and said that, I will always be with you in all of your trials ... [and] a feeling come over me when I heard that voice, that told me that it was God that spoke to me, and the people told me if I always listened to that voice, I would be right in everything."[34]

William grew up on the plantation with a decent master who allowed him to make speeches and preach of good things to come. He was excited about the mood of the country as the word "freedom" became more pronounced. He also had an uncanny ability to change people's hearts. He called it "sleight of hand" and told unbelievers that his sleight of hand "would cause [people] to live more happy than they had been living." To put this gift to the test, he asked where the meanest master lived and he was told about a Kentucky plantation (his master having moved from Mississippi to Kentucky) where the master was so cruel even his slaves were not respected because they belonged to that plantation. He was taken to the plantation and introduced at night to all the people (his master, uncommonly accommodating, permitted him night freedom, trusting him completely). Using his power of imagination and intention and energy of spirit, he convinced them that he was the good person they had all been waiting to see. The slaves were so pleased they brought a lamb, sacrificed it and cooked it for supper. William asked for the restoration of peace on the plantation. He walked back to his plantation that evening and prayed to God.[35]

Transformation on the "meanest" plantation manifested itself within a week. The slaves prayed, asking for the evil surrounding the plantation to be lifted. William brought bags of roots "to gain their attention." The bags were no larger than his thumb and he sewed the ends together. Using the biblical magic of the number "twelve," William gathered twelve men together and asked them to shake the bags of roots each morning in the direction of the master's house and say, "Lord, peace be with us this day." They were not to tell the others about the bag ritual but they were to ask all the slaves to say, each morning, "Peace be unto us to-day." The master of that plantation came to see William and asked if he was the stranger who had been stirring up his slaves. A bit frightened, William had to say he was and that his master had moved there from Mississippi. The cruel master said he had felt changes in the past two weeks. He had been troubled in his mind, even thinking his Negroes were trying to poison him. William boldly suggested that maybe the Lord was working on his mind. The master continued, saying he had nightmares that his slaves were all standing around him in the night, so he decided he needed to treat them better to save his own life. The slaves were unnerved thinking William had used those roots to "conjure old master" or "to draw master down." No, William said, the roots were to remind them they were always talking to the Supreme Being.[36]

William's "Aunt Mary" dreamed she saw "great hosts of men drawn up together and heard a voice say 'this is to free you.'" William told her he had heard that voice since he was born and that he was sure he would live to see freedom. "This is my purpose, to warn you all to be ready to receive your prize that is coming. I would tell you more, but I can not at the present time."[37]

When the war began William had his freedom. He dreamed he was traveling to the West and came across some strange people who took him in. An officer arrested him and placed him in a guardhouse for reasons not fully understood by William. He had been offered the opportunity to enlist and had refused. A Colonel Bond decided there was no reason to hold him and released him. William looked to his dream of the West for his next move. He had been working in the "wood business" and saw no future in that so he followed his dream, heading West "as God directed." He took the train to Monroe City, stayed a while with a Quaker family, set off for Detroit where he worked again in the wood business, and lived alone in the woods.

Then William dreamed of a wife and knew he would meet her soon[38]:

I dreamed that night about three yellow snakes, and I thought the smallest one of the three was trying to bite me, and I thought that one of the other snakes got between me and the one that was trying to bite me, and I thought the largest one of all stood and looked on at the other two. I thought the first two snakes came in contact and fought awful, and I thought the one that was taking up for me whipped the other one badly, and I thought the largest one that had been looking on parted the two that were fighting. I thought the one that got whipped crawled off and the other two followed him, and I thought I went on after them. The largest one of all told the other two snakes that they had better make friends and say no more about it. And the smallest one said he would tell it, for I would be sure to tell it, and he would tell it himself. I thought the largest one told me not to tell. I said to the smallest one, if they would make friends and settle the matter, I would leave that place. He agreed to settle it and they all made friends, and I thought I left the place. After I awoke I studied that dream over. I always knew that if you dreamed about a snake, it was a sure sign some one had ill will against you. I did not think anyone out there had any ill will against me, for they always said I was a pious man, for nobody but a pious man could live in the woods alone as I did.

At daybreak three men William knew came to measure the wood he had cut. The smallest of the three did not want to pay William, and a fight among the three broke out. To settle the fight, William said if they would pay him he would take the train and leave. On the train William remembered the snake dream and thought if that dream had taken place then surely the dream of the woman who would be his wife would follow.[39]

William went back to Detroit to a boardinghouse he had rented earlier on Cass Street and returned to his whitewashing job. There he met the woman he had seen in his dream. He allowed the courtship to come slowly and eventually asked her to marry him. They became engaged, and William bounced around the eastern states and into Canada, and from there to Vermont and on to Albany, New York. He visited Niagara Falls and then went back to Detroit, where he married his dream woman on October 20, 1867.[40]

William had a son who died and a daughter who lived. One night after the death of his son he had a dream in which he "was carried up on a high pillar, and I thought I saw four pools of water, and I saw a man standing by me, and he said come up a little higher, and he asked me if I saw those four pools of water":

> I told him I did.... He said those four pools of water were kingdoms, and he pointed down to one kingdom ... and said that kingdom was richer than all the rest, and said it was able to buy kingdoms to go with it. And one kingdom stood off by itself, and a great jealousy arose against it in the other kingdoms.... Then the man told me to look down, and I thought I saw the sea, and thought it looked blue, and I thought that all kinds of boats and fleets you could mention were in the sea. I thought I saw a great army, and I thought that great army was going against that kingdom that had grown so strong. I thought there was a very strong fort at one end of the kingdom, but the great army went around the fort and entered the city, and I heard a voice sound in the city, saying, "woe, woe, to thy happiness.[41]

William, upon waking, recalled the great shout of joy that went up throughout the South the day Lincoln was elected president, and the greater shout of freedom tempered by Lincoln's death and the disappointment of unfulfilled promises in Andrew Johnson, turned around once again in the election of Ulysses S. Grant. He reported no additional dreams. His freedom was his reward for years of dreaming well.

Escaping from Charleston on the Steamer Planter: Robert Small

On September 30, 1862, the *Charleston Mercury* reported the story of Robert Small, a Negro man who ran the steamer *Planter* from the Charleston wharf. He successfully made a trip to freedom, escaping from Charleston "with the greatest pleasure in the world." Robert had thought about escape so much that he finally dreamed how he would accomplish it and acted on the dream, sharing it first with his shipmate. Together they decided to do it. Several families met at Robert's house on May 12, took stock of their assets, and made a plan to escape on the steamer where they worked. There were four heavy guns on the boat. On the day of their escape, they hid the women and children in the engine room of another boat nearby. A man named Abraham kept watch until midnight. Under a bright moon a fire started in the city, and the men were afraid people would think the fire was at the wharf. However, no one from the city came, so the men, feeling like it was time, moved out from their assigned positions, manned the boat, picked up the women and children, and steamed to Fort Johnson. Not wanting to come in front of the fort in the dark, Robert gave a signal—two long blows and a short one. He donned the captain's straw hat and stood so that the sentinel could not see his color. Passing the range of guns at the fort, they "put on plenty of steam. I hoisted a white sheet, taken from the bed, and reached the blockading vessels in safety, and we were received with cheers."[42]

Dreaming of Lincoln: A Dangerous "Omen"

Dreaming could be dangerous. One report noted that slaves didn't share dreams or visions of Abraham Lincoln. If they had such dreams, they would gather in the woods and talk alone about those. A young slave named Charlotte had such a dream, told her dream and was nearly beaten to death.[43]

Chaplain Joseph Twichell shared a story of a "contraband" former slave in the Union camp who saw President Lincoln, who was accompanied by Secretary of War Edwin M. Stanton, when they appeared in a surprise visit to the camp. The event began in the middle of the afternoon, July 9, 1862, and was first announced by a salute fired by gunboats and by the excited news shared by "Ben whom we "stole out of Maryland": "He was out foraging and came in, his black face all shining and cloven with a mighty grin, and with keen delight informed me, 'Ise seen ole Uncle Linkum!'" Twichell had been told by the contraband slaves in the camp that they had heard of Lincoln described only in derogatory terms, as a "monster," but they had taken that to mean he was a good man for them. In fact, they had built Lincoln up in their minds to be a mythological creature, not a real man but an "omen ... of good, which some day would break the clouds above them." Twichell wrote that they saw "*persons* rather than *principles*." Ben said that when Twichell's "division came to the Lower Potomac the slaves did not regard it as the *Union Army* but as a visible sign of the coming of the long expected, benign reign of "ole Uncle Linkum."[44]

More Views of Omens

Hoodoo and spells were used but were viewed as unreliable. They even backfired unless they were used carefully. Signs were a part of living and dying. Dreams and visions were reported calmly, without disbelief, as simple, straightforward, "just so" experiences. Whether foretelling a simple event, bearing an introduction to the Divine and the Spirit, or presaging death, visions were actively sought as a part of life and provided hope for survival from the most cruel of existences. Most remembered dreams foretold death;

others, no matter the content, were viewed as possible warnings of death or bad things happening. These, like visions, were "sho' nuf going to happen."

A Note on the Soldier

Most of the collected letters written by black soldiers patiently and beautifully subscribed to a perfection of form and an elegance of presentation that seemed determined to prove their ability to write as well as, if not better than, any white soldier. Only generic mention of dreaming appeared in most of these letters but they were still eloquent.

Sergeant John H.W.N. Collins, Co. H, 54th Massachusetts Infantry, shared news of the movements of the 54th from Jacksonville to the islands near Charleston and of the continual transfers from place to place, which made life hard, especially with no pay. Describing a steamer leaving a landing, he wrote that the 8th U.S. Colored Troops cheered them as the band struck up a song: "The night on the water passed off very pleasantly. Here and there lay the brave members of the 54th, scattered all over the decks of the steamer—some dreaming of those at home, some humming a hymn of praise, some reading the Testament—thus we passed the solitary night on the water." He wrote about the disconnect between Lincoln's signing of the Emancipation Proclamation and the real treatment of the Negro, and he scribed a haunting tale of an elegant white Confederate woman riding a white horse "like a ghost" across the rise of a hill as firing began. She was still seen riding away as the mists of gunfire ceased.[45]

The End of Slavery

A former slave, name and sex unknown, balked at casting blame and reliving old memories best left buried. It was time to move on: "I think it is against the race to tell about how the white people done us back in slavery. I don't want to do anything to tear down; I want to build up. These white people that used to be here before the war, it is just now and then that you can run upon them, and if you do they are about as old as I am. The law says white and black shan't mix. Now, who made that law? They made that law. I made a law with my hoe that all those weeds must die that I hit."[46]

CHAPTER 18

Many Are the Hearts That Are Weary Tonight: Wishing for the War to Cease

> *Our night has been long, its hours dark, its dreams troubled and its watchings most weary, but it has had its stars too, and they have led on the morning whose twilight is already on the hills. Our day is at hand, the nation is to live, it has gone through severe trial, it has been tested in fire and has come out safe.*[1]

Poignant pleas for a dreamed loved one to stay just a while longer; harsh visions of death; sumptuous feasts in a starved and otherwise hopeless prison landscape; practical advice on surviving a burned-over beloved landscape; and images of humor and hope in a landscape ravaged by desolation, disease, and war—all of these found a place in the soldiers' dreams, offering consolation, healing, warning, and a means of survival for those who made it back home. Often there were nightmares that would not forgive or allow forgiveness. For those who did not come home, their dreams found their way in letters back to their families and friends, offering a glimpse of the soldiers' interior lives.

The crisp and exacting reality of the Union soldier's dreams presented an often nononsense acceptance of the sleep dream as useful and as trustworthy as waking reality in the camp or on the battlefield. In the letters of the Southern dreamer, reaching one more time for his beloved as she vanishes, one might glimpse Celtic roots, as wistful and romantic as the mountains where they were born, fully accepting dreams as agents of hope and survival.

Through it all, especially as the days, weeks, months and years dragged out a war that all thought would be brief—some even thought would be bloodless—the soldier wished for an ending. Guy Taylor may have said it best as he gazed on the North Star in the last year of the war and wondered if even the most exquisite music could compare to the "wild cry of peace":

> I take my seat by the ... desk with pen in hand to write you a few lines to let you know that I am well. As I was out with the regiment this evening I cast my eyes up towards the Heavens, and looked through the pine tops, and saw the same bright Glittering Star (the North Star) that I have often gazed upon when you have been by my side, and I wondered in my mind if I ever would see that time again, and when if I ever do (God only knows) I hope that I may soon see that time again. As I sit a writing, the Brigade Band is filling the air with Music, and as we listen to the music ... we lend a listening ear to their voices for it is far pleasanter music to our ears then that of the Drums & Horns, for it says victory in every sound and we know that ... we will have peace ... and what music could sound so sweet as the wild cry of peace.[2]

Dreaming of Home Today

John Tidd, a private in the 109th New York Regiment, wrote, "[T]he absent ... soldier ... often thinks and meditates on the past pleasures of home.... [S]ometimes [they] even think they are enjoying the pleasures of the home circle ... [and] these thoughts are ... felt in midnight dreams."[3] The families dreamed of their soldier home, dreamed of the conditions of their home in war and dreamed in deep grief beside the graves of lost loved ones.

Dreaming of home was, as Henry Graves wrote, an angel "of mercy" to the "soldier mortal." Recounted in thousands of letters to and from home, Civil War dreams reflected the personality and experience of their writers, offering vivid examples of hope and tangible expressions of love coming from deep sorrow, loss, and pain—for some, disappointment or terror, for others warnings of danger or death or a glimpse of humor, yet always with a sense of reality. These letters recorded a time when the American culture accepted dreams as valued indicators of life and death, of hope and sorrow, of a hold on humanity that *could* allow soldiers and families to survive horrible living conditions, loneliness, depression, and the bodily deprivations of a lost home, war, and even prison.

In these letters there was rarely a sense of unreliability in their dreams, even when the writer awoke to find it was "just a dream." "Just a dream" was not disbelief; it was more an expression that the dream had ended and left the soldier on the battlefield or in camp longing for home or left those at home dreaming of the home terror of war or grieving for a dead family member. If the soldier or family member could not integrate the dream with the waking reality, the nightmare took over.

These dreams speak to every generation from the first man to defend a piece of ground to those returning home from more technologically brutal modern wars. Brian Turner, recounting a recurring dream of home in Iraq, writes of home with the same sense of reality as soldiers writing from camp in the Civil War—or from any war, past, present or future:

> And finally the dream shifts to where it often goes, a dream I started having when I was in Iraq—I'm back home in the San Joaquin Valley, about 20 miles north of Fresno, out in the country, and I'm sort of a disembodied hovering version of myself, floating over my family's property where I was raised, drifting in and out of the eucalyptus trees, the ground everywhere—for as far as I can see—covered with red bark (like the bark chips you get from a home and garden store for planter boxes and ground cover).... It's a dream I like, one that I always want to last longer, drifting between those trees. The clarity of this dream is far beyond most of my dreams, which are often murky, convoluted, fragmented, disjointed.[4]

I read two of the dreams from the Civil War in a workshop for women vets. When I looked up from reading the letters, a young woman who had returned from Iraq said, with tears in her eyes, "I thought I was the only person who dreamed of home in the middle of a nightmare." I realized in that statement that there were no boundaries separating the language of letters written in war. Even letters filled with loneliness and terror shared the "realness" of a dream that brought them home in the common language of the night.

Recognizing the power of dreams of home and family and of the gifts of the imagination could still be the angel of mercy—the missing piece—to returning today's soldiers safely home and to offering families healing from the nightmare of war. Just as in the Civil War, dreams and imagination could offer a place where hearts and souls mend and find humanity, even when the hardships of war have forced their way into the most protected and private of places that struggle to keep body and spirit together and whole. Our culture is not so far removed from the Civil War that we cannot reclaim the power of dreaming as a vital part of healing soldiers and families experiencing home after a physical nightmare.

Chapter Notes

Introduction

1. Abingdon, Virginia, *The Richmond Daily Dispatch*, "Local Matters," August 10, 1864.
2. Mark Nesbitt, ed. *Through Blood & Fire: Selected Civil War Papers of Major General Joshua Chamberlain* (Mechanicsburg, PA: Stackpole Books), 1996. 24 (letter 6th), Head Quarters 20th Me. Camp near Antietam Ford, October 10th, 1862, to "My dear Fanny." Major General Chamberlain was born in Brewer, Maine, studied in both military school and for the ministry, married Frances Caroline Adams [Fanny]. He enlisted in July, 1862 and was Major General of Maine Volunteers.

Chapter 1

1. Marc Newman (ed.). *Potomac Diary, a Soldier's Account of the Capital in Crisis, 1864–1865, Diary of Richtmyer Hubbell.* (Town of Jefferson, NY: self-published), 2000. 90. Richtmyer Hubbell was with the 1st Wisconsin Heavy Artillery Company M., stationed as company clerk at Fort Weed in northern Virginia, across the Potomac River from Washington, D.C., entry dated April 15, 1865.
2. Ward Hill Lamon. *Recollections of Abraham Lincoln, 1847–1865.* (Washington, D.C.: published by Dorothy Lamon) (Project Gutenberg) 1911 Chapter VII, Dreams and Presentiments, 122. Byron's "Dream" was one of Lincoln's favorite poems. Ward Lamon, aide, friend, and biographer, often heard him quote the lines above.
3. Arthur Brooks Lapsley (ed.). *Abraham Lincoln. The Papers and Writings of Abraham Lincoln.* (Project Gutenberg: Constitutional Edition), volume 6, 1862–1863, Telegram to Mrs. Lincoln, Executive Mansion, Washington, June 9, 1863. To "Mrs. Lincoln, Philadelphia, Pa.
4. Quoted in William H. Herndon & Jesse W. Weik. *Abraham Lincoln* (Project Gutenberg), Volume 2. 1888.
5. Lamon, 110.
6. Herndon & Weik. *Abraham Lincoln*, Volume 1. 1888. mad-stone visit.
7. Lamon, 111–113.
8. Herndon, Volume 2.
9. Robert Moss blog, "The Real History of Lincoln's Dreams," http://mossdreams.blogspot.com/2008/12/real-history-of-lincolns-dream.html.
10. *Ibid.*, http://mossdreams.blogspot.com/search?q=Lincoln.
11. Lamon, 113–116. Genesis 28: 10-15: "Jacob left Beersheba and set out for Harran. When he reached a certain place, he stopped for the night because the sun had set. Taking one of the stones there, he put it under his head and lay down to sleep. He had a dream in which he saw a stairway resting on the earth, with its top reaching to heaven, and the angels of God were ascending and descending on it. There above it[c] stood the Lord, and he said: "I am the Lord, the God of your father Abraham and the God of Isaac. I will give you and your descendants the land on which you are lying. Your descendants will be like the dust of the earth, and you will spread out to the west and to the east, to the north and to the south. All peoples on earth will be blessed through you and your offspring.[d] I am with you and will watch over you wherever you go, and I will bring you back to this land. I will not leave you until I have done what I have promised you."
12. *Ibid.*, 116–117.
13. *Ibid.*, 118.
14. *Ibid.*, 118–119.
15. See "The Terrible Times That Haunt Me" under "Just So dreams."
16. Charles M. Segal, ed. *Conversations with Lincoln.* (New York: G. P. Putnam's Sons), 1912. pp. 391–395, compiled interviews and first person accounts of Lincoln. Various versions of the cabinet meeting and dream, all similar, appear in Montgomery C. Meigs MS. Diary (Apr. 14, 1865, in Montgomery C. Meigs MSS, Library of Congress; Welles MS Diary (Apr. 14, 1865); Beale ed., II, 280–283. For another version of the cabinet meeting, see F. W. Seward, *Reminiscences of a War-Time Statesman and Diplomat*, 254–257. Also Hugh McCullock, *Men and Measures of Half a Century* (New York, 1889), 409.
17. Honore Willsie Morrow. *International-Cosmopolitan*, "Lincoln's Last Day" (Hearst), Feb. 1930. Mary Lincoln to F.B. Carpenter, April 14, 1865. Also see Allan Nevins and Milton Halsey Thomas, ed. *The Diary of George Templeton Strong, the Civil War, 1860–1865* (Vol. 3). George Templeton Strong attended the Lincoln funeral and recorded memoirs.
18. Dr. John Hugh Bowers. *Life of Abraham Lincoln* (Girard, Kansas: Haldeman-Julius Company), 1922. Project Gutenberg.
19. Lord Charnwood. *Abraham Lincoln* (Garden City, NY: Garden City Publishing Co. Inc.; Henry Holt and Company), 1917. Chapter XXIX, 583: Dreams.
20. Lamon, 119–120.
21. Gideon Welles. *Diary of Gideon Welles: Secretary*

of the Navy Under Lincoln and Johnson (Boston & New York: Houghton Mifflin Company), 1911; Frances Fisher Browne. *Revision of the Everyday Life of Abraham Lincoln. Biography with Pen-Pictures and Personal Recollections by Those Who Knew Him* (Chicago: Browne & Howell Company), 1913. Project Gutenberg.

22. Lamon, 121.

23. See Robert Moss on Dream reentry, a core technique of Active Dreaming, explained in several of Robert Moss' books, including *The Three "Only" Things* and *Active Dreaming*, with examples of how it can be used to clarify possible future events and change the future for the better. Lincoln's dreams: http://blog.beliefnet.com/dreamgates/2012/11/lincolns-dreams.html#ixzz2GIv5D9Hy.

24. *Recollections and Letters of General Robert E. Lee by Captain Robert E. Lee, His Son* (on-line), letter from Mary Custis quoted in the Recollections. http://www.fullbooks.com.

Mary Custis Lee DeButts (ed.). *The Journal of Agnes Lee, Growing Up in the 1850s.* (Chapel Hill, NC: UNC Press, published for the Robert E. Lee Memorial Association Inc.), 1984. 116: Feb. 5, 1884, letter from daughter Mildred Lee. In 1884, Lee's fifth child, Eleanor Agnes Lee, died and was buried next to her father in the chapel, where Mary Custis was laid to rest next to her husband soon after Agnes. Agnes had begun a journal in December, 1852, when she was twelve, and had penned charming memories of Arlington and of West Point. Roses, gathered from the rosebush planted by General Lee, were placed on Agnes' heart.

25. Blog: Historic Valley Forge, http://www.ushistory.org/valleyforge/washington/vision.html.

26. Frank Moore (ed.). "The Strange Dream of John C. Calhoun," *The Civil War in Song and Story* (New York), 1889. Also printed in *The Florida Home Companion* (Ocala, Florida), January 21, 1860, Digital image available in the Bonds Conway Papers, 1763–1907. (University of South Carolina, South Caroliniana Library), http://www.sc.edu/library/digital/collections/sk12.html. See also: http://wesclark.com/jw/calhoun.html.

27. *The Evening Courier.* (Portland, Maine), March 8, 1862; reprinted in *The Individual Christian Scientist*, Vol. XI, No. 2.

28. The Richmond, Virginia, *Daily Dispatch.* See: [http://imls.richmond.edu/cgi/t/text/text-idx?c=ddr;cc=ddr;type=simple;rgn=div2;q1=dream;view=text;subview=detail;sort=occur;idno=ddr0531.0023.017;node=ddr0531.0023.017%3A4.1.

29. *Journal of the American Society for Psychical Research*, Section "B" of the American Institute for Scientific Research (York, PA: American Society for Psychical Research), 1906, 353–355, Volume XI, No. 1, January, 1917. The society declared the McClellan dream a fitting companion to the widely disseminated "Washington Vision." To prove their point the society wrote to George McClellan's son, Professor George B. McClellan, Jr., of Princeton University, who replied on May 12, 1917, that the McClellan dream was written by someone "whose patriotism seems to have been more admirable than his literary ability," intended obviously as "an allegory." He was surprised that anyone had ever accepted the story as truth. He had never read the manuscript, had never seen it referenced in any of his father's papers and wrote that his father's "...inspiration was his own genius and the valor of the now much-abused American Volunteer, rather than the advice of the Father of our Country, whose largest command never exceeded in size one of the divisions of the most magnificent body of men eve brought together, the Army of the Potomac. http://books.google.com/books?id=ongYAQAAIAAJ&pg=PA353&lpg=PA353&dq=general+mcclellan's+dream&source=bl&ots=k3YnGyrKC1&sig=kred20CwrF1bkRa_MRzgUQ1V3lY&hl=en&sa=X&ei=izmiUsSSHMS2kQeehIGgBg&ved=0CGoQ6AEwBw#v=onepage&q=general%20mcclellan's%20dream&f=false.

30. John Y. Simon, ed. *The Personal Memoirs of Julia Dent Grant* (Mrs. Ulysses P. Grant) (Carbondale and Edwardsville: Southern Illinois University Press), 1975. 49–50 and Footnote 22: p. 63: Julia Grant gave a more detailed account of the marriage proposal to a journalist in 1890. Foster Coates, "The Courtship of General Grant," *Ladies' Home Journal*, VII (October, 1890), 4.

31. *Ibid.*, 54; 318, they were accompanied by General and Mrs. Sheridan as they entered New Orleans.

32. *Ibid.*

33. *Ibid.*, 76.

34. *Ibid.*, 78.

35. *Ibid.*

36. *Ibid.*, 84.

37. *Ibid.*, footnote p. 114, possible contradiction in time of commission from spring to fall, but, since these reminiscences were written later, times may have become distorted. The dream memories themselves might have added or subtracted details; but the feeling and general content of the dreams could still be entirely accurate.

38. *Ibid.*, 90–92.

39. *Ibid.*, 93. Footnote 11 on p. 115: In his *Memoirs*, I, 277–79, Grant described his narrow escape from enemy bullets while supervising the departure of his troops after the Battle of Belmont on November 7, 1861.

40. *Ibid.*, 99.

41. *Ibid.*, 155–157, footnote 6: the man trying to overhear the luncheon conversation was also the man who rode up alongside the carriage—John Wilkes Booth. In Philadelphia, Grant received a telegram about Lincoln's death, sent Julia on to Burlington, and returned.

Julia also enjoyed sharing her children's precognitive dreams, one of them dreaming their papa would come into the room. When told he would not be there that evening, she pointed to the door. He had just walked in. On another occasion little Nellie announced that someday they would live in a great house like "the picture in my geography of the ... Capitol in Washington." 157.

42. *Ibid.*, 234. "I was just where Cortez makes that gallant and cruel dash upon the capital when I was interrupted by the entrance of a servant making some inquiry. I sat back in my chair to rest, I do not know how long, when directly I saw a mountain with cliffs and precipices, draped in overhanging clouds. Moving out of this cloud came a cavalcade of miniature horsemen with silver helmets, spears, and pennants and bright flags fluttering in the breeze. I saw them all so clearly, these horses and men, scarcely more than eighteen inches high, the horses champing their bits and tossing their tiny heads to loosen their reins as they wound up the rugged mountain road in solemn procession.

And now I saw the same again as we crossed the valley of Ajalon and wound our way up the mountainside. But now my husband, General Grant, was in the advance, escorted by this gorgeous, gleaming pageant, entering Jerusalem. Every detail of this brilliant sight before me was so exact in every feature—the rugged mountain, the cliffs, the overhanging clouds, the silver helmets, the glittering lances, and gay banners—all, all were so exact with my daydream of long years ago that I cannot help but tell it here." ... In Jaipur, spelled "Jeypore" in her journal, Julia and Ulysses were met by His Highness, the Maharajah of Jaipur [Ram Singh] and the small group, with attendants, struck out for Amber [or Amer], the former capital. Julia was riding an elephant and delighting in her view from such a height. In her Memoirs, Julia shared a story, told by the Maharajah, that the former capital, Amber, was abandoned by the Maharajah's great-grandfather [Maharaja Pratap Singh], who was told in a dream to move his city. Julia described the palace—"with its columns and long line of walls following over hill and dale, away down into the valley and appearing again, passing on and on..."

43. It was unclear whether or not she thought she was dreaming about the possible presidency of her son Frederick. No further notes accompanied this dream.

44. Bill Potter (ed.). *Beloved Bride, the Letters of Stonewall Jackson to His Wife* (San Antonio, TX: The Vision Forum, Inc.), 2002–2012. 15, April 25, 1857.

45. *Ibid.*, 20, March 1859; 21–24, May 7, 1859.

46. *Ibid.*, 34, February 19, 1861.

47. *Ibid.*, 61, August 22, 1861.

48. James I. Robertson. *Stonewall Jackson: The Man, the Soldier, the Legend* (New York: Macmillan Publishing), 1997. 628.

49. *Beloved Bride*, 115–117, November, 1862.

50. *Ibid.*, 136, April 18, 1863.

51. *Ibid.*

52. *Ibid.*, 141–147.

53. Jeff Toalson (ed.). *Mama, I Am Yet Still Alive, a Composite Diary of 1863 in the Confederacy* (Bloomington: IUniverse, Inc., Butternut Series), Volume 3, 142, May 10th, Hamilton's Crossing, Virginia, 2nd Lt. George D. Buswell, Co. H-33rd Virginia Infantry, near Chancellors house; 156, May 21, 1863, Sergeant Benjamin F. Porter, Richmond, Virginia, Co. E-11th Alabama Infantry, written from Winder Hospital, Ward 35 where he lay wounded but "OK."

54. Robert Lewis Dabney, D.D., *Life and Campaigns of Lieut.-Gen. Thomas J. Jackson* (Harrisonburg, Va.: Sprinkle Publications), 1983, 565.

55. For an excellent article on the debate see David I. Holmes, Lesley J. Gordon, and Christine Wilson. "A Widow and Her Soldier: A Stylometric Analysis of the 'Pickett Letters.'" *History and Computing*, Volume 11, p. 159–179; DOI 10.3366/hac.1999.11.3.159, ISSN 1753-8548, Available Online 1999.

56. 1851 and 1856, both wives dying from complications of childbirth.

57. George Edward Pickett, LaSalle Corbell Pickett. *The Heart of a Soldier as Revealed in the Intimate Letters of Genl. George E. Pickett CSA* (New York: Seth Moyle [Incorporated]), 1908–1913. 21.

58. John Garraty and Mark Carnes, eds., *American National Biography* (New York: Oxford University Press), 1999.

59. *The Heart of a Soldier*. 50, "Your Soldier, In Camp, June 27, 1862; 77, "Your Soldier, Headquarters, September 25, 1862.

60. *Ibid.*, pp. 73–76, In Camp, April 15, 1863.

61. *Ibid.*, 81–83, Greencastle, Pennsylvania, June 24, 1863.

62. *Ibid.*, 86–87, Your Soldier, Chambersburg, June 27, 1863; p. 88, XVII, "Your soldier," In Camp, June 29, 1863; 91: Charge at Gettysburg, Gettysburg, July 3, 1863.

63. *Ibid.*, 100, "Your sorrowing Soldier." In Camp, July 4, 1863.

64. *Ibid.*, 127: The Wilderness Before Cold Harbor, "Your Soldier" In Camp, June, 1864.

65. *Ibid.*, 131, Cold Harbor, June 3, 1864; 134, "Your Soldier" Headquarters, June 18, 1864.

66. *Ibid.*, 138–143, the destruction of Turkey Hill, "Your Soldier" Headquarters, June, 1864; 149, birth of son, July 17, 1864; 152, visit with wife and son, In Camp, July 19, 1864; 169–170, Five Forks, Exeter Mills, April 2, 1865.

67. *Ibid.*, 179, "Your Soldier" Appomattox, April, 1865.

68. *Ibid.*, "Your lonesome Soldier" No date.

69. William W. Hassler with a foreword by Brian Wills. *One of Lee's Best Men; The Civil War Letters of General William Dorsey Pender* (Chapel Hill & London: The University of North Carolina Press), 1965. Cited from letters in the William Dorsey Pender Papers, #1059, Southern Historical Collection, The Wilson Library, University of North Carolina at Chapel Hill. 11: Montgomery, Ala. March 16th, 1861, to my dearest wife.

70. *Ibid.*, 21: Garysburg, NC, May 14th, 1861, "My dear Wife."

71. *Ibid.*, 40, Suffolk, Va., June 26th, 1861, "My dear Wife"; 42, Suffolk, Va., June 30th, 1861, "My dear Wife"; 42, Good Spring, June 30th, 1861, to "My dear Husband.

72. *Ibid.*, 69: Camp Hill, Va., Sept. 28th, 186, to "My precious Wife."

73. *Ibid.*, 24, Garysburg, NC, Sunday, May 19th, 1861 to "My dear wife"; 38: Suffolk, Va., June 23rd, 1861. "My dear Wife"; Good Spring was Fanny's family home. See also Mrs. Cicero W. Harris (ed.). *South-Atlantic: A Monthly Magazine of Literature, Science and Art*, Volume 1, #1 (November 1877). Published by Jackson and Bell, Wilmington, NC, 1877: Samuel Turner Pender, "General Pender." 228–35. Copy in The William Dorsey Pender Papers, #1059, pp. 8–10, Southern Historical Collection—University of North Carolina (Chapel Hill), as S. T. Pender, "Life of General Pender."

The full reference reads: "...At the battle of Sharpsburg, General A. P. Hills Division, of which General Pender was a Brigade Commander, arrived at an important crisis, checked the advance of the enemy, and contributed materially to their total repulse. In the [ ] he had obtained a short leave of absence which he spent with his family, near Salem, N. Carolina. Never had the brave soldier seemed in better health or spirit, enjoying, to the fullest degree, the few moments of a repose so seldom accorded him. In this delightful retreat—far from the noise and bustle of war, he threw off for a time, the constant responsibilities of his rank. Lying on the grass under the trees, surrounded by those he loved best with the song of birds and the air laden with the sweet odor of flowers, he exclaimed—This is the happiest day of my life; never have I felt such perfect content! What a fortunate soldier I have been any how—with every wish gratified. My heart, as a boy, was fixed upon going to West Point. At my own request I was transferred to the Dragoons. I married the woman I loved best. My promotion in the Confederate Army has been as rapid as any reasonable man could expect and even those little fellows (pointing to the children, who, with the nurse, were playing nearby) are all a fond father's heart could desire. But (with a sigh) there is no rest for a poor soldier."

74. *One of Lee's Best Men*, 138–139, Camp near Yorktown, Va., April 27th, 1862; Pensacola boy dream, Richmond, *Daily Dispatch*, April 11, 1862. http://imls.

richmond.edu/cgi/t/text/textidx?c=ddr;cc=ddr;type=simple;rgn=div3;q1=dream;view=text;subview=detail;sort=occur;idno=ddr0447.0021.086;node=ddr0447.0021.086%3A7.1.2].

75. *Ibid.*, 245–247: Hamilton's Crossing, June 12th, 1863, "My dear Wife."
76. *Ibid.*, 216: Camp Gregg, Va., April 1st, 1863, "My dearest Wife."
77. *Ibid.*, 116: Camp Fisher, Va., Feb. 26, 1862, to "My precious Wife."
78. *Ibid.*, 254–255: Fayetteville, Pa., June 28th, 1863, "My dearest Wife."
79. *Ibid.*, xi, xiv; 259–262; Afterword.
80. *Ibid.*
S. A. Ashe. Civil War Collection. Military Collection. State Archives of North Carolina; MilColl box 71 folder 45, S. A. Ashe served under William Pender and wrote a post-war report that included references to Lee's and Hill's words of commendation on Pender: "General Lee wrote in his official report: 'The loss of Major-General Pender is severely felt by the Army and the country. He served with the Army from the beginning of the war, and took a distinguished part in all of its engagements. Wounded on several occasions, he never left his command in action until he received the injury that resulted in his death. His promise and usefulness as an officer were only equaled by the purity and excellence of his private life.' General A. P. Hill wrote: 'No man fell during the bloody Battle of Gettysburg more regretted than he, nor around whose youthful brow were clustered brighter rays of glory.'"

Chapter 2

1. Cecil D. Eby, Jr. (ed.). *The Diaries of David Hunter Strother, a Virginia Yankee in the Civil War* (Chapel Hill, NC: The University of North Carolina Press), 1961. Introduction. Most of his early work was landscapes and other outdoor scenes. His art pertained mostly to Virginia and the Southern United States. Prior to the American Civil War, his art was published in books titled *The Blackwater Chronicle* (1853) and *Virginia Illustrated* (1857)." https://archive.org/stream/virginiayankeein000891mbp/virginiayankeein000891mbp_djvu.txt
2. *Ibid.*, 201, September 28, Monday (1863).
3. *Ibid.*, 5.
4. *Ibid.*, 79, description of Captain Nalle's house, then General Pope's headquarters, 1862.
5. *Ibid.*, August 17, Sunday.
6. *Ibid.*,164, April 7, 1863.
7. *Ibid.*, 78, August 9, Saturday [1862].
8. *Ibid.*, 99: August 20, Friday.
9. *Ibid.*, p. 131, December 3, Wednesday.
10. *Ibid.*, 147, "With Banks in Louisiana," January 22, Thursday (1863).
11. *Ibid.*, 213, February 16, Tuesday (1864), "With Sigel at New Market."
12. *Ibid.*, 281, July 21, Thursday (1864).
13. *Ibid.*, 287, August 9, Tuesday (1864).
14. Both the notebook and diary are available as a digital sesquicentennial exhibition through the Smithsonian Archives of American Art: http://civilwardiary.aaa.si.edu/; 43. Henry Mosler's illustrated notebook entry from December 19, 1862. Henry Mosler Civil War diary, Henry Mosler papers, 1856–1929, Archives of American Art, Smithsonian Institution.
15. *Ibid.*

16. *Ibid.*; An embedded artist in the American Civil War worked in a fashion not unlike those on modern battlefields. Mosler drew his sketches in the field, in positions of danger, and then sent the sketches through the mails via sutlers to his editor, John Bonner, who was hundreds of miles away. The Mosler website quoted the process from Mosler's diary entry on October 8, 1862, referencing his sketch of the Battle at Perryville and the town of Perryville. Mosler wrote that he made the sketches in about "3 hours and sent them to be mailed at Louisville by our sutler of the 9th Indiana." Mosler website notes on "sutlers," speculated that this reference might be to one that may have served as a go-between for Mosler when he was in the field. Mosler wrote poignant notes about each scene, this one from the 1862 battlefield at Perryville, also from the October 8, 1862 entry: "*In the Evening Col Blake Cotton and Myself Went Out to View the Battlefield Which Was a Sight That I Have Not the Power to Express We Where Also at the Hospital Where About 200 Wounded Where Lying Suffering Some Crying Oh! Mother Oh! Doctor Oh Give Me Some Water. Enough to Make Any One Feel the Terror of This War We Encamped Again Under a Large Tree with but a Blanket Over...*" Mosler's sketches appeared in *Harper's Weekly* on November 1, 1862. Battle of Perryville sketch.
17. Bryan F. Le Beau. *Currier and Ives: America Imagined* (Smithsonian Institution Press), 2001. This piece printed in http://www.common-place.org/vol-09/no-02/lebeau/. LeBeau explored the "revolution in print" contributions of Nathaniel Currier and James Ives.
18. *Ibid.*
19. *Ibid.*
20. LeBeau stated that much of what was included in the on-line Commonplace article was drawn from research for his book *Currier and Ives: America Imagined* (Washington, D.C., 2001). The most complete collection of information on Currier and Ives prints is Bernard F. Reilly, Jr.'s *Currier and Ives: A Catalogue Raisonne* (Detroit, 1984). Other useful publications include: Russell Crouse, *Mr. Currier and Mr. Ives* (Garden City, NY, 1936); Harry Peters, *Currier & Ives: Printmakers to the American People* (Garden City, NY, 1929–31); Walton Rawls, *The Great Book of Currier & Ives' America* (New York, 1979); and Colin Simkin, *Currier and Ives' America* (New York 1952).
21. Lydia Minturn Post (ed.). *Soldiers' Letters, from Camps, Battlefield and Prison* (New York: U.S. Sanitary Commission; Bunce & Huntington, Publishers; 540 Broadway, 1865. University of Michigan; Michigan Historical Reprint SeriesC. 125, Hatch Smith, 8th Illinois Cavalry, May 3d, 1862, Shipping Point, Letter LII.
22. *Ibid.*, p. 170: Letter LXXV, Shiloh, no location or date.
23. Oklahoma Historical Society blog: http://www.freewebs.com/minstreltune/civilwarhistory.html.
24. *John Dooley's Civil War*, 186. July 15, 1863; again on April 22, 1864: "...Feel quite fatigued but at night we have music and dancing which does much towards driving away fatigue and sorrow and chasing the gloomy shadows from our hearts."
25. John Lockwood. *Our Campaign Around Gettysburg: Being a Memorial of What Was Endured, Suffered, and Accomplished by the Twenty-Third Regiment (N.Y.S.N.G.) and Other Regiments Associated with Them in Their Pennsylvania and Maryland Campaign, During the Second Rebel Invasion of the Loyal States*. 1908. June-July 1863.
26. *Ibid.*, July 3, 1863, Gettysburg.

Chapter 3

1. Frances Clarke. "So lonesome I could die: Nostalgia and Debates over Emotional Control in the Civil War North." *Journal of Social History* (Sydney NSW, Australia: University of Sydney, Department of History, School of Philosophical & Historical Inquiry), 2007. 1.

2. Mills Lane (ed.). *Dear Mother: Don't Grieve About Me. If I Get Killed, I'll Only Be Dead, Letters from Georgia Soldiers in the Civil War* (Savannah, GA: A Beehive Press Book, Library of Savannah, letters from the Georgia State Department of Archives and History, Atlanta), 1990. xxv–xxvi, John Tilley to his wife, 10-6-61, GAH; John Swann to his wife, 6-30-62, GAH; William Stanley to his family, 7-30-62, GAH; William Stillwell to his wife, 8-9-63, GAH; John Swann ltr., 1-15-64, GAH; 101, Theodore Montfort to his family, Fort Pulaski, Georgia, Feb. 23, 1862, GHS.

3. Kevin Alderson and Patsy Alderson (eds.). *Letters Home to Sarah, the Civil War Letters of Guy C. Taylor, 36th Wisconsin Volunteers* (Madison, Wisconsin: The University of Wisconsin Press), 2012. 72, Camp near Petersburg, July 25, 1864, "My dear wife."

4. Stephen E. Ambrose (ed.). *A Wisconsin Boy in Dixie—Civil War Letters of James K. Newton* (Madison, Wisconsin: The University of Wisconsin Press), 1961. Abel Newton Papers—State Historical Society Library, Madison, Wisconsin. 24, Pittsburg, June 2,/62; p. 26, Pittsburg, June 18th/62.

5. Kenneth M. Jones (compiler). *Never Forsake the Flag, The Letters of Captain George A. Turnbull, Captain Company A; 134th NY Volunteers.* (Self-published), 1998, p 88, Lookout Valley, Tennessee, December 7, 1863; p. 34, Camp near Germanstown, Va., November 25, 1862. Letters were found in Duanesburg, NY.

6. *Dear Mother: Don't Grieve about me.* note 26, xxxi: J.M. Davis letter., 9-26-63, Malcolm Collection, UGA; Tullius Rice to his wife, 7-21-61; Benjamin Moody to his family, 10-20-61; Jack Felder to his sister, April, 1862; Jack Felder to his sister; 9, Jack Felder to his Father, Portsmouth, VA, May 1, 1961.

7. Carlton McCarthy. *Detailed Minutiae of Soldier Life in the Army of Northern Virginia, 1861–1865* (Richmond, Va: Carlton McCarthy and Company), 1882; Cambridge: The Riverside Press, H.O. Houghton and Company. Edward Stevens McCarthy, Captain First Company Richmond Howitzers, fell at Cold Harbor, June 4, 1864. Chapter XI, "Camp-fires of the Boys in Gray." Gutenberg Press.

8. Mary Jordan & Joyce Hatch with Ronald E. Ostman & Harry Littell (eds.). *The Civil War Letters of Private John Tidd* (Ithaca, NY: Six Mile Creek Press), 2011. 73, Savage Switch, April 26, 1863, John Tidd to "Dear Friend Amelia."

9. *Ibid.*, 158. "Home," October 13, 1865. Letter written by "Pam," one of John Tidd's "watchers," addressed to "Dear Friend Amelia" while he was ill.

10. Lucille Griffith (ed.). *Civil War Letters of John W. Cotton, Yours Till Death* (University of Alabama Press), 195. 105, Tunnelhill Ga, Aprile 28th 1864.

11. Neil Kagan and James Robertson (eds.). *The Untold Civil War: Exploring the Human Side of War* (Washington, DC: National Geographic), 2011. 122.

12. *Ibid.*
13. *Ibid.*
14. *Ibid.*
15. *Ibid.*
16. *Ibid.*

17. *Ibid.*, 122; dreaming of home, Joel of Virginia responding to his wife, Mary Ann.

18. Kathleen S. Hanson (Ed.) *Turn Backward O Time: The Civil War Diary of Amanda Shelton; Papers of the Shelton Family, 1864–1866* (University of Iowa); http://beta.worldcat.org/archivegrid/record.php?id=226449112&contributor=164&archivename=University+of+Iowa. 126: Address of Amanda Shelton Stewart On Her Experiences As A Civil War Nurse. First delivered at the reunion of Spanish-American War Veterans and Nurses in Chicago in 1908; and later before the Mississippi Valley Historical Society in 1911.

19. Christian Nix. Letters and photos, National Park Service on-line archives, http://www.nps.gov/stri/historyculture/nix.htm.

20. Jean Powers Soman & Frank L. Byrne, eds. A Jewish Colonel in the Civil War; Marcus M. Spiegel of the Ohio Volunteers) (Lincoln & London: University of Nebraska Press), 1995. 37, Camp Paw Paw, Va., Feb. 13, 1862, My dear beloved Wife, My faithful Caroline!; 39, Paw Paw, Va., Feby. 17/62, My dear and much beloved Wife, My good and sweet Children!.

21. *Ibid.*, 69, Near Winchester Va., March 13/62, My lovely and good Wife, Good Children and dear Brother.

22. *Ibid.*, 99–100, Near Woodstock Va., May 2/62, My dear good lovely and sweet Wife, disturbing dream; 148, Camp in the field in front of the Breastworks, Aug 6/62, My dear dear Wife!, standing before him laughing; 299, Big Black Miss., July 1/63, My dear dear Wife, Spirits meeting.

23. *Ibid.*, 341.

24. Joseph G. Foster. "Homesickness and the Location of Home: Germans, Heimweh, and the American Civil War" (2012). All GraduateTheses and Dissertations. Paper 1333. http://digitalcommons.usu.edu/etd/1333 (Utah State University); quoting Kamphoefner and Helbich, Carl Anton Ruff to his family, January 12, 1865. 39, quoting Carl Anton Ruff to his family, January 12, 1865, in Walter D. Kamphoefner and Wolfgang Helbich, *Germans in the Civil War: The Letters They Wrote Home* (Chapel Hill, NC: The University of North Carolina Press), 2006. 366, Valentin Bechler to Leokadia Bechler, October 25, 1861, in "A German Immigrant in the Union Army," 152; Joseph Hotz to Maria Hotz, December 14, 1861, M710 Box 1, Joseph Hotz Collection, Indiana Historical Society, Indianapolis; Joseph Hotz to Maria Hotz, January 3, 1862, Joseph Hotz Letters; Joseph Hotz to Maria Hotz, August 4, 1862, Joseph Hotz Letters.

25. Foster, 46, quoting *Germans in the Civil War, 323*, Friedrich Martens to his parents, December 3, 1862.

26. *Ibid.*, 69, quoting *Germans in the Civil War*, 137, Wilhelm Francksen to his father, August 4, 1862.

27. Quoting *Germans in the Civil War: The Letters They Wrote Home*, 112, Wilhelm Albrecht to his family, August 22, 1864.

28. Susan J. Matt, "You Can't Go Home Again: Homesickness and Nostalgia in U.S. History." *Journal of American History* 94, no. 2 (September 2007). 469–471.

29. Susan J. Matt, *Homesickness: An American History* (New York: Oxford University Press), 2011. 99–100.

30. Foster, 53.

Chapter 4

1. Calvin Shedd. *The Civil War in Florida: Letters of a New Hampshire Soldier* (Miami, FL: The University of Miami Libraries, Special Collections, The Calvin

Shedd Papers). Letter dated Feb. 26, 1863, from St. Augustine, Florida, Calvin Shedd to his "Dear Wife & Bairns."

2. *Dear Mother: Don't Grieve About Me*, 176–177. Letter to Aunt Hattie, August 7, 1862, Petersburg, VA. See Graves Family Papers, UNC, Collection Number: 02716; http://www.lib.unc.edu/mss/inv/g/Graves_Family.html. Chiefly letters to and from Henry Lea Graves. Letters from Graves discuss routine military life, maneuvers, camp life, and requests for mail; letters to Graves chiefly discuss life on the home front, family news, illnesses, etc., 1861 letters found Henry in the vicinity of Norfolk, Va.; letters in January–September 1862 found him in Wilmington, N.C., and Petersburg, Va.; October 1862–January 1863 letters found him in Petersburg and Richmond, Va.; and letters, 1864–1865, were received by him at Savannah, Ga., and Charleston and James Island, S.C.

3. Lydia Minturn Post. *Soldier's Letters, from Camps, Battlefield and Prison* (Published for the U.S. sanitary commission; University of Michigan; University Library; Michigan Historical Reprint Series. Reprint from: NY: Bunce & Huntington, Publishers; 540 Broadway), 1865. 169: No author, no date, near a letter dated Dec. 1862.

4. Odin's Castle, http://www.civilwarhome.com/letters.htm. "Civil War Home" Collection, Thomas D. Newton.

5. Thomas B. Booth. Confederate 3rd Virginia Cavalry Soldier's Letter. July 13, 1861, Cockletown. Published on-line, http://www.soldierstudies.org/blog/2010/06/confederate-3rd-virginia-cavalry-soldiers-letter/.

6. Civil War Letters between Two Brothers. (Warren County, NY: Rootsweb), http://www.rootsweb.ancestry.com/~nywarren/military/civilwarletters.htm, September 1, 1861; November 29, 1861, Upton Hill, Virginia.

7. J. Gregory Acken. *Inside the Army of the Potomac: The Civil War Experience of Captain Francis Adams Donaldson* (Mechanicsburg, PA: Stackpole Books), 1998. 397, Camp 118th Regt. P. V., 3 miles South of Kelly's Ford, Va., November 29th, 1863, to My dear Brother.

8. Richard T. Van Wyck, Virginia Hughes Kaminsky, ed. *A War to Petrify the Heart: The Civil War Letter of a Dutchess County, N.Y. Volunteer, Richard T. Van Wyck* (Hensonville, NY: Black Dome Press), 1997, 347, Belger Barracks, Baltimore, May 16, 1863, "Dear Cousin [Sarah]."

9. Valgene Dunham (ed.). *Allegany to Appomattox. the Life and Letters of Private William Whitlock of the 188th New York Volunteers* (Syracuse, NY: Syracuse University Press). 2013. 213, Wednsday Evening Jan. the 25th ... 65 "Dear Lide."

10. William Walton (ed.). *A Civil War Courtship, the Letters of Edwin Weller from Antietam to Atlanta* (Garden City, NY: Doubleday & Company, Inc.), 1980. 19–20, letter from Edwin Weller to Nettie Watkins, from Camp near Fairfax Station, Virginia; January 6th, 1863; 107 N.Y.V.

Edwin and Nettie were both from Havana, a small town in south-central New York, two miles south of Watkins Glen and 20 miles north of Elmira. Edwin's regiment, Company H of the 107th New York Volunteers, was formed quickly in 1862, in response to Lincoln's call for 300,000 men, and all were from Havana (later renamed Montour Falls). Edwin wished Nettie "pleasant dreams" and imagined himself "home, tonight on a sofa with my arms full of calico or any other kind of goods, only that it contained a nice young lady..." 69, letter from Edwin Weller to Nettie Watkins, from Camp of Detachment 107 N.Y.V, near Wartrace, Tennessee, Feby 10th, 1864. Edwin survived. On November 15, 1865, Edwin Weller and Antoinette Watkins were married.

11. Kevin Alderson and Patsy Alderson (eds.). *Letters Home to Sarah, the Civil War Letters of Guy C. Taylor, 36th Wisconsin Volunteers* (Madison, Wisconsin: The University of Wisconsin Press), 2012. 156, letter #28, In Camp near Petersburg, Va., November the 27th 1864, "My Dear Wife."

12. Monroe F. Cockrell (ed.). *Gunner with Stonewall, Reminiscences of William Thomas Poague* (Jackson, Tennessee: McCowat-Mercer Press, Inc. Jackson, Tennessee), 1957. 11.

13. *Ibid.* 124.

14. Frank Alexander Montgomery. *Reminiscences of a Mississippian in Peace and War*, Electronic Edition. (Chapel Hill, NC: University of North Carolina), 1999. © This work is the property of the University of North Carolina at Chapel Hill. It may be used freely by individuals for research, teaching and personal use as long as this statement of availability is included in the text. Call number 973.78 M78r 1901 (Davis Library, UNC-CH) Reminiscences of a Mississippian in Peace and War; Montgomery, Frank A. Cincinnati The Robert Clarke Company Press1901 The electronic edition is a part of the UNC-CH digitization project, Documenting the American South, Beginnings to 1920. Dream reference in entry of October 20, 1864.

15. Dena Croft Sullivan (ed.) *The Civil War Diaries and Letters of a Confederate Soldier* (Dickson, Tennessee: self-published), 2010. Roysdon Roberson Etter, Private, 16th TN Infantry Regiment, Co. H., C.S.A., 141, December 27, 1861.

16. David J. Coles and Stephen D. Engle (eds.). *Powder, Lead and Cold Steel: Campaigning in the Lower Shenandoah Valley with the Twelfth Pennsylvania Cavalry, the Civil War Letters of John H. Black.* (Charles Town, West Virginia: The Magazine of the Jefferson County Historical Society), Volume LV, December 1989. 30–31, Pope's Head Run, Headquarters of Company G, June 12, 1862. Also printed in David J. Coles and Stephen D. Engle, eds. *A Yankee Horseman in the Shenandoah Valley: The Civil War Letters of John H. Black, Twelfth Pennsylvania Cavalry* (Knoxville, TN: The University of Tennessee Press), 2012. Note: p. 13, "There is nothing that will bring a person to the grave so soon as homesickness, and how easy it is kept off if only time is taken by the forelock. The only cure for such disease is to form the unbroken resolution to take the world as it comes, and that too as cheerful as nature will allow one to do." John Black to Dear Jennie, Pope's Head Run, Headquarters of Co. G, June 12, 1862.

17. *Ibid.*, 87, Camp, 12 Pa. V. Cavalry, Charlestown, Virginia, December 26, 1864.

18. *Ibid.*, 87.

19. *Ibid.*, 89, Camp 12 Pa. V. Cavalry, Charlestown, Virginia, Camp 12, December 28, 1864, to "My dear Wife." Also in *A Yankee Horseman*, 88.

20. *Ibid.*, 92, Camp 12 Pa. V. Cavalry, Charlestown, Virginia, January 5, 1865, "My Dear Wife."

21. *Ibid.*, 103–104, Charlestown, Virginia, March 31, 1865. About his wounding to "Miss Jennie Black" from P. H. McAteer; Capt. Co. G., 12th Paa. Vol Cavalry.

22. Edward K. Cassedy. *The Civil War Letters and Diaries of Sergeant Charles T. Bowen, Twelfth United States Infantry, 1861–1864* (Baltimore, MD: Butternut & Blue, Army of the Potomac Series), 2001. 243, "soul on paper" reference; 24, Fort Hamilton Sept. 15th, 1861, to "My ever beloved wife, Katie"; 80, Camp Winfield Scott

near Yorktown Va., April 28, 1862, My dearest wife Katie, dream of her and baby.

23. *Ibid.*, 208, In camp near Falmouth, Va. Dec. 28th, 1862, to Katie Darling.

24. *Ibid.*, 236, Camp near Falmouth Va. Feb 22nd/63, My ever darling wife Katie.

25. *Ibid.*, 540, Camp of the 12th Regulars, near Petersburg, Va. July 23/64, to Dear wife. Charles died nine years later from consumption, August 8, 1874. Kate and Charles had five more children, four more daughters and one son. Kate was left destitute after Charles' death. She moved first to Troy, NY, and then to Gloversville, NY, where she worked in the factories.

26. Jeff Toalson (ed.). *Send Me a Pair of Old Boots & Kiss My Little Girls, the Civil War Letters of Richard and Mary Watkins, 1861-1865* (Bloomington, NY: IUniverse, Inc.), 2009. 29–30: Letter from Private Richard Watkins to Mary Watkins.

27. ix–xi; 54, Bio: The letters between Richard H. Watkins and Mary P. Watkins of Prince Edward County, Virginia begin June 27, 1861, and end October 4, 1864. Richard's brother, Nathanial was in the 34th Virginia Infantry.

28. *Ibid.*, 7, Letter from Mary Watkins to Private Richard Watkins; 26, Letter from Mary Watkins to Private Richard Watkins, Linden August 13th, 1861, "My dear Mr. Watkins"; 39: Letter from Private Richard Watkins to Mary Watkins, Halfway House. Oct 15 1861, to "My own dear Mary."

29. *Ibid.*, 60: Letter from Private Richard Watkins to Mary Watkins, Camp Shields, Janry 14th 1862, to "My Precious One."

30. *Ibid.*, 116: Letter from Lt. Richard Watkins to Mary Watkins, Richmond, Aug 21st 62, to "My Precious Mary"; 125: Letter from Lt. Richard Watkins to Mary Watkins, Aug 29th 1862, to "My Darling Mary."

31. "magnetic chain letter" quoted in part on 136: Letter from Mary Watkins to Lt. Richard Watkins, Linden Sept. 24th 1862, to "My dear dear Husband"—full letter used with permission granted by the Virginia Historical Society; 428 North Boulevard, PO Box 7311; Richmond VA 23221-0311; with thanks to Katherine Wilkins, Assistant Librarian.

32. Nathaniel V. Watkins Family Papers, 1846–1889, Special Collections, College of William and Mary, Earl Grey Swem Library, Box 1, Folder 3, Item 10: Nath[aniel] V. Watkins, at camp "Stonewall Jackson," to [Nannie V. Watkins], June 22, 1862.

33. *Ibid.*, 132: Letter from Pattie Watkins to Nannie Watkins, Mt Pleasant, Sep 16th 1862, to "My Dear Sister"; 186: Letter from Mary Watkins to Captain Richard Watkins, May 1st 1863, to "My dear Husband"; 195, Letter from Captain Richard Watkins to Sgt. Nathaniel Watkins, Camp near Orange CorHo, May 14th 1863, To "Dear Bro Nat."

34. *Ibid.*, 127, Letter from Mary Watkins to Lt. Richard Watkins, Linden Sept. 5th 1862; 132, Letter from Pattie Watkins to Nannie Watkins, Mt Pleasant, Sep 16th 1862, to "My Dear Sister"; 186: Letter from Mary Watkins to Captain Richard Watkins on the deaths of the children, May 1st 1863.

35. Letter from Captain Richard Watkins to Mary Watkins, Camp near Culpeper Coho, Feby 19th 1863. With permission to use granted by the Virginia Historical Society; 428 North Boulevard, PO Box 7311; Richmond, VA 23221-0311; with thanks to Katherine Wilkins, Assistant Librarian.

General William Dorsey Pender, one of Lee's generals, wrote to his wife, Fanny: "You say you dreamt that you were riding in a hearse and that it was a bad sign. I thought dreams were interpreted by contraries; that hearses indicated a wedding or something of that sort." "Contraries" as dream interpretation led to false significance of dream imagery. General Pender was mortally wounded less than four months later at the Battle of Gettysburg, leading to the probability of Fanny's dream being precognitive of her husband's death. "To my dearest Wife," March 1863. William W. Hassler, Brian Wills, and William Dorsey Pender (eds.). *One of Lee's Best Men: The Civil War Letters of General William Dorsey Pender* (The University of North Carolina Press, 1965) Originally published as The General to His Lady, 1965.

36. Letter from Mary Watkins to Captain Richard Watkins, Linden, Apr 5th 1863, to "My dear, precious Husband"; with permission to use granted by the Virginia Historical Society; 428 North Boulevard, PO Box 7311; Richmond VA 23221-0311; with thanks to Katherine Wilkins, Assistant Librarian.

37. *Send Me a Pair of Old Boots*, 180: Letter from Captain Richard Watkins to Mary Watkins, April 7th 1863, to "My Precious Mary."

38. *Ibid.*, 208, Letter from Mary Watkins to Captain Richard Watkins, Linden July 27th 1863, to "My Dear Husband"; 244: Letter from Mary Watkins to Captain Richard Watkins, Linden, Dec. 24th 1863, to "My darling Husband"; 250–251: Letter from Captain Richard Watkins to Mary Watkins, Camp near Charlottesville, Jany 12th 1864, to "My Own Dear Mary."

39. *Ibid.*, 286: Letter from Mary Watkins to Captain Richard Watkins, Linden June 25th 1864.

40. *Ibid.*, 294–295: Letter from Mary Watkins to Captain Richard Watkins, Linden July 1st 1864, to "My darling Husband."

41. *Ibid.*, 307: Letter from Captain Richard Watkins to Mary Watkins, Camp near Smithfield, Aug 31, 1864, to "My own Dear Mary."

42. *Ibid.*, 329: Letter from Richard Watkins to Nathaniel Watkins, Home. Aug 29th 1865.

43. Arch Fredric Blakey, Ann Smith Lainhart, and Winston Bryant Stephens, Jr. (eds.). *Rose Cottage Chronicles, Civil War Letters of the Bryant-Stephens Families of North Florida* (Gainesville, FL: University Press of Florida), 1998. Preface. Florida seceded from the Union on January 10, 1861. Winston Stephens' company was organized in September and mustered into service in November, 1861. He served in the state of Florida, but his visits were still brief and not as frequent as either he or Octavia wished. Enhancing the preserved correspondence between Octavia, called "Tivie," editors included journal entries and letters between Octavia's parents, James and Rebecca; her brothers, Willie, Davis, Henry, and George; and aunts and uncles. The family was divided in their loyalties. Octavia's father supported the Union; most of the other male members supported the Confederacy.

44. *Ibid.*, 40, Octavia Bryant to Winston Stephens, White Cottage Jan 29, 1859; 44–45, Winston Stephens to Octavia Bryant, Pine Grove June 27, 1859.

45. *Ibid.*, 65: Octavia Stephens to Winston Stephens, Nov. 5, 1861, to "My dear Husband."

46. *Ibid.*, Winston Stephens to Octavia Stephens, Camp Porter Nov 10 1861, to "My Dear Wife."

47. *Ibid.*, 81: Octavia Stephens to Winston Stephens, Christmas Eve 1861, to "My dear Husband"; 92: Winston Stephens to Octavia Stephens, Fernandina Jan 14, 1862,

to "My Dear Good Wife"; 103: Octavia Stephens to Winston Stephens, March 9, 1862, to "My dear Husband."

48. *Ibid.*, 117: Octavia Stephens to Winston Stephens, May 23, 1862, to "My dear Winston"; 145–146: Octavia Stephens to Winston Stephens, Sept 9, 1862, to "My own husband"; 172: Octavia Stephens to Winston Stephens, Rose Cottage Nov 21, 1862, to "My dear husband."

49. *Ibid.*, 180: Journal: [Rebecca] Dec 14, 1862; 206: Octavia Stephens to Winston Stephens, Rose Cottage Feb 21, 1863, to "My own dear husband."

50. *Ibid.*, 225: Winston Stephens to Octavia Stephens, Camp Finegan May 4, 1863, to "My Dear Wife."

51. *Ibid.*, 227: Octavia to Winston Stephens, Rose Cottage May 14, 1863, to "My dear husband."

52. *Ibid.*, 235: Winston Stephens to Octavia Stephens, Camp Finegan June 1, 1863, to "My Dear Wifey"; 239: Winston Stephens to Octavia Stephens, Camp Finegan June 15, 1863, to "My Dear Wifey."

The "representative," would be born in March, 1864, days after Winston's death. Tivie would name it Winston, Jr., in Winston's memory and honor.

53. *Ibid.*, 243: Octavia Stephens to Winston Stephens, June 19, 1863, to "My own dear husband."

54. *Ibid.*, 253: Winston Stephens to Octavia Stephens, Camp Cooper July 27, 1863, to "My dear Wife."

55. *Ibid.*, 282–283: Octavia Stephens to Winston Stephens, Nov 6, 1863, to "My very dear husband."

56. *Ibid.*, 296: Winston Stephens to Octavia Stephens, Camp Cooper Dec 19, 1863, to "My Dear Wife"; 301: Octavia Stephens to Winston Stephens, At Home Jan 1, 1864, to "My dear husband."

57. *Ibid.*, 299, Winston Stephens to Octavia Stephens, Camp Cooper, Dec 29, 1863; p. 304: Octavia Stephens to Winston Stephens, At Home Jan 8, 1864. "My dear husband."

58. *Ibid.*, 305; Winston Stephens to Octavia Stephens, Camp Cooper Jan 11, 1864, to "My Dear Wife"—the magic of a word; 306: Octavia Stephens to Winston Stephens, At Home Jan 17, 1864, to "My dear dear husband."

59. *Ibid.*, 307: Winston Stephens to Octavia Stephens, Camp Cooper Jan 18, 1864 to "My Dear Wife"; 312: Octavia Stephens to Winston Stephens, Jan 29, 1864, to "My dear husband"; 313: Winston Stephens to Octavia Stephens, Camp Cooper Feb 2, 1864, to "My Dear Wife."

60. *Ibid.*, 316: Octavia Stephens to Winston Stephens, Feb 12, 1864, to "My very dear husband."

61. *Ibid.*, 317: Winston Stephens to Octavia Stephens, Lake City Feb. 13, 1864, to "My Dear Wife"; 326: Octavia Stephens to Willie Bryant, Mar 2, 1864, "Dear brother Willie" about their mother; 327: Willie Bryant to Rebecca Bryant, Atlanta Ga. Mar 8, 1864, "My dear Mother" about Winston's death; 328: Willie writes to his brother Davis from Aunt Julia's on March 12, 1864, that "Mine is not a grief that can relieve itself in words."; Tivie writes in her journal: Near Thomasville, Mar 15, 1864; 329: Swepston Stephens to Octavia Stephens; Ocala Oct 20, 1866, to "My Dear Sister Tivie."

62. Hudson Hyatt (ed.). *Captain Hyatt, Being the Letters Written During the Years 1863–1864 to His Wife, Mary by Captain T. J. Hyatt, 126th Ohio Volunteer Infantry* (Ohio History, The Scholarly Journal of The Ohio Historical Society), Volume 53. 166, Letter dated January 8th, 1863. http://www.webring.org/l/rd?ring=cwarchring;id=1;url=http%3A%2F%2Fwww%2Efrontierfamilies%2Enet%2Ffamily%2Fhome%2Ehtml.

63. *Ibid.*, 171, Captain Thomas Hyatt, HdQrs. 126th Ohio Vols, March 6th, 1864, to "Dear Wife."

64. *Ibid.*, 181, Wednesday morning, August 31st.

65. *Ibid.*, 183, from J. Lamb. October 15, 1864, Winchester.

66. *Dear Mother*, 43, Manassas, Virginia, August 3, 1861, Hiram to his Mother, GAH.

67. *Ibid.*, 288, Azra Bartholomew to Frank; Murfreesboro, TN; January 5, 1863; 288: Grant Carter to his Sister, Madison Station, Virginia, March 24, 1864; 296: Blanton Fortson to his Mother, Pumpkin Vine Creek, June 3, 1864; 300: Bolton Thurmond to Frances Porterfield, Cobb County, Georgia, June 10, 1864.

68. William Ross Stilwell. *The Stilwell Letters: A Georgian in Longstreet's Corps, Army of Northern Virginia* (Mercer University Press), 2002. 49, Antietam, Virginia side, September, 18, 1862, William Stilwell to Molly.

"William Ross Stilwell was wed to Mary Fletcher Speer (known as Molly) on 8 September 1859 in McDonough, Georgia, in Henry County. William was twenty and Molly was eighteen. Having moved to northwestern Louisiana and having their first child, they returned to Georgia in 1861 so Molly and their son Tommy could stay with the family while William joined Company F of the 53rd Regiment Georgia Volunteer Infantry in May 1862." "The 53rd Georgia, on reaching Virginia, was immediately assigned to the brigade commanded by Paul Jones Semmes, a wealthy Columbus banker. The brigade was later commanded by Goode Bryan and then by James Philip Simms. The 53rd Georgia was in the Corps of James Longstreet and fought at Antietam, Chancellorsville, Gettysburg, the Wilderness, and Cedar Creek." Stilwell maneuvered for a special position and consecutively held positions of brigade headquarters guard, assistant to the brigade quartermaster, and finally brigade courier. Throughout the war, he maintained daily contact with company F."

69. *Ibid.*, 58, Antietam, Camp near Martinsburg, N.W. Virginia, September 23, 1862.

70. *Ibid.*, 14–15, General Semmes' Headquarters, July 15, 1862, William Stilwell to Molly.

71. *Ibid.*, 122, place missing, probably March 1863. William Stilwell to Molly; *Dear Mother,* William Stilwell to his wife, 8-9-63.

72. *The Stilwell Letters*, 182, Gettysburg, William Stilwell to Molly, July 10, 1863.

73. *Ibid.*, 18, Headquarters, General Semmes, 4 miles east of Richmond, Virginia, July 22, 1863; 157, Chancelorsville, Same old Camp Fredericksburg, May 10, 1863, William Stilwell to Molly.

Song in William Stilwell's letter—1863—I Will Watch for Thee.

   1.—I watch for thee when parting day sheds on the earth lingering ray when his blushes o'er the rose a richer tint of crimson throws, and every flower's leaves are curled like beauty shrinking from the world. When silence reigns o'er lawn or lea, then dearest love, I watch for thee.

   2.—I watch for thee when eve's first star shines dimly in the heavens afar, and twilight mists and shadows gray upon the lake's broad water play. When not a breeze or sound is heard to startle evening's lonely bird but hushed is even the humming bee. Then, dearest love, I watch for thee.

   3.—I watch for thee when on the eyes of childhood slumber gently lies when sleep has stilled the noisy mirth of playful voices round our hearth and each young one's fancy glows with dreams that only childhood knows of pleasures past or yet to be then dearest love I watch for thee.

74. *Ibid.*, 252, The Wilderness; William Stilwell to Molly, Camp near Gordonsville, Virginia, April 25th, 1864.
75. *Ibid.*, 245, William Stilwell to Molly, Greeneville, East Tennessee, March 23rd, 1864.
76. *Ibid.*, 287, Cedar Creek; Nov. 17th, 1864; General Hospital No. 1, Savannah, Georgia.
77. Joan Metzger (ed.) *The Griffith Letters: The Story of Frank Griffith and the 116th New York Volunteer Infantry in the Civil War* (Westminster, MD: Heritage Books), 2007. 14, Camp Chapin, October 23, 1862, "Dearest wife."

On bio: 1: "I came here to serve my country," Baltimore, MD—Fall 1862: Frank E. Griffith enlisted in Company K of the 116th on September 2, 1862. His brief note of September 9 informed his wife Thankful that he (and the men of Co. K) would be leaving Buffalo the next day. In the next six letters written from camp in Baltimore, MD, Frank expressed his loneliness, and explained what life was like in camp. As he put it "this Soldier life makes [us] tough if we do not die seasoning." Frank had six sisters and two daughters, Carrie Annette, "Nettie," born June 5, 1860, and Gertrude Mary, "Gertie," born April 7, 1862.

78. *Ibid.*, 20, Fort Monroe, December 2, 1862.
79. *Ibid.*, January 12, 1863.
80. *Ibid.*, 31, Camp Love, Greenville, Louisiana, Jan. 24th, 1863; 33, January 31, 1863.
81. *Ibid.*, 59, Thursday morning, April 9th [1863].
82. *Ibid.*, 55, April 7, 1863: "…it must have been a splendid building if we can judge from its present appearances … it was lighted with gass for we can see the gass pipes all over the inside, and some of the most splendid stone cornice around the rooms, but they are all in ruins now, and all blacked with smoke and shored timber. The tower is used as a signal station by our forces. But the yard which covers about two acres is the most beautiful place I ever saw in my life. The unusual shade trees abound here in all there magnificence, nice shady walks, and the most beautiful shrubs and flowers of this southern climate here greet the eye. It is like our May or June here now, only the nights are cool … there were once nice fountain and every thing pleasant here, but it has all been sacrificed to the demen of secession. The city is about as large as Springville. Now the most of it was burned when we took the place by our shells, and you can see the ruins of the once splendid stores and palaces of the southern aristocracy. I tell you we talk of making sacrifices to carry on this war, but they are nothing when compared with what the men and women of the south have sacrificed to their Confederacy. The Old State Prison is standing yet, but is used for the use of the army to hold their prisoners and for military stores." The remaining walls became part of an 1882 restoration.

83. *Ibid.*, 75, Baton Rouge, July 11, 1863.
84. *Ibid.*, 86, Camp Misery, Bayou Teche, Louisiana, "in the mud knee deep," St. Mary's Parish on the road to Texas, October 2, 1863.
85. *Ibid.*, 121–122, Camp Emory near Franklin, Louisiana, January 17, 1864; "war over" dream, 124, same location, January 20, 1864; "likeness," 135 and 142, Camp Emory, January 30, 1864, to "Mein Leiber Frow," February 4, 1864; dream, 143, Camp Emory, February 7, 1864.

Frank described the "ornaments" in their camp at Camp Emory, apparently so well known that they were noted as a special army curiosity: "…there is some talk of our going to New Orleans in a few days, but I do not know how true it is. We have got the best camp here that I ever saw any where and we are fixing it up nice. Ev[e]ry Co are making some kind of an ornament at the end of their Co street. I have been at work all the week making an arch in our street. There is the letter of our Co on the top and under that 116, and then in the arch I took some vines and made this sentence, "Our Country and Our Flag." It is all trimed with moss and is high enough for the Co to march through. I heard the Col say that it was the neatest thing he has seen yet. There, is not that complimentary? but then I don't feel very proud of it myself for I have had all the Co mad at me all the time that I have been at work on it…" (147, February 12, 1864). Camp Emory was located on level ground with a few scattered trees, according to Orton Clark, quoted in The Griffith Letters. He states it was the way the different companies of the 116th decorated the camp which attracted attention and visitors to the camp, and quotes from the record of the 114th N.Y.S.V.: "The camp of the One Hundred and Sixteenth New York was a place of especial resort, being regarded as one of the greatest curiosities in the army. Situated in a very romantic spot, its inmates had, with a great amount of pains and pride, enhanced the natural beauty of the location. By the use of moss and evergreens, they constructed arbors, bowers, and arches, resembling architecture of every kind. Their grounds were laid out with exquisite taste. Flower beds, miniature forts and monitors, rustic seats and shrubbery, every where met the delighted eye. In the evening, when the camp was lit up by the fires the effect was perfectly enchanting, resembling one of the fabled scenes of oriental magnificence." Clark, 139–141.

86. *Ibid.*, 150, No. 13, Camp Emory, La., Feb. 14, 1864.
87. *Ibid.*, 273, Washington, May 14, 1865. Groves Theatre was located at Pennsylvania and East near the President's mansion.
88. Charles F. Larimer. *Love and Valor; Intimate Civil War Letters Between Captain Jacob and Emeline Ritner* (Western Springs, Illinois: Sigourney Press), 2000. Author Query.
89. *Ibid.*, 72, Camp Near Helena, Arkansas, December 2, 1862, to "Dear Emeline"; 258, Chattanooga, Tennessee, December 1, 1863, "Dear Wife"—Jacob had a boil on his hand.
90. *Ibid.*, 96, Mount Pleasant, Iowa, January the 5th, 1863, Monday night, "Dear Jake."
91. *Ibid.*, 103, Letter No. 5, Napoleon, Arkansas, January 15, 1863; 134, Young's Point, Louisiana, March 15, 1863, "Dear Emeline."
92. *Ibid.*, 154, Greenville, Mississippi, April 17, 1863, to "Dear Emeline."
93. *Ibid.*, 163 & 165, Mount Pleasant, Iowa, May the 6th, 1863, "Dear Jake."
94. *Ibid.* 308–309, Mount Pleasant, Iowa, July the 19th, 1864, "Dear Wife"; 335, Jacob to Emeline's mother, Camp near Atlanta, Georgia, August 14, 1864; 344, Near Atlanta, Georgia, August 29, 1864, "My dear Wife."
95. *Ibid.*, 373, Bivouac in the Field near Rome, Georgia, October 13, 1864, "My dear Wife"; 386, Mt. Pleasant, Iowa, Nov. 10th, 1864, "Dear Husband"; 403, Savannah, Georgia, January 4, 1864, "My Dear Wife,"; 405, Camp 25th Iowa Infantry, Savannah, Georgia, January 8, 1865, "My Dear Wife"; 426, February 17, 1865, letter written to Emeline after the capture and burning of Columbia, SC.
96. *Ibid.*, 448, from the obituary of Capt. J. B. Ritner.

97. Andrea R. Foroughi (ed.). *Go If You Think It Your Duty: A Minnesota Couple's Civil War Letters* (Minnesota Historical Society Press), 2008, http://muse.jhu.edu/books/9780873516716; Project Muse Bowler manuscripts. http://www.mnhs.org/library/findaids/00792.xml; Manuscript finding aide—Minnesota Historical Society. JMB to ECB, 27 April 1861 and 27 September 1862, Bowler Papers; ECB to JMB, 2 September 1864, Bowler Papers.

98. *Ibid.*,30, Fort Snelling, May 2, 1861, 1½ o'clock p.m.; 42, Nininger, Minn., Dec. 23/1861, Lizzie to Madison.

99. *Ibid.*,100, Murfreesboro, TN, Thursday, June 5, 1862, Madison to Lizzie; 101, Nininger, June 17, 1862, Lizzie to Madison.
This is explained further in the next few letters—men in JM's regiment were out to get him and pulled a dangerous prank involving forged documents. JM was court martialed and cleared of the charges. Nothing, apparently, to do with the event described in this letter. On page 161, further explanation in a letter from Columbus, Ky., April 30, 1863; Madison to "Libby." Footnote read: "Madison's 'little trouble' was a charge of "Conduct prejudicial to good order and military discipline," which resulted in a trial before a court-martial on May 5 and 6, 1863, in Columbus. Madison was accused of "knowingly and intentionally" carrying $50.00 of "worthless Bank Currency of various amounts and denominations … with the intention of fraudulently using and disposing of the same for their pretended or some other value." Although the charge was submitted by Major Hans Mattson and proceeded up the chain of command to be referred to the court-martial, it was instigated by Sergeant David Morgan and Sergeant William Allison in Company F, both of whom Madison had referred to unfavorably in earlier letters. The transcript of James M. Bowler's court-martial file [LL-600] can be found at the national Archives and records Administration, Washington, D.C."

100. *Ibid.*, 133; Notice of their marriage appeared in the *Hastings Independent*, 4 December 1862: "MARRIED.—On the 30th ult., by Rev. T.F. Thickstun, at the residence of the bride's father, Lieut. James M. Bolar, of the Third Regiment Minnesota Volunteers, and Miss Lizzie Caleff, eldest daughter of Mr. Samuel Caleff of Nininger."

101. *Ibid.*,159, Nininger, April 23, 1863, Thursday evening, Lizzie to "Dear Hubbie."

102. *Ibid.*, 170: Steamer Izetta, Columbus, Ky., June 4, 1863, Madison to Lizzie; 176: Snyder's Bluff, Miss., Wednesday, July 1, 1863, Running journal entries, Madison to Libby.

103. *Ibid.*, 208, Head Quarters, Post of Little Rock, Arkansas. (letterhead), October 23d, 1863, Madison to Libby.

104. *Ibid.*, 211–212, Little Rock, Ark., Nov. 14, 1863 Madison to Lizzie; quoted in *Go, If You Think It Your Duty*, 216 Stephen Berry argued in the mind of a Southern soldier "so long as a man could see himself through the idealized eyes of a woman, he would continue to fight. If ever he could not, romance and patriotism, love of woman and love of country, might become disaggregated, and then he would be forced to choose between them" [*All That Makes a Man*, 192, 216]. The editor argued, that, although a Northerner, "Madison, too, needed Lizzie's approval so that his sense of duty to her and to the Union could be one and the same and not competing obligations."

105. *Ibid.*, 261: Nininger Oct 25, 1864, Lizzie to Madison.

106. *Ibid.* 277: Nininger Minn. Feb 5th, 1865, Saturday evening, Lizzie to Madison; 280: Little Rock, Ark., Feb'y. 18th 1865, Madison to Lizzie; 290: April 21st, 1865, Lizzie to Madison; 297: Little Rock, Ark., June 3rd, 1865, Madison to Lizzie (Saturday).

107. Robert W. Glover (ed.). "The War Letters of a Texas Conscript in Arkansas," Arkansas Historical Quarterly, XX (Winter, 1961). 358, August 27, letter from Washtaw County, Arkansas; 361, September 7 letter from "Perrairie Co., Arkansas.

108. *Ibid.*, 369, letter from Camp Nelson, Arkansas.

109. *Ibid.*, 358; 387, William E. Stoker to Elizabeth Stoker, August 27, 1862.

Chapter 5

1. James Martin. "Fatherhood in the Confederacy: Southern Soldiers and Their Children"; *The Journal of Southern History*, Volume LXIII, No. 2, May 1997. Mr. Martin is an associate professor of history, Marquette University.

2. Walbrook D. Swank (ed.). *Confederate Letters and Diaries, 1861–1865* (Shippenburg, PA: Burd Street Press, a division of White Mane Publishing), 1988.
Benjamin Moody; Arch Fredric Blakey, Ann Smith Lainhart; and Winston Bryant Stephens Jr. (eds.). *Rose Cottage Chronicles, Civil War Letters of the Bryant-Stephens Families of North Florida* (Gainesville, FL: University Press of Florida), 1998. 69.

3. Jeffrey D. Marshall (ed.). *A War of the People, Vermont Civil War Letters* (Hanover, NH: University Press of New England), 1999. 238, George G. Howe to "Dear Lorette, Near Cold Harbor, Va., June 12th, 1864. Lt George Howe was a captain by the time he mustered out on June 24, 1865. He wrote to Lorette to "start for Vermont" and married her on Feb. 20, 1866. They had one child, Edith; and Lorette died of typhoid fever on September 19, 1868, just one year after the birth of her baby. Letters between Howe and Wolcott are in the collections of The Henry Sheldon Museum in Middlebury, VT.

4. Posted by a descendant in genealogy records: *Civil War Letters*, http://fanflower.com/2009/05/12/civil-war-letters/. Richard E. Richards to "Dear Wife," March 20, 1864, Headquarters, Co. C 125th Regiment Illinois Volunteer Inf., Camp at Lee and Gordon's Mills.

5. *Ibid.*, March 26, 1864, to My Dear Wife, no location but probably Gordon's Mills, Georgia.

6. *Ibid.* Richard Richards "To Eddy and Freddy, my very dear little boys," from the Marine Hospital, Chicago, Illinois, Dec. 21, 1864.

7. John C. Oeffinger (ed.) *A Soldier's General; the Civil War Letters of Major General Lafayette Mclaws* (Chapel Hill & London: The University of North Carolina Press), 2002. 91, Willliamsburg, Virginia, June 8th 1861, My dearly beloved wife.

8. *Ibid.*, 113, Camp 2nd Division; Youngs Mill, Virginia; October 23, 1861, Wednesday, to "My dearly beloved wife.

9. *Ibid.*, 117, birth letter, Camp Young Mill, December 8th, 1861, Sunday.

10. *Ibid.*, 148; Head Quarters Division, Culpeper Court-House, Virginia, Nov. 16th/62, Sunday, My dearly beloved wife; 173, Fredericksburg, Virginia, April 2, 1863, Thursday.

11. *Ibid.*, 181, Fredericksburg, May 9th/63 Saturday.

12. *Ibid.*, 186, Head Quarters Division; Raccoon Ford on the Rapidan, Virginia, June 5th/63, Friday.

13. *Ibid.*, 206: Head Quarters Division, Camp Near Chattanooga [Tennessee], October 14th/63 [Wednesday]; 251: Ft. Stevens Depot, [St. Stephens Depot, South Carolina], February 22nd 1865 [Wednesday], My dear Sweet Wife.

14. John D. Miller, Editor and Transcriber. "An Alabama Merchant in Civil War Richmond: The Harvey Wilkerson Luttrell Letters, 1861–1865." (The University of Alabama Press: The Alabama Review), July, 2005. 176–206; 183, Oxford, Alabama, July 30, 1861, Harvey to Dear Father.

15. *Ibid.*, 187: Second Alabama Hospital, Richmond, Virginia, Saturday, May 16th 1863, Harvey to My Dear Sue.

16. *Ibid.*, 197, Howd Grove Hospl., Richmond May 30th. 1864. Harvey to My dear Sue.

17. *Ibid.*, 200, Howard Grove Hospital, Richmond, Virginia, September 3, 1864, Harvey to My Dear Sue.

18. *Ibid.*, 206, Camp near Petersburg, October 14th 1864, Harvey to My Dear Sue.

19. http://freepages.genealogy.rootsweb.ancestry.com/~connectville/military/jeycw/700.htm June 1, 1862, John Yates to "Dear Wife," Elizabeth Roberson Yates, Columbia, TN.

20. Jennifer Cain Bohrnstedt. *While Father Is Away: The Civil War Letters of William H. Bradbury* (Lexington, KY: University Press of Kentucky), 2003. 29: Headqrts. 38 Brigade 10 Div. A.G., Bowling Green, Ky, Nov. 6, 1862, to "My dearest wife"; 45: Head Quarters U.S. Forces, Bowling Green Ky, Dec. 12th 1862, "My dearest wife."; "A Chapter on Dreams," *Harper's New Monthly Magazine* 2, No. 12 (May 1851), 768–74; Samuel Osgood, "Mental Health," *Harper's New Monthly Magazine*, 28, No. 166 (March 1864), 496.

Chapter 6

1. http://freepages.family.rootsweb.ancestry.com/~bowen/hobbys8thTexas.html (Bowen Family Papers). W. L. Fagan. W. L. Fagan. *Southern War Songs Camp-Fire, Patriotic & Sentimental* (On-Line songbook). http://www.traditionalmusic.co.uk/southern-war-songs/southern-war-songs%20-%200403.htm; see also http://shortstories.ucgreat.com/read/010/983.htm-poem/song written in Galveston, Texas, 1864.

2. Pat Elliott family blog. *Civil War Letters of William (Billy) A. Elliott*: http://www.civilwarhome.com/elliott letters.htm. Billy was nineteen. He wrote to his father from Top Sails Inlet, twenty-one miles below Wilmington, North Carolina. Letter 1, "Dear Father." 11 Reg company ANN Troops."

3. *Ibid.*, family folklore.

4. Edmund J. Raus, Jr., ed. *Ministering Angel:The Reminiscences of Harriet A. Dada, a Union Army Nurse in the Civil War* (Gettysburg, PA:Thomas Publications), 2004. 55, dream of lemons; 50, statement of hope. William H. Bright, Company C, 22d Wisconsin Infantry, was the young man who wrote a tribute to Harriet after the war, recalling that he owed his life to her telling him to "bid me live."

5. Bob Blaisdell, ed. *Civil War Letters from Home, Camp & Battlefield* (Mineola, NY: Dover Pubications, Inc., 2012, 178, Chauncey H. Cooke, U.S.A., 25th Infantry, Wisconsin, Pine Woods of Georgia, June 6, 1864, Dear Parents.

6. John H. Worsham. *One of Jackson's Foot Cavalry: John H. Worsham* (New York: Neale Publishing Company), 1912. 147.

7. Richmond: *The Daily Dispatch*. December 21, 1864. Story titled "The Dream of Home and its Results."

8. Richmond, Virginia, *Daily Dispatch* on November 24, 1863, *Hid Away in the Smokehouse*, http://dlxs.richmond.edu/cgi/t/text/text-idx?c=ddr;cc=ddr;type=simple;rgn=div2;q1=dream;view=text;subview=detail;sort=occur;idno=ddr0949.0025.121;node=ddr0949.0025.121%3A3.1.

9. William D. Turner. *Some War-Time Recollections. the Story of a Confederate Officer Who Was at First One of Those in Charge of and Later a Captive in Libby Prison*, printed in the "The Libby Lion."

10. Jeffrey C. Lowe and Sam Hodges (eds.). *Letters to Amanda; "The Civil War Letters of Marion Hill Fitzpatrick, Army of Northern Virginia* (Macon, GA: Mercer University Press), 1998. 199. 34: Near Guiness Station, Va. (Letter Number 17), Dec. 4th, 1862, Dear Amanda; 181: 45th Ga. Near Petersburg, Va. (Letter Number 89), Oct. 23rd, 1864, Dear Amanda; 209–211, letter from William Fields, Co. 1, 48th Va. Infantry, to Mrs. Fitzpatrick, Jackson Hospital, Richmond, Va., June 8, 1865.

11. John Beauchamp Jones. *A Rebel War Clerk's Diary* (Philadelphia, PA: J. B. Lippincott & Co.), 1866. http://www.cw-chronicles.com/blog/1861/06/; 56, A Rebel War Clerk's Diary at the Confederate States Capital by a Clerk in the War Department of the Confederate States Government; Project Gutenberg.

12. *Ibid.*, 337.

Robert Tyler, eldest son of the rather unpopular President John Tyler and his first wife, Letitia, never aspired to the presidency. He was the Confederate Register of the Treasury during the Civil War, his father's private secretary, and, after the war, editor of the *Montgomery Advertiser*. www.en.wikipedia.org/wiki/Robert_Tyler.

13. Jones, Jenkin Lloyd. *An Artilleryman's Diary* (Wisconsin History Commission: Original Papers, No. 8; Wisconsin History Commission), February, 1914. Project Gutenberg.

14. Michael B. Chesson (ed.). *J. Franklin Dyer, the Journal of a Civil War Surgeon* (Lincoln and London: University of Nebraska Press), 2003. 46: dream of home, Rectortown, November 7, 1862; 72: dream of rebel conversation, Falmouth, April 23, 1863; 70: Falmouth, April 13, 1863, evening, journal entry, on rebels; 164: Totopotomoy Creek, June 1, 1864.

Jonah Franklin Dyer, the surgeon of the Nineteenth Regiment of Massachusetts Volunteer Infantry, surgeon in chief of the Second Division, and acting medical director of the II Corps, Army of the Potomac, was born April 15, 1826, in Eastport, Maine. He was the fourth of seven children of Charles Dyer, a Maine native, and Hannah Snow, who was born in Granville, Nova Scotia. After obtaining his medical diploma, Frank moved to Annisquam, one of the villages in the town of Gloucester on the northwest side of Cape Anne Peninsula in Essex County, Massachusetts. After becoming settled in his career, Frank married Maria Haskell French in Boston on May 4, 1853. She died within a month. Frank then married Maria Davis of Hancock, New Hampshire, on September 7, 1854. Franklin [Frankie] was born on August 29, 1856. This is a remarkable example of a surviving surgeon's journal. Frank chose to remain in the field, treated both sides equally; wrote one of the earliest and best reports on scurvy among the soldiers and had both professional and political skill. He survived. One of many of his wry comments concerned seeing Custer in camp: 114: Banks' Ford, Rappahannock September 1, 1863, "...Saw Kilkpatrick yesterday at his quarters near Hartwood Church. He may be a smart man, at any rate is a smart talker. General Custer, who has a brigade of cavalry near, is a gorgeous-looking young man—smart though—his dress a black velvet jacket and pants, double knot of lace on sleeves, and two gold stripes on the legs, and light flaxen hair falling in curls on is shoulders. Some men can dress like circus riders without making themselves ridiculous." A photograph exists of Custer in this dress.

15. George A. Lawrence. *Border and Bastille, the Author of "Guy Livingstone"* (New York: W. I. Pooley & Co., Harpers' Building, Franklin Square: Wynkoop, Hallenbeck & Thomas, Printers, Fulton Street, New York). Chapter 1, "A Foul Start." Gutenberg Press.

16. J. M. Addeman. *Reminiscences of Two Years with the Colored Troops* (Providence, RI: N. Bangs Williams & Co.), 1880. Reprinted in Project Gutenberg.

17. Sam R. Watkins. *Co. Aytch, a Confederate Memoir of the Civil War* (Chattanooga, TN: Chattanooga Times), 1900, 17, Romney. The weekend of February 9, 2013, brought an enormous nor'easter into Boston, Connecticut, New York, and other areas. Long Island experienced this same phenomenon known as "thunder snow."

18. Rebecca Blackwell Drake and Margie Riddle Bearss, editors and introductions. *My Dear Wife, Letters to Matilda; the Civil War Letters of Sid and Matilda Champion of Champion Hill* (Self published), 208 August 27, 1864, Camp near Atlanta "My dear Wife."

19. *Ibid.*, 40, Camp in Vicksburg, September 26, 1862, "My Dear Wife."

20. *Ibid.*, 87–88, Camp Kelsoe, April 30, 1863, "My Dear Wife."

21. *Ibid.*, 91: Vicksburg, May 12, 1863.

22. *Ibid.*, 146: Refuge Home, June 14, 1864, "My Precious Husband"; 152, Refuge Home, June 24, 1864, "My Precious Husband."

23. *Ibid.*, 261, epilogue based on memoirs written by Matilda's grandson, Sid Champion III, prior to his death in 1957.

24. Mary Jeffreys Bethell. *Diary, January 1st 1861–Dec. 1865* (Chapel Hill, NC: University of North Carolina at Chapel Hill), Electronic Edition. Jan 29th, 1864, It may be used freely by individuals for research, teaching and personal use as long as this statement of availability is included in the text. MARY JEFFREYS BETHELL DIARY: January 1st 1861–Dec. 1865 Mary Jeffreys Bethell, Call number 1737 (Manuscripts Dept., Southern Historical Collection, University of North Carolina at Chapel Hill). In other dreams warm baths were either advised or played additional roles for Aelius Aristides; International Journal of Dream Research, Volume 5, No. 1, "The Dreams of Aelius Aristides, a Psychological Interpretation," by J. C. Stephens, Oakland, CA, 2012—discusses Aristides and dreams of bathing, JStor.

25. Virginia Jeans Laas. *The Civil War Letters of Elizabeth Blair Lee—Wartime Washington* (Urbana & Chicago: University of Illinois Press), 1991. Introduction; 348, letter about Elizabeth's run on sentences.

26. *Ibid.*, 70, Philadelphia, July 28, 1861, Lizzie to Dear Phil.

27. *Ibid.*, 77, Bethlehem, September 10, 1861.

28. *Ibid.* 134, on "rack of anxiety"—journal—May 1, 1862; 135, Silver Spring, April 27, 1862, Dear Phil; 136, Silver Spring, April 29, 1862.

29. *Ibid.*, 138, Silver Spring, May 6, 1862, Dear Phil; 151, Silver Spring, May 26, 1862.

30. *Ibid.*, 267, Washington, May 8, 1863.

31. *Ibid.*, 273, Silver Spring, June 12, 1862, Dear Phil.

32. *Ibid.*, 334, Washington, January 7, 1864, Dear Phil.

33. *Ibid.*, 425, Silver Spring, August 23, 1864.

34. *Ibid.*, 448, Washington, December 10, 1864, Dear Phil.

35. *Ibid.*, 471, Washington, February 1, 1865.

36. *Ibid.*, 479; 485, Washington, March 21, 1865, My dear Phil; 496, Washington, April 17, 1865, My dear Phil; 497, Washington, April 19, 1865, My dear Phil; 498, Washington, April 20, 1865; 499, Washington, April 22, 1865, My dear Phil.

37. *Ibid.*, 500, Washington, April 25, 1865.

38. Brooks D. Simpson (ed.) *The Civil War; the Third Year Told by Those Who Lived It* (The Library of America: Penguin Groups), 2013. 569 and 573: Battle of Chattanooga: Tennessee, November 1863; William Wrenshall Smith: Journal, Monday, November 16; p. 578: Tuesday Nov 24, 1863.

39. *Ibid.*, 611, A soldier at Mine Run: Virginia, November-December 1863.
Wilbur Fisk to The Green Mountain Freeman [Second Vermont Regiment].

40. Lucienne Grace Oppenheimer Guyot. "Fighting My Way Through: Northern Rural Women in the American Civil War," a thesis submitted in partial fulfillment of the requirements for the degree of Bachelor of Arts (Honours) in History; University of Sydney; October 2012, quoting from the R. Dutton Silsby *Civil War Letters 1862–1863* (Barre, Vt.: Vermont Historical Society) (MSA 521:01–07. Called the Silsby Collection. 5, Russell Dutton Silsby to Marinda Brown Silsby, November 12, 1862 Russell Dutton Silsby to Marinda Brown Silby, November 12, 1862.

41. *Ibid.*, 17 in the thesis; Marinda Brown Silsby to Russell Dutton Silsby, undated c. April 1863. Silsby Collection.

42. *Ibid.*, Russell Dutton Silby to Marinda Brown Silsby, March 1, 1863; 37 in thesis.

43. *Ibid.*, Marinda Brown Silsby to Russell Dutton Silsby, June 26, 1863. Silsby Collection. 62 in the thesis.

Chapter 7

1. John Brown Gordon. *Reminiscences of the Civil War, 1832–1904* (Chapel Hill, NC: University of North Carolina Press), 1999, Electronic Edition. © This work is the property of the University of North Carolina at Chapel Hill. It may be used freely by individuals for research, teaching and personal use as long as this statement of availability is included in the text. Call number E470.G66 1904c (Davis Library, UNC-CH) *Reminiscences of the Civil War* Gordon, John B. New York Charles Scribner's Sons Atlanta The Martin & Hoyt Co. 1904. Chapter IV, The Spring of 1862—Battle of Seven Pines or Fair Oaks.

2. *Letters of James Parrott* (Rootsweb, Ancestry. com.), by descendants Gary Norris for Mrs. Dorris Parrett Wilford, great-granddaughter of the writer. Sergeant James Forrester Parrott of the 28th Consolidated Infantry to his wife, Mahala Bowman. Parrott was wounded in the lower leg at Franklin, Tennessee. This injury required the amputation of his lower leg. After the war, Mr. Parrott was murdered on his own property in 1868. He was buried at the Officer Cemetery in Overton

County. http://www.rootsweb.ancestry.com/~tnoverto/docs/CivilWarLettersParrott.html; letter about eating dinner, Letter #2, April 12, 1863, Tennessee; letter of little John, Letter #3 May 1863, State of Georgia; continuation of Letter #3; "fat" letter, second half of May, 1863, State of Georgia; "dream of you," Letter #5, June 15, 1863.

3. *Dear Mother*, William Herrick to his Wife; Carrollton, Georgia: September 18, 1864; 332, GAH.

4. Sam Watkins, Co. Aytch. *A Confederate Memoir of the Civil War* (Feather Trail Press via Amazon.com.); 44. Saltwater mussels cling to coastlines using the byssal threads part of their body while freshwater mussels use their foot to burrow into the beds of rivers and streams. The different methods of movement result in a tender muscular foot for saltwater mussels and a much tougher foot for river mussels. The rougher texture of river mussels does not make river mussels inedible, but you may not like the tough texture. Read more: Can You Eat River Mussels? | eHow.com http://www.ehow.com/facts_6870678_can-eat-river-mussels_.html#ixzz2Dq0cMhmp.

5. Roger S. Durham. *High Seas and Yankee Gunboats: A Blockade Running Adventure from the Diary of James Dickson* (Columbia, SC: University of South Carolina Press), 2005. p. 54.

6. Letter printed in the Richmond *Daily Dispatch*, to George Lucas of Fairfax, Virginia, from Emma Wilson, Providence, Rhode Island, July 9, 1861.

7. Company Aytch, 70, ten dead mourners, 73, Zack's tale.

8. *Ibid.* 99.

Chapter 8

1. Jenkin Lloyd Jones, Private, Sixth Wisconsin Battery, *An Artilleryman's Diary* (Wisconsin History Commission: Original Papers, No. 8; Wisconsin History Commission; February), 1914. Project Gutenberg. Letter of August 23, 1863.

2. *Ibid.*, en route, Thursday, December 24, 1863.

3. *Ibid.*, Sunday, January 31, 1864.

4. *Ibid.*, Huntsville, Saturday, March 12, 1864.

5. *Ibid.*, Huntsville, Monday, March 14, 1864.

6. *Ibid.*, Nashville, Tuesday, November 29, 1864.

7. William C. Davis & Meredith L. Swentor, editors, *Bluegrass Confederate, the Headquarters Diary of Edward O. Guerrant* (Louisiana State University Press), 1999. 53.

8. *Ibid.*, 55.

9. *Ibid.*, 310, Friday, July 31st, 1863.

10. *Ibid.*, 312, school dream, Thursday, 6th August, 1863; 318, wrong lady dream, Friday, 28th August, 1863.

11. *Ibid.*, 418, Sunday, May 1st, 1864; 492, Thursday, June 23rd, 1864; Saturday, 27th Aug'st 1864.

12. *Ibid.*, 526, home dreams, Wednesday, 14th Sept. 1864; 549, more Yankees in his dream, Tuesday 4th October, 1864; 579, setting a dream intention, Saturday, 12th November, 1864.

13. *Ibid.*, happy dreams of home, 596, Monday, 5 December, 1864; Tuesday, 6th December, 1864.

14. *Ibid.*, ice dreams, 620–624, December 29th & 31rst, 1864; January 1–3, 1865.

15. *Ibid.*, 644, Saturday, 18th February 1865.

Guerrant survived the war, married the sweetheart of his February, 1865, dreams; became a physician; and, after a serious illness, became a minister, traveling into Appalachia to minister to churches, schools, and orphanages. His travels and missions fulfilled a vow to God when he survived typhoid fever. He had been near death in the summer of 1873 and then miraculously survived. Part of the vow manifested in his founding a sect, The Society of Soul Winners. [*Beginning at Jerusalem in the Regions Beyond: Edward O. Guerrant and the Southern Home Mission Movement* (Project Gutenberg); J. Gray, McAllister, and Grace Owings Guerrant. *Edward O. Guerrant: Apostle to the Southern Highlanders* (Richmond, Va.: Richmond Press), 1950. 52.

16. Christopher Columbus Burns. Dege Didear private family letters. *Civil War Letters of Christopher Columbus Burns*. Permission to use granted by family member Dege Didear. Dege Didear transcripts unless noted as BLN (Bess Lipscomb Nichols); photocopies and original transcripts provided by BLN. Letter from C. C. Burns to "Dear Georgia," Camp near Nacogdoches, May 23, 1862; Letter from C.C. Burns to "Dear little Georgia, Camp near Nacogdoches, May 27, 1862.

Men of the 24th Cavalry Regiment were recruited in Nueces, Comanche, Waller, Montgomery, and Karnes counties. It was soon dismounted and sent to Arkansas. Here the regiment was captured at Arkansas Post in January, 1863. After being exchanged, it was consolidated with the 17th, 18th, and 25th Texas Cavalry Regiments (dismounted) and assigned to Deshler's, J.A. Smith's, and Granbury's Brigade. This command fought with the Army of Tennessee from Chickamauga to Atlanta, endured Hood's winter operations in Tennessee, and ended the war in North Carolina. The 24th was organized with about 900 men and reported 54 casualties of the 587 engaged at Arkansas Post. The 17th/18th/24th/25th reported 200 disabled at Chickamauga and totaled 690 men and 520 arms in December, 1863. Few surrendered on April 26, 1865. The field officers were Colonels William A. Taylor and Franklin C. Wilkes, and Lieutenant Colonels Robert R. Neyland and Patrick H. Swearingen.

17. *Ibid.*, C.C. Burns to "Dear Georgia," P.S. June 29th, 1862.

18. *Ibid.*, Letter from C.C. Burns to "My Dear Georgia," Pine Bluff Ark Sept 1st 1862; Letter from C. C. Burns to "My Dear good sweet little Georgia," Arkansas Post Tuesday Oct. 21st, 1862.

19. *Ibid.*, Letter from C.C. Burns to "Dear Georgia," Shreveport Sept the 19th 1863; letter from C.C. Burns to "My Dear Georgia," Camp near Coldsprings, Polk Co, Texas Feb 12 1865.

20. *Ibid.* Letter from C.C. Burns to "My dear Georgia," Camp Near Coldsprings, April 28th 1865.

21. Charles McDowell. Lisa Saunders (ed. and descendant), *Ever True: A Union Private and His Wife; Civil War Letters of Private Charles Mcdowell; New York Ninth Heavy Artillery* (Bowie, MD: Heritage Books), 2004. 79, "To Nancy from Charles, Near Cold Harbor," June 6, 1864.

22. Samuel T. Reeves Correspondence, 1864–1870, the bulk 1865. University Libraries of Notre Dame. Letter Groups. MSN CW 5012-9; Civil War some envelopes; MSN/CW 5012-1 to MSN/CW 5012-31, Samuel T. Reeves; March 22–24, 1865; Camp Dennison, Ohio; To Huldah Reeves; pages 1–5.

23. Marti Skipper and Jane Taylor (editors). *A Handful of Providence: The Civil War Letters of Lt. Richard Goldwaite, New York Volunteers, and Ellen Goldwaite. Jefferson, North Carolina* (McFarland & Company, Inc., publishers), 2004. 14, "Your ever Affectionate Wife Ellie Goldwaite To Her Husband Richard Goldwaite," first verse of a poem Ellie wrote for Richard. They had been

married only days when he left with the army. Her poem was to the tune and lines of a popular hymn called "The Parting Hands."

24. *Ibid.*, 5–13.

25. *Ibid.*, 18, To Lieutenant R. M. Goldwaite, Camp Hamilton, Fortress Monroe, Virginia, 3rd Regiment, New York Volunteers; from Ellie, Rexford Flats, May 25, 1861.

26. *Ibid.* 23, To Mrs. R. M. Goldwaite, Rexford Flats, Saratoga County, New York, from Camp Hamilton, Virginia, June 12, 1861.

27. *Ibid.*, 24, Lieutenant R. M. Gold waite, Camp Hamilton, Fortress Monroe, Virginia, 3rd Regiment, New York Volunteers, from Ellie, Clifton Park, June 19, 1861.

28. *Ibid.*, 27, Letter to Mrs. R. M. Goldwaite, Rexford Flats, Saratoga County, New York, from Richard at Camp Hamilton, Virginia. June 24, 1861.

29. *Ibid.*, 31, July 2, 1861, to My Dear Richard.

30. *Ibid.*, 36, to My Dear Wife.

31. *Ibid.*, 44, Ellie to My Dear Husband, August 24, 1861.

32. *Ibid.*, 48, accident, letter from Frances Hill to Richard, September 8, 1861; 51, Ellie to Richard on her ghostly dream, September 29, 1861; 53, report of Tom's death, September 28, 1861.

33. *Ibid.*, 68, Richard to Ellie, December 3, 1861, Hampton Roads on Board Steamboat Adelaide.

34. *Ibid.*, 70, Richard to Ellie, from Head Quarters, 3rd Regiment, Fort McHenry, Baltimore, Maryland, December 22, 1861.

35. *Ibid.*, 72–73, Ellie to "Dick" with Merry Christmas wishes, December 25, 1861.

36. *Ibid.*, 75–76, Ellie to Richard, January 3, 1862, with wishes for a "Happy New Year Dick."

37. *Ibid.*, 78. Ellie to My Dear Husband, January 9, 1862.

38. *Ibid.*, 80–81, Richard to Ellie, Fort McHenry, January 14, 1862.

39. *Ibid.*, 82, Richard to My Dear Ellie, January 23, 1862.

40. *Ibid.*, 84, Richard to My Dear Wife, February 10, 1862.

41. *Ibid.*, 85, Ellie to My Dear Husband, February 16, 1862, longing for him to come home; 88 & 91, resignation of commission and reenlistment, March 19, 1862.

42. *Ibid.*, 94–95, Ellie to My Dear Husband, April 3, 1862; 96, Richard to My Dear Ellie, April 5, 1862; 98, Ellie to My Dear Husband on rocking chair dream, April 10, 1862.

43. *Ibid.*, 128–129, Ellie to Richard, June 24, 1862.

44. *Ibid.*, 135, Ellie to My Dear Husband, July 14, 1862.

45. *Ibid.*, 144, Ellie to My Dear Husband, August 7, 1862; 151, Ellie to My Dear Husband, September 5, 1862.

46. *Ibid.*, 169, Richard to My Dear Wife, December 10, 1862. New York Volunteers, Camp Mansfield; Deep Creek, Virginia.

47. *Ibid.*, 170, Ellie to My Dear Husband, December 10, 1862; 173, Richard to My Dear Wife, Camp Mansfield, Norfolk, Virginia, December 17, 1862.

48. *Ibid.*, 179, Ellie wishing My Dear Husband a "happy new year," January 2, 1863.

49. *Ibid.*, 182, Ellie to My Dear Husband, January 8, 1863.

50. *Ibid.*, 185, Richard to My Dear Ellie, January 24, 1863.

51. *Ibid.*, 189, Richard to My Dear Wife, February 8, 1863.

52. *Ibid.*, 195–196. Ellie to My Dear Husband, March 21, 1863.

53. *Ibid.*, 200–201, Richard to My Dear Wife, April 4, 1863; 211, discharge.

54. J. Michael Welton (ed.); John K. Gott and John e. Divine, annotations. *My Heart Is So Rebellious, the Caldwell Letters 1861–1865* (Warrenton, Virginia: The Fauquier National Bank), no date listed. 7–8, 10.

55. *Ibid.*, 23. Warrenton, Virginia, Tuesday, July 2nd, 1861, Dearest Papa; 55–56: Warrenton Fauquier, Thursday Sept. 12th 1861, Dearest Papa.

56. *Ibid.*, 34, Warrenton, Va., Saturday Night, July 20th, 1861, Dearest Papa; 43, Warrenton, Va., Tuesday Night, August 13th, 1861, Dearest Papa.

57. *Ibid.*, 47–48: Emeline Jeffords Caldwell to Lycurgus Washington Caldwell Warrenton, Via, Thursday, August 22nd, 1861; Monday morning ... [August 26]; 49–50: Warrenton Fauquier, Sunday, Sept. 1st, 1861, My Dearest Papa.

58. *Ibid.*, 104, Susan Emeline Jeffords Caldwell to Lycurgus Washington Caldwell, Warrenton Fauquier Co, April 27th 1862, Dearest Papa; 113, Warrenton Fauquier Co., Sunday May 11th 1862, Dearest Papa.; 138, letters about dreams of Emeline's parents, Wednesday June 25th 1862.

59. *Ibid.*, 142–143, Undated, 1862, fragment.

60. *Ibid.*, 145, Warrenton Fauquier Co., Monday August 12th 1862, Dearest Papa (candy letter); 147, Monday August 18th 1862, Dearest Papa (dream of you by night); 148–49, Warrenton Fauquier, Saturday August 23rd 1862, Dearest Papa (pleasant dreams).

61. For another use of dreams by contraries see under "Dreaming at Home with a Smile"—A Richmond *Daily Dispatch* story of October 22, 1861, titled "Spicy Letter from a Yankee Girl,"—"I am thinking of you all the time and dreaming at night, but dreams do go by contraries. Sometimes I dream of being at fishing frolics, but, alas! Awake disappointed—though in hope it will not always be so."

62. *Ibid.*, 155: Warrenton Via, Tuesday Night Sept 30th/62, Dearest Papa (furlough); 166, Warrenton, Sunday Dec. 28th, Dearest Papa (pants dream).

63. *Ibid.*, 172, Undated 1863 but before January 16 and just a few weeks after the dream of ragged pants.

64. *Ibid.*, 192–193, Warrenton Via, Tuesday July 13th 1863; July 19th 1863—troubled dreams; 201, Warrenton Via, Saturday Sept 26th 1863, Dearest Papa (good dreams); 202, Friday Nov 27th 1863, Dearest Papa (mother's death).

65. *Ibid.*, 220–221, Warrenton Fauquier, Monday April 25th 1864, Dearest Papa (Frank's dreaming); 225, Lycurgus Washington Caldwell to Emeline Emelline Jeffords Caldwell, Richmond, Va May 25 1864, My Very Dear Daughter.

66. *Ibid.*, 231, Richmond August 6th 1864, My Dear Daughter.

67. *Ibid.*, 238, Lycurgus to Emeline, Richmond, Sept. 16 1864, My Dear Daughter; 239, Tuesday night Sept. 27, 1864.

68. *Ibid.*, 240, Warrenton Via, Sunday Oct 2nd 1864, Dearest Papa; 241, Warrenton Via, Sunday Oct 9th 1864; p. 242, Mary Humbert Jeffords to Emeline Emeline Jeffords Caldwell, Blackville October 17 1864, My Own Dearest Daughter.

69. *Ibid.*, pp. 253–255, Warrenton via, Jany 15th 1865, Dearest Papa; p. 258 (hat story), Warrenton Fauquier, Friday night Jany 27th/65, My dearest Papa.

70. *Ibid.*, 263, *The True Index*, Volume I, Number 1.

"Lycurgus published and edited *The True Index* through much of the remainder of the 19th century, and eventually sold it to his son, Frank, who in turn would sell it in 1899. Emeline Caldwell would live in relative peace and happiness after the war, bearing two more children—Charles and Harry—and would eventually enjoy a number of grandchildren. The Caldwells would live, together with the Finks, in their home on Smith Street in Warrenton until their deaths. In 1879 John finks died; in 1910, Lycurgus; in 1911, Lucy Finks; and in 1913, Emeline Caldwell."

Chapter 9

1. David Lane. *A Soldier's Diary*, 1862–1865 (self published), 1905. 192, Field Hospital, August 23d, 1864. Limited numbers of this journal were privately published and signed in 1905; original privately owned and generously shared by descendant Rosemary Pierce and her husband, Delbert, Fonda, NY. Rosemary Pierce wished to share David's extraordinary experiences in dream journeying. David noted in his opening pages that "The events recorded were written down on the date of their occurrence…" [p. 5, enlistment details]. David Lane was 38 years old and lived in Blackman, Michigan. He referred to his wife, Jane, as "my darling"—never revealing her name in the journal. Once he mentioned the name of one child, Nell, the baby. He addressed her as growing older as her face peered at him from the pages of his journal where her photo bookmarked her progress and growth.
2. Eudora Welty. *Some Notes on River Country* (University Press of Mississippi), 2003. 7.
3. *A Soldier's Diary*, 151–52: February 11th, 1864.
4. *Ibid.*, 11, Maryland Heights, Virginia, September 21st, 1862.
5. *Ibid.*, p. 19, Pleasant Valley, October 17th, 1862.
6. *Ibid.*, 22, Camp near Fredericksburg, Virginia, Dec. 9th, 1862.
7. *Ibid.*, p. 25, December 29th, 1862.
8. *Ibid.*, p. 27, January 15, 1863, Camp Pittman, Virginia.
9. *Ibid.* 61–62, Haines Bluff, Mississippi, June 27th, 1863.
10. *Ibid.*, pp. 81–82: Camp Parks, Ky., August 22d, 1863.
11. *Ibid.*, 178, July 2d, 1864.
12. *Ibid.*, 218, Peebles House, October 15th, 1864.
13. *Ibid.*, 269–279: June 8th, 1865.
14. Levi Bird Duff; Jonathan E. Helmreich (ed.). *To Petersburg with the Army of the Potomac, the Civil War Letters of Levi Bird Duff 105th Pennsylvania Volunteers* (Jefferson, NC and London: McFarland & Co. Publishers; Jefferson, NC), 2009. 11, June 28th, 1861, Harriet's fear and saying good-bye.
15. *Ibid.*, 56: Levi Duff, Williamsburg, Va., May 8th, 1862—Battle Of Williamsburg; 57: Allegheny City, May 16th/62 "Dear Bird." Bird is a name Harriet uses for Levi.
16. *Ibid.*, 43: Levi Duff, March 16, 1862.
17. *Ibid.*, 60, Hospital near the battlefield, June 2nd, 1862, "Mr. Samuel Duff, Clarion, Pennsylvania; 62–63: letter on Harriet's fragile nerves.
18. *Ibid.*, 72: Sept. 26th, 1862; 100, Dec. 26th, 1862.
19. *Ibid.*, 33, note and letter of December 21st, 1861; p. 34, Allegheny City, Dec. 24th, 1861, "My Dear Levi." Harriet saved the flora mementos that Levi forwarded, most pressed in a 1008 page volume by Thomas H. Prescott, *The American Encyclopedia of History, Biography and Travel, Comprising Ancient and Modern History: The Biography of Eminent Men of Europe and America, and the Lives of Distinguished Travelers*, Columbus: J. & H. Miller, 1857. Some she carefully mounted and labeled. Others were simply inserted between the pages without record of their origin (courtesy Allegheny College). This note is from the editor, 129.
20. *Ibid.* 119, May 10th, 1863.
21. *Ibid.*, 129, Allegheny City, July 4th, 1863, from Harriet to Levi; 131, July 6, 1863, Harriet fears for Levi's life; July 9th, 1863, Allegheny City, Harriet to Levi, "sad anxiety" letter.
22. *Ibid.*, 136, Camp near Warrenton, Virginia, July 26th, 1863.
23. *Ibid.*, 187, May 1st, 1864, apple bud; May 2nd, 1864, flower from garden.
24. *Ibid.* 188, Chancellorsville, Va. 4 p.m., May 4th, 1864.
25. *Ibid.*, 197: Camp (near) New Castle, Va. May 29th, 1864; corrected his location to Camp 3 miles South of Salem Church, May 30th, 1864.
26. *Ibid.*, 206, Allegheny City, June 21st 1864; Telegraph, Washington 22 1864, to "Mrs. H. Duff, Allegheny"; June 23rd—Harriet wrote to "Mother" that the limb is doing splendidly—is a terrible sight—is taken off about 3 inches below the joint; 209, Epilogue.
27. *Ibid.* 209.

Chapter 10

1. Julia Johnson Fisher, *Diary*. May 15, 1864. Chapel Hill, NC: "This work is the property of the University of North Carolina at Chapel Hill: Southern Historical Collection, University of North Carolina at Chapel Hill. "It may be used freely by individuals for research, teaching and personal use as long as this statement of availability is included in the text; call number 1757."
2. Sarah Morgan, Charles East (ed.). *The Civil War Diary of a Southern Woman*. New York: Touchstone/Simon & Schuster & Athens, Georgia; University of Georgia Press, 1991. Project Gutenberg., Journal entry of June 18, 1862.
3. *Ibid.*, Entry of August 21, 1862.
4. *Ibid.*
5. *Ibid.*, entry of August 12, 1862, Linwood.
6. *Ibid.*
7. *Ibid.*, entry, September, 1862.
8. *Ibid.*, entry, Saturday, September 6, 1862.
9. *Ibid.*, entry, Wednesday, March 25, 1863.
10. *Ibid.*
11. *Ibid.*, 584–586, entry, December 25, 1863.
12. On Naming the Bedposts: See a similar reference in Julia Dent's journal in her precognitive dream about her future husband [Ulysses]. Both Sarah Morgan and Julia Dent use the same phrase, "as is the custom" in naming the bedposts. According to a 19th century issue of the American Folklore Society, the "custom" is: in a strange place or a new place or when a young woman receives a new bed, to name the bedposts if she desires a dream to come true and that this technique is usually used by young women wishing to dream of their future husbands. Another version would be to place a garter on the bedpost and ask for a dream of the one you are to marry. *The Journal of American Folk-Lore*. Boston and New York; Houghton, Mifflin and Company & London: Trubner & Co., 57 Ludgate Hill; Leipzig: K.F. Koehler's Antiquarium, Universitatsstrasse, 26, MDCC–XCII. Copyright 1892. Volume V. Also: Cambridge, Mass: The

Riverside Press, Printed by H. O. Houghton and Company. Vol. v.—JANUARY–MARCH, 1892.—No. XVI. A similar story of precognitive dreaming by naming the bedposts appeared in a 1913 Bicknell family genealogy: [NI4523] [Usa.ftw] From T.W. Bicknell's 1913 genealogy book page 330 and 331 "Harriet (Bicknell) Grange is a woman of strong personality, of fine intellectual powers, with unusual social qualities and a strongly religious character.... It is said that Harriet Bicknell was one of the prettiest girls in Ontario before her marriage, and that she and Dr. Grange were a very handsome couple. The Grange family moved from Napanee, Ontario, to Chattanooga about 1890. There is a fine bit of romance in the love-making of James Grange and Harriet Bicknell which will help to give flesh and life to the dry bones of genealogical facts and figures. One Hallowe'en, having a friend spending the night with her, Harriet Bicknell decided, with her companion, to do all the Hallowe'en stunts, such as eating a teaspoonful of salt, going down cellar backwards with a mirror in one hand and a lighted candle in the other, naming the bedposts, etc., etc., after which each was supposed to dream of her future husband. In the morning, on awakening, Harriet was in high glee, and said: "Whom do you suppose I dreamed of last night? Jimmie Grange." She thought that she drove into Napanee with her father and drew up in front of Grange's drug store; that Jimmie, the son of the proprietor, was standing near the door, and, seeing Mr. Bicknell's carriage, came out and asked Mr. B. what he could do for him. Mr. B. introduced James to his daughter, and all went into the store together. So much for the Hallowe'en dream. The girls laughed over the dream, as neither knew "Jimmie Grange," save by name. A few days after Mr. Bicknell had occasion to go to Napanee for some paint for his barn, and asked Harriet if she would like to ride in with him, an invitation which she gladly accepted. At the town Mr. B. stopped in front of Grange's drug store and the Hallowe'en dream was literally fulfilled. James and Harriet again met, and a few days after he got a friend to show him the way to Bicknell's Corners, and thereafter Jimmie had no need of a guide or companion to the Bicknell mansion, the scene of the Hallowe'en dream. James Grange and Harriet Bicknell were married Dec. 24, 1851. Soon thereafter Mr. Grange decided to study medicine, sold his store at Napanee to his cousins, moved to Coburg, Canada, and attended Victoria College. Afterwards he completed his medical studies at the College of Physicians and Surgeons, New York City. He was a successful practitioner at Napanee, Ontario, and at Chattanooga, Tenn., where he died, in 1906, at the age of 80. It is not a matter of surprise that the fine physical charms and excellences of character should be transmitted to succeeding generations. Nature's gifts are distributed by natural laws." http://genealogy.bicknell.net/notes/not0020.htm; The full story is repeated originally in the Bicknell family history: http://www.archive.org/stream/historygenealogy1913bick/historygenealogy1913bick_djvu.txt].

13. *Ibid.*, entries, July 27, 1863.
14. *Ibid.*, entry, June 15, 1865.
15. Sarah Lois Wadley. Diary, August 8, 1859—May 15, 1865. Chapel Hill, NC: Manuscripts Dept, Southern Historical Collection; The University of North Carolina at Chapel Hill. This work may be used freely by individuals for research, teaching and personal use as long as this statement of availability is included in the text. Call number 1258. Diary entry, Thursday, August 6, 1863, Oakland, Georgia.

16. Guy R. Everson & Edward W. Simpson, Jr. (eds.). *Far, Far from Home: The Wartime Letters of Dick and Tally Simpson, 3rd South Carolina Volunteers.* New York; Oxford: Oxford University Press, 1994. 258: Letter 106, Tally Simpson to Caroline Virginia Miller, Bunker's Hill Va. Saturday, July 18 /63: "...Savannah will follow, and then Mobile, and finally Richmond. These cities will be a loss to the Confederacy. But their fall is no reason why we should despair. It is certainly calculated to cast a gloom over our entire land. But we profess to be a Christian people, and we should put our trust in God. He holds the destiny of our nation, as it were, in the palm of his hand. He it is that directs the counsel of our leaders, both civil and military, and if we place implicit confidence in Him and go to work in good earnest, never for a moment losing sight of Heaven's goodness and protection, it is my firm belief that we shall be victorious in the end. Let the South lose what it may at present. God's hand is certainly in this contest, and He is working for the accomplishment of some grand result, and so soon as it is accomplished, He will roll the sun of peace up the skies and cause its rays to shine over our whole land. We were a wicked, proud, ambitious nation, and God has brought upon us this war to crush and humble our pride and make us a better people generally. And the sooner this happens the better for us."

17. Sarah Lois Wadley Diary entry, September 26, 1863.
18. *Ibid.*, 168, diary entries, February 16, 1864 (music); 173, February 26, 1864.
19. Mary Octavia Smith Tabb. *Love and Loss: A Virginia Girl's Civil War Diary, 1863–1868.* Smithville, York County, Virginia. Hampton, Va.: Paxton Press, 2009. Introduction, Monday, September 20, 1863.
20. *Ibid.*, 5, Monday, January 12, 1863.
21. *Ibid.*, 54–55, Wednesday, March 11, 1868.
22. *Ibid.*, 72, Friday, July 3, 1868.
23. *Ibid.*, 82, Monday, September 7, 1868.
24. On Otterburn from Wikipedia: Otterburn is a Palladian-influenced Greek Revival house near Bedford, Virginia. The original house was built in 1828 for Benjamin A. and Sally Camm McDonald, but burned in 1841 and was reconstructed by 1843. At this time the final form of the house was created with the introduction of a loggia, cross-gable roof and Greek Revivial detailing. The house was the seat of a 1,651-acre (668 ha) estate by 1825, with a mill, sawmill, and dependent structures. After McDonald's death in 1871 the property passed through several owners until 1950, when the house became the Hines Memorial Pythian Home, an orphanage operated by the Knights of Pythias. A detached dormitory was added at this time. The orphanage ceased operations in the early 1960s, but operated for two years in the late 1960s as the Otterburn Academy, a private school for white children created as a response to court-ordered desegregation. In later years the property was operated as a rest home for the elderly.[2] The house is presently being restored.
25. Letitia M. Burwell. *A Girl's Life in Virginia Before the War.* Dahlonega, Georgia: Frederick A. Stokes Co., The Confederate Reprint Company, 1895. 125–127.

Robert Moss, writer of numerous books on dreams and the imagination, notes that "the first book F.W.H. Myers prepared (with Gurney and Podmore) for the SPR, *Phantasms of the Living*, is full of incidents of this kind. There's a reason the Scots Gaelic word for seer (taibshear) literally means "seer or ghosts of doubles." Astral travel in a subtle body, confirmed by sightings of this kind, is one of the great categories of evidence that consciousness is not confined to the physical body and must therefore be presumed to survive it.

26. John Hammond Moore (ed.). *A Plantation Mistress on the Eve of the Civil War, the Diary of Keziah Goodwyn Hopkins Brevard, 1860-1861*. Columbia, SC; The University of South Carolina Press, 1991. 105, 28 of March—Thursday [1861].

27. Ibid.
28. Ibid., 47: [Lincoln's election] Nov. 1st [1860].
29. Ibid., 22, 31st Last day of July 1860.
30. Ibid., 24, August 7, Tuesday, 1860.
31. Ibid., 28, August 27.
32. Ibid., 33, Thursday, 20th/1860, September.
33. Ibid., 53, November 19th, 1860, Monday; 76, 20th January 1961.
34. Mrs. Campbell Bryce, wife of a well-to-do planter, lived at the southwest corner of Blanding & Pickens streets. One of the founders of Columbia's Wayside Hospital during the Civil War, she died in Philadelphia in 1901. Two other ladies mentioned in this dream sequence—Mrs. Bell and Mrs. Staunton—cannot be identified.
35. Benjamin M. Palmer (1818-1902), Charleston native and ardent secessionist, was pastor of Columbia's Presbyterian Church from 1843 to 1855, also serving briefly on the faculty of the Theological Seminary before moving to New Orleans in 1856.
36. Ibid., 108-109: April 2nd [1861].
37. Ibid., 115, 15 April, 1861; 116.
38. Amelia Akehurst Lines, Thomas Dyer (ed.). *To Raise Myself a Little; the Diaries and Letters of Jennie, a Georgia Teacher, 1851-1886*. Athens, GA; University of Georgia Press, 1982. ix, 1-8; p. 9, Marietta quote.
39. Ibid., 22-23: February 2nd Clinton, 1855.
40. Ibid., p. 87, Thursday 24th (possibly June, definitely 1858).
41. Ibid., 98: Friday [July] 23rd 1858.
42. Ibid., 165-66: In Atlanta, Thursday [September] 19th 1860—dreamt while Sylvanus was away at a lodge meeting.
43. Ibid., 187-188 Jennie to Maria, Atlanta, April 30th 1862, "My Dear Sister."
44. Ibid., 126 Tuesday 4th January, 1859.
45. Ibid., 224-225.
46. Ibid., 271-272: Daisy to Anna Maria Akehurst Barham, Macon Ga May 17th 1886, "Darling Auntie."
47, Kate Plake. *The Southern Husband Outwitted by His Union Wife*. Chapel Hill, NC: The University of North Carolina at Chapel Hill. Electronic Edition. This work may be used freely by individuals for research, teaching and personal use as long as this statement of availability is included in the text. Call number CT275.P66 A3 1867 Philadelphia Printed for the Authoress, Moore & Brother 1867. Chapter IX.
48. Ibid., Chapter X.
49. Ibid., Chapter XII.
50. Ibid.

Chapter 11

1. George Root, composer. *Tramp, Tramp, Tramp* (Chicago: Root & Cady), 1864.
2. Yancey Hall, *U.S. Civil War Prison Camps Claimed Thousands* (National Geographic News), July 1, 2003 http://news.nationalgeographic.com/news/2003/07/0701_030701_civilwarprisons.html].

3. Overmire, Laurence, "The Ancestry of Overmire, Tifft, Richardson, Bradford, Reed" (Laurence Overmire, RootsWeb World Connect Project), 2000-2014, permission to cite David Kennedy's letter of July 9, 1864. http://wc.rootsweb.ancestry.com/cgi-bin/igm.cgi?op=GET&db=glencoe&id=I52885.
4. Lyman H. Needham, *The Civil War Letters from Danville Prison* (Genealogy Website: http://fanflower.com/2009/05/14/civil-war-letters-from-danville-prison/.
5. John McElroy, *Andersonville, a Story of Rebel Military Prisons, Fifteen Months a Guest of the So-Called Southern Confederacy, a Private Soldier's Experience in Richmond, Andersonville, Savannah, Millen, Blackshear and Florence*, 1879, Project Gutenberg EBook. There is an excellent description of a dream house in Saint-Exupery's *Wind, Sand, and Stars*. A character, an airline pilot, driven down into the arid wasteland of the Sahara, lost in the middle of a great desert, explores his dream memory of a house where he discovers a reality greater than the waking reality of the Sahara and gives himself over to its magic: "I was the child of this house, filled with the memory of its odours, with the cool breath of its vestibules, with the voices that had animated it, even to the very frogs in the pools that came here to be with me. I needed these thousand landmarks to identify myself."].
6. Ibid.
7. Ibid.
8. Ibid.
9. Comrade William N. Tyler, *The Dispatch Carrier and Memoirs of Andersonville Prison* (Port Byron, Illinois: Port Byron "Globe" Print), 1892, reprinted by Gutenberg Press. http://www.gutenberg.org/files/40046/40046-h/40046-h.htm. 30-31, story of Jim.
10. Ibid., Memoirs, 1.
11. Ibid., 9-11.
12. Ibid., 12, 19.
13. Ibid. There are other accounts of this miraculous spring called Providence, including private letters recounting the Andersonville imprisonment of Daniel James Meals of The 7th Tennessee Volunteer Cavalry (Susan Morgan family letters).
14. Ibid., 29-30.
15. Ibid., 38.
16. Ibid.
17. Ibid., 54-56, 59.
18. Ibid., 56.
19. Ibid., 61.
20. John L. Maile, *Prison Life in Andersonville with Special Reference to the Opening of Providence Spring* (Project Gutenberg: http://www.gutenberg.org/files/39584/39584-h/39584-h.htm), 91-114, with a sketch by John Maile.
21. John Ransom, with an introduction by Bruce Catton, *John Ransom's Andersonville Diary* (New York: Berkley Books), 1986-1994. First published Auburn, NY, 1881, Preface and p. 3, Belle Island, Richmond, Virginia, November 22, 1863.
22. William Marvel, "Johnny Ransom's Imagination"; *Civil War History* (Volume 41, Number 3, September 1995), pp. 181-189 | 10.1353/cwh.1995.0030, p. 182: William Marvel compared dates and events in Ransom's journal with that of other prisoners' diaries and found abundant errors. Marvel maintained that no Ransom journal ever existed but was a postwar memoir created from memory, from imagination, and from other published sources. Marvel "attributes Ransom's purpose for publishing his account to the promotion of a congressional

bill designed to provide pensions for former prisoners. In fact, Ransom's first edition was published with the text of the proposed bill included. In addition Ransom had filed a pension claim in 1879, for the loss of teeth from scurvy, at about the time he began writing. Marvel concluded with the statement that because of the success of Ransom's book, despite his "exaggerations and misrepresentations," he and many other prisoners received pensions for many years. Ransom's first edition was published as *Andersonville Diary, Escape, and List of the Dead* (Auburn, NY: 1881)."

23. Ransom, p. 10, Dec. 1, on dreaming; p. 12, Dec. 3, on "sure death."

24. Ibid., p. 100, June 29, 1864; 109, July 8, 1864; 110–111, July 9, 1864; p. 124, July 19, 1864.

25. Ibid., 80, May 17, 1864.

26. THE GRAYBACKS SO TENDERLY CLINGING (Words: Anonymous, Music by Henry Clay Work).

> There were companions on the march, as every soldier found,
> With ceaseless zeal in digging deep in every spot around,
> And though each hero killed a lot, still thousands more abound,
>   The graybacks so tenderly clinging.
> CHORUS: O! ho! no! no! we never can forget.
> Ow-ow! ow-ow! we almost feel them yet;
> The busy little grayback teeth in us so firmly set,
>   Who went with us Marching Through Georgia.
> The visitors were never big, in fact were very small.
> In silence they put in their work, no sound they made at all;
> They thought it was full fun enough to hear the comrades bawl
>   While graybacks were busily biting.—CHORUS.
> And never partial were those bugs, no mortal would they spare,
> No dignity could keep them off, they just bit everywhere,
> And generals could not deny but what each had a share
>   Of graybacks so constantly nibbling.—CHORUS].

http://www.civilwarpoetry.org/union/songs/greybacks.html.

27. Thomas Wentworth Higginson, "Army Life in a Black Regiment," *The Atlantic Monthly* (Project Gutenberg), 1869. Thomas Wentworth was commander of a regiment of former slaves writing about picket duty in 1863 in the thoroughfare of land between Beaufort and Charleston, SC, known as the 'Shell Road,' nine miles from Beaufort.

28. Ibid., 174, November 23, 1864, "in the woods near Doctortown Station, No. 5, Georgia.

29. Louis N. Beaudry, ed., *The Libby Prison Chronicle*, #2, August 21, 1863.

30. Ibid., *The Libby Chronicle*, "devoted to facts and fun"; editor-in-chief, Louis N. Beaudry, Chaplain, Fifth NY Vol. Cavalry, Richmond, Va., August 28, 1863, #2. *The Libby Chronicle, Lights and Shades in Libby*, #2— excerpt: "The earliest skirmishers have not finished their bloody task before' you hear much pounding and grating, and no little rumbling and rattling. You need not wonder; the cooks have commenced their work. The stoves fairly groan under their loads of pots and kettles for soup and coffee, while their ovens are pregnant with the accustomed hash and toast. Glad as we are to have our scanty rations brought to us in gross, thus furnishing us needed employment both in cooking, and in cutting and carving the bones, there is, nevertheless, great annoyance, these hot summer days, from the extra heat of the stoves. There is pounding on the floor for water from below, when the faucets have been closed; there is haste to secure the best pots, kettles. and pans for public and private uses; there is gouge game and grab game from head cooks to young apprentices, and from those who are not cooks at all, while selfishness and profanity mingle too frequently in shameful confusion.

…Happy is the man who can secure even a rusty or broken piece of tin for a plate, or the half section of a canteen! Some are compelled to eat *À La Turkie*, that is, with their fingers, and when it comes to soup, their scanty mess is gulped with rough wooden spoons, carved out with dull jack knives. And yet all this would be considered a royal assemblage of table furniture, if there were only food enough to satisfy the tithe of your hunger!

The morning meal dispatched, we greet the "General," a colored prisoner whose chief employment is to disinfect the rooms by means of his "union smoke," as he calls his fumigations made from burning tar, carried here and there in a small iron skillet. Groups gather around the "General," enjoying his spicy Union talks quite as well as his disinfectant.—*Editor*"

31. Ibid.

32. James R. Knight, ed. *Letters to Anna: The Civil War Through the Eyes and Heart of a Soldier* (self published), 2007. 116, Johnson's Island near Sandusky, Ohio, Sept. 6th, 1863, My Dear Anna; 120, Johnson's Island near Sandusky Ohio, Oct. 15, 1863, My Dear Anna.

33. Robert Emmett Curran, editor, *John Dooley's Civil War, An Irish American's Journey in the First Virginia Infantry Regiment*. (Knoxville, TN: The University of Tennessee Press, 2012), "Voices of the Civil War," Peter S. Carmichael, Series Editor, 2012. p. 18, August, 1862.

34. Ibid., Prison Notes 2, p. 236, December 8, 1863. See also Calvin Goddard Zon, *the Good Fight the Didn't End, Henry P. Goddard's Accounts of Civil War and Peace* (Columbia, SC: University of South Carolina Press, 2008), p. 148 referenced on p. 127: Falmouth, Va., Feb. 14, 1863: Excerpt from 14th C. V.: *Regimental Reminiscences of the War of the Rebellion*, by Henry P. Goddard (Middletown, CN: C. W. Church, 1877): "What a winter it was that followed in camp at Falmouth with no field officer…. Ah, what punches Fred Doten used to mix in that winter, as we gathered in each other's Sibleys: "When every officer seemed a friend, and every friend a brother." It was at some of these gatherings that Capt. [Henry] Lee used to give swan-like imitations and that G's officers used to trot out little "Uncas," the stuttering teamster as a spiritual medium, who used to go into trances and therein deliver addresses on didactic subjects, but who got mad when Lt. Fred Seymour asked him to take a drink in his spiritual, not material, character. Qt. Mr. [Charles F.] Dibble used to say that when Uncas got mad at his mules, he could swear in the most unspiritual manner without stuttering at all, p. 12.

35. *John Dooley's Civil War*, Prison Notes 1, p. 224. 1863.

36. Ibid., Prison Notes 1, p. 210. Sept. 22nd, 1863.

37. Ibid., Prison Notes 2, p. 258, April 14, 1864.

38. Ibid., p. 186, Prison Notes 1, July 15th, 1863; p. 259, Prison Notes 2, April 22nd, 1864.

39. Ibid., p. 317, November 24, 1864.

40. *Ibid.*, p. 353, April 4, 1865; p. 401, May 6th, 5 a.m., 1865.
41. George H. Jones, ed. James Parks Caldwell, *Northern Confederate at Johnson's Island* (Jefferson, NC: McFarland & Company, Inc., Publishers), 2010, 207, poem "written while a Confederate soldier, undated, excerpt, Johnson's Island.
42. *Ibid.*, 96.
43. *Ibid.*, 98. Journal, Monday, March 28, 1864. Edward Bulwer-Lytton, *A Strange Story—An Occult Fantasy*. Edward George Earl Bulwer-Lytton, 1st Baron Lytton (1803–1873) was an English novelist, playwright, and politician. Bulwer-Lytton's literary career began in 1820, with the publication of his first book of poems. He wrote in a variety of genres, including historical fiction, mystery, romance, the occult, and science fiction. Lord Lytton was a florid, popular writer of his day, who coined such phrases as "the great unwashed," "pursuit of the almighty dollar," "the pen is mightier than the sword," and the infamous incipit "It was a dark and stormy night." On trances, Bulwer-Lytton wrote about experiences of conjuring oneself into "beautiful lands far away from earth; flowers and trees not like ours." He defined "trance" as a "cerebral activity, a projectile force given to the mind, distinct from the soul, by which it sends forth its own emanations to a distance in spite of material obstacles, just as a flower, in an altered condition of atmosphere, sends forth the particles of its aroma.... Your thought travels over land and sea in your waking state; thought, too, can travel in trance, and in trance may acquire an intensified force. There is, however, another kind of trance which is truly called spiritual, a trance much more rare, and in which the soul entirely supersedes the mere action of the mind." http://www.gutenberg.org/ebooks/7701.
44. *Ibid.*, Journal, October 2, 1864. James returned home to fulfill an interrupted path as lawyer, and he became a vibrant newspaper editor. He remained a bachelor. Ginny was arrested and imprisoned in New Orleans but escaped with the help of her equally interesting sister Charlotte Moon. Ginny returned to Memphis, where the Moons had settled after the war. She became a philanthropist, particularly helping with the yellow fever epidemics of the 1870s. She died in New York City in 1925.
45. *Ibid.*, 199, Journal, Thursday, June 1, 1865.
46. Peter Cozzens. http://opinionator.blogs.nytimes.com/2014/04/24/humanity-and-hope-in-a-southern-prison/?ref=opinion April 24, 2014, Disunion Blog, *New York Times*.
47. Bell Irvin Wiley, editor, *W. W. Heartsill, Fourteen Hundred and 91 Days in the Confederate Army, a Journal Kept by W. W. Heartsill for Four Years, One Month, and One Day. Or, Camp Life, Day by Day, of the W. P. Lane Rangers from April 19, 1861, to May 20, 1865* (Jackson, Tennessee: MCowat-Mercer Press, Inc., Reprints from the Collection of the University of Michigan Library), 1954. XIX, Heartsill's preface to his journal; XVII, Introduction.
48. *Ibid.*, 135, June 29th, 1863.
49. *Ibid.*, 270, Heartsill's Manuscript Journal, original version, Appendix I, The Chickamauga Campaign.
50. The realness of battlefield dreams crosses time and space and is an ever-renewing story, as reliable as the nature of wars in human society. In a "Backstory" interview, a soldier, David B. Rasch, who had served in today's army for 3 years and overseas 2½ years, spoke to me of the "realness" of soldiers' dreams. After his friend "Ski" was killed, he talked to him in dreams as though he were awake and ate "real" food in dreams on the battlefield.
51. Walbrook D. Swank, owner, *Letters and Diary of a Confederate Prisoner of War, Private William W. Downer, Company I, 6th Virginia Cavalry*. (Mineral, Virginia: Colonel Swank, Colonel USAF, retired, Route 2, Box 433), Letters from 1864.
52. *Ibid.*, February 5, 1865.
53. *Ibid.*, June 9, 1865.
54. John W. Alexander, *A Personal Narrative of Life in Union Prisons, 1864–1865*, submitted by Hudson Alexander, great-grandnephew for inclusion in Diane Janowski, *In Their Honor: Soldiers of the Confederacy: The Elmira Prison Camp* (Elmira, NY: New York History Review Press), 2009. 39, letter of August 17, 1864.
55. Private G. W. Nichols. *A Soldier's Story of His Regiment (61st Georgia) and Incidentally of the Lawton-Gordon-Evans Brigade, Army Northern Virginia*, Jesup, Georgia (Self-published), 1898. 229–235, W. H. Bland's Prison Life.
56. Lydia Minturn Post, *Soldiers' Letters, from Camps, Battlefield and Prison* (New York: Bruce & Huntington, U.S. Sanitary Commission; Reprint, University of Michigan, Michigan Reprint Series), 1865, Letter C, p. 214, Fort Anderson, MD., April 14, 1863.
57. *Ibid.*, 382, Letter CLXXXI, The Prison Camp, Elmira, NY, July 1864.

Chapter 12

1. Project Gutenberg. Clara Barton to "My dear Cousin Vira." Head Quarters 2nd Div.; 9th Army Corps-Army of the Potomac; Camp near Falmouth, Va.; December 12th, 1862—2 o'clock a.m. http://masterworld.org/out/491212/Red-Clara-Barton-Ame-Civil-War-Women-American-Red-Cros.html?PHPSESSID=3b919bf8c2a61333326bdaaa77ec0686.
2. Jane Stuart Woolsey, with an introduction by Daniel John Hosington. *Hospital Days; Reminiscence of a Civil War Nurse* (Roseville, Minnesota: Edinborough Press), 1996–2007, Preface Note: In the autumn of 1865, when the new Peace on all the hills and fields made them seem so sweet and fair, we found ourselves, a family long parted, exploring the by-roads in the north New Hampshire country. Following, one day, a winding green wagon-track, far from the main road, we came upon a desolate rough farm half way up the lower slopes of the Bartlett mountain. 'A dozen sheep were scattered over the stony fields, and among them sat a man in the full uniform of a Zouave, bagging trowsers, gay-braided jacket, cap, tassel, and long bright crimson scarf, complete. He had but just got home from some distant post, with very little back pay in his pocket for the sick wife, and none at all to spend in sober clothes, and had gone at once to work upon the obstinate farm, all in his gay attire. He seemed a little stunned by the silence round him. He missed the drums, he said.

We had a little talk over the old days already so distant although so near, and left him, the sun touching the red and the blue of his bright garments, tending his sheep under the solemn hills. One who sits and listens for the drums to-day seems like the Zouave among the sheep-crofts; the flags and the music have marched so far away. And yet there may be some, in these times of gain-getting, pleasure-seeking, and reaction who are not sorry to look backward a little, now and then, and refresh from the old fountains their courage and their love of country.

3. Georgeanna Woolsey Bacon; Eliza Woolsey Howland; Daniel John Hoisington (ed.). *My Heart Toward Home, Letters of a Family During the Civil War* (Roseville, MN: Edinborough Press), 2001. 357, Mother to Georgy.

4. *My Heart Toward Home*, 10, Abby to Eliza, December 17, 1959.

5. *Ibid.*, 202, A.H.W. to G. and E., Friday, May 16, 1862; 245, June 17th, 1862.

6. *Ibid.*, 326.

In similar fashion Francis Bacon, confidante to Georgeanna, penned a story with an ending that was designed to surprise:

I reluctantly confess that I am subjugated and crushed by a woman who sings The Star Spangled Banner copiously through all the wards of my hospital.... She weighs three hundred pounds. She comes every morning, early. She wears the Flag of our Country pinned across her heart. She comes into *My* room, my own office, unabashed by the fact that I am the Surgeon in charge, and that an orderly in white gloves stands at the door. She looks me in the eye with perfect calmness and intrepidity. She takes off her sunbonnet and mantilla and lays them upon my table, over my papers, as if they were rare and lovely flowers of the tropics. She knocks off three of my pens with her brown parasol, worn out in the joint, and begins to exude small parcels from every pocket.... She nurses tenderly, and feeds and cries over the bad cases. Poor Martin Rosebush, a handsome, smooth-faced, good boy from New Hampshire, desperately wounded and delirious, would start up with a cry of joy when she came, and died with his arms around her neck, calling her his mammy.

Jerry Cammett, a peaceful giant, grown as they grow them in Maine, with pink cheeks, bright-yellow beard, and handsome blue eyes as free from guile as a baby's, lies with his right thigh amputated. After each visit she makes him, I hear the effect it has upon Jerry in about three hours of steady quiet whistling to himself of funny, twiddling Methodist hymns. Of course I do not encourage the visits of this creature with the Flag of our Country and the National Anthem. On the contrary, they encourage me. [308, Francis Bacon to Georgeanna Woolsey, July 6th, 1863].

7. *Hospital Days*, 95.

8. *Ibid.*, 55–56.

9. *My Heart Toward Home*, 95–96, dream; 336–337, Request for dream.

10. *Hospital Days*, 8, 11.

11. Jean V. Berlin (ed.). *A Confederate Nurse: The Diary of Ada W. Bacot 1860–1863* (Berlin; The University of South Carolina Press), 1994. 24, Tuesday, Jan. 1st, 1861.

12. *Ibid.*, 28, Sunday, Feb. 24th, 1861; 28, Friday Noon, March 15th, 1861; 29, Sunday night, March 17th, 1861.

13. *Ibid.*, 31, Thursday afternoon, April 25, 1861; 33, Wednesday night, Roseville, May 2st, 1861; 38, Tuesday Night, May 28th, 1861.

14. *Ibid.*, 40, Roseville, Sunday morning, June 1st, 1861, dressing the child; 43, Friday forenoon, June 21st 1861 and Sunday after dinner June 23d, 1861; 131, Monticello, Friday morning, July 18th 1862.

15. *Ibid.* 92–95: Charlottesville, Tuesday Night March 18th 1862.

16. Myrta Lockett Avary. *A Virginia Girl in the Civil War, Being a Record of the Actual Experiences of the Wife of a Confederate Officer* (Torrington, WY: The Narrative Press), 2004. The text for this book was obtained from an original edition published in February 1903 by D. Appleton and Company, NY, 10, 38–39.

17. John R Brumgardt (ed.). *Civil War Nurse, the Diary and Letters of Hannah Ropes* (Knoxville, TN: The Tennessee Press), 1980. 67, September 18–30, 1862, Hannah to My Dear Mother.

18. Ednah D. Cheney (Ed.). *Louisa May Alcott, Her Life, Letters, and Journals* (Boston, MA: Little, Brown, and Company), 1898. *Copyright, 1889*, By J. S. P. Alcott. (Cambridge, MA: University Press, John Wilson and Son, Cambridge; Project Gutenberg. 45, 64.

19. *Ibid.*, pp. 123, 126, 197, flannel petticoat.

20. *Ibid.*, 51—Imagination book reference—1843, Wednesday; December 27; 89, March 14, 1858, Beth's death.

21. *Ibid.*, 139, 143, Journal kept at the Hospital, Georgetown, D.C., 1862.

22. *Ibid.*, 117, December 27, 1862, Lewie; 119, same date, roll call.

23. *Ibid.*, 128, Brookline, Massachusetts, January 27, 1863, Alice to her brother; manuscript letters recorded on dream; Edward Ropes to Alice Ropes, Jan. 28, 1863. This brief missive was followed the next day by another, in which Edward told his sister the dream, Edward Ropes to Alice Ropes, Jan. 29, 1863; Skinner-Ropes Manuscript Collection, Special Collections Division, General Library, University of California.

24. *Ibid.*, 145, Journal Kept at the Hospital. LMA, "Mrs. R." is Hannah Ropes.

25. *Ibid.*, 147–147.

26. *Ibid.*, 247, January 1885; 311; 328, white flower dream; 332; death. The practitioners of the mind cure believed that since the spirit was superior to the body, cleansing one's mental state would result in a corresponding improvement in one's physical state. LMA's unsuccessful visits to Anna B. Newman at 17 Boylston Street in Boston are reported in "Miss Alcott on Mind-Cure" in the 18 April 1885 Woman's Journal and in her letter 15 March [1885] to Maggie Lukens, in SL, 287–188 [*The Selected Letters of Louisa May Alcott*, Myerson & Shealy].

27. Mr. A. P. Erving, publisher. *Reminiscences of the Life of a Nurse in Field, Hospital and Camp, During the Civil War, Annie Priscilla Zerbe Erving. Army Nurse, Medical Dept.; US Volunteers* (Newburgh, NY: Daily Press, reprint), 1904. 46, Preface.

28. Mrs. Fannie Beers. *Memories: A Record of Personal Experiences and Adventures During Four Years of War* (Philadelphia, PA: Press of J.B. Lippincott Company, 1888), Project Gutenberg. 36, 45, 67–68.

29. Richard Barksdale Harwell (ed.). *Kate Cumming, the Journal of a Confederate Nurse* (Baton Rouge, LA: Louisiana State University Press), 1959. 75, poem by Kate Cumming's mother, Kate Cumming; *Gleaning from Southland*; 56, cited by Kate Cumming, Mobile, July 16. Jed Marum wrote his song, *Chickahominy River*, from Kate's poem, released on *South Wind*.

30. *Ibid.*, 13, April 10, 1862.

31. *Ibid.*, 3, quote; 4, Thomas Hood, "The Lady's Dream," stanza 16; 14, first visit to a ward, April 11, 1862; 16, Sunday, April 13, 1862, sleeping on a shelf.

32. *Ibid.*, 28, April 30; 74–74, October 29.

33. *Ibid.*, 99, April 13; "Somebody's Darling," a poem by Miss Marie Ravenel LaCoste of Savannah. It was set to music by John Hill Hewitt and published in Macon and Savannah in 1864. Harwell, *Confederate Music*, 143; "long home," Ecclesiastes 12:5: "*When they shall be*

afraid of *That Which Is* high, and fears *Shall Be* in the way, and the almond tree shall flourish, and the grasshopper shall be a burden, and desire shall fail: because man goeth to his long home, and the mourners go about the streets"; 137, Kingston, Cherokee Springs, Sunday, September 6, vacant dreams.

34. *Ibid.*, 155, October 6; Edward Monro. *The Journey Home: An Allegory* (London, Eng.), 1854. A dream allegory.

35. *Ibid.*, 183.

36. Kathleen S. Hanson (ed.). *Turn Backward O Time, the Civil War Diary of Amanda Shelton* (Edinborough Press), 2006. Papers housed at the University of Iowa as part of the Shelton Family Papers, donated by daughters, Helen and Lucy S. Stewart, in 1956. Consists of 3 diaries, one from Ortus Carnifax, one from Mary, and one from Rhoda Amanda. 111, Iowa Hospital for the Insane, Sept. 11th, 1866.

37. *Ibid.*, 49, Friday, April 22nd; 70, Monday May 16th.

38. *Ibid.*, 111, Iowa Hospital for the Insane, Sept. 11th, 1866.

39. *Ibid.*, 75, Monday, May 23rd; 136.

40. *Ibid.*, 111.

41. Frank E. Vandiver, [ed.]. "Letters from the Confederate Medical Service in Texas, 1863–1865," *Southwestern Historical Quarterly*, LV (April, 1952), 467. Edward A. Pye to Molly Pye, December 16, 1864.

42. Thomas S. Hawley, M.D., edited by Dennis W. Belcher. "This Terrible Struggle for Life," The Civil War Letters of a Union Regimental Surgeon (Jefferson, NC: McFarland & Company, Inc. Publishers), 2012. 16, Thomas Hawley to "Dearest Friends," St. Louis, Mo., July 2, 1861.

43. *Ibid.*, 48, Camp Fremont, December 9, 1861.

44. Discussed in chapter titled "Soldier's Heart." Thomas Hawley describes one case in detail: "I formed several pleasant acquaintances during my short stay in Rolla among which was Dr. Burnes, a graduate of some school in Canada. Was not over 30 years of age. No family, no relations, had removed from Arkansas to Rolla in April. Soon after coming to Rolla commenced drinking and had been under the influence of stimulants to a greater or lesser degree ever since until last Thursday night. Was attacked with premonitory symptoms of *mania a potu*. He continued to grow gradually worse. Was not wild and raving at any time. Dr. Fuller and I called in on Sunday. He was then one mass of living, dying, jerking, quivering flesh. Eyes glaring wildly, his pulse was feeble and irregular, limbs cold and clammy. The Dr. had prescribed for himself the first two days of his sickness. He then called in Dr. Thrallkill. He took large quantities of stimulants opiates. When we saw him we knew he must die but sent over a vial containing equal parts of tine, opiates and viratril. Nothing did any good. He died Monday morning." 32, St. Louis, August 2, 1861, Thomas Hawley to "Dearest Friends."

45. *Ibid.*, 60, Camp 11th Regt. Mo. Vols. July 20 [1862]., to "Darling sister Myra."

46. *Ibid.*, 170, Camp near Memphis, Tennessee, January 29, 1864.

47. *Ibid.*, 226–27. No. 13 Camp 11th Mo. Inf. V.V., Near Blakely Fort, Sunday Night, April 9, 1865, "Dear Darling Wife."

48. *Ibid.*, 238, Demopolis, Alabama, December 22, 1865.

49. Bill Martin and Jon Curtis' study earned them first place in team competition at the 2001 Intel International Science and Engineering Fair, http://mentalfloss.com/article/30380/why-some-civil-war-soldiers-glowed-dark.

50. College of Physicians of Philadelphia, Mutter Museum. Collections, Letter to S. Weir Mitchell, February 10, 1906.
Joseph Brin. (Hidden City Philadelphia), September 11, 2013. http://hiddencityphila.org/2013/09/philadelphia-during-the-civil-war-a-medical-perspective-opening-at-the-mutter/. For additional information on the exhibit: http://www.collegeofphysicians.org.
College of Physicians of Philadelphia, Mutter Museum. Collections, Letter to S. Weir Mitchell, February 10, 1906.

51. http://en.wikipedia.org/wiki/Phantom_pain, Dr. Mitchell quote, "thousands of spirits." He also wrote novels and a short story about a doctor who lost all four limbs in the Civil War: "The Case of George Dedlow,"Atlantic Monthly, Vol. XVIII, No. CV, July, 1866.

Chapter 13

1. W. Eric Emerson and Karen Stokes. *Faith, Valor, and Devotion: The Civil War Letters of William Porcher Dubose* (Columbia, SC: The University of South Carolina Press), 2010. xxiv, ftnt 45 on the skull; 48, Holcombe Legion, March 4, 1862; 52, Holcombe Legion, letter about Dick, March 24th, 1862.

2. *Ibid.*, 67, Sunday, May 25th, 1862.

3. *Ibid.*, 85, Camp Clover, Aug. 7th 1862.

4. *Ibid.*,139, Holcombe Legion, Febry. 24th 1863.

5. *Ibid.*, 144, Holdombe Legion, March 4th 1863.

6. *Ibid.*, 186, 4 miles from Brownsville, July 1st 1863.

7. *Ibid.*, 202, Holcombe Legion, Aug. 3rd 1863.

8. *Ibid.*, 328: letter of March 25th, 1865—also pleased that their house had not been burned.

9. Peter Messent & Steve Courtney (eds.). *The Civil War Letters of Joseph Hopkins Twichell, a Chaplain's Story* (Athens, GA: The University of Georgia Press), 2006. 1, Joseph Twichell to his father, April 22, 1861.

10. *Ibid.*, 51: In Camp—Washington, Sunday, Aug 4th '61, to My dear Father.

11. *Ibid.*, 143 &145: Before Richmond. June 19th 1862. Dear Father. The Yale class of 1859 had scheduled its first reunion, the triennial, for 31 July.

12. *Ibid.*, 148: In Camp before Richmond. June 25th 1862, Dear Father.

13. *Ibid.*, 159: In Camp Near Harrison's Bar—on James River July 5th 1862, My dear Father.

14. *Ibid.*,192: In Camp, near Falmouth, Va., Sunday Evening, Dec. 7th 1862, Dear Father.

15. *Ibid.*, 212: In Camp,near Falmouth, Va. Feb. 22nd 1863, My dear Father.

16. *Ibid.*, 237: Camp near Falmouth, Va., 3 o'clock p.m. June 11th 1863.

17. *Ibid.*, 275: Near Rappahannock Station, Va., 10½ o'clock a.m. Sunday, Nov. 8th 1863, Dear Mother.

18. *Ibid.*, 288: 2nd Regt. Excelsior Brigade. Dec. 31st 1863.

19. *Ibid.*, 300.

20. *Ibid.*, 311–312; 6; Note, 314: Joseph provided Twain a view of life on both sides of the track, and Twain accompanied Joseph to his speaking engagements after the war and heard his stories and, with Joseph's delighted permission, used them. In one, related by the editor of Joseph's letters, Twain recounted a tale of pulling a howling patient's tooth in a medical tent. There

was an audience. The proud patient remained quiet while the audience each grabbed their jaws, hop around and howl at each extraction. Mark Twain had a special gift for the wit needed to bring out both the horror and humor in Joseph's stories and scattered them among his own.

Note 2: There were considerably more instances of dreams that did not beg the question, "Which is the Dream." Dr. Seth Rogers served with a colored regiment as Surgeon of the First South Carolina Volunteers, under Colonel Higginson in 1862-1864. The regiment was renumbered in February, 1864, as the 33rd U.S. Colored Infantry, the first regiment of colored troops formed in the United States.

In March of 1863, Dr. Seth Rogers reported dreaming realistically and peacefully of a prayer meeting when a rebel bombshell burst in the middle of the town. He had to race from his dream of a prayer meeting to caring for his South Carolina "hospital" which Providence had abandoned. Humorously reminding people that the Lord "was on the side of our big guns" he crawled on top of the observatory and watched until a shell passed over his head "with a note so shrill "that I began to think of Gabriel's trumpet and crawled down again." Dreams for Seth Rogers were practical and often awakened to deadly surroundings. [JStor. February Meeting. Quarter-Centenary at Geneva; Channing and John Brown; *Letters of Dr. Seth Rogers, 1862,1863*; Proceedings of the Massachusetts Historical Society, Third Series, Vol. 43 (Oct. 1909–Jun. 1910), pp. 282–411. Published by: Massachusetts Historical Society Stable URL: http://www.jstor.org/stable/25079, 379.

21. New York State Library, CEC Building, Albany, NY: Charles Hagar Papers (1862–1865). 1 box (0.25 cu. ft.). Collection Call Number: SC22915. Acquisition from David Greene, Auburn, New Hampshire; Box 1, Folder 1, Item 1; no date, 1862?; Box 1, Folder 1, Item 12,. Friday evening 6 o'clock (nd 1862?), Charles to his children Emma and Charly.

22. *Ibid.*, Folder Three, Item 4; Camp of 118th in Va., Jan. 29th, 1863, Thursday morning.

23. *Ibid.*, Folder Three, Item 7; Saturday evening, Feb. 21st 1863, Sunday morning.

24. Folder Three, Item 14: Suffolk VA, May 18th, 1963, Monday morning; Charles Hagar to "Dear Loved Ones."

25. Folder Three, Item 13, Suffolk VA, May 10th 1863, Fort Union—Sunday morning; Charles Hagar to "My dear wife."

26. *Ibid.*, Folder Five, Item 21: Point of Rocks Hospital, Bermuda Hundred, VA; Charles Hagar to Elizabeth, Tuesday evening, May 30th, 1865.

27. *Ibid.*, Folder Five, Item 3 & Item 8, Point of Rocks Hospital, Bermuda Hundred, VA; Wednesday morning, February 23, 1865; Charles Hagar to Elizabeth.

28. *Ibid.*, Folder Five, Item 28, Adam's Landing, October 13th, 1865, Thursday eve 10 o'clock.

29. poem, Folder Seven, Miscellaneous.

I created a battlefield itinerary in the spring of 2012 and followed the dreams recorded in the letters of three of the soldiers: Charles Hagar, Henry Lea Graves, and William Stilwell. At the location of Point of Rocks, we read the markers for the location of the Civil War hospital and followed general directions from the original letters, behind a modern picnic area, down a wooded path and along the river to a location that approximated the location of the hospital. Coming back up along a steep path from the river, I tripped over roots that could have been the location of the stairs in Charles' letter. The moment gave me a shiver of recognition: "I have dreamed of her every night for a week...." The past is often not past.

Chapter 14

1. J. David Hacker, associate professor of history at SUNY Binghampton, NYTcivilwar, drawing from the following Sources: Drew Gilpin Faust, *This Republic of Suffering: Death and the American Civil War*; Joshua B. Howard, *North Carolina Civil War Death Study*; Francis Amasa Walker, Report of the Superintendent of Census to the Secretary of the Interior, Dec. 26, 1871; Henry Gannett, "The Alleged Census Frauds in the South"; Francis Amasa Walker, Documents Relating to the Taking of the Census of South Carolina, Oct. 5, 1880; Robert P. Porter, Henry Gannett and William C. Hunt, "Progress of the Nation, 1790 to 1890"; William F. Fox, "Regimental Losses in the American Civil War, 1861–1865"; Thomas L. Livermore, "Number and Losses in the Civil War in America, 1861–65"; Steven Ruggles et al., "Integrated Public Use Microdata Series."

2. Drew Gilpin Faust. *The Civil War Soldier and the Art of Dying*: The Journal of Southern History, Vol. 67, No. 1 (Feb., 2001), pp. 3–38. Published by: Southern Historical Association Stable URL: http://www.jstor.org/stable/3070083 "Courtesy of JSTOR." 3–4.

3. *The Stilwell Letters,* 12–13; letter from William Stilwell to Molly, "three miles below Richmond, Virginia, July 14, 1862.

4. Frank Anderson Chappell (ed.). *Dear Sister, Civil War Letters to a Sister in Alabama.* (Huntsville, Alabama: Branch Springs Publishing), 2002. 111: Letter # JZB 30, July 15th 1862.

5. *Ibid.*, 191: Letter # LSB 15 [Lewis Sylvester Branscomb], Camp Terrill Apr 15th [1864], to "Beloved sister"; 203–04: Letter #LCH 2 [Lucinda Caroline Hunter (Sister); 205: Letter #JWB 7 [John Wesley Branscomb—married], Camp Nichols July 9th. 64.

6. Culbertson Family Genealogy Pages, Internet: http://sonic.net/~fredd/cwl.html, Letters from Y.J. Culbertson, Columbia, SC, from his brother-in-law to James' wife, August 10, 1863; to his mother, May 7, 1861.

7. Mary D. Robertson (ed.). *Lucy Breckinridge of Grove Hill: The Journal of a Virginia Girl, 1862–1864* (Columbia, SC: University of South Carolina Press), 1994. 54, Wednesday, Sept. 17th, 1862.

8. *Ibid.*, 60, Sunday, Sept. 28th, 1862.

9. *Ibid.*, 38, Monday, August 25th, 1862.

10. *Ibid.*, 106, Monday, January 19th, 1863.

11. *Ibid.*, 90–91, Friday, Dec. 19th, 1862.

12. Ella Jane Bruen and Brian M. Fitzgibbons, editors and introduction. *Through Ordinary Eyes; the Civil War Correspondence of Rufus Robbins, Private, 7th Regiment, Massachusetts Volunteers* (Westport, CT: Praeger Publishers), 2000. 19, July 15, 1861.

13. *Ibid.*, 61, August 25, 1861, Sunday, Washington, D.C., "Dear Mother."

14. *Ibid.*, 62–63, August 28, 1861, Washington, D.C., to Henry.

15. *Ibid.*, 98, December 17, 1861, Washington, D.C., to his brother on falling to sleep.

16. *Ibid.*, 108–109, February 2, 1861, Washington, D.C. "Dear Brother," with a history of illness.

17. *Ibid.*, 120–121, March 23, 1862, Washington, D.C., "Dear Brother,"; 137–138, June 14, 1862, Seven Pines, Virginia, "Dear Brother."

18. *Ibid.*, 161, August 24, 1862, Camp near Yorktown,

Virginia, "Dear Brother," 167, dream of home and "Mother," September 5, 1862, Camp near Chain Bridge, Virginia, "Dear Brother."

19. *Ibid.*, 189-190, February 16, 1863, Philadelphia, Pennsylvania, "My dear Mrs. Robbins." Rufus Robbins, Jr., Private, age 34 years and 7 months at his death. He was buried in his hometown of South Abington, now Whitman, Massachusetts.

Psalm 91: 1 Whoever dwells in the shelter of the Most High will rest in the shadow of the Almighty.[a] 2 I will say of the Lord, "He is my refuge and my fortress, my God, in whom I trust." 3 Surely he will save you from the fowler's snare and from the deadly pestilence. 4 He will cover you with his feathers, and under his wings you will find refuge; his faithfulness will be your shield and rampart. 5 You will not fear the terror of night, nor the arrow that flies by day, 6 nor the pestilence that stalks in the darkness, nor the plague that destroys at midday. 7 A thousand may fall at your side, ten thousand at your right hand, but it will not come near you. 8 You will only observe with your eyes and see the punishment of the wicked. 9 If you say, "The Lord is my refuge," and you make the Most High your dwelling, 10 no harm will overtake you, no disaster will come near your tent. 11 For he will command his angels concerning you to guard you in all your ways; 12 they will lift you up in their hands, so that you will not strike your foot against a stone. 13 You will tread on the lion and the cobra; you will trample the great lion and the serpent. 14 "Because he[b] loves me," says the Lord, "I will rescue him; I will protect him, for he acknowledges my name. 15 He will call on me, and I will answer him; I will be with him in trouble, I will deliver him and honor him. 16 With long life I will satisfy him and show him my salvation."

I was typing notes from this journal when Civil War music began playing in the background on my computer: "Come Dearest the Daylight is Gone"—an interesting coincidence, and an even more interesting omen to Rufus' fated death in a culture that believe in omens and signs.

20. Guy R. Everson & Edward W. Simpson, Jr. (eds.). *Far, Far from Home: The Wartime Letters of Dick and Tally Simpson, 3rd South Carolina Volunteers* (New York; Oxford: Oxford University Press, 1994). 41, Letter 18, RWS to Caroline Virginia Taliaferro Miller, Vienna Va., August 4th [1861].

21. *Ibid.*, 136: Letter 57, TNS to Caroline Virginia Taliaferro Miller [aunt], Camp Jackson [Va.], Monday July 14th 1862.

22. *Ibid.*, 160, Letter 67, TNS to Mary Simpson, In Camp near Fredericksburg, Tuesday, Dec. 2nd 1862.

23. *Ibid.*, 217: Letter 88, TNS to Caroline Virginia Taliaferro Miller, Freder'sburg, Va, April 24th, 1863.

Gaillard's blacksmith shop: In Pendleton, SC, James Hunter opened a blacksmith shop on Mechanic Street in the 1850s. Mr. Hunter continued the blacksmith shop at that location until 1889. He began the operation of a store with a Mr. Long in 1870. The store known as Hunter and Long was located in a two story brick building which was built about 1850 on Queen Street. The building is still known as Hunter's Store. In 1873 Mr. Hunter bought full interest in the store and it was known as James Hunter—Dealer in General Merchandise. Later he and two of his sons, James T. Hunter and Miles M. Hunter, ran the store as James Hunter and Sons. After his death in 1889 it became James Hunter's Sons—Dealers in General Merchandise. Later Miles M. Hunter bought full interest and ran the store as M. M. Hunter—General Merchandise, Fertilizers and Cotton and about 1916 it became M. M. Hunter—Dealer in General Merchandise and Cotton. In 1929 a new building was built across a side street and the original building was used as a warehouse. After the death of Miles Hunter in 1939 three of his sons, Benjamin Gaillard (B.G.) Hunter, Ralph Hunter and Miles Hunter, operated the store as Hunter's Store, Inc. until 1962 when the assets were liquidated. In 1967 the property of the original Hunter's Store which was located across from the town square in Pendleton was purchased from H. L. Dunlap by the Pendleton District Historical Commission in order to be used as a tourist center, museum and its *Headquarters*. There is no surviving evidence of the location of Fannie's family and who she was remains a mystery. She was probably sixteen or seventeen years old and her family was probably from Charleston, SC, and not well-to-do. She apparently moved to Pendleton in the summer or fall of 1862, which explained why Tally had never met her—see page 281 for more speculation.

283-284. As a part of Kershaw's Brigade of McLaws' Division of Longstreet's Corps, Tally's Third South Carolina was in the portion of Robert E. Lee's Army of Northern Virginia sent west to reinforce Braxton Bragg's Army of Tennessee in September of 1863.... The fighting around Chickamauga Creek had been going on for a full day when Longstreet arrived, and his men were marched directly from the railway station into the line of battle. The next morning—the 20th of September—it was Longstreet's men who made the difference.... Longstreet threw his troops against the exposed right flank of the Union army in one of those sledgehammer attacks he had come to be known for, and drove it from the field.

...General George Thomas—"the Rock of Chickamauga"—rallied remnants of the demoralized Union army ... made a stand—on a small knoll near the Snodgrass farm—and there he waited for Longstreet.... Longstreet sent them up Snodgrass Hill in repeated attempts to dislodge Thomas from his position. Kershaw's men in particular, Longstreet would later write in his report, "made a most handsome attack upon the heights at the Snodgrass house." But it was to no avail. Thomas held on until seven o'clock that night, when he quietly withdrew into the safety of Chattanooga, the last of the Union army to leave the field.... Kershaw's Brigade ... had been especially hard hit, suffering over 500 casualties ... including nine officers and fifty-six enlisted men killed action. One of those enlisted men was Corporal Taliaferro N. Simpson—struck down at the foot of Snodgrass H ill while "gallantly pushing forward in the front rank of his company"—and it fell to the old family friend and pastor, the Rev. John M. Carlisle, to write to Tally's father those all-too-familiar words that have brought sorrow and grief to many a home in many a war, "It is my mournful duty to communicate to you and your dear family the fact that your son and my dear young friend, Tally, fell on the bloody field of Sunday last, [the] 20th inst. He was shot through the heart by a minnie ball, his left arm was broken, and either a grape or canister shot passed through his head, supposed to be after he fell. He was doing his duty and met his fate as a brave soldier. He fell with his face to the foe. This was letter 114 the Rev. John M. Carlisle to Richard Franklin Simpson; Ringgold Georgia R R; Sept. 22nd 1863.

24. *Confederate Letters and Diaries, 1861-1865*, 56-57.

25. C. Vann Woodward (ed.). *Mary Chesnut's Civil War* (New York: Yale University Press), 1994. 429-430

[drawing room]; 440–441 [dream vision], winter of 1863. James Chesnut, Jr. (January 18, 1815—February 1, 1885) of Camden, South Carolina, was a planter, lawyer, United States Senator, a signatory of the Constitution of the Confederate States of America, and a Confederate States Army general. His wife was Mary Boykin Chesnut, born March 23, 1823, at Mount Pleasant; she became notable for her diary of the Civil War years, first published in 1905 nearly 20 years after her death.

26. Judith W. McGuire. Diary of a Southern Refugee During the War by a Lady of Virginia. (Lincoln, Nebraska: University of Nebraska Press), 1995. 166–168, Richmond, October 15, 1862. At the Battle of Pea Ridge, General James McIntosh commanded a brigade in the division of Ben McCulloch, who was killed by Union infantry fire. Shortly after assuming division command, McIntosh was leading an advance when he was struck and killed by a bullet, less than fifteen minutes after McCulloch's death [Wikipedia].

27. Franklin R. Crawford. *Proud to Say I Am a Union Soldier: The Last Letters Home from Federal Soldiers Written During the Civil War, 1861–1865* (Natchez, Mississippi: Heritage Books), 2005. 71–72, Natchez, Mississippi, August 20/1863. Edward Y Adkinson from John H Adkinson; Co K—95 Regiment Infantry." John H. Adkinson Collection—Boone County Historical Society. Belvedere, Illinois.

28. Included in "Strange Tales of Floyd County, VA" edited by—and quoted by permission—Patricia Robin Woodruff; originally in Rand Dotson "The Grave & Scandolous Evil Infected to your People." 404, in *The Virginia Magazine of History and Biography*.

29. John Beatty. *The Citizen Soldier: Or Memoirs of a Volunteer* (Digital Scanning Inc.), 2008. July 1862, John Beatty. John Beatty (1848–1914) left his work and his home to join the Ohio volunteers in 1861. He began as a private, but rose through the ranks to become a Brigadier General by 1862. Beatty recorded his daily life and experiences as a Union soldier during the Civil War.

30. Kenneth Jones. *Never Forsake the Flag, the Letters of Captain George A. Turnbull*, Captain Company A; 134th NY Volunteers (Self-published), 1998. 59, Camp 134 Reg. N.Y.S. Vols; Hope Landing Va April 16 (1863), "Dear Beck."

31. *Ibid.*, 34: Camp near Germanstown, VA, Nov. 25th, 1862, "Dear Beck."

32. *Ibid.*, 88: Lookout Valley Tenn. Dec 7/63, to "Dear Beck."

33. Jim Derr. On Line Blog, http://www.jwdletters.com/2012/11/letter-26-georgetown-college-hospital_12.html; Letter #27, John W. Derr to his parents, Georgetown College Hospital, Ward No. 2, Nov. 11, 1862; charm, http://braucher.webs.com/healingcharms.html].

Jim Derr, John's great great grandson, posted John's letters and detailed information concerning references in each letter, including photographs and facsimiles of letters. Jim researched Dutch Paper and found that it would be an amulet on the brown wrapping paper constructed and used in this fashion. "Headache" is used in this example, John could write whatever condition that needed mending and tending:

On a piece of brown paper, preferrable the type used for wrapping meats, write the following:
HEADACHE.
HEADACH.
HEADAC.
HEADA.
HEAD.
HEA.
HE.
H.

Soak the paper in vinegar for three minutes. When ready, let it drip-dry then place on the head of the individual with the headache. Lay your hands on the person's head and repeat three times:
Up Jack Got and Home Did Trot.
As Fast as He Could Caper.
He Went to Bed to Mend His Head.
With Vinegar and Brown Paper.

Some may notice right away that this charm is actually the sequel to the ever-popular "Jack and Jill" rhyme...

Brown paper and vinegar was an old Amish cure-all, most especially for wounds. The paper was wetted with vinegar then placed directly on the wound. This acted as a disinfectant and the brown paper helped the blood clot faster.

34. John Q. Anderson, ed. *Brokenburn, the Journal of Kate Stone, 1861–1868* (Baton Rouge, LA: Louisiana State University Press), 1955. 58, 60. Also in on-line archives; E. and M.A. Bedford (eds.) *Encyclopedia of Superstitions*, ed. (New York),1949. 48, dream cake.

35. *Brokenburn*, 61, journal. October 17, 1861.
36. *Ibid.*, 179.
37. *Ibid.*, 182.
38. *Ibid.*, 186.
39. *Ibid.*, November, 1864, day not listed, "On the way to Texas," 304.
40. *Ibid.*, 364, "Brokenburn, Nov. 16 [1865]."

Chapter 15

1. John Brown Gordon, *Reminiscences of the Civil War*. Electronic Edition. Chapter V, "Presentiment and Fatalism among Soldiers."
2. *On a Skirmish Line Behind a Friendly Tree*, 186.
3. *Reminiscences of the Civil War*, Chapter V.
4. *Ibid.*
5. *Ibid.*
6. *Ibid.*
7. *Ibid.*
8. *Ibid.*
9. Sam Watkins, *Company Aytch, a Confederate Memoir of the Civil War* (CreateSpace Independent Publishing Platform), 2009, 55.
10. Robert Hunt Rhodes (ed.). *All for the Union: The Civil War Diary and Letters of Elisha Hunt Rhodes* (New York: Vintage Civil War Library; Vintage Books; A Division of Random House, Inc.), July, 1992. 156. Also see, Dave Shampine, *New York's North Country and the Civil War Soldiers, Civilians and Legacies* (Charleston/London: The History Press), 2012. 16–17.
11. Dave Shampine (ed.). *New York's North Country and the Civil War*.
Soldiers, Civilians and Legacies (Charleston/London: The History Press), 2012. 16–17.
12. Rufus R. Dawes. *Rufus R. Dawes, Brevet Brigadier General U.S. Volunteers* (Dayton, Ohio: Press of Morningside Bookshop), 1996. reissued reprint. Full text also available on-line at the Internet Archive; original at Cornell University: http://www.archive.org/stream/cu31924030918944/cu31924030918944_djvu.txt, 6 on name of regiment; 15, Journal, on presentiment, July 6.
13. *Ibid.*, 20, Camp Atwood, Patterson Park, August 5th, 1861, Dawes to his sister; 32, January 9, 1862.

14. *Ibid.*, 138, Journal, Monday, May 4th, 1863; 180, Journal, retreat and holding Cemetery Hill.
15. *Ibid.*, 202, Journal, September 6, 1863.
Dawes married and survived a horrible injury and amazingly successful surgery on his jaw. He had been shot in the face and recovered under the skillful and unusual surgery at the Officers' Hospital in Nashville, Tennessee, 287, record of surgery by J.H. Greene.
16. Charles N. Tenney Civil War Letters, 1861–1863. Accession number 11616, Special Collections, University of Virginia Library, Charlottesville, Va. Folder "1862 January–June Letters of Charles Tenney." Charlie Tenney to Adelaide Case, August 11, 1862. Illustration and poem appear as the letterhead.
17. *Ibid.* Letter, January 19, 1861, from Adelaide E. Case to Charles Tenney. "Dear Brother,"; p. 1, ALS 1861-10-03 NC61j03; Letter from Adelaide E. Case to Charles N. Tenney, 3 October 1861; Manuscript letter.
18. *Ibid.*, 4, Letter from Adelaide E. Case to Charles N. Tenney, 12 October 1861; ALS October 12, 1861 NC61j12.
19. *Ibid.* Charles N. Tenney to Adelaide E. Case, October 1861.
20. *Ibid.*, 2–3, Letter from Charlie to Addie, Parkersburg, Virginia, Dec 11th 1861; 2–3, 3–4, Adelaide Case to Charles Tenney, January 26, 1862.
21. *Ibid.*, 2–3, Mecca, January 1st, 1862 NA62a01, Letter from Adelaide E. Case to Charles N. Tenney; ALS 1862-02-19 NA62b19; Letter from Adelaide E. Case to Charles N. Tenney, February 19, 1862.
22. 4., Mecca, ALS February 09, 1862 NA62b09 Letter from Adelaide E. Case to Charles N. Tenney; Dreaming on the hillside, Maple Grove, March 14, 1862, Adelaide E. Case to Charles N. Tenney; pp. 1–2; Bible vision, p. 2, Letter from Adelaide E. Case to Charles N. Tenney, Thursday evening. May 6th 1862; sweet dreams/horrific dreams, Letter from Adelaide E. Case, to Charles N. Tenney, April 20th, 1862, Maple Grove. April 20. 1862; 2–3, Letter from Adelaide E. Case to Charles N. Tenney, May 18, 1862; May 18, 1862 NA62e18.
23. 1–3 Case, Adelaide E.. Letter from Adelaide E. Case to Charles N. Tenney, May 26th 1862.
24. *Ibid.*, 7–8, Letter from Charles N. Tenney to Adelaide E. Case, 18 August 1862; Culpepper Court House. Virginia, Aug 18th 1862; fragment, undated, Addie to Charlie on his "funny dream."
25. *Ibid.*, 2, ALS 31 August 1862 NA62h31, Letter from Adelaide E. Case to Charles N. Tenney, East Clarindon August 31st 1862.
26. *Ibid.*, Harpers Ferry, Virginia, ALS October 21, 1862 NC62j21, Letter from Charles N. Tenney to Adelaide E. Case.
27. *Ibid.*, Letter from Adelaide E. Case to Charles N. Tenney, 2 November 1862 ALS 2 November 1862 NA62k02; 1–4, Tenney, Charles. Letter from Charles N. Tenney to Adelaide E. Case, 25 November 1862.
28. *Ibid.*, 1–2, ALS 8 December 1862 NA62m08, Letter from Adelaide E. Case to Charles N. Tenney, Farmington Dec. 8th 1862.
29. *Ibid.*, 1–6; ALS 15 January 1863 NA63a15; Letter from Adelaide E. Case to Charles N. Tenney; 15 January 1863, Farmington, Ohio.
Hundreds of Union soldiers died at Harpers Ferry from disease and most were buried on Bolivar Heights. Their remains were removed after the war and reinterred at the Antietam National Cemetery.Reference: http://www.nps.gov/resources/place.htm?id=105.
Adelaide [Addie] Case, born June 11, 1844, married George Benson Woodworth, a musician in the 12th Pennsylvania Infantry, Company H. Sources: [S104] DAR *DAR Lineage Book*, Vol. 26: Pg. 214/Item 25580; Ancestry.com; U.S. National Cemetery Interment Control Forms; http://www.pa-roots.com/pacw/infantry/12th/12thcoh.html. http://www.pacivilwar.com/cwpa12h.html.

Chapter 16

1. The Walt Whitman Archive. On-Line: http://www.whitmanarchive.org/published/LG/1891/poems/282.
2. http://backstoryradio.org/civil-war-call-in-show/ Wanda Burch interview; Comment by Mark Huber, Vietnam combat veteran; J. R. R. Tolkien, Book Six, Chapter Three. "Mount Doom," *The Lord of the Rings*.
3. Judith Pizarro, M.A., Drs. Roxane C. Silver and JoAnn Prause. "Physical and Mental Health Costs of Traumatic War Experiences among Civil War Veterans"; *The Archives of General Psychiatry* (Feb 2006, Vol. 63, No. 2), 193–200).
4. Kathleen Logothetis graduated in May 2012 with an M.A. in History from West Virginia University. Her thesis, *"A Question of Life or Death: Suicide and Survival in the Union Army,"* examines wartime suicide among Union soldiers, its causes, and the reasons that army saw a relatively low suicide rate. © http://emergingcivilwar.com/2012/08/15/to-the-breaking-point-mental-stress-in-the-union-army/.
5. *The Civil War Diary and Letters of Elisha Hunt Rhodes*, 33, July 30th, 1861; 198, Thursday January 5, 1864, 248. For additional accounts of cases of insanity see Dr. Byron Stinson, "Battle Fatigue" and how it was treated in the Civil War, *Civil War Times Illustrated* v 4, no. 7 (November 1965), 248 pp. 40–44.
6. *Mania a Potu* is defined in the 1913 Webster dictionary as "Violent derangement of mind; madness; insanity." Cf. *Delirium*.
7. *John Dooley's Civil War*, 191, August 10, 1863.
8. *Ibid.*, 332, Prison Notes 4, February 8, 1865.
9. *The Griffith Letters*, 192–193: Marine Hospital, New Orleans, La., May 30th [1864].
10. Mark Nesbitt. *Through Blood & Fire*, 176–177, Appomattox C.H., April 11th 1865, Head Quarters 1st Brig. 1st Div. 5th Corps.
11. Stacy Dale Allen (ed.), *On the Skirmish Line Behind a Friendly Tree, the Civil War Memoirs of William Royal Oake, 26th Iowa Volunteers*. Helena, Montana: Farcountry, 2006. 320.

Chapter 17

1. Frederick Douglass. *Life and Times of Frederick Douglass* (Electronic edition), http://docsouth.unc.edu/neh/dougl92/dougl92.html, 201.
2. *Ibid.*, 213.
3. *Ibid.*, 250.
4. *Ibid.*, 713–714.
5. Solomon Northup. *Twelve Years a Slave; Narrative of Solomon Northup, a Citizen of New-York, Kidnapped in Washington City in 1841 and Rescued in 1853 from a Cotton Plantation Near the Red River in Louisiana* (Auburn: Derby and Miller), 1853. 27–28.
6. Sarah H. Bradford. *Scenes in the Life of Harriet Tubman* (Auburn: W.J. Moses, Printer), 1869. Project Gutenberg. 1, 79; 80, flight like a bird.
Robert Moss. *The Secret History of Dreaming* (Novato,

CA: New World Library), 2010, read Chapter 9, "The Underground Railroad of Dreams" for the remarkable full account of Harriet Tubman's dreams and visions.

7. Bradford, *Scenes in the Life...*, 56.
8. Moss, Chapter 9, "not only in this world..."; Bradford, 14–16, vision of horsemen.
9. Bradford, 19.
10. Bradford, 50–51.
11. *Ibid.*, 82–83.
12. Moss, Chapter 9, 240.
13. Bradford, 82–84, Sanborn, Beaufort, South Carolina, June 30, 1863.

Robert Moss wrote that she "endured for almost half a century, moving back and forth from fame to obscurity, always living in poverty, struggling to feed her parents and brothers and numberless homeless people who sought sanctuary with her on her little farm in Auburn." She lobbied for a war pension but never received it. She found "a biographer in Sarah Bradford, a writer of children's book and Sunday school teacher who had read Bible stories to Harriet's elderly parents.... The later version of the Bradford biography was read by Queen Victoria, who invited Harriet to her birthday party, and earned enough money to pay off the mortgage on the Auburn place." [Moss, Chapter 9.].

14. *The Civil War, the Third Year Told by Those Who Lived It.* 560–561: Cornelia Hancock to an Unknown Correspondent, Contraband Hospital, Washington, Nov. 15th, 1863. Henrietta Stratton Jaquette, ed. *Letters of a Civil War Nurse, Cornelia Hancock, 1863–1865* (Lincoln, Nebraska: University of Nebraska Press), 1998. 31–32, same letter.
15. William Andrews (ed.). "The Representation of Slavery and Afro-American Literary Realism" (*African American Autobiography: A Collection of Critical Essays* (Englewood Cliffs, N. J: Prentice Hall), 1993. Campbell, Donna M. "The Slave Narrative." *Literary Movements.* http://www.wsu.edu/~campbelld/amlit/slave.htm. The narrative prefaces in the lesser known books and pamphlets attested to their writers' authenticity and to the sufferings described within. On-line.
16. Andrea Ball and PG Distributed Proofreaders. (Charlottesville, VA: Bruce Fort, Corcoran Department of History, Randall Hall, University of Virginia. Produced from images provided by the Library of Congress, Manuscript Division). WPA on-line collection: http://www.fullbooks.com/Slave-Narratives-A-Folk-History-of-Slaveryx10183.html.
17. Ophelia Settle Egypt, J. Masuoka, and Charles S. Johnson (eds.). *Unwritten History of Slavery: Autobiographical Accounts of Negro Ex-Slaves* (Nashville, TN: Fisk University, Microcard Editions, Washington, D.C.), 1968. 37, "Massa's Slave Son." The interviews were with ex-slaves, telling their stories from childhood memories. They were conducted during 1929 and 1930 by Ophelia Settle Egypt, then a member of the Research Staff of the Social Science Institute at Fisk University. The subjects resided, for the most part, in Tennessee and Kentucky.
18. *Ibid.*, 38.
19. George P. Rawick (ed.). *The American Slave: A Composite Autobiography* (Westport, CN: Greenwood Press, 1972–79). Lucinda Davis, Tulsa, Oklahoma, WPA Narrative.
20. Charles Ball. *Slavery in the United States: A Narrative of the Life and Adventures of Charles Ball, a Black Man* (New York: Documents in the History of Slavery), 1837. On-line. http://www.digitalhistory.uh.edu/modules/slavery/documents.html.

21. WPA narrative. American Life Histories: Manuscripts from the Federal Writers' Project, 1936–1940, Item 1 of 100, Project #1655, interviewer: Cassels R. Tiedeman, Charleston, S.C. (Verbatim Conversation), Source:, Addison Court, Charleston, S.C. "A dream dat rest heaby on you mind in a wisitation ob do sperrit. Look on it wid concern."
22. *Ibid.* WPA narrative. *Memories of Childhood's Slavery Days*: Electronic Edition. Annie L. Burton, b. 1858? Text scanned (OCR) and corrected by Katharyn Graham. Text encoded by Natalia Smith. First edition, 1996, Academic Affairs Library, UNC-CH, The University of North Carolina at Chapel Hill, NC 1996. 16.
23. WPA on-line collection. Part 5, prepared by the Federal Writers' Project of the Works Progress Administration for the State of Arkansas. Interviewer: Miss Irene Robertson; Person interviewed: Malindy Maxwell, Madison, Arkansas. Age: Up in 80's.
24. *Ibid.*, Name of Interviewer: Martin & Barker, Information given by: Maggie Perkins, Pine Bluff, AK, W. 6th. St.
25. *Ibid.*,, Interviewer: Pernella Anderson, Information given by: Mose Minser—Farmer—Age—78; Place of Residence: 5 miles from El Dorado—Section 8.
26. *Ibid.*, Interviewer: Mrs. Bernice Bowden, Person interviewed: A.J. Mitchell, 419 E. 11th Avenue, Pine Bluff, Arkansas, Age: 78; Name of Interviewer: Irene Robertson, information given by: Tom Wylie Neal, Hazen, Arkansas—Near Green Grove Age: 85.
27. *Documents in the History of Slavery.* "Narrative of the Life and Adventures of Henry Bibb, An American Slave" (New York), 1849.
28. *Unwritten History of Slavery: Autobiographical Accounts of Negro Ex-Slaves.* 107 and 158. I grew up in the South, familiar with the "belief" that one never shared a dream before breakfast or it would not come true.
29. *Documents in the History of Slavery.* Source: The Interesting Narrative of the Life of Olaudah Equiano or Gustavus Vassa the African (London), 1789.
30. WPA slave narratives. "When it's Right to Steal from your Master," 15; on turning down the pot, "Slaves Have no Souls"—testimony by "Mr. Reed," 21; "Every Thursday Was 'Whipping Day' for Slaves," slave narrative, speaking to ants and birds, 112.
31. One wonders if she was dreaming a spiritual dream of the Emancipation Proclamation and the White House.
32. WPA slave narratives, "Sold from Block at Four Years Old"—testimony by "Vergy," 30.
33. William Webb. *The History of William Webb, Composed by Himself* (Detroit, Michigan: Egbert Hoekstra, printer), 1873. © This work is the property of the University of North Carolina at Chapel Hill. It may be used freely by individuals for research, teaching and personal use as long as this statement of availability is included in the text. Call number E444.W36 (Library of Congress), 3.
34. *Ibid.*, 9.
35. *Ibid.* 20–21.
36. *Ibid.*, 22–25.
37. *Ibid.* 27.
38. *Ibid.*, 41–44, living in the woods; 57, dream of a wife.
39. *Ibid.*, 58–59.
40. *Ibid.*, 60.
41. *Ibid.*, 63–64.
42. Daily Chronicles of the American Civil War, blog:

http://www.cw-chronicles.com/blog/the-running-off-of-the-steamer-planter-from-charleston/, The Charleston Mercury, September 30, 1862.

43. *WPA Slave Narratives,* "They Would Tie you Up and Whip You," p. 126.

44. *The Civil War Letters of Joseph Hopkins Twichell, a Chaplain's Story.* 165: In Camp—Near Harrison's Landing, Va. July 9th 1862, "Dear Father."

45. Edwin S. Redkey (ed.). *A Grand Army of Black Men* (Cambridge University Press), 1992. 61–62: South Carolina II, Letter 24: John H.W.N. Collins, Sergeant, Co H, 54th Massachusetts Infantry, Fort Green, Folly Island, SC [May 1864].

The same story of the woman on the white horse was repeated by David Lane of Company G, 17th Regiment of the Michigan Volunteer Infantry: City Point, August 9th, 1864:

A fearful tragedy was enacted here today. A barge, laden wit ammunition, was blown to atoms, scattering death and destruction around.... Near as can be ascertained at this time, about two hundred were killed and wounded. A vast amount of property was destroyed. Blocks of timber, shells, grape shot and other missiles were thrown over a mile. We are situated about a mile and a half from the landing. I was on my way to the Point; had covered, perhaps, one-half the distance. As I looked toward the landing I saw a lady, mounted on a white horse that belonged to the Commission, ride up the bank from the river and turn in the direction of Grant's headquarters. I recognized her as a member of the Michigan Relief Society. The horse was a spirited one, and I could but admire the case and grace with which she restrained him and compelled him to do her bidding. He tossed his beautiful head and spurned the ground beneath his feet as he lightly galloped over the plain.... They had reached a point perhaps half a mile from the landing, when a violent concussion rent the air. From the landing fire, smoke and innumerable missiles were being hurled upward, in a whirling eddy, as from the mouth of a volcano. Heavy timbers and other debris flew over and around me. I looked for the lady on horseback. For an instant I could see nothing in that direction but a swirling cloud of dust; in another instant I saw, through the dispersing gloom, a white horse clearing the ground with rapid strides, and on his back, cool and erect, a lady.

I was afterward informed the lady was Mrs. Wheelock, of Jackson, Michigan, a member of the Michigan Relief Society.

A Soldier's Diary, David Lane, 188–89.

46. Andrea Sutcliffe (ed.). *Mighty Rough Times I Tell You, Personal Accounts of Slavery in Tennessee* (Winston-Salem, NC: John F. Blair, Publisher), 2000. 180. WPA, Social Science Dept. project, Fisk University, 1929–30, Nashville, Tennessee.

Chapter 18

1. R. G. Plumb. *Letters of a Fifth Wisconsin Volunteer, Correspondence of James H. Leonard, Company a of the Fifth Wisconsin Infantry* (JStor), Written from Havenwood Hospital; Washington, Dec. 13th, 1863. James Leonard was a school-teacher at Branch, Manitowoe County.

2. *Letters Home to Sarah,* 218, In Camp on Comstock Farm, February 21th 1865, "My Dear Wife."

3. *The Civil War Letters of Private John Tidd,* 73.

4. Brian Turner served seven years in the Army, most recently in 2004 as an infantry team leader in Mosul with the Third Stryker Brigade Combat Team, Second Infantry Division. His 2005 book of poems, "*Here, Bullet,*" challenges others to record and share their dreams, many of those responding by sharing the dreams of home that got them through the most difficult days. A young soldier reported on Turner's blog dreams of home mixing with scenes in Baghdad but bringing him back home again in the terror of war.

Bibliography

Primary

Addeman, J.M. *Reminiscences of Two Years with the Colored Troops*. Providence, RI: N. Bangs, Williams, 1880. Project Gutenberg.

Alcott, Louisa May. *The Journals of Louisa May Alcott*. Edited by Joel Myerson and Daniel Shealy. Athens and London: University of Georgia Press, 1997.

_____. *Louisa May Alcott: Her Life, Letters, and Journals*. Edited by Ednah D. Cheney. Boston, MA: Little, Brown, 1898 (Copyright 1889 by J.S.P. Alcott). Cambridge, MA: University Press, John Wilson and Son, Cambridge. Project Gutenberg.

Alexander, John W. "A Personal Narrative of Life in Union Prisons, 1864–1865." [Submitted by Hudson Alexander, great-grandnephew for inclusion] In *In Their Honor: Soldiers of the Confederacy; The Elmira Prison Camp*. Elmira: New York History Review Press, 2009.

Alleman, Mrs. Tillie Pierce. *At Gettysburg; or, What a Girl Saw and Heard of the Battle*. New York: W. Lake Borland, 1889.

Andrews, Eliza Frances. *The War Time Journal of a Georgia Girl, 1864 to 1865*, 1908. Whitefish, MT: Kessinger, 2005.

Ashe, S.A. Civil War Collection. Military Collection. State Archives of North Carolina. MilColl box 71, folder 45, S.A. Ashe served under William Pender and wrote a postwar report that included references to Lee and Hill's words of commendation on Pender.

Avary, Myrta Lockett. *A Virginia Girl in the Civil War, Being a Record of the Actual Experiences of the Wife of a Confederate Officer*. Torrington, WY: Narrative, 2004.

Bacon, Georgeanna Woolsey, Eliza Woolsey Howland, and Daniel John Hoisington, ed. *My Heart Toward Home: Letters of a Family During the Civil War*. Roseville, MN: Edinborough, 2001.

Bacot, Ada W. *A Confederate Nurse: The Diary of Ada W. Bacot, 1860–1863*. Edited by Jean V. Berlin. Columbia: University of South Carolina Press, 1994.

Ball, Andrea, and PG Distributed Proofreaders. *WPA Slave Narratives: A Folk History of Slavery in the United States*. Charlottesville, VA: Bruce Fort, Corcoran Department of History, Randall Hall, University of Virginia. Produced from images provided by the Library of Congress, Manuscript Division. WPA, http://www.fullbooks.com/Slave-Narratives-A-Folk-History-of-Slaveryx10183.html. *American Life Histories: Manuscripts from the Federal Writers' Project, 1936–1940*,

Ball, Charles. *Slavery in the United States: A Narrative of the Life and Adventures of Charles Ball, a Black Man*. New York: Documents in the History of Slavery, 1837. http://www.digitalhistory.uh.edu/modules/slavery/documents.html.

Barlow, Francis C. *"Fear Was Not in Him": The Civil War Letters of Major General Francis C. Barlow, U.S.A.* Edited by Christian G. Samito. New York: Fordham University Press, 2004.

Barton, Clara. Project Gutenberg, Letter of December 12, 1862. http://masterworld.org/out/491212/Clara-Barton-Ame-Civil-War-Women-American-Red-Cros.html?PHPSESSID=3b919bf8c2a61333326bdaaa77ec0686.

Beale, Jane Howison. *A Woman in a War-Torn Town, The Journal of Jane Howison Beale*. Edited by Kerri S. Barile and Barbara P. Willis, with contributions from John Hennessy and Pula S. Felder. Fredericksburg, VA: 1850–1862, Donning, 2011.

Beatty, John. *The Citizen Soldier; or, Memoirs of a Volunteer*. Digital Scanning, 2008.

Beaudry, Louis N. Chaplain, Fifth New York Volunteer Cavalry, Richmond. *The Libby Chronicle*. "Devoted to facts and fun." Richmond, VA, August 21, 28, 1863.

Beers, Mrs. Fannie. *Memories: A Record of Personal Experiences and Adventures During Four Years of War*. Philadelphia: J.B. Lippincott, 1888. Project Gutenberg.

Berkeley, Henry Robinson. *Four Years in the Confederate Artillery: The Diary of Private Henry Robinson Berkeley*. Richmond: Virginia Historical Society, Documents, Volume 2, 1961.

Berry, Carrie. *A Confederate Girl: The Diary of Carrie Berry, 1864*. Edited by Kerry Graves. Mankato, MN: Blue Earth, 2000.

Bethell, Mary Jeffreys. *Diary, January 1st 1861–Dec. 1865*. Chapel Hill: University of North Carolina. Electronic Edition. "It may be used freely by individuals for research, teaching and personal use as long as this statement of availability is included in the text. MARY JEFFREYS BETHELL DIARY: January 1st 1861–Dec. 1865, Mary Jeffreys Bethell, Call number 1737 (Manuscripts Dept., Southern Historical Collection, University of North Carolina at Chapel Hill)."

Biddlecom, Charles. *No Freedom Shrieker: The Civil War Letters of Union Soldier Charles Biddlecom, 147th Regiment NY State*. Edited by Katherine M. Aldridge. Ithaca, NY: Paramount, 2012.

Billings, John D. *Hardtack and Coffee: The Unwritten Story of Army Life*. Lincoln and London: University of Nebraska Press, 1842.

Black, John H. "Powder, Lead and Cold Steel: Campaigning in the Lower Shenandoah Valley with the Twelfth Pennsylvania Cavalry; The Civil War Letters of John H. Black." Edited by David J. Coles and Stephen D. Engle. *Magazine of the Jefferson County Historical Society* 55 (December 1989), Charles Town, WV.

———. *A Yankee Horseman in the Shenandoah Valley: The Civil War Letters of John H. Black, Twelfth Pennsylvania Cavalry*. Edited by David J. Coles and Stephen D. Engle. Knoxville: University of Tennessee Press, 2012.

Blaisdell, Bob. *Civil War Letters from Home, Camp and Battlefield*. Mineola, NY: Dover, 2012.

Booth, Thomas B. 3rd Virginia Cavalry Soldier's Letter (Confederate). July 13, 1861. Cockletown, http://www.soldierstudies.org/blog/2010/06/confederate-3rd-virginia-cavalry-soldiers-letter/.

Bowen, Sergeant Charles T. *Dear Friends at Home: The Civil War Letters and Diaries of Sergeant Charles T. Bowen, Twelfth United States Infantry, 1861–1864*. Edited by Edward K. Cassedy. Baltimore: Butternut and Blue, 2001.

Bowen Family Papers. http://freepages.family.rootsweb.ancestry.com/~bowen/hobbys8thTexas.htmlRootsweb: Freepages.

Bowers, Dr. John Hugh. *Life of Abraham Lincoln*, Girard, KS: Haldeman-Julius, 1922. Project Gutenberg.

Bowler, Madison. *Go, If You Think It Your Duty: A Minnesota Couple's Civil War Letters*. Edited by Andrea R. Foroughi. Minnesota Historical Society Press, 2008.

Bowler Papers. Profect Muse Bowler manuscripts. http://muse.jhu.edu/books/9780873516716; http://www.mnhs.org/library/findaids/00792.xml; Manuscript finding aide, Minnesota Historical Society. JMB to ECB, 27 April 1861 and 27 September 1862, Bowler Papers; ECB to JMB, 2 September 1864, Bowler Papers.

Boyd, Cyrus F. *The Civil War Diary of Cyrus F. Boyd, Fifteenth Iowa Infantry, 1861–1863*. Edited by Mildred Throne. Baton Rouge: Louisiana State University Press, 1953.

Bradbury, William H. *While Father Is Away: The Civil War Letters of William H. Bradbury*. Edited Jennifer Cain Bohrnstedt. Lexington: University Press of Kentucky, 2003.

Bradford, Sarah H. *Scenes in the Life of Harriet Tubman*. Auburn: W.J. Moses, 1869. Project Gutenberg.

Breckinridge, Lucy. *Lucy Breckinridge of Grove Hill: The Journal of a Virginia Girl, 1862–1864*. Edited by Mary D. Robertson. University of South Carolina Press, 1994.

Brevard, Keziah Goodwyn Hopkins. *A Plantation Mistress on the Eve of the Civil War: The Diary of Keziah Goodwyn Hopkins Brevard, 1860–1861*. Edited by John Hammond Moore. Columbia: University of South Carolina Press, 1991.

Broadhead, Sarah M. *The Diary of a Lady of Gettysburg, Pennsylvania, from June 15 to July 15, 1863*. Hershey, PA: Reprinted by Gary T. Hawbaker, 2012.

Bryant-Stephens Families. *Rose Cottage Chronicles: Civil War Letters of the Bryant-Stephens Families of North Florida*. Edited by Arch Fredric Blakey, Ann Smith Lainhart, and Winston Bryant Stephens, Jr. Gainesville: University Press of Florida, 1998.

Buck, Lucy Rebecca. *Shadows on My Heart: The Civil War Diary of Lucy Rebecca Buck of Virginia*. Edited by Elizabeth R. Baer. Athens and London: University of Georgia Press, 2012.

Burns, Christopher Columbus. *Civil War letters of Christopher Columbus Burns*. Dege Didear private family letters, permission granted Dege Didear. Dege Didear transcripts unless noted as BLN (Bess Lipscomb Nichols); photocopies and original transcripts provided by BLN.

Burstein, Andrew. *Lincoln Dreamt He Died: The Midnight Visions of Remarkable Americans from Colonial Times to Freud*. New York: Palgrave/MacMillan, 2013.

Burton, Annie. *Memory of Childhood's Slavery Days*. Boston, MA: Ross, 1909. Photo of Annie Burton. © "This work is the property of the University of North Carolina at Chapel Hill. It may be used freely by individuals for research, teaching and personal use as long as this statement of availability is included in the text. Call number E444.B97 (Wilson Annex, UNC-CH)."

Burwell, Letitia M. *A Girl's Life in Virginia Before the War*. Dahlonega, GA: Frederick A. Stokes, 1895.

Butler, Ovid Family. *The Civil War Home-Front Letters of the Ovid Butler Family: Affectionately Yours*. Edited by Barbara Butler Davis. Indianapolis: Indiana Historical Society Press, 2004.

Caldwell, James Parks. *Northern Confederate at Johnson's Island*. Edited by George H. Jones. Jefferson, NC: McFarland, 2010.

Caldwell, Lycurgus Washington, and Susan Emeline Jeffords. *My Heart Is So Rebellious: The Caldwell Letters, 1861–1865*. Edited by J. Michael Welton. Annotated by John K. Gott and John E. Divine. Warrenton, VA: Fauquier National Bank, n.d.

Carpenter, Francis B. *Six Months at the White House with Abraham Lincoln: The Story of a Picture*. New York: Hurd and Houghton, 1867.

Chamberlain, Joshua. *Joshua L. Chamberlain, A Life in Letters*. Edited by Thomas Desjardin. Long Island City, NY: Osprey, National Civil War Museum, 2012.

———. *Through Blood and Fire, Selected Civil War Papers of Major General Joshua Chamberlain*. Edited by Mark Nesbitt. Mechanicsburg, PA: Stackpole, 1996.

Champion, Sid, and Matilda Champion. *My Dear Wife: Letters to Matilda; The Civil War Letters of Sid and Matilda Champion of Champion Hill*. Edited by Rebecca Blackwell Drake and Margie Riddle Bearss. Self published.

Chappell, Frank Anderson, ed. *Dear Sister: Civil War Letters to a Sister in Alabama*. Huntsville, AL: Branch Springs, 2002.

Charnwood, Lord. *Abraham Lincoln*, Garden City, NY: Garden City; Henry Holt, 1917.

Chesnut, Mary C. *Mary Chesnut's Civil War*. Edited by Vann Woodward. New York: Yale University Press, 1994.

Civil War Letters Between Two Brothers. Warren County, NY: Rootsweb. http://www.rootsweb.ancestry.com/~nywarren/military/civilwarletters.htm, September 1, 1861; November 29, 1861, Upton Hill, Virginia.

Coates, Foster. "The Courtship of General Grant," *Ladies' Home Journal* 7 (October 1890).

Coddington, Ronald S. *Faces of the Civil War: An Album of Union Soldiers and Their Stories*. Baltimore and London: Johns Hopkins University Press, 2004.

———. *Faces of the Confederacy: An Album of Southern Soldiers and Their Stories*. Baltimore and London: Johns Hopkins University Press, 2008.

Comstock, Cyrus B. *The Diary of Cyrus B. Comstock*. Edited by Merlin E. Sumner. Dayton, Ohio: Morningside, 1987.

Cotton, John W. *Civil War Letters of John W. Cotton:*

Yours Till Death. Edited by Lucille Griffith. University of Alabama Press, 1951.

Crawford, Franklin R. *Proud to Say I Am a Union Soldier: The Last Letters Home from Federal Soldiers Written During the Civil War, 1861-1865*. Natchez, MS: Heritage, 2005.

Culbertson, Y.J. Culbertson Family Genealogy Pages. http://sonic.net/~fredd/cwl.html.

Cumming, Kate. *Kate Cumming: The Journal of a Confederate Nurse*. Edited by Richard Barksdale Harwell. Baton Rouge: Louisiana State University Press, 1959.

Dada, Harriet A. *Ministering Angel: The Reminiscences of Harriet A. Dada, a Union Army Nurse in the Civil War*. Edited by Edmund J. Raus, Jr. Gettysburg: Thomas, 2004.

Daily Chronicles of the American Civil War. Blog. http://www.cw-chronicles.com/blog/the-running-off-of-the-steamer-planter-from-charleston/.

Davis, Chaplain. *Chaplain Davis and Hood's Texas Brigade*. Edited by Donald E. Everett. Baton Rouge: Louisiana State University Press, 1999.

Derr, John W. *John W. Derr: Civil War Letters*. "To the memory of Private John W. Derr of the 48th Pennsylvania Volunteer Infantry Regiment, Company D (1861-1865)," http://www.jwdletters.com/2012/11/letter-26-georgetown-college-hospital_12.html.

Dickson, James. *High Seas and Yankee Gunboats: A Blockade Running Adventure from the Diary of James Dickson*. Edited by Roger S. Durham. Columbia: University of South Carolina Press, 2005.

Donaldson, Francis Adams. *Inside the Army of the Potomac: The Civil War Experience of Captain Francis Adams Donaldson*. Edited by J. Gregory Acken. Mechanicsburg, PA: Stackpole, 1998.

Dooley, John. *John Dooley's Civil War: An Irish American's Journey in the First Virginia Infantry Regiment*. Edited by Robert Emmett Curran. Knoxville: University of Tennessee Press, 2012.

Dougherty, Michael. *Michael Dougherty Prison Diary, Late Co. B, 13th., Pa., Cavalry*. "While confined in Pemberton, Barrett's, Libby, Andersonville and other southern prisons. Sole survivor of 127 of his regiment captured the same time, 122 dying in Andersonville." Bristol, PA: C.A. Dougherty, 1908.

Douglas, Henry Kyd. *I Rode with Stonewall*. Greenwich, CT: Fawcett, 1961.

Douglass, Frederick. *Life and Times of Frederick Douglass*. Documenting the American South. http://docsouth.unc.edu/neh/dougl92/dougl92.html.

Downer, William W. *Letters and Diary of a Confederate Prisoner of War, Private William W. Downer, Company I, 6th Virginia Cavalry*. Edited by Walbrook D. Swank, USAF, ret. (owner), Route 2, Box 433, Mineral, VA.

Drennan, William A. *Lieutenant Drennan's Letter: A Confederate Officer's Account of the Battle of Champion Hill and the Siege of Vicksburg*. Edited by Matt Atkinson. Gettysburg: Thomas, 2009.

Dubose, William Porcher, *Faith, Valor, and Devotion: The Civil War Letters of William Porcher DuBose*. Edited by W. Eric Emerson and Karen Stokes. Columbia: University of South Carolina Press, 2010.

Duff, Levi Bird. *To Petersburg with the Army of the Potomac: The Civil War Letters of Levi Bird Duff, 105th Pennsylvania Volunteers*. Edited by Jonathan E. Helmreich. Jefferson, NC: McFarland, 2009.

Dyer, J. Franklin. *J. Franklin Dyer: The Journal of a Civil War Surgeon*. Edited by Michael B. Chesson. Lincoln and London: University of Nebraska Press, 2003.

Early, Jubal A. *A Memoir of the Last Year of the War for Independence in the Confederate States of America: Jubal A. Early*. Edited by Gary W. Gallagher. Columbia: University of South Carolina Press, 2001.

Eaton, Harriet. *The Birth Place of Souls: The Civil War Nursing Diary of Harriet Eaton*. Edited by Jane E. Schultz. New York: Oxford University Press, 2011.

Egypt, Ophelia Settle, J. Masuoka, and Charles S. Johnson, ed. *Unwritten History of Slavery: Autobiographical Accounts of Negro Ex-Slaves*. Microcard ed. Nashville: Fisk University; Washington, D.C., 1968.

Elliott, William. *Civil War Letters of William A. Elliott*. Pat Elliott family blog. http://www.civilwarhome.com/elliottletters.htm.

Erving, Annie Priscilla Zerbe. *Reminiscences of the Life of a Nurse in Field, Hospital and Camp, During the Civil War: Annie Priscilla Zerbe Erving, Army Nurse, Medical Dept., U.S. Volunteers*. Newburgh, NY: A.P. Erving, reprnt, Daily Press, 1904.

Etter, Roysdon Roberson. *The Civil War Diaries and Letters of a Confederate Soldier: Roysdon Roberson Etter, Private, 16th TN Infantry Regiment, Co. H., C.S.A*. Edited by Dena Croft Sullivan. Dickson, TN: Self-published, 2010.

Favill, Josiah Marshall. *Diary of a Young Officer: Josiah Marshall Favill,. 57th New York Infantry*. Chicago, Illinois: R.R. Donnelley and Sons, 1909. Blog entries: http://dotcw.com/category/diary-of-a-young-officer-josiah-marshall-favill/.

Fisher, Julia Johnson. Diary. Chapel Hill, NC: "This work is the property of the University of North Carolina at Chapel Hill: Southern Historical Collection, University of North Carolina at Chapel Hill. It may be used freely by individuals for research, teaching and personal use as long as this statement of availability is included in the text; call number 1757."

Fitzpatrick, Marion Hill. *Letters to Amanda: The Civil War Letters of Marion Hill Fitzpatrick, Army of Northern Virginia*. Edited by Jeffrey C. Lowe and Sam Hodges. Macon, GA: Mercer University Press, 1998.

Fleet, Maria Louisa Wacker. *Green Mount After the War*. Edited by Betsy Fleet. Charlottesville: University Press of Virginia, 1978.

Fletcher, William A. *Rebel Private: Front and Rear: Memoirs of a Confederate Soldier*. Self published, n.d.

Forten, Charlotte L. *The Journals of Charlotte Forten Grimké, 1854-1892*. Edited by Brenda Stevenson. New York and Oxford: Oxford University Press, 1989.

Glover, Robert W., ed. "The War Letters of a Texas Conscript in Arkansas." *Arkansas Historical Quarterly* 20 (Winter 1961).

Goddard, Henry P. *The Good Fight That Didn't End: Henry P. Goddard's Accounts of Civil War and Peace*. Edited by Calvin Goddard Zon. Columbia: University of South Carolina Press, 2008.

_____. *Regimental Reminiscences of the War of the Rebellion*. Middletown, CT: C.W. Church, 1877.

Goldwaite, Richard, and Ellen Goldwaite. *A Handful of Providence: The Civil War Letters of Lt. Richard Goldwaite, New York Volunteers, and Ellen Goldwaite*. Edited by Marti Skipper and Jane Taylor. Jefferson, NC: McFarland, 2004.

Gordon, John Brown. *Reminiscences of the Civil War, 1832-1904*, Chapel Hill: University of North Carolina Press, 1999. Electronic Edition. © "This work is the property of the University of North Carolina at Chapel Hill. It may be used freely by individuals for research, teaching and personal use as long as this statement of availability is included in the text. Call number E470.G66 1904c (Davis Library, UNC-CH), *Reminiscences of the Civil War* Gordon, John B., New York Charles Scribner's Sons Atlanta The Martin and Hoyt Co. 1904."

Grant, Julia Dent. *The Personal Memoirs of Julia Dent Grant (Mrs. Ulysses P. Grant)*. Edited by John Y. Simon. Carbondale and Edwardsville: Southern Illinois University Press, 1975.

Grant, Ulysses S. *The Man Who Saved the Union*. Edited by H.W. Brands. New York: Doubleday, 2012.

Graves, Henry. Family Papers. University of North Carolina. Collection Number: 02716. http://www.lib.unc.edu/mss/inv/g/Graves_Family.html.

Griffith, Frank. *The Griffith Letters: The Story of Frank Griffith and the 116th New York Volunteer Infantry in the Civil War*. Edited by Joan Metzger. Westminster, MD: Heritage, 2007.

Guerrant, Edward O. *Bluegrass Confederate: The Headquarters Diary of Edward O. Guerrant*. Edited by William C. Davis and Meredith L. Swentor. Baton Rouge: Louisiana State University Press, 1999.

Hagar, Charles. Charles Hagar Papers, 1862–1865. Albany: New York State Library. CED Building, 1 box. Collection Call Number: SC22915. Acquisition from David Greene, Auburn, New Hampshire.

Hancock, Cornelia. *Letters of a Civil War Nurse, Cornelia Hancock, 1863–1865*. Edited by Henrietta Stratton Jaquette. Lincoln: University of Nebraska Press, 1998.

Harris, Mrs. Cicero W., ed. *South-Atlantic: A Monthly Magazine of Literature, Science and Art* 1, no. 1 (November 1877).

Hawley, Thomas S. *"This Terrible Struggle for Life": The Civil War Letters of a Union Regimental Surgeon*. Edited by Dennis W. Belcher. Jefferson, NC: McFarland, 2012.

Heartsill, William Williston. *W.W. Heartsill, Fourteen Hundred and 91 Days in the Confederate Army: A Journal Kept by W. W. Heartsill for Four Years, One Month, and One Day; or, Camp Life, Day by Day, of the W.P. Lane Rangers from April 19, 1861, to May 20, 1865*. Edited by Bell Irvin Wiley. Jackson, TN: MCowat-Mercer. Reprints from the Collection of the University of Michigan Library, 1954, xix, Heartsill's preface to his journal; xvii, Introduction.

Hedrick, John A. *Letters from a North Carolina Unionist; John A. Hedrick to Benjamin P. Hedrick, 1862–1865*. Edited by Judkin Browning and Michael Thomas Smith. Raleigh: Division of Archives and History, NC Department of Cultural Resources, 2001.

Herndon, William H., and Jesse W. Weik. *Abraham Lincoln*. Vol. 2. Project Gutenberg, 1888.

Higgenson, Thomas Wentworth. "Army Life in a Black Regiment." *Atlantic Monthly*. Project Gutenberg, 1869.

———. "An excerpt from the Complete Civil War Journal and Selected Letters of Thomas Wentworth Higginson." Edited by Christopher Looby. *Civil War Journal* 19 (June 2005). http://press.uchicago.edu/Misc/Chicago/333302.html.

Historic Valley Forge. Blog: http://www.ushistory.org/valleyforge/washington/vision.html.

Hubbell, Richtmyer. *Potomac Diary: A Soldier's Account of the Capital in Crisis, 1864–1865; Diary of Richtmyer Hubbell*. Edited by Marc Newman. Town of Jefferson, NY: self-published, 2000.

Huntington, George W. *Diary of 1864*. Pdf Private Collection. GW Huntington mustered into "A" Co. of the 7th Indiana Cavalry. He was transferred out on 8/1/1864. On 8/1/1864 he transferred into Veteran Reserve Corps (date and method of discharge not given). http://www.soldierstudies.org/index.php?action=article_04.

Hyatt, T.J. "Captain Hyatt, Being the Letters Written During the Years 1863–1864 to His Wife, Mary, by Captain T.J. Hyatt, 126th Ohio Volunteer Infantry." Edited by Hudson Hyatt. *Scholarly Journal of the Ohio Historical Society* 53.

Jackman, John. *Diary of a Confederate Soldier: John S. Jackman of the Orphan Brigade*. Edited by William C. Davis. Columbia: University of South Carolina Press, 1990.

Jackson, Thomas. *Beloved Bride: The Letters of Stonewall Jackson to His Wife*. Edited by Bill Potter. San Antonio, TX: Vision Forum, 2002–2012.

Jennie. *To Raise Myself a Little: The Diaries and Letters of Jennie, a Georgia Teacher, 1851–1886*. Edited by Amelia Akehurst Lines and Thomas Dyer. Athens: University of Georgia Press, 1982.

Jones, Jenkin Lloyd. *An Artilleryman's Diary*. Wisconsin History Commission: Original Papers, No. 8; Wisconsin History Commission. February 1914. Project Gutenberg.

Jones, John Beauchamp. *A Rebel War Clerk's Diary*. Philadelphia: J. B. Lippincott, 1866. http://www.cwchronicles.com/blog/1861/06/.

Journal of the American Society for Psychical Research 11, no. 1 (January 1917), 353–355. Section "B" of the American Institute for Scientific Research, York, PA: American Society for Psychical Research, 1906. http://books.google.com/books?id=ongYAQAAIAAJandpg=PA353andlpg=PA353anddq=general+mcclellan's+dreamandsource=blandots=k3YnGyrKC1andsig=kred20CwrF1bkRa_MRzgUQ1V3lYandhl=enandsa=Xandei=izmiUsSSHMS2kQeehIGgBgandved=0CGoQ6AEwBw#v=onepageandq=general%20mcclellan-'s%20dreamandf=false.

Katz, Harry L., and Vincent Virga. *Civil War Sketch Book: Drawings from the Battlefront*. New York: W.W. Norton, 2012.

Kemble, Frances Anne. *Journal of a Residence on a Georgian Plantation, 1838–1839*. Project Gutenberg.

Kennedy, David. Letter by permission of Laurence Overmire. "The Ancestry of Overmire, Tifft, Richardson, Bradford, Reed." Laurence Overmire, RootsWeb World Connect Project, 2000–2014.

Knight, James R. *Letters to Anna: The Civil War Through the Eyes and Heart of a Soldier*. Self-published, 2007.

Lamon, Ward Hill. *Recollections of Abraham Lincoln, 1847–1865*. Washington, D.C.: Dorothy Lamon, Project Gutenberg, 1911.

Lane, David. *A Soldier's Diary, 1862–1865*. Self published, 1905.

Lane, Mills, ed. *Dear Mother, Don't Grieve About Me; If I Get Killed, I'll Only Be Dead: Letters from Georgia Soldiers in the Civil War*. Savannah, GA: Beehive. Library of Savannah, letters from the Georgia State Department of Archives and History, Atlanta, 1990.

Lassen, Coralou Peel. *Dear Sarah: Letters Home from a Soldier of the Iron Brigade*. Bloomington and Indianapolis: Indiana University Press, 1999.

Lawrence, George A. *Border and Bastille: The Author of "Guy Livingstone."* New York: W.I. Pooley. Gutenberg Press.

Lee, Agnes. *The Journal of Agnes Lee, Growing Up in the*

1850s. Edited by Mary Custis Lee DeButts. Chapel Hill: University of North Carolina Press, 1984.

Lee, Elizabeth Blair. *The Civil War Letters of Elizabeth Blair Lee: Wartime Washington*. Edited by Virginia Jeans Laas. Urbana and Chicago: University of Illinois Press, 1991.

Lee, Robert E. *Memoirs of Robert E. Lee*. Edited by A.L. Long. Secaucus, NJ: Blue and Grey, 1983.

_____. *Reading the Man: A Portrait of Robert E. Lee Through His Private Letters*. Edited by Elizabeth Brown Pryor. New York: Penguin, 2007.

_____. *Recollections and Letters of General Robert E. Lee by Captain Robert E. Lee, His Son*. http://www.fullbooks.com.

Leonard, James H. *Letters of a Fifth Wisconsin Volunteer: Correspondence of James H. Leonard, Company A of the Fifth Wisconsin Infantry*. Edited by R.G. Plumb. JStor.

Leupp, Laura. *Auction Selections of Civil War and Other Major Collections*. Catalogue #64. January 6, 2015, Cohasco, Yonkers, NY.

Lincoln, Abraham. *Abraham Lincoln. The Papers and Writings of Abraham Lincoln*. Edited by Arthur Brooks Lapsley. Project Gutenberg, Constitutional ed. Vol. 6, 1862–1863.

Lincoln, Mary Todd. *The Dark Days of Abraham Lincoln's Widow as Revealed by Her Own Letters*. Edited by Myra Helmer Pritchard and Jason Emerson. Carbondale: Southern Illinois University Press, 2011.

_____. *Mary Todd Lincoln Her Life and Letters*. Edited by Justin G. Turner and Linda Levitt Turner. New York: Alfred A. Knopf, 1972.

Livermore, Mary A. *My Story of the War: The Civil War Memoirs of the Famous Nurse, Relief Organizer and Suffragette*. Edited by Nina Silber. New York: Da Capo, 1995.

_____. *My Story of the War: Woman's Narrative of Four Years' Personal Experience as Nurse in the Union Army, and in Relief Work at Home, in Hospitals, Camps, and at the Front, During the War of the Rebellion, with Anecdotes, Pathetic Incidents, and Thrilling Reminiscences Portraying the Lights and Shadows of Hospital Life and the Sanitary Service of the War*. Hartford, CT: A.D. Worthington, 1888. http://www.ourstory.info/library/1-roots/Livermore/storyTC.html#TC.

Lockwood, John. *Our Campaign Around Gettysburg: Being a Memorial of What Was Endured, Suffered, and Accomplished by the Twenty-Third Regiment (N.Y.S.N.G.) and Other Regiments Associated with Them in Their Pennsylvania and Maryland Campaign, During the Second Rebel Invasion of the Loyal States. June–July 1863*. 1908.

Logsdon, David R., ed. *Eyewitnesses at the Battle of Shiloh*. Lyles, TN: Kettle Mills, 2011.

Lowell, James Russell. *The Biglow Papers*. 1890. Whitefish, MT: Kessinger, 2004.

_____. "The Biglow Papers." *The Poetical Works of James Russell Lowell in Five Volumes*. Second Series. Vol. 3. In *The Complete Writings of James Russell Lowell in Sixteen Volumes*. Vol. 11, 1866. Boston and New York: Houghton, Mifflin, 1905.

Luttrell, Harvey Wilkerson. "An Alabama Merchant in Civil War Richmond: The Harvey Wilkerson Luttrell Letters, 1861–1865." Edited by John D. Miller. *Alabama Review* (July 2005).

Maile, John L. *Prison Life in Andersonville; with Special Reference to the opening of Providence Spring*. Project Gutenberg. http://www.gutenberg.org/files/39584/39584-h/39584-h.htm).

Makely, Wesley. *I Fear I Shall Never Leave This Island: Life in a Civil War Prison*. Edited by Dr. David Bush. Gainesville: University Press of Florida, 2011.

Marshall, Jeffrey D., ed. *A War of the People: Vermont Civil War Letters*. Hanover, NH: University Press of New England, 1999.

Matrau, Henry. *Letters Home: Henry Matrau of the Iron Brigade*. Edited by Marcia Reid-Green. Lincoln and London: University of Nebraska Press, 1993.

Maynard, Nettie Colburn. *Was Abraham Lincoln a Spiritualist?; or, Curious Revelations from the Life of a Trance Medium*. Chicago: Progressive Thinker, 1917.

McAllister, J. Gray, and Grace Owings Guerrant. *Beginning at Jerusalem in the Regions Beyond: Edward O. Guerrant and the Southern Home Mission Movement*, Project Gutenberg.

_____ and _____. *Edward O. Guerrant: Apostle to the Southern Highlanders*. Richmond: Richmond Press, 1950.

McCarthy, Carlton. *Detailed Minutiae of Soldier Life in the Army of Northern Virginia, 1861–1865*. Richmond: Carlton McCarthy, 1882; Cambridge: Riverside, H.O. Houghton. Project Gutenberg.

McDowell, Charles. *Ever True: A Union Private and His Wife; Civil War Letters of Private Charles McDowell, New York Ninth Heavy Artillery*. Edited by Lisa Saunders (descendant). Bowie, MD: Heritage, 2004.

McElroy, John. *Andersonville: A Story of Rebel Military Prisons, Fifteen Months a Guest of the So-Called Southern Confederacy; A Private Soldier's Experience in Richmond, Andersonville, Savannah, Millen, Blackshear and Florence*. 1879. EBook. Project Gutenberg.

McGuire, Judith W. *Diary of a Southern Refugee During the War by a Lady of Virginia*. Lincoln and London: University of Nebraska Press, 1995.

McKnight, William. *Do They Miss Me at Home?: The Civil War Letters of William McKnight, Seventh Ohio Volunteer Cavalry*. Athens: Ohio University Press, 2010.

McLaws, Lafayette. *A Soldier's General: the Civil War Letters of Major General Lafayette McLaws*. Edited by John C. Oeffinger. Chapel Hill and London: University of North Carolina Press, 2002.

Meals, Daniel James. Private letters owned by Susan Morgan. Daniel Meals served with the 7th Tennessee Volunteer Cavalry.

Mitchell, Weir. Letter. Philadelphia: College of Physicians of Philadelphia, Mutter Museum, exhibit: "Broken Bodies, Suffering Spirits," 2013. Article by Joseph Brin. "Hidden City Philadelphia," September 11, 1913. http://hiddencityphila.org/2013/09/philadelphia-during-the-civil-war-a-medical-perspective-opening-at-the-mutter/. Additional information on the exhibit: http://www.collegeofphysicians.org.

Montgomery, Frank Alexander. *Reminiscences of a Mississippian in Peace and War*. Electronic ed. Chapel Hill: University of North Carolina, 1999.

Moore, Frank, ed. *The Rebellion Record: A Diary of American Events with Documents, Narratives, Illustrative Incidents, Poetry, Etc*. New York: D. Van Nostrand, 1895.

_____. "The Strange Dream of John C. Calhoun." In *The Civil War in Song and Story*. New York, 1889. Also printed in *Ocala Florida Home Companion*, January 21, 1860. Digital image available in the Bonds Conway Papers, 1763–1907, University of South Carolina, South Caroliniana Library. http://www.sc.edu/library/digital/collections/skl2.html. See also http://wesclark.com/jw/calhoun.html.

Morgan, Sarah, Charles East, ed. *The Civil War Diary*

of a Southern Woman. New York: Touchstone/Simon and Schuster; Athens, GA; University of Georgia Press, 1991. Project Gutenberg.

Morley, Frank, Austin Perkins and Nathan Perkins. *Morley CW Letter, Austin and Nathan Perkins Letters.* (1) Camp Cacey, Washington, D.C., 16 October 1861 (2) Headquarters Ret't R.I., Co. B Camp California, 1861, 19 December (3) Hatteras Inlet, 19 January 1862 (4) Camp Opposite Fredericksburg, VA, 17 January 1863 (5) Washington, 21 September (?), 29 July 2002. http://www.genealogy.org/~ajmorris/cw/perkins.htm.

Morrow, Maud E. *Recollections of the Civil War from a Child's Point of View.* Lockland, OH: John C. Morrow, 1901.

Mosler, Henry. Henry Mosler Civil War Diary, Henry Mosler Papers, 1856–1929. Smithsonian Archives of American Art. http://civilwardiary.aaa.si.edu/.

Needham, Lyman H. *The Civil War Letters from Danville Prison.* http://fanflower.com/2009/05/14/civil-war-letters-from-danville-prison/.

Newton, James K. *A Wisconsin Boy in Dixie: Civil War Letters of James K. Newton, Madison, Wisconsin.* Madison: University of Wisconsin Press, 1961. Abel Newton Papers. State Historical Society Library, Madison.

Newton, Thomas D. Civil War Home Collection. Odin's Castle. http://www.civilwarhome.com/letters.htm.

Nichols, G.W. *A Soldier's Story of His Regiment (61st Georgia) and Incidentally of the Lawton-Gordon-Evans Brigade of Northern Virginia.* Self-published, 1898.

Nix, Christian. Letters and photos. National Park Service. http://www.nps.gov/stri/historyculture/nix.htm

Northup, Solomon. *Twelve Years a Slave: Narrative of Solomon Northup, a Citizen of New-York, Kidnapped in Washington City in 1841 and Rescued in 1853 from a Cotton Plantation Near the Red River in Louisiana.* Auburn: Derby and Miller, 1853.

Oake, William Royal. *On the Skirmish Line Behind a Friendly Tree: The Civil War Memoirs of William Royal Oake, 26th Iowa Volunteers.* Edited by Stacy Dale Allen. Helena, MT: Farcountry, 2006.

Page, James Madison. *The True Story of Andersonville Prison: A Defense of Major Henry Wirz.* Confederate Reprint Company. www.confederatereprint.com.

Paine, Halbert Eleazer. *A Wisconsin Yankee in Confederate Bayou Country: The Civil War Reminiscences of a Union General.* Edited by Samuel C. Hyde, Jr. Baton Rouge: Louisiana State University Press, 2009.

Palmer, S.A. *The Story of Aunt Becky's Army Life.* New York: John F. Trow, 1867.

Parrott, James. *Letters of James Parrott.* Ancestry.com: Rootsweb. http://www.rootsweb.ancestry.com/~tn overto/docs/CivilWarLettersParrott.html.

Partridge, George W., Jr. *Letters from the Iron Brigade, George W. Partridge, Jr., 1839–1863.* Edited by Hugh L. Whitehouse. Indianapolis: Guild Press of Indiana, 1994.

Patterson, John V. *As Near Hell as I Ever Expect to Be; The Civil War Letters of Lieutenant John V. Patterson of the 21st Regiment, Ohio Volunteer Infantry.* Edited by Paul G. Tremewan. XLibris, 2011.

Pender, William Dorsey. *One of Lee's Best Men: The Civil War Letters of General William Dorsey Pender.* Edited by William W. Hassler. Foreword by Brian Wills. Chapel Hill and London: University of North Carolina Press, 1965. Cited from letters in the William Dorsey Pender Papers, #1059, Southern Historical Collection. Wilson Library. University of North Carolina.

Pickett, George Edward, and LaSalle Corbell Pickett. *The Heart of a Soldier as Revealed in the Intimate Letters of Genl. George E. Pickett, CSA.* New York: Seth Moyle, 1908–1913.

Plake, Kate. *The Southern Husband Outwitted by His Union Wife.* Chapel Hill: University of North Carolina. Electronic ed. 1867. "This work may be used freely by individuals for research, teaching and personal use as long as this statement of availability is included in the text. Call number CT275.P66 A3 1867 Philadelphia Printed for the Authoress, Moore and Brother 1867."

Poague, William Thomas. *Gunner with Stonewall, Reminiscences of William Thomas Poague.* Edited by Monroe F. Cockrell. Jackson, TN: McCowat-Mercer, 1957.

Polley, J.B. *A Soldier's Letters to Charming Nellie.* Edited by Richard B. McCaslin. Knoxville: University of Tennessee Press, 2008.

Portland (ME) Evening Courier, March 8, 1862; reprinted in *Individual Christian Scientist* 11, no. 2.

Post, Lydia Minturn. *Soldiers' Letters, from Camps, Battlefield and Prison.* New York: Bruce and Huntington, U.S. Sanitary Commission; 1865. Reprnt, University of Michigan.

Prey, G. G. *Late of the 104th N.Y.V., Wadsworth Guards: Recollections of Three Rebel Prisons—Libby, Salisbury, Danville.* Warsaw, NY: Western New-Yorker, 1896.

Quintard, Charles Todd. *Doctor Quintard, Chaplain, C.S.A., and Second Bishop of Tennessee: The Memoir and Civil War Diary of Charles Todd Quintard.* Edited by Sam Davis Elliott. Baton Rouge: Louisiana State University Press, 2003.

Radison, Garry. *Last Words of the Civil War: The Moment of Sacrifice.* Yorkton, SK: Smoke Ridge, 2001.

Rajoppi, Joanne Hamilton. *New Brunswick and the Civil War: The Brunswick Boys in the Great Rebellion.* Charleston, SC: History Press, 2013.

Ransom, John. *John Ransom's Andersonville Diary.* Introduction by Bruce Catton. Auburn, NY, 1881. New York: Berkley, 1986–1994.

Redkey, Edwin S., ed. *A Grand Army of Black Men.* Cambridge, MA: Cambridge University Press, 1992.

Reeves, Samuel T. *Correspondence, 1864–1870, the Bulk Being 1865.* University Libraries of Notre Dame. Letter Groups. MSN CW 5012-9; Civil War envelopes; MSN/CW5012-1 to MSN/CW 5012-31.

Remley Brothers. *Southern Sons, Northern Soldiers, The Civil War Letters of the Remley Brothers, 22nd Iowa Infantry.* Edited by Julie Holcomb. DeKalb: Northern Illinois University Press, 2004.

Rhodes, Elisha Hunt. *All for the Union: The Civil War Diary and Letters of Elisha Hunt Rhodes.* New York: Vintage, 1992.

Richards, Richard E. *Civil War Letters.* http://fanflower.com/2009/05/12/civil-war-letters/.

Richmond Daily Dispatch. Abingdon, Virginia.

_____. "The Dream of Home and Its Results." December 21, 1864.

_____. "Hid Away in the Smoke House," November 24, 1863.

_____. "Local Matters," August 10, 1864.

_____. "McClellan Dream," See http://imls.richmond.edu/cgi/t/text/text-idx?c=ddr;cc=ddr;type=simple;rgn=div2;q1=dream;view=text;subview=detail;sort=occur;idno=ddr0531.0023.017;node=ddr0531.0023.017%3A4.1

_____. "Spicy Letter from a Yankee Girl," July 9, 1861.

Ritner, Jacob, and Emeline Ritner. *Love and Valor: Intimate*

Civil War Letters Between Captain Jacob and Emeline Ritner. Edited by Charles F. Larimer. Western Springs, IL: Sigourney, 2000.

Robbins, Rufus. *Through Ordinary Eyes; The Civil War Correspondence of Rufus Robbins, Private, 7th Regiment, Massachusetts Volunteers*. Edited by Ella Jan Bruen and Brian M. Fitagibbons, eds. Westport, CT: Praeger, 2000.

Rogers, Seth. *Letters of Dr. Seth Rogers, 1862, 1863*. Edited by Channing Brown and John Brown. JStor. *Proceedings of the Massachusetts Historical Society* 43 (October 1909–June 1910). February Meeting. http://www.jstor.org/stable/25079.

Ropes, Hannah. *Civil War Nurse, The Diary and Letters of Hannah Ropes*. Edited by John R. Brumgardt. Knoxville: Tennessee Press, 1980.

Sears, Stephen W. *The Civil War: The Second Year Told by Those Who Lived It*. Library of America. Penguin, 2012.

Segal, Charles M., ed. *Conversations with Lincoln*. New York: G.P. Putnam's Sons, 1912.

Sessarego, Alan. *Letters Home: A Collection of Original Civil War Soldiers' Letters*. Gettysburg, PA: self-published, private collection, n.d.

_____. *Letters Home, II*.

_____. *Letters Home, III*.

_____. *Letters Home, V*.

Shaw, Robert Gould. *Blue-Eyed Child of Fortune: The Civil War Letters of Colonel Robert Gould Shaw*. Edited by Russell Duncan. Athens and London: University of Georgia Press, 1999.

Shedd, Calvin. *The Civil War in Florida: Letters of a New Hampshire Soldier*. Miami: University of Miami Libraries. Special Collections, Calvin Shedd Papers.

Shelton, Amanda. *Turn Backward, O Time: The Civil War Diary of Amanda Shelton; Papers of the Shelton Family, 1864–1866*. Edited by Kathleen S. Hanson. University of Iowa. http://beta.worldcat.org/archivegrid/record.php?id=226449112andcontributor=164andarchivename=University+of+Iowa.

Silber, Nina, and Mary Beth Sievens. *Yankee Correspondence: Civil War Letters Between New England Soldiers and the Home Front*. Charlottesville and London: University Press of Virginia, 1996.

Simonds, Henry C. Of 20th ME Regt Company C, 20 letters to his wife, Lizzie Simonds, of North Turner and Wilton, Maine. http://www.soldierstudies.org/blog/2010/06/new-20th-maine-letters-found/.

Simpson, Brooks D., ed. *The Civil War: The Third Year Told by Those Who Lived It*. Library of America. Penguin, 2013.

Simpson, Brooks D., Stephen W. Sears and Aaron Sheehan-Dean, ed. *The Civil War: The First Year Told by Those Who Lived It*. Library of America. Penguin, 2011.

Simpson, Dick, and Tally Simpson. *Far, Far from Home: The Wartime Letters of Dick and Tally Simpson, 3rd South Carolina Volunteers*. Edited by Guy R. Everson and Edward W. Simpson, Jr. New York and Oxford: Oxford University Press, 1994.

Singleton, William Henry. *Recollections of My Slavery Days*. Edited by Katherine Mellen Charron and David S. Cecelski. Raleigh: Office of Archives and History; North Carolina Department of Cultural Resources, 2007.

Sneden, Robert Knox. *Eye of the Storm: A Civil War Odyssey*. Edited by Charles F. Bryan and Nelson D. Lankford. Free Press, October 2000. Originally written and illustrated by Private Robert Knox Sneden, 1863.

Spiegel, Marcus. *A Jewish Colonel in the Civil War: Marcus M. Spiegel of the Ohio Volunteers*. Edited by Jean Powers Soman and Frank L. Byrne. Lincoln: University of Nebraska Press, 1985.

Stephens and Bryant Families. *Rose Cottage Chronicles: Civil War Letters of the Bryant-Stephens Families of North Florida*. Edited by Benjamin Moody, Arch Fredric Blakey, Ann Smith Lainhart, and Winston Bryant Stephens, Jr. Gainesville: University Press of Florida, 1998.

Stewart, Salome Myers. *The Ties of the Past, The Gettysburg Diaries of Salome Myers Stewart, 1854–1922*. Edited by Sarah Sites Thomas (descendant). Gettysburg: Thomas, 1996.

Stillwell, Leander. *The Story of a Common Soldier of Army Life in the Civil War, 1861–1865; Late of Co. D, 61st Illinois Infantry*. Franklin: Hudson, 1920.

Stilwell, William Ross. *The Stilwell Letters: A Georgian in Longstreet's Corps, Army of Northern Virginia*. Mercer University Press, 2002.

Stone, James Madison. *Personal Recollections of the Civil War by One Who Took Part in It as a Private Soldier in the 21st Volunteer Regiment of Infantry from Massachusetts*. Boston: Self-published, 1918.

Stone, Kate. *Brokenburn: The Journal of Kate Stone, 1861–1868*. Edited by John Q. Anderson. 1972. Baton Rouge: Louisiana State University Press, 1995.

Strong, George Templeton. *The Diary of George Templeton Strong, the Civil War 1860–1865*. Edited by Allan Nevins and Milton Halsey Thomas. New York: Macmillan, 1962.

Strother, David Hunter. *The Diaries of David Hunter Strother, A Virginia Yankee in the Civil War*. Edited by Cecil D. Eby, Jr. Chapel Hill: University of North Carolina Press, 1961.

Sutcliffe, Andrea, ed. *Mighty Rough Times I Tell You: Personal Accounts of Slavery in Tennessee*. Winston-Salem, NC: John F. Blair, 2000.

Swank, Walbrook D., ed. *Confederate Letters and Diaries, 1861–1865*. Shippensburg, PA: Burd Street, 1988.

Tabb, Mary Octavia Smith. *Love and Loss: A Virginia Girl's Civil War Diary, 1863–1868*. Smithville and Hampton, VA: Paxton, 2009.

Tarbell, Doctor, and Mary Conant Papers. Manuscripts Division, William L. Clements Library, University of Michigan. Finding aid for Doctor Tarbell and Mary Conant Papers, 1864–1881, James S. Schoff Civil War Collection.

Taylor, Guy. *Letters Home to Sarah: The Civil War Letters of Guy C. Taylor, 36th Wisconsin Volunteers*. Edited by Kevin Alderson and Patsy Alderson. Madison: University of Wisconsin Press, 2012.

Taylor, Susie King. *A Black Woman's Civil War Memoirs; Reminiscences of My Life in Camp with the 33rd U.S. Colored Troops, Late 1st South Carolina Volunteers*. Edited by Patricia W. Romero and Willie Lee Rose. Princeton: Markus Wiener, 2009.

_____. *In My Own Words: The Diary of Susie King Taylor, Civil War Nurse*. Edited by Margaret Gay Malone. 1902. New York: Benchmark, 2004.

Tidd, John. *Dear Friend Amelia: The Civil War Letters of Private John Tidd*. Edited by Mary Jordan and Joyce Hatch with Ronald E. Ostman and Harry Littell. Ithaca, NY: Six Mile Creek, 2011.

Toalson, Jeff, ed. *Mama, I Am Yet Still Alive: A Composite Diary of 1863 in the Confederacy*. Butternut Series, Volume 3. Bloomington: IUniverse.

Trask, William L. *Civil War Journal of William L. Trask,*

Confederate Sailor and Soldier. Edited by Kenneth A. Hafendorfer. Louisville, KY: KH, 2003.

Turnbull, George A. *Never Forsake the Flag: The Letters of Captain George A. Turnbull, Captain Company A; 134th NY Volunteers.* Edited by Kenneth Jones. Self-published, 1998.

Turner, Brian. *Here, Bullet.* Bloodaxe, 2011.

Turner, Columbus Lafayette. *Worthy of Record: The Civil War and Reconstruction Diaries of Columbus Lafayette Turner.* Edited by Kenrick N. Simpson. Raleigh: Office of Archives and History, North Carolina Department of Cultural Resources, 2008.

Turner, William D. *Some War-Time Recollections: The Story of a Confederate Officer Who Was at First One of Those in Charge of and Later a Captive in Libby Prison.* Printed in the "The Libby Lion."

Twichell, Joseph Hopkins. *The Civil War Letters of Joseph Hopkins Twichell: A Chaplain's Story.* Edited by Peter Messent and Steve Courtney. Athens: University of Georgia Press, 2006.

Tyler, Comrade William N. *The Dispatch Carrier and Memoirs of Andersonville Prison.* Port Byron, IL: Port Byron "Globe", 1892. Reprinted by Gutenberg Press. http://www.gutenberg.org/files/40046/40046-h/40046-h.htm.

Tyrel, James, and Charles Tyrel. Letters. Warren County, NY: Rootsweb. http://www.rootsweb.ancestry.com/~nywarren/military/civilwarletters.htm,

Vandiver, Frank E., ed. "Letters from the Confederate Medical Service in Texas, 1863–1865." *Southwestern Historical Quarterly* 55 (April 1952).

Van Wyck, Richard T. *A War to Petrify the Heart: The Civil War Letters of a Dutchess County, N.Y. Volunteer.* Edited by Virginia Hughes Kaminsky. Hensonville, NY: Black Dome, 1997.

Velazquez, Loreta Janeta. *The Woman in Battle: The Civil War Narrative of Loreta Velazquez, Cuban Woman and Confederate Soldier.* Madison: University of Wisconsin Press, 2003.

Wadley, Sarah Lois. *Diary, August 8, 1859—May 15, 1865.* 1865. Chapel Hill: Manuscripts Department, Southern Historical Collection, University of North Carolina at Chapel Hill. "This work may be used freely by individuals for research, teaching and personal use as long as this statement of availability is included in the text. Call number 1258."

Wakeman, Sarah Rosetta. *An Uncommon Soldier: The Civil War Letters of Sarah Rosetta Wakeman, alias Pvt. Lyons Wakeman, 153rd Regiment, New York State Volunteers, 1862–1864.* Edited by Lauren Cook Burgess. New York and Oxford: Oxford University Press, 1994.

Watkins, Nathaniel V. Family Papers. Richard and Mary Watkins. Family Papers. 1846–1889. Special Collections, College of William and Mary, Earl Grey Swem Library. Special thanks to Katherine Wilkins, Assistant Librarian.

Watkins, Richard, and Mary Watkins. *Send Me a Pair of Old Boots and Kiss My Little Girls: The Civil War Letters of Richard and Mary Watkins, 1861–1865.* Bloomington, NY: IUniverse, 2009. See entry for Watkins Family papers.

Watkins, Sam R. *Co. Aytch: A Confederate Memoir of the Civil War.* Chattanooga: Chattanooga Times, 1900.

Webb, William. *The History of William Webb, Composed by Himself.* Detroit, MI: Egbert Hoekstra, 1873. © "This work is the property of the University of North Carolina at Chapel Hill. It may be used freely by individuals for research, teaching and personal use as long as this statement of availability is included in the text. Call number E444.W36 (Library of Congress)."

Weller, Edwin. *A Civil War Courtship, The Letters of Edwin Weller from Antietam to Atlanta.* Edited by William Walton. Garden City, NY: Doubleday, 1980.

Welles, Gideon. *Diary of Gideon Welles, Secretary of the Navy Under Lincoln and Johnson, 1910.* Boston and New York: Houghton Mifflin, 1911.

Whitlock, William. *Allegany to Appomattox: The Life and Letters of Private William Whitlock of the 188th New York Volunteers.* Edited by Valgene Dunham. Syracuse, NY: Syracuse University Press, 2013.

Whitman, Walt. "Old War Dreams." Walt Whitman Archive. http://www.whitmanarchive.org/published/LG/1891/poems/282.

Willard, Van R. *With the 3rd Wisconsin Badgers: The Living Experience of the Civil War Through the Journals of Van R. Willard.* Edited by Steven S. Raab. Mechanicsburg, PA: Stackpole, 1999.

Woodruff, Patricia Robin, ed. Diary quote in "Strange Tales of Floyd County, Va." Rand Dotson. *Virginia Magazine of History and Biography.* Permission by Patricia Woodruff.

Woolsey, Jane Stuart. *Hospital Days: Reminiscence of a Civil War Nurse.* Roseville, MN: Edinborough, 1996–2007.

Worsham, John H. *One of Jackson's Foot Cavalry.* New York: Neale, 1912.

Yates, John, and Elizabeth Robert Yates. http://freepages.genealogy.rootsweb.ancestry.com/~connectville/military/jeycw/700.htm. Rootsweb: Freepages.

Secondary

Andrews, William, ed. "The Representation of Slavery and Afro-American Literary Realism." In *African American Autobiography: A Collection of Critical Essays.* Englewood Cliffs, NJ: Prentice Hall, 1993.

Armadon, George F. *Rise of the Ironclads.* Missoula, MT: Pictorial Histories, 2004.

Ash, Stephen V. *A Year in the South, 1865.* New York: Perennial, 2002.

Backstory Radio. Wanda Burch interview. http://backstoryradio.org/civil-war-call-in-show.

Blog, Oklahoma Historical Society. http://www.freewebs.com/minstreltune/civilwarhistory.html.

Brady, Lisa M. *War Upon the Land: Military Strategy and the Transformation of Southern Landscapes During the American Civil War.* Athens and London: University of Georgia Press, 1971.

Browne, Frances Fisher. *Revision of the Everyday Life of Abraham Lincoln; Biography with Pen-Picuites and Personal Recollections by Those Who Knew Him,* Chicago: Browne and Howell, 1913. Project Gutenberg.

Bulwer-Lytton, Edward. *A Strange Story: An Occult Fantasy.* Project Gutenberg, 1864. http://www.gutenberg.org/ebooks/7701.

Carlson, Peter. *Junius and Albert's Adventures in the Confederacy: A Civil War Odyssey.* New York: Public Affairs, 2013.

Carnton Plantation and Battlefield. Franklin, TN: Battle of Franklin Trust, n.d.

The Carter House. Franklin, TN: Battle of Franklin Trust, n.d.

Civil War Handbook. Eastern National: National Park Service Commemorative Series, 2011.

Clarke, Frances. "So lonesome I could die: Nostalgia and Debates over Emotional Control in the Civil War North." *Journal of Social History*. University of Sydney, Department of History, School of Philosophical and Historical Inquiry, 2007.

Clinton, Catherine. *Southern Families at War: Loyalty and Conflict in the Civil War South*. New York: Oxford University Press, 2000.

Cozzens, Peter. http://opinionator.blogs.nytimes.com/2014/04/24/humanity-and-hope-in-a-southern-prison/?ref=opinion. Disunion Blog, *New York Times*, April 24, 2014.

Dabney, Robert Lewis. *Life and Campaigns of Lieut.-Gen. Thomas J. Jackson*. Harrisonburg, VA: Sprinkle, 1983.

Donald, David Herbert, *Lincoln*. New York: Simon and Schuster, 1995.

Durham, Roger S. *High Seas and Yankee Gunboats: A Blockade Running Adventure from the Diary of James Dickson*. Columbia: University of South Carolina Press, 2005.

Ekirch, Roger. "Sleep We Have Lost: Pre-Industrial Slumber in the British Isles." *American Historical Review* 106, no. 2 (April 2001), 343–386.

Emerson, Jason. *The Madness of Mary Lincoln*. Carbondale: Southern Illinois University Press, 2007.

Fagan, W.L. *Southern War Songs: Camp-Fire, Patriotic and Sentimental*. http://www.traditionalmusic.co.uk/southern-war-songs/southern-war-songs%20-%200403.htm.

Fahs, Alice Fahs. *The Imagined Civil War: Popular Literature of the North and South, 1861–1865*. Chapel Hill and London: University of North Carolina Press, 2001.

Faust, Drew Gilpin. "The Civil War Soldier and the Art of Dying." JStor. *Journal of Southern History* 67, no. 1 (February 2001), 3–38. http://www.jstor.org/stable/3070083.

_____. *This Republic of Suffering: Death and the American Civil War*. Vintage, 2009.

Foote, Shelby. *The Civil War: A Narrative*. 1958–1974, 3 vols. New York: Vintage, 1986.

Foster, Joseph G. "Homesickness and the Location of Home: Germans, Heimweh, and the American Civil War" (2012). All Graduate Theses and Dissertations. Paper 1333. http://digitalcommons.usu.edu/etd/1333 (Utah State University).

Freud, Sigmund. *Le mot d'esprit et sa relation à l'inconscient*. 1905. Translated by Denis Messier. Paris: Editions Gallimard, 1988. Translation of *Der Wirtz und seine Beziehung zum Unbewussten*.

Garraty, John, and Mark Carnes, ed. *American National Biography*. New York: Oxford University Press, 1999.

Garrison, Webb. With Cheryl Garrison. *The Encyclopedia of Civil War Usage*. Nashville: Cumberland House, 2001.

Guyot, Lucienne Grace Oppenheimer. "Fighting My Way Through: Northern Rural Women in the American Civil War." A thesis submitted in partial fulfilment of the requirements for the degree of Bachelor of Arts (Honours) in History. University of Sydney. October 2012. Quoting from R. Dutton Silsby, *Civil War Letters, 1862–1863*. Barre, VT: Vermont Historical Society (MSA 521:01–07. Called the Silsby Collection).

Hall, Yancey. "U.S. Civil War Prison Camps Claimed Thousands." *National Geographic News*, July 1, 2003. http://news.nationalgeographic.com/news/2003/07/0701_030701_civilwarprisons.html.

Holmes, David I., Lesley J. Gordon, and Christine Wilson. "A Widow and Her Soldier: A Stylometric Analysis of the Pickett Letters." *History and Computing* 11 (1999). Online. DOI 10.3366/hac.1999.11.3.159, ISSN 1753-8548.

Holtzworth, Jerry. *Stonewall Jackson and Winchester, Virginia*. Charleston, SC: History, 2012.

Journal of American Folk-Lore. London, Boston and New York: Houghton, Mifflin, 1892.

Journal of the Civil War Era. William Blair, editor. Chapel Hill: University of North Carolina Press in association with the George and Ann Richards Civil War Era Center, Pennsylvania State University, 2010–2013.

Kagan, Neil and James Robertson, ed. *The Untold Civil War: Exploring the Human Side of War*. Washington, D.C.: National Geographic, 2011.

Kingseed, Cole C. *The American Civil War*. Westport, CT, and London: Greenwood, 2004.

Lakoff, George, and Mark Johnson. *Metaphors We Live By*. Chicago: University of Chicago Press, 2003.

LeBeau, Bryan F. *Currier and Ives: America Imagined*. Smithsonian Institution Press, 2001. Printed in http://www.common-place.org/vol-09/no-02/lebeau/.

Logothetis, Kathleen. "A Question of Life or Death: Suicide and Survival in the Union Army" ©. http://emergingcivilwar.com/2012/08/15/to-the-breaking-point-mental-stress-in-the-union-army/.

Long, Lisa A. *Rehabilitating Bodies: Health, History, and the American Civil War*. Philadelphia: University of Pennsylvania Press, 2004.

Marlantes, Karl. *What It Is Like to Go to War?* New York: Atlantic Monthly, 2011.

Martin, Bill, and Jon Curtis. "Nematode Study for Angel's Glow." Intel International Science and Engineering Fair, 2001. http://mentalfloss.com/article/30380/why-some-civil-war-soldiers-glowed-dark.

Martin, James. "Fatherhood in the Confederacy: Southern Soldiers and Their Children," *Journal of Southern History* 58, no. 2 (May 1997).

Martinez, Susan B. *The Psychic Life of Abraham Lincoln*. Franklin Lakes, NJ: New Page, 2007.

Marvel, William. "Johnny Ransom's Imagination." *Civil War History* 41, no. 3 (September 1995).

Matt, Susan J. *Homesickness: An American History*. New York: Oxford University Press, 2011.

_____. "You Can't Go Home Again: Homesickness and Nostalgia in U.S. History." *Journal of American History* 94, no. 2 (September 2007), 469–471.

Mauro, Charles V. *A Southern Spy in Northern Virginia: The Civil War Album of Laura Ratcliffe*. Charleston, SC: History, 2009.

McPherson, James M. *Battle Cry of Freedom: The Civil War Era*. 1988. New York: Ballantine, 1989.

_____. *For Cause and Comrades: Why Men Fought in the Civil War*. Oxford and New York: Oxford University Press, 1997.

McSherry, Frank, Jr. *Civil War Women*. Edited by Charles G. Waugh and Martin Greenberg. New York: Touchstone, 1988.

Miller, Chris. *A Domestic Nation: The Relationship Between Nation and Family in the Confederacy*. Georgetown University, Senior Honors Thesis in History, HIST-409-01, Mentored by Professor Chandra Manning, May 4, 2009. Focus is the correspondence between Octavia and Winston Stephens. See *Rose Cottage Chronicles*.

Morrow, Honore Willsie. "Lincoln's Last Day" *International-Cosmopolitan*, February 1930.

Moss, Robert. "The Real History of Lincoln's Dreams." http://mossdreams.blogspot.com/2008/12/real-history-of-lincolns-dream.html, http://blog.beliefnet.com/dreamgates/2012/11/lincolns-dreams.html#ixzz2GIv5D9Hy.

_____. *The Secret History of Dreaming*. Novato, CA: New World Library, 2010. Chapter 9, "The Underground Railroad of Dreams."

National Geographic. Civil War Issue. Washington, D.C., May 2012.

Norris, David A. *Life During the Civil War*. Niagara Falls, NY: Moorshead, History Magazine, 2009.

Perry, John. *Mrs. Robert E. Lee: The Lady of Arlington*. Sisters, OR: Multinomah, 2001.

Pizarro, Judith, Roxanne C. Silver and JoAnn Prause. "Physical and Mental Health Costs of Traumatic War Experiences Among Civil War Veterans." *Archives of General Psychiatry* 63, no. 2 (February 2006), 193–200.

Prescott, Thomas H. *The American Encyclopedia of History, Biography and Travel, Comprising Ancient and Modern History*. Vol. 6, *The Biography of Eminent Men of Europe and America and the Lives of Distinguished Travelers*. Columbus: J. and H. Miller, 1856 [used for pressing flowers sent by Levi Duff to Harriet Duff].

Rawick, George P., ed. *The American Slave: A Composite Autobiography*. Westport, CT: Greenwood, 1972–79.

Robertson, James I. *Stonewall Jackson: The Man, the Soldier, the Legend*, New York: Macmillan, 1997.

Roper, Robert. *Walt Whitman and His Brothers in the Civil War: Now the Drum of War*. New York: Walker, 2008.

Segal, Charles M. ed. *Conversations with Lincoln*. 1961. London and New Brunswick, NJ: Transaction, 2002.

Selby, John G. *Virginians at War: The Civil War Experiences of Seven Young Confederates*. Wilmington, DE: Scholarly Resource, 2002.

Sheehan-Dean, Aaron. *The View from the Ground: Experiences of Civil War Soldiers*. Lexington: University Press of Kentucky, 2007.

Shively, Julie. *The Ideals Guide to American Civil War Places*. Nashville: Ideals, 2011.

Simon, John Y. and Michael E. Stevens, ed. *New Perspectives on the Civil War: Myths and Realities of the National Conflict*. 1998. Lanham, MD: Rowman and Littlefield, 2002.

Southern Cultures. "Remembering the Civil War." Chapel Hill: University of North Carolina Press, 2013.

Speer, Lonnie R. *Portals to Hell: Military Prisons of the Civil War*. Lincoln and London: University of Nebraska Press, 2005.

Stephens, J.C. "The Dreams of Aelius Aristides, a Psychological Interpretation." Oakland, CA. *International Journal of Dream Research* 5, no. 1 (2012). JStor.

Stone, DeWitt Boyd, Jr., ed. *Wandering to Glory: Confederate Veterans Remember Evans' Brigade*. Columbia: University of South Carolina Press, 2002.

Summers, S. Thomas. *The Journals of Lt. Kendall Everly: A Story of the American Civil War*. Tucson: Anaphora, 2013.

Thacher, Joseph M. *Confederate Coal Torpedo: Thomas Courtenay's Infernal Sabotage Weapon*. Fredericksburg, VA: Keith Kenerly, 2011.

Tolkien, J.R.R. *The Lord of the Rings*. Book Six. New York: Mariner, 2012.

Twain, Mark. *The Best Short Stories of Mark Twain*. Edited by Cynthia Brantley Johnson. New York: Simon and Schuster, 2004.

Walker, Keven. *A Guide to the Battlefield Landscape: Antietam Farmsteads*. Sharpsburg: Western Maryland Interpretive Association, 2010.

Wellman, Judith, Kelly Yacobucci Farquhar et al. *Uncovering the Underground Railroad: Abolitionism, and African American Life in Montgomery County, New York, 1820–1890*. Fonda, NY: Montgomery Co. Dept. of History and Archives; Preservation League of NY State and the NYS Council on the Arts, 2011.

Welty, Eudora. *Some Notes on River Country*. University Press of Mississippi, 2003.

Wiley, Bell Irvin. *The Life of Billy Yank, the Common Soldier of the Union*. Baton Rouge: University of Louisiana Press, 2008.

_____. *The Life of Johnny Reb, the Common Soldier of the Confederacy*. Baton Rouge: University of Louisiana Press, 2008.

Index

Numbers in ***bold italics*** indicate pages with photographs.

Addeman, J.M. 88, 246*n*16, 263
Adkinson, Johnny 193–194
Adkinson, Mary (mother) 194, 258*n*27
Albrecht, Wilhelm 47, 239*n*27; *see also* homesickness
Alcott, Louisa May 165–167; transcendentalism and *Little Women* 166, 254*n*18, 254*n*19, 254*n*20, 254*n*21, 254*n*22, 254*n*23, 254*n*24, 254*n*25, 254*n*26, 263
Alexander, Charles W. 13; *see also* Bradshaw, Wesley; *The Soldier's Casket*
Alexander, John 159, 253*n*54
amputations 30, 32, 89, 124, 180, 246*n*2
Angel's Glow (*Photorhabdus luminescens*) 174, 175, 255*n*49, 271
Antietam 11, 17, 22, 24, 31, 37, 50, 67, 69, ***209–210***, 235*n*2, 240*n*10, 242*n*68, 242*n*69, 259*n*29
Appomattox 13, 36, 117, 237*n*67, 240*n*9, 259*n*10
Arlington 13, 72, 236*n*24
Army of Northern Virginia 3, 17, 22, 30, 96, 117, 192, 239, 242, 246, 265, 267, 269
Army of the Potomac 31, 40, 51
Avary, Myrta 165, 254*n*16, 263

Bacot, Ada 161, 164–165, 254*n*11, 263
Ball, Charles 224, 260*n*20, 263; *see also* slave narratives
Banks, Gen. Nathan 31, 238*n*10
Bartholomew, Azra 67, 242*n*67
Bartholomew, "Frank" 67, 242*n*67
Barton, Clara 161, 253*n*1, 263
Beatty, John 195, 258*n*29, 263
bedposts 7, 18, 125, 128, 196, 249–250*n*12
Beers, Fannie 169, 254*n*28, 263
Bethell, Mary Jeffreys 90, 91, 246*n*24, 263
Bibb, Henry 225; *see also* slave narratives

The Bible 8, 9, 10, 28, 67, 152, 171, 189, 205, 215, 221, 259*n*22, 260*n*13
Birney, Gen. David 31
Black, Jennie 53–54, 240*n*16
Black, Jennie 53–54, 240*n*16
Bland, W.H. 159–160, 253*n*55, 266
Booth, John Wilkes 11, 236*n*41
Booth, Thomas 50, 240*n*5
Bowen, Charles T. 54–55, 240*n*22, 245*n*1, 264
Bowen, Kate (Katie) 54–55, 240*n*22, 245*n*1, 264
bowers 245*n*85
Bowers, John Hugh 11, 235*n*18, 264
Bowler, Elizabeth 75–77, 244*n*97, 244*n*98, 244*n*99, 244*n*100, 244*n*101, 244*n*102, 244*n*103, 244*n*104, 244*n*105, 244*n*106, 264
Bowler, James 75–77, 244*n*97, 244*n*98, 244*n*99, 244*n*100, 244*n*101, 244*n*102, 244*n*103, 244*n*104, 244*n*105, 244*n*106, 264
Bradbury, Mary 83, 220, 245*n*20, 264
Bradbury, William 83, 220, 245*n*20, 264
Bradshaw, Wesley 13, ***14***, 15, 16, 17
Branscomb, James 186, 256*n*5
Branscomb, Lewis 186, 256*n*5
Breckinridge, Lucy 187, 188, 256*n*7, 256*n*8, 256*n*9, 256*n*10, 256*n*11, 264
Brevard, Keziah Goodwyn Hopkins 133–135, 251*n*26, 251*n*27, 251*n*28, 251*n*29, 251*n*30, 251*n*31, 251*n*32, 251*n*33, 251*n*34, 251*n*35, 251*n*36, 251*n*37, 264
Bryant, Willie 242
Bull Run 11, 32, 52, 161, 179, 195
Burns, Christopher Columbus 104, 247*n*16, 247*n*17, 247*n*18, 247*n*19, 247*n*20
Burton, Annie 224, 264; *see also* slave narratives
Burwell, Letitia 132–133, 250*n*25, 264

Caldwell, James Parks 154–156, 253*n*41, 253*n*42, 253*n*43, 253*n*44, 253*n*45, 264
Caldwell, Lycurgus 112–117, 248*n*57, 248*n*58, 248*n*59, 248*n*60, 248*n*61, 248*n*62, 248*n*63, 248*n*64, 248*n*65, 248*n*66, 248*n*67, 248*n*68, 248*n*69, 248–249*n*70, 264
Caldwell, Susan Emeline Jeffords 112–117, 248*n*57, 248*n*58, 248*n*59, 248*n*60, 248*n*61, 248*n*62, 248*n*63, 248*n*64, 248*n*65, 248*n*66, 248*n*67, 248*n*68, 248*n*69, 248–249*n*70, 264
Caldwell, Willie 112, 114, 116
Calhoun, John C. 13, 15, 16, 17, 236*n*26
Camp, Hiram 66, 242*n*66
cannon 19, 37, 52, 67, 79, 94, 123, 137, 215
Cannon, Col. LeGrand 8
Carter, Grant 67, 242*n*67
Case, Adelaide (Addie) 201–211, ***206***, ***209–210***, 211, 259*n*16, 259*n*17, 259*n*18, 259*n*19, 259*n*20, 259*n*21, 259*n*22, 259*n*23, 259*n*24, 259*n*25, 259*n*26, 259*n*27, 259*n*28, 259*n*29; *see also* presentiment; Tenney, Charles (Charlie)
Chamberlain, Gen. Joshua 4, 216, 235, 264, 235*n*2
Champion, Matilda 89–90, 246*n*18, 246*n*19, 246*n*20, 246*n*21, 246*n*22, 246*n*23, 264, 265
Champion, Sid 89–90, 246*n*18, 246*n*19, 246*n*20, 246*n*21, 246*n*22, 246*n*23, 264, 265
Chancellorsville 22, 69, 123, 179, 182, 192, 242*n*68, 249*n*24
Chesnut, Mary Boykin Miller 192, 193, 257–258*n*25
Clark, Mary 97
Clarke, Frances 41, 239*n*1
Clarke, James E. Henry 164, 165

273

Cold Harbor 24, 26, 66, 105, 237n65, 239n7, 244n3, 247n21; *see also* Gaine's Mill
Collins, John H.W.N. 231, 261n45
contraband 222, 230, 260n14
Cooke, Chauncey 85, 245n5
Cottage Home (North Carolina home of Jacksons) 22
Cotton, John W. 42, 239n10, 264
Cotton, John (prisoner of war) 44
Crawford, J.B. (38th Mississippi) 44
Culbertson, Young James 187, 256n6, 265
Cumming, Kate 169–172, 254n29, 254n30, 254n31, 254n32, 254–255n33, 255n34, 255n35, 265
Curtis, Newton 200; *see also* presentiment
Custis, Mary Anna Randolph 12, 13, 236
Currier and Ives (Nathaniel Currier & James Merritt Ives) *4*, 9, *10*, 34, 35, *36*, 238n17, 238n20

Dabney, Robert Lewis 24, 237n54
Da Costa, Dr. Jacob 213
DaCosta's Syndrome 213; *see also* PTSD
Dada, Harriet 84, 245n4, 265
Davis, Jefferson 15, *33*, 35, 73, 192
Davis, J.M. 42, 239n6
Davis, Lucinda 223, 260n19
Davis, Mrs. William A. 65, 69, 247n7
Dawes, Brevet Gen. Rufus 200–201, 258n12, 258n13, 259n14, 259n15
Dawson, Sarah Morgan 125–129, 131, 249n2, 249n3, 249n4, 249n5, 249n6, 249n7, 249n8, 249n9, 249n10, 249n11, 249–250n12, 250n13, 250n14, 251n13, 267–268; *see also* Linwood Plantation
Documenting the American South 2, 240, 265
Dooley, John 40, 152–154, 215, 238n24, 252n32, 252n33, 252n34, 252n35, 252n36 252n37, 252n38, 252n39, 253n40, 259n7, 265
Douglass, Frederick 218–219, 223, 259n1, 259n2, 259n3, 259n4, 265
Downer, Willie 158–159, 265
dreams, by "contraries" 7, 29, 30, 46, 47, 52, 53, 57, 58, 68, 71, 79, 80–96, 98, 112, 113–116, 118–119, 121, 124, 125, 131, 132, 145, 149, 158, 166, 186, 187, 191, 194, 220, 230, 235n1, 236n41, 241n35, 244n1, 248n61, 271
DuBose, Anne Barnwell Peronneau ("Nannie") 177–179, 255n1, 255n2, 255n3, 255n4, 255n5, 255n6, 255n7, 255n8, 265
DuBose, William 177–179, 255n1, 255n2, 255n3, 255n4, 255n5, 255n6, 255n7, 255n8, 265

Duff, Harriet 121–124, 249n14, 249n15, 249n146, 249n17, 249n18, 249n19, 249n20, 249n21, 249n22, 249n23, 249n24, 249n25, 249n26, 249n27, 265, 272
Duff, Levi 121–124, 249n14, 249n15, 249n146, 249n17, 249n18, 249n19, 249n20, 249n21, 249n22, 249n23, 249n24, 249n25, 249n26, 249n27, 265, 272
Dutch paper 195–196, 258n33
Dyer, J. Franklin 87, 88, 245n14, 265

80th Indiana Infantry, Company C 105
Elliott, William 84, 245n2, 265
Equiano, Olaudah 223, 226, 260n29; *see also* slave narratives
Erving, Annie 168, 254n27, 265
Etter, Private Roysdon 52, 240n15, 265
Evans, Lt. Jonathan 44

Faust, Drew Gilpin 186, 256n1, 256n2, 271
5th Indiana Cavalry 139
Fisher, Julia Johnson 125, 249n1, 265
Fisk, Wilbur 94, 246n39
Fitzpatrick, Marion Hill 86, 245n10, 265
Ford's Theatre 11
Fort Monroe 8, 71, 179, 243n78
Fort Sumter 11, 35, 135
Francksen, Wilhelm 47, 239n26; *see also* homesickness

Gaine's Mill (Cold Harbor) 24
Gemütlichkeit 45–47; *see also* homesickness
Gettysburg 11, 24, 26, 27, 30, 40, 69, 84, 123, 153, 179, 182, 187, 202, 222, 237n62, 238n25, 238n26, 241n35, 242n68, 242n72, 245n4
Giles, Valerius (Fourth Texas) 44
Gillis, Malcolm (Georgia volunteer) 41
Goldwaite, Ellen Trice Hill 106–112, 247–248n23, 248n24, 248n25, 248n26, 248n27, 248n28, 248n29, 248n30, 248n31, 248n32, 248n33, 248n34, 248n35, 248n36, 248237, 248n38, 248n39, 248n40, 248n41, 248n42, 248n43, 248n44, 248n45, 248n46, 248n47, 248n48, 248n49, 248n50, 248n51, 248n52, 248n53, 265
Goldwaite, Richard Matthew 106–112, 247–248n23, 248n24, 248n25, 248n26, 248n27, 248n28, 248n29, 248n30, 248n31, 248n32, 248n33,

248n34, 248n35, 248n36, 248n237, 248n38, 248n39, 248n40, 248n41, 248n42, 248n43, 248n44, 248n45, 248n46, 248n47, 248n48, 248n49, 248n50, 248n51, 248n52, 248n53, 265
Gordon, John Brown 96, 198, 199, 200, 246n1, 258n1, 265–266; *see also* presentiment
Grant, Julia Dent 12, 17, 18, 20, 21, 93, 236n30
Grant, Ulysses S. 8, 11, 13, 15, 17, 18, 20, 21, 24, 25, 36, 89, 93, 94, 174, 175, 182, 229, 236n39, 236n41, 236n42, 261n45
graves 86, 123, 128, 180, 181, 225, 233
Graves, Henry Lea 1, 4, 5, 49, 50, 142, 184, 233, 240, 256, 266
Griffith, Frank 70–73, 216, 243n77, 243n78, 243n79, 243n80, 243n81, 243n82, 243n83, 243n84, 243n85, 243n86, 243n87, 259n9, 266
Griffith, "Thankful" 70–73, 216, 243n77, 243n78, 243n79, 243n80, 243n81, 243n82, 243n83, 243n84, 243n85, 243n86, 243n87, 259n9, 266
Guerrant, Edward O. 101–104, 247n7, 247n8, 247n9, 247n10, 247n11, 247n12, 247n13, 247n14, 247n15, 266, 267

Hagar, Chap. Charles 182–184, 256n21, 256n22, 256n23, 256n24, 256n25, 256n26, 256n27, 256n28, 256n29, 266
Hagar, Elizabeth 182–184, 256n21, 256n22, 256n23, 256n24, 256n25, 256n26, 256n27, 256n28, 256n29, 266
Hancock, Cornelia 222–223, 260n14, 266
Harper's New Monthly Magazine 31, 245n20
Harper's Weekly 238n16
Hawley, Dr. Thomas 174, 255n42, 255n43, 255n44, 266
hay 86
Hay, John 9
Heartsill, William Williston 157–158, 253n47, 253n48, 253n49, 266
Henderson, Col. Henry A.M. 156–157
Herndon, William H. 9, 235n4, 235n6, 235n8
Herrick, William 97, 247n2
Hill, Gen. A.P. 13, 17, 27, 30, 40, 82, 237n73, 238n80
Hill, Lt. Gen. D.H. 199
Hobby, Col. A.M. 84, 245n1, 264
homesickness 39, 41–47, 50, 53, 56, 67, 72, 90, 115, 127, 157, 190, 213, 214, 239n24, 239n29, 240n16, 271

Hooker, Gen. Joseph 40
Hotz, Joseph 47, 239n24; see also homesickness
Howe, Capt. George 79, 244n3
Huber, Mark 212, 259n2
Hunter, Gen. David 31
Hunter, James 257n23
Hunter, Mary 31; see also Strother, David Hunter
Hyatt, Capt. Mary 65-66, 242n62
Hyatt, Capt. Thomas J. 65-66, 242n62

Illinois, Springfield 9, 11, 157
Indiana 8, 47, 73, 105, 120
Indiana Historical Society 239n24

Jackson, Julia 22-23
Jackson, Mary Anna Morrison 22-23
Jackson, Thomas (Stonewall) 22-24, 30, 52, 57, 237n44, 237n45, 237n46, 237n47, 237n48, 237n49, 237n50, 237n51, 237n52, 241n32, 245n6
Jeffords, Mary Humbert 248n68
Jemison, Ophelia 224; see also slave narratives
Johnson, Gen. R.W. 11, 33, 236n21
Jones, Jenkin 87, 100, 101, 103, 245n13, 247n1, 266
Jones, John Beauchamp 87, 245n11, 266
Jung, Carl 2

Kagan, James Robertson 44, 239n11, 239n12, 239n13, 239n14, 239n15, 239n16, 239n17, 271
Kagan, Neil 44, 239n11, 239n12, 239n13, 239n14, 239n15, 239n16, 239n17, 271
Kennedy, David 140, 141, 251n3, 266

Lamon, Col. Ward Hill 8, 9, 11, 235n2, 235n5, 235n11, 235n20, 236n22
Lane, David 118-121, 249n1, 261n45, 266
Lane, Jane 118-121, 249n1, 261n45, 266
Lawrence, George 88, 246n15, 266
Lee, Eleanor Agnes 236n24
Lee, Elizabeth Blair (wife of Samuel Phillips Lee) 11, 91-93, 246n25, 246n26, 246n27, 246n28, 246n29, 246n30, 246n31, 246n32, 246n33, 246n34, 246n35, 246n36, 246n37, 267
Lee, Henry "Light Horse Harry" 12, 252n34
Lee, Mary Custis 13, 236n24
Lee, Mildred 236n24
Lee, Capt. Robert E. Lee (son of Robert Edward Lee) 12, 236n24
Lee, Gen. Robert Edward 12, 13, 17, 22, 24, 30, 36, 38, 57, 80, 105, 117, 182, 192, 198, 199, 216, 236n24, 238n80, 241n35, 257n23
Lee, Samuel Phillips 11, 91-93; see also Lee, Elizabeth Blair
Leupp, Laura 36, 267
The Libby (Prison) Chronicle 151, 252n30, 252n31, 263
Lincoln, Abraham 7, 8, *10*, 12, 35, 230, 235, 236, 264, 266, 267, 270, 271
Lincoln, Mary Todd 8, 9, 10, 11, 12, 21, 93, 235
Lincoln, Robert 8
Lincoln, Tad 8, 11
Lincoln, Willie 8, 11
Lines, Jennie 135-138, 251n38, 251n39, 251n40, 251n41, 251n42, 251n43, 251n44, 251n45, 251n46, 266
Lines, Sylvanus 135-138, 251n38, 251n39, 251n40, 251n41, 251n42, 251n43, 251n44, 251n45, 251n46, 266
Linwood Plantation 126, 128, 249n5; see also Dawson, Sarah Morgan
Lockwood, John 40, 238n25
Louisiana, New Orleans 8, 19, 21, 73, 88, 92, 169, 216, 222, 236n31, 243n85, 251n35, 253n44, 259n9
Lucas, George 97, 247n6
Luttrell, Harvey 81-82, 245n14, 245n15, 245n16, 245n17, 245n18, 267
Luttrell, Sue 81-82, 245n14, 245n15, 245n16, 245n17, 245n18, 267

Maile, John 148-149, 251n20, 267
Mangham, W.H. 79
mania a potu 174, 255n44, 259n6
Martens, Friedrich 47, 239n35; see also homesickness
Mary (aunt of William Webb) 228
Mary Ann (responding to husband Joel of Virginia) 239
Maryland, Baltimore 8, 43, 108, 159, 168, 240n8, 240n22, 243n77
Maxwell, Malindy 224, 260n23; see also slave narratives
McCarthy, Carlton (private, 2nd Co., Richmond Hoitzers, Cutshaw's Battalion Artillery, Second Corps) 42, 43, 239n7, 267
McClellan, Gen. George 13, *14*, 15, 16, 17, 20, 24, 31, 35, 36, 92, 186, 199, 236n29
McCoy, William Kenneth 192
McDowell, Private Charles 105, 247n21, 267
McDowell, Nancy 105, 247n21, 267
McElroy, John 142-145, *143*, 158, 216, 251n5, 267
McGuire, Judith 193, 258n26, 267
McLaws, Emily 80-81, 244n7, 244n8, 244n9, 244n10, 244-245n11, 245n12, 245n13, 257n23, 267
McLaws, Maj. Gen. Lafayette 80-81, 244n7, 244n8, 244n9, 244n10, 244-245n11, 245n12, 245n13, 257n23, 267
Meade, Gen. George 40, 183
Miller, Mary Boykin see Chesnut, Mary Boykin Miller
Minser, Mose 225, 260n25; see also slave narratives
mirror, in superstition, visions and dreams 9, 12, 17, 19, 20, 139, 144, 250n12
Mitchell, Dr. S. Weir 175, 176, 255n50, 255n51, 267
Montfort, Theodore 42, 239n2
Montgomery, Frank 52, 240n14, 267
Moody, Benjamin 79, 239n6
morphine 60-63, 173, 192
Morrison, Mary Anna 22; see also Jackson, Thomas (Stonewall)
Mosler, Henry 33, *34*, 238n14, 238n15, 238n16
Moss, Robert 10, 12, 221, 235n9, 235n10, 236n23, 250n25, 259n6, 260n8, 260n12, 260n13
music 24, 26, 28, 31, 32, 37, *38*, *39*, 40, 52, 71, 75, 87, 89, 103, 116, 136, 138, 153, 154, 162, 170-172, 173, 178, 183, 187, 192, 204, 205, 232, 238n24, 245n1, 250n18, 252n26, 253n2, 254n33, 257n7, 259n29

National Tribune 15
Needham, Sgt. Lyman H. 141, 251n4, 268
Newton, James K. 42, 239n4, 268
Newton, Mary 50
Newton, Thomas D. 50, 240n4, 268
9th Indiana Volunteer Regiment 33, 238n16
Nix, Christian (6th Regiment, Wisconsin Volunteers) 45-46, 239n19, 268
North Star (steamer) 32
Northup, Solomon 219-220, 223, 259n5, 268

Oake, William 216-217, 259n11, 268
Ohio, Springfield 198
omens 7, 168, 194, 195, 223, 230, 257n19

Parrott, James 96, 246-247n2, 268
Parrott, Mahalo 96, 246-247n2, 268
Peel, William 152
Pender, Mary Francis Sheppard ("Fanny") 27-30, 237n69, 237n73
Pender, Gen. William Dorsey 27-30, 237n69, 237n73, 238n80, 241n35

Pensacola soldier dream 29, 237n74
Perkins, Maggie 225, 260n24; see also slave narratives
Pickett, Gen. George 24–27, 40, 152, 237n55, 237n57
Pickett, LaSalle Corbell 24–27, 40, 152, 237n55, 237n57
Pickett, Tom 102
Plake, Kate 138–139, 251n47, 251n48, 251n49, 251n50, 268
Poague, Col. William Thomas 52, 240n12, 268
Pope, Gen. John 31, 238n4
Porte Crayon 31; see also Strother, David Hunter
Prescott, William H. 21
presentiment 1, 2, 7–9, 11–12, 21, 24, 66, 71, 100, 107, 122, 124, 198–205, 235n2, 258n1, 258n12
PTSD 212–216, 259n3, 259n4, 259n5, 259n6, 259n7, 259n8, 259n9, 259n10, 259n11, 271, 272
Pye, Edward 173, 256n41, 270

Ransom, John 149–151, 251n21, 251–252n22, 252n23, 252n24, 252n25, 252n26, 268, 271
Rapidan River 3, 159, 182
Ratliff, John A. 194; see also presentiment
Reeves, Huldah 105–106, 247n22
Reeves, Samuel T. 105–106, 247n22
Rhodes, Elisha 200–201, 215, 258n10, 259n5, 268; see also presentiment
Rice, Mary 79, 239n6
Rice, Tullius 79, 239n6
Richards, Richard 79, 244n4, 244n5, 244n6, 268
Richards, Sarah Walford 79, 244n4, 244n5, 244n6, 268
Richmond Daily Dispatch 3, 17, 29, 97, 235, 237n74, 247, 248, 268
Ritner, Emeline 73–75, 243n88, 243n89, 243n90, 243n91, 243n92, 243n93, 243n94, 243n95, 243n96, 268–269
Ritner, Capt. Jacob B. 73–75, 243n88, 243n89, 243n90, 243n91, 243n92, 243n93, 243n94, 243n95, 243n96, 268–269
Robbins, Rufus 188, 189, 256n12, 256n13, 256n14, 256n15, 256n16, 256n17, 256–257n18, 257n19, 269
Ropes, Hannah Chandler 165, 166, 167, 254n17, 254n23, 254n24, 254n25, 269
Ruff, Carl Anton 47, 239n24

Sand, George 19
2nd Co. Richmond Howitzers, Cutshaw's Battalion Artillery, Second Corps 42
7th Indiana Regiment 202, 266n

Seward, William 11, 105
Shakespeare, William 8, 9, 127, 154, 178
Shelton, Rhoda Amanda 44, 45, 172–173, 239n18, 255n36, 269
Sheridan, Gen. 31, 236n31
Sherman, Anthony 16
Sherman, William Tecumseh 11, 15, 73, 93, 135, 159, 214, 217
Sigel, Gen. Franz 31, 238n11
Silsby, Russell and Marinda 94, 246n40, 246n41, 246n42, 246n43, 271
Simpson, Mary 257n22
Simpson, Richard ("Dick") 131, 190–191, 250n16, 250n17, 250n18, 257n20, 257n21, 257n22, 257n23, 269
Simpson, Taliaferro Calhoun ("Tally") 131, 190–191, 250n16, 250n17, 250n18, 257n20, 257n21, 257n22, 257n23, 269
slave narratives 223–227; see also slavery
slavery 73, 112, 130, 136, 137, 158, 161, 164, 192, 218–231; see also slave narratives
Small, Robert 229
Smith, Mary Octavia (Tavey) 131–132, 250n19, 269
Smith, William Wrenshall 93–94
Sneden, Robert **141, 142**, 269
The Soldier's Casket 13
Spiegel, Marcus 46, 239n20, 269; see also homesickness
Stanley, William 41, 239n2
Stephens, Davis 62, 64, 65, 241n43, 242n61
Stephens, Octavia 60–65, 241n43, 241n44, 241n45, 241n46, 241–242n47, 242n48, 242n49, 242n50, 242n51, 242n52, 242n53, 242n54, 242n55, 242n56, 242n57, 242n58, 242n59, 242n60, 242n61, 244n2, 264, 269, 271
Stephens, Willie 64, 65, 241
Stephens, Winston 60–65, 241n43, 241n44, 241n45, 241n46, 241–242n47, 242n48, 242n49, 242n50, 242n51, 242n52, 242n53, 242n54, 242n55, 242n56, 242n57, 242n58, 242n59, 242n60, 242n61, 244n2, 264, 269, 271
Stilwell, Mary Fletcher Speer ("Molly") 67–70, 242n68, 242n69, 242n70, 242n71, 242n72, 242n73, 243n74, 243n75
Stilwell, William 67–70, 242n68, 242n69, 242n70, 242n71, 242n72, 242n73, 243n74, 243n75
Stoker, Betty 78, 244n109
Stoker, William E. 78, 244n109
Stone, Sarah Katherine (Kate) 196–197, 258n34, 258n35, 258n36, 258n37, 258n38, 258n39, 258n40, 269

Stones River 11, 45
Strother, Ann Doyne Wolff 31
Strother, David Hunter 31–33, 238n1, 238n2, 238n3, 238n4, 238n5, 238n6, 238n7, 238n8, 238n9, 238n11, 238n11, 238n12, 238n13; see also Porte Crayon
Strother, Emily (daughter of David Hunter Strother) 31
Strother, Mary Hunter (second wife of David Hunter Strother) 31
Swann, John 41, 239n2

Taylor, Guy 42, 52, 232, 239n3, 240n11, 269
Tenney, Charles (Charlie) 201–211, **209–210**, 259n16, 259n17, 259n18, 259n19, 259n20, 259n21, 259n22, 259n23, 259n24, 259n25, 259n26, 259n27, 259n28, 259n29; see also Case, Adelaide (Addie); presentiment
3rd West Virginia Cavalry 31
38th Indiana Infantry Volunteers 82
Thurmond, Bolton 67, 242n67
Tidd, John (109th NY, 1st Brigade, 3rd Division, 9th Army) 43, 233, 239n8, 239n9, 261n3, 269
Tilley, John 41, 239n2
Toombs, Robert 16
Tubman, Harriet 220, 220, 221, 259n6, 259n7, 259n8, 259n9, 259n10, 259n11, 259n12, 259n13, 264
Turkey Hill 26–27, 237n66
Turnbull, Capt. George (134th Regiment, NYS Volunteers) 42, 195, 239n5, 258n30, 270
Turner, Brian 233, 261n4, 270
Turner, William D. 86, 245n9, 270
27th Indiana 17
Twichell, Chaplain Joseph Hopkins 179–182, 230, 255n9, 255n10, 255n11, 255n12, 255n13, 255n14, 255n15, 255n16, 255n17, 255n18, 255n19, 255–256n20, 261n44, 270
Tyler, William N. 145–147, 158, 251n9, 251n10, 251n11, 251n12, 251n13, 251n14, 251n15, 251n16, 251n17, 251n18, 251n19, 270
Tyrel, Charles 51, 270
Tyrel, James 51, 270

Van Wyck, Richard T. (150th NY Volunteer Infantry) 51, 240n8
Vermont, Washington County 94
Vicksburg 11, 47, 71, 89, 100, 126, 129, 147, 157, 194, 196, 217, 246n19, 246n21
Virginia, Richmond 1, 5, 8, 21, 24, 25, 29, 31, 32, 41, 43, 49, 66, 81, 82, 85, 86, 113, 115, 117, 124, 140, 141, 152, 154, 155, 159, 161, 169, 179, 180, 183, 186, 192, 193, 198, 201, 215, 235n1, 236n28, 237n53,

239n3, 239n7, 240n2, 240n11, 241n25, 241n30, 241n31, 242n69, 242n73, 245ch5n14, 245ch5n15, 245ch5n16, 245ch5n17, 245ch5n18, 245ch6n7, 245ch6n8, 245ch6n10, 247ch7n6, 247ch8n15, 248n61, 248n65, 248n66, 248n67, 249n14, 250n16, 251n21, 252n30, 255n11, 255n12, 256n3, 258n26; see also Belle Isle; Libby Prisons
Virginia Military Institute (VMI) 32

Wadley, Sarah Lois 129–131, 250n15, 250n16, 250n17, 250n18, 270
Washington, Pres. George 13, 15, 16, 17, 21, 36, 126, 236n25, 236n29
Washington D.C. 12, 13, 31, 36, 43, 73, 91, 113, 124, 159, 166, 167, 188, 195, 215, 217, 219, 222, 235n2, 236n41, 238n20, 243n87, 244n99, 246n25, 246n30, 246n31, 246n32, 246n33, 246n34, 246n35, 246n36, 246n37, 249n26, 255n10, 256n13, 256n14, 256n15, 256n16, 256n17, 259ch17n5, 260n14, 260n17, 261n1
Washington Mounted Riflemen 102
Watkins, Willie 59
Watkins, Mary Purnell Dupuy 55–60, 241n26, 241n27, 241n28, 241n29, 241n30, 241n31, 241n32, 241n33, 241n34, 241n35, 241n36, 241n37, 241n38, 241n39, 241n40, 241n41, 269, 270
Watkins, Richard 55–60, 114, 241n26, 241n27, 241n28, 241n29, 241n30, 241n31, 241n32, 241n33, 241n34, 241n35, 241n36, 241n37, 241n38, 241n39, 241n40, 241n41, 269, 270
Watkins, Sam 89, 97, 98, 200, 246n17, 247n4, 258n9, 270
Webb, William 227–229, 260n33, 260n34, 260n35, 260n36, 260n37, 260n38, 260n39, 260n40, 260n41, 270
Weller, Edwin 51, 52, 240n10, 270
Welles, Secretary Gideon 12, 235n16, 235n21
West Virginia, Harpers Ferry 50, 67, 186, 208, **209**, 210, 211, 221, 259n26, 259n29

Winston, Colonel 85
Whipple, Lt. John 160
White House 9, 11, 21, 36, 227, 260n31
Whitlock, William 51, 240n9, 270
Whitman, Walt 212, 259n1, 270, 272
Wirz, Capt. Henry 146, 147, 148, 268
Wolff, Ann Doyne 31; see also Strother, Ann Doyne Wolff
Woolsey, Carry 162
Woolsey, Charles 161, 162, 163, 253n2, 270
Woolsey, Eliza 162, 254n3, 263
Woolsey, Georgeanna 162, 163, 254n3, 254n4, 254n5, 254n6, 254n7, 254n8, 254n9, 254n10, 263
Woolsey, Hatty 162
Woolsey, Jane 161, 162, 163, 253n2, 270
Woolsey, Mary 162
Worsham, John H. 85, 245n6, 270

Yankees 3, 58, 59, 60, 61, 81, 86, 103, 153, 164, 186, 247
Yates, Elizabeth 82, 245n19, 270
Yates, John 82, 245n19, 270

www.ingramcontent.com/pod-product-compliance
Lightning Source LLC
Chambersburg PA
CBHW081544300426
44116CB00015B/2751